Charity and Correction in New Jersey

Charity and Correction in New Jersey

A HISTORY OF
STATE WELFARE INSTITUTIONS

by
JAMES LEIBY

RUTGERS UNIVERSITY PRESS
New Brunswick *New Jersey*

Library of Congress Catalogue Card Number: 67-13078

Manufactured in the United States of America
by Quinn & Boden Company, Inc., Rahway, N. J.

The account of Mrs. Caroline Wittpenn is based on an article prepared for *Notable American Women, 1602–1950,* a biographical dictionary to be published by the Belknap Press of Harvard University Press.

To

Jean

Foreword

My purpose in this book is to tell how the State of New Jersey established and organized its services for the "dependent, defective, and delinquent classes." I have tried to get behind the details of administration, as set forth in official documents, to discover what the services meant to the various individuals and groups who were interested in them.

Simple as this program sounds, it has often seemed beyond my skills and scope. The subject is ramified and complicated, and the secondary literature on the history of social welfare provides no models of interpretation. To keep my research within practical limits I restricted it for the most part to published records, supplemented in the recent period by interviews, but I have become painfully aware how misleading the document may be, and how unreliable the hearsay. Conversations sometimes brought out confidences that I felt inhibited about divulging—a grave embarrassment for a historian.

In looking for the groups and interests that bore upon welfare institutions I assumed that New Jersey was typical of states in the Northeast that were industrialized after the Civil War. I found no general historical interpretation of its social structure, economy, or polity that brought out fundamental differences. It seems obvious that state services developed in a matrix of municipal, county, and private agencies, but secondary works scarcely mention these local arrangements and relevant primary sources are scattered and hard to manage. I have perforce considered local provisions from the viewpoint of state institutions and policies, but I believe that they will appear differently, and significant in many other ways, when they are studied in connection with other community affairs so as to bring out their "latent functions," as sociologists put it, as well as the informal alternatives to their "manifest functions."

In the first seven chapters I recount the origins of state welfare institutions before 1918. The two following chapters show how men came to perceive the lot of them as part of an apparatus of state government, a development that culminated in 1918 in the establishment of a central organization that was peculiar to New Jersey and put it in the van of welfare administration for many years. The new department brought all sorts of services under common guidance and relied on unpaid or honorary boards to manage the several institutions and the whole. This structure gave form to the plausible ideas that the services had common interests in management and in meeting needs of people in trouble or danger, and that citizen boards would minimize political exploitation and encourage professional expertise and scientific progress.

Later chapters take up problems of theory, policy, and administration as they appeared to people in the central office and in the field. My story ends in 1959 when, after men had explored and tested the system for forty years, a study commission pronounced it a mixed success and partly obsolescent, and I offer an interpretation, somewhat different from that of the commission, about how and why its promise was unfulfilled. I conclude with reflections on the relation between this history and the national "war on poverty" that developed rapidly, and unexpectedly, in the years after I had completed my major research for the book, during which I was writing it.

JAMES LEIBY

Berkeley, California
October, 1966

Acknowledgments

My work was made possible by a grant from Mrs. Geraldine L. Thompson to the Rutgers Research Council for the preparation of a history of the Department. Professor Richard P. McCormick arranged for me to undertake the project under conditions that guaranteed autonomous scholarship. A grant from the Institute of Social Science Research at The University of California, Berkeley, paid for typing the manuscript. My study also benefited substantially if indirectly from research on the history of public assistance in California which I have carried on during the last three years with the aid of grants from the California State Department of Social Welfare.

For assistance in my library research I want in particular to thank Francis X. Grondin and Donald Sinclair of the Rutgers University Library, Kenneth W. Richards of the New Jersey State Library at Trenton, Miriam V. Studley of the Newark Public Library, and the staff of the libraries at the University of California, Berkeley, especially of its Institute of Governmental Studies.

Much of my research was in interviewing departmental personnel and other interested parties, and I hope my story reflects the candid and generous spirit with which they reviewed their problems and controversies, as well as their patience in delivering me from ignorance. I conversed and corresponded at length with three former commissioners: Sanford Bates, Dr. F. Lovell Bixby, and John Tramburg, and with Dr. Lloyd McCorkle, who became commissioner upon Tramburg's untimely death, and also with the division chiefs, Dr. V. Terrell Davis, Dr. Maurice Kott, and Irving Engelman. Among those whose long acquaintance with the Department made them especially valuable sources were Edward L. Johnstone, Dr. Emil Frankel, Dr. Douglas MacNeil, Marc Dowdell, Eugene Urbaniak, and Donald Rice, and three remarkable secretaries, Agnes Trier, Elizabeth Feehan, and Rose O'Brien. Mrs. Thompson regaled me with her unparalleled knowledge of people, events, and progress in the state, and Lloyd Wescott and Archibald Alexander gave me the impressions and judgments derived from their association with the Department's work. Harold F. Goldmann, the Department's public relations officer, facilitated my work with an enthusiasm and objective spirit that reflected in part his own historical training.

I shall not list all my other interviewees, but those who may recognize their observations or ideas, with or without attribution, include: John C. Bonnell, Raymond Ring, Cantwell Walsh, Gertrude Hutchins, Irene Ladlie, Edwin F. Hann, Jr., Pauline Thyfault, Mrs. Leonard Shiman, Donald Goff, Edna Mahan, Albert Wagner, R. Royle W. Eddy, Harry Elmer Barnes, Edward Cass, Dr. Paul Haun, Dr. Harold Magee, Milton Brown, Howard Prettyman, Mildred Hurley, Letitia Roe, Dr. Phyllis Greenacre, Dr. George Stevenson, Harry Von Bulow, Miriam Lernerd, Joseph Parneke, and Elizabeth Boggs.

Dean Wayne Vasey and Dr. Juanita Luck Cogan, my colleagues at Rutgers, took time from the business of setting up its School of Social Work to talk over my research with me; Dr. Hasseltine Taylor and Professor Walter Friedlander, my colleagues in the School of Social Welfare at Berkeley, read the manuscript and offered many suggestions to improve it; I was fortunate that Frank Bane, during his tenure as Regents' Professor at Berkeley, shared with me his unique acquaintance with public welfare administration and also read the manuscript, as did Professor Oscar Handlin of Harvard, the reader I most want to please. Daniel Warshaw and Joseph White were capable research assistants; Florence Myer was an expert typist. Jean Griest Leiby helped me endure the trials of scholarship and assisted in preparing the manuscript for the press.

J. L.

Contents

Contents

Charity and Correction in New Jersey

1

Public Welfare and the Rural Democracy

New Jersey took form as an English colony, and its welfare institutions developed from such English precedents as the common law, the poor law, the machinery of legal justice, and the fabric of family and community rights and duties. But in the new world traditional ways encountered new conditions. Throughout the seventeenth and eighteenth centuries the mother country had a labor surplus; the colony was a wilderness desperately short of workers. Colonists came mostly from somewhat disadvantaged groups; some settlements were not English at all. Consequently, the class structure was confused and unstable by English standards. Most colonists were religious dissenters; the Church of England, traditionally the resource of the unfortunate, was of minor importance.

The early settlements were diverse and uncongenial, but just beyond their clearings stood the wilderness, an immense native fact that would, as threat, refuge, or challenge, draw them into unimagined common ways of life. Land policy and the labor shortage encouraged agriculturists and artisans to work for themselves, and their economic self-sufficiency supported their social democracy and local autonomy. So long as Jerseymen enjoyed a rude rural prosperity, their local institutions were more or less equal to the tasks of public welfare, and they had neither the need nor the inclination to look to the state government for service or leadership.

Colonial New Jersey

Whatever their antecedents, the colonists soon fell into a common class structure. It was English more in appearance than in fact. In political affairs the most prominent people were the proprietors and their associates, the rich families that held or claimed legal title to the land. Many of them were not residents; all of them were, in effect, real estate promoters, who stood to gain as *rentiers* and land speculators by encouraging others to settle their land. At first they ruled their lands somewhat as independent principalities, but in 1702 they surrendered their political authority to the Crown, which thereafter appointed royal governors and other colonial officials. This was not much of a surrender, in fact, for the proprietors continued to have large influence in the appointments and in the policies of the Crown. Whatever the technicalities, they were, or aspired to be, aristocrats like those of England.[1]

The names and claims of these worthies fill the history books, but it was clear from the start that the crucial character in the colony was the man who actually brought his family and servants to the wilderness. It was he whom the proprietors tried to attract, encourage, and protect by "grants and concessions," although once the settlers had established themselves on the land they needed no legal documents to recognize and assert their rights. These actual settlers had various backgrounds, interests, and degrees of dignity, but taken together they were called "freemen" or "freeholders." In traditional legal language the names denoted citizens or townsmen with political and civil liberty, who held their land on a lifetime tenure, and it was they who supported the local governments and churches by their contributions in money and service.[2]

Apart from the freeholders and their families was a class of unfree people—apprentices, indentured servants, and outright slaves. Ideally, and often in fact, these humble people were part of their master's family. An apprentice was, traditionally, a boy who agreed to serve a master for a number of years in order to learn a trade. His contract was the "indenture." He lived with the master, like one of the family. The arrangement was analogous to secondary education today, and not dishonorable.

In the colonies, however, this traditional pattern of indentured servitude changed. The institution became a device for recruiting labor. Poor people in Europe would sign an indenture for a merchant or sea captain who agreed to take them across the Atlantic and sell the contract to a colonist. In effect, the person mortgaged his labor for several years to finance his trip.

There were many variations of this pattern. Sometimes immigrants moved as families and became tenant farmers on the master's land. In other cases the migrants were convicts, deliberately transported from jail to the colonies. Sometimes they were individuals kidnapped or spirited away; sometimes they were actually slaves.[3]

There are no recorded statistics on the number and kinds of unfree servants in New Jersey, but some evidence suggests that they were plentiful. Many Dutch settlers had large land holdings and used slaves in the fashion of the New York Dutch. Most settlers had small holdings, however, and preferred a well-chosen servant or two, rather than gang labor, to work with them, and Quakers were willing to pay a premium to get white servants and avoid the moral quandary of slavery.[4]

In any case, this class of unfree labor was the most distinctive feature of the problems of dependency and crime in colonial New Jersey and for a generation after independence. In fact, it is helpful to think in terms of two systems of welfare and justice during these years, one for the freeholders, the established families, and their superiors, the other for the unfree population.

Helping Dependents

When people in established families suffered misfortune, they could turn to "kith and kin," as the many Scottish settlers in Jersey put it. That is, established families generally had relatives or neighbors who felt a special bond of mutual consideration or an obligation based on mutual respect. Often the churches, founded and supported by the freeholders' families, organized and directed this mutual aid. Any of the congregations whose church had *ever* been established—including Dutch Reformed, Yankee Congregationalists, Scottish Presbyterians, and Anglicans—expected that their officers would give charity in their parishes; Quakers expected to relieve all the needy in their fellowship without recourse to the public, and so did many Baptist groups. Religious and neighborly aid was not a matter of law and record, but the expression of a natural sentiment of solidarity that was especially strong among those who shared the ordeal of pioneering. And long after the congregation and neighborhood lost their initial cohesion and vitality, the ideal of mutual aid persisted as an assumption about what all "charity" should be.[5]

By contrast, the poor law itself, the formal public procedure for meeting the needs of the helpless, applied mostly to people who had no home, family or friends, no church membership, toward whom no one felt a special obligation. Sometimes people from established families could sink into this unhappy situation—the dangers and temptations of settlement were terrible—but for the most part "the poor" were strangers and outcasts, somehow outside the normal circles of family, neighborhood, and church. Strangers and wanderers made up the burden of public poor relief.

The most prevalent problem of public welfare arose from sexual misconduct involving servants. Except for slaves and "redemptioners," who moved as families to become tenants, most unfree laborers were forbidden to marry, since family responsibilities were supposedly incompatible with devoted service to the master's family. This enforced celibacy was unnatural and difficult to maintain among lusty people whose inhibitions were weak from the start. Whether as tempted or temptress, whether with master or apprentice, the maidservant was a source of trouble. Sometimes the lovers ran away to take their chances among strangers. Sometimes they left a broken and needy family behind them. Often the result was a bastard child in the community. In any case this was an occasion for action under the poor law.

A second welfare problem involved people, usually former servants, who were free but who could not support themselves because of age or infirmity. Sometimes masters deliberately emancipated servants or slaves to avoid caring for them. Sometimes the servant survived a misfortune that killed or incapacitated his master. Sometimes respectable freemen lost the sympathy or exceeded the charity of their peers and fell into this group; war, disease, and accident took a heavy toll among them as well as among their inferiors.

A third recurring problem was needy strangers, sick or hurt or somehow stranded. If they were respectable migrants or clergymen or in transportation and commerce, they generally found some private resource. But often they were refugees or runaways, doubtful or downright sinister characters. If they found no help they came to the attention of public authorities.

The poor law itself was copied from a series of parliamentary acts of the sixteenth and seventeenth centuries. In England it had replaced the medieval system of religious charity, and for many years congregational officials, churchwardens of the parish, took part in its administration. Even when secularized it gave form to the tradition that in a Christian society no one should helplessly starve; in England it also carried on the tradition that the church—the organized parish and particularly its leading and well-to-do members—was especially responsible.[6]

New Jersey had neither an established church nor a class of gentlefolk who felt a traditional responsibility for charitable functions. Instead there was the obvious requirement of mutual aid in the pioneer communities; to judge from early legislation on the subject, little else was needed. The colonies did not have the large groups of depressed proletarians who raised chronic problems for English poor law officials. Not until 1683, seventeen years after its settlement, did Newark make public provision for the poor, and then for a single person. That same year Gawen Lawrie, the governor of East Jersey, wrote the proprietors that there were no poor in Elizabeth, the provincial capital. When, in 1702, Queen Anne gravely commissioned the first royal governor of New Jersey to build workhouses to put the poor to work, the very idea of a workhouse in the wilderness revealed how different the situation was between the homeland and the settlements.[7]

The first comprehensive poor law in New Jersey appeared in 1709, a generation after the first settlements. It was simple and general, evidently intended to formalize existing practice as part of a codification of laws which the new royal government undertook. The law said that the towns should appoint "overseers of the poor" who were "to take care that all Poor were supplied with Necessary Maintenance and not suffered to wander abroad." Overseers had also to "put forth" (indenture) poor orphans and children whose parents were unable to support them. Since helping cost money, the law provided for assessors, who figured out a poor rate, or tax; the overseers themselves were to collect the funds and pay them out. The overseers were not paid; in fact, there was a fine levied on those who would not serve. The central government—the royal governor—supervised these acts in the person of a local justice of the peace, who was to authorize the election and to attend to legal aspects of the affairs, for example, the contract of indenture for children.[8]

As long as cases were few, the overseer simply gave a small grant to help a needy family stay together until it prospered again or was finally broken, or he arranged to pay a local family to take care of the needy person, if dependent. This was a reasonable and practical arrangement. Families who wanted an extra income and who could make space—and there were many such—were willing to take money for a public service. Often the householder could turn the orphan or the sick into a helpful hand. Often a family would take care of several unfortunates, especially as the number of cases rose.[9]

Problems in the system came as side effects of prosperity. As the eighteenth century passed, better roads and more commerce encouraged migration and the rapid spread of settlement. The central fact in the evolution of the poor law was people moving from village to village, making homes, occupying and improving the countryside. These families came to be the core of the rural democracy, but among them was a small and indefinite proportion of helpless or dangerous undesirables, "very vexatious and chargeable" to the established families. As more and more people swelled the movement, the number of undesirables rose. Since the settlements were losing their original isolation and self-sufficiency, it became harder to recognize the undesirables and to keep track of them, or, to put it differently, it became easier to ignore them in the crowd. Consequently, they probably increased disproportionately in the whole number.

In any case, the wanderers provoked three lines of legislation during the eighteenth century. One law, in 1720, dealt with the large numbers of servants, paupers, and transported convicts who were coming from Europe. Essentially a passenger act, it required two justices of the peace to check incoming vessels for "old Persons, . . . maimed, Lunatic or any Vagabond or Vagrant Persons"; if the justices discovered any who appeared unlikely to support themselves, or who had a criminal record, the masters who brought them were to post a bond before they were landed.[10]

This act aimed to restrict immigration; the settlement laws of 1740 and 1758 dealt with migration within and between colonies. Settlement laws set up residence requirements for public aid and an administrative procedure for handling undesirable transients. The law of 1740 gave "settlement" to persons born in the community and to families who lived there for a year on land they owned or rented for £5. Servants and apprentices got settlement after serving one master for a year. Other eligible classes included those who paid a poor rate for a year (whether residents or not) and persons who served as town officials for a year (whether meeting property qualifications or not).

The law required town overseers to summon those who might become charges, but had no legal settlement, for examination by two justices of the peace. If justices and overseers agreed that such people were likely charges and unsettled, the magistrates were to order the constable to take them to constables of the next town "and so from Constable to Constable until . . . conveyed to the Place of . . . their former Settlement." [11]

The 1758 law obliged every person coming into a community to inform the local overseers, in writing, within ten days, of his address and the names of members of his family. Presumably, no notice meant no settlement, and the responsibility for notice lay on the migrant.[12]

The third effort to handle undesirable transients was the workhouse. Apparently, there were two workhouses in colonial New Jersey, authorized by laws of 1748 and 1754. Why special acts were necessary is not clear, since a general statute of 1713 allowed the erection of such institutions. In any case, the acts tell us all we know about them. The 1748 act authorized Middlesex county officials to build in Perth Amboy; the 1754 act applied to municipal officials of Elizabethtown. The verbal formula—"a Poorhouse, Workhouse and House of Correction"—indicated that the buildings were to house several classes of destitutes: the poor or helpless who did not fit into the system of outdoor relief and boarding out; vagrants and petty misdemeanants; and misbehaving servants, sent there for punishment. The lawmakers, expecting that these institutions would serve several communities, authorized officials to charge for these commitments.[13] The workhouse institutionalized a distinction between "deserving" and "undeserving" poor; it was supposed to punish and suppress the undeserving. For the most part the deserving were local people, the undeserving were the flotsam on the currents of migration.

Few people paid attention to these laws that attempted to apply English institutions to American conditions. The poor law was in one aspect a regulation of labor on mercantilist principles, supported by notions of economic planning as well as by a real danger of high poor rates on local property owners. Colonists were dubious about regulation that hindered their freedom and they were not burdened by a high poor rate; important economic interests favored a labor supply not restricted by settlement laws.[14]

As the economic situation favored the mobility of labor, so did the administrative machinery. Often the laws seem directed as much at local authorities as at the transients. The work of overseers and constables was neither pleasant nor rewarding; they had to go on call to take charge of all sorts of pitiful or threatening situations—abandoned babies, raving maniacs, travelers struck down by sickness or violence, helpless people left without families. Sometimes the system of boarding out paupers meant that more or less shiftless families were employed to care for the more or less helpless—both supported by a single grant, as it were. The law that gave settlement to public officials after a year's service, regardless of their property holdings, suggests that some public officers—very possibly the overseers of the poor and the constables—did not meet the property requirement for settlement. The act of 1758, noting the failure of previous legislation, put the burden of establishing residence on the *migrant*, not the official.[15]

Finally, in 1774, came a comprehensive poor law, summarizing the colonial legislation. Its occasion was frankly administrative neglect: An important section stated that whereas

> Overseers . . . frequently neglect or refuse to deliver a true and fair Account of Monies received . . . [and] leave considerable Sums of Money assessed for Maintenance of the Poor uncollected, [they had henceforth to keep records of assessments and collections; they also had to account for expenditures, lest they] may frequently, upon frivolous Pretences, and for their own private Ends, grant Relief to what Persons they think fit, and may continue the same longer than there may be a real Occasion.[16]

This law of 1774 summed up the experience of a century and remained virtually unchanged for over a century more; its provisions show how public poor relief was supposed to work.[17] Relief was, in the first place, the job of the municipality, which was, in New Jersey, the "town" or "township" and the incorporated borough. The towns elected unpaid "overseers of the poor" to bear this responsibility. Since their decisions often involved judicial determinations, they worked with the local justice of the peace, who was also a judge on the county court and a member of the county governing board.

When some wretch seemed to need—or likely to need—public help, the overseer took him to the magistrate, and together they raised three questions: Does the party have settlement—i.e., is the municipality really responsible? If so, does he have relatives who are legally liable? If not, what sort of help is appropriate?

In each respect the lawmakers in 1774 tried to clarify and strengthen existing practice. Regarding settlement, the basic requirement was a year's residence on a freehold estate worth £50; apprentices and indentured servants were eligible after a year with a local family. Two new provisions, reflecting the increase in commerce and immigration, gave settlement after a year to unpropertied "mariners" and "every . . . healthy Person directly coming from Europe into this province." The law intended to exclude vagrants from other provinces—unless they gave notice in writing of their abode and family relations—and, specifically, servants from workhouses, jails, and hospitals of neighboring colonies.

These provisions are the clearest attempt to define, by inclusion and exclusion, the group of undesirable transients of the time. The law was harsh on them; if local officials found them to lack settlement, they were sent in the direction of their previous residence. If they failed to leave in a day, they were punished (men by ten to fifteen lashes "on the bare back," women by a night in jail on bread and water) and sent away again. Inhabitants who "received or entertained" such transients and failed to notify the overseers were made responsible for their care.

The distinction between desirable and undesirable migration appeared also in other provisions. Those deemed unsettled could appeal the decision to the county court; they could post a bond of £50 for their own security; or they could produce a "certificate of settlement" whereby the overseer of their last residence agreed to take them back if they needed public help. Very few could meet these conditions, but the law-makers obviously wanted to encourage desirable migrants in every conceivable way. Furthermore, if the needy person was too sick to return to his place of settlement, local authorities were obliged to care for him and if necessary to bury him; the responsible municipality also paid for this service.

In the case of settled persons, local officials tried to find responsible relatives—parents, children, grandparents, and grandchildren. This procedure formalized and perhaps elaborated existing practice; it aimed to forestall irresponsibility of kin and a quick indiscriminate action by the overseers.

Once local officials found themselves obliged to help, they had to fix on a plan. If the helpless were "deserving"—genuine victims of misfortune—but able to look after themselves, they got a grant in money or kind. If they needed physical care or supervision, they were boarded with an established family at public expense. If there were several persons in this category, the overseers might "farm them out" by public auction to the family that bid lowest on the contract. The public pauper was required, under the law, to wear a scarlet or blue letter on his sleeve, "P" for pauper and the initial of the town. This "badging the poor" was supposed to strengthen the public authorities by identifying the poor who belonged to the community. The "undeserving poor"—who were thought too irresponsible to support themselves—went to jail as misdemeanants or perhaps to the workhouse, and presently joined—or rejoined—the stream of undesirable transients.

Infants and children were clearly not responsible in any case, and the law provided separately for them. An illegitimate child was settled with the mother. Two overseers or justices appointed themselves "guardians" over abandoned, orphaned, or neglected children; they had to provide and supervise the care of the children and in time arrange their indenture. The overseers could separate "neglected" children from their parents—if the latter were disabled or in custody, for example—and the law allowed parents three months to bind out children to masters of their own choice before the overseers made an arrangement. Furthermore, the law bound masters to teach the indentured children to read and write, and required the appointed guardians "to take care that the terms of Indenture be fulfilled, and that children be not abused or ill-used."

After the authorities decided on appropriate relief and agreed on its costs, the justice gave the overseer an order authorizing a weekly allowance or whatever was called for, and the overseers had to keep records of the occasion and amount of expenditures. These records were not case records, related to individual needs, but an administrative check on the overseers.

Municipalities paid the entire cost of relief by a property tax called the "poor rate." At first this was assessed and collected as problems arose, but when there were enough cases to require regular annual provision, the overseers and justices met to determine it. Presumably they estimated costs for the coming year, as indicated by the auction of the poor plus a contingency fund; "farming out" the permanent poor in one or two sizable groups, which became a common practice, was clearly a help in preparing this budget as well as in reducing the work of supervision.[18]

Punishing Criminals

The first settlers of New Jersey thought about social security in terms of the security of person and property under law. This was the great theme of Hobbes and Locke; it was the purpose of the "grants and concessions" that the proprietors offered the settlers, which became the written constitution of the new communities.[19] The rights of Englishmen that the proprietors thus agreed to respect were embodied in the common law and in the machinery of justice by which it was enforced.

The principal instrument of justice was the county court. The proprietors quickly "erected"—mapped out—counties, which were the boundaries of the jurisdiction of county courts. The courts were simply the local justices of the peace meeting together periodically—every three or six months—to try cases that exceeded their authority as individual magistrates. The court was an important place for the freeholder. It held the official record of his real property and its disposal by sale, will, and bequest. It was at court that he won compensation from the party who damaged his property, broke his contract, or slandered his good name. There the king's officers tried people charged with serious crimes.[20]

"Keeping the peace" was the business of the local constable, who served the local justice of the peace. If the justice could not dispose of the case, the constable took the offender to the county jail, which stood next to the county court. The jail was the responsibility of the sheriff, who took charge of the culprit until the court acted, then executed the court's judgment. Constables—like justices and sheriffs—were compensated for their services by fees. In emergencies, private citizens acted in the name of the law or served as temporary officers.

The legal procedures were sometimes complicated, but in a functional view the problem of justice, like the problem of mercy, involved the distinction between freeholders and servants. The settlers rooted out and punished sin wherever they discovered it—the first criminal code of East Jersey was based on Deuteronomy—and technically the penalties applied to all classes. Distinctions appeared because the classes committed different kinds of crimes and suffered different kinds of punishment.

Established families—property owners—had little reason for the violent crimes of rootless unemployed men. They occasionally appeared in court charged with "theft" or with some illegal business. The theft often involved livestock, an important product of the frontier economy, which usually wandered at large and unclearly marked. The illegal businesses included smuggling, the "salvage" of wrecked vessels, outright piracy (Captain Kidd himself found Cape May a good base of operation), receiving and selling stolen goods, and counterfeiting.[21]

Servant crimes were a different matter. The foremost were fornication, petty theft, "disturbing the peace," and running away (violation of contract). Others were crimes of revenge—arson and murder. Sometimes runaways organized themselves into bands of desperadoes in the wilderness, or became part of the labor force in the illegal businesses, such as smuggling and the trade in stolen goods.[22]

Most servant crimes were misdemeanors, for which local magistrates dealt out summary justice. Since the servants' work time was valuable, punishment was generally "corporal"—whipping or mutilation. The law that demanded these penalties was brutal by later standards, but in context it seems to have protected servants from the entirely arbitrary brutality of their masters. Death was a common penalty, for example, but masters could not inflict it privately, and other serious punishments were also a public responsibility. Serious crimes involved indictment and trial in the county court, and while the juries, made up of freeholders, were not apt to sympathize with servants against masters, they could take a somewhat detached view of justice in the situation.[23]

Punishment of servant crimes was conditioned by the labor shortage. If a servant put the master to trouble or expense, by having a baby or running away, all the costs, including legal costs, were simply calculated as an extension of the period of indenture. The master took the servant and the contract (indenture) to court, and terms were quickly adjusted.[24] In the case of slaves, the state made a payment to masters whose slaves were executed for crime; this policy was intended to keep masters from protecting their slaves against the claims of justice, and incidentally to keep slaves from thinking that they could get away with anything serious. Slaves were thought to be particularly thievish and especially involved in petty theft and the trade in stolen goods. They were not subject to special legal punishments, but in fact they were punished more harshly than white offenders.[25]

The freeholder-entrepreneur in illegal business got better treatment. He might avoid the indignity of jail by posting bond and escape physical punishment by paying a fine. Moreover, the jury of his peers might look upon his illegal business with understanding or even approval, or the judges might temper the brutal punishment as they saw fit.

On the other hand, respectable people who belonged to religious congregations were subject to church discipline, which went beyond the formal demands of the law and involved the action of the congregation, the threat of excommunication, and some sort of confession and penance. It exercised a significant social control throughout the eighteenth century.[26]

Men did not find much occasion to worry about crime in New Jersey, as they did in England. The commonest offense on court dockets, except perhaps for assault and battery, was fornication. Prosecution was relatively easy and there were good reasons for prosecution, since the convicted father became liable for his bastard child under the poor law and if he were a servant this cost plus any fine would be calculated as an addition to the term of indenture for the master's benefit.[27] In the 1750's fornication was charged to about one person in 4,000; the courts took cognizance of only a dozen illegitimate births a year in a population of over 80,000.[28]

On the other hand, law enforcement was difficult and the opportunities for crime certainly increased during the century, along with the opportunities for pauperism. The wilderness and the labor shortage made a getaway easy—Ben Franklin crossed New Jersey as a runaway apprentice in 1723 without difficulty—and when imperial authorities ordered a crackdown on the illegal businesses the offenders were inclined to turn their minds and hearts to constructive thoughts of treason.

The Rise of the Rural Democracy

Early in the eighteenth century it became evident that there was a gap between the inherited traditions of English society and the ways of life which survived the ordeal of settlement. The evidence appeared in two important and related trends—the erosion of the authority of church and state and the spread of humanitarian ideas. Both had large consequences for the history of social welfare.

The erosion of authority lay not in the working of government but in the attention paid to a common good and in the respect for legal authority. Perhaps the clearest case is the fate of the Swedish and Dutch settlements in New Jersey. Certainly the founders of these communities wanted to keep their traditional customs, to be law-abiding and God-fearing citizens in the ways they recognized as right. The Swedes were few in number, but they had a subsidy from their king, with which they imported a Swedish clergyman to maintain their language and Lutheran faith. They were in an economic backwater, without pressure from other communities to change, but change they did. The Dutch, by contrast, were numerous and prosperous; they likewise wanted to keep their tie with Holland. When that failed they established Queen's College (now Rutgers) to supply themselves with a distinctive ministry, and that effort also failed. In both cases the children drifted away or ran after new forms.[29]

The same sort of thing happened to the other religious groups among the settlers. The Quakers, for example, did not lose their sense of difference from the "people of the world" but they lost their enthusiasm and rather self-consciously retreated into a complacent formalism. At first Quakers and Baptists had regarded Congregationalists and Presbyterians, and especially Anglicans, with suspicion and hostility; but as the century wore on these distinctions seemed unimportant.[30]

That religion was lax and indifferent was the cry of the preachers who, in 1731 in the Dutch Church of New Brunswick, began the "great awakening" of faith in the colonies. They outspokenly opposed a general decline in religious conviction, but their purpose was not to build an organization. They held that the spirit of religion was more important than its form, and that sectarian differences, upheld by a learned clergy, were not important. They thought that personal faith and religious experience outweighed an authoritative exposition of scripture. They wanted men to have this experience, which they thought of as salvation.[31] The bitter division they made between "new lights" and "old lights" doubtless distracted congregations from developing their charitable institutions. By multiplying denominations they undermined the idea of a single religious organization for everyone. They thus contributed to the erosion of religious institutions. But in the long run their most important influence was to awaken a lively sense of the importance of each individual soul, no matter how humble, and to emphasize again that suffering and sin, mercy and justice, were more central to religion than were formalities of doctrine and organization. Humanitarian movements developed these views.

Meanwhile, political events of the eighteenth century brought into focus a constitutional conflict between central authority and local autonomy. The central authority was the royal governor, who represented the Crown in theory and the large landed interests in fact. His policies aimed, whether correctly or not, at farsighted common objectives, in trade, transportation, defense, and fiscal arrangements, as set forth by authorities in the mother country. His agents were the legislative council, an aristocratic upper house which he appointed, the justices of the county court, who were also justices of the peace, and the sheriffs and constables, all of whom he appointed. In short, he controlled the courts and the machinery of justice, with all that this implied for men of property and substance.

Local autonomy, on the other hand, was vested in the self-governing towns, which elected their own officers—overseers of the poor, for example—and which also chose certain freeholders to meet with the County Court for matters of county business. The "Board of Chosen Freeholders" became the Jerseyman's county commissioners. The principal county business was to finance the courthouse and jail and certain roads that the governor wanted built. Also the townsmen elected representatives to an assembly or lower house of the legislature. Resistance to the governor took the form of protests and arguments in the assembly, or sometimes of riots that closed the courts or opened the jails when the sheriff tried to enforce an unpopular law.[32] Ultimately it took the form of organized armed resistance, led by the assembly—the Revolution. But this was only a final step in a long continued challenge to political authority.

The erosion of religious and political authority had, of course, a constructive side. It was the French aristocrat Crèvecoeur who set forth the ideals of the rural democracy in his *Letters from an American Farmer,* written before the Revolution and published shortly afterward. Crèvecoeur's "American farmer" was the freeholder of the central colonies, particularly the Delaware valley. The Frenchman was well acquainted with Jersey types. He knew and loved the Quakers (like them he opposed the Revolution); he knew and respected the Dutch, among whom he lived for years; the Scotch, like "Andrew the poor Hebridean," who, in his story, rose to the status of freeholder; the Germans; and the French. The pride and joy of the American farmer, Crèvecoeur observed, was his home, which he inherited from his father and passed on to his children. The feudal hierarchy and established church that held European society together, the authorities of the old world, meant nothing to him. *His* church and state were friendly and rather casual associations with his neighbors. His aspirations were merely a simple wholesome life, lived with good cheer about the family hearth, bathed in neighborly good will.[33]

The portrait was idyllic and sentimental, but it had an unmistakable spiritual quality. Its spiritual aspect was a version of pietism, and the Quaker Jerseyman John Woolman most clearly expressed the constructive side of the rural democracy. Woolman was as free of sentimental fancies as of sectarian polemics. The message he brought—and lived—was a heartfelt sympathy with and concern for suffering people, an earnest hope and rational confidence that they might be helped and that good men could be brought to help them. Like the revivalists, he was concerned for men's souls, but his concern was distilled into universal fellow feeling and humane responsibility. His journal of travel and labor in the rural democracy is the testament of that time and place to all who would understand the nature of democratic ideals.[34]

In the long run, however, the authentic spokesman of the rural democracy in New Jersey was neither a romantic Frenchman nor a pious Friend; it was the author of a minor classic, *The Story of an Old Farm,* in which Andrew D. Mellick, Jr., set forth, with ingenuous garrulity, the story of how his German forebears settled the Raritan valley and lived and prospered across the generations. His best passages have the gusto and charm of genre painting. He shows considerable community spirit of a sort, local and even state pride. He hoped to write a history of the state as its great events appeared to his kinsmen and bore upon them. The author is admittedly an amateur and writing for friends rather than for a scholarly public, but the idea moves him to diligence, care, and often to insight.

In the large, however, Mellick's book is significant because he cannot make the connection. Too often the great events and small stand apart, linked by anecdotal garrulity and folksy nostalgia. It is significant that the narrative drifts to a close in the early years of the nineteenth century, for the author wrote in the 1880's, when things were changing. If the pleasures of his ancestral past had any relevance for his present, he did not choose to mention it.

What stands out in his reflections is the freeholder or yeoman farmer, improving the family estate, carefully looking out for his own, responsible and self-reliant, sharing his interests with his neighbors and taking part in mutual concerns. He is an upright man, generous and public-spirited in his own terms. But the terms are narrow. When the wilderness is plowed and the Revolution fought he does not see much occasion to look beyond his private affairs and local government.[35]

It was amid such tendencies and ideas that Jerseymen tried to develop their welfare institutions after the Revolution. When people came much later to find fault and to want change, to create an enlightened public spirit and a bold public policy, they would often complain about apathy, localism, and complacent conservatism, not realizing how close these lay to the historic roots of their ideals.

After the Revolution

New Jersey was the "cockpit of the Revolution" as regards both battles and propaganda. It was a scene of civil war. Tom Paine wrote the first and greatest of the *Crisis* papers in Newark and later fought at Trenton and Princeton (in 1802 he made his home on a farm near Bordentown). Paine's writing, like other radicals' doctrines, gave a political and secular emphasis to the notion that all men, however humble, are equal and precious. His purpose was to establish the idea of political and civil rights as part of the revolutionaries' constitutional argument, but there was a decidedly humanitarian and religious quality to his thought. In fact, the ideals of the Enlightenment had become a substitute for traditional religion among many upper-class people. Princeton, for example, founded by new-light revivalists, had become a hotbed of Deism by the time of the Revolution.

The organized churches, which had to face this intellectual challenge, had generally lost ground during the war. Quakers and Anglicans suffered because they opposed it; non-English congregations had to identify themselves with one side or the other. Presbyterians were strengthened, in the long run. But it is significant that when the passion of revivalism returned in the nineteenth century it was not Presbyterians who organized and developed it, nor any of the important colonial churches; Methodist circuit riders were the ones who then won the hearts of the rural democracy. In the years after the fighting, churchmen struggled to attend to their organizational needs. Church discipline declined sharply as a means of social control.[36] Congregations showed little concern for or organized initiative in the provision of charity.

Society at large was as disorganized as the churches. Upper-class families that were closest to the royal government fled; some returned, but at a disadvantage. Meanwhile the war cut off the importation of bound servants; they seem to have come again sporadically when peace returned, but neither the supply nor the demand was at the earlier level, and presently the class disappeared.[37] Considering the importance of the would-be aristocrats in politics and of unfree labor in social problems, their disappearance changed the situation greatly.

In every respect, these developments enhanced the power and the localism of the rural democracy. Politically, the Revolution made the state legislature supreme. The legislature, not the governor, now appointed the justices of the peace, among other officers; sheriffs were elected by popular ballot. This meant that the machinery of justice, like the making of law, was in local hands. Politics were not managed, in the early decades, by parties; local cliques took charge. Legislators appointed justices of the peace; justices were likely candidates for the legislature. The sheriff ran the elections—an ill-organized and tricky business. The result was that a new office-holding class emerged, somewhat like the colonial office-holding class, but responsible, ultimately, to the local electorate.[38]

These factors—an expansive humanitarianism, an absence of religious leadership to channel it, a democratizing of the social structure and political order—shaped three significant developments in welfare institutions after the Revolution: the move to abolish slavery; the establishing of almshouses; and state provision for education. All bore in some way upon the operation of the poor law.

Slavery was a long-time concern among Quakers. As early as 1696 their Yearly Meeting for Pennsylvania and the Jerseys had recommended against importing slaves; twenty years later it expressed a cautious disapproval of buying them. But the spirit languished. In 1737 one Jerseyman in twelve was a Negro slave, and yet the protest had died out; indeed, masters feared slave revolts, like those which had occurred in New York. Then, in 1742, John Woolman began to clarify and press the moral issue. By 1758 the Yearly Meeting recommended that Friends free their Negroes; by 1776 it was ready to disown slave-owning members.[39]

There were two sides to the problem of freeing slaves. One was the master's loss of his property. The other and more difficult, early and late, was what to do with the freedmen. A law of 1714 held that "free negroes are . . . idle, slothful people and prove very often a charge to the place where they are"; therefore any master who freed his slaves had to give enough security to pay them an annuity of twenty pounds a year. To overcome this obstacle, bills in the legislatures of 1773 and 1775 allowed manumission without security, on grounds "of humanity and tenderness," but they were defeated.[40]

A law of 1786 allowed masters to free able-bodied slaves aged twenty-one to thirty-five without security (two justices had to certify the action, however) and forbade the importation of more slaves. Slaves confiscated by the state during the Revolution were freed in 1790, without security.

An act of 1804 provided for the gradual abolition of slavery. Children were born free, but made "servants," as if bound out by overseers of the poor, until age twenty-one for women and twenty-five for men. The law required the master to support these free children of slaves for a year, but after that he might, by giving notice, "abandon" them. Negro children so "abandoned" were considered paupers of the township, whom the overseers would bind out in the usual way. But the law also provided that the state would pay maintenance for these children, so masters often refused to support the free Negro infants and local overseers of the poor charged the cost of their support to the state. One-third of the state treasurer's disbursements were for this purpose in 1807, two-fifths in 1809. Lawmakers repealed the provision in 1811, noting that "in some cases the money drawn for maintenance amounts to more than [the child] would have brought if sold for life." [41]

The masters might gladly have supported the infants in order to command their later services; the fact that they did not suggests that the demand for unfree labor was much diminished since colonial days. The episode shows how humanitarian and economic motives combined in the formulation of a liberal state policy, how local interests took advantage of the policy and frustrated it, and how the state, unable to sustain the policy, simply returned the problem to local hands.

The decade after 1789 saw two significant trends in poor law administration: frequent litigation over settlement and the institution of public almshouses, or "indoor relief." These developments came when the federal Constitution and the wars of the French Revolution had restored the commerce of New York and Philadelphia. In this relative prosperity and security local authorities were inclined to take a long-run view of their situation and prospects. The state government undertook the codification of state laws in the decade and the establishment of the state prison, to be discussed later; but within the municipalities the spirit of planning also found expression.

Litigation over settlement arose in the efforts of local officials to rid themselves of unsettled charges and to get a judicial determination on the bearings of the law (we know only of cases that were appealed to courts of record).[42] The litigation and process of transporting the unsettled poor were paid for by fees to local justices and constables, so an element of self-interest was involved; these men did not try to get the state to formulate a more enlightened policy on settlement which would end their tiresome and expensive bickering and its incidental cruelty to the poor.

In the colonial period, problems of "settlement" had involved undesirable transients, more or less sturdy vagrants, who were run out of town in the direction of their last settlement. This class was not so prominent in the 1790's—probably as a consequence of reduced immigration—and the litigation often involved helpless people who needed long-term care, infants, and the aged.

In the general codification of laws in the 1790's, an act of 1798 authorized counties to build almshouses and an act of 1799 authorized them to build workhouses.[43] The institution of public almshouses after 1800 showed a humanitarian motive. The "workhouse," which in colonial times had served as an almshouse and might have developed in this direction, was, traditionally, a substitute for jail. It connoted undeserving paupers forced to work. The "almshouse" suggested private religious charity; Quakers in Philadelphia and Dutch Reformed congregations in New York had "almshouses."[44] Perhaps the post-Revolution weakness and distraction of the churches were a reason for public, rather than private, almshouses. The churches might have provided, but did not. In any case, the public almshouse was a substitute for the inhumane act of "auctioning the poor" as well as for the often cruel treatment of farming them out. A public almshouse and poor farm offered a regular provision for the unfortunate (and, incidentally, jobs for local politicians).

West Jersey counties moved first to establish almshouses: Salem in 1796, Burlington in 1798, Gloucester in 1799; then Cumberland in 1809 and Cape May, sometime before 1818. In East Jersey only rural Monmouth acted, in 1801; more populous counties considered the matter, but would not act, and here the towns finally took action. The cost of the enterprise was clearly the great obstacle, but there was also a question of jurisdiction: Should less populous townships have to contribute to a county almshouse which more populous towns would use? If towns went ahead and built for themselves, would they be taxed again later for a county institution? Clearly the answer to both questions was free local initiative and autonomy, a policy spelled out in an act of 1820, which said that towns that built almshouses would not have to contribute to a county almshouse built later, except on their own terms. Newark acted in 1816, Paterson before 1825, Orange and Bergen townships in 1826, Elizabeth before 1833.[45]

By the 1840's the almshouse, or "indoor relief," had largely replaced the auctioning and boarding out of the helpless poor. Sometimes the county, other times one or several municipalities, acted, according to the principle of local autonomy and self-determination. "Outdoor relief" was always municipal. In general these policies and institutions were supposed just and efficient by the rural democracy. The poor law revision of 1874 eliminated whipping and badging, but otherwise remained unchanged.[46]

Public Education and Public Welfare

During the colonial period there had been two systems of education, just as there had been two systems of poor relief. Families who could afford it sent their children to tuition schools, often conducted under church auspices. Many families were unchurched, however, and many children were bound out as orphans or neglected children. For these there were "charity schools" and an elementary public provision, since the overseers of the poor were supposed to see that children under their guardianship got some education.

Churchmen had a practical interest in education. It was a means of proselytizing among the unchurched, of confirming children in their faith, and of recruiting clergy. Churches established colleges and also the preparatory schools or academies intended to bridge the gap between elementary education and college. These institutions were definitely religious and for the well-to-do. Often clergymen taught in them, thus piecing out their incomes; this was particularly true in the non-English congregations, where the teacher was supposed to maintain a tie with the ethnic heritage.[47]

Tuition as well as endowments and gifts supported the church schools; charity schools were supported entirely by philanthropy. Sometimes benefactors paid the fees for a few poor scholars; often the charity students were kept separate. Some schools were organized specifically for Negroes and Indians, others for the poor. Quakers and Anglicans, drawing on English models of philanthropy and proselytizing, were active promoters of educational charity.[48]

Where congregations did not form their own schools, parents joined together to establish "common schools," temporary and informal arrangements. The best organized of these were in towns settled by New Englanders, such as Newark, Woodbridge, and Piscataway. They foreshadowed the public school, because part of their support came from the town, which set aside certain of the common lands as a sort of secular endowment fund. The town also collected tuition from the participating families on a regular basis, like taxes. In fact, there was a good deal of clerical interest and control in these institutions, and participating families had to pay a sizable part of the cost—enough so that many poorer families were excluded. Where these schools existed, overseers of the poor often subsidized them by providing therein for the education of their wards.[49]

There was more interest in education in the first generation of settlers than later; after royal governors took charge, in 1702, the central government was in sympathy with the Church of England and its Society for the Propagation of the Gospel, and it was not inclined to help other religious or municipal institutions, which were left on their own. The religious revival brought a renewed interest, a competition for proselytes and clergymen, and this led to a notable development of secondary and higher education. At the same time, some people expressed humanitarian and social concern about the neglect of education of the poor. The poor laws of 1758 and 1774 reflected this general trend by making overseers responsible in a somewhat more explicit and definite way for the education of poor and bound children.

The Revolution delayed this development; it sanctified the sovereignty of local authorities in the matter. Nevertheless, there were advances. An Orphans' Court was set up in 1784 to give more dignity to the process by which justices had protected dependent children. In 1794 the Assembly passed an act which allowed the incorporation of societies to promote learning. These were schools or benevolent societies that supported charity schools or nondenominational "free schools" for poor children, or libraries. A statute of 1798 required owners of slaves and servants to teach them how to read before they were twenty-one.[50]

These signs of interest did not change the fundamental situation, which stood in 1800 as it had for a century. Education was a matter of private, religious, or local initiative, except for laws requiring some sort of schooling for the poor, in charge of the overseers, and for servants and slaves. The poor might learn the rudiments in charity schools or in the common schools, where their parents could avoid the burden of the school rate, or part tuition, by declaring themselves to be paupers. In general, the common schools were a minimum provision, associated with boors, paupers, and servants. The teachers were at best clergymen, college students, or rather fancy indentured tutors from Scotland or France; at worst they were charlatans and scoundrels who showed up with dismaying frequency in the county jails.

Then began the long effort to increase the state's interest in education, until it finally guaranteed all its children, not just paupers, a free education. The effort took longer in New Jersey than in any neighboring state. It was difficult and complicated; in the present context it is relevant insofar as it was part of the provision for dependents, defectives, and delinquents, and insofar as it shows the difficulty of rallying public opinion for any sort of reform.

The problem was always money, and the first step was to accumulate a state fund—a state endowment, as it were—which could help the local common schools. This campaign took some five years, 1812–1817, although the first appropriation from the fund was not made until 1829. Meanwhile, in 1820 towns were authorized to raise school taxes for the education of their poor children—a provision that plainly identified public education with impoverished children.[51]

In 1821 the Assembly established a fund (taken from funds "not otherwise appropriated," i.e., a surplus) to educate deaf and dumb persons. Under this act a county's Board of Chosen Freeholders applied to the governor on behalf of a resident who was twelve years old, indigent and "of good natural capacity," and the governor might send him to an out-of-state school for three years; the expense could be no more than $160 a year. In 1825 a group of citizens, incorporated as the New Jersey Institution for the Deaf and Dumb, planned a state school for these unfortunates that would be free to the poor but would charge tuition to those who could afford it. The idea was not realized until 1882, but meanwhile the Assembly did its bit by asking the federal government for funds and continuing and enlarging the support of handicapped students in out-of-state schools. In 1836 the state similarly provided for poor blind children, who at the age of seven became eligible for five years' schooling.[52]

The record does not reveal much about the administration of the law—about how poor the parents were or even how many children were helped—but the conditions were liberalized from time to time. In 1838 a law eliminated the Board of Chosen Freeholders from the process of application and required the children's guardians or the overseers of the poor to pay part of the costs of transportation and clothing, at least; the law also required the governor to review the list to eliminate ineligibles. These are signs that the need was growing and that the local authorities had been taking advantage of slack administration to get the state to pay.[53] (The notion of a state institution that would charge fees to those able to pay and help paupers at the expense of the local overseers appeared later in the plan for the state lunatic asylum.)

Meanwhile, in 1829 the state distributed an appropriation from the school fund, but many local authorities, instead of adding this amount to their funds, used it to pay their share of common school costs for educating the poor, and continued the school rate-bill for families that were able to pay. This was particularly true of "poor and thinly settled townships where improvement was most needed." In 1831 the private church-related schools succeeded in diverting some of the funds to themselves; they kept alive the principle that those who could afford education should pay for it and that state funds should apply to the education of the poor.[54] Then followed a long, bitter contest to make taxation compulsory, to make the common, public schools free, without rate-bills and pauper students, to establish state supervision, and to found state teacher-training institutions. Compulsory taxation and state supervision came, after a fashion, in a law of 1846, which replaced township school committees by elected and paid superintendents and provided for licensing of teachers and for reports; a hired state superintendent replaced the school fund officials and exercised control by allotting the state fund. In two years local appropriations for schools doubled and enrollment increased by 60 percent. The state normal school came in 1855. But the victories were partial. New Jersey did not end aid to sectarian schools until 1866 and it was the last state to abolish the rate-bill, or tuition charge, in 1872, when a state tax was enacted to supply the necessary additional funds.[55]

The long struggle to extend the principle of public education from paupers and indigent handicapped to all children has a large significance for the history of public welfare. It was clear from the start that there was a need for an educated citizenry in a democracy. James Parker, a leading advocate of the cause for fifty years, was a Federalist from Perth Amboy, but he took his ideas on the subject from Thomas Jefferson, and many conservatives came to see the need for improved and widespread education. City people supported the movement—Newark was especially prominent—and their newspapers gave it strong support. It had a great popular appeal and was without question the state's largest, most persistent, and most effective reform movement between 1820 and 1860. Its lobby was well-recognized and effective. No movement for adult paupers, criminals, or insane had such support.

What was perhaps more interesting than the support, however, was the opposition. Some people, of course, doubted the need. Once, when a legislator argued that good common schools had favored the intelligence and enterprise of Connecticut, a member from Sussex replied that back where he came from people guarded their pockets when a Yankee appeared, and if that was the result of common schools, Jersey could do very well without them. Others doubted the wisdom of public schools. For example, in the 1830's men said that education would reduce crime. The state was engaged in developing a new prison system at the time, and the prison keeper made a study which indicated that convicts were indeed poorly educated. But those who favored sectarian schools argued that only religious schools could furnish the appropriate moral education that would decrease crime; and sure enough, crime did not decrease with increasing budgets for public schools. Later the issue came up when some larger towns wanted the state to set up industrial and reform schools, such as other states had, which would take problem children out of their burgeoning school systems and give them a special moral discipline and industrial training. Rural localities opposed the appropriation of funds for this purpose because they did not think they would share in the benefits, and defenders of sectarian schools objected that public schools could not give the proper moral training.[56]

Money and supervision were the central issues, because those who doubted the need and those who doubted the wisdom of particular measures could always join to defeat proposed legislation, albeit for different reasons. And in the end money was the lever by which reformers moved the obstacles of local and private interest. When the state established a school fund to aid the local authorities, it set up a device which could, in the long run, induce them to meet standards of finance and administration that they would not otherwise have chosen to maintain.[57] In the case of adult poor relief, almshouses, and jails, there was no such device, and state supervision was much slower to make itself felt. The story of the public schools suggested the plight of those who would reform the institutions of a rural democracy when these became unenlightened and reactionary.

2

The New Jersey State Prison, 1797–1869

Until 1797 provision for paupers and criminals was entirely the work of local agencies. The prison authorized by the legislature in that year, the earliest state "welfare" institution, was part of a general reform of the criminal law, intended to undertake a new job that the masters of the county jails felt they could not handle. Visions of industrial development led its founders to think that it would largely support itself, for they looked upon it not as an inevitable expense of social disorganization, but as a school for hard labor and an investment in useful manufactures. The notion of making criminals into productive workers was sound, and so was the vision of an industrial future. But as matters turned out, neither prison officials nor the state government could bring these ideas into focus.

The County Jail and Penal Reform

The primary purpose of county jails was to hold people accused of crime lest they escape the law. Suspects were held pending indictment by a grand jury; if indicted they remained until the court met in its regular session to try their case. The indictment and trial might come at one session of the court, otherwise the case might be laid over for three or six months. The accused remained a prisoner during his trial and, if found guilty, until the sentence was executed. Witnesses were sometimes held until and during trial. Prisoners in transit and recaptured runaways were detained there.

The jail was also a convenient lockup for other dangerous or sinister characters: drunks and maniacs, unruly servants and slaves, anyone who needed discipline or, in some cases, simply help. Creditors might, on complaint, have debtors incarcerated until they paid their debts.

Security was the great problem of colonial jails. At first they were simply log cabins; a determined man could easily break out of them, especially if he had confederates. It was "the universal complaint of the sheriffs" who managed these log jails "that they were unable to keep the prisoners in, and the universal complaint by the prisoners that they would not stay in, unless the sheriff would keep the sheep out."[1] Wooden buildings were easily set afire, but men condemned to brutal punishment or death had nothing to lose, and stone structures often could not hold them.

A second problem was costs. It was unthinkable that honest men should support criminals, so, following English tradition, jail officials expected to collect fees from the prisoners, including witnesses and those proved innocent. These unfortunates remained until their fees were paid, piling up greater debt every day. If they had no money, they might beg or borrow it; if their credit was bad (and since they were not out on bail that was likely the case) they might indenture themselves to someone willing to take a chance on a jailbird as a "bargain servant." Sometimes officials would accept a promissory note; sometimes they might let the prisoner go—or bury him—and get the county to pay their fees.[2]

Both problems—security and costs—fell upon the executive officer of the county, the sheriff. He had many affairs to manage, including elections, and the jail was not his most important job. Often he appointed an assistant, or deputy, to keep it for him. There were two lines of legislation about sheriffs and jails during the eigtheenth century. One attempted to make the sheriff do his job, and suggests that his job was not very desirable; the other aimed to keep him from taking advantage of his position in the matter of fees and supplies for the prisoners.[3]

The central fact about the county jail was that prisoners were few. There are no available statistics, but the mere size of the institutions is indicative. A few rooms in the cellar constituted the provision in many counties. The jail and courthouse were not set up to supply food and drink; these were usually procured at a neighboring tavern, and it often appears that the tavern keeper and sheriff had mutual interests or were the same man—which was one reason for the deplorable drinking that went on in jails.

As the colony became more populous and civilized, the jail population rose. In a way this was good for the sheriffs, since it increased their business and their fees. In another way it was bad, since escapes became commoner, and sheriffs were personally liable for losses and damages caused in breaks. By the mid-eighteenth century a number of laws related to this situation: Two acts of 1748 fixed in detail the duties and fees of sheriffs and other officers; and numerous acts authorized counties and cities to rebuild their courthouse and jail.[4]

During the colonial period, sheriffs and local magistrates often had to take the part of the rich worthies who appointed them; sometimes they found themselves opposed to their neighbors in the rural democracy. At times there were "land riots"; occasionally crowds would raid or destroy jails to release prisoners.[5] The Revolution made the shrievality elective, however. It quickly became, and long remained, the most eagerly sought and hotly contested county political office. Sheriffs were influential in the election machinery and prominent in the office-holding class of legislators and officials who dominated public affairs until the rise of organized political parties.[6] So, while the problems of the local jail were becoming more pressing, the sheriff, who was responsible for the jail, was becoming influential in politics, and he had a definite interest in the reform of colonial criminal law and the institution of a state prison.

A second interest in a state prison was humanitarian. Its chief supporters were Quakers. William Penn had held enlightened views about prisons; the criminal laws in Pennsylvania and West Jersey were notably less cruel and more constructive than the punitive codes of the English and Puritans. But these early efforts fell under the shadow of the traditional code, by 1700 in West Jersey, by 1718 in Pennsylvania.[7] John Woolman felt a concern for the slaves, the Indians, and the poor, but penal reform did not attract his attention.

There were, however, signs of a general revulsion against the vindictiveness of the law. In England it found expression in the application of "benefit of clergy" to anyone who could read and in the transportation of convicts to the colonies. In New Jersey governors became more and more lenient in granting pardons and reprieves, especially if the prisoner enlisted for military service against the French and Indians; juries and courts frequently hesitated to demand the full legal punishment, particularly for first offenders.[8]

Patriots spoke out for the rights of man during the Revolution; respectable people who had been imprisoned then for political or military reasons sympathized with the rights of all offenders and prisoners. Soon after the peace in 1783 some citizens of Philadelphia, the new nation's largest city, organized to reform the criminal code. A law of 1786 substituted "hard labor, publicly and disgracefully imposed," for death as punishment for many felonies. The failure of public work drew attention to the jails, where prisoners were held, and in 1787 there appeared "The Philadelphia Society for Alleviating the Miseries of Public Prisons," which gave leadership in reform.[9]

The Philadelphia Society included many Quakers; Thomas Eddy, the leading reformer of New York laws and prisons, was a Friend and so were many of his associates. It is reasonable to suppose, in the absence of definite evidence, that Quaker humanitarianism supported the movement in New Jersey. But the sentiment was very general. The Philadelphia Society drew more on John Howard, the English reformer, than on William Penn; Thomas Eddy studied Beccaria, Montesquieu, and Howard as well as Penn.[10] Similar movements appeared in New England, Virginia, and Kentucky, where direct Quaker influence was negligible.

The objectives of reformers were to substitute imprisonment at hard labor for corporal punishment, to end the idleness and depravity of jailbirds, and to separate the various kinds of inmates so that the worse did not corrupt or victimize the better. In short, they wished to protect prisoners from laws, officials, and influences that made them worse, and to appeal to their better natures and their hope for a better life.

The substitution of imprisonment at hard labor for corporal punishment was humanitarian, but it did not break with existing ideas about crime. The criminology that informed both practices was a deduction from a pervasive religious heritage. The new view held, as did the old, that if men obeyed God's laws there would be no crime. Every life was a struggle between God-fearing and sinful motives. The criminal, diverted by lust and selfishness, had given way to lawless desires and hence was guilty. Legal guilt was the formality; sin, and ultimately damnation, was the substance.

Somber sermons had always pointed out that God's judgment was just, terrible, and inevitable. Popular revivalists in the eighteenth century drew lurid pictures of the severity of God's punishment. Law-abiding citizens were justified in any steps that would protect the godly here on earth and deter the sinner from ultimate damnation. If they did not teach the culprit the evil of his ways, so much the worse for him. Mutilation, branding, flogging, and death were not so terrible as eternal hell fire.

But other elements of the religious heritage modified its severity. Jesus had suspected the righteousness of the Pharisees and found virtue in the poor, the humble, the afflicted, even in outright sinners. He preached forgiveness, brotherhood, self-sacrifice, and service. He asked who should cast the first stone, and He suffered and died between common criminals. Revivalists who preached hell fire also held out the hope of widespread, even universal, salvation: the humblest sinner might be sanctified. This more cheerful side of Christianity awakened a lively response in the humble and hopeful democracy.

In this perspective, the logic of corporal punishment was dubious. The criminal was made in God's image, brother to God's other children. Should he be whipped, branded, tormented like a beast? Would Jesus flog or mutilate prisoners, or bless the mocking hilarity that accompanied degrading punishment? Traditionally, corporal punishment was too brutal for the aristocrat or gentleman; was it suitable then for a humble man? Did not the Savior ask for sympathy and forgiveness to help the suffering and correct the erring brother?

In the ideological contradiction between divine vengeance and divine mercy lay the roots of humanitarian prison reform. Pious Quakers were sensitive to the issue, but many sects were represented in the movement and there was no organized religious opposition.

The First State Prison

Such were the forces for reform when William Paterson undertook to revise and codify the criminal law of New Jersey in 1793. The new criminal code, ratified in 1796, substituted imprisonment at hard labor for offenses that hitherto had called for corporal punishment or death. Since county jails were not equipped to employ convicts and county workhouses were not intended for dangerous lawbreakers, some new institution was needed. Accordingly a state prison, near Trenton, was authorized in 1797 and opened in 1799.[11]

Inasmuch as lawmakers have often merely embalmed their humanitarian intentions in legislation, particularly when unprecedented and large public expenditures were at stake, it appears that some practical interest supported the new prison. The people who gained most from the new institution were the sheriffs and other local officials. Sheriffs gained because they no longer had to be responsible for the unpleasant business of public corporal punishment, and because they could send their most dangerous prisoners to the state institution. Technically, all convicts sentenced to more than six months were automatically sent there, but in fact the judge made the decision. Since the criminal code specified maximum penalties, the judge might fine rather than imprison, or he might keep harmless convicts at the local jail where the sheriff and other officials could continue to charge fees. Not only did the sheriff send off his most dangerous prisoners, but the state paid him for transporting the convict and for the legal costs of prosecution. So he, or his deputy, got another fee and a free trip to the state capital, the center of state-wide political activity.[12]

The founders hoped that the profits of prison labor would pay this expense in addition to the costs of maintenance and production and even of prosecution; each prisoner had an account of his particular debts and credits, with the possibility of accumulating a surplus toward his discharge. While the institution thus exacted its fiscal support from the wrong-doer, its discipline would show him the error of his ways and lead him to penitence. If not—second offenses for many crimes were punishable by death.[13] Such was the rationale of the new criminal law and the state prison. Everyone gained, no one lost, and humanity was served.

The success of the prison in realizing these hopes rested on its efficiency as a "manufactory." There was no provision for prisoners raising their own food or for employment on public works, despite the fact that Jerseymen were increasingly engaged in building roads, bridges, and turnpikes. (Convicts at Philadelphia had at first worked on the city streets, but spectators had mocked and provoked them, and the keepers were unable to maintain discipline without chaining the prisoners and threatening them with heavy weapons.)[14] Consequently, officials favored intramural manufactures of a crude sort: nail-making, "cordwaining" (leather working, especially making shoes), picking and carding wool and hair, weaving, and chairmaking. The executive officer, or principal keeper, was looked upon as primarily a businessman and plant manager; until 1820 he received a 5 percent commission on sales of prison-made goods, in addition to his regular salary ($600 a year and maintenance). His work was quite different from that of the undersheriffs and turnkeys who administered county jails, and who had only to attend to the security and maintenance of a few inmates. The keeper had a much larger institution, and he also had to oversee the employment of convicts, arrange the purchase of raw materials, and market the product of convict labor. To help him he appointed an assistant, a clerk, and three guards.[15]

The keeper's establishment dominated the physical structure of the prison. It included his living quarters, the main entrance and offices, also a kitchen, bakery, dining room, and store rooms. On either side of this central building, adjoining it to the rear, were wings which included dormitories for sixty inmates, guard rooms, and work shops. Women, segregated in one wing, were supposed to wash and cook for the prison as well as work at industrial tasks. The buildings included a chapel and an infirmary (there was a part-time physician). Behind the buildings was a yard enclosed by a twelve-foot wall. The women's wing was not completed, but in general the physical plant was like the recently built Newgate Prison in New York (although the latter was built to house 432 inmates and boasted an industrial superintendent at $1,500 a year as well as a resident principal keeper at $875).[16]

The organic law directed how prisoners were to be received and made various sanitary regulations for their protection. It limited their daily labor to eight or ten hours, depending on the season. The prison was to provide such work and compensation as would give them an incentive to earn their maintenance, plus a surplus to cover the cost of their prosecution and transportation and for their own benefit during and after confinement. Sick prisoners whose sentences had ended could demand to be kept until cured. The law allowed the governor, on recommendation of the prison authorities, to forgive debts of prisoners who had no property to attach and who were obviously unfit to earn their keep.

General supervision of the prison was the business of eight "inspectors," appointed annually by a joint session of the legislature. The inspectors did for the prison what the sheriff did for the county jail. The inspectorship was modeled on that of the New York and Philadelphia prisons; originally it was supposed to give a voice to the citizens organized for prison reform, and perhaps to give the keeper the advantage of business advice and connections. New Jersey paid the inspectors a dollar a day while on prison business. The inspectors appointed the keeper and passed all administrative regulations. They met quarterly for general policy decisions; two of them visited the prison weekly or oftener.[17]

Why the Prison Failed

The prison set up with such forethought and at such expense (£9,842, or $41,158.55) proved a failure. The keeper was often unable to find work for his charges; if he went ahead without orders he had difficulty in marketing their product. An increasing number of aged or decrepit convicts were unproductive. Most prisoners did not earn a surplus over maintenance. Accounts proved mystifying and misleading. Following the model of Philadelphia, each prisoner and each industry had a separate account, but there was no summary. Bad debts, due from prisoners or from buyers of prison goods, were carried as credits, and it was hard to appraise the value of the improvements and the inventory of unsold products. Legislative committees appointed annually to settle the accounts of the prison contemplated them with bewilderment and disappointment.[18]

Some of these problems were common to any business enterprise of the period, others were peculiar to prison conditions. The management presently discovered aggravating and ultimately insurmountable problems of discipline. The design of the prison protected the inmates from the surveillance of the guards, and the guards from the eye of the keeper, while the prisoners could easily communicate among themselves and, through windows, with the outside. The design was based on the Walnut Street jail in Philadelphia, which had been built in 1773 and was essentially a large, old-fashioned county jail converted into a place of residence and labor for dangerous prisoners. Instead of one or two large rooms in which everyone was locked up all the time, the converted prison had separate rooms for sleeping, eating, and working; but the facilities were mostly "congregate," with only a few cells set aside for isolating and disciplining troublemakers. The plan worked for a time in Philadelphia and New York, and also in New Jersey. Eighteen years passed before a legislative committee inquired into the need for more solitary cells. The first substantial addition to the original prison, in 1820, provided many cells for isolating difficult convicts.[19]

In time, the convicts, closeted in their living rooms, learned to organize gangs to exploit other prisoners and take advantage of their guards. In 1830 a committee of legislators, making a "thorough investigation," revealed a state of affairs that was obviously of long standing. A new keeper testified to "the general prevalence of insubordination and the pre-existence of a perfect familiarity and almost unrestrained intercourse among the prisoners, and between the prisoners and the assistant keepers." There was "extensive indulgence of a system of traffic, between the prisoners and their keepers, in which articles made by them, and property over which they had no control, were exchanged with the keepers, for other commodities in a secret and covert manner." Prisoners testified about a "staunch gang" of inmates who "will lie and swear to it; . . . steal provision and carry it off; . . . steal other men's provisions. . . . They have rules by which they are bound to each other; one rule is, if a man tells anything, they will fall a foul of him and beat him." [20]

Unable and often unwilling to maintain control by regular surveillance and discipline, the keepers had to resort to severe punishments. The clerk, who had been at the prison for twenty years, named ten men supposed to have died from such punishment. More than one prisoner in twelve had broken out of the prison; of these more than half escaped permanently. The prison was evidently no deterrent, but a school for crime with a high rate of recidivism.[21]

These unhappy consequences make the plans of the founders seem shortsighted indeed. The question occurs, why were they so far wrong in their calculations? The investigators of 1830 laid everything to the design of the prison. The design frustrated discipline, and lax discipline made the work inefficient. But this explanation ignores certain facts that bear upon the story. It is noteworthy that Americans were generally overoptimistic about industrial possibilities during these years, nowhere more than in New Jersey. The legislators who authorized the prison and the inspectors who supervised it at first were often identical with the capitalists who set up the ill-fated million-dollar Society for the Establishment of Useful Manufactures (SUM). Moore Furman, the merchant, was a patron of the SUM, a member of the legislature, and president of the prison's Board of Inspectors. William Paterson was governor when the state gave the SUM its marvelous charter and invested state funds in its stock (the Society named the site of its mills Paterson, the forerunner of the present city). The prison cost less than a quarter as much as the bridge over the Delaware at Trenton, which was built shortly afterward. In this expansive atmosphere the industrial employment of prisoners seemed a sound state investment.[22]

Moreover, there was a certain plausible early success in manufacture. In 1804 Moore Furman, then president of the Board of Inspectors, made an unusually detailed report answering specific questions about the prison management. Neither questions nor answers suggest any criticism of the institution or any possible improvements.[23] During the embargo the prison sold its inventory and it made a considerable profit for several years. A committee headed by the critical-minded James Parker in 1812 noted that the large losses of the first five years arose because relatively few people were employed and the staff was unacquainted with the work; the following year there was a loss because, Parker said, some prisoners, unable to earn a living, were actually paupers maintained by the state. In 1812 Henry Bellerjeau, who had served the prison as assistant keeper from 1798 and keeper from 1804, resigned to become a director of the Trenton Banking Company.[24]

There was reason still to believe, after fifteen years, that the prison might be solvent. The long-run failure of prison industry came after the War of 1812. The embargo and the war, which helped the prison, were a much greater stimulus to private industry; when peace came the competition of British manufactures and the depression bankrupted many private businesses. Under these conditions the prison needed extraordinary leadership merely to hold its own.

But it was about this time that serious disciplinary problems arose. To some extent these resulted from crowding; inmate population, under seventy during the first decade, reached 112 by 1818. The inspectors were by then looking for means to reduce it; they asked that courts send no convicts for less than a year, and that they, the inspectors, be given authority to pardon prisoners whose sentences expired before they had earned their maintenance and costs. The fact was, inspectors said, that the institution had to pay large costs for prisoners it received, which it was unable to recover from them.[25]

A new building in 1820 took care of the overcrowding. In any case population declined to fifty-six in 1825; when the legislative committee drew up its critical report of 1830, there were only ninety inmates. The discipline problem of that year did not, therefore, arise simply from the design or from overcrowding. Eight of the ten deaths from punishment occurred after 1820. Part of the problem, certainly, was that the staff was less able or less interested than in earlier days. Far from giving the prison better leadership, the personnel was getting worse.

In short, when the committee of 1830 laid the problem to the architectural design, it ignored three other significant aspects of the administration. First, the prison continued to pay local officials for the cost of trial and transportation even when it was clear that the prisoners would not be able to pay back this sum. These charges were a considerable portion of prison "losses." Second, it would have taken resourceful leadership and staff to make prison industries profitable in any layout. Third, the system of inspection and reporting was at fault, since there was no indication of serious trouble in the regular reports.

What this adds up to is politics, for local officials profited from charging the cost of transportation to the state prison, and local officials, represented in the legislature, chose the keeper and the inspectors. But to have criticized any of these points would have laid the blame on the legislature itself. There was, moreover, a substantial argument in the committee's favor. There were prisons that maintained good discipline and paid their way. This fact was brought home to the committee by the Reverend Louis Dwight, secretary of the Boston Prison Discipline Society, whose help the committee publicly acknowledged. It is clear that Dwight told them what to look for, if not what to find.

Theories of Prison Discipline

A dedicated man who made himself a leading authority on prisons, Dwight advocated a mode of discipline called the "Auburn system," after the New York prison where it took form. Officials there thought that it was essential to prevent inmates from organizing for mischief by keeping them each in a separate cell. The trouble with existing prisons, they said, was that they retained the congregate living rooms of the old jails. But mere solitary confinement was expensive and bad for the inmates' health, and it much reduced the efficiency of their labor. So working and eating continued as "congregate" activities, but only under conditions of strict silence. Hard work and perpetual silence were the features of the system. Dwight wrote about the Auburn prison in 1826, three years after its opening.

> The unremitted industry, the entire subordination, and subdued feeling among the convicts, has probably no parallel. In their solitary cells, they spend the night with no other book than the Bible, and at sunrise they proceed in military order, under the eye of the turnkey, in solid columns, with the lock march to the workshops, thence in the same order at the hour of breakfast to the common hall, where they partake of their wholesome and frugal meal in silence. Not even a whisper might be heard through the whole apartment.

The "lock march," or lockstep, meant that prisoners walked with one hand on the shoulder of the preceding convict, all heads turned toward the guard. Convicts ate in silence, usually all facing in the same direction; they gave hand signals to waiters. At the ringing of a bell "of the softest sound" the men rose and marched back to the workshops. "There is the most perfect attention to business from morning till night, interrupted only by the time necessary to dine—and never by the fact that the whole body of prisoners have done their tasks and the time is now their own, and they can do as they please." [26] Those who got out of step or line, turned their heads, or whispered were whipped, put in solitary, or otherwise punished. Terror made the system work.[27]

This satisfying spectacle of regimented and terrorized convicts gave moral justification to the important observation that prisons conducted in this fashion were profitable. The committee of 1830 noted that the new prison at Wethersfield, Connecticut, had saved the state enough money in three years to pay the cost of its construction.[28]

Later committees and governors called for a new prison, like Auburn or Wethersfield. They showed no interest in the county jails or in abandoning a state prison entirely. What was wrong with the penal system, they assumed, was buildings and discipline—in short, prisons and prisoners—and the solution lay in a new departure. But by 1833 a second and different system of prison discipline had won strong support. This was the "Pennsylvania" or "separate" system. Its warmest advocates were Quakers and other reformers around Philadelphia, who carried the tradition of the first prison reform society. They had won their case with the Pennsylvania legislators. The great institution at Cherry Hill, near Philadelphia, opened in 1829, was their star exhibit.[29]

The principle of the separate system was complete separation, or isolation, of the inmates from each other. Like the Auburn or silent system, it was supposed to end the bad associations and influences of congregate living. In both systems prisoners slept in individual cells, but the Auburn system allowed congregated labor, which its principle of silence rendered harmless and efficient. The separate system was more radical; prisoners lived and worked in isolation in their cells. Therefore, individual cells had to be much larger and better equipped than in Auburn-type prisons, and the building had to be larger and more expensive.

By 1833 proponents of the separate plan had won over New Jersey legislators; a committee that year decided against the system of Auburn and for the system of Cherry Hill. The separate system was less brutal, the committee said, because it offered no occasion for flogging or other corporal punishment of the sort that already had disgraced Auburn. It was more deterrent because it made the inmate confront his guilt. In *"solitude,"* the committee observed, "the mind of man is necessarily cast upon itself." The convict surveys "his life . . . with a scrutiny that it never encountered before." Conscious that escape is hopeless, "he continues the unwelcome task of self-examination, till his obduracy is subdued." [30]

Opponents of the system argued that the severity was too great. Solitary confinement was a fearsome punishment in ordinary prisons; as a permanent condition it would be debilitating and maddening. But, it was answered, the convict did talk to people—the guard who brought his food, the warden, the "moral instructor" or clergyman, the teacher, the trade instructor who supervised his labor, the inspectors, his county sheriff, who visited when he brought new convicts, and so forth. Moreover, these associations were all beneficial, directed toward moral improvement.

Preaching was particularly effective: "If any circumstances can be imagined, calculated to impress the warning, the encouragements, the threats and hopes of religion on the mind," the committee said, "it must surely be those of the convict in his cell." There he hears "the voice which must come to him as it were from the other world," telling him "of God, of eternity, of future reward and future punishment." These instructions may "frequently discover to the guilty tenant . . . what seems often not to have occurred to him," that "he has a spiritual nature." This discovery "alone may and does effect a great change in a man's whole character." The guilty man feels that he is "a being superior to what he had thought himself"; his new self-respect awakens a new ambition to improve, which the mild and helpful associations can encourage.[31]

While separate labor is generally less efficient than congregate labor, the committee continued, the isolated prisoner works with "avidity . . . to alleviate his solitude." Experience has shown that to deprive him of work is a severe punishment; if the warden also darkens his cell, the "most hardy . . . prisoner has been found broken down in his spirit, begging for his work and his Bible to beguile the tedium of absolute idleness in solitude." Evidence indicated that most prisoners working in isolation could earn their maintenance, and the committee was willing to ignore the economic advantage of congregate labor. Their object was not merely to convert "a penitentiary into a manufactory." They thought convict labor was "simply a mean, dictated by the wisest benevolence, for the health of [the convict's] moral and physical powers." A penal system should promote reform, the "best good of the convict and that of . . . society," whatever "labour and profit be lost." [32]

For a generation, "humanitarian reformers" debated which kind of grim monastery was most salubrious and which mode of brainwashing would best convert the guilty. Well-meaning people took sides with incredible zeal; they bitterly accused one another of misrepresentation and falsehood. Always the focus was on the system. The Pennsylvania or separate system had the better argument in the abstract, and appealed to a more humanitarian sentiment. The New Jersey Prison Instruction Society, organized in 1833 to encourage Sunday schools and good preaching in the prisons of the state, was evidently inspired by Louis Dwight but swung over to the Pennsylvania system. European travelers, like Beaumont and Tocqueville, favored it; so did Dorothea Dix, in her *Remarks on Prisons and Prison Discipline* (1845).

The Second State Prison

Somewhat to their credit, New Jersey legislators, given a choice between economy and reform, chose reform. A new state prison, designed by the architect of Cherry Hill, was authorized in 1833 and opened in 1836. It is still in use. Originally a central building which housed the keeper and various service rooms opened into a large circular observatory, from which two cell blocks radiated in a large V. The cells rose in two stories along a central corridor fourteen feet wide. Individual cells measured twelve feet by seven and one-half feet. Each had running water and a toilet. Its opening to the world—to the corridor—was a heavy double door, wood sheathed with iron, which had a small hole for observation.[33]

Hopes ran high for the new prison. Governor Vroom in 1834 did not doubt that when completed it would be the most perfect in the nation. The state should not expect it to be a source of profit, he said, but only to meet expenses. In 1836 Joseph Yard, a Methodist clergyman, secretary of the New Jersey Prison Instruction Society, became warden and supervised the transfer. "I had for some years past been in the habit of visiting the prisons . . . for religious instruction," he wrote to a friend after he had been in office for seventeen months. "In that capacity I acquired but very little knowledge of a prison, or its proper discipline. . . . I have had . . . everything to learn." He thought the new system was a decisive improvement over the old. Religious instruction was more effective "where every prisoner . . . can distinctly hear the minister without seeing him or being seen by . . . other [prisoners]." Prisoners give less trouble and need less punishment. "In my office as Warden, I have sometimes had my temper and patience put to a severe trial, by the most refractory and intractable offenders, some of whom could only be subdued by force; but with the spirit of a christian, with no other instrument than the gospel of peace, I have succeeded in reducing others to perfect subjection." The warden did not think that "hard usage" ever reformed anyone; he believed that of his 139 charges "about forty . . . appear to be determined to lead a new life; they are, I believe, as sincere as the pious who visit them; but how strong their resolutions may be when exposed to temptation, I cannot tell." [34]

The inspectors were also enthusiastic. In its first year the prison earned $1,741.41 over its expenses, including the salaries of officers, compared with a loss of $1,352.31 during the last year of congregate work. But even more impressive was its reformatory effect. The convict's isolation "affords the keeper the very best opportunity to study . . . his character and . . . propensities, and to regulate . . . treatment . . . accordingly." Sooner or later "the 'monitor' placed within [the convict] will speak. In proof of this, we have witnessed (in a visit . . . but a few days since), the powerful athletic frame tremble in agony, and the big pearly drops steal down the manly cheek, whilst the conscience-stricken convict . . . related to us his first departure from the path of duty, in 'despising a mother's advice,' and 'disregarding a father's authority'; and this, the small commencement of a career of crime, which has terminated in the lonely cell of a prison." [35]

Pious visitors, thoughtful warden, sobbing convict, "monitor within": such were the happy days at the prison, when "benign and gracious Providence" was pointing the way to the finest penal system known to "civilized society." The sad days came quickly. The architect underestimated costs: he had estimated $150,000 for three hundred cells; the legislature allowed, at first, $130,000; in 1837, with only two of five blocks completed, the cost was $193,012, and less than two hundred cells were in use.[36] Clearly, the legislature had to cut some corners. The Cherry Hill prison had small exercise yards opening from each cell, but Trenton did not; Cherry Hill provided regular paid moral instruction, but Trenton relied, as in the past, on volunteer preaching and visiting.

The effect of these omissions on body and spirit soon became evident. By 1839 the prison physician noticed that convicts, who never got into the sun, were very pale and showed unusual glandular developments; they showed a marked weakening of "muscular fiber" and a languid will. Prisoners were, literally, marked men. Even worse were the mental effects. Prisoners "indulge in the amusements of the child, wasting their time, after the daily task is over, upon toys," observed the physician in 1839, "engaged in no thought that is not immediately associated with the things about them." If they show any abstract reflection, "it is more the wandering of a visionary, than the operation of a well-balanced mind." There were "many cases of insanity"; the doctor traced those which developed in prison to "onanism," a frequent problem. These sad results usually appeared within a year of confinement, despite benevolent management. "Were another course pursued, and the superintendent possessed of no sympathy for the convict, in less than a year the . . . prison would be a bedlam." [37] The doctor was strengthened in these observations by deductions from phrenology, and George Combe, the master phrenologist, quoted them to mutual satisfaction in his *Moral Philosophy*.[38]

A new group of inspectors reported in 1840 that the prison showed a deficit, as it had every year after 1837. This was partly because of the depression, they said, but they thought prison industry, particularly marketing, needed a special manager, apart from the keeper; as it was, "either the money interest, or the discipline must be neglected." As for the discipline, they thought that "the solitary system is the best," but they said that "this system cannot . . . produce the unnatural results that have frequently been claimed." They could report "but few known changes for the better among the convicts"; in some instances convicts who "were received young, and for crimes the result of rash propensities," who showed "good conduct while in prison," left prison only to commit "crimes that evince a settled depravity."

The inspectors complained that they had to receive lunatics, who were "subversive of all system"; they supported the physician's report on the convicts' physical and mental health. Sentences were too long for the system, they said. "Ten years confinement . . . would be a terrible punishment"; experience made them doubt "whether the best constitution could endure that term, without being seriously injured, if not completely destroyed." The prison was then four years old.[39]

The obeisance to a system grew perfunctory and a concern for suffering convicts led to many changes. In 1841 the physician said that he had helped prisoners who were predisposed by masturbation to insanity, by putting a second convict in the cell and by "prescribing tobacco," the "best remedy for those suffering under despondency." He confessed that he allowed more tobacco than the law permitted, but he did not think it should be withheld. "Many cases" showed "its certain utility" in preventing madness.

Perhaps tobacco-chewing or pipe-smoking helped kill the awful stink of the cells. They were heated by a hot water pipe an inch and a half in diameter and had vents in the outer wall, but at best the air moved little, and in cold weather prisoners closed the vents. When the doctor turned inmates "suffering from want of air" into the yard for a few hours a day, he noted that they "gained in health and strength rapidly" from this indulgence.[40]

Within a few years partisans of the separate system in New Jersey were on the defensive. The prison was not a fair test because prisoners did not get the separation, the appropriate exercise, or the moral instruction the theory called for. "The best advantages of the system are not . . . fully possessed here," Dorothea Dix wrote in 1845. "There is less attention to suitable instruction than can in any way be excused or accounted for. Heretofore the inspectors have given apparently little thought or influence to the subject, confining their attention to the general direction of the prison and to financial concerns." [41]

Miss Dix did not at that time find the prisoners notably debilitated, but she thought the discipline was uneven—both observations pointing to a relaxation of the original discipline.[42] In 1845 there were more convicts than cells, so double and triple occupancy became necessary. There was no strong effort to restore the original principle. In 1848 the legislature provided for a moral instructor, the Reverend Samuel Starr; he became the moving spirit of the New Jersey Prison Reform Association, organized in 1849. The Association was mild in criticizing the state prison; in 1852 it observed that nearly thirty cells had double occupancy and prisoners had found ways to communicate between the other cells, "thus violating the very principle" of the discipline; it also noted that in the severe winter of 1851–1852 several prisoners "had been frosted in their hands and feet," which not only soured their dispositions but disabled them from manual labor. "In all other respects," however, the situation was "what justice and humanity require." [43]

The real interest of the Prison Reform Association lay elsewhere; it was very critical of the county jails, which its members inspected, and it wanted a separate institution for youthful offenders. *"Youth"* and *"manhood"* were obviously different, the reformers said, and *youth* needed "gentler measures" of punishment and reformation than "the hardened adult"—something like "a school or asylum rather than a place of ultimate punishment." The reformers also tried to help discharged prisoners find employment.[44]

Nothing came of these ideas. Legislators did not enlarge the prison until 1860; county officials did not reform the jails; and discharged convicts found little help. In 1850 the state began work on a "House of Refuge" for juveniles, but the project stirred so much opposition that the legislature abandoned it in 1853, after which the New Jersey Prison Reform Association ceased its annual reports, and doubtless its activity.[45]

Meanwhile the prison piled up deficits; in 1857 Governor Rodman Price called it a complete failure, inhumane in its discipline, unable to reform, more expensive even than "the old system of the workhouse." He asked that the officials establish congregate workshops, like those of the Auburn system; these would be more productive than work in the cells. A committee responded that the separate system was superior in principle, and made a strong defense of it. They did not defend its practice in New Jersey, where "parsimonious appropriations" compromised its operation; they asked that the state erect a new cell wing on the Pennsylvania plan and a new hospital.[46]

In accounting for the prison's failure, the committee stated explicitly and at length a theme which other observers had suggested before and which men would elaborate for almost a century: The "greatest evil" in the management of the prison was politics. The "great qualification" for the keeper, the committee said, was his "political tenets," not "the fitness . . . requisite for an office in which so much depends upon its executive." [47]

In short, between 1830, when legislators noted the failure of the first state prison, and 1857, when they conceded the failure of the second, men recognized a new factor in prison administration, the "greatest evil," politics. The evidence of increasing political influence is not spelled out in official documents about the prison, but many events make sense if they are related to political motives.

Politics and the Prison

The spoils system held the attention of legislators in 1857. The practice of rewarding party service with government jobs was a function of political organization, and it is a notable coincidence that the failure of the first state prison and the sad history of the second were contemporary with the rise of organized parties. In general, these parties, as they developed in the 1820's, were coalitions of local political clubs largely for the purpose of influencing the appointment of state officials. Under the constitution of 1776, the legislature appointed *most* state officials; consequently more was at stake than merely the selection of the prison keeper and his assistants.

What was new in the parties of the 1830's was organized and persistent competition in local elections. In the generation after the Revolution there were often rival candidates in local elections, but they arose from the ambitions and contention of local families, cliques, and factions. There were no established groups of "outs" and "ins"; there were individuals who held office and others who wanted office. This was the nature of the "office-holding class" and its rivals for well over a generation. General conflicts of interest, class conflicts, were realized in disagreement between localities, rather than within localities.

But great forces were working to change the character of politics. The largest social needs and most exciting business speculations of the early nineteenth century were banking and transportation; banks, turnpikes, canals, and railroads needed charters from the state legislature. Groups of capitalists, competing for its favors, became interested in its membership. Politicians discovered that they had powers undreamed of in the colonial days, and power gave a special prestige to fellowship in the local political club. Many local clubs and societies gave form in this period to a desire to join, to associate for mutual benefit—the reformers' associations were examples—but of them all the political club was perhaps the most interesting and lucrative. Inexpensive printing and a growing number of local newspapers amplified and spread these organized interests, especially the political. As men took sides, they often discovered that grave issues dignified their contests: majority rule, minority rights, aristocracy, democracy, executive tyranny, monopoly—these were subjects that men came to debate as they appealed for votes.[48]

Political partisanship—political participation—was, therefore, no mere joust for office, not merely a matter of calculated self-interest. It was friendship, loyalty, and dedication to great ends. It was a caucus, a handshake, a parade, and a gamble. The party was a team. The spoils system was an instrument of team spirit.

Between 1830 and 1832 Jersey legislators enacted laws which polarized their politics for forty years. They chartered a group of capitalists to build a railroad between Camden and Perth Amboy. These towns were not impressive centers of commerce, but in fact the route linked Philadelphia and New York—and the corporation was given a monopoly of railroad traffic between them. In return the company guaranteed the state an annual payment of $30,000, more than enough to pay its operating expenses, on 2,000 shares of stock, which promised sizable additional dividends and a rapid appreciation in value.[49]

Railroading was a risky business, but in this case the company and the state government profited handsomely by the arrangement. Its success introduced a great complication into state politics, since the company had a vested interest with wide ramifications. It was aggressor or defender in all sorts of legislative actions. The net result was to raise the ante for playing politics and to increase the importance of party management.

Meanwhile, the slow increase of municipal and county functions in the establishment of almshouses, the rebuilding of courthouses and jails, and the development of roads, for example, gave parties a larger stake in local affairs. Neighborhood interests and organizations, the building blocks of statewide parties, were important in their own right. Local political leaders accordingly wanted respectful consideration of the sensibilities and interests of their constituents and a fair share in the disposal of whatever perquisites the statewide organization could offer them.

It was a sign of the times when the legislature, revising the criminal code and related laws in 1829, took upon itself the appointment of the principal keeper of the prison, as well as the appointment of prison inspectors. (It reduced the number of inspectors to five, but increased their compensation to $1.50 a day while on prison business.)[50] The appointments were annual; after 1840 there began the frequent changes of administration which the committee of 1857 criticized. These not only broke the continuity of management, but also led to a neglect of the work; when the committee of 1857 reported, officials were spending as much as three months a year working for their reappointment.

Changes in political life, summarized then as the progress of democracy, led to a constitutional reorganization in 1844. This hardly touched the prison directly, although the new constitution mentioned the office of keeper in a way that would complicate matters years later. Indirectly it enshrined the autonomy of local party officials.

One evidence of local interests appeared in the history of the Prison Reform Association of 1849–1852. The Association began its work with frank criticism of the jails, which were under political control, and local officials opposed and finally defeated the Association's effort to establish a juvenile reformatory or "House of Refuge" in 1850–1852. The arguments against the House of Refuge were inconsistent: A hostile committee of the legislature put the cost at $100,000, a large advance upon the estimates, which ranged from $42,000 to $72,000, and said that this expense would lay equally upon citizens of all counties, regardless of how much they used the institution.

The committee suggested that the several counties, separately or together, build appropriate institutions. In this way "counties which have few or no juvenile offenders . . . would not have to contribute for those which have"; moreover, the expenses of transportation would be less, "officials in the immediate neighborhood of the offenders" could provide a better-adapted "mode of treatment," and "the expenditure drawn from the pockets of the people of the counties would, in a measure, be restored by its outlay among themselves."

Furthermore, although the state revenue promised to be more than adequate to support a juvenile reformatory, it might better be used to support free schools in the local communities. "Shall it be said that the income of the state is not sufficient to satisfy this just demand [for free schools] . . . whilst [the legislature] authorizes the expenditure . . . in a manner not asked for by the people?" If the state did invest its revenue in free schools, "the necessity of a House of Refuge would be much diminished, if it not be rendered entirely unnecessary." [51] Whatever the merit of these arguments—the question rose again in 1864—it is clear that local officials were the heart of the opposition and that, as usual, they had their way.

Meanwhile, a new interest began to exert political influence in the conduct of the prison: capitalists who thought it profitable to employ prison labor. The original plan to employ convicts envisioned the keeper as a sort of business manager organizing production of goods for sale in the open market. This arrangement, later called the "public account" system, placed great reliance on the keeper, who had to be a salesman and bill collector as well as an industrial manager and disciplinarian.

This was asking too much, and the inspectors, who set these policies, began after 1820 to contract for convict labor with entrepreneurs who would provide the materials and buy the products at a set price per piece. This "piece-price" system had the advantage that the contractor took the business risks and left the keeper free to attend to prison management. Its disadvantages were that contractors offered very low wages for prison labor, and, when business was bad, simply did not supply materials. As a result, earnings were low and intermittent. Well-drawn contracts would have made contractors liable if they did not supply work and thus wasted convict labor time. The legislative investigation of 1830 observed that poor contracts, along with poor oversight, were "evils demanding a speedy remedy." [52]

When the new prison opened, the old-fashioned congregate workshops were perforce eliminated, and the inspectors seem to have returned to the public account system. Ideally the new discipline required close industrial supervision; the instructor was an important influence in the convict's life. In fact, it was hard to employ good supervisors as deputy keepers, and difficult to oversee the work of so many scattered individuals; in any case the old problems of business management, marketing and bad debts reasserted themselves, especially during the depression of 1837–1840. In 1841 the inspectors reverted to the piece-price system, which worked reasonably well for a decade while the market for convict labor was better. (During this period the Auburn-type prisons were very profitable.)[53]

Then a decline set in, as overcrowding and the spoils system weakened discipline and cut down efficiency. In 1856 a loss of $18,322 was an occasion for criticism. Governors complained regardless of party. In 1858 the legislature authorized the establishment of congregate workshops, but none was built. In 1859 the governor advised building workshops and allowing contractors to operate them. The next year he reported that *the contractors themselves had built some workshops in the prison yard* and the inspectors said that even this partial employment of congregate labor had more than paid the cost of maintaining the prisoners. Then the legislature appropriated sums totaling over $19,000 for building workshops, and the prison went practically on the Auburn plan.[54]

The crucial fact about this development is that contractors saw profits in employing convict labor; it was in their interest that congregate workshops were established—otherwise they would neither have built any on their own initiative nor offered profitable contracts to the inspectors. Certainly the spoils system did not diminish in the years 1857–1861, when the new Republican Party first came into power in New Jersey. What changed was the market for prison labor, in the eyes of potential contractors.

By 1861 the great experiment with the separate system was abandoned. The change to congregate labor was said to benefit the prisoners, who had suffered, mentally and physically, from isolation. It was said to be more productive than the labor of separate convicts, which it probably was. In fact, however, the new order helped the prison administration more than the convicts: it got prisoners out of the overcrowded cells, where they could not have worked if they had wanted to; it gave them something to do; it removed the necessity of asking for large new expenditures to make the old system work, and it allowed management (for a time) to show good returns on the work. Above all it profited the contractors who employed the prisoners, and the politicians who could influence the letting of contracts and the employment of new personnel, who were hired rapidly as the institution made money. A committee investigating prison scandals in 1869 was more outspoken about the evils of politics than was the committee of 1857.[55]

And yet there was a fog around the development; the historian of the prison noted that "as late as 1868 . . . officials were scarcely aware that there had been a change of systems" and official reports indicated "a haphazard and slovenly attitude" toward administration.[56] Between the crises of 1830 and 1857 it was disorganized by social changes which would have swamped any system of discipline and industry. At best its importance was much diminished in the public eye. Between 1797 and 1829 the prison accounted for over a third of the total cost of state government; until the Civil War it was the most prominent item of state administration. The edifice completed in 1836 was a great expense, but it cost under $200,000; by 1840 the Camden and Amboy Railroad Corporation alone had invested well over $3 million in facilities. By 1861, when the contractors prevailed upon the legislature to put up $19,000 for new workshops, the investment of the Camden and Amboy was some $10 million, and it had been the patron of dutiful politicians for decades, during which time there was no state tax at all.[57] In this situation the gain or loss of a few thousands was hardly a matter of concern unless something else was at stake—an election, a contract, or a job. Everybody won, nobody lost, and party government was served.

But the signs were foreboding. In the prison crisis of the 1830's, something was done: there was discussion, debate, action—a new prison, a bold experiment. After 1856, when there was a crisis, very little was done: one system ended, another began, but no one seemed to know or care. The trouble now was "politics," and it would get worse before it improved. After the Civil War, reformers practically wrote off the old prison. They forgot the great debate about systems of prison discipline. They put their faith in different institutions, organized—it was hoped—on different principles.

3

The State and the Mentally Disordered, Before 1872

New Jersey was later than neighboring states in building public institutions for the mentally ill and retarded, perhaps because it had no metropolis where problems and professional interest concentrated. Until 1848 its provision for "lunaticks," idiots, and imbeciles was unspecialized in the rural pattern; cases were handled by analogy with normal people who were somehow dependent, like paupers and orphans, or dangerous, like thieves and murderers. The "asylum" it established then was a new departure in organization—it had an unpaid board of managers, like a private hospital, which was intended to protect it from spoilsmen—and its original purpose was cure rather than custody. But by 1872, when county asylums appeared, its mission was indefinite. The state institution helped a minority of the mentally ill who needed care; for the host of mentally deficient there was no institution at all.

The Feeble-minded in Rural Society

There was—and still is—a large practical problem about specialized provision: it is difficult to define abnormal or deviant behavior. Common sense calls so much ordinary activity "crazy" and "foolish" that it is hard to decide where pathology begins. Conspicuously stupid or bizarre behavior may indicate either mental deficiency or mental illness. In 1764 the eminent New Jersey lawyer James Parker, whose *Conductor Generalis* gave practical advice to rural justices for decades, noted that "*Non compos mentis* is of four kinds": First, idiots, "who are of *non sane* memory from their nativity, by a perpetual infirmity"; second, people who are born normal but "lose their memory and understanding by a visitation of God, as by sickness, or other accidents"; third, "Lunaticks [,] who sometimes have their understanding and sometimes not"; and finally "Drunkards [,] who by their own vicious act for a time deprive themselves of their memory and understanding." [1]

Philosophical Jerseymen learned from John Locke, who was a physician and educator, among other things, that "the difference between Idiots and Madmen" is that "Madmen put wrong ideas together, and so make wrong propositions, but argue and reason right from them; but idiots make very few or no propositions, and reason scarce at all." [2] Physicians distinguished "amentia," the absence of normal mental powers, and "dementia," the derangement of normal mental powers.

All definitions pointed to a fact of practical importance: the mentally retarded child suffered a primordial handicap, like congenital blindness or deformity; he required special consideration from early years. The suspicion that the child was different arose in the family, but it is hard to find documents that describe the dawn of recognition. Often, parents and their advisers did not know what was happening; usually their understanding was shaped by shame, guilt, fear, and desperately unrealistic denial.

Dr. Edouard Seguin, in his classic treatise *Idiocy* (1846), described the situation as it appeared to a sympathetic and clinically minded physician. Sometimes one could distinguish idiocy at birth, he said, by the "monstrous shape" of the head. But sometimes months passed before casual observers recognized "the head hanging back, or rolling on the pillow automatically; the eyes unlighted and playing the pendulum in their sockets, fixed, or upward and sideways." Sometimes the infant fell into coma or had convulsions. Gradually matters became plain: "a continuance of the isolation and helplessness of babyhood under ampler forms and obsolete proportions . . . a sickening sight indeed." [3]

Besides "the confirmed idiot" the doctor recognized a much more numerous group who by degrees approached ordinary physical, mental, and moral powers. The most difficult was the "imbecile," who had no muscular or sensory deficiency (unless induced by "self-abuse"). He lacked "the gentleness, . . . the timidity, the obedience, the affection" of the confirmed idiot; he was "self-confident, half-witted, and ready to receive immoral impressions, satisfactory to his intense egotism." Another type developed outward symptoms of idiocy in later life and then got worse; others suffered a sort of "incipient insanity." [4]

Whatever parents saw, they had no Dr. Seguin to advise them. If they had turned to a local physician, he was likely to observe that whereas insanity might be treated, idiocy and imbecility were not illnesses and not his business. If the child could attend school, his teachers tried to communicate a rote knowledge; the schools were too haphazard to provide formally for bright or dull students. Discipline, not understanding, was the purpose of primary education. If parents turned to a clergyman, he could have sifted his library and found only scattered references to the problem. Traditionally, religious thinkers had seen the retarded in two opposite ways, as special children of God or as children of the Devil, punishment for sin. Both attitudes were plausible and might shape parents' views. In either case the practical conclusion was the same: the retarded child was a sign of God's providence, a special obligation laid upon them.[5]

Whichever way they turned, parents were thrown back on their own resources, if indeed they ever looked beyond them. Experts today think that perhaps 1 percent of all babies are severely retarded, and another 2 percent are distinctly handicapped. A proportion of babies born on the isolated farms must have been "nonambulatory," but one can only imagine their fate. For the higher types a practical solution was not impossible. The problems of normal infancy and childhood were well recognized, and the retarded child of middle or high grade in a way prolonged these stages of his growth. Under favorable conditions he might find in the family a sort of life like the "farm colony" which later seized the imagination of reformers. On the other hand it was difficult for parents to protect normal children from open fires, dangerous tools and weapons, and ornery beasts, to keep them from wandering or running off to the woods or another settlement. A retarded child faced prolonged and aggravated risks.

Thus, even where there were understanding and favorable circumstances, mere survival was dubious. Where there was no understanding, a neglected and overgrown child could easily slip away. Sooner or later, at best, the responsible family would break up and the child would have to find some new arrangement.

At this point public policy came into play. If the child's family had property, he was a legal heir. Whether a will provided for him or not, he was legally like an orphan. He became, technically, the ward of the chancellor, who was supposed to protect the orphan—to see that he was cared for out of the estate—and, since the idiot could not make a will, to see that his survivors received their appropriate inheritance. In fact the chancellor (until 1844 the governor himself) delegated the work of investigation, appointment of a guardian, and supervision to the "ordinary," the judge of probate in the county court, who was simply a county judge acting in a special capacity. All these officers collected fees for their services.[6]

Most people who were mentally deficient came to public attention as neglected children or vagrants falling under the poor and vagrancy laws. In practice, a citizen or constable brought them to the attention of the local justice of the peace, who wanted to learn three things: Were they dangerous? Were they responsible for their acts? If not, what persons or jurisdictions were responsible for them? On the basis of his findings he might commit the person to a jail, if dangerous, or to overseers of the poor or relatives, with or without restraint, with or without charge to the person or his relative (actually two justices had to sign the order). In cases where the person in question was disorderly and destructive, plaintiffs might enter civil suits, for damages, against idiots, but there was no criminal prosecution. Drunkards were criminally liable, and lunatics might be, depending on their sanity at the time.[7]

The law and the tenor of administration clearly intended to relieve normal people from the vagaries of the afflicted person, so that they would not pay taxes to support him, or lose their inheritance by his indiscretion, or suffer damage by his acts. Doubtless the high-grade retarded could find an inconspicuous place more easily in a rural society than in cities. Some got help in the out-of-state training schools for blind, deaf, and dumb which the state began to patronize in 1821. The others remained a burden of hopeless grief and mystification to their families, or they joined the motley parade of vagrants and presently came to the poor farm or almshouse or jail, depending on their luck. Dorothea Dix extended her sympathy to them, as to the criminals and insane, and she included them in her reports on suffering. But the founders of the New Jersey State Lunatic Asylum were quick to exclude those that they could distinguish.[8] They hoped to cure people; they did not feel that they could cure idiocy, any more than teachers felt that they could instruct it. On all sides the case was hopeless. And so just men punished the innocent and good men passed by the afflicted.

Changing Ideas about Insanity

As a practical matter, people identified the lunatic by his obvious delusions and hallucinations, bizarre beliefs and visions. Madmen were mysterious because at times they seemed to be normal (the word lunatic points to the phases of their affliction); at other times their behavior was bestial; but sometimes the strange moods and ideas came when they showed a penetrating insight which was akin to genius. The insane appeared to be superhuman or subhuman, in a word, "possessed." The Bible testified that an unholy demon or a holy spirit could enter people's bodies; such possession was an everyday fact of religious revivals.

In any case, the enduring attitudes of those who had to deal with recognized madmen were fear, suspicion, and impatience. The horror stories of cruelty and neglect that recur in every period of this history stemmed from these attitudes. Usually the lunatic's family first undertook his care, but whereas the retarded were often tractable and manageable, the insane were often noisy, difficult, and violent. When the family could not provide, public authorities had to step in. *Conductor Generalis* made the fear and suspicion explicit: "Any person may justify confining and beating his friend being mad," Judge Parker observed; vagrants who were "furiously mad" and dangerous might be confined as seemed suitable, by chains if necessary. Since lunatics were not liable to criminal process, wrongdoers might plead insanity to escape justice, and it was up to the judges and sheriff to determine whether they were feigning.[9]

Violent and dangerous cases were put in jails. (Often the acts of the insane were criminal for normal men.) Others were confined for their own safety. Those who were harmless but dependent or nuisances were treated as paupers and vagrants.

Keepers of the insane quickly learned that their wards would rebuff, misinterpret, or cunningly use attempts to help them. Lunatics might hurt themselves or others; they would certainly bother others, if they got the chance. Their caretakers had, therefore, to keep them out of harm's way and trouble, where their excitements and manners would least annoy and offend others. It was unpleasant enough to watch over ordinary criminals and paupers; the insane were an extra and trying burden, and it was unthinkable, usually, to do more than one had to for them. Their caretakers were handed a task which is perhaps the most trying and least rewarding in the world for anyone without trained understanding and sympathetic skill.

The central question for the caretakers, accordingly, was, simply, what had to be done. The answer was that their wards needed food, shelter, and restraint. If possible it was well that they be isolated, neither distracted by nor distracting others. Hence the locked rooms, cages, dungeons, and chains (they could cut or bite through ropes). The insane might be kept clean and comfortable, if they behaved themselves. Often, however, they seemed to prefer offensive talk and habits, and they considered their keepers to be tyrants and villains. Then their care became harsh and cruel and their miseries increased. Their treatment in the poor farms, almshouses, and jails was dictated by the convenience and protection of normal people.

The move to improve the lot of the insane in New Jersey came primarily from physicians. If insanity was an illness, like a fever, which it sometimes resembled, it might be treated. The insane were not, in this view, possessed, and they were like patients, not paupers or criminals. Benjamin Rush, the eminent Philadelphia practitioner and teacher, gave a focus and direction to this interest in the decades around 1800. Humane and intelligent as he was, this "father of American psychiatry" looked for the physical or material conditions of mental illness and cure; his prescriptions were murderous bleeding and purging and a "tranquillizer," a super-strait jacket that worked by reducing the patient's circulation. He also favored a device which spun the patient until calm.[10]

Rush saw mostly pauper patients in the insane wards of the Pennsylvania General Hospital. Meanwhile, European physicians were working along other lines. Their practice was primarily among the wealthy, and it was hard for the family of a rich man to submit him to the fate of a pauper or criminal because he was sick. Gentlefolk deserved better care. Consequently some doctors took mental patients to live in their homes or established private sanitaria for the rich. King George III was so cared for during his attacks; Philippe Pinel, the distinguished French physician who is sometimes said to have begun the modern epoch of care for the insane, had originally conducted a private asylum.[11]

In the United States a few private asylums or retreats appeared after 1800 to serve this upper-class clientele. Often they received some public support and cared for some paupers, but costs were high and fell mostly on the patients. Their mode of therapy was named "moral treatment." It called for soothing and diverting the patients in a healthful, wholesome routine. It was clearly more promising than the misunderstanding and neglect of the public caretakers, and it was more wholesome than the purges and bleedings which were conventional "medical" treatment for mental symptoms. In fact, moral treatment was perhaps best practiced by English Quakers at the York Retreat, established in 1796 for Friends who suffered mental illness, where the officials were not physicians and frankly opposed "medical" procedures. When properly carried out, moral treatment was more successful than any therapy devised until recently. Its well-advertised results bolstered the case for humane and therapeutic treatment, and raised the cry for a state institution to make these benefits more widely available. The State Lunatic Hospital at Worcester, Massachusetts, was the first result (1831) of this new movement; eight other states followed suit in the next decade, among them Pennsylvania in 1841 (when the insane department of the original Pennsylvania Hospital became a separate state institution) and New York in 1843.[12]

Dorothea Dix and the Trenton Asylum

The early history of the New Jersey institution has several interesting features. The initiative came from organized medicine. The campaign was the first deliberate effort to rally public opinion in the state for a welfare institution. It was one of the series of efforts which made Dorothea Dix a national celebrity. The hospital itself was the first full-blown example of the "Kirkbride hospital," the architectural type for asylums for fifty years. And in the end the founders' hopes were frustrated by the same forces which compromised and defeated the purpose of the state prison.

The New Jersey Medical Society was the oldest in the country, organized in 1766. It prevailed upon the legislature to pass a licensing law in 1772, and for years its primary concerns were fee-setting and the education and certification of physicians. Surviving the Revolution with surprising vigor, it was incorporated in 1790. Then sectarian and other rivalries began to divide the doctors, and their attention shifted to local affairs. County medical societies appeared in 1816.[13]

Not until 1837 did physicians take up the question of a state asylum, which was pressed upon them by Dr. Lyndon Smith, of Newark, when he took office as president. His colleagues supported the idea, and in 1839 the legislature appointed a committee to look into it. The committee did not look very hard; they deduced on the basis of statistics collected for Massachusetts that there were eight hundred insane and idiotic people in New Jersey, of whom four hundred were suited to asylum care. They disagreed with the notion that these people were incurable, and, in any case, they held that much of their suffering could be alleviated by proper asylum care. Having expressed these enlightened sentiments, the committee passed the ball back to the doctors, naming a commission which included four of them to get more facts.[14]

The commissioners divided the state among them, intending to visit shelters for lunatics or to inquire among doctors and local officials.

Their inquiry was incomplete and haphazard, but it revealed 695 lunatics and idiots. Moreover, a few of these busy men did take time to inspect the condition of the afflicted, for the report included some horror stories: a woman, aged twenty-eight, chained by the ankle for twelve years; a lunatic, harmless in the doctor's eyes, chained hand and foot, and others. Two hundred and seventy-eight of these cases were supported by friends and family, 273 in poorhouses, twenty-two by "charity," twenty-three were "occasionally insane from drink" and thirty-seven "in confinement [jail?]." (The commission's figures didn't tally.)[15]

For the most part, the commissioners emphasized the danger of maniacs to the community—violence, theft, arson, murder. Peace and safety required their custody; but jails, dungeons, and other provision only made "the cause of their confinement remediless, and . . . confinement itself terminable only by . . . death." The commissioners all agreed that evidence showed that proper treatment in an asylum could cure insanity. They estimated that $20,000 would cover the cost of the building.[16]

The following year a legislative committee reported on these recommendations. After some new horror stories, it emphasized that a state asylum would bring a real saving: As it was, towns supported two hundred pauper lunatics at an average cost of $1.75 per week—a sum equal to $18,200 per year. This expense, if applied to an asylum for two years, would pay for land and buildings; over a ten-year period, the committee thought, a well-regulated asylum would be the cheapest method of supporting pauper lunatics.[17] State prison officials also raised questions about the provision for insane prisoners: Did they not need medical care? Should they be released when their terms expired?[18]

Legislators felt the weight of these arguments, but decided against incurring a state debt even in this good cause.[19] An act of 1843 obliged county officials to study the condition of pauper lunatics in their towns and to send those deemed curable to asylums in neighboring states. Naturally, there was no penalty attached to the law.[20]

There matters stood when Dorothea Dix arrived on the scene in the fall of 1844. Encouraged by success in New England, she worked up memorials to the legislatures of New Jersey, Pennsylvania, and New York during the same season. She did not say anything that advocates of an asylum had not already said. Her technique was simple. First of all, she insisted on seeing things for herself—not just a few lunatics and a few keepers, but a careful survey—poor farm, almshouse, and jail, town after town, until she knew more about conditions than anyone else. Then she confronted the legislators with her "memorial," the harrowing evidence of need. She made a direct appeal to conscience. She did not see why "New Jersey with ample means, unembarrassed by state debts and prosperous in all . . . channels of business, should fail to take an honorable . . . position" by establishing "such state institutions as the wants of her citizens require." Throughout the state she had heard "but one and the same opinion and wish, 'We need a hospital, and desire its immediate establishment.' " She avoided foolish promises of specific economies, but she asked why Jerseymen should pay for out-of-state care for their insane, when they could better spend that money at home.[21]

Senator Joseph Dodd, of Essex County, presented the memorial on January 23, 1845. Miss Dix did not stop at that point, but stayed in Trenton to rally friends of the proposal and persuade its opponents. Often she would invite legislators to her rooms to discuss the question. "You cannot imagine the labor of converting and convincing," she wrote a friend at the time. "Some evenings I had at once twenty gentlemen for three hours' steady conversation." One evening she invited "a rough country member who had announced . . . that 'the wants of the insane . . . were all humbug' "; after discussing matters with her for an hour and a half he "suddenly moved into the middle of the parlor" saying, "Ma'am, I bid you good-night! . . . *I am convinced;* you've conquered me out and out; I shall vote for the hospital. . . . The Lord bless you." [22]

In short, Miss Dix confronted conditions and legislators at first hand; the famous memorials were only a formal record of her real work. She did not create the groups that were directly interested in a lunatic asylum—the medical society, the families who could not afford expensive private retreats, the poor-law officials who had to put up with pauper insane, the sheriffs who were responsible for the local jails, the authorities of the state prison; indeed, she does not seem to have worked deliberately with these groups or for them. But she dramatized the situations that bothered them; she made men face a choice between action and neglect. In time she convinced all the rough country members and they blessed her: The bill for an asylum passed unanimously.

So a neurotic spinster succeeded where committees, commissions, and well-meaning reports had failed. She felt that the Trenton asylum was her special creation, her "first-born child," for previously she had worked to improve existing institutions. She helped to plan the asylum. She visited it frequently and often sent its residents books and exotic flora from her travels. (Some of these still live, including a great yew tree which was a slip of the shrub mentioned in Gray's "Elegy in a Country Churchyard.") In 1882 she became ill during a visit. The managers asked her to stay, since she had no home. They gave her an apartment with an inspiring view, just below the cupola, and looked after her until her death in 1887.[23] One wonders if she realized then how the hopes of the 1840's had been disappointed.

Establishing the Asylum

The original Trenton asylum has grown long wings and a thick body, and buildings to house its overflow and its servants clutter its site. It is still handsome and imposing, however, and justifies the pride of its founders. They designed and built it with great care to give form to an exciting and important idea: that it was possible, at last, after ages of neglect and misunderstanding, to cure some kinds and degrees of insanity. The first reports of Dr. Horace A. Buttolph, its superintendent, and the influential book *On the Construction, Organization and General Arrangements of Hospitals for the Insane,* by Dr. Thomas S. Kirkbride, its designer, show how the building gave shape to their ideas about mental illness and its treatment.

Certainly these men were well chosen for their work. Dr. Kirkbride, the designer, was born of a Quaker family in Morrisville, Pennsylvania, in 1809. He attended preparatory school across the Delaware in Trenton; he was apprenticed to Dr. Nicholas Belleville, of that city, for two years. He then studied in Philadelphia at the Pennsylvania Medical School, the country's largest, for four years. In 1832 he accepted a residency at the nearby Quaker "Asylum for the Relief of Those Deprived of Their Reason," which was modeled after the famous York Retreat in England.[24]

Dr. Kirkbride was interested in mental patients, but he returned to the general practice of medicine. The next year he began residency at the great Pennsylvania Hospital, where the insane were confined in the basement and generally ignored, except as they interfered with the medical and surgical patients housed above them. He tried to treat some of them by the traditional medical methods of bleeding and purges, with the traditional lack of success.[25]

From 1835 to 1839 he practiced in Philadelphia. Then in 1840 two jobs opened for him, as attending surgeon at the Pennsylvania Hospital and as superintendent of the new institution for the insane which the Pennsylvania Hospital was erecting on a farm in West Philadelphia. He chose the latter. In 1844 he was one of the thirteen founders of the Association of Medical Superintendents of American Institutions for the Insane, the first national society of medical men, which is now the American Psychiatric Association.[26]

Dr. Horace Buttolph, the first superintendent, was born in Duchess County, New York, studied at Stockbridge Academy, then served as apprentice to an uncle who was a physician. He attended Berkshire Medical College, where he took an M.D. in 1836. In 1842, after several years' practice in New York and Connecticut, he became assistant to Dr. Amariah Brigham, superintendent of the Utica State Hospital which opened the next year. He worked with Dr. Brigham for six years before coming to Trenton. The managers chose him for the new post from among seven candidates; he was one of two candidates from outside the state. In short, Dr. Buttolph was well-trained, familiar with developments in New England and New York, and had assisted in establishing a new hospital. Before assuming his duties at Trenton in 1847, when he supervised much of the construction of the asylum, he toured institutions in England, France and Germany.[27]

These men planned an asylum in order to cure mental illness by moral treatment. "Moral treatment" had two meanings: to physicians it meant treating the "moral," "affective," or emotional causes of mental illness; to Quakers, who employed it effectively, it meant a nonmedical treatment related to their religious doctrines. The practice was similar, but the medical view was scientific and rationalistic in spirit.

Dr. Buttolph based his view of insanity on the phrenology of Dr. George Combe. The brain, he thought, was the seat of various distinct aptitudes or propensities (sometimes called "faculties"). These were located in specific regions—animal and selfish propensities here, moral and religious propensities there, and so on. In normal brains these parts —and propensities—developed in balance or harmony, but in lunatics they had become unbalanced or deranged. Insanity was an overindulgence of normal feelings, like a sense of loss, or shock, or religious exhilaration, or melancholy, all of which might be appropriate when properly harmonized or balanced.[28]

The problem of diagnosis was to find the predisposing and exciting causes of the overindulgence. Predisposing causes were physical weaknesses in the brain. Perhaps it was defective, its parts (or bumps, as it were) too large or small from birth; perhaps it was damaged by injury or somatic illness. In any case, exciting causes—circumstances and events —had aggravated this weakness by stimulating the organ too much or too little. Once the doctor had discovered the predisposing and exciting causes of derangement, the treatment was to remove the exciting cause and to make the brain sound, by restoring health to the body or by re-educating the person so he could compensate for his weakness. Insofar as the predisposing and exciting causes were physical—somatic illness or injury, for example—treatment was "medical," like that for any sick person; insofar as the causes arose from circumstance and "stimulation," treatment was "moral," intended to soothe, divert, and cheer the patient.

In practice, therefore, moral treatment meant "removal from home and [its] sources of irritation," and care by "strangers, who should be intelligent, kind and conscientious, and who have tact and experience . . . in the performance of their particular duties." The asylum setting encouraged patients to enjoy "such occupations and amusements as are adapted for their benefit, in view of their previous habits and pursuits, and the form and stage of [their] disease." In fact "any and all moral motives may be presented . . . as a means of enlisting their feelings, and of directing their attention from themselves and [their] morbid trains of thought." As Buttolph describes them the "occupations and amusements for patients" sound like a present-day vacation resort—something otherwise unheard of in that time and place. Patients needed plenty of physical exercise to restore their appetite and digestion, he said, to give them "cheerfulness and contentment during the day and quiet and refreshing sleep at night." For exercise the doctor recommended walking, riding, and mild games. Amusements were theatricals, musicals, and "popular and scientific lectures." (Buttolph himself lectured on phrenology.) [29]

An isolated community, peaceful surroundings, plenty of room, a wholesome way of life: the site chosen for the asylum promised all these to near perfection. A tract of 112 acres on a rise beside the Delaware River two and a half miles north of Trenton, it had good farm land and meadow, thirty wooded acres, and a fine spring—important for a large medical institution. At its foot was a feeder of the Delaware and Raritan Canal, over which came the native red sandstone used for construction, and other bulky supplies. A road to Trenton ran along the top of the rise.

The original plan was to house two hundred patients and their keepers. There was an imposing central building with pillars at the entrance and a large handsome dome. It had rooms for administration, services, and the superintendent's apartment. Wings, set slightly back, longer and narrower than the central building, stretched out to each side of it. Here the patients lived, men on one side, women on the other. The edifice faced the Delaware on the west, so that it took advantage of sun and breeze. Newfangled gas jets gave illumination at night; gaslight was expensive, but clean, safe, and very bright—all important considerations in a place designed for people apt to be melancholy and careless. Ventilation received much thought. Special closets were provided for soiled laundry and housecleaning equipment, in an effort to avoid the unpleasant smell of institutions. The water supply was plentiful and pressure good; the great dome housed the water tank. The considered needs of the patients shaped windows, doors, locks, furniture, and every detail of the building.

With regard to treatment, the most important architectural feature was the arrangement of the wings into wards, each fixed up for a particular class of patients. Classification of patients was, Dr. Buttolph thought, "the foundation of successful treatment," the "prominent difference between the . . . asylum and ordinary poor house management of the insane." In a well-ordered asylum, he said, patients are "associated as near as practicable, with those who from the form and stage of their disease, and from their peculiar mental and moral constitution and social standing, are adapted to help, or at least, not to hinder their recovery." Proper classification separated "the noisy and vociferous, . . . the violent, the vulgar and filthy" from "the harmless, the cleanly and the timid classes." This was necessary to proper diversion: obviously materials suitable to divert one class would bore a second and become destructive weapons for a third; amusements suitable to one illness—or one social class—would likewise annoy others.

The original plan provided six or seven wards for each sex. Accommodations varied according to the group's symptoms and its status. Quieter patients lived close to the center, more disturbed patients in remote sections where they would be less disruptive. Each ward had its own dining room; food, prepared in a common kitchen in the basement of the central building, was moved to the dining rooms by means of a basement railway and dumbwaiters. Thus diet and dining became part of the classification and therapy.[30]

In view of later history, it is a striking fact that the recruitment of staff received little attention during the institution's first forty years. For many years there was only one physician, the superintendent. Superintendencies rarely go begging today, but the job was even more attractive in the early days. Dr. Kirkbride recorded his reasons for preferring an asylum: "a comfortable residence, a rather liberal salary, the opportunity of . . . developing new forms of management . . . and possibly securing . . . a reputation as desirable" as that of a leading doctor "in the City." "Besides," he adds, "my parents viewed my accepting this new office as putting a certainty in place of an uncertainty" and "beyond all else my young wife approved the plan, knowing, as she did, [that] a successful City practice must necessarily keep me most of my time from home while the care of a Hospital would . . . keep me somewhere on the premises." [31] A country doctor's practice was even more taxing. An obituary of Dr. John Kirby, assistant physician at Trenton from 1876 to 1897, noted that his first twenty-four years of practice in rural Salem county were "unusually arduous," requiring "long rides and much work at night." [32]

The superintendent received $1,500 a year; he was assisted by a matron and nurse (in fact his wife), who earned $300; an "assistant superintendent"—an apothecary—who got $500; a steward and a treasurer, who handled business matters and made $600 and $200 respectively.[33]

The asylum's bylaws spelled out at length the duties of attendants. They were, first of all, enjoined to respect the officers and "receive instructions kindly." With regard "to each other and themselves" they had to exhibit self-respect and "avoid all gross and vulgar habits" such as "loud talking and laughing." Other desirable qualities were politeness, a "high sense of moral obligation" and "a calm, cheerful deportment." Their "duty to the institution" was to keep wards clean and in a "perfect and systematic neatness"; to keep doors locked at night, so that there was no visiting from ward to ward; to get permission before leaving grounds; and to give thirty days' notice before leaving the job. Finally, the "duty to patients" was to address them with a "mild persuasive tone of voice, and never . . . coarsely or by a nickname." Attendants had to eschew roughness and violence; even, the bylaws added, "when [they] receive insult and abusive language, they must keep cool, forbear to recriminate, threaten, or dictate in the language of authority."

Attendants lived on the wards with the patients. Their regular duties were to see that their charges were washed and neatly dressed and to supervise the round of daily life. They were to "prevent improper conduct" and even "bad postures" and to "instruct, comfort and amuse" the patients by "talking to them, reading to them, and the like." To preserve order they were allowed to segregate the noisiest. They also had to protect their patients from dangerous implements and to keep them from dangerous places.[34]

Evidently, the superintendent had no difficulty in filling these jobs and there was little turnover. His report for 1856 gives a table of employees and their monthly wages. There were fifteen male attendants (for 124 patients); they earned $14, except for one at $15 and one at $16. Twenty-one female attendants cared for 139 patients; they made $9, except for two at $10. These wages were in addition to maintenance. The ratio of attendants to patients was better than one to eight. In addition there were forty other employees. A carpenter and a gardener each got $25, a tailor $18, and a baker $16; three people worked in the kitchen, at $14, $12 and $11. The other thirty-three were not identified.[35]

Doubtless the documents that pertain to the early years of the asylum are biased toward high hopes and good appearance, but even under critical examination they suggest that the institution's central problem did not lie in its theory, structure, or staff. The superintendent himself defined the central problem, rather obscurely, in terms of "public confidence" and, later, as a contradiction in public policy.[36]

Custody or Cure?

The original policy was that the institution was a hospital to cure people. Obviously it could accommodate only two hundred patients, whereas the state had almost seven hundred "insane and idiotic" according to the admittedly incomplete census of 1850. Under the organic act the board of managers could restrict admission to curable patients and limit their stay to three years.[37] In his first report, Dr. Buttolph went into some detail about who should be institutionalized for treatment. Persons whose illness "obviously depends upon bodily disease of a temporary character" should remain at home; so should aged persons and those partially paralyzed, who "have no dislike of their friends, and are quiet and manageable." Also, "very delicate females . . . only partially insane," who "cherish a strong attachment to home and friends" are "sometimes unfavorably affected" by separation.[38]

When he wrote, in January 1849, the asylum had been open for almost eight months and had eighty-three patients; it ended 1849 with 110 patients and 1850 with only 162. Dr. Buttolph reported then that of the first 292 patients sent to him, 105 had returned to the community (he doesn't say what happened to the other twenty-five). But it is plain that most of the insane in the state were still in private homes, poorhouses, and jails. The great demand for asylum care had not materialized.[39]

Two reasons kept the patients away: skepticism about results and, of course, the cost. Dr. Buttolph tried to allay skepticism by discussing, in his reports, the character of insanity and the advantages of asylum treatment; clearly he intended his words to reach more people than the governor and legislature. The question of costs was complicated. The general idea, as stated in the organic act, was that the state put up the building and paid the officers' salaries, but that families or communities paid the cost of maintaining patients. The act recognized four types of patients: (1) paupers, who were in effect taken out of the poorhouse and whose maintenance was paid by the township responsible for them under the poor law; (2) indigent patients, who were not paupers but who could not afford treatment, who were supported at public expense, and in effect, kept out of the poorhouse; (3) private patients, who paid their own way; and (4) prisoners in the state prison or county jails, whose expenses were charged to the appropriate authorities.[40]

Then, as wards remained empty, there were significant changes in the law. Originally the managers were authorized to set the charge for maintenance at its cost, but a law of 1849 limited the charge to $2 a week. When this did not prove adequate, the state paid the balance—in effect, a subsidy. Even more important, a law of 1850 made the county, rather than the township, liable for support, a change which gave a "motive to the officers of townships to extend the benefits of the institution to many cases long deemed incurable." By the end of 1851 the townships were unloading chronic and violent cases on the asylum, and the state was subsidizing them at the rate of 75 cents a week per patient.[41]

This change made things difficult for asylum officers in two ways. First, it threatened overcrowding that would destroy the classification system and the hopes for therapy built around it. Second, it made the hospital an annex of the county poorhouse and tended to reduce the number of private patients.

Already, by the end of 1850, Dr. Buttolph saw a dilemma approaching. Soon the managers would have to choose between refusing and discharging private patients to make place for those sent by public authorities, or discharging chronic and incurable cases to make place for those of recent or hopeful nature, or asking that facilities be expanded, particularly to handle violent, noisy, and excitable cases, who were already overcrowded.[42]

If the managers had followed their original policy, their decision would have been easy. The asylum was intended as a place of cure, not custody; the managers had the power to admit only promising cases (with some exceptions) and to discharge those that did not improve in three years. But to carry out the policy strictly would have disappointed and alienated groups on which they relied for support. Hence the dilemma, and hence the talk about "public confidence."

To discharge public patients, for example, would alienate the poorhouse keepers who were unloading their tough cases; these people, influential with the legislature, would ask why the asylum wasn't curing patients, and thus reinforce the idea that insanity was incurable. Moreover, the legislature was already bemused by the fact that the building alone cost over $80,000, much more than any estimates. In fact, the managers had themselves paid $24,000 for furniture and other fittings, after the appropriations were exhausted, for which they were later reimbursed. When the legislators agreed that the state would subsidize county patients for charges above $2, they opened themselves to a large and increasing liability.[43] Since the managers wanted to go to the legislators for improvements and expansion, they could hardly afford to say either that they had been too optimistic about cures or that they were not interested in helping the local officials except for taking the most promising cases. Dorothea Dix had not hedged her appeal with that kind of qualification.

On the other hand, the managers were very solicitous about private patients. Doctors had first realized the possibilities of moral treatment in private retreats for the well-to-do, and the asylum was organized under a board of managers, like a private charitable hospital, not like a poorhouse or jail. Since private patients paid their full maintenance, the managers were not obliged to ask the state for a subsidy for them and thus to emphasize the expense of asylum care; moreover the patients' families were likely to be rich enough to give significant gifts to the institution. To discharge these patients would, in short, make the asylum more dependent on the legislature for funds and perhaps lose it the active sympathy and support of influential families.[44] It was for the sake of respectable people that the legislature, at the managers' urging, amended the organic law to keep out the criminal insane, that is, convicts who became insane in prison.[45]

It was to respectable families that Dr. Buttolph addressed his discussion about admission. Poorhouse keepers did not need to know that senile gentlefolk and "delicate females" might better stay with their families and friends. The theme that gentlefolk were separated and treated appropriately for their social position ran through his discussion of classification. The fact was not published, but private patients lived in the best rooms, located near the superintendent's quarters. In short, it was a matter of interest as well as pride that the asylum cater to private patients and not disappoint their families.

Furthermore, as the officers said, it would have been cruel to send inmates back to private care or to the poorhouse. From every point of view, the solution was to expand the asylum to handle both jobs—humane custody and cure. This was, of course, a much greater expense than the legislature had originally bargained for. Hence the managers chose to play up overcrowding and ask for more facilities, without, however, raising the fundamental question of what provision the state should make. By 1854 Dr. Buttolph was ready to admit publicly that his previous reports had ignored evils of inadequate classification "from motives of policy, not wishing to lessen public confidence in the institution, on account of defects that I hoped would soon be corrected." Meanwhile, in the same report, the managers interpreted a number of recent gifts to "show that confidence is reposed in the institution, and that a growing interest in its prosperity is beginning to be felt by the public." They hoped that Dr. Buttolph's reports would "tend to elevate the character of the institution and enlist in its behalf the sympathy and support of every portion of the community." [46]

The institution was expanded in 1855, 1863, and 1866, to accommodate five hundred patients. But in the end nobody was fooled. Events supported skeptics who said that the asylum could not cure, skeptics who asked where the cost would stop, skeptics who pointed out that many insane still lived in private dwellings and poorhouses.[47]

Meanwhile, as the institution was pushed into custodial care, it was clear that some people found advantages in the situation. During the 1860's the number of "indigent" patients rose, and in 1869 the managers pointed to a practice that was probably of long standing. "Respectable" families, not paupers, would go to county authorities and get themselves adjudged "indigent"; the authorities would arrange to place their insane ward in the asylum at the county rate, considerably lower than the private rate, and the families would reimburse the county for its costs of maintenance. By this device the asylum lost the higher fee paid by private patients, the state lost the cost of its subsidy ($1 per week at the time), the family gained by the lower rate, and the county authorities gained because the family reimbursed them, whereas pauper families did not.[48]

On their part, the officers found certain advantages in the situation. The institution was crowded, but not unprosperous; not only did it live within its income, but it managed to finance important repairs and minor improvements without having to beg additional funds.[49] Accordingly, the institutional farm and other uses of inmate labor grew in importance. Originally, the farm, or "garden," had seemed to be more of a convenience and a pleasant diversion, like walking and riding, than an economic enterprise.[50] But increased population, especially from the poorer and laboring classes, made it necessary to look for some easily managed group employment, especially for men (women could sew and do household chores). Work details, and especially farm labor, were a plausible solution that could also contribute substantially to the institution's support. In 1868 Dr. Buttolph asked the legislature to buy more farm land on which to employ more of his 520 charges.[51]

At any time during these years the managers might have raised the policy question simply by refusing to accept more patients and discharging those whom they could not help. From time to time they did ask local authorities to be more discriminating in commitments.[52] But their hope and expectation was that the state would adopt the policy of caring for all insane, not just curable ones, in state asylums.[53] By October 1871 there were seven hundred patients in the buildings designed for five hundred; the superintendent frankly criticized the legislature for not acting on a new hospital and he threatened to discharge numbers of chronic cases in favor of those supposed curable. Finally, in July 1872, the managers told Dr. Buttolph to receive no more patients until the overcrowding was reduced. "The action . . . was the result of long and anxious waiting for some change that might reduce the number of inmates or . . . increase the facilities," they said; but plans to remove milder cases to counties or to discharge harmless chronics had failed. They did not describe these plans or their failure; their disappointment was, plainly, that the state had not provided more facilities. When they did order that the increase stop, there were 732 patients and many of the sitting rooms had been filled with beds, "with scarcely sufficient passageway between them." [54]

By this time the state had begun a large new asylum at Morris Plains, but it was not to be opened for four years. It was planned to serve the great new cities of North Jersey, the source of the increasing patient load. Meanwhile something had to relieve the need, and the more populous and politically active counties began, in the 1870's, to provide county institutions of their own.

The story of these developments belongs to a later chapter. In the present context they show the disappointment of the original hopes for the state asylum. By the 1870's men felt disillusioned about the efficacy of moral treatment and the curability of insanity; presently they would speak of the early hopes as "the cult of curability." [55] The managers were justified in assuming that sooner or later the state would provide asylum custody of all its insane; such was the pattern in most states. But in New Jersey the county asylums came—and stayed. Experts considered them a step backward, because they were frankly custodial and political, more like a specialized almshouse than a hospital. County asylums developed and flourished in New Jersey because they gave shape to what most interested people had really wanted. They provided specialized custodial care for people too difficult to keep at home or in the poorhouse; this was a service to people who had to take care of "lunatics." They were located near where they were needed. They opened new jobs and contracts for local politicians. Withal, they were notably cheaper in the short run (and perhaps in the long run) than the state institutions. In short, they served the sane, rather than curing the insane.

So the policy question—whether the state should provide hospitals for cure or asylums for custody—was resolved, after a fashion. The state would try to do both, but its medical treatment would be ineffective and its custodial care expensive, and for a generation men would not seriously hope for improvement; progress, such as it was, would come from private hospitals and doctors serving the rich, not from public institutions.

Policy and Public Responsibility

In retrospect it seems that the disillusion about "moral treatment" and curability was as mistaken as the illusion. Asylum officials never had a proper chance to test their original ideas; from the first they were caught between a fear that they could not deliver on their promises and a fear that they would offend any of the groups to which they had to appeal. The result might have been a frank confrontation of the risks, expense, and possibilities of asylum care and public responsibility toward the insane. Instead the managers and officers of the asylum made policies and pronouncements intended to reconcile parties and ideas that were vaguely compatible but also vaguely hostile. In this way, they engaged in politics.

Their problem was ironic because the asylum was deliberately organized to avoid politics. Its responsible authority was an unpaid board of ten managers with overlapping terms, who were appointed by justices of the supreme court. The purposes of the board were, as Dr. Buttolph observed, citing the recommendations of the Association of Medical Superintendents of Institutions for the Insane, "to protect [the asylum] from all influences connected with political measures or political changes" and to encourage "public confidence" by virtue of board members' "liberality, intelligence and active benevolence." [56] This arrangement contrasted with the poorhouses, jails, and state prison, where political control was lending itself to graft and the spoils system.

The board of managers certainly secured a stable administration for the asylum and freed it from the grosser evils of political management. In fact, its autonomy amounted to a kind of irresponsibility; it was difficult for the governor or legislators to discover exactly what its situation or policy was. Its annual reports did not present a full and candid picture. Even its financial affairs were obscured by dubious accounting. Was it proper that the managers should finance improvements out of their own pockets, as they did at first, or by fiscal juggling, as they did later on? Was it proper that they should shift the state's policy from "cure" to "humane custody" without a candid assessment of each function, in the hope that they would somehow by indirection get a definite mandate that they were unwilling to demand directly? Did they not, in avoiding the spoils system, ignore political responsibility?

As they saw it, their problem was not, how can we make the asylum work as an agency for curing the insane? It was, rather, how can we hold what "public confidence" we have and win more for our institution? Their unspoken argument went something like this: To care for the insane in private homes and public almshouses is inhumane and impractical. (That was the message of Dorothea Dix, which, on her evidence, no one would deny.) A state asylum was humane and would cure people. (That was the idea of the asylum.) But experience belied the optimism about cures. It might follow that the state should abandon the enterprise. This would, however, be cruel to the people who already enjoyed the advantages of asylum care. It would re-establish the conditions that the asylum was intended to remedy. It would, incidentally, involve conceding errors in judgment that were understandable but embarrassing. When the managers did ask that the counties handle chronic custodial cases, the counties were unwilling, and the managers would not force the issue until 1872. Of course nothing suggested that county asylums, if they were established, would be any more effective than the notorious local poorhouses and jails, and, if the counties did establish asylums, then what would become of the state institution?

Presumably, it would return to its original purpose—curing people.

It is significant, therefore, that throughout the 1850's and 1860's asylum officials were not saying, by word or deed, "Take these chronics off our hands so we can get to work at what we really want to do, curing people." They did not plead for a chance to show what they could do because they were not sure what they could do. Their mention of cures did not emphasize the fact that two out of three people who entered the asylum stayed there. Instead, their plea was for facilities to give humane custody to those who did not benefit from their treatment. That way they did not have to criticize or challenge local authorities, nor give up the hope of cures. The proposed state custodial care was certainly, in their eyes, better for the patients than local custodial care, and it was the pattern that was developing in the other states. In time, therefore (they expected), they would keep their original function, such as it was, and acquire a large new one, and humanity would be served. So they could afford not to draw the issue, but they could not risk any loss of "public confidence."

Defining the problem as they did then, as holding on to public confidence and increasing it, did their policy succeed? Yes and no. Yes, because the new state asylum at Morris Plains was the old state asylum writ large, with Dr. Buttolph himself in charge. No, because the county asylums, which institutionalized a doubt about the propriety, efficiency, and sufficiency of state care, were here to stay and indeed persisted long after their disappearance in most states.

But if the state asylum entered the 1870's with a dubious public support, the state prison, managed by political appointees, had lost the confidence of everyone, and the local institutions—the poor-law administration, the almshouse, and the jail—gave no indication that they could handle their problems in any way that would enlighten the citizenry, or arouse its sense of responsibility and honor its ideals.

In the 1830's and 1840's the founders of the public schools had managed to capture the imagination, arouse public responsibility, and honor public ideals; so, in a way, did the men who established the silent system in the state prison and so did Miss Dix and the founders of the state asylum. The schools were close enough to the interests and aspirations of local communities to win a persistent, if uneven, support, and the next developments in welfare institutions, such as reform schools for delinquents and training schools for the handicapped and retarded, would capitalize on the prestige and professional expertise of "education." But the state prison and state lunatic asylum could not maintain and develop the force of their original ideals. Both institutions represented a genuine insight into the problems with which they dealt; both deserved a fairer trial than they got.

Why did the legislature fail to give adequate support to policies it had itself established? Those familiar with the prison said the difficulty lay in "politics," by which they meant the spoils system and other perverse influences on management. Those familiar with the asylum thought the trouble was apathy, the absence of public confidence and support. In either case, there were obviously fatal gaps between politics and policy, between the means and ends of welfare programs. When every man votes his interest as he sees it, how many voters stop to speak and act in behalf of the pauper, convict, and lunatic? Very few. In the 1830's and 1840's people tried to overcome the gap between needs and responsibilities by humanitarian appeals, appeals to sympathy and conscience and to the ideal of moral reform. These sentiments inspired the "separate system" and "moral treatment." Politics, apathy, and even costs were decidedly secondary, in this train of thought, to the sense of moral obligation.

When it developed that these grand projects disappointed some people, alienated others, bored others, and cost much more than anyone expected, the appeal of sympathy and moral rectitude began to need qualification. Perhaps, if circumstances had remained more or less constant, the qualifications could have been made; the moral imagination and the sense of responsibility could have again found appropriate vehicles.

But circumstances changed. The homogeneous New Jersey of the decades before 1850, the rural democracy, was displaced in many localities by a different order. A man who traveled from the Palisades to Camden in 1820 and again in 1880 would see marvelous changes: huge swarms of strange people speaking strange languages, moving around strange buildings, doing strange things. If it was hard to enlighten the moral imagination and compose the sense of responsibility in a homogeneous society with common institutions, a common heritage and common moral ideals, it was much harder for men to discover a public good and a common good among the diverse groups that later came upon the scene.

In all these respects the history of welfare in New Jersey was fundamentally like that of other states in the Northeast. In all of them the groups and interests of industrial cities arose within the framework of older institutions and ideas. For the most part this development has impressed historians of public welfare as an unmanageable increase in the volume and complexity of deviation and suffering. It was that, but it also widened the existing gap between the ends and means of welfare programs. It raised, in short, a problem of leadership. The difficulty became acute wherever rural and urban, native and foreign, rich and poor, moralistic and scientific, came into conflict. But perhaps it was unusually troublesome in the land between Philadelphia and New York where the rural democracy was a law unto itself, a congeries of towns that had no aristocracy, no established church, no really coherent statewide political parties, not even a metropolis to bring wealth, power, and culture into focus.

4

Public Welfare in an Urban Setting, 1866–1917

In ninety years of statehood, New Jersey had built two institutions for deviants—the prison and the lunatic asylum. In the next five decades it opened seventeen, the framework of its present system, and they stood beside a large network of municipal and private agencies that were also established during the period.

These developments were similar to those in neighboring states. Differences were in timing and in details of management and supervision. The similarity did not result from coercion; no one required that New Jersey establish training schools for retarded children or the deaf and dumb like those in Pennsylvania, a "state charities aid association" like that in New York, or a reform school like that in Ohio. In every instance Jerseymen followed precedents set elsewhere, but they were free to do quite differently, as men did in Georgia, Wisconsin, or Ontario. The private, entirely voluntary institutions were more like those of neighboring states than were public agencies. The similarity arose partly from the colonial heritage and partly from the situation and problems of urban life, with its characteristic groupings of people. In general, urbanization tended to magnify the importance of the state government, to elaborate the earlier distinctions between public and private institutions, and to increase the problems called "political."

Social and Political Change

The basic fact was the growth of population. Between 1790 and 1840 the number of Jerseymen increased steadily but much more slowly than during the colonial period or the later decades. It grew mostly by natural increase, which was diminished by emigration to Western states. In 1840, New Jersey had 373,000 residents; a few years later mass immigration began and after 1850 the population doubled every thirty years until 1920, when it numbered over 3.1 million. But this staggering increase was not evenly distributed. Much of it came to unsettled places and upset the balance of social and political forces that had existed before 1840.[1]

The state may be divided into four sections: the northeast, between the Raritan and Hudson rivers; the northwest, which turns toward the upper Delaware; the center, a narrow waist of land; and the south, lying between the Delaware estuary and the Atlantic. In 1840, the northwest had the largest population, followed closely by the center; the northeast was a poor third, not far ahead of the south. By the end of the century this had all changed. The most marvelous growth was in Jersey City, made self-governing only in 1838, which by 1900 numbered 206,000 inhabitants, almost a hundredfold increase; its enclave, Hoboken, and its appendage, Bayonne, grew at similar rates. These were the notable municipalities of Hudson County, created only in 1840. North of them lay the old county of Bergen, more notable then for Hackensack than for the communities that faced upper Manhattan. The Hudson Tubes, opened in 1910, brought large groups of commuters to these places.[2]

The metropolis of the state, if there was one, was Newark, with almost 250,000 people in 1900. It was the county seat of Essex County; west of it lay the Oranges, Montclair, Maplewood, and the other towns that became typical of suburbia. Essex County had been twice divided; to its north was Passaic County and the towns along the Passaic River, of which Paterson was the greatest. To its south, on the main line between New York and Philadelphia, was Union County, created as recently as 1857, where the centers of population were the old city of Elizabeth and the new one of Rahway. Beyond these communities lay the old towns of Plainfield and New Brunswick, all part of the economy centered in New York. Even the countryside north of them, west of Essex, was dotted with estates belonging to rich people of the metropolitan community.[3]

Beyond New Brunswick the urban centers were Trenton and Camden on the Delaware. Both grew with the railroads; both were the seats of new counties—Mercer, organized in 1838, and Camden, in 1844. Neither had great incursions of immigrants as did the communities near New York; each had a population of nearly 80,000 by 1900. They served hinterlands that were relatively in decline. Once the Delaware valley north of Trenton and the lowlands east of Camden had supported a thriving economy based on cattle, lumber, and, in the latter case, products of the sea, but richer frontiers had taken their place. Once capitalists in both sections had managed to put together ore, fuel, and flux in proportions sufficient for a primitive iron industry, but it could not compete with richer fields to the west. The result in these rural areas was not only economic stagnation, but an apparent decline in vigor; in the twentieth century the piney-woods people of the south were among the notorious groups of inbred degenerate families in the nation, and somewhat similar enclaves appeared in the northern hills. Perth Amboy and Burlington, the colonial capitals, lost prestige and power in state affairs. To some extent the shore communities grew prosperous by catering to vacationers from neighboring states, but this was a seasonal and risky business.[4]

Such were the urban and rural parts of the state. Transportation was the great factor of the differences between them and the core of political issues that divided them. Railways, and later streetcars and other urban utilities, were a convenience and an almost indispensible condition of local prosperity. Places that did not have them wanted them. But the companies that provided them needed a special charter from the state legislature until 1874, and rival groups of capitalists spent huge sums to create and maintain charter privileges. Often the corporations became great vested interests, exploiting those whom they were supposed to serve. Once communities got their services, their interest was somehow to control the companies. One persistent issue was that between those who wanted the company to expand in their direction and those who wanted it controlled where it was.[5]

Two facts complicated the issue. The utilities were as important in the public economy, as tax sources, as they were in the private sector. Taxes and fees from corporations paid most of the cost of state government during this period, including the cost of new state institutions. This kept local taxes down for rural areas. But it kept local taxes high for the urban places, because, according to their charters, the corporations—at least the railroads and street railroads—paid less than the going municipal rate. A second complication was that the municipalities themselves were incorporated by the state legislature, and often they found their charters changed or construed by state officials to their disadvantage. In short, urban places were beholden to the legislature in the fields of both corporate privilege and municipal autonomy; in both cases they had trouble because the rural regions were grossly overrepresented in the legislature. This meant simply that the state government was neither truly representative nor truly democratic.[6]

This was the main political division, but there were others. In 1900, the proportion of people with at least one immigrant parent in the twelve largest cities of the state was between three-fourths and four-fifths. Their religion and customs were alien and suspect to the natives, as the persistent issues of temperance and sabbath-keeping showed. But there were also divisions among natives on these questions, for many well-to-do and better-educated people allowed themselves urbane opinions. To an increasing extent the residential sections of the cities and the suburbs gave shape to ethnic and class divisions.[7]

Finally, of course, the rival political parties constituted a division in the community. As the stakes of government rose, so did the efficiency of party organization. There were rural and county machines, although city organizations attracted more attention. In general the Democratic Party represented the poor man and the foreigner, but there was no definite class alignment. Camden was Republican, like Philadelphia; Jersey City was Irish Democrat, like Manhattan; Newark was Democratic but Essex County was Republican. In any case the party strength was in county machines, and it often appeared that there were as many parties as there were counties.[8]

The result of this confusion of interests and organizations was triviality and corruption—"politics" in the worst sense—as corporations, municipalities, parties, and other groups bargained for votes and favors. But while politics had much to do with welfare institutions, it is significant that social services were rarely subjects of political debate. The connection between politics and welfare was that the public institutions were particularly vulnerable to mismanagement in matters of construction, personnel, and maintenance. But the relation was considerably complicated by the fact that there were, with reference to their sponsors, four kinds of welfare institutions: (1) local public agencies—the jail, almshouse, hospital, and outdoor relief; (2) private "nondenominational" charities supported by middle-class philanthropists; (3) private "sectarian" charities, established by immigrants to care for their own; and, finally, the state institutions. The full story of these institutions is beyond the scope of this book, but it is necessary to sketch in their relations.

Agencies and Problems

In the colonial period and the decades following the Revolution, respectable families looked to relatives, friends, or church for help, while public agencies took care of the friendless poor who had no other resource. In part the multiplication of institutions in the cities elaborated these early patterns. The differences were that, while there was no period of unfree servitude to allow nineteenth-century immigrants to adjust, their numbers were large enough and their group feeling strong enough to encourage them toward measures for mutual benefit and self-help. These were never sufficient, but the wealth and philanthropy of the cities could also support a variety of charitable institutions to meet the need. Voluntary agencies took the place, in part, of informal neighborhood help, although they had a formal organization and served a special clientele—schools for poor children, or homes for sailors or unwed mothers or aged clergymen and their widows. Public agencies continued to care for those who had no other resource.

Private charitable societies developed to meet needs that people thought were most appealing or promising. The souls and minds of children, especially orphans, were most frequently the object of attention, or even rivalry, among religious groups; charitable institutions for pregnant girls were also appealing—two for the price of one, as it were. So were the aged. But the most dramatic development came with regard to the sick. Sickness and injury touched all classes and places; the sick presented the danger of contagion if they were not segregated; and the improvement of medical science gave hope for cure. Everything pointed to the need for hospitals, and since hospitalized people were in particular need of spiritual help, the churches were interested. The result was an endowment of dispensaries and hospitals, most of them under religious auspices.[9]

These genteel charities ignored the needs of the able-bodied unemployed and vagrants, an old problem but new in its industrial setting and, as a large-scale phenomenon, in America. These people should have been breadwinners or preparing themselves as breadwinners, but they were not; instead it generally appeared that they were deserting their wives, neglecting their children, and ignoring their parents, in addition to being unable to support themselves. Some of them were honestly looking for work, really out of luck, but it was difficult to distinguish these deserving poor from those who chose to loaf around the saloons, drinking and gambling when they could, available for all sorts of criminal or political mischief. To help these idlers was to confirm their evil ways and to divert charity from the deserving, and thoughtful people recognized that it was wrong in every way.

Tramps followed the railroads out of the big cities. Their presence showed the breakdown of the settlement law. If it had worked properly, they would have been returned to their place of settlement and kept there. Instead the local authorities—constables, police, overseers of the poor—were satisfied to put them up overnight and then push them along. In many cases private citizens helped them, and they did not see the public officials except when they got into trouble. The problem grew steadily in importance, especially during depressions.

A study of poor relief in Elizabeth during the nineteenth century presents some suggestive details. Although the poor law required that overseers keep records, those that have survived are reasonably full only from 1843 until 1854, when they become perfunctory. They show that the number of transients receiving public aid grew from 50 in 1844 to 453 in 1850. The help was minimal. "A man and sick Woman going to Easton, wanting to stay till Monday, gave them Dinner and Paid their passage to Westfield which was cheaper," wrote the overseer on one occasion. For the most part his attention was directed toward eccentric behavior or the plight of women: "I was Called on by some . . . citizens in respect to a man that was deranged. I gave him refreshments and paid his fare to New York," reads a characteristic entry; again, "Paid a womans fare to Rahway in the Cars. She was deranged. She said she Escaped from the lunatic assilam in Mass., and was now on her way to Bordentown."[10]

The tramp proper—the more or less able-bodied man—was passed over in summaries. At first the overseer evidently tried to investigate his plight, as he was supposed to do under the poor law, but by 1856 the numbers were too large; that year the city opened a "station-house" for overnight lodging. It was simply an empty room, "the soft side of a wooden plank." The depression of 1857 brought a new class, not only persons "ruined . . . by . . . drink, leading abandoned, worthless lives," but "intelligent respectable people who are 'driven to the wall' by the hard times," as a local newspaper noted.[11]

The problem diminished during the Civil War, but by 1870 it was increasing. During the depression of the mid-1870's the Elizabeth City Council debated the policy of free lodging. On the one hand, it seemed to encourage tramps; perhaps a workhouse would scare them off or employ them in a profitable way. But a workhouse was expensive and was more appropriately a county function. Perhaps the station-house should be closed; but if public doors are closed to tramps, a councilman observed, they "are sent back to private doors"—a worse nuisance. Or, another councilman suggested, "they will go into a barn . . . then we will have fires." A third councilman took the humane view: "These tramps are human beings, and the question should be carefully handled. We don't expend any money and the place may as well be kept open. It is the duty of the citizens to protect these outcasts and take care of them." Finally, the council decided to put the station-house under the police instead of the overseer of the poor; presumably the police would be tougher. Perhaps for this reason, or perhaps it was only the return of prosperity, the number diminished for several years.[12]

Tramps were beggars, but when people denounced beggary they had in mind professionals who displayed themselves to exploit the sympathy of well-meaning people. Often, it appeared, beggars were organized and "worked" in a systematic way. Nothing stirred philanthropists to righteous indignation more than

THE MAN ON THE FLOOR

> The Sunday car from Elizabeth to Newark was crowded, when at the city line a crippled man hobbled in on crutches. A seat was given up near the door, and the compassionate passengers watched the unfortunate man place his crutches on the floor, which was interpreted as a somewhat self-conscious, but at least delicate, consideration for his sound-bodied fellowmen.

Compassion changed to wonder when the man

> lowered his maimed body to the floor and hutched himself to the front of the car, and with affected composure took a long breath and waited. Soon the conductor walked to the front, like the man who steps into the shell game convinced of the certainty of an honest guess, and gave the man on the floor five cents, receiving in exchange three pencils.

Then the procession began.

> When passengers were looking out of the windows, the man on the floor touched them and held up his empty hand. It seemed to the person in the high hat that every person in the car gave something but himself. . . . But the reflection that the beggar was making it harder for the deserving poor of Newark and Elizabeth to obtain assistance they sorely need, prevented him from giving just for the sake of appearing generous to a number of strangers.[13]

The worst problems, however, were more feckless and numerous. "Paupers," according to the head of the New Jersey Bureau of Labor Statistics, who made an extensive investigation of them in 1883, were "a class of persons obtaining their subsistence, either wholly or partly, through public relief." The fact of public relief was essential, but the significance of the word was its connotation. It was, he observed, a "term . . . of reproach . . . associated with moral and social degradation." Pauperism was a "loathsome disease and disgrace of our civilization." He reported that there were some 16,000 paupers in the state, exclusive of the insane and defective who were in special institutions and veterans in special homes, and also exclusive of vagrants. The proportion of public paupers he estimated at about one person in seventy-six—the same as that calculated by authorities in Massachusetts, much lower than comparable figures for Europe, but growing ominously.[14]

A third of the public paupers were fully supported on indoor relief; these were "in nearly every case . . . more or less completely disabled by sickness, infirmity, old age or some other visitation." The state had forty-one poorhouses, serving 196 townships; twelve were supported by county taxes, twenty-nine by township taxes; there were also five "private" almshouses maintained by overseers of the poor on their own property. Seventy-one other townships—more than a quarter of the whole number—did not yet have any sort of almshouse, but boarded out the poor in the old way. The township or city institution appeared where there was a long history of need and where New England traditions were strong—in Essex and Middlesex counties, for example. County institutions appeared in the old Quaker section of South Jersey and in the fast-growing new counties of Hudson and Camden. Hudson County was decidedly the most afflicted, with the municipalities of Essex second; together they spent a fifth of all relief funds, apart from their large expenditures for private charity.[15]

Horror was the theme that ran through descriptions of the poorhouse. A "professor" who studied the township institutions of Monmouth County reported in 1883 that "The general feeling . . . favors the poor house as a last resort, when temporary relief fails" because "once in the poor house" the inmates "lose all energy and make no efforts for self support." [16] Another observer said of the indoor pauper, "Commonly, his misfortunes or his vices are stowed away in a remote poorhouse on a muddy road. Politicians do not concern themselves with his fate, for he has no vote; benevolent people have their hands full in helping the poor who are not yet sunk into paupers; the very newspapers seek him only when his woful [sic] lot has acquired the lurid attraction of 'a horror.' " [17]

Two characters symbolized the misery of the almshouse in these descriptions. One was the almshouse baby, illegitimate, sometimes mulatto, sometimes born to a feebleminded woman who was herself born in the almshouse; gathered together in misery, the paupers were left "to propagate a race of paupers." [18] Even sadder was the old man dying in the attic. A narrative in the 1883 report tells how the visitors, climbing the steps to the attic, "for the moment . . . imagined ourselves suddenly transported into a vault among decomposing bodies."

As usual on these visits, a doctor was present; he pointed out that the particular stench arose from a sore on the man's leg which, because of long neglect, had rotted the flesh and even the bone. Nothing could be done for the man, the doctor observed, and the patient himself uttered a pitiable prayer for speedy death. (In a similar case, recounted on the preceding page of the report, the doctor left indignantly, outraged by such medical ineptitude.) The visitors noticed a half cup of dubious brew, cold and "covered with scum," by the man's head; also a "crust of dry bread." Before they left they discovered a second man, curtained off in the attic corner; he was dying too, but quietly; they noticed only the "nauseatingly filthy" bedclothes and, again, the "poisoned atmosphere" that was in itself enough to kill a healthy man.[19]

Such were the sights, sounds, and smells that the poorhouse called to mind. If the scenes and props were stereotyped, it was partly because the visitors were trying always to state "the lurid attraction of 'a horror.'" The horror of the poorhouse is the key to much of the history of welfare institutions during the period. The dying pauper who was literally rotting away in the attic, his covers stinking, clotted with fecal dust and yellow-stained, or perhaps slick and redolent of fresh deposits, a man without hope, neglected beyond repair, with the scum-smooth drink and brittle crust to satisfy his needs—this man was for his time and place an absolute: no further misery or degradation was imaginable. But all the poor and afflicted stood next to pauperism; all paupers stood next to the poorhouse; those who went to the poorhouse died there. That logic brought the horror home.

Every charitable provision other than the poorhouse was, in the eyes of people of that time, a device to save and protect people from this horrid fate. Public outdoor relief was supposed to spare the more deserving poor its ignominy. The work of the private charities was like outdoor relief, helping the more respectable poor in their homes. Homes for the orphaned and aged and hospitals were places where people in need could go and still keep some self-respect. But if there was no one to help you or look out for you or send you to other people who were supposed to care about you, then you went to the poorhouse. That was the end of the line. "Benevolent people" had "their hands full" helping "the poor who [were] not yet sunk into paupers."

So long as "benevolent people" thought that the important questions about a needy person were whether he was deserving or not and whether their charity would help him toward self-sufficiency or pauperize him, they could easily ignore the impersonal causes of dependency. In time their attention would turn from pauperism to poverty, and they would support measures to improve the general conditions of working-class life in terms of "social welfare."[20] Then the older concern with pauperism and charity would seem complacent and self-righteous. But in the post-

Civil-War years "benevolent people" in New Jersey simply did not see the alternatives as either helping paupers or preventing poverty. They saw the increasing host of tramps, beggars, and paupers and they asked how they might improve the charities that were already confronting the problem. Their question was not whether charity could solve social problems, but how to make charity more helpful.

In short, the point of the distinction between deserving and undeserving was, in their minds, as much to help the former as to deter the latter, and sponsors of private charities felt an obligation to take initiative in helping the worthy. Policemen and poor-law officials did not establish the city mission; that was the inspiration of the forerunners and followers of the Salvation Army. Policemen and poor-law officials did not build the YMCA's, to give deserving country boys a city home and keep them from the saloons and gambling halls; that was the work of Protestant laymen. (The Newark YMCA, organized in 1857, wrote clergymen for fifty miles around, asking that they put the Y in touch with city-bound boys from their congregations.)[21] Catholic laymen were the mind and heart of the Society of St. Vincent de Paul, which appeared in New Jersey in 1857 and gave many kinds of help to those who were, as its leaders observed, victims of prejudice as well as poverty.[22] Policemen and poor-law officials had nothing to do with organizing or directing the efforts of the Ladies Aid or the Female Benevolent societies which occupied middle-class and church women. When disaster struck—war, pestilence, or depression—the clergy and private philanthropists organized and administered relief and reflected on the means and ends of helping.

Charity Reformers

People associated with private agencies therefore began to think critically about the organization and efficiency of all charitable work. No sooner did they try to survey the whole picture than they realized that charity was disorganized and inefficient. This was plainest with regard to the public agencies. Obviously the poor-law officials and the police were merely passing responsibility for transients to other jurisdictions; not only did they condone irresponsibility, but in some respects they encouraged it. Jailers, for example, liked to see their jails full of relatively manageable vagrants, because they collected public funds for their support and generally managed to turn a sizable profit on the deal.

To some extent, the same was true of almshouse keepers. Their work was entirely inefficient because it was "indiscriminate"—men and boys (and even women and girls) were herded together, treated alike, without regard to their individual needs or problems or the risks of their association. What could be more self-defeating, from any point of view, than the almshouse baby and the pauper dying from medical neglect? Public outdoor relief was a notorious political dole (reformers succeeded in getting rid of it for a time in New York, but not in Jersey City or Newark).[23]

But, these critical-minded people noticed, private agencies also left much to be desired. Philanthropists, unlike political job-holders, did not as a rule stand to gain from mismanagement, but they might be satisfied with perfunctory service, or misled by foolish ideas, or gulled by crafty mendicants; in any case their services were likely to duplicate themselves in some ways and to ignore other, less obvious, needs.

If these were the problems, the solution was clearly supervision and better organization. Regarding private agencies, the critical spirit took the shape of the Charity Organization Society (COS), which appeared in at least twelve New Jersey cities by 1898.[24] With regard to public agencies the critical spirit took the form of the State Charities Aid Association (SCAA), which began as an organization of well-meaning Episcopalians in Morristown in 1881. They were so successful in improving the Morris County almshouse that the movement spread to other counties. In 1886, its annual report was subsidized by the state government and it became a semi-official inspection agency, like its prototype in New York.[25]

But organization and supervision were not the only interests of the critical spirit. Another was method. With regard to private charities, reformers wanted a discriminating individual approach to each person and family in need; they recognized that mere almsgiving was not enough, that the poor often needed counsel and good example as much as material help, and that the help had to have a personal, direct, and friendly quality to be effective. "Not alms, but a friend" was the motto of their visitors.[26] With regard to public institutions, the constructive idea was specialized institutions to segregate and classify different kinds of problems, so that the authorities could aim at rehabilitation rather than mere custody. The models for these new state institutions were schools and hospitals, which were traditional vehicles of private philanthropy and more recently were associated with professional training and scientific ideas. These models contrasted with old-fashioned catch-all institutions for custody, like the public almshouse and jail.[27]

The general relation among the four kinds of welfare institutions that developed in this period was as follows: The universal institutions of last resort were the public jail and poorhouse and public outdoor relief. To spare paupers the indignity and danger associated with them, people set up a variety of private charities. Some of these were definitely sectarian and ethnic; others were nondenominational (in fact, Protestant and middle-class) and directed toward especially appealing sorts of problems. It was within this last group, for the most part, that a critical spirit arose, which tried to introduce more rational methods into welfare work. The critical spirits were the people who supported the COS and the SCAA. They were also the people who inspired and promoted most of the state institutions established during the period.[28] They had plenty of opposition from the politicians who directed the local agencies and also from philanthropists who disagreed with them. In the end they had their way, in form if not in spirit. That is why the state institutions were "nonpolitical," organized under more or less autonomous boards of managers, like private charities; that is why they were conceived as schools or hospitals and not as custodial institutions; that is why, for all their faults, they did not rest easily in their failure.

State Institutions

The various services assigned to divisions and bureaus of the modern Department of Institutions and Agencies began as vague discriminations in what was called "charities and corrections." As people saw special needs they created special institutions; in time they came to think of these as falling into categories with rather distinctive and separate problems. But there was nothing inevitable about the order of their appearance and the details of their management.

The first institutions created after the Civil War were for veterans: a Soldiers' Children's Home (incorporated 1865) and a Home for Disabled Veterans (1866). These were explicitly intended to spare indigents the indignity of the almshouse. A similar institution took shape during the Spanish American War—the New Jersey Memorial Home for Disabled Soldiers, Sailors and Marines and their Wives and Widows (1898).

The state also provided a reform school for boys (1865) and for girls (1871). Partly, these were unfinished business from before the war, partly they reflected the increasing problems of neglected and delinquent children in the cities. In the 1870's there was a great development of local charity, both private and public: seven private hospitals were organized between 1871 and 1875, and the county almshouses expanded, with state aid, for the custodial care of the insane. All this was in addition to the organization of private charity in the depression following 1873. Between 1873 and 1876 the state was building its huge asylum at Morris Plains (now Greystone Park).

Once established, all these institutions required expansion and improvement. In the 1880's the state established three institutions to perform services that it had previously farmed out to out-of-state agencies. These were the School for the Deaf and Dumb (1882); Vineland Training School (1888), a private school for the retarded that took care of state cases; and the Vineland State School for Feeble-minded Women (1888), modeled after a similar institution in New York and intended to keep the girls from reproducing. In this decade also state officials began to experiment with supervisory agencies. A State Council of Charities and Corrections, established in 1885, quickly went into limbo, but the State Charities Aid Association began to publish reports the following year and became the focus of enlightened thought.

In general, however, philanthropic and civic spirits in the state turned toward the grand question of "labor reform" and the flagrant corruption of elections: between 1886 and 1894 demagoguery and corruption probably reached an all-time high, or low, in the state government. During the depression of the 1890's the initiative in service lay with local agencies, public and private. Then, as prosperity returned and problems piled up, there were developments in many directions. Doctors and caretakers of the retarded were interested in the State Village for Epileptics (1898), which put some trying cases in a more hopeful environment. The State Tuberculosis Asylum (1907) was intended to relieve local hospitals and state institutions of a class of patients that taxed ordinary means, although this work was ultimately left mostly to county sanatoria.

State reformatories, for adult first offenders, were established after long agitation, the men's in 1901, the women's in 1913. Both were occasioned by overcrowding at existing institutions. A prison farm (1913) and a "colony" for retarded men (taken over from private sponsors in 1916) gave shape to more modern ideas of institutional treatment. Meanwhile, there were a variety of "agencies" that dispensed with institutional care. One of these, probation (1900), remained attached to the county courts and did not become a centralized state service;[29] others were the Board of Children's Guardians (1899), which took children out of the almshouses, and the Commission for the Blind (1910), which helped sightless people in their homes. In 1905 the legislature created the office of Commissioner of Charities and Correction, a step toward systematizing and integrating the separate organizations.

Helping Veterans

In some ways the state's provisions for veterans foreshadowed its other policies. There were no homes for veterans' children or for disabled veterans before the Civil War. When, in 1811, a committee of the Assembly considered the plea of a "superannuated revolutionary soldier" for relief, it was satisfied to grant the merit of his claim but to deny relief because of the large number of similar cases. "Taking into consideration . . . the ample provision that is made in the different townships . . . for the support of the poor," the committee said flatly that a general law granting pensions to needy soldiers would be beyond the means of the state.[30]

This policy was upheld until 1831, when the legislature began to grant individual pensions to Revolutionary War veterans and their dependents. The usual grant was $60 a year for the veteran or $30 for his unremarried widow. Perhaps the humanitarianism and patriotism of the decade encouraged the new policy; perhaps the poor-law machinery seemed less adequate then; perhaps political representatives became more solicitous about their constituents, for the passing of so-called private or special legislation, such as individual pensions or charters of incorporation, became a great problem in these years. Certainly the state found itself relatively affluent because of its interest in the Camden and Amboy Railroad. In any case the effect of these pensions was to help deserving people escape the status of pauper. There were a few pensions granted to veterans of the War of 1812 before 1857, but the depression brought many new petitions and many others were granted during the 1860's. In 1874, after another depression, the state passed a general law granting pensions to veterans of that war.[31]

Meanwhile, the state itself went into the orphanage and hospital business, for that is what its two institutions for Civil War veterans were. The Soldiers' Children's Home was, in fact, the sixth incorporated orphanage in the state.[32] Like all state institutions, its building was the responsibility of a commission; ultimately it cost $48,000 and housed some two hundred children. The incorporators were all ladies, and the charter gave them an entirely free hand to support and educate their charges. The state paid $150 per year per child. (In fact, the legislature often had to make additional appropriations.) The payments were limited by statute to an interval of a decade. So, in 1876, the institution closed, the legislature thanked the lady officers and authorized them to give away the school's bedding, much worn after ten years, to the worthy poor.[33]

The Home for Disabled Soldiers was the pet of the popular war governor, Joel Parker; three of the six members of its first board of managers—appointed by the Supreme Court—were or would be governors. The "commandant" was to be a physician and surgeon; admission was by certificate of the Court of Common Pleas, stating that the applicant had an honorable discharge and was disabled by wounds incurred in service. The officers were authorized to grant temporary relief and out-patient relief; later, eligibility was extended to soldiers from other states and soldiers who were disabled after discharge. Also, the facilities were made available as a hospital for surgery, at the discretion of the commandant.[34]

The founders appropriated $50,000 for land and construction; they limited annual appropriations to $10,000 and expected the veterans to pay part of their disability compensation toward their support. By 1868 they had to appropriate an extra $25,000; then the federal government began to subsidize domiciliary care of disabled veterans. As the federal government expanded its own institutions, governors began to talk of closing the home. Increased demand for its service during the depression of 1873–1877 sustained it.[35] In 1888 it was relocated; between then and 1896, when a new but similar home was being considered, the thought occurred that the state should also provide for veterans' wives and widows.[36]

These institutions touched upon important welfare problems—dependent children, disability, chronic illness, and old age—and might have shown the way toward more constructive views of them and their treatment. The idea of pensions for veterans and their families might have expanded to include other classes, somewhat as California in 1883 subsidized outdoor relief for "veterans" of the gold rush.[37] In Iowa, Kansas, and Illinois, "soldiers' children's homes" became state orphanages, taking pauper children from almshouses.[38] The home for disabled veterans might have become a model specialized hospital—there were in 1866 only two incorporated hospitals in the state—with a selected clientele and strong public support, that would have set new standards for treatment and service for all disabled and elderly people, as the Veterans Administration mental hospitals led the way after World War II.

Veterans had greater risks of dependency after the Civil War than after previous wars partly because of factors that affected the entire labor force in modern society—diminished obligation of kin outside the nuclear family, weakened neighborhood ties, impersonal economic roles and forces.[39] But veterans remained a privileged class and the provision for them did not inspire a general review of welfare programs and services. Veterans claimed special treatment because they were especially deserving, and consequently their case ignored the extent to which their needs were a result of common social factors. A social science that could have explained this point did not gain currency until the twentieth century, but in any case the charity reformers never mentioned that provision for veterans and their dependents had any relevance for the "dependent, defective, and delinquent classes" at large. The foundations of state welfare services in New Jersey, as in the nation, were laid by those who wanted to reform charities and corrections, rather than by anyone who could see that the needs of veterans and their families were, after all, common human needs.

5

Dependent and Delinquent Children, 1850–1918

Children, not veterans, were the focus of progressive thinking about welfare in the decades after the Civil War. It was wrong to treat little boys and girls like mature paupers and criminals, and it was easy to imagine ways of helping them. Since private charities took the initiative in child-saving, questions of method received prolonged and fruitful discussion. Moreover, the plight of children interested those who wanted better schools and those who wanted labor legislation; it was a subject on which many kinds of reformers could get together. In fact the case for the various child welfare agencies seems so obvious that it is harder to account for the delay than for the progress in their development.

However complicated the story of child welfare services, they all were related somehow to the breakdown of traditional poor relief. Poor-law officials under the old system helped children, along with their parents, by indoor and outdoor relief, but they were often able to put orphaned or neglected children in foster homes by the process of indenture. This practice, formalized in the poor law of 1774, remained unchanged in the poor-law revision of 1874. It was akin to apprenticeship, and like apprenticeship it declined during the nineteenth century. It was a form of unfree servitude that offended democratic sensibilities; moreover, its economic advantage diminished as employers could hire children and even adults as needed without the obligation of long-term support and freedom dues.[1]

Indenture did not disappear, however, and the demand for children continued much higher on farms than in the city, much higher for children over twelve than under, and much higher for normal children than for the handicapped. Problems were gravest in the cities, where poor families suffered from special physical, economic, and moral hazards that increased the proportion of orphaned, abandoned, or simply "neglected" offspring.

Around this pool of distress appeared a variety of "child-saving" institutions that tried to help the delinquent, dependent, or defective.

All these classes needed what people often referred to as parental care and guidance, but ideas about providing it were confused and contradictory. Some people favored institutional care, but disagreed on who should run the institutions—a private society, a church, poor-law officials, public school officials, or the state—and how to run them. Other people rejected institutions in favor of foster homes, but they disagreed on who should place the children and under what conditions. The question of finance cut across every issue; since poor-law officials were ultimately responsible, they might subsidize or supervise private institutions, but such proposals stirred political and religious controversy.

No single program met all needs (the poor-law officials had had a choice of indoor or outdoor relief or indenture, keeping the family together or separating it); therefore comprehensive thinking had to combine several ideas. Moreover, discussions about child care were often subordinated to more general issues of pauperism, crime, and social justice: Prohibitionists, Socialists, and others could easily argue that the real problem lay far from the perplexities of child-saving.

Amid this confusion, legislators established state agencies for child welfare. If they had followed the logic of child care they would have dealt first with the host of dependents and then with the special difficulties of defectives and delinquents. Instead the correctional institutions came first and the State Board of Children's Guardians last. Legislators, sizing up proposals for change, looked for advice to local public officials and philanthropists. Since local situations varied greatly, representatives from Cape May or Trenton could simply fail to see the situation in Hudson County or Newark, or to understand the difference between child-care work in the two urban counties.

The State Reform School

The first agitation for a state correctional institution for children, in 1850–1853, came from people who didn't want to see youngsters put with vicious companions in local jails, much less the state prison. They were strongly supported by the state commissioner of education, who looked upon the reform school as a place to send truants and disciplinary cases. What defeated the agitation was a question of policy rather than of principle. Small counties objected to the state investing its funds in a school that, as things stood, would mostly benefit Essex County and its neighbors. The alternative was to allow counties where the need existed to build regional reformatories, as Essex County did in 1857.[2] This was the way almshouse care had developed and the way county insane asylums would develop in the 1870's.

In this case, however, the expansion of public education, with state aid and supervision, kept the issue of a state reform school alive, while delinquency increased and local provision continued to be disappointing. A legislative commission of 1864 expressed no doubt about either the problem or the need and won over those who had earlier opposed state action.[3] In little more than a decade the special and growing problems of city children had impressed themselves upon the legislators.

The fact was, the commission thought, that the occasions for neglect and the opportunities for delinquency were greater in the city than in the country. "In our towns and cities, and even in the villages of our agricultural districts, a large number of children are growing up without proper parental control. . . . They become accustomed to the use of tobacco and intoxicating drinks . . . ; hazard their little possessions in various games of chance; hang about low theaters and taverns." They "absent themselves from the daily and sabbath school, congregate at the corners of streets, insult the passers by with ribald jests or profane language . . . and become prepared for a continual progression of evil." [4]

It was wrong to steal fruit or produce from a neighbor's farm; was it wrong for a ragged child to walk through a railroad yard, pick up lumps of coal that lay half-buried and useless on the ground, and take them to his family's tenement flat to burn? Would the railway, rich and powerful, miss the pieces of coal? But it was easier and more fun to kick coal from the cars and pick it up, and it was more profitable to steal tools or common machine parts and sell them to unscrupulous junk dealers. So, the clerk of Hudson County Court observed, "children of the tenement, deprived not only of the luxuries, but of the necessities of life, too young to work, too young to care to work, wanting money and what money buys . . . soon learn to take greater chances." [5]

At common law, a child under seven was incompetent to commit a crime; children from eight to fourteen were only contingently competent. Whatever the law, people often declined to complain of young criminals; grand juries ignored bills against them, petit juries found them not guilty, judges suspended sentence. This was demoralizing, but it was perhaps better than sending the children to jail; as a warden told the commissioners who studied the subject in 1864, "boys are taught much evil here, and go out thinking it is not such a bad thing, after all, to be in jail." [6]

Clearly, the commission of 1864 thought, there should be some alternative to letting the boys off with a warning and sending them to the jail; there ought to be a reform school. Moreover, the state should assume the task: "Experience has demonstrated that, if left to the counties, it is left to be utterly neglected." They proposed not one but three institutions: reform schools for boys under fourteen and for girls, and a "nautical school ship" for boys over fourteen. They estimated the cost at $100,000, a large burden in addition to the debt of the Civil War. But it was only a fraction of the value of the riparian lands beside Jersey City, to which the state had just established a claim, and the commissioners tried to link the reclamation of the land with the reclamation of the children.[7]

The reform school at Jamesburg, to which these suggestions led, embodied two constructive ideas. Since delinquency began in parental neglect, it was thought, the institution should be a substitute family;

to this end its inmates were separated "into families and classes," groups of thirty to fifty, each under "a judicious man and his wife as parental caretakers; the several families to be united in chapel and in a common graded school." Moreover, since farm life "developes the bodily and mental powers naturally and healthfully," its influences being "far more exhilarating and ennobling than those of the workshop," the institution was to be a farm school. In both respects the school departed from the large congregate "Houses of Refuge" in New York and Philadelphia which reformers of 1850 had wanted to copy.

The family system farm school was copied from the new reform school at Lancaster, Ohio. The commissioners expected that it would be without "that ignominious restraint of grate and lock which sickens the heart of many a refuge boy, and impels him to risk his life in efforts at escape." It "*must* rely" on "the power of truth and love and right, . . . a wonderful lever in lifting degraded children up to a level where the light of science and morals and religion can reach them." Another constructive idea was to make a separate provision for boys over fourteen; the idea of a "nautical school ship" for these boys was borrowed from Massachusetts.[8]

So the school went up on a farm of 490 acres on high land two miles east of the village of Jamesburg—water abundant and pure, soil good and varied, site "elevated and healthy, and commands a fine view of distant hills in almost every direction." Trustees were appointed, officers hired, the boys filled their places; reports were filed, slow year after slow year. After two decades a committee of the legislature looked into the management of the institution; it did not compare what it saw with the hopes of the founders, but only applied its own common sense. It found no scandals, but it observed that something was missing.

There were then about three hundred boys at Jamesburg, distributed in families of fifty, each with its own building. The buildings—called cottages—had three stories. The basement held dining rooms, play rooms, and bath; the first floor was arranged as a school room; the upper floor was a congregate sleeping room. Each family was under an officer and his wife, who had an apartment in the building. The family lived together day and night. The officer supervised work and instructed in a trade; his wife, usually, served as teacher in the school. The boys got up at 5:30 and breakfasted on coffee, milk, and bread at 6:15. Then they went to work for almost five hours, with a short recess. At lunch, from noon until 12:45, they ate "as much soup as they will and the meat and vegetables that were boiled in it"; then they returned to work. At 2:15 they had a recess; then came school, from three until six; then supper, "devotions" at 7:45 and bed at 8:00. The food was "honest and wholesome," the legislators said, having sampled it twice.

At first, farming had largely occupied the boys, plus whatever work was needed to maintain and improve the plant; then, in 1875, the trustees contracted with shirt makers, and a factory appeared on the premises. Authorities measured the progress of the boys in two ways.

Work assignments were defined as tasks; when a boy finished his particular task, he could amuse himself until the next scheduled activity. More generally, there was a merit system, which rewarded good behavior for a month with a badge; a series of badges brought privilege and the hope of indenture.

To the committee this all looked mechanical and routine. "It is not enough for a school to prevent, repress and forbid what is evil. It must draw out latent powers, direct growing activities, encourage honest desires and build up character." In short, the reform school should reform. In fact, the boys' life was "hard, routine, and monotonous," especially for boys under twelve. Neither work nor school offered any challenge. The tasks were dull and unpromising: neither shirt-making nor the "plain sort of agriculture" practiced on the farm was profitable. The school, scheduled after hours of labor, was ungraded and elementary. When the day, "given up altogether to task work," was done, the boys were "locked up at night by fifties, cut off from books, newspapers, and . . . civilization." Jamesburg was not a family, nor a reformatory, but a boys' prison. The wholesome food was "served like prison messes, in silence." [9]

The committee did not ask how things had fallen into such a state; it was generally respectful of the management and the trustees. Part of the problem was to find people who could combine supervision, trade instruction, and parental guidance. Moreover, the institution began to be crowded in the mid-seventies with older boys (half the inmates were over thirteen in 1886). The difficulty of finding suitable families to whom to bind out the boys steadily increased.

Public Opinion and Reform Schools

External as well as internal conditions were a handicap. The founders did not foresee that anyone would object to nightly "devotions" or to the notion that the inmates' "families" should be "united in chapel." But since a large proportion of the children came from the city poor, many were Catholic, and their spiritual guardians had definite ideas about "chapel," devotions, moral instruction, and the rest of it. Furthermore, they were generally skeptical about Protestants, public reformatories, and most child-saving agencies. As neighbors and friends of the children and as defenders of the faith, they were interested in promoting parochial schools. Under the education act of 1846 they had claimed a share of school funds for their institutions; this riled nativists and led to a long, bitter argument that had led the legislature, in 1866, definitely to deny the claim.[10] The argument did not end then, of course, and meanwhile it spread to charity and correction.

The problem, in the Catholic view, was that most of the private charities engaged in child-saving work were either frankly Protestant or nondenominational middle class—that is, vaguely Protestant. These agencies took children in distress and usually tried to place them in good rural homes—mostly Protestant, of course. The situation was clearest across the Hudson in New York, where needs were greatest, the system best developed, and Catholic responses clearest. Catholics were skeptical of foster home placement. They favored putting orphaned, neglected, and "delinquent" children in church-sponsored institutions, in the European tradition.

That pattern afforded religious control and education and was also more convenient for temporary dependency—when a parent went to a hospital or jail for a short period. Ideally Catholics looked forward to a restoration of the family, not its separation. They could not have found enough suitable foster homes if they had wanted to. The result, in New York, was a number of Catholic orphanages (mostly for children under twelve) and industrial schools and protectories, for children over twelve. The Catholic Protectory of New York, established in 1864, the largest of these institutions, handled the sort of children that came to Jamesburg.[11]

Catholics in Jersey City and Newark hoped to establish a similar institution in their diocese, aided, as New York's was at first, with state funds. A bill looking toward this end was offered in the New Jersey legislature of 1874, at the same time that the legislature was debating certain constitutional amendments, several of which involved the relation between church and state. An assemblyman from Hudson argued "that there were 300,000 Catholics in the State, and that they would not submit to having their children sent to an institution [Jamesburg] where the love for their religion was likely to be crushed out." He insisted that the act did not really call for state aid to religion, and pointed to similar arrangements in New York, Massachusetts, and England. Despite angry opposition, the measure passed the lower house and went to the Senate. There the rural counties ruled; the examples of New York, Massachusetts, and England did not win a warm response. A committee reported an "emasculated" version of the bill, which was easily defeated. The senator from Hudson County offered a "Liberty of Conscience" bill, aimed at the admission of priests to state institutions; his colleagues defeated that too.[12]

But electoral majorities were fickle, and it was plain that the Catholic population was increasing. Interest therefore turned to the constitutional amendments, which would bind subsequent legislators. On the Sunday before the election, the Bishop of Newark advised the faithful to vote against the "antichurch" amendments; he suggested that they vote against all amendments, to avoid confusion, although for the discriminating he prepared ballots with three offensive items crossed out. Numbered one, two, and eleven, they prohibited the use of public money for sectarian purposes, guaranteed free schools, and forbade special (private) legislation. The result was decisive; not only did the electorate approve the amendments by large majorities, but they defeated almost all the legislators who voted for the protectory bill.[13]

The implications of the controversy went far beyond the question of a Catholic protectory to serve alongside Jamesburg, but the result was that Catholics were disposed to be skeptical and even hostile where the reformatory was concerned. Events had made it a symbol of grave divisions in the state.

Where, then, could the reform school find support? Who knew or cared whether it worked or not? Lawyers and judges, educators and conscientious wardens, and people in private charitable work had supported it at first; after 1886 the State Charities Aid Association might have been a vehicle of criticism and help, although its concern was local public, not state, institutions. But none of these groups had any responsibility for the conduct of the institution, or any direct channel of information about it. Moreover, it simply did not solve the problems that interested them. It did not keep children out of the jails, for example; children went to jail pending trial and sentence as usual, and Jamesburg received only those whose sentences might run a year or more. (A law of 1888 required jail keepers to separate children over sixteen from those below that age.) [14] Furthermore the reform school did not receive children under eight and, because it took so many over fourteen, judges were reluctant to send younger children there.

This matter became serious when the state passed a compulsory education act in 1874 and truancy became a legal offense. On the one hand, truants were crowded into the institution; on the other hand, judges and teachers saw that it was no place for wayward schoolboys.[15] What Jamesburg did, as matters turned out, was take older or more incorrigible offenders who otherwise might have served ordinary jail or prison sentences.

So the interest of the original supporters of the reformatory went on to new ventures: detention homes or special quarters in the jails, special courts, an effective probation system, parental schools (special disciplinary schools in the school system itself and under direct supervision of school authorities), and a new state reformatory, to take charge of the older and tougher inmates at Jamesburg. The relationship among these proposals was not clear but in any case they diverted attention from the reform school. Moreover, the people who recognized the additional needs came from the cities where Catholic influence was growing stronger, especially in the police and the lower courts, which were closest to the problem of juvenile delinquency.

From the viewpoint of the trustees and officials of the reformatory, the people they had to please were the legislative committees that doled out the appropriations. The legislators cared most about what the institution spent. If they looked at the institution at all—they didn't have to—they wanted to see something clean, well-kept, and smooth-running—no trouble, no scandals. And this is what the management tried to give them: this was the meaning of the discipline of outer conformity, the employment of boys at task work (the tasks got done), the repressive routine, the silent suppers. The program may have helped the boys in the authorities' view (it *was* better than putting them in the jails or the state prison, wasn't it?), and it certainly helped the institution. Throughout the years, the official reports did not say: "We are supposed to be like families, but we are not; we are supposed to reform, but we do not." Instead they said that things were generally satisfactory and improving, but there was a pressing need for this and that, ultimately for more money.

The drift of the situation appears in the first legislative investigation of Jamesburg, in 1880. The occasion was not cruelty or misconduct. A shirt-making firm that had leased the labor of the boys complained that the trustees had neglected them to favor a rival. The aggrieved entrepreneurs calculated their loss at $12,500, not to mention their anxiety; they insinuated that the trustees had had some ulterior motives for their preference. Legislators thought the matter serious; a committee took 175 pages of testimony and reported that the "trustees have acted honorably, and with a view to promote the welfare of the youth committed to their care." [16]

No one raised the question, then, whether shirt making was an appropriate activity. It was not the ennobling exhilarating farm life that the founders had foreseen, and it did not teach a trade. But it was a profitable enterprise and grew accordingly. The committee of 1886, criticizing the routine institutional character of the place, allowed that the purpose of the school's program was to "be as nearly self-supporting as possible," but submitted that "the primary purpose of the school is not so much to make money as it is to make good citizens." No one took them up on the idea.[17]

At the girls' reformatory—The State Industrial School for Girls at Trenton, established in 1871—the situation was no more hopeful. The school was small and its population grew slowly; it was evidently cheaper to enlarge it by additions to the main building rather than by building new cottages, so it grew into a congregate institution. The inmates included a larger age range than Jamesburg and the grounds were more cramped, as the city of Trenton grew up around them. The institution escaped notice for years, but in 1899 there were scandals about cruelty and slipshod administration. An investigating committee ignored the cruelty and traced the administrative difficulty a long way back to the original plan of incorporation.[18] A friend of reform on the committee thought a more liberal regime and better classification would reduce the need for punishment, and he hoped that the proposed parole law might remove half the population in a year.[19]

The parole law and a new organic act did not improve the situation.[20] An observer described it in 1904: "Take a hundred girls (good or bad, it doesn't much matter); shut them up in an institution; keep them idle about half the time; give nothing to play with, no physical exercise, no recreation, no fun, nothing to work off steam; keep them carefully from all contact with the real world; feed them poorly; play 'favorites' with some and jump on others; let big and little, good and bad, black and white, the normal and the abnormal, mix together indiscriminately; and if the whole lot are not spoilt for life, it is because, after all, human nature has more power of moral resistance than we give it credit for." [21]

New trustees and officers and new facilities improved matters, but well-meaning people were losing interest in reform schools. The secretary of the State Charities Aid Association, commenting on Jamesburg in 1914, said that to send boys there was to brand them as criminals and to reduce their opportunity to find positions of trust and responsibility; army, navy, and civil service would not knowingly employ them, for example. Reformers should make "every effort . . . to prevent . . . commitment" there. Reformers (following the lead of big cities) must encourage "special schools . . . , truancy schools, parental homes and the like," and improve and extend probation. "Many boys are committed . . . simply because there is a lack of proper probation . . . in rural communities and the smaller cities of the state." He suggested that if counties paid the cost of caring for the boys they sent to Jamesburg, they would take more interest in probation.[22]

Women's clubs were particularly interested in the "George Junior Republic" in New York, a private institution for delinquent children where they learned "self-government." In 1903 the ladies considered building a New Jersey cottage there or perhaps at the similar "Carter Junior Republic" near Easton, Pennsylvania.[23] Caroline Bayard Colgate, when she turned her notable means and zeal to correctional work in 1912, found an appropriate object not in Jamesburg but in the Newark Parental School; together with the judge of the Juvenile Court in Newark she fostered Bonnie Brae, a private farm home for "dependent delinquents" of the sort that were often sent to Jamesburg. When she was appointed to the Jamesburg board in 1917 her "first reaction was . . . breathless panic, because the institution . . . had such an unsavory reputation." An old friend told her it would be "like cleaning the Augean stables." She knew that juvenile court judges "did not sentence boys to Jamesburg unless their crimes were of a serious nature. They would, if possible, send them to Bonnie Brae or place them on probation." [24]

So matters stood by the time the first Jamesburg boys were men of sixty or seventy. On the one hand, people felt that what was needed to improve Jamesburg was a great system of detention homes, special courts, probation, and parental schools—how long would that take? On the other hand, men felt that what was needed to improve Jamesburg was a little more of this and that, in effect, a little more money. Nor could one deny the force of the argument; as the critical committee of 1886 concluded, "the appropriation for the school should be much enlarged" to give the trustees "liberal means for the improvement of the school in such direction as may be best." But the committee had begun its report by acknowledging that its own inquiry was handicapped "for want of the appropriation . . . passed by the legislature at the last session, but . . . not approved by the Governor." [25] Whether they looked within or without, the people who ran reform schools in New Jersey could see little prospect that they would soon get the support to do the job they were supposed to do.

The State Board of Children's Guardians

As indenture became difficult and pauper children crowded the poorhouses, reformers had to devise substitutes either for binding out young people or for almshouse care. Poor-law officials might have risen to the challenge by devising better ways to find homes and place children, or they might have built orphanages alongside the almshouses. Public welfare departments, handling children among other problems, might have developed as rapidly as schools, police, fire and health departments.

To some extent, in some places, this happened. Some states, like Ohio, established a system of county orphanages; others, like Michigan, provided a state orphanage and child-placing agency. A delegate from New Jersey to the National Conference of Charities and Corrections in 1881 favored the Michigan system.[26] On the other hand, the Morris County Charities Aid Association, organized in that year, campaigned successfully for a county-supported orphanage to get children out of its almshouse (which had become crowded when a local iron works had closed). The state commissioner of labor approved this institution in his report on pauperism in 1883, and the Children's Committee of the SCAA approved it in 1887.[27] Mrs. Emily Williamson, the secretary of SCAA and for years a leader in movements for child welfare, at first favored a new state industrial school to get children out of the almshouses.[28]

But in general, voluntary charities developed the alternatives. Private orphanages took the place of almshouse care, private child-placing agencies offered a substitute for indenture by poor-law officials. Once established, they reduced the cost of public provision, because they were subsidized by churches and rich philanthropists instead of by taxpayers. They were also supposed to be less corrupt and more efficient.

There were several difficulties with the private agencies, however. One was that they simply didn't do the job. The census of 1890 showed that New Jersey stood fourth highest in the proportion of its children in almshouses, far higher than any neighboring state.[29] Moreover, private agencies divided sharply on how to do the job. Some, thought progressive, favored putting children with foster families; others, Catholics and Lutherans in particular, favored church-connected institutions.

Probably the relative strength of the private agencies in New Jersey as well as the rivalry among them delayed a state program. People actively interested in child-saving looked to an improvement of their own work and feared an advantage to their rivals. For whatever reason, a state agency for dependent children was not proposed until thirty years after the reform school appeared; even then it provoked the most bitter and prolonged opposition of any state institution, and, perhaps as a result of the controversy, it was the most progressive institution of the period.

The agency was first proposed in the report of a "Commission on Defective, Delinquent and Dependent Children" in 1897. Legislators were unenthusiastic about the Commission and did not give it an appropriation or the power to subpoena witnesses and take testimony, but Hugh Fox and Emily Williamson, the commissioners (and SCAA officials) who wrote the report, were both so rich they did not need public funds, and in retrospect it seems that they made their comments on existing provision as inoffensive as possible. "The private charities of New Jersey are in every respect excellent," they reported, "especially those for children." They counted thirty-five homes caring for 3,005 children; 1,439 of these were in Catholic institutions. Their primary interest was the 445 children reported in almshouses; 252 of them were in the Hudson County almshouse, forty and twenty in the municipal institutions of Paterson and Elizabeth. In all of populous Essex County there were only ten almshouse children, they noted, because of the admirable work of the Children's Aid Society of Newark (supported by "citizens of every sect") and the Charity Organization Societies of the Oranges. In rural places the largest collection by far was in Burlington County, the home of the piney-woods people. The other pauper children were scattered through the state.[30]

Clearly, Hudson County was the trouble spot, with more than half of the unfortunate children. Almshouse care was bad in itself—it had no defenders, the commissioners said—but many children in the Hudson County almshouse simply should not have been there. Some had relatives who were able to support them but unwilling; others were kept when they should have been placed out. Hudson County spent almost twice as much as the nonsectarian agencies to maintain a dependent child. "The taxpayer's money is nowhere spent as freely as it is in this county. . . . It is a blot upon the escutcheon of the state." (Commissioner Hugh Fox was president of the Bayonne COS and a large taxpayer in Hudson County.)[31]

For the most part, the commissioners talked about the possibilities of the future. "We find at least this consolation for New Jersey's tardiness . . . , that we are in a position to profit by the mistakes . . . made in other states." Two mistakes seemed clear. One was to allow parents to keep guardianship of their pauper children or to regain it at request. This practice encouraged irresponsible parents to surrender children who were a burden and then to reclaim them when they were old enough to work; it allowed irresponsible parents to exploit either the taxpayers or the children, without regard to what was best for the little ones. To avoid this mistake the commissioners proposed, as their central idea, that a state agency investigate every commitment of a pauper child to see whether it was necessary, and, if it was, to become the legal guardian of the child in his own interest. This procedure was intended to reduce the number of commitments and protect the helpless child from abuse by almshouse keepers or by parents or foster parents who might remove him.

A second mistake, the commissioners believed, was institutional care, particularly care in private institutions subsidized by public grants, as in New York. The alternative, supported by the best authorities, was to place the children with foster families. "Place out" did not necessarily mean "indenture," which legally bound a child to a master for many years; the commissioners wanted the state agency to supervise the child and transfer him as seemed best. It would try to place children in free homes, under these conditions, but it could pay the foster parents up to $1.50 a week for board.

Such were the essential ideas of the State Board of Children's Guardians. To administer the program the commissioners proposed a board of guardians in each county, appointed by the orphan's court, serving without salary and hence "nonpolitical." A state board would supervise the county boards. The arrangement was somewhat like that between the State Charities Aid Association and its county branches. The state would pay the cost of administration; counties or municipalities would pay the cost of board, clothing, and medical care for the wards (since they were responsible for these charges under the poor law). The commissioners, who had studied the subject carefully, borrowed their ideas mostly from Massachusetts and the District of Columbia.[32]

The proposals, submitted to the legislature in 1898, were opposed on several grounds. Local poor-law officials, the most influential critics, objected to the nonpolitical county boards, which would remove all pauper children from their authority. Moreover it appeared to the commissioners that these boards had not worked well in Indiana, so they agreed, in their second report, that a single state agency should take children upon commitment by local overseers of the poor.[33]

Argument then turned to the fundamental issues of state guardianship and placing out. Opposition came from three sources, for quite different reasons: the chosen freeholders of Hudson County; the Catholic bishops; and the Children's Home Society, a private child-placing agency in Trenton that served the rural counties.

An overseer of the poor for Hudson County, who had spent twenty-five years in relieving the poor, put his own construction on the situation at the almshouse. He acknowledged that most of the children did have a living parent, but it was plain that he sympathized with the parents. In most cases they had put in the poorhouse children who were mentally or physically handicapped and "of no use at home." He did not believe that the parents were irresponsible, or think it right that they should lose their parental rights simply because they had had to put their children in the almshouse, and he thought they had a right to take their children back when they were able. In effect, he looked upon the almshouse as a free asylum for the children of distressed parents, and not as a form of punishment for irresponsibility. The almshouse warden did find homes for children who were really orphans and who were healthy; he had more requests than he could fill for them.[34]

Furthermore, he observed, the almshouse children were not the real problem, not a drop in the bucket of childhood misery. "I can take you to 20 tenements in Jersey City in which are 200 children over ten years old who don't know one letter from another," he said. They live amid "bad sanitation, bad air and all that would tend to dwarf a child mentally and physically." The almshouse children were only the obvious "mental and physical wrecks among the children of the poor." To get at the roots of the matter he urged stricter laws on education (opposed by employers of child labor) and stricter laws on housing and sanitation (opposed by landlords).[35]

Catholic bishops, for their part, opposed state guardianship and family placement. They thought that parents who had to send their children to the poorhouse should not lose their sacred rights as parents. They favored the arrangement in New York, where municipal poor-law authorities committed pauper children to private institutions and subsidized their board. This idea failing—the commissioners thought that it was plainly unconstitutional and that it worked badly in New York—the bishops seemed to favor local public orphanages. They thought that institutional officials, whether private or public, could be trusted to operate satisfactorily when subject only to general state supervision. On the other hand, they were skeptical about the commissioners' proposal to place children in families of like religion; it was evident that they did not want to entrust a state agency with this responsibility.[36]

The Children's Home Society, the third source of opposition, was one of a number of affiliated agencies which received children from poor-law officials (and relatives and friends) and placed them with families. It was technically nonsectarian, simply a charitable society, and authorized, along with similar private bodies, to deal with the poor-law officials under a state law of 1881 (ch. 196). It was in fact supported by Protestant women's groups; its officers were Protestant clergymen. The Society thought that present arrangements were satisfactory. It said it had "emptied the almshouses already" and had more requests for children than it could fill. This was largely the case in the rural counties it served, although even here many undesirable children could not be placed and the society chose to ignore the situation in Paterson and Hudson County.[37]

The Society of course favored the policy of placing children in foster homes, for that is what it did. It received requests from families for children (perhaps through an affiliate in the Middle West), found a suitable child, and placed him. Private charity financed its work, without cost to poor-law officials. After the child was placed the Society did ask the local officials for a "voluntary donation," in view of the fact that it had saved them money. Donations varied. Camden County usually gave $50; in Warren County, a tame frontier on the upper Delaware, authorities thought $30 per child was about right.

But the Society opposed the ideas of state guardianship and subsidized foster home care, which would make matters difficult for it in two ways. If the state took and kept guardianship of the waifs, it would be harder to find foster homes, especially at a distance. Families would think twice about taking a little almshouse child to their bosom if state agents would presently come snooping around, criticizing, able to remove the child at will. This was all a grave violation of the privacy of the home and the rights of parents (foster parents, in this case); the state supervisor would fatally disrupt the ties of trust, discipline, and love that bound families together.[38]

Furthermore, the subsidies would amount to an enormous expense. Families would be unwilling to take children "free" if they could get the state to subsidize the child's board. As matters stood, when overseers placed children through the society they paid neither the administrative cost of placement nor any charge for board, but according to the commissioners' proposals a tax-supported agency would take over the work of placement and it would commit the local officials to pay $1.50 per week for board plus other expenses, without the local authorities having any say in the matter. Patriots from the pastureland recognized an ancient evil, taxation without representation. And there were other doubts. Would not the state open itself to liability for all the three thousand children supported by private charities, an enormous expense? Would it not take children permanently, if it chose, from parents in temporary straits? Was not some sort of institutional provision a necessary and desirable supplement to foster family care (as a dissenter among the commissioners said)? [39]

These arguments were the occasion for a grand impugning of motives all around. Protestants and Catholics had no difficulty discerning each other's hostile and subversive intentions. The Children's Home Society was called a trafficker in human flesh. Responsible public officials (or political hangers-on) pointed gravely to elementary considerations that philanthropic reformers (or enthusiastic busybodies) ignored (and vice versa). A Jersey City editor raised the question whether Mrs. Williamson was trying to get herself a state job on the proposed board. Observers in the hinterland noted that Hugh Fox was secretary of the American Brewer's Association, a spokesman for the saloon interests.

To this exchange of thoughts the New York *Herald* added a mighty voice. One of the *Herald*'s owners was a Jerseyman whose interest in his home state created a New Jersey edition of the *Herald* that, in the view of another journalist turned historian, "was for years the most potent single force in New Jersey's affairs." The paper took up the case of ten-year-old Johnny Pfeiffer. Little Johnny had lost a leg under a trolley car; his mother, thinking him dead, had lost her mind. When mother and child were reunited they found that the husband and father had deserted. Mrs. Pfeiffer and Johnny got along as best they could, but finally she had to lead him to the Hudson County almshouse on Snake Hill. Johnny somehow made off from the almshouse, however, and tried to support himself, without success. When the police finally picked him up for vagrancy and told him friendly that they knew a home for him, Johnny protested. "You don't mean the almshouse again, do you?" he is reported to have cried. "Don't send me there! I want to make my own living. . . . If you send me back to Snake Hill, I won't be nothin' but a bum, nor I won't, neither." [40]

Following up the story, newshawks from the *Herald* brought Snake Hill into the view of their readers. It rose out of mosquito-ridden marshes by the sluggish Hackensack River. In this wasteland, miles from a settlement, were the county penitentiary and insane asylum, grimly crowded, and between them the almshouse with its hundreds of children. Conscientious sensationalism gave the old horror a fine statement: "the abode of filth," noted the journalists; "indescribably degraded, abandoned and dissolute," with "every kind of communal nastiness and vice"; sexual propriety gone; here were families "reared by parents who had themselves been born there." Human bodies "covered with vermin"; minds "even fouler than their limbs." The *Herald* would protect little Johnny from all this.[41]

This was the pabulum of popular sensation, but it is notable that the SCAA ladies who visited Snake Hill during these years were respectful of the management and thought the inmates, particularly the children, were clean and orderly. "Much has been said of the demoralizing influence on children from their contact with the adult paupers," a visitor reported in 1897; but it was unfair, she thought, to hold that paupers were necessarily vicious. "Let it be said in behalf of the women [paupers, who looked after the children], that they take personal pride in the room and the children placed in their care, entering into a sort of rivalry, especially in regard to the cleanliness and behavior of their child-charges." [42] The commissioners who proposed the state board never argued that the children at Snake Hill were abused, but rather that the management admitted too many, placed out too few, too carelessly, and that the formal education that the almshouse offered was perfunctory. Reformers worried about the children's future, not their present.[43] When Mrs. Williamson finally removed the children from Snake Hill she specifically denied stories about their mistreatment. "I found the children here in better physical condition than those of any other place," she said. "They were clean and well kept." [44]

Bemused by such contradictions, the legislature acted indecisively. On the last day of the 1899 session, it voted to establish the Board of Children's Guardians, but it made no appropriation for the work. Moreover, the act allowed poor-law officials to continue to place children with the Children's Home Society, and it was not even clear about the responsibility of county officials.[45]

The Guardians in Action: Foster Care and Home Life

Nevertheless, the governor appointed the Board—seven members, unpaid, including by law two women—and it went to work. The Bayonne COS offered the Board a desk in its quarters above the police station.

Mrs. Williamson herself began the work of visiting the almshouse children, to determine whether they had relatives who could take them or what kind of foster home placement was appropriate. Board members themselves financed the cost of administration and even underwrote the subsidies to foster homes; Mrs. Williamson alone is said to have contributed $10,000 to the work.[46]

Acting first with friendly public officials, the Board showed that its policies worked. It did find relatives to take many children; it even found children who could claim an inheritance; it worked effectively with private charities to keep or bring deserving families together, out of the almshouse; it did find free homes for many children; it did correct the abuse of foster children and yet its supervision proved to be tactful and welcome; it did scrupulously respect the religious affiliation of its wards. It did, in short, get children out of the almshouse and substitute casework for perfunctory relief.

Ahead lay two obstacles: the Hudson County freeholders and the Children's Home Society. Hudson County, refusing to cooperate, challenged the Board's authority by a "friendly suit," which was not in fact at all friendly. County elections presently brought more reasonable freeholders into office, however, and in April, 1901, they agreed to release their almshouse children to the Board. Their questions on this occasion show the substantial doubts that the Board had to satisfy. What would happen to the twenty-three deaf and dumb and severely handicapped children? The Board would place them in appropriate state institutions for treatment or care, or in medical institutions. What would happen to families in the almshouse, mother and children together? The Board would try to rehabilitate them, with the help of private charities. It would not separate them unless necessary. How about costs? Orphan children under four could be placed for adoption, along with some others; children from four to ten were usually boarded out; those over ten usually went to free homes. How did the Board ascertain the child's religious affiliation? By careful study of family records. Evidently nothing in the Board's record of two years led the freeholders to doubt its good faith. The newspaper account noted that when children finally left, five or six almshouse employees would lose their jobs.[47]

The following year the Board took on the Children's Home Society. The issue was whether poor-law officials could continue to place pauper children with the Society, where they were not under state supervision. The argument was partly whether the Society's work was adequate and partly what the state's responsibility was toward its unfortunate children. The Board proposed a law that it, alone, should take responsibility for children committed to almshouses as public charges. In this case the religious question helped it, for testimony of the Society's officials indicated that they were not solicitous about placing children in homes of their ancestral faith. This gave the politicians a chance to affirm their respect for everybody's ancestral faith, and the Board won its case.[48]

It is clear in retrospect that the prolonged and frank, if bitter, debate over the Board was a benefit to all concerned. COS people learned that they needed to get together with local public officials and institutional officers in a constructive way, and even that they might learn something from them. This was a motive of the State Conferences of Charities and Corrections, which began in 1902.[49] Private child-care agencies were forced into a wholesome review of their methods and differences.[50] Protestants and Catholics learned more respect for each other's interests and ideas; the Catholic Children's Aid Society of Newark, established in 1903 under Father Francis R. Foy, was a significant departure in Catholic child-placing, the first outside New York.[51]

The founders of the Board of Children's Guardians quickly acknowledged that institutional provision was necessary for some kinds of children, and they acquired a well-informed view of the private and public institutions that cared for their wards; this led to an exchange of ideas about various programs, particularly for defective children and probationers, and to strong support for improving and expanding them.[52] As the agency improved its casework it became more respectful of the needs and interests of pauper parents. At first it had insisted on retaining guardianship of its wards even when they were returned to their parents, but a law of 1902 (ch. 160) allowed it discretion to surrender guardianship to one or both parents.

So it was that in 1910 New Jersey pioneered in what became a major public welfare program: aid to dependent children in their own homes. When the Board had taken charge of the children in the Hudson County almshouse in 1901, a reporter noted that more than sixty children had been removed by "parents and friends who were willing to endure even greater privations than their poverty was already forcing on them," rather than see their children placed in homes "from which they feared they could not remove them when they might be in a position to care for them." Someone suggested at the time that the guardians might board the pauper waifs with their own indigent mothers. Mrs. Williamson observed that the idea seemed reasonable and humane, but it might "encourage some mothers to throw their children upon the public with the purpose of having them sent back to them as boarders." [53] In fact, the Board did refer such cases to private family agencies, which often did help mother and child; Mrs. Williamson was only voicing the well-established COS belief that public outdoor relief—in this case, a public subsidy to the indigent mother—was dangerously liable to abuse.

Mother's aid—a public subsidy to help poor mothers keep their families together—became an issue in many states, between, usually, politicians who found it popular and charity organizers who thought it unwise. But in New Jersey the State Board of Children's Guardians anticipated the plan in 1910 by asking the attorney general to rule that aid to mothers was within its legal power. Moreover the Board persuaded overseers to make "paper commitments" of these families so that they could remain outside the almshouse until the child was boarded out to its own mother.[54] Another law of 1910 (ch. 13) gave judges the power to commit delinquent children to the Board rather than to a correctional institution. These laws are signs of a flexible policy and public confidence, the result of the long debate in which many shibboleths were confronted: public versus private care, institutions versus foster homes, the rights of parents, children and foster parents, the state's responsibility and local control.

In form the guardians' work was simple. When overseers of the poor committed a child to the almshouse, the warden notified the Board; an agent took the child and placed it, in all but a few cases, in a private family. But those few words contained "volumes of experience," as Frances Day, the agency's executive, remarked in 1911. Only experience could bring out all the practical details of studying the child's needs, finding a suitable family, and exercising supervision, the details of what to look for, where to find, what to do and how to do. Only practice knit together all the families, relatives, friends, public officials, institutions, social workers, teachers, clergymen, doctors, nurses, and others who had somehow to be met and whose interest and services had somehow to be brought to bear on the fate of hundreds, then thousands, of girls and boys, each of them a different case.[55]

Frances Day had learned all these things at first hand, for she had helped Mrs. Williamson almost from the start, had become "general agent" in 1904 and continued as chief executive until 1930. The Board got its own office, a year or so later, in Jersey City, where the trouble was endless and the transportation good. There Miss Day got around by trolley, but often she had children to visit or trouble to shoot in other parts of the state, for she did run a state-wide agency. Then she took a train, her bicycle in the baggage car. She was energetic and liked the work, which was good because the agency was chronically understaffed. She often talked about pioneers and pioneering.[56] So the stories go, a good deal too cheerfully, for Miss Day grew old in the work: her job, especially in the first years, was responsible and demanding child care, with misunderstanding and controversy hovering over every decision; and even an energetic and zealous woman might find drawbacks to riding a bicycle a couple of miles through the rain in a long dress and petticoats.

The significance of the origin of the State Board of Children's Guardians is not only the fight over its founding, or the constructive services to children which it developed or helped foster by its presence, or Miss Day on the trail. One does not look far into the campaign for any social legislation during the "progressive period" in New Jersey without seeing some Board member in action, perhaps as an official, perhaps as an individual, for all the laws bearing on schooling, truants, tenements, child labor, police, courts, sanitation, food, playgrounds, hospitals, anything involving not just children but mothers and fathers, took on a special meaning for the fine ladies and gentlemen who served on the Board and who learned, hard case after hard case, how the odds ran against the children of the poor.

Indeed, matters pushed ahead so rapidly in so many aspects of child care that the agency's practice in 1901 seemed antiquated and amusing by 1911, as Miss Day remarked. But large new responsibilities were in the offing. Widow's pensions came to New Jersey in 1913. Indigent mothers could thereafter appeal to the Court of Common Pleas for a pension, without going to the poor-law officials and without commitment to the almshouse. The Board was not enthusiastic about this plan; its own informal policy of mother's aid gave it more freedom of action. It feared (with reason) that the case load would increase very rapidly and that casework with the mothers would be more difficult.[57]

On the other hand, because poor-law officials, to reduce the charges for the maintenance of pauper children, had often found devices to avoid committing them to the almshouse and hence to the Board, a law of 1915 empowered judges to commit neglected children directly to the Board, over the heads of the local overseers.[58] Both these developments radically increased the case load. By 1918, the agency supervised over 6,000 children, two-thirds of them in the new "home life" program, the others in the older foster-care program. At that time it had only fifteen agents, and its perennial plea for more adequate resources was more urgent than ever. Meanwhile the flu epidemic tripled the number of petitions for aid and the World War snarled parenthood and childhood, as wars will.[59] In 1918 the Board came under the new state department which controlled all charitable and correctional institutions. The questions of its future resources, and of its relation to what was envisioned as a comprehensive state welfare program, were matters to be determined anew.

6

State Provision for the Handicapped, to 1917

The new institutions that offered special help to deaf, blind, and feebleminded were in part a consequence of the general specialization of educational facilities after 1850. But because their precedents and partisans were associated as much with "charity" as with "education," they raised questions, which grew in importance, about the nature and sponsorship of their service. At first, it seemed obvious that the state government had to step in and save the handicapped from the pauperizing neglect of their families and local communities. As the dimensions of problems became clearer and local services improved in the big cities, after 1900, it seemed that the public school system and local services were in a better position to help—if they had the means and inclination.

State institutions gave form in different ways to these ideas. The School for the Deaf, placed under the State Board of Education in 1891, never became part of the state welfare department. The Commission for the Blind, which worked in the community and never developed a residential school, was included in the State Department of Institutions and Agencies rather than Education. A private "training school" for feebleminded children, patronized by the state, furnished leadership in creating three custodial institutions as experience undermined hope for its charges and scientific inquiry revealed that mental deficiency was an unrecognized cause of much pauperism and crime.

Special Education for the Deaf and the Blind

New Jersey first provided for its deaf and blind children in schools in New York and Philadelphia. These institutions, among the earliest in the country, were humanitarian and charitable ventures, and it was expected that they would draw students from neighboring states. Their founders were clergymen or physicians who thought of the afflicted as deprived of the dignity of independence and the inspiration of religion. Pity and hope struck a common chord, and the founders succeeded so well in raising money that it seemed for a time that the provision would exceed the demand; hence students from out of state were actively sought.

The first schools were for the deaf, the largest group. The New York Institution for the Deaf and Dumb opened its doors in 1818 and the next year received a subsidy from the legislature. The Pennsylvania institution was a private charity in Philadelphia which the legislature incorporated and subsidized in 1821.[1] The presence of schools convenient to both East and West Jersey doubtless encouraged legislators from both sections to grant a subsidy so their constituents might attend them. The first law (1821) allowed the governor to grant $160 per year for three years to an indigent deaf person of good natural ability. Later acts extended the term of benefit and lowered the age requirement.[2]

Provision for the blind followed a similar course. The New York Institution for the Blind opened as a private charity in 1832 and received state subsidy in 1834; the Pennsylvania institution, opened in 1833, received public aid from the start.[3] New Jersey began to subsidize students in both schools in 1836. (In 1860 the state began to pay the tuition of indigent retarded children in a school near Philadelphia.) [4]

By 1872 the state had established and expanded its lunatic asylum and reform schools for juveniles, and reformers had carried the battle for public education far beyond the idea of free schools for the poor. Consequently in that year parents of deaf children asked for a state residential school to afford their children a more convenient public education as a matter of right.[5] Their plea led the legislature to authorize a commission to investigate the plight of all "defective" classes. Its report (1873) gives a picture of the situation then.

In general, the commissioners said that the state provided well for a few of its handicapped, but it met only a fraction of the need. Specifically, the state maintained 121 students in out-of-state schools, at a cost of $36,600 (about the statutory limit, at that time, of $300 apiece). The deaf ("and dumb") numbered fifty-three; blind, forty-one; feebleminded, twenty-seven. The commissioners had nothing but praise for the schools. But handicapped people without special provision were pitiable, "inevitably gravitating lower and lower in the scale of humanity" and meanwhile "subjected to want, pitiless exposure and shameful outrage." Many were "scattered among our almshouses, filthy, diseased, untaught, in many cases treated with shocking indifference, and in others with still more shocking cruelty." Others were "in the nominal care of ignorant, or poor, or heartless relatives, to whom they are a burthen and a shame, and by whom they are permitted to descend to a level lower than that of the beast. . . . These sightless eyes, deaf ears, mute tongues and vacant minds are a perpetual witness against us," the commissioners said; "hereafter we cannot escape our responsibility by pleading ignorance of the facts." [6]

But the facts about the overall need were not at all clear. The commissioners put no trust in the federal census of 1870; they guessed that

New Jersey had five hundred deaf, six hundred blind and over a thousand feebleminded, and they calculated that the state ignored sixteen unfortunates for each one it chose to help. What was the state's responsibility? Surely, the commissioners thought, the state should provide education and training in special institutions for those of school age (eight to twenty-one—about one-third of the total); and clearly the feebleminded should be housed separately from the other classes. In general, then, the state should act to reduce the number of dependents or the degree of their dependence. It should require the counties to protect and care for unimprovable defectives, especially the feebleminded. Specifically, the commissioners recommended that the state immediately establish schools—not mere asylums—for 150 deaf, one hundred blind, and one hundred feebleminded.[7]

The governor, Joel Parker, an old friend of education and a resident of Monmouth County, whence the petition in behalf of deaf children had come, supported the recommendations, observing that the income from riparian lands might pay the bill.[8] The commissioners, reappointed to make plans, chose a site near New Brunswick, but the legislature refused to buy it, and later a governor vetoed a bill that allowed citizens to buy it as a gift.[9]

The ostensible reason for rejecting the plans was economy; in 1874 the comptroller dismissed the whole matter by observing that the new state lunatic asylum rising at Morris Plains (Greystone Park) would take any surplus in the treasury and perhaps occasion a tax, and that the interest on the cost of the proposed construction would be more than the expense of maintaining students out of state.[10] Moreover, the bill was doubtless caught up in the politicking over the school fund and state aid to private institutions. Rural districts wanted the income from riparian lands to go into a state fund that would keep down school taxes, not expand services, and Catholics wanted the state to subsidize students in church institutions (in 1871 New York had authorized public aid to St. Mary's School for the Deaf, the second permanent school in New York).[11]

In any case, nothing more was done for the handicapped until 1882, when the former Soldiers' Children's Home, vacant since 1876, was fitted out as "The State Institution for the Deaf and Dumb." [12] (The state continued to support students in New York and Philadelphia, presumably when the location was more convenient.) Meanwhile ideas about an "institution" were changing. People who had agitated for an institution in the 1870's had conceived of it as both a charity and a school, like those the state already patronized. But the developing notion of a right to free public education, dissociated entirely from the idea of charity, led those interested in special education of the handicapped to emphasize pedagogical rather than charitable aspects of the "institution." Consequently, in 1891, following the example of New York, the legislature renamed the institution a school and put it under supervision of the state superintendent of education. In 1911, a law authorized public school districts where there were ten afflicted students to establish special classes as part of their program, and Newark and Jersey City began day school classes.[13]

Such was the pattern of progress—from a subsidy for selected indigents in out-of-state charity schools to special day classes in a public school system. However effective the provision in fact, the transition in thinking showed plainly the change from nineteenth- to twentieth-century notions of need and right.

New Jersey never did build a residential school for its blind. In 1895 it was offered a gift of land for an asylum, but the legislature did not accept.[14] Later in the decade the blind had to compete for public assistance against veterans, epileptics, dependent children, and the grave need for a new reformatory. Meanwhile, Catholics created two asylums for the adult blind, St. Joseph's in Jersey City and The House of Our Lady of Perpetual Help in Bayonne (both in 1890). In 1910 some philanthropic ladies established the Arthur Home and Kindergarten for the Blind at Summit, sponsored by the International Sunshine Society, which had its roots and model in England.[15]

But progressive thinkers were dubious by then about asylums and favorable to giving handicapped people an experience as normal as possible. In 1908, after many appeals, the legislators appointed a temporary Commission for the Amelioration of the Condition of the Blind, modeled after an agency in Massachusetts, which was made permanent and quickly expanded its services. It combined notions of "friendly visiting" and social casework with home instruction in braille and industrial work and other services.[16] Its executive, Lydia Hayes, herself blind and a graduate of Perkins Institute, was instrumental in winning state support and supervision for braille classes in public schools, which began in 1910 in Newark and 1911 in Jersey City. In 1912 the state subsidized the college education of indigent blind students.[17] The Commission and the braille classes in public schools put the state, which had hitherto neglected its blind, among the leaders in this work.

Provision for the Retarded and the Epileptic

Efforts to help the deaf and blind led to hopes that they might, despite their affliction, lead reasonably normal lives. Efforts to help the "feeble-minded" led men to believe that, despite their pathetic innocence, the retarded were a social menace and that segregation, not rehabilitation, was the answer to their condition.

From the first, efforts to help them were tinged by hopelessness. Dorothea Dix sympathized with the poor idiot in the almshouse, but the state lunatic asylum denied him entrance. When Senator Stephen Garrison asked the legislature for a state training school in 1845—even before it had established the asylum—other matters seemed more important. In 1852, however, philanthropists in Pennsylvania organized the celebrated Training School at Elwyn, near Philadelphia, and New Jersey began to send indigent retarded there in 1860.[18]

Schools for the handicapped solicited support by "exhibitions" of their students, and there is a record of a performance that helped persuade New Jersey legislators to send students to Elwyn. One of the exhibits was "Grubb," a twelve-year-old orphan, "moral idiot," and behavior problem afflicted with St. Vitus' dance. When he had come to the school his "honest face covered the most mature dishonesty," but he had made fine progress in classes and Sunday school. After his visit to Trenton he was helped to write a letter about the event. He tells how he took "the train of cars" up the Delaware, crossed the "big bridge" to Trenton, and then "went to a tavern, and staid [sic] there all night.

> We showed the people what we could do; all the boys and me sung, and did the dumb-bell exercises; some geography and did some sums. A whole lot of people was in, and ladies, and they stamped their feet. The Governor of New Jersey talked to us, and I made him a present of a smoking-cap. . . . Next day we . . . went up on top of a big State House, and saw the whole country. We saw a great many men in the State House writing, and a good many women was looking at them. Dr. Wm. A. Newell [the governor] took me into his room, and showed me a big pair of scales, made of gold; . . . he took me into another room, and I saw, oh! a great large map of Massachusetts, as big as our new map of Pennsylvania.[19]

Grubb's letter appears in a volume dedicated to Dorothea Dix, a "Faithful Friend of Elwyn." Dr. Joseph Parrish, of a distinguished Quaker family of physicians, who was superintendent of Elwyn for years and who in 1875 opened a private home for "nervous patients" in Burlington, says in the introduction that he is sure that "idiots may be redeemed" from "their sorrowing night of ignorance and degradation." He observes, doubtless from experience, that "feeblemindedness comes not to the poor alone," but also to "the mansions of the rich," where it looks "all the more ghastly, in the midst of the luxury with which it is surrounded." His reflections are as much moral as medical. Idiots teach the wise, he says,

> how foolish is their wisdom; the lofty, how easily the pride of man may be made ashamed; the rich, that moth and rust will corrupt their treasure, if it is not bestowed upon the poor; . . . that idiotcy [sic] with all its loathsome characteristics, is not the fault of those who bear its mark, but that it comes . . . as the result either of Providence or accident, over which short-sighted men seem to have no control.[20]

In general, he believes, "idiotcy" manifests a violation of the "moral law," a general miscarriage in "our modes of life and social arrangements" which are, he thinks, arranged to encourage the "race for riches" or the quest for fame.[21]

The training the school offered was partly academic, partly moral. One visitor was astonished by James, "a most pitiable object, whose ponderous jaws, set with irregular teeth, were always wide open, his eyes fixed on vacancy or staring at the ceiling, and his gaunt body incessantly swaying from side to side"; poor James, "apparently the lowest and most unpromising case in the room," was able to name several geometric figures when drawn on the blackboard, to read all the letters of the alphabet and a half-dozen words, and to count to thirty; he proved to have "a remarkably sensitive and reflecting mind, for this class of children" and to be "a very promising case." As moral training the children learned to recite and sing psalms, they listened to sermons, and they participated in "experience meetings" or public confessions. "The work may seem repulsive," the visitor concluded, but "when a sense of Christian charity and duty actuates a mind, any work for the amelioration of human suffering becomes a pleasure." The testimony of the teachers in the institution, he says, "is almost enthusiastic; their hopes are not chimerical." [22]

Such was the spirit that led the New Jersey legislature, in 1860, to authorize the governor to subsidize a few poor children at the school. The provision did not begin to meet the need. The commissioners who reported on the deaf, blind, and feebleminded in 1873 guessed that there were almost as many feebleminded as deaf and blind together and called their plight "especially pitiable." But their specific recommendation was only for a school for one hundred, and it was entirely ignored.[23]

The Vineland Schools: Stephen Olin Garrison

The story of New Jersey's leadership in work with the retarded begins with the economic revival of the southern part of the state. The railroads and large-scale immigration that brought prosperity to the vicinity of New York and the routes to Philadelphia had passed by the shore counties and the pine belt. The wilderness had reconquered the outposts of lumbermen and miners; the little wharves had rotted; forgotten roads and ghost towns, curious and charming to antiquarians now, were in fact symbols of defeat.

In part, these economic ruins were vacated because the resources of the countryside were not rich enough to match the brimming treasures of the West. Given strong social discipline, the inhabitants might, like Puritans or Mormons, have overcome this difficulty, but their moral enthusiasm waxed and inevitably waned in compensatory religious revivals, while the able and ambitious quietly left. The situation was somewhat like that in the "burnt-over district" of New York (there were similar places in Maryland and New England). In and around the pine woods many families lived primitive and dissolute lives. Their neighbors, who were proper Baptists, Methodists, and Quakers, despised them, but both the demoralized and the proper classes were responding to a pervasive frustration; both were set in their ways, conservative and complacent. A few idealists from the cities tried to make a go of little communities in the region, where land was cheap and the location convenient, but they were dispersed. Not idealists but vacationers, coming by train from the big cities, were the salvation of South Jersey.

The founder of the Training School at Vineland, the Reverend Stephen Olin Garrison, was a Methodist minister at Millville, in the heart of the region. A native of the town, a graduate of Wesleyan University and Drew Seminary (1878), he was the son of that Stephen Garrison who had first asked New Jersey to build a school for its retarded, but he had a personal interest in the problem: one of his own children was afflicted. In 1887 he opened his home as a private school. Needing more room after a few months, he moved to neighboring Vineland, where he had received an advantageous offer of a mansion and grounds and where the Board of Trade offered other inducements. Meanwhile he had enlisted the support of State Senator Philip P. Baker. Baker, a merchant, banker, and railroad man who with his brothers had literally created the resort town of Wildwood, succeeded in winning a state subsidy for indigent students at the new school and helped it in other ways.[24]

But Garrison wanted his new institution to be more than a training school. He dreamed of a "village," a little community on marginal land where the retarded might live and be made more or less self-sustaining in a world suited to their needs and capabilities. His dream was a humane version of the "cottage plan" and "farm colony" that were to dominate thinking about custodial care for the retarded in the coming generation.[25]

As time passed, the spirit of humanitarian pity and hope, such as Dr. Parrish had expressed, which encouraged men to build the first training schools, was giving way, in the 1880's, to fears of hereditary pauperism. In 1875, Richard Dugdale had begun publishing his study of "the Jukes," a "degenerate" family of paupers in rural New York. Charity reformers in that state soon publicized his conclusions as part of their battle against outdoor relief and for almshouse reform. Their agitation led New York to set up an experimental asylum for feeble-minded women of child-bearing age, which in 1885 was made into a permanent custodial asylum.[26]

The founders of the New Jersey State Charities Aid Association, who began public reports in 1886, were of course aware of the situation in New York, and with their assistance the Reverend Mr. Garrison and Senator Baker prevailed upon the legislature, in 1888, to establish the Vineland State Institution for Feeble-minded Women, across the street from their new training school and with Mr. Garrison himself temporarily in charge. Like the Training School, it was to be a village, but its object was frankly "to relieve the State from perpetuating a race of feeble-minded paupers," said Mrs. Emily Williamson, secretary of its board of managers and also of the SCAA; as an example she pointed to one girl, "the mother of four illigitimate [sic] children born in the almshouse, the youngest . . . six weeks old." [27]

The two institutions grew in different ways. Because it was a private establishment with some paying students and some wealthy friends, the Training School could finance its own expansion, and by 1897 it had grown large enough to accommodate all the indigents the state was willing to support. (Hitherto the governor had continued to send students to Elwyn and to Lakewood, Connecticut.) The State School, on the other hand, really a custodial institution for pauper girls, depended upon legislative appropriations for its growth, and evidently many legislators thought there were better ways to segregate the girls or to spend the state's funds, for expansion was slow. In its tenth year Dr. Mary Dunlap, its superintendent, reported that its population had just risen to 103, including forty who were epileptic as well as retarded.[28]

Epileptics were a problem there, and at the Training School too, and at the state and county mental hospitals, and, of course, in the almshouses. Their violent seizures were unsettling and left them amnesic and stupid, and it was supposed that they never recovered completely but got progressively worse. They were also supposed to be especially difficult. Mr. Garrison's last service to the state was to round up medical support for a separate institution for this class. He found his greatest help among doctors, who were energized by the scientific revolution in their ancient craft. In 1896 Garrison was secretary of a commission of doctors who reported to the legislature that there was a pressing need for a colony for epileptics, such as New York had just opened. The legislature agreed, but the governor thought other needs, in the state hospitals and correctional institutions, more pressing, and vetoed the bill. Then "the medical society . . . took up the matter in earnest," and the State Village for Epileptics, at Skillman, near Princeton, was created in 1898.

Like the institutions at Vineland, Skillman was conceived as a rural "village" where afflicted people could live a wholesome life and contribute by their labor to their own support. But the village did not prosper. After five years its managers complained that niggardly appropriations failed to provide even for "pressing necessities" and certainly failed to "accomplish what the legislature in creating the village intended and the public have a right to expect." [29]

Edward R. Johnstone and H. H. Goddard

The Reverend Mr. Garrison died in 1900 after an illness of two years. His successor, Edward R. Johnstone, was distinguished by imagination, energy, and practical wisdom. Johnstone was born in Galt, Ontario, December 27, 1870. He studied at the University of Cincinnati, worked in a reform school, and later taught in the public schools. In 1893 he became a teacher at the Indiana School for the Feeble-minded, where his half-brother, Alexander Johnson, was principal. He himself was principal when he left to help Garrison in 1898; he was twenty-nine when he became superintendent.[30]

"When I came here," he wrote his half-brother much later, "this was a little South Jersey private school with no standing in its own town and the farmers around hating it because Garrison had thrown freedom from certain taxes in their faces." [31] Johnstone was rarely so acerb—never in public—but it is characteristic that he could not understand how a man could deliberately offend anyone. He once wrote a series of articles on institutional management, later published with the significant title "Dear Robinson:—Letters on Getting Along with Folks." The articles reveal how remarkably sensitive he was to personal relations: what the parents felt and feared and needed to know, and how to reassure them; what employees knew and needed to know and how they shared in what men would much later call a "therapeutic milieu"; how the younger and older staff members felt and how to handle them (always ask junior members to give their opinions first, he advised); and above all how the children, rejected by the world, could be accepted and made happy in "the village of happiness," as he called Vineland. "Happiness first, all else follows," was not simply the slogan he repeated over and over, but the key to mutual confidence and to successful administration.[32]

For Johnstone had learned to respect and like his charges. They taught him that "the apparently trivial things of life" are momentous. One's voice should never sound harsh or unkind; appearance and dress should be pleasant but not conspicuous; praise and appreciation create energy, but fault-finding destroys it; and all these qualities may become matters of habit. In fact, his principles were popular clichés—boost, don't knock; it's the little things that count—but his practical experience in teaching and living with the retarded and running a school gave them a shining significance. He had learned too that what succeeded with the retarded also succeeded with normal people; in dealing with parents, employees, professionals, and board members one had to see things in their way and work with them, guiding and helping and leading but not driving or fault-finding.

Johnstone had a youthful, even childlike, quality, playful, imaginative, full of enthusiastic visions, quick to organize teams and devise expediencies. He saw his work as a great challenge and delighted in it. What a wonderful place an institution for the retarded could be, he thought! What a variety of children and problems, what an opportunity to study them, day in and out, year in and out, with an expert staff to help; how free, relatively, of the belligerent stupidities of normal life! "Where in all the wide, wide world . . . is there such a wonderful opportunity within such a small compass, covering such a stretch of time, and directed and practically controlled by one man—the Superintendent?" [33]

So he threw himself into all sorts of tasks. To win over the Vineland farmers he promoted a local club which in turn promoted a rural phone system; he turned his institution into a demonstration farm and got help from Trenton and Washington to revive the viniculture that had given the community its name, and to attract attention to possibilities in sweet potatoes, fruit trees, and poultry vaccines. He was the moving spirit of the State Conference of Charities and Corrections, which he hoped—correctly—would bring together people who talked and people who acted and would bring to light common interests and unmet needs.

One factor of Johnstone's success was his connection with people of various points of view. His half-brother and mentor, Alexander Johnson, was a charity organizer in Cincinnati, secretary of the Indiana Board of Charities, and executive secretary of the National Conference of Charities and Corrections (1890–1893, 1905–1913); he was a strong link to the burgeoning profession of social work.[34] Johnstone looked upon himself as a teacher and part of the expanding profession of educators.

In December 1901, returning from a child-study meeting in Newark, Johnstone proposed that his companions on the train get together occasionally for informal discussions, and he offered Vineland as a meeting place. His thought took hold and the men organized a "Paidological Staff," which met twice a year at various places but presently settled at Vineland, calling itself "The Feeble-Minded Club,"—a characteristic Johnstonian whimsy. Most members were educators or administrators from around Philadelphia, but other professions and interests were represented and people came from North Jersey and New York. Without formal organization or agenda the group flourished through the years and was the source of many interesting ideas and innovations.[35]

One thing that interested these gentlemen was the movement toward special public school classes for slow learners. The classes seemed a good idea, but, as a practical matter, who was to teach them? In 1903 the Training School instituted a summer program of teacher training. The trainees soon raised questions that Professor Johnstone, an honest man, could not answer. His friends in the Feeble-Minded Club thought that of course "research" was the answer. They took up the matter with the Training School trustees, some of whom contributed to a fund to establish a researcher and encourage him to study.[36]

The man Johnstone picked for this unprecedented job was Henry H. Goddard. A psychologist, Goddard had earned his doctorate at Clark University under G. Stanley Hall and taught at West Chester State Teachers College; he was a member of the Feeble-Minded Club and in 1906 he happened to be due for a sabbatical. When he came to Vineland he discovered that he did not know how to make psychological studies of the retarded, and his "S.O.S. calls to . . . psychologists, asking for suggestions and literature, brought almost no response." G. Stanley Hall, who was engaged in genetic studies, suggested that he inquire into early attempts at vocalization.[37]

Early in 1908 Goddard spent two months in Europe. "I expected to find them far ahead of us," he reported on his return, but he discovered that there was "more dissatisfaction and more inquiry after better methods with us than abroad." In Europe only a few "leaders of thought" were interested and "to them the situation seem[ed] almost hopeless at times." He was especially disappointed in France, supposed to be the leader.[38]

Even as Goddard stated these views, his assistant was translating material on a standardized intelligence test devised by the French psychologists Binet and Simon. He had already dismissed their work because he thought it was "impossible to measure intelligence in any such way." [39] Nevertheless, he gave the tests to the children at Vineland and he observed, with interest, that the results corresponded with the staff's intuitive judgment of the students. Other tests, on school and institutional populations, confirmed the favorable impression; teachers and administrators quickly caught a glimpse of the implications of testing for their programs. And so began the development of intelligence tests and all the later psychological tests that would presently classify, interpret, and harrass the organization man.

The tests refined the idea of a continuum of "intelligence," from genius to idiocy. As for the subnormal, men had hitherto made a distinction between the "idiot," more or less helpless, the "imbecile," an overage and often nasty child, and the "feebleminded," a generic name that applied particularly to conspicuously stupid but otherwise normal people. The tests made it possible to classify the groups by definite scores and brought out the great number of the higher grade, for whom Goddard, in 1910, coined the word "moron" (from the Greek word for foolish). Obviously, Goddard thought, this multitude of morons could learn very little and were not really responsible for their failures and deviations; the demands of normal autonomy and responsibility were simply beyond them. The tests provided a precise measurement that confirmed cruder distinctions and gave them new vitality, for wherever the testers looked, in poorhouses and prisons and among all sorts of problem people, they found the morons and "borderline" cases.

Living at the Training School, close to people who were concerned in many ways with welfare institutions and social work, Goddard could not miss the ramifications of the new knowledge, and neither could his coworkers. He himself was carried away by the idea—in 1931 he interpreted the World War and the great depression as catastrophic manifestations of mental defect—but even without exaggeration it was plain that people in education, social work, medicine, and many other enterprises had somehow to come to terms with these new insights.[40]

Meanwhile, Goddard had begun studying the family histories of children at Vineland, following the model of the charity reformers' studies of hereditary pauperism. The forebears of a moronic piney-woods girl named Deborah were especially interesting. Goddard's assistant, Elizabeth Kite, searched public records and the memories of living people until she put Deborah's story together. Miss Kite was a good person for the job, a friendly, serious woman of Quaker descent, native to the region, a trained historian who had published researches on colonial and French history (it was she who translated Binet and Simon), who could not only see meaning in a story but also tell it in an interesting way. She discovered that Deborah's great-great-great-grandfather was a revolutionary militiaman, wild and thirsty as a young soldier away from home for the first time, but of good family. As it happened, he fathered two very different family lines. One stemmed from a bastard son born to a feebleminded maidservant whom he had met in a tavern; the other, from the son of a woman of good Quaker family whom he had married and who helped him get and keep large land holdings.

Both families inherited a touch of wildness and a thirst, but the children of the good Quakeress had practically all controlled it, becoming respectable, sometimes illustrious, citizens, generation after generation. Deborah's ancestors were harder to trace, but most were feebleminded paupers and many were depraved and incestuous. Miss Kite diligently traced them, and as she went over the evidence with Dr. Goddard, drawing complicated diagrams of little squares and circles, black and white, marked with N's and F's (normal and feebleminded), and connected by lines of relationship, there emerged from the variegate mass of historical detail a pattern approximating that predicted by Mendelian laws of heredity, assuming that mental defect was a hereditary character.[41] (Goddard named Deborah's family the Kallikaks.)

This work furnished impressive studies of hereditary pauperism, based on diligent historical research and well-informed clinical judgment about the reported behavior of the subjects, cast in formidable scientific language and graphs. Excited, Miss Kite began to publish some results in the *Survey,* a remarkable journal, part scholarly, part popular, supported by reformers and social workers. Her articles won a quick response; within a year the magazine devoted an issue to the problem of feeblemindedness, with contributions from Goddard and Johnstone as well as Miss Kite.[42]

Research had paid off, and the excitement down at Vineland had many consequences. The researchers gave a new urgency to Johnstone's belief that segregation was the only suitable way to help the really defective (and help their parents and neighbors). The alternatives were a painless death, which he would not consider, and sterilization, a popular idea which he feared would make girls "a safe centre [sic] of vice, toward which . . . libertines would gravitate" and a "menace to the community." Of course he expected that segregation would lose its grim and repressive character and the institutions would become "an asylum, a school, a shop, and a laboratory," like Vineland. Since institutions were not considered in this happy light, his problem was to educate professional people, parents, and teachers, in the advantages of suitable institutional placement.[43] The problem was, he might have added, to educate taxpayers and philanthropists to provide suitable establishments as well as special classes in the schools and guidance for those who were mentally subnormal but not physically defective.

Johnstone worked patiently to educate everyone he could, and soon there were results. In 1904 the state forbade the marriage of feebleminded individuals.[44] In 1909 it required medical examinations in the schools, which it later extended to mental as well as physical conditions.[45] In 1910 Johnstone organized a "Committee on Provision for the Feebleminded" which rallied friends of children on waiting lists to write legislators and which fed stories to the press. This agitation led to laws in 1911 requiring special classes in public schools and authorizing eugenic sterilization. The New Jersey Supreme Court struck down the sterilization law in 1913 and the other laws were not effective, but they were evidence of growing interest.[46]

In 1914, a Commission on the Care of Mental Defectives, appointed by the legislature, endorsed Johnstone's argument for permanent custodial care and "farm colonies." Meanwhile, in 1913 the Training School had opened a colony for its older and stronger boys in a waste land of scrub oak, knotty pine, and thornbush. In 1914, Johnstone got the state to provide land for a second colony in Burlington County; he persuaded some public-spirited citizens of the county to finance a few improvements; he took responsibility for administration and sent older children who were state wards to help clear the land. The first colony, called Menantico, became the center of the Training School's agricultural enterprises and experiments; the second, at New Lisbon, was taken over by the state in 1916. So Johnstone, on his own initiative, had put together "waste land and waste people"—and public officials, philanthropists, foresters, and agricultural experts of several kinds and especially his own efforts—to "let the soil bloom." [47]

More exciting still, members of his informal "Committee on Provision" financed an "Extension Department" of the Vineland Training School, which sent Alexander Johnson and others to lecture and testify in many states. Its efforts, from 1914 to 1917, capitalizing on the great interest in the subject aroused by the tests, *The Survey* and *The Kallikaks,* led directly to fourteen new institutions and substantial additions to existing provision. The coming of war ended this progress, but created new opportunity. As the nation tried to mobilize its resources, the army arranged to give its recruits psychological as well as physical examinations. Six men working at the Training School devised the psychological tests, which were administered at Fort Dix, and which were certainly the most extensive and valuable psychological tests made to that time.[48]

Meanwhile, the state commissions that studied New Jersey institutions in 1917 with a view to their reorganization were much influenced by these developments. They proposed their unique reorganization partly because of the importance they were led to attach to the problem of feeblemindedness, and it was clear that as the new department took shape Johnstone and the men around him would play a decisive role in it.

7

State Hospitals for the Insane and Tuberculous, 1866–1917

The new kinds of institutions that appeared between 1866 and 1917 were mostly for children, and their names—reform school, foster home, veterans' home, training school, village—had hopeful connotations. Meanwhile the words "lunatic asylum"—like the unfortunate inmates themselves—lost their promise. Provision for the insane during these years raised two significant points: a disagreement over the auspices of custodial care and a somewhat contradictory effort to earn the name "hospital" with its newly hopeful associations in somatic medicine. Forward-looking people advocated state care and medical treatment of the insane, which they contrasted with non-medical custody in local asylums. The discussion affords an instructive comparison, however, with emerging opinions about the state's role in providing for the tuberculous, who, like the mentally ill, required a lengthy, expensive, and unpromising hospitalization.

Insane Asylums: State Versus County Care

By 1866, most people agreed that the insane required attention in special asylums, rather than in attics, almshouses, or jails. No one proposed extra-mural or foster-home programs. But the experience of a generation had disappointed the hopes for cure; lunatics crowded the asylum and many were left in private homes and almshouses, no better off than before. Indeed they were more irksome because their caretakers knew that more humane provision was possible and others were already benefiting from it. The problem was, therefore, to get the insane into a place where they really belonged.

At first the solution seemed obvious: bigger state asylums. So men expanded the Trenton institution and, in 1873, began a great new asylum near Morristown. (Its postal address was "Morristown" until 1893, then "Morris Plains" until 1924, when it was called "Greystone Park.") Like Trenton, it was a Kirkbride hospital; it housed various classes of patients in separate wards, each having dining and exercise rooms. Like Trenton, it gave patients the benefits of a peaceful, wholesome, beautiful rural setting. (Neighboring hills were presently occupied by country residences of rich people who also sought these advantages.) Of course the primary consideration in its location was its proximity to metropolitan Newark and Jersey City.

The distinctive feature of the new asylum was its size. People who work there say it was the largest building under one roof until the building of the Pentagon (a sobering thought, if true). The original edifice, built of gray stone (hence the name), four stories high, stretched along an elevated site. Vast and imposing, it testified to the interest, vision, and pride of its founders. Its interior arrangements were planned with all the care that Dr. Buttolph could summon from his experience of twenty-six years at Trenton.

The asylum opened in mid-August 1876. In five years it was filled to capacity—600—and the managers converted the fourth floor, the attic, into wards, adding 200 beds. These were filled by 1885. In 1887 the exercise rooms attached to the wards were made into domitories, which increased capacity to 1,004, but "restricted" the patients "seriously" in cold or inclement weather. That year the managers asked for two congregate dining rooms, near the kitchen, that would vacate the ward dining rooms for dormitory use (and, they mentioned in passing, expedite the food service).[1]

But the institution never caught up with the need. The asylum population of the state in 1880 was 1,632, divided about equally between Trenton, Morris Plains, and the five county asylums then in operation. In 1914, when a state commission studied the subject, Morris Plains alone had a capacity of 1,600 and actually housed 2,412 patients; Trenton had almost 1,600 and there were then nine county institutions with 3,133 inmates. By 1914 there were more than four insane people under public care for every one in 1880. Such were the outer dimensions of a problem that had reached a crisis. This was by far the largest state enterprise in public welfare.[2]

The question of state versus county care was neatly dramatized by the large asylums that Essex and Hudson Counties built during the period within twenty miles of the state asylum at Morris Plains. The crux of the question was cost. It happened that as Morris Plains was under construction men were beginning, with entirely honorable motives, to criticize extravagance in building state asylums. The governor of New York, Samuel Tilden, gave voice to this opinion at the National Conference of Charities and Corrections in 1876, and those who supported him pointed as an example to the New Jersey institution, which cost more than $3,500 per bed.[3]

Costs of construction had caused the legislature to postpone a decision to build, particularly since it was not clear where the burden would fall. Since the state would erect the building and pay the physicians' salaries, and since the institution was planned to serve the metropolitan communities, it might seem that they would benefit, because revenues from the whole state would pay for service to one section. On the other hand, these revenues came mostly from franchise taxes on corporations and (during the construction of Morris Plains) from a small state property tax, and the urban counties paid most of them, so it occurred to representatives of these rich counties that they might very well collect and pay out the money themselves, without sending it through state officials.[4]

In any case, the pressure to do something fell mostly on the political leaders of the urban counties, because their poorhouses took in more and more lunatics. The first county asylums, opened by Essex in 1872 and Hudson in 1873, were technically poorhouses, since county officials had no legal authority to build insane asylums. Hudson County's institution adjoined the county almshouse on Snake Hill. Essex County, which had no county almshouse but relied on municipal institutions, built its asylum on the outskirts of Newark and received most of its first inmates from the Newark almshouse. These establishments were inexpensive temporary barracks that looked like poorhouses, in charge of an officer whose duties were substantially those of the poorhouse warden. He was a political appointee, of course, as were his helpers. His "board of managers" was a committee of the Board of Chosen Freeholders (the county commissioners). The only medical feature of the institutions, periodic visits by a physician, was similar to the arrangement for almshouses.[5]

Essex had the larger and better organized of the two asylums, but it is clear that its officials undertook the job without stopping to learn much about it. Their first plan made no provision for segregating disturbed cases and provided no quarters for nurses or attendants (these facilities had quickly to be added). At the start the officials looked upon the quarters as temporary, pending the completion of Morris Plains, but by 1877 they had made many additions and improvements and began to plan a permanent institution.[6]

Ostensibly, their reasoning was that they could keep their insane much more cheaply in their own institution. The Essex asylum, with all additions to 1880, cost about half as much per bed as Morris Plains and maintenance costs were much lower. Of course the construction was frankly cheap—no imposing gray stone fortress here—and "maintenance" did not include a resident physician or specialized medical care. It was cheap, in short, because it was a poorhouse. In fact, its operation was sometimes actually profitable. In 1882–1883 the officials spent $2.50 per week per patient but collected $2.84. The state paid them a subsidy of a dollar a week per patient, and they were free to seek contributions from relatives and friends of the inmates, although they had no legal claim.

At that rate, county officials could afford to pay the whole cost of construction and enjoy the benefits of a convenient and responsible local institution, not to mention the political advantage of handling its jobs and contracts. If, on the other hand, they sent their insane to Morris Plains, they paid the state two dollars a week to maintain them. In fact, their county asylum never met the demand and they seem to have sent three kinds of patients to Morris Plains: those who could not claim settlement in the county, for whom they did not have to pay maintenance; people whose families could afford better care (this was also an opportunity for favoritism), and difficult cases.[7]

However valid the arguments for economy, it is true that Morris Plains was planned and built by a bipartisan commission that included George Halsey, the most popular Republican in Republican Essex County, and that it was supported warmly by Joseph Bedle, a Supreme Court justice and leading Democrat from Hudson County who won over Mr. Halsey in the gubernatorial campaign of 1874.[8] Not until 1877 did Essex County officials begin to talk about a permanent asylum, a step probably inspired by officers of their institution, the warden and (part-time) physician, who had been disappointed in their hope to be put in charge at Morris Plains. Certainly Essex officials were hostile to Dr. Buttolph, who got the job.[9]

In short, the question of whether the state or the counties should provide for the insane arose because, when the state was slow to act, county officials, more sensitive than legislators to pressure from beleaguered families and poorhouse keepers, had to act. Their first response was an emergency measure in the tradition of poorhouse care, but county asylums created a vested political interest, which soon found a rationale in arguments against elaborate state institutions like Morris Plains.

One possible solution was to recognize two kinds of insane, who required different kinds of treatment. Insanity often seemed to come in a more or less violent seizure that later subsided or passed entirely. If patients were not cured in this "acute" phase, they often fell into a lasting but rather mild eccentricity. The "harmless chronics," as they were called, constituted much of the asylum population and a great custodial problem. Therefore it was proposed that the state build elaborate reception centers for acute cases, while the county maintained simple accommodations for the harmless chronics. Since, under this arrangement, the state subsidized the county care of patients, it might properly inspect and supervise the local asylums; or it might simply bear the entire cost of care and the whole responsibility of management.[10]

Separation of acute and chronic, state supervision, or state care—these were the possibilities. New York, in a similar but much more critical situation, adopted state supervision in 1873 and state care in 1890. New Jersey adopted a perfunctory supervision (by the managers of the state asylums) in 1891 and never adopted state care.

In New York the question took shape in the deliberations of the State Commissioners of Public Charities (organized 1867) and the State Commissioner in Lunacy (appointed 1873).[11] In New Jersey the issue took shape in the investigations of legislative committees. In 1880, the joint committee on lunatic asylums reported that per capita cost of care in the state institutions ($5.00–$5.50 per week) was twice that in the county asylums; it criticized the "ambition of architects, the pride of commissioners and superintendents," and general "extravagance," and recommended the separation of chronics into institutions where the cost of care would not be more than in the Essex County asylum. (The committee also questioned why the salary of the superintendent should be $4,000 at Morris Plains and $2,500 at Trenton.) [12]

The following year the Philadelphia *Times* charged a scandal at the Camden County asylum (established 1879) and a joint committee investigated the county establishments. The inquirers found that the Camden institution was run by incompetent appointees and badly designed, but nevertheless favored county care for chronics and commended the Essex asylum. A minority who expressed the views of Essex officials went beyond favoring county care for chronics, to hold that asylums in large counties could equal the state asylums in medical care, and it feared that to make all county institutions, large and small, strictly custodial would "so degrade" the larger institutions that "no proper medical care would be insisted upon, and there would be none of that incentive to the best of treatment . . . which arises from the fact that cures are aimed at." The minority favored a state "advisory" commission, like that in Massachusetts, to visit county asylums and "stimulate them to the highest attainments." The state would thus develop county care along both medical and custodial lines, instead of building more institutions.[13]

The Medical Demiurge

In effect, the minority conceded that specialized poorhouse care for the insane was not enough, that even harmless chronics deserved an asylum that aimed at cures. Friends of the state asylums objected to the distinction between "acute" and "chronic" cases. To them the issue was between medical care under trained physicians or almshouse care under political appointees, between an effort to cure and a relegation to custody that was more expensive in the long run. But the dramatic advances in medical science and medical education during these years and the rise of general hospitals put the asylums, and asylum doctors, under criticism from a new quarter. The question arose, not whether medical care in a state asylum was better than custodial care in a poorhouse annex, but whether medical care in a state asylum approximated medical care in a general hospital.[14]

This newer, more professional spirit among physicians was especially prominent in Newark. Doctors there criticized political mismanagement of the county asylum, but supported the establishment of a permanent asylum and in particular favored its direction by a full-time, qualified medical superintendent. Such was the character of the new Essex asylum that opened in 1884. (Its first chief, Dr. Livingston Hinkly, formerly at Ward's Island, New York, a Democrat, served under Republican freeholders until he resigned in 1901.) [15]

Newark doctors also supported the ouster of Dr. Buttolph from Morris Plains in 1884. The institution's managers wanted it run like a general hospital, by a business executive, so that the chief medical officer could devote his energies to strictly medical work. Dr. Buttolph had argued that an insane hospital was not like a general hospital: its patients were committed differently, for long terms, and it did not have a staff of advanced medical students to serve as residents, under supervision of visiting physicians from the community. His remarks went unheeded; perhaps the managers thought that his views were as dated as the phrenology he had discoursed upon at mid-century.[16]

The medical demiurge worked on the old asylums in many ways. In 1893, at the behest of Dr. Britton Evans, a bright young man who had just become medical director at Morris Plains and who was supported by the Newark doctors, the legislature officially designated the "insane asylums" as "state hospitals for the insane." (A law of 1894 allowed the Essex "asylum" to become a "hospital.") Essex in 1886 and Morris Plains in 1894 organized a training school for nurses after the fashion of those in general hospitals. By 1895, both Essex and Morris Plains had laboratories and pathologists, whose work was mostly performing autopsies, dissecting brains looking for lesions in the fashion of pathologists in general hospitals.[17]

But these steps were the form rather than the substance of scientific medicine. The undeniable fact was that asylum doctors could neither diagnose nor cure mental illness and that their custodial problems, growing inexorably more difficult, preoccupied them. Official reports and inspections say little about the inner life of these institutions; occasional scandals say much, but their sensations distort the truth. Certainly the patients were a cranky, freakish lot, whose condition varied from violently troublesome ("acute") to hopeless ("chronic"). Certainly this unpromising herd was more than usually vulnerable to the risks of life in large institutions—epidemics, fire (the wards were mostly locked), and cruel indifference. Certainly their caretakers had to arrange some routine that would satisfy the necessities of life and maintain a minimal decorum in the madhouse.

People who lived in the institution year in and year out—patients and caretakers—formed themselves into a hierarchy of authority and privilege. At the bottom were the patients, who, because they were legally committed, technically had no rights, no liberty or property, no power of self-determination except to conform or to rebel and sabotage. Above them stood the attendants, then the supervisory staff and artisans, the "non-coms" who kept the organization going, and then the professional staff topped by the medical director and warden and their assistants.[18]

This hierarchy was, inevitably, a parody of normal society. At its best it might be like a big family in the authoritarian style of nineteenth-century paternalism. When possible the patients, like docile children, were assigned chores. Many patients, burdensome and homeless people, did find a secure asylum crudely suited to their needs and aspirations. For the higher ranks the life might be relatively pleasant. The superintendent was lord of a substantial manor and enjoyed running it (few resigned). In opposing a dual head for Morris Plains (medical director and business manager), Dr. Buttolph argued that the superintendent benefited from administrative duties and their "variety of thoughts, feelings, and interests." He said his own health had deteriorated noticeably when his work was "restricted entirely to the routine and details of professional work, within the house" and he lost the "mental change and bodily exercise connected with some attention to outside affairs." (In other words, when he had to live more like the patients in the wards.)[19]

Often professional and supervisory staff took their parents' occupations or married their associates. There were asylum families just as there were army and church families. Dr. John Wesley Ward, who succeeded Dr. Buttolph at Trenton when the latter moved to Morris Plains in 1876, had been apprenticed to Dr. John Kirby of Salem and later graduated from the University of Pennsylvania medical school; he came to the Trenton asylum in 1867 and a few years later married the daughter of Caleb Sager, its first and long-time steward. In 1876 he found a place for his erstwhile mentor, Dr. Kirby, who remained as assistant physician until his death in 1897. A biographical sketch of Dr. and Mrs. Ward, published in 1907, noted that "in their beautiful home [they] . . . feel the intellectual part of man as only a few can wish." The Wards satisfied their intellectual part by filling their beautiful home with collections of books, engravings, minerals, and shells. Their son, John, Jr., attended Bordentown Military Academy, not Trenton High School.[20]

Familial paternalism was difficult to maintain as the asylums grew. The patients became too numerous, the staff too large, for close personal supervision. Moreover, the character of the staff changed. At first most helpers, even on the wards, had been more or less permanently identified with the institution. But increasingly after the Civil War the attendants were recruited from "floaters" who made their way from institution to institution. The phenomenon first appeared in big county asylums; reformers often complained that their officers were hiring incompetent people and paying them too much. The reformers attributed this practice to political corruption and intended to contrast it with conditions at the state asylums, which were still in rural settings. The earliest candid statement of the problem in state institutions was during an investigation at Trenton in 1901, when, among other things, attendants complained about the food, and the warden made angry statements about "renegades from other hospitals." The committee of managers that investigated the complaints concluded that "there are always some dissatisfied and complaining employees," especially among the attendants.[21]

Often scandals turned on relations between doctors and administrative staff. Dr. Buttolph charged that the managers who ousted him had listened to the steward, whom he described as "a man with early dissipated habits . . . who for years had proved himself highly unsatisfactory in performing [his] duties." [22] This was Warden Martin Monroe, and in 1886 Dr. E. C. Booth, Buttolph's successor at Morris Plains, charged Warden Monroe with disrespect toward doctors and encroachment on their prerogatives. The charges, made to the managers, failed, but the problem festered. In 1889 a legislative committee supported Warden Monroe, arguing that if things were as bad as Dr. Booth said, he should have complained to the managers. Dr. Booth said he had complained to individual managers, but that after the failure of his charges in 1886 he felt "diffident." [23]

The scandal at Trenton in 1901 turned in part on the charge made by an assistant physician that an attendant had choked a patient to death. The managers' committee that investigated reported that the assistant physician had been "derelict for some six or seven years" and had been trying to blackmail Dr. Ward, but that Dr. Ward had not informed the managers because "he did not want any controversy." [24] Meanwhile, in 1901 the Essex Freeholders replaced the superintendent of their institution with Dr. Daniel Dill, one of their own number who had been for several years on their lunacy committee. Under Dr. Dill the Essex mental hospital grew rapidly (along with the county's population) and a farm called Overbrook, originally for harmless chronics, became the site of a great new county mental hospital opened in 1908.

But two years later Dr. Dill was dismissed for incompetence. Workers demolishing the old county asylum—the one built in 1884—found evidence of an unreported fire and the skeleton of a woman in the attic, and Dr. Dill could not supply the names of women who died or were discharged during the interval when the fire was thought to have occurred. Worse, he did not report a fire in 1910, and it appeared that he had failed to investigate it properly, or to investigate employee absences, or to discipline employees for drunkenness, or to carry out fire drills—among other faults.[25]

The truth about asylum life lay between the official reports and inspections that recorded careful management and tolerable service and the occasional scandals that confirmed popular notions about a bedlam. (Parents in Trenton around 1900 warned naughty children that Dr. Ward would get them if they didn't behave.) Both official report and scandal pointed to the practical solution: paramilitary discipline. Discipline would keep the patients in line, and the attendants, and the staff. It would keep the organization going, keep costs down, eliminate the occasion for criticism. And so the fences, gates, and guards outside the institutions were reinforced by the authoritarian hierarchy within. When it worked, as it often did, it spelled No Trouble.

At Morris Plains, Dr. Britton Evans took the helm from 1892 to 1920. Aged thirty-four when he arrived, he had graduated from the College of Physicians and Surgeons in Baltimore and served five years as assistant superintendent at the asylum at Catonsville, Maryland, and for a brief stretch as superintendent of an institution for the feebleminded. An articulate, confident man, he frequently testified in court, notably at the sensational trials for the murder of Harry Thaw and the subsequent habeas corpus proceedings.[26] At Trenton, after 1907, Warden Samuel Atchley exercised a firm grip, keen eye, and political savvy (he was sometime sheriff of Mercer County) that kept that institution in perennial high standing with the legislature.

Good administration in terms of housekeeping and No Trouble were indispensable achievements, and yet they did not make asylums into hospitals or elevate asylum doctors to the peerage of scientific medicine. Perhaps the fact that asylum doctors couldn't diagnose or cure contributed to their concern with paramilitary discipline. The asylum doctors might have looked at custodial care as Ed Johnstone did, and proclaimed, as he did, "Happiness first, all else follows." [27] They might have viewed their operation as a wonderful experiment in congregate living and tried to learn from the mad as Johnstone tried to learn from the fools. They did not. Granted that Johnstone ran a private school for children and not a great public asylum, one cannot in any case imagine the asylum doctors conceiving of their communities as a "village of happiness" and making this principle the foundation of administration. Johnstone was first of all a teacher, an amiable, enthusiastic, rhetorical, not very efficient man who liked to help people and wanted to help them. The asylum doctors were, after all, physicians, who could not afford to ignore the authoritarian tradition of their craft or its occult science. If their science led them to dissect dead brains and regiment living wretches, that was compatible with their dignity.

Real research and the men who run it are no friends of smooth administration. When Ed Johnstone blithely brought H. H. Goddard to Vineland in 1906 he had some lessons to learn. "You know the type of man," he confided to a friend much later about the beginning of research, "what its organization and almost disorganization and reorganization . . . meant." [28] Research is people asking questions that prick complacent authorities, trying things that upset practical-minded routines. It did not fit easily into the paramilitary discipline of the well-run asylum.

Some evidence for this thesis appears in the history of Skillman Village for Epileptics. This institution had the support of doctors and an M.D. superintendent, Henry Weeks, who in a few years moved to greener pastures and was succeeded by his son David. Young Dr. Weeks was therefore to the manner born. His patients, epileptics, were a trying lot, but many of them came from institutions for the retarded, and the ideal of a "village of happiness" for them had certainly been in the mind of the Reverend Mr. Garrison when he had led the campaign for the institution.[29]

In 1910, Dr. Weeks asked Dr. J. E. Wallace Wallin to establish at Skillman the first psychological laboratory in an institution for epileptics and the first state-supported psychological laboratory in New Jersey. Wallin had been a "demonstrator" of experimental psychology at Princeton (1903–1906), who had turned to "applied" (clinical) psychology and, like Goddard, had taught in teachers' colleges. When Dr. Weeks approached him he was spending the summer at Vineland Training School ("a little oasis of contentment and unworried calm," he called it); and at Johnstone's urging he took the position at Skillman.[30]

Wallin had many complaints about the job. It was mostly psychological testing, and he had no clerical help; he had to furnish his own office typewriter and even his own stationery. But these burdens were minor, he said, compared with "the over-regimentation and over-militarization" of the place. He also suffered from the "low professional status" accorded him "in comparison with the dentist and the physicians, and even the nurses (highly restricted as they were)." He could not enter a cottage or leave the grounds without the superintendent's approval. He had to submit scholarly papers for approval before presenting them and to list the superintendent as co-author.[31]

Presently Dr. Weeks undertook to set Dr. Wallin straight on how institutions operated, "to intimidate or cajole [him] into . . . sycophantic servility." He explained patiently that although Wallin was "not an officer or a physician" and had only the "rank of an attendant," Dr. Weeks had "permitted [him] to reside" in the cottage that "housed the physicians and the dentist and had permitted [him] to use their dining room as well." Wallin resented this condescension (he was a Ph.D. and none of the four institutional physicians had a baccalaureate, he observed) and he thought such regimentation would "ruin any scientific enterprise." He left shortly afterward. Granted that both he and Weeks were flinty characters, there is no reason to doubt his contrast between "the friendly, genial, permissive" atmosphere at Vineland and the "stifling, repressive, overregimented" atmosphere at Skillman, and there is no doubt that the professional ideals of Mr. Johnstone and Dr. Weeks had something to do with the success of research at their respective institutions.[32]

Dr. Henry Cotton

The possibility of scientific research under medical auspices took shape in New Jersey's mental hospitals in the person of Dr. Henry Cotton, who succeeded Dr. Ward at Trenton in November 1907. Cotton, born at Norfolk in 1876, attended public schools, the Polytechnic Institute at Baltimore, and Johns Hopkins before serving as a private in the medical corps during the Spanish American War. After the war he earned an M.D. at the University of Maryland medical school and joined the staff of the Baltimore city asylum, Bay View. From there he went to Worcester and later Danvers state hospitals in Massachusetts, and put in two years of research in Germany. He was assistant superintendent at Danvers when, aged 31, he came to Trenton.[33]

Shortly after his arrival in New Jersey, he addressed the state medical society on "the progress of modern psychiatry." For years, he said, psychiatry had lagged behind medical science. "Asylum physicians . . . were regarded in a somewhat pathetic light, and, to a large extent, this attitude seemed justified. They were surrounded by patients with a hopeless malady, loaded down with executive and administrative duties, usually isolated from medical centers, and, without the leaders so necessary to stimulate and guide them, they naturally followed the path that offered the least resistance." The theme of his story was that psychiatry, inspired by laboratory research and formal presentation in regular medical education, notably in Germany, was re-entering the main stream of medical progress. He pointed especially to Kraepelin's analyses of the manic depressive cycle and "dementia praecox" (schizophrenia), and to the studies of his own mentor, Adolph Meyer, on "habit psychoses." These researchers showed that mental illness was a deteriorating state. It was obvious that the asylums got only the end stages of the illness, and that there were large possibilities for early diagnosis and prevention—if asylum doctors and general practitioners could work together.[34]

It was clear that the Trenton Hospital was due for a change under Dr. Cotton and Warden Atchley, and that is what the managers wanted. In 1907, typhoid had struck and inspectors from the State Department of Health discovered an accumulated crust of dirt where hands touched the kitchen and dining room doors, and other faults. Neither the medical superintendent nor the warden felt responsibility for the faults, and there was other evidence of bad relations. When Dr. Ward contradicted himself before the managers they considered his usefulness at an end.[35] Dr. Cotton, for his part, made his view on administration clear to the managers before he came. He wanted "to devote his whole time to the treatment and care of the patients" and he thought a businessman could handle business affairs better than a physician.[36]

As the new team took over they discovered that the patients' records were unsatisfactory. From the first, patients' names had been entered at the top of a page in a large ledger book, together with some detail about who committed them, their behavior, periodic medical examinations (once or twice a year) and treatment. When these entries reached the bottom of the page the clerk flipped past pages for later patients until he came to a blank side on which to continue. The record of a long-term patient (many stayed for decades) was on a number of pages scattered through several bulky ledgers. For this system Dr. Cotton substituted a file of individual envelopes, like that in the Danvers hospital.[37]

In his first two months, he ended restraint for the one Trenton hospital patient in thirteen who had wrestled with a muff or strait jacket while Dr. and Mrs. Ward had pondered their engravings and shell collection. (Ninety women and six men were under restraint when Cotton took over. Restraint was less necessary for men because their male attendants found other methods of "discipline" that were just as effective.) In all he relegated 707 "restraining devices" to the museum.[38]

To replace male attendants on the wards Dr. Cotton hired more nurses and reorganized and improved a training program for nurses in cooperation with the local general hospital, so that in 1915 its graduates became eligible for registration. He improved laboratory facilities, established a surgery, and engaged local physicians as consultants; he built up a collection of current medical literature, instituted regular staff conferences to discuss it, and established the policy of educational leaves of absence. He encouraged his colleagues to publish; the hospital proudly collected their publications in two sizable bound volumes by 1913.[39]

People who shared the excitement of these innovations often thought of Dr. Cotton as a *real doctor.* "We thought we were the best state hospital in the country," said Donald Rice, who became Warden Atchley's assistant in 1923, when the excitement was at its highest. "We had more doctors running around the place, and better doctors, and more nurses, and more professional staff generally, than any state hospital I knew about." Dr. Harold Magee, who joined the staff in 1929 and became medical director in 1945, recalls that "Even though Dr. Cotton had begun to draw back on his theories when I came here—they have since been discredited, of course—he was still a famous man, and I thought I had something to learn from him. What he taught his staff was simple, but very important. He believed that you should take a good hard look at the patient, not just write him off as crazy. He was no bughouse doctor, not one of those fellows that knew the routine and that's all. He was a *real* doctor. He wanted you to *study* the patient's condition." [40]

At first young Dr. Cotton stuck closely to what he had learned. He introduced hydrotherapy in 1909. In 1911, when salvarsan became available for the treatment of syphilis, and hence of general paresis, a frequent cause of insanity, he began to give his patients routine Wasserman tests to discover latent and incipient cases. (Both the Wasserman test and salvarsan had been developed in Germany a few years before his visit there.) His interest in the early stages of disease and prevention, and in the patient's general health were results of the teaching of Dr. Adolph Meyer, the dean of American psychiatrists. Prepared in this way, Cotton was quick to see the potential importance of the studies of hereditary mental defect going forward at Vineland, and in 1910 he hired social workers to collect case histories on his patients. He also had stenographers transcribe the ravings of psychotics, for purposes of study.[41]

As he studied the patients, he realized that quite apart from their mental disturbance they were often unhealthy people, full of foci of infection—bad teeth and tonsils, for example. Was it not possible that these infections produced toxins that somehow corrupted the brain? Might not medical treatment and surgery, by eliminating the source of the toxin, get at the root of the "mental" symptoms? Dr. Cotton was not the only one to suspect a relation, but he was in a position to act on the idea. Treatment led to good results and confirmed his hunch. If he were right, he realized, he would bring psychiatry closer to the main stream of medical progress than it had been in his lifetime.[42]

As the significance of this insight struck him, World War I interrupted the life of the hospital. Meanwhile, there was the added excitement that men were organizing a new state department, which was supposed somehow to give state institutions, including state mental hospitals and even county institutions, a kind of effective leadership and enlightened spirit that were unexampled in the nation. Inevitably, Dr. Cotton's hopes and works were an inspiration to the founders of the department, and he would become, for a time, a public symbol of their hopes and their cause.

The State Tuberculosis Sanatorium at Glen Gardner

Physicians had promoted the village for epileptics and were interested in the work of the mental hospitals, and they were also the principal influence in favor of the state tuberculosis sanatorium. The sanatorium idea was supported by two scientific discoveries about TB. In 1882 Robert Koch identified the tubercle bacilli and recognized some paths of infection. The discoveries meant that, contrary to earlier ideas, the disease was communicable, and therefore its victims should be isolated. It proved, however, that there was no simple public control, such as had arrested typhoid, no effective immunization, and no quick therapy. Therefore the only treatment was to recognize the disease early and to arrange a generally healthful regime as a long convalescence.[43]

It took time for these ideas to sink in—some doctors doubted the fact of contagion, others hoped for dramatic countermeasures—but gradually it was realized that the situation called for two kinds of action. First, doctors had to alert people to the symptoms of the disease and the importance of personal hygiene in limiting contagion; and second, they had to provide hospital or sanatorium care to isolate cases and treat them. Both jobs, alerting the public and providing sanatoria, involved public relations, and in the 1890's several organizations were formed to carry on the work. The most active were in New York and Philadelphia.[44]

As men faced up to the problem they found that they were dealing with a veritable plague, which killed almost four thousand persons a year in New Jersey alone. Moreover, it was a social as well as a medical problem: it raged in urban slums and its convalescence was far beyond the means of slum dwellers. The logic of an anti-TB campaign led to tenement reform on one hand and to a public health and medical program on the other. Accordingly, in 1902 New York doctors organized themselves and their lay allies in a committee of the Charity Organization Society and later sought the help of the State Charities Aid Association.[45]

The question of state care in New Jersey was first raised in 1902 in an address by the president of the state medical association, who was supported by the State Charities Aid Association. There was a flurry of excitement, encouraged by events in New York; the legislature quickly passed a bill, drawn by a committee of the state medical society, to establish a state sanatorium, and the governor appointed Dr. Charles Kipp, of Newark, as president of the managers who were to oversee its erection.[46]

Then there were second thoughts. The managers planned an edifice costing $400,000 for two hundred patients and portending a large annual charge for maintenance. This investment would preclude other developments that SCAA officials and doctors were interested in—for example, the reformatories and the village for epileptics; furthermore, it would at best handle only a few cases. Were there not cheaper, more extensive and preventive measures, such as school sanatoria for consumptive children, farm colonies where incipient cases could be cured at their own expense, agencies to promote home nursing and advise on nutritious diet or even help provide it?[47]

So the matter hung fire. Meanwhile, the New York committee had combined with other groups to organize the National Tuberculosis Association, which attained a degree of stability and an energetic executive in 1905; with his assistance a New Jersey Tuberculosis Association was organized in March, 1906, and the State Board of Health renewed its activity.[48] Helped by this push, the sanatorium at Glen Gardner was completed and opened in 1907, somewhat reduced from the original plan in its size and expense.[49]

The new sanatorium only made the question of state policy clearer. Should the state provide for all TB cases? If not, what other provision was appropriate? In any case, since the New Jersey Tuberculosis Association was in fact only a few people interested in charitable reform and public health, how could the public be aroused to the danger and the need? In 1909, the governor appointed a commission to study the situation. It reported that the state sanatorium took care of 121 cases, and municipal and county institutions provided after a fashion for 660, equally divided between incipient and advanced cases. The commission favored some expansion of Glen Gardner, in the form of remodeled farmhouses and "shacks"; it specifically opposed a single state hospital for advanced cases and favored instead municipal and county sanatoria at local expense, along lines that New York had recently adopted; it favored an expanded program by the State Board of Health, including education and the provision of nurses in rural districts.[50] In general the state institution was to take only curable cases and to serve as a model and training center for the others.

Following these recommendations, the legislature passed a law that authorized counties and municipalities to establish sanatoria; when this did not bring results it *required* them to establish sanatoria and offered them a subsidy for indigent patients.[51] Hudson County not only built a sanatorium but worked out a model system of clinics and visiting nurses and fresh-air schools. Other urban places responded more slowly, partly because of the cost, partly because of the difficulty of finding sites: people did not want a host of lungers living in their neighborhood.[52]

Meanwhile, many questions went unanswered. Why should the state subsidize the care of the insane and tuberculous, but not other long-term patients? A law of 1911 offered a dollar a week toward hospital care of the chronic ill, but the next legislature quickly repealed it on the grounds that it would undermine private philanthropy and put an unthinkable burden on state finance.[53] Why should the state TB sanatorium accept only as many patients as it could properly treat, regardless of a waiting list, while the state mental hospitals received patients regardless of the overcrowding that so frustrated their care? Why should the state subsidize patients in any sort of county (or private) institution without saying how the money should be spent or supervising the care? Why should Glen Gardner get a better break on appropriations than the state mental hospitals, and why, for that matter, should Morris Plains be so much more crowded than Trenton? A commission to investigate the state charitable institutions, appointed in 1917, concluded that the solution lay in a new departure in organization and supervision.[54]

The commission's recommendations will be considered in a later chapter. If its members had paused to take a historical view of the situation, they would have been struck by how the discussion of state care differed as regards the tuberculous and the insane. In 1872 reformers had wanted to keep the counties out of the asylum business; in 1912 they wanted to get them into the sanatorium business. Why? In the first place, county asylums were founded as annexes to the poorhouse, not hospitals, and such they continued to be in rural and smaller counties. TB sanatoria, however, were conceived as annexes to general hospitals, for patients whose care did not fit the developing pattern of short-term hospital treatment. (The act authorizing them required that they be organized like general hospitals, with five unpaid directors serving revolving terms to minimize political interference.)

The prognosis for advanced TB in 1907 was as poor as that for advanced mental illness (the type of cases the mental hospitals got), but TB was a contagion that doctors and the public could understand, and its treatment was more hopeful than psychiatry. The State Tuberculosis Association, which led the campaign for education and care, was small, but it was more single-minded and effective than the Charity Organization Societies and the State Charities Aid Association that undertook to speak to general welfare problems. In fact, its successes, like those of the "extension department" of the Vineland Training School with regard to provision for the feebleminded, foreshadowed new ways to organize reform.

In part, the difference between attitudes toward county asylums in 1872 and county sanatoria in 1912 lay in the improvement of scientific medicine and of the professional organization of doctors. In the 1870's, and for decades thereafter, county asylums were identified with the spoils system whereas the state asylums were identified with nonpolitical and medically directed care. In 1912, however, the county sanatoria were linked with the urban general hospitals that were centers of medical progress, and the state institution was conceived as a demonstration clinic. Hudson County, under the notorious boss Frank Hague, was to develop excellent medical institutions. As regards care of the mentally ill, the Essex County institution was acknowledged to be the equivalent of state institutions, despite political control and dual management.[55] The difference was not better politics or nonpolitical organization as such, but better doctors and higher standards of hospital care.

Public policy toward illness would confront later generations in many different contexts, but in 1917 people who thought about state services could not get much beyond the peculiarities of providing for the mentally ill and the tuberculous. They were aware that the state's responses to the two problems were different and inconsistent; they saw clearly the threat of partisan politics, the increasing cost of institutional care, and the terrific liability that the state might incur in subsidizing it. Local communities took care of schools, police, and fire service, they thought; urban hospitals, supported by philanthropy or local taxes—usually both—provided short-term treatment and clinics; local health departments and schools were central to preventive medicine and case-finding. Therefore, it seemed that the problem was to get these communities to expand and develop their facilities, especially at the county level, since that was the practical unit of service for rural places.[56]

On this view, men might have proposed a state subsidy to induce local authorities to act; payments for patients in county asylums and sanatoria did that, and the idea that the state supervise institutions receiving aid might provide a means to improve standards. But instead men chose to look upon a state subsidy as likely to negate local initiative and responsibility. They were willing to continue it for the mentally ill, but they proposed to withdraw it from the tuberculous, and for other chronic illness they rejected it. They thought that the State Tuberculosis Sanatorium should be a model for training and research, somewhat as teacher-training institutions set up model schools for emulation.

The argument was not consistent—why not apply it also to state mental hospitals, correctional institutions, and the Board of Children's Guardians? But it was premised on three observations that seemed obvious: (1) The insane asylums, which the state either managed or subsidized, were an increasing burden if not a scandal. (2) Urban hospitals and health services, which had developed under local sponsorship, philanthropic and public, without state finance or supervision, were progressive and increasingly effective. (3) State subsidy to private agencies, whether charity or health, where it was tried, in New York, Pennsylvania, and the District of Columbia, for example, had created pernicious vested interests and diminished local responsibility and philanthropy.[57] Consequently, in the 1920's the leaders of the new department would seek to encourage the organization of social service by counties, but they would have neither the means nor the inclination to devise a "grant-in-aid" as an inducement.

8

Prison Reform, 1869–1917

Everyone who studied New Jersey prisons between 1869 and 1917 agreed that they were failing. They did not deter crime; they seemed to corrupt and brutalize inmates instead of reforming them. They were costly; the time and energy of convicts was invested neither in profitable work nor in useful instruction. The reformers all proposed similar improvements, but changes were slow to come and didn't work. Everyone who inspected the jails said that there ought to be some official inspection and supervision of them, but the state never established an effective guide or control. Reformers repeatedly scandalized the community with accounts of cruel punishment and brutal officers; the inquiries of 1869 and 1917 both began with scandals, and both concluded by recommending radical changes of the system—the same system.

Pardon and parole policy was consistently frustrated. It took twenty-five years' agitation to establish the reformatories for adult first offenders, and they succeeded no better than the reform schools for children. The sense of a cumulative development, such as animated partisans of the state's institutions for dependent children, the blind, the retarded and the mentally ill, was absent. "A reading of the reports of previous investigating commissions," said the Prison Inquiry Commission in 1917, "gives the impression that none . . . laid any stress on the fact that almost the identical conditions investigated by them had been officially studied and reported upon by a prior investigating body." [1]

No one had a good word for the county jails. A distinguished lawyer, asked to comment in 1867, felt "his indignation rise" as he contemplated the "disgraceful outrages" inflicted in them. Persons charged with crime, or merely witnesses to crime, were incarcerated with convicts and hardened criminals; "inexperienced youths, male and female, and respectable men and women, . . . sometimes obliged to be put into the sheriff's custody," suffered alongside the desperate and dissolute, "subjected to dirt, vermin, offensive air and darkness; without a chair or table in the room; fed like a felon behind the bars; associated with the depraved and disgusting criminal; eating, sleeping and living with the wicked and profane. . . ." [2] Commissioners who reported in 1869 set forth in detail the perennial demands: classification and segregation of inmates, to avoid demoralization; "clean, well-ventilated" cells in place of the dark, dirty apartments, cold, damp, fetid, and infested with vermin, which became "implements of torture"; workhouses or houses of correction to employ short-term convicts at healthful and productive work; and supervision by an official "Inspector of the Jails," empowered to inspect, recommend, convene the county governing board "for prompt relief," and report annually to the governor or legislature.[3]

Moved perhaps by this report, and certainly by the growing problem of vagrancy and petty offenses, Hudson County erected a workhouse or penitentiary in 1869, Essex County in 1873, and Mercer County (Trenton) in 1892. These were sizable institutions, intended not only for the petty misdemeanants who crowded the jails, but also for some offenders who might have gone to the state prison. The larger municipal and county institutions, forced to expand, did provide some modern quarters and classification, but the commissioners of 1917 found that demoralizing congregation, idleness, and improper living conditions still characterized most jails.[4]

It is doubtful whether any physical improvements would have impressed reformers much, however, because the jails were so involved in politics. The jail was the responsibility of the sheriff, who collected fees for its inmates, arranged its contracts, and hired its staff, and who was open to influence and favoritism in his administration. The sheriff was also a key man in the law-enforcing team of policeman, prosecuting attorney, and judge. He selected the grand jury, that had to indict serious offenders, and the petit jury, that tried cases. Hence he was in a position to protect people engaged in organized crime or illegal business, as well as political buddies guilty of bribery or fraud.

Because of his political connections with people who made and administered laws, the sheriff was an important target in the war against bossism and political corruption that absorbed progressives in New Jersey, as elsewhere. When, in 1902, a "progressive civic organization" of Morristown conducted an essay contest on the qualifications of a sheriff, the New Jersey Review of Charities and Corrections suggested that contestants look around at present incumbents to see what qualities ought to be rejected. Suppose, the editor said, writers discovered that the sheriff was *not*

> a man whom prisoners can respect; nor a temperate man; nor fastidious as to methods of paneling juries; nor puritanical about overlooking crime here and there for certain considerations; nor a believer in probation and the juvenile court; nor desirous of any reforms that will diminish the number of prisoners; nor in favor of abolishing the present method of speculating on prisoners' food; nor a believer in prison work; nor an advocate of cleanliness and good reading for prisoners; nor averse to bargaining privileges for "better prisoners"; nor picayune in his restrictions on visitors or attendants; well, then,

> there is, as you see, little left except this conviction, that prisoners, law, taxpayers, and the State of New Jersey are made for the sheriff, whose fees are the only divine right still canonized.[5]

Politics was also supposed to be the core of the state prison's problems. The commission of 1869 laid the difficulty to the fact that the legislature appointed the keeper and the inspectors (managers) annually. "Political influences secure the appointment of the Keeper, and . . . his deputies," they observed. "Hence, it is not surprising that pot-house heroes should sometimes be found" as guards. Moreover, the frequent change of officers led to disciplinary problems. "The prisoners are ever ready and quick to test [a new officer's] capacity to govern, his patience to endure annoyances, his power to resist temptation to passion, his firmness and ability to restrain insubordination." [6] Accordingly, the revision of the constitution in 1875 gave the governor (instead of the legislature) the power to appoint the principal keeper, for a term of five years. This made for more stable administration, and later investigators did not complain of the turnover of personnel. But the change did not end the suspicion that political influences led the authorities to condone or encourage practices that frustrated the purpose of the prison.

On their part, prison officials could always put the responsibility for their problems on the legislature or the public, for clearly the prison institutionalized contradictions in the public view of crime and punishment. The law said that convicts should each have a separate cell, but legislators never provided enough cells; the law sentenced convicts to hard labor, but legislators never provided enough means of employment. These contradictions were literally built into the edifice. The plan of the prison, when it opened in 1836, was that the convict would live, work, and receive industrial and moral training in individual and entirely separate quarters. When, in 1858, authorities introduced the "Auburn system" of congregate workshops, they did not build the dining or assembly halls needed for that regime, and they never provided enough shops or work to do in them.

This meant that the prisoner spent his time either in one of the original cells, measuring 7½ x 12 feet, together with one or as many as four other men, or in a newer cell, measuring 4 x 7 feet, in which case he was usually, but not always, alone. Meals were served in the cells, the food carts moving slowly down the long wings. In effect, he lived and ate in a room the size of a small bathroom, with a noisome bucket for a toilet and a cot narrower than a bathtub. He bathed occasionally in a bathhouse in the yard, which was closed in bad weather. Should he die he might be laid to rest in a well-cultivated, well-limed plot where arrivals caused a reshuffling of the old skeletons.[7]

A more fundamental contradiction lay in the question of "prison discipline," as it was called, between a regimen that looked toward the convict's past, his punishment, and his threat to security, and one that looked toward his future and his rehabilitation, that tried to win his cooperation rather than terrorize him. In the reform of the 1830's a clergyman, Joseph Yard, had become keeper, and he had called for plenty of moral instruction for the sinners. The commissioners who reported in 1869 testified that "the preaching of the Gospel and the counsels of the Moral Instructor" were the most important and powerful agencies of reform, and that education and good habits of industry came next. But they doubted that preaching in the halls (because the institution had no chapel) was effective, and they doubted that the counsels of a moral instructor were well received with eavesdroppers in the cell or in the next cage.[8]

In any case, it was obvious in 1869 that a Christian spirit was absent from discipline, and even that the law forbidding corporal punishment was ignored. On one visit to the prison the commissioners found five men stretched flat on the cell floor, bound by leather thongs attached to iron rings. This arrangement allowed "very little movement of the person, obliging the condemned to void his excrements in his clothing and rendering the air of the cell nauseatingly offensive." The treatment lasted twenty-two days for one prisoner, ten for another. Another punishment was to suspend troublemakers by the wrists, with the feet just touching the floor.

The commissioners thought that such punishments impaired the health of the prisoner, not just by torturing his muscles but by his "protracted inhalation of foul and noxious gases"—they specified hydrogen sulphide—and the encrustations of "filth" on his skin. The commissioners were gratified that the governor had "protested" against the punishments "herein disclosed" and that the keeper and the inspectors had abandoned them.[9] But in 1878 a legislative committee investigated charges of cruelty against the keeper, General Gershom Mott, after it became known that a convict named Jacob Snook had died of "meningitis" while being stretched on a sort of rack. The committee denied that the torture had killed Snook and exonerated the General on the grounds that, finding the device in the prison, he naturally thought that its use was entirely legal. (Nor did the committee take exception to the practice of pouring alcohol on inmates during epileptic seizures and then igniting it, to detect shamming.)[10]

There were later protests about cruelty, including those which led to the inquiry in 1917, but the warmest proponents of punishment and opponents of converting a "receptacle for criminals . . . into a playhouse" conceded that in theory the commission of 1869 (and those who later repeated its arguments) were correct in saying that "the wise prison keeper" should try to win the "affectionate respect and confidence" of the convicts and to "recognize and encourage their efforts at self-control and reformation." The program implied by this idea was "to encourage good behavior by appropriate rewards, and to discourage misconduct by deprivation of privileges." Specifically, the commissioners of 1869 (like those who later studied the problem) favored granting convicts social privileges, such as attendance upon religious services, Sabbath School, and other edifying lectures; incentive pay for faithful labor and good deportment at labor, with a bonus for overtime; and a plan of commuting sentences for good behavior.[11]

No one opposed these ideas, and yet their realization was slow and half-hearted. The fact was that to put them into practice required more patience, insight and self-discipline than the guards and their supervisors were apt to have. To appeal to incentives—to recognize rights in the prisoner and give him responsibility—involved, inescapably, a risk; to offer him diversion and education, whether moral, academic, or industrial, involved an expense that the legislators would not make.

Furthermore, the questions of program, of privileges, rewards, and training, were related to convict labor. When the prison was first established, in the dawn of the factory system, men believed that the inmates would be a valuable labor force who could maintain themselves and also pay the costs of their apprehension and management and leave a surplus. This idea died hard, but it was clear that whatever the state lost on prisoners' maintenance would discourage further expenditure on their "welfare"; moreover the availability of privileges, rewards, and training, and the elimination of demoralizing idleness, depended on there being a variety of productive employment for the prisoners.

The problem became urgent when, during the depression of the 1870's, mass unemployment and the increase of vagrancy testified to a labor surplus. The workers who joined the Knights of Labor in that decade began to agitate the question, should the state put convicted criminals in competition with law-abiding workers? Should the state allow capitalists to profit from exploiting convicts, at the expense of free labor?[12]

In 1879, the state legislature appointed a commission to ponder the questions. It met with commissions from Connecticut, Massachusetts, and New York, with famous wardens, businessmen and economists, and even with a labor leader or two. It concluded that of course the state could not support prisoners in idleness like pensioners, and so they had to work. Furthermore, the work had to be "penal"—a punishment and a deterrent. It had to be hard, safe, and healthy. It had to be reformatory, that is, it had to give the prisoner good work habits and if possible some mechanical skill ("The man who has learned a useful trade, is far on the way towards becoming a good citizen. . . . The man who has broken stones for years . . . has learned little which will be useful to him when he becomes free").[13]

Finally, the commissioners said, prison labor had to be productive—the prisoner had to work at something that could be used or sold. Therefore he had to compete with free labor; even menial chores around the prison "might be done by free men and women, and no doubt would be done very gladly by some of them." There was no doubt, therefore, that prisoners had to work and had to compete with free labor. But the state might minimize competition in two ways: Most obvious was to limit the number of workers employed at any one occupation; but whatever the restriction upon occupations in its own prisons, the commissioners observed, there remained competition from institutions in other states, for prison goods moved freely in interstate commerce. The solution to this problem was an interstate agreement or a federal law—both substantially beyond anyone's control.[14]

The commission's report led to a law in 1881 that restricted the number of prisoners employed in any particular trade to one hundred, but the agitation did not end, and in 1883 a committee of legislators looked into the question again. Assuming that convicts had to be employed, it asked what was the best system of managing the enterprise. Specifically it contemplated three systems—piece-price, public account, and state use. Under the piece-price system, prison authorities arranged with businessmen to put prisoners to work on goods that the businessmen hoped to sell. The businessmen put up the capital, sometimes supplied instructors, bought the finished product at a set price per piece, and of course marketed it. This system differed from the older way of leasing convict labor in that under the old plan businessmen had actually conducted the prison industries and the keepers were responsible only for discipline, whereas under the piece-price system the keepers were responsible for both industrial production and discipline.

The new arrangement was supposed to eliminate the confusion and corruption that outside contractors might bring into the prison, and to strengthen the penal and reformatory purposes of the labor. On the other hand, the businessmen, since they bought finished products, not labor time, could reject anything that did not meet their standards. Under the public account system the prison authorities went into business for themselves, supplying all the factors of production and marketing the product; under the state-use system they sold their products only to institutions of government—a captive but supposedly quite limited market.[15]

Pondering these alternatives, the committee decided that the piece-price system was the most practicable, and it was written into law. Prison authorities opposed it, arguing that it would neither benefit free labor nor save the state money; they favored, by implication, the old lease system, whereby the state did not bear the cost of inefficient labor. It seemed that nobody benefited from the new dispensation except the contractors, and this may have been a leading consideration in the committee's decision, as the historian of the prison asserts. But the legislators' immediate problem was somehow to satisfy the demands of labor leaders, and labor was satisfied with the new arrangement, for the time, at least.[16]

In any case, these reports on prison labor are doctrinaire and unrealistic. The commission of 1879 took for granted that the agitation had sprung from "the ignorant and interested efforts of demagogues" to take advantage of "the general distress and depression to exalt their own importance and further their own selfish ends," and in straightening out the demagogues, it stuck close to the theory of wages and of penal labor. It did not, for example, ask whether any convict labor was in fact "hard, safe, healthy, reformatory, and productive"; it did not observe that in fact many prisoners were demoralized pensioners; it said that authorities should diversify occupations, but it made no practical recommendations as to what diversification was economical or even possible.

The committee of 1883 confined itself to considering the three alternatives, ignoring the obvious and fatal gap between any theory and practice. The most charitable interpretation of these events is that both groups of men recognized that they had to make the best of a bad situation: if society said on one hand *give prisoners reformatory labor* and on the other, *don't let convicted criminals burden free labor, let alone taxpayers*—what were they to do?

There was, however, another reward to offer prisoners, the best of all, that might both induce good behavior and reduce overcrowding and its problems—early release. According to the deterrent theory of imprisonment, there were two ways for a prisoner to get out, either by serving his term or by winning a pardon. A pardon was an act of executive clemency, granted, in New Jersey, under the constitution of 1846, by the governor and a Court of Pardons that included the "lay judges" of the State Court of Errors and Appeals. Because the procedure of criminal courts was often inept and the procedure of review complicated and expensive, there was considerable justification for many pardons.[17] But as the commissioners observed in 1869, when there were half again as many pardons as ordinary releases, the authorities were granting pardons as much to relieve overcrowding (and, presumably, in response to political influence) as to rectify the miscarriage of justice.

"It is a grave error," the commissioners said, to suppose that "the pardoning power" should "sit as a court of general jail delivery." This abuse obviously undermined the penal theory which held that the sentence solemnly pronounced in open court should be strictly carried out. As things were, the approach of the court's session produced "a feverish excitement in every cell, where each man longs for freedom, and labors for a continual presentation of his case. . . . Crimes are covered up; falsehood and deceit take the place of penitence and frank confession." Not only did this situation disrupt discipline, but it was "a hindrance to any valid reformation." [18]

It was the hope of these commissioners, and of later observers who reiterated the argument, that authorities could "give a new and better direction to the convict's hopes and efforts by opening to him a path by which he can *earn* his liberation." Their idea, simple and obvious, was that the authorities should commute the prisoner's sentence in reward for good conduct and faithful labor. A law to this effect had passed in 1868, but then, as later, it was administered mechanically; authorities began by reducing the convict's term by his possible "good time," and then added to the sentence for bad conduct. The procedure became another occasion for deprivation rather than a discriminating reward for good behavior.[19]

The good time allowed—five days a month—simply did not clear the prison fast enough, so wholesale pardoning continued as needed. Then, in 1889, the warden of the state prison got through a parole law. Like the commutation of sentence, parole was an effort to relate discharge to good behavior and rehabilitation rather than to the old idea of executive clemency. The difference was that the prisoner got out sooner—he became eligible after serving only half his sentence—but his release was, unlike a pardon or commuted sentence, conditional, and the parolee remained under supervision until the term of sentence expired. Furthermore, prison officials, not the court of pardons, granted the conditional release. This proved to be a sticking point; the attorney general decided that it interfered with the power of the courts to sentence, so the law had to be rewritten to give the parole power, as well as the pardoning power, to the Court of Pardons.[20]

But even the parole law did not clear the prison fast enough; half the sentence was too long, and the parole law did not apply to recidivists or to certain major crimes (during especially crowded periods, a lifer might serve only five to eight years). In 1898, the business of parole was put back in the power of the warden and inspectors, but the Court of Pardons, with its more lenient rules, continued to discharge more prisoners. This confused situation, with two paroling authorities, was further complicated in 1914 when a law granted the courts the power to recall and resentence prisoners committed by them.[21]

The details of the situation were complicated, but by the time the Prison Inquiry Commission studied it in 1917 the general result was clear. If imprisonment were punishment for violating the law, the dignity of the law required that it be strictly administered, and wholesale discharges by the Court of Pardons were a flagrant abuse. If, on the other hand, imprisonment and parole were to be agencies of reform, the parole should be granted with discrimination and carefully supervised, and a mechanical disposition was futile. In fact, men seemed to lack the will to make either view effective, and policies of early discharge, rationalized as humanitarian and reformatory, continued to be merely an expedient to relieve overcrowding.[22]

The Reformatory Idea

The efforts to introduce a more humane discipline and a more constructive program succeeded better at the reformatories for men at Rahway (opened 1901) and for women at Clinton (1913). The founders of the state prison had hoped to reform convicts by discipline and hard labor, but, as it turned out, the prison undertook to guard desperate characters by terror; security and punishment, rather than reform, came to be its rationale. This much was clear when the legislature, moved by stories of cruel treatment, established the commission that reported on prison discipline in 1869. The commissioners criticized jails and the prison, as we have seen, but their central thought was that, since overcrowding was going to force some new construction anyhow, the state should build a new type of institution, which they called an intermediate prison or house of correction.[23]

By "intermediate" they meant between the jail and the state prison. Jails would continue, in their view, to hold vagrants and disorderly persons for short sentences; the prison would continue to hold recidivists and people guilty of serious crimes. The proposed institution would house adult first offenders whose crimes were "of lesser turpitude." The commissioners envisioned it as something like the workhouse or penitentiary that Hudson County was even then building at Snake Hill; they thought the state might well take over the Hudson County institution, which was well-located, they observed, at a great mass of trap rock for breaking, and which offered a variety of healthful outdoor employments, with easy transportation by river to a great urban market.[24]

The model the commissioners had in mind was the House of Correction at Boston. Their suggestions about discipline drew heavily on the "Irish" system that had begun to influence prison reformers. In general, they wanted each inmate of the new prison to pass through four phases of treatment. The first or "penal" phase, would be strict cellular confinement on "low diet," at monotonous work (like oakum picking) except for one or two hours of school. Good behavior, appropriately graded and tallied, entitled the convict to enter the second phase, in which he enjoyed congregate labor during the day, an increasing scale of "gratuities" for his efforts, improved diet, and other privileges. The third stage would offer considerable liberty, in shops, farms, and other employments outside the walls—"moral confinement" but "very little, if any, prison restraint of bolts and bars." The final stage would be, in effect, parole, during the last part of the sentence.[25]

Such was the reformatory idea, advanced even before New York State finished, in 1870, the "reformatory" at Elmira that gave the new type of institution a name. The plan, like Jamesburg's, emphasized reform and some formal education, but whereas Jamesburg embodied the idea of "family life" in "cottages" under parental supervision, the proposed house of correction was a modified prison for adults; whereas Jamesburg received juveniles who were committed until their majority or indenture or discharge by the board of managers, the proposed reformatory was to house criminals sentenced for definite terms. Nevertheless, both institutions embodied a common attitude, that detention should be correctional rather than penal, and the commissioners explicitly recommended that the new institution be managed, like Jamesburg and unlike the jails and state prison, by an unpaid board appointed by the governor, chancellor, and chief justice, to minimize political interference.[26]

The reformatory idea did not appeal much to the legislators in 1869; their practical decision was to expand the state prison and to let

Hudson and Essex County officials build their own workhouses. The prison commission that reported nine years later, in 1878, showed no enthusiasm for these moves. Absorbed by the problem of vagrancy in the depression still under way, they laid their emphasis on a new state reformatory modeled on the Elmira institution, which they described at length. Elmira provided three grades of confinement, they noted. Newcomers entered the middle grade, whence they might fall or rise as their behavior merited. The commissioners described at length the way of tallying credit. Each inmate, they said, "has his own little *bank* book in which [his] monthly credits are entered. Ungentlemanly behavior at table or elsewhere" and otherwise unsatisfactory performances reduced his balance. This banking of creditable behavior appealed to the commissioners. So did the indeterminate sentence, according to which prison authorities might parole convicts at any time before the maximum term set by law. They thought this "indefinite sentence" was analogous to commitment to an insane asylum, where the objective was "cure," not "vengeance." [27]

The commissioners of 1878 had the support of Governor George McClellan (1878–1880) and of people influenced by the successes of prison reform in New York. But as the depression passed, public interest turned away. In 1886, the legislature considered a report urging a female reformatory, but the only result was an improved administration of the women's wing at the state prison.[28]

Nevertheless, in 1886 well over half the convicts in the state prison were eligible for reformatory discipline. As crowding there increased and led to wholesale pardons and, incidentally, to increasing industrial losses, and as it appeared, too, that some expansion or supplementary institution was needed for the older Jamesburg boys, the legislature authorized a new commission to consider an intermediate reformatory. Its report, in 1890, noted that there were then only three reformatories in the country, at Elmira (1870), Concord, Massachusetts (1885), and Huntington, Pennsylvania (1889).

The commissioners were interested in the Concord institution, which allowed its highest class unprecedented liberty and privilege; they also applauded the probation work in Massachusetts. Experience there, and even more in England, convinced them that the reformatory idea, given form in law and institutions, could bring about a substantial reduction in crime. They favored Elmira as a model for the proposed reformatory, however; they did not discuss administration, except to emphasize that habitual or serious offenders should be excluded and that the program should emphasize formal education.[29]

The legislature did not act on the report for five years (years of unprecedented political turmoil and corruption, by all accounts), and the reformatory at Rahway did not open until 1901. Its location was a state-owned farm property near the metropolitan centers, swampy and undeveloped except for a clay-pit and brickyard. The edifice boasted a great dome, larger than the national capitol's, from which radiated two wings. Only one was completed in 1901, however, and the board of managers had no luck in getting more appropriations. In 1904, its president, Charlton Lewis, said in a public letter that judges had to send several hundred offenders to the state prison or county institutions because Rahway was unfinished.

The *New Jersey Review of Charities and Corrections,* noting that state prison officials were also asking for construction to relieve overcrowding, commented that withdrawing federal prisoners and those eligible for reformatory discipline would reduce the prison population by half. Were contractors for prison labor the effective influences for expanding the prison instead of the reformatory? asked the editor. As it turned out, the prison got an expensive new wing of 350 cells, opened in 1907; the second wing at Rahway was not authorized until 1908.[30]

As to program, Rahway was like Elmira—three grades, inmate entered in the middle grade, employment at outdoor work (mostly to improve the institution) and various shops, and of course a system of grading creditable behavior; the discipline was described as "semimilitary," with plenty of drill. In 1909, Dr. Frank Moore became superintendent and introduced ideas based on his experience in administering public schools. He simplified and rationalized the grading system; introduced various placement tests and improved the schooling; adjusted other aspects of institutional life to approximate the outside life of the parolee; introduced an honor system of discipline and even a degree of inmate self-government (which didn't work, he found). Moore was not only an energetic administrator but was also interested in public relations. He sponsored "illustrated lectures" around the state to clarify the reformatory idea and to encourage public support. By 1917 he was a well-known spokesman for enlightened penology.[31]

It was ironic that Moore's enlightened ideas included a proposal to convert Rahway into a state prison and build a reformatory elsewhere. The architect had conceived it as an intermediate prison, not a true reformatory, he complained, and it was unsuited to the more liberal ideas about discipline and reform that were gaining influence.[32] For their part the Prison Inquiry Commission of 1917 praised Rahway's schooling and its progressive ideas, but they called it "a prison with reformatory features, . . . too much like its famous prototype, the Elmira reformatory, to be altogether admirable." They also thought it had "more than a touch of the severity of spirit" of prison management, resulting in part from the construction "with its inside cells and depressing prison atmosphere." [33]

Clinton Farms: The New Reformatory Idea

Until a men's reformatory was established there was not much hope for one for women, but it happened that the founding of Rahway came when New Jersey's women's clubs were federating and turning their attention to provision for delinquent children and women. Clubwomen of the Oranges, led by Mrs. J. R. Paddock and Mrs. Caroline B. Alexander, gave new force and direction to the old demand for a women's reformatory. Their campaign was different from that for Rahway, however, insofar as their purpose was less to reform criminals than to help erring sisters go straight; it was the same spirit that led them in these years to support probation and private "junior republics" for delinquent boys.[34]

When the ladies began their agitation there were four places to send female offenders. Girls under sixteen could go to the State Home for Girls in Trenton. The workhouses of Hudson and Essex Counties had separate quarters and some work for females. The state prison had a place for more serious offenders. Otherwise, women and girls were simply put in the county jails. None of these alternatives was likely to reform them. The State Home was under a cloud at the time; workhouses were for habitual offenders; the prison was severe and punitive. The jails were scandalous. Visitors to the jail in Atlantic City in 1902 reported their experience under the title "Can you believe it?":

> As we approached the jail we heard shouts of laughter and loud talking, male and female, such as would have justified condemnation of the place as a public nuisance. We did not ask whether the prisoners were usefully employed. Out in the kitchen and in the halls were the "trusties," two men and one woman, preparing the afternoon meal—the second and last of the day. . . . The supper was taken to the woman prisoners by a young man, successsor to another young trusty who had recently sawed his way out of jail, after he had been brought back from the home of a girl prisoner whither he had escaped with the sheriff's horse and buggy. He [the present trusty] had fallen in love with [a] girl of seventeen, while he was waiting upon her at jail. . . . She and one other of sixteen were the youngest among the thirteen women. Neither of the girls was smoking as were some of the others, nor did they ask for tobacco or money. The foster mother of one, serving sentence for keeping a disorderly house, had practically no clothing above the waist when we first went in, nor did she hurry to complete her toilet. A colored women [sic] had just taken a bath, and while her clothes were soaking in the dirty bathtub full of dirty water, she loafed about with a blanket drawn around her. A girl of twenty-four had decided a few months before that streetwalking would be more endurable than her shop work. Most of these women had been sentenced by the Mayor of Atlantic City acting as a magistrate. He could not send the girls to the State Home, there was no reformatory, he was not acquainted with the practice of . . . probation, and he sent them to this dreadful place to maintain the dignity of the law.[35]

The governor appointed a commission on a women's reformatory, which reported in 1904. It recommended an institution like that in Massachusetts, then twenty-five years old, which had three grades of confinement, a credit system for promotion, and industrial training, in the typical reformatory pattern. But the commission favored altering this plan to use the "cottage system" of housing, as did the new institution at Bedford, New York. The commission also noted (in a second report, a year later) that judges in Hudson, Essex, and Union counties sometimes suspended sentence for women offenders who agreed to enter private houses of correction, missions, or homes, as a form of probation; the report does not describe these places, but their existence testified to the recognized need for a reformatory.[36]

Nevertheless, the idea made slow progress. The legislators invested first in expanding the prison and then in completing Rahway before they authorized a women's reformatory in 1910. It finally opened in May 1913, on a farm near Clinton, far out along the old road from Newark to Easton. It was then little more than a few farm buildings somewhat refurbished as dormitories. Its small size and rustic features precluded a typical reformatory discipline. Instead, its authorities embraced with zest the newer ideas of an honor system and family life in the cottages.

Clinton's first superintendent, May Caughey, formerly on the staff of the House of Refuge for girls at Darlington, Pennsylvania, hoped to develop in her charges "a strong spirit of self-reliance and helpfulness," and she thought the best way to train the girls to "withstand temptation" was to give them "the opportunity to choose between right and wrong while here." Many of her charges were illiterate and foreign-born, and because she had only one teacher, who doubled as psychologist and parole officer, academic training was minimal. Her program, farm work and training for domestic service, suited the separate cottage families.[37]

As Mrs. Caroline Alexander (now Mrs. H. O. Wittpenn), who had led the campaign to establish the institution and who became the leader on its board of managers, put it, the problem of the program was "to impress the necessity for discipline and obedience" on the girls, "for it is a lack of these which has largely brought [them] . . . to Clinton Farms." The solution was a healthful and regular life, training in household skills, and preaching and worship. (Mrs. Wittpenn herself gave the institution a large, handsome chapel; it was certainly the best-equipped state correctional institution in that respect.) The keys to reform, she said, were to give the girls liberty "where it is not being abused" and to build in them loyalty to the officers, the institution and to each other.[38]

To the secretary of the State Charities Aid Association, a visit to Clinton in 1915 was "a revelation":

> Here is a farm house remodeled into a comfortable, home-like house, with rugs on the floor, a fire in the grate in the living room where there are rockingchairs, curtains at the windows, and a canary and other household pets. There are rooms, clean and neat in their appointments, where the women sleep. There are no clanging steel or iron doors except the two in the basement for the temporary confine-

ment of the women who develop a nervous tendency to temporarily rebel at authority. . . . There are no indications from the dress of these women that they are different from others. They wear khaki bloomers while at work in the laundry and at various outdoor occupations, but within the house they dress in neat garments and live very nearly a normal life. . . . It is a far cry from the old institutional management of cells and strict supervision to the comparative freedom and opportunity for self-expression afforded the women offenders . . . by this new type of institution.[39]

The inmates were not classified in grades with a complicated system of tallying credits, but by age and color. The first cottage built for the institution was for Negro girls, because by segregation the management could put Negro matrons in charge of them. The visitor in 1915 noticed that the cottage for colored women was "a distinct division of Clinton Farms . . . a quarter of a mile, at least, from the main farmhouse," but he found that it had "neat rooms, one for each of the women, a very attractive sitting room and a large veranda . . . , a neatly appointed dining room and an admirable kitchen."[40]

Clinton was also a revelation to the Prison Inquiry Commission of 1917. They criticized its "slackness of administration" and "rather easy-going" and even undisciplined life, but the place struck them as "a tolerant, good-natured, co-operative family, or group of related families, rather than a 'correctional institution.'" In general they applauded the "vigorous spirit of co-operation" within the families and the "wholesome rivalry" between them; they praised the "spirit of sympathy and understanding" and the "attitude of trust and sympathy" in the institution, which they attributed largely to the insight and energy of its board of managers. The problem of prison discipline, they thought, was somehow to combine the "fine spirit" of Clinton and the "order, system and efficient administration" of Rahway. Clearly it was the reformatory idea that gave them their perspective on reorganizing the state's correctional institutions.[41]

The Prison Inquiry Commission of 1917

The report of the Prison Inquiry Commission, which summed up fifty years of prison reform in New Jersey, was organized around four problems: convict labor, discipline, parole, and administration.

Prison labor attracted the most attention, partly because of its economic failure and partly because of its political interest, for the progressive coalition of middle-class humanitarians and labor sympathizers could agree that the state ought not to expose free labor to the competition of unpaid and sweated convict labor, but rather ought to aim at education and reform.

In 1911, these pressures had led the legislature to discard the "piece-price" system of contracting for prison labor and to adopt the state-use system in its place. To direct the development and control the operation of the new system, the legislature established a Prison Labor Commission, which consisted of representatives of the prison, the reformatory, and the public. The agency was a step toward a common policy in the several institutions, with authority to channel the purchases of all state and local governmental institutions for the state-use enterprise. It had an impressive look, but its history was disappointing. It was not organized until fourteen months after the act was passed, and then began a "discouraging record of 'orders' and 'directives' . . . to the . . . correctional institutions and of appeals for appropriations, nearly all of which were ignored or met with the conclusive formula, 'no funds.' " [42]

The simplest explanation of this record was that the businessmen who profited from prison labor had opposed state use and had influenced prison authorities and legislators to side with them. Officially, prison officials feared that when the contracts were withdrawn the convicts would be left idle, with disastrous effects on discipline. They doubted whether the state-use market could keep the prisoners employed. In any case, to institute it would require new and different machinery and organization and extensive provision for "recreation" during the transition, in a prison yard already much too crowded. They set the cost of installing the system at half a million dollars.[43]

When, in the event, the existing contracts expired, there was nothing to take their place, so the legislators rushed through a law to renew them. The law, looking forward to the termination of the contracts, provided that authorities could not renegotiate them nor replace them with new ones, with the ironic result that, as wages rose during the prosperity of 1914–1917, the contracts became more profitable than ever.[44]

Advocates of state use were, however, somewhat more gratified in their hopes for extramural employment of prisoners. The example of the county workhouses and the reformatory idea of a schedule of increasing privilege and responsibility joined in this case with the persistent problem of overcrowding and a lively interest in conservation. Set up prison farms, reformers said, with cheap barracks and minimum security; set up road camps, where work gangs would live while working on the public highways, along which passed the files of horseless carriages; let prisoners work to prevent forest fires, clear public parks for tourists, and campaign against the Jersey 'skeeter on the Jersey beaches. Away from stone walls, the prisoners would grow as healthy as Rough Riders, while the state would save on construction and develop its resources. The combination seemed irresistible.[45]

To realize these hopes the Prison Labor Commission bought a one-thousand-acre farm near Leesburg in 1913 and opened two road camps (it opened others in 1915 and 1917); Rahway boys also worked on the roads, although they lived at the institution, and in 1917 they set up an "honor camp" on a state-owned farm called Annandale. Superintendent Moore, at the Reformatory, strongly supported the state-use program, as long as it did not interfere with his program of schooling.

But prison authorities, worried about escapes, demanded that extramural work have a numerous and expensive guard and obstructed the enterprise in other ways.[46]

It seemed to the Prison Inquiry Commission that division of authority and responsibility had crippled state use, and that the division took root in the old-fashioned discipline enforced by the prison authorities. The inspectors and keepers were appointed by the governor or the legislature according to various organic acts. The inspectors were, by law, apportioned equally among the two political parties, and subordinate jobs were divided equally among the party faithful.

The principal keepers were primarily politicians, but two of them served ten years and made some reputation for enlightened policies. They were John H. Patterson (1886–1896), a prosperous farmer and shipper and a prominent Democrat, formerly sheriff of Monmouth County and doorkeeper of the (U. S.) House of Representatives, and George O. Osborne (1902–1912), a Republican from Hudson County who had previously held appointments as a manager of almshouses and hospitals. Their chief deputies were practically career men. Thomas Madden, appointed principal keeper by Woodrow Wilson in 1912, had been a subordinate official at the prison for most of his life; his son, Dr. Walter Madden, was a leading Democrat of Mercer County and sheriff at the time.[47]

These men encouraged some improvements in the lives of the convicts: a prison school, begun in 1887; a library; better clothes and more money for discharged men. Keeper Osborne eliminated the traditional prison stripes, haircut and lock step when he discovered, at a meeting of the National Prison Congress in 1902, that most other states had dropped them.[48] But long tenure did not usually make officers humanitarian and after a point it made them inefficient. A commission reported in 1908 that "Many . . . officers have spent their lives in the service, and have become aged and unfit to properly and fully discharge their duties," and it recommended retiring them on half-pay.[49] In 1917, the Prison Inquiry Commission, observing that the discipline of the prison expressed "a general attitude of severity toward the inmates and an indifference as to the conditions under which they . . . live," had "no doubt" that many of the officers "who [had] passed years . . . in controlling prisoners under . . . repressive conditions" had "by their very training become temperamentally unfitted to serve." [50]

Scandals about prison conditions and discipline brought the Prison Inquiry Commission into being. Official documents reveal little about the inner life of the prison, but there are suggestions that Keeper Osborne was too lenient and that Keeper Madden was, by necessity and perhaps by choice, much more strict. While he was tightening discipline the problems of changing to state use and guarding convicts outside the walls would have seemed especially difficult to him. In any case, he came to represent what an editorialist in the *Newark News* would call the "hard-shell standpat element in prison control, satisfied with the old-type system of dealing with prisoners—keeping them behind high walls, with strong guards on the outside, and compelling them to work for contractors in the making of goods for private profit." [51]

When the *News* made this comment the *New York Post* was publicizing sensational charges about conditions in the prison, made by Patrick Quinlan, who had done time there as a leader of the Paterson strike of 1913. Stories about a brutal, corrupt, and plague-ridden institution were echoing through the land.[52] The truth was worse than the stories, in the view of Caroline Bayard Colgate, who visited the institution during these days. Just before the visit her cousin, Mrs. Caroline (Alexander) Wittpenn, told her to ask to see a man named Bailey, who was being kept in the Dog Kennels, the solitary dungeons. "You will find opposition," Mrs. Wittpenn said, "so wait until you are in the wing." The keeper was "visibly annoyed" by the request, but since Mrs. Colgate was accompanied by a judge of the Criminal Court and by Mrs. James Fielder, wife of the governor—the Fielders were old family friends—he could not refuse.

"As we made our precarious way down the steep, dimly-lit, narrow stone stairs," she recalled, "my heart sank." She touched the cold stone wall for support. "As I heard the warden coming down behind me," she continues, "I thought, 'Just one push, and this would be the end of me.' " The visitors wound their way underground until they came to the Dog Kennels, "small whitewashed cells, with narrow slits up near the ceiling at ground level for light and air." Near the foot of one wall were "shackles to which men could be bound hand and foot."

She did not see Bailey, but the judge later went back and talked with him. The story was that he had witnessed the beating and death of another prisoner, who "had been buried with quicklime . . . to destroy all evidence." The authorities had kept Bailey in solitary to keep him from talking until relatives outside the prison began to inquire. After the judge talked to him, Bailey was quickly freed, Mrs. Colgate said, "obviously . . . to keep us quiet." The governor had the Dog Kennels closed, she said, but what struck her about the situation was that, while the governor meant well, "because he *was* Governor everything possible was done to keep him from knowing" the facts. His action antagonized the keeper, but it was "a very polite fight on the surface,—quiet and hushed for fear the newspapers would get interested." [53]

Such were the views of one interested party and the suspicions that fed upon Mr. Quinlan's sensations. The situation played into the hand of the incoming governor, Walter Edge, a Republican, who, like the Republican legislature, was happy to bring out evidence of laxity under the preceding Democratic administration. The first resolution of the new legislature was for a Prison Inquiry Commission, which the governor appointed on January 26, 1917, shortly after his inauguration. William B. Dickson was its chairman; Seymour Cromwell, president of the New York Stock Exchange and also president of the State Charities Aid Association, and the eminent Dwight Morrow, a Morgan partner, were among the five members.

The Commission visited the prison and held hearings during the next week, while the convicts busied themselves with a riot.[54] On February 5 the commissioners issued a preliminary report saying, among other things, that the prisoners had inadequate medical examinations, and facilities for segregating those with contagious disease were wanting; that food was poorly prepared and served—in the cells; that the bath house—in the yard and inaccessible in winter—was inadequate; that exercise space was "entirely inadequate"; that facilities for education were lacking and dungeons were used for punishment; that there was no system of grading prisoners by conduct and achievement; that parole procedure was inequitable, and that laws regulating contract labor were violated. The Commission recommended improvements, but asked for authority to make a comprehensive report on or before January 1, 1918, which was readily granted to it.[55]

Newspapers called the Commission's preliminary report an indictment, but some people did not think it went far enough. It criticized prison facilities, but prison officials themselves had been saying as much for years. Its references to the prison staff were general; it named no names and it ignored the more lurid charges of brutality and corruption. These charges were kept alive by a "Citizens Union," an organization of progressive spirits and social workers with branches in many North Jersey suburbs, who found a loud trumpet in the *New York Post*.[56] Accordingly, the Commission interviewed many inmates, ex-prisoners, and guards and held a public hearing on April 17, 1917; as a result Chairman Dickson, who had been appointed to the prison's Board of Inspectors, preferred charges on June 12 to the Board against four deputy keepers.

The Board, considering the character of the witnesses, would not take action, and Dickson resigned from it. Two weeks later the Citizens Union charged that an insane convict had died after guards had beat him with clubs and blackjacks, and they made other charges, naming names. The Commission considered these charges and finally recommended that the governor turn them over to a grand jury in Mercer County. In the end, the grand jury did not indict, holding that the keepers had used no more force than was necessary in any of the cases.[57]

Meanwhile, on July 17 Mr. Dickson resigned as chairman of the Prison Inquiry Commission, saying that he suddenly had to go to Washington on business.[58] But it appears that he and Dwight Morrow, who replaced him, took different views of the Commission's work. Dickson had first sent his colleagues a memorandum that he wanted to hear from "intelligent, thoughtful men among the prisoners" who might have suggestions to end the mental stagnation and repressive regime at the prison.[59] Morrow had replied that he favored a preliminary report about immediate problems followed by a "large constructive program" for reorganizing the correctional institutions.[60] During Dickson's tenure the Commission did hear inmates and in general addressed itself to the scandals agitated by the Citizens Union, but it made no moves toward the more general study.

Dwight Morrow was not interested in investigating criminal acts; he told J. A. H. Hopkins, a leader of the Citizens Union, that he did not look upon the organization as "unofficial publicity agents" for the Commission, as they assumed; he did not reply to Hopkins' charge that of course the Mercer County grand jury had whitewashed the prison officials, who of course were in solid with both political parties.[61] (Newspapers reported that one of the keepers named before the grand jury was a brother of the public prosecutor of Mercer County.)[62]

Morrow moved ahead with his own plans. He asked Professor George Kirchwey, of Columbia University and the New York School of Social Work, to outline a study and make recommendations for background information.[63] Subsequently he engaged experts to study the laws governing institutions, commitments, and parole, and he commissioned investigations of prison labor, the prison system of the Philippines (supposedly a model system set up by the United States government), and local jails and workhouses; he also commissioned a history of the state's correctional institutions, which was published later as a second volume of the Commission's report.[64] Morrow financed much of this work himself and took great interest in it; in mid-September he was recommending books published by the Russell Sage Foundation to Governor Edge.[65]

The Commission report that drew on these resources was a comprehensive and lucid document, written largely by George Kirchwey.[66] With regard to prison labor, it strongly recommended that the contracts end; it favored centralization that would end the conflict of authority in state use and it looked forward to a large expansion of extramural employment. As for discipline, it favored improved living conditions, a mild, reformatory-style discipline, with formal merit-grading, and better schooling. Moved by the psychiatric studies by Dr. Bernard Glueck at Sing Sing and intelligence testing, it emphasized the importance of mental and psychiatric testing and classification of inmate population, as well as better medical examinations. It favored leaving parole to institutional boards of managers and linking it to behavior.[67]

The criticisms followed enlightened opinion and included no sensations or surprises. The Commission allowed that the correctional system was, "on the whole, fairly abreast of the penal systems of other states"; the "most serious defect," it said, was the lack of a centralized authority able to coordinate and improve the management of the several institutions, and its recommendations were mostly toward correcting that defect.[68]

The Balance of Forces in Prison Reform

Because these constructive recommendations became the basis of the state's unique organization for social welfare, they will be considered at length in later chapters. But to see them in historical perspective it is worth asking how the commissioners themselves saw their history and understood its lessons. What struck them most forcibly was the diversity of management among the institutions, and their leading historical question was how this came about. Their answer was that as problems increased men built new institutions that made a gross classification of offenders by age, sex, and character of offense, so as to give them special treatment. The newer institutions were of a reformatory nature, characterized by a more humanitarian spirit and a more scientific understanding than the old jails and the state prison.

The contrast between the punitive and the reformatory institutions led to efforts to give them some sort of common policy and direction. Humanitarians wanted to level the management of all the institutions up to that of the most enlightened; public officials wanted to unify them in the interest of administrative efficiency—to make better use of prison labor, for example. This historical perspective supported, if it did not embody, the commissioners' judgment that the need of the day was administrative reorganization.[69]

The history Morrow commissioned turned out to be a weighty volume, put together under great pressure, with prodigious energy, by Harry Elmer Barnes, then a graduate student at Columbia (it became the foundation of his well-known later studies of penology and criminology). Drawing upon laws and public documents, Barnes organized his history around the formalities of institutional organization and administration. His business was to describe these formalities rather than to interpret them as human acts and situations.

Barnes' account therefore supported without qualification the commissioners' thought that the significant history of a state's institutions told how they were formally set up and how the administrative set-up changed. One could read the commissioners' pronouncements and Barnes' redaction of documents and never learn that in two generations the social structure of the state had changed greatly, that Dr. Frank Moore and Mrs. Wittpenn, Patrick Quinlan and the editor of the *New York Post,* Governor Edge (an enormously successful advertising man from Atlantic City), Dwight Morrow, Professor Kirchwey and Professor-to-be Barnes were members of an urban society, or that their problems and solutions were in any way linked to the social changes that had brought them to the fore.

This consideration—how their work related to changes in the society around them—did come up, in a way, when the commissioners and their advisers paused to reflect on why progress had been so slow, why investigation after investigation made the same points with the same futility. If the equation of progress was that effective reform was the product of humanitarian sympathy, scientific understanding and administrative efficiency, why didn't the factors combine? Who opposed humanitarian sympathy, scientific understanding, and administrative efficiency?

The commissioners and their advisers did not pause over this consideration because the answer seemed so obvious to them that they could take it for granted. Partly, of course, administrative schemes were at fault: a divided authority over parole or prison labor was an inherent source of misunderstanding and trouble. But the core of the problem was politics. It unbalanced the equation of progress in two ways. On one hand, it was the vehicle of special interests—prison contractors or organized labor, for example—and of course politicians themselves were well-organized special interests who made laws and employed personnel with prior regard to party considerations.[70] On the other hand, politicians represented the public, and the public itself was ignorant and apathetic about prison reform.

"The fundamental difficulty in the past," Harry Elmer Barnes remarked, "has been that society has not understood the nature of the causation of crime and has believed that its interests were at an end when the prison gates were closed upon the offender and the revenge of society was thereby inflicted." The case of prison reform, in New Jersey as elsewhere, was, on this view, "simply one manifestation of the indescribable tardiness of the evolution of social intelligence and the almost unbelievable inertia in the public mind." [71]

The confident reference to "the nature of the causation of crime" rested upon developments in behavioral science that gave an authentic glimpse of impersonal forces and unconscious factors. The commissioners referred to mental and psychiatric testing as "a new basis for the understanding and classification of . . . criminal elements." Barnes thought that recent studies brought out that "the problem of criminality is not an isolated metaphysical, theological, and juridical phenomenon, but is an inevitable product of defects in the social environment produced by abnormal biological and psychological forces and influences." [72]

So, almost in passing, the commissioners and their advisers recognized that the moral basis of prison reform had changed. For the reformatory idea, from its root in imprisonment at hard labor to its flowering at Clinton, had grown from the assumption that criminals were guilty people whose reform was essentially moral regeneration and moral instruction, and the reformers' motive was not to diagnose pathology but to help fallen sinners, as their faith demanded. The commissioners who reported in 1869 thought the reformatory spirit was essentially "Christian kindness," and they believed that the "use of the Scriptures" and other "religious books and tracts," the "preaching of the Gospel and the counsels of the Moral Instructor" were "first in importance and in power" in reaching "the heart and conscience" of the convict.[73] The genteel ladies who took up the cause of girls gone wrong felt a religious obligation, and Mrs. Mary Cory of the Citizens Union thought that its plans, endorsed, she said, by Bishop Lines of the Episcopal church, were "God's way of working." [74] But neither God nor Christian kindness is named in the report of the Prison Inquiry Commission, and Barnes held that "The Binet-Simon test and the Freudian theory of the neuroses are rocks upon which the old theological dogmas of 'free will' and the 'free moral agent' have been hopelessly disintegrated." [75]

To imply that criminals were sick, defective, or specimens of social pathology was to challenge not only the theology of free will and responsibility but also the assumptions of the criminal law, which were entirely punitive, and this moral revolution is as important as the social revolution in analyzing the course of prison reform. For who could be its leaders? Who could play the role here that psychiatrists took in the mental hospitals or professional educators and psychologists took in institutions for the retarded?

In the rural society clergymen and lawyers had led prison reform. But in the urban society the clergy were sharply divided, among the confessions and within their own minds; they did not speak with a single voice or unchallenged authority, even on ethical subjects; they were notably absent among the commissioners of 1917 and their advisers. Lawyers did gain in influence during these years; the three leading prison reformers of the period, Samuel Allinson, Charlton Lewis, and Judge Harry V. Osborne, were lawyers; so was George Kirchwey.

Charlton Lewis advocated the reformatory and the indeterminate sentence on the legal ground that the purpose of criminal law was to protect society, rather than to punish offenders, and tried to direct attention from the moral deserts of the crime to the rehabilitation of the lawbreaker and to prevention.[76] But lawyers spoke with no single voice on prison reform. Many were ardently engaged in the political shenanigans that reformers deplored; many were bound to the assumptions of the criminal law; judges were political appointees and they were dubious about the "indeterminate sentence" that underwrote reformatory discipline but undermined their power to sentence. They were not much interested in the juvenile court, in which they were cast as a kind of social worker.

Conceivably, the sheriffs and wardens might have led prison reform, but they were, in New Jersey, career men in politics, not penology. Could their subordinates, who often served for many years, have fostered an enlightened view and policy? Not likely; they learned their jobs by rote and could not boast of professional expertise or spirit. In any case they looked to political bosses, not reformers, for leadership; the reformers, for their part, were inclined to think them brutal and indifferent.

Not only did prison reform in this period lack a definite class interest, a coherent moral appeal, or an effective leadership, but its partisans could not see that even in the prisoners' view the situation had possibilities. The outsiders involved with prison industries, the irrational ways of pardon and parole, the arbitrary power of the guards, sanctioned by torture, the genial politicians in ultimate authority—all the notorious occasions for favoritism and corruption in administration—were in a way opportunities for the convicts as well as the staff. The convict was not, after all, a lucrative person to exploit; he was generally a desperate man, with nothing to lose, as prison officials emphasized whenever he offered testimony against them. There was not much to take away from him, as advocates of reformatory privileges observed. So long as he did not make trouble, the guards were likely to let him alone; if he were docile, and especially if he had money or influence beyond the walls, "favoritism" brought him favors, even freedom, and "corruption" pandered to his vice.

Lady reformers thought the Atlantic County jail was "a dreadful place," but they themselves observed that it was full of fun and even romance (the better sort kept out on bail, of course). Lady reformers believed that the reason men delayed building a women's reformatory was that women prisoners sometimes had sexual relations with male convicts; Caroline Bayard Colgate recalled that after they opened the reformatory at Clinton and transferred the women there from the prison "one old colored woman screamed day and night. They could not quiet her. She kept saying, 'I certainly do miss the men.'"[77]

While brutal but corruptible disciplinarians and enlightened but pious lady reformers confronted one another over a screaming old colored woman—ultimately over the form and substance of punishment—and while the story of prison reform in New Jersey impressed its graduate-student historian with "the indescribable tardiness of the evolution of social intelligence," the commissioners of 1917, masters in the brave new world of business administration and corporate reorganization, were investing their hopes in an administrative reorganization that would, if it worked, get politics out of all state welfare, not just the correctional institutions, and give scientific understanding its appropriate professional voice. The idea of some centralized state administration was almost as old as the diversity of state institutions, of course, but the commissioners' deliberations scarcely touched on that history, and, as it happened, they bypassed its central issue.

9

Centralization: Supervision or Control?

It seemed to the Morrow Commission—as the Prison Inquiry Commission of 1917 came to be called—that previous advocates of central supervision had wanted to promote either humanitarian service or efficient financial management. Since no one would oppose these goals in principle, the commissioners were disposed to blame the halting progress on self-seeking politicians who took advantage of public ignorance and apathy. In part, at least, this conclusion was obvious, but it overlooked the fact that people engaged in helping dependent, defective, and delinquent individuals saw the situation and problems in different and often antagonistic ways.

In the proliferation of charitable and correctional institutions that attended urban growth, the philanthropic public spread its interest over three types of enterprise. Some people wanted to reform local public agencies that were abused under the spoils system. Others wanted to improve local private charities by "charity organization" and better methods; still others were interested in state institutions. The resulting conflicts between charity organizer and political spoilsman were usually clear, but they were of little interest to the multitude who neither sponsored charities nor sought a spoilsman's employment. Insofar as these people had a charitable interest, it was mutual aid or self-help—their church's aid to its parishioners and its missionary work, a fraternal organization, a labor union, or the YMCA. Insofar as they had to choose between charity organizers and spoilsmen, they were closer to the spoilsmen; indeed, the political machine was a kind of self-help and welfare organization for many of them.

Moreover, genteel charity and vulgar mutual aid were characterized by differing ideas about helping. The traditional—and vulgar—notion of humane sensibility was uncomplicated sympathy with and mercy toward a suffering person. Charity, in this view, was direct aid: alms for a beggar, a meal for a tramp, a basket for the poor, a home for a waif. People supposed that it was a wholesome exercise of fellow-feeling, an imitation of God's bounty and mercy, good for both giver and receiver. Of course they recognized that it was often a mere formality: the helper gave a coin or basket instead of himself, the client exploited his patron. Solid citizens could easily see that handouts that confirmed pauperism were a vicious waste, and that well-intentioned help often came in the wrong way at the wrong time.

These thoughts, encouraged by what the solid citizens were learning about science, medicine, and education, inclined them toward a "scientific charity" which, like scientific penology, was intended to reform, rehabilitate, or discipline its objects. These critical notions struck the wealthier citizens with particular force, because it was they who largely supported, by taxes and gifts, both public and private agencies that looked after deviants.

In the end, the difference of emphasis often led to antagonism. To the vulgar, "scientific charity" seemed unsympathetic or suspicious, exhibiting snobbery rather than fellow-feeling. Ordinary people, and especially politicians, felt obliged to be generous; they deplored the rascality of pauperdom, but they were inclined to err on the side of tolerance in particular appeals and to respect church charity; they felt little call for complicated ideas of scientific charity and charity organization. To the genteel, or at least the progressive spirits among them, indiscriminate handouts and most of the old-line religious and patrician charities did more harm than good, however laudable their original purpose.

The Charity Organization Society (COS), which gave form to the critical spirit, was originally an English idea; Episcopalians and Quakers often sponsored it in New Jersey. There was some sort of association of private charities in the Oranges as early as 1869; Newark and Salem were organized in 1881, Trenton in 1883, New Brunswick in 1884. The idea thrived best in suburbs, and by 1902 the state had twelve local societies and stood third among states in that regard.[1]

The "charities aid association" came to New Jersey in the same spirit and at the same time as "charity organization." Whereas charity organization related to private almsgiving, the charities aid association helped inmates of public poorhouses and jails. Charity organizers wanted to supplement or supplant public outdoor relief, relief to the poor in their homes; charity aiders wanted to visit, protect, and encourage the poor in public institutions. The Charities Aid Association was modeled on the English "workhouse visiting society." Its first appearance in America was in New York, when, in 1872, Louisa Lee Schuyler arranged to visit the Westchester County almshouse with her friends. Her efforts led to a statewide organization that led in agitating for a better law governing pauper children. The New Jersey organization began in Morristown, when some Episcopalian ladies and their rector, concerned about pauper children in the county almshouse, invited a speaker from the New York association. The resulting organization became a model for several other Jersey counties.[2]

The State Council of Charities and the SCAA

Meanwhile, other states had established official agencies to inspect public institutions, collect facts, and make recommendations. The first was organized in 1863 in Massachusetts, which already had a variety of asylums and training schools and which was also directly involved in poor relief. Its board was "supervisory," that is, it reported and advised rather than issued orders. It was unpaid, but it had a paid staff. Its impressive reports led other states to create analagous agencies: New York and Ohio in 1867; Illinois, North Carolina, Pennsylvania, and Rhode Island in 1869; Wisconsin and Michigan in 1871; Kansas and Connecticut in 1873. The New York board, composed of eight unsalaried members who served revolving terms of eight years, had to inspect all charitable institutions that received state aid and all local almshouses. Its purpose was to determine whether state funds were being spent carefully and wisely, and to furnish facts and advice to the legislature.[3]

In New Jersey the state did not contribute to poor relief, and its subsidy to county insane asylums, begun in 1872, appeared at first to be a temporary measure. Here the first recommendation for central supervision came from a commission of doctors appointed in 1866 to inquire into sanitary conditions in charitable institutions (and, incidentally, into the means of preventing pauperism and treating insanity). Its recommendations had no effect, but a similar commission in 1874 led to the founding of the State Board of Health, which was empowered to inspect sanitary conditions in public institutions. The Board experienced difficulty in this work and recommended other state supervision.[4]

The Prison Commission of 1878, which pointed to bad conditions in local jails as part of its argument for a state reformatory, recommended a state board of charities like those in neighboring states, with advisory power over publicly supported penal and charitable institutions.[5] Nothing was done, but in 1881 the state began to send official delegates to the National Conference of Charities and Corrections, an annual meeting of members of state boards, then in its eighth year. The delegates in 1881 came back thinking that the inspectors of the state prison should inspect all jails and lock-ups; in 1882 the delegation reported that a state agency ought to supervise jails and almshouses, but not state institutions. (Its members were all associated with state institutions.)[6]

No one voiced a dissent to these repeated suggestions, and in 1883 the increasing agitation of the "labor question" gave significance to the sensational report on pauperism by the State Bureau of Labor Statistics, which pointed out the need for better information. That year the legislature authorized a "Council of Charities and Corrections" composed of the governor and six members whom he appointed and who served without pay. The Council was empowered to investigate all public charitable and correctional institutions (state and local), but its main business was to prescribe a common register of statistics of inmate population (relevant to the claims for state subsidies, among other things), productive labor (relevant to the question of convict labor), and costs of maintenance (relevant to charges of waste and graft).[7]

When the Council got to work, in 1884, it prepared a statistical form. It was authorized to pay local officials for collecting data, but its appropriation was insufficient, and the functionaries, who looked upon its inspection and recommendations as "an unwarranted interference," refused to co-operate. The Council duly reported this situation and its own need for clerical help. The legislature might have solved the problem simply by either providing compensation or making returns mandatory. It did neither. The Council managed nevertheless to compile some useful information and its inspections, cursory as they were, revealed some worthy institutions (the Hudson County penitentiary and the Essex County jail) and some shockers (the Hudson County almshouse). Given energetic leadership it might have made interesting reports even with very limited means, but after three accounts of frustration, it lapsed into silence.[8]

As this first attempt at official supervision failed, the legislature in 1886 incorporated the Morris County Charities Aid Association and similar groups into a State Charities Aid Association, authorized to inspect jails and almshouses and to make annual reports. Its work was entirely voluntary; not until 1892 did it receive a nominal subvention of $600 a year. The State Association was simply a "board of managers" chosen to represent the county societies. Local groups did the actual work, organizing committees for visitation, inspection, and whatever other functions struck them as appropriate.

Some societies were active, others not; some made perfunctory visits, others (like Morris) were as broad as Charity Organization Societies. However valuable their help to inmates, or their reports to the public, they certainly did not even try, at first, to provide a comprehensive picture of public welfare. Their efforts gave form to a patrician interest and responsibility in local affairs, not to a notion of far-sighted administration.[9]

The record does not reveal much about the way these people worked. They were considered "representative of the prominent families of the state," as a correspondent to the *New York Times* once put it.[10] Mrs. Emily Williamson, a leader for many years, complained that when she tried to get people to work at the state level they usually replied "I am too busy with my private affairs and local charitable work to do more than I am doing." [11]

Another lady, discussing twenty-four years of work by the Provident Savings Committee of the Morris County chapter, mentioned that its monthly meetings were "enlivened by the collectors, who relate many incidents, some amusing, some sad, with which they meet in their work." The purpose of this committee was to "induce those who have no bank account to lay aside weekly savings," and the collectors brought the bank to the people, as it were, entering their deposits of nickels and dimes. The ladies learned that their friends suffered from curious illnesses like "compound indigestion" and "brown cheetus," and they remarked on the "poor woman" who said "with pride that her husband had 'pot-mane poisoning.'" Another "poor woman" told a visitor that she was "much troubled by her husband's politics," because she had been reading the Bible a great deal and she could not find any good word in it for the "publicans."

The ladies were interested in the reasons for saving—to purchase sewing machines, organs, and carpets, for example. They were pleased that some people saved by cutting down on tobacco and beer; "one of the most encouraging reports" was about a saver who "gave up her liquor saloon," partly because "she was ashamed to have the young ladies come collecting and know that she was connected with such a business." The collectors were amused by people who were so anxious to deposit money that they borrowed from neighbors to save, and by those who were found to withdraw money from the bank to hand it to the collector as a new deposit.

The ladies were particularly thankful that the collectors "who for the love of helping others [had] risked contagion" in their visits, had escaped illness and accident. It seemed to them that such faithfulness and zeal, often at "considerable sacrifice of time and pleasure by those who have many social duties" was evidence that "in blessing others [the collectors] themselves [were] being blessed." [12] It did not fall to the Provident Savings Committee to visit jails and almshouses, but this account shows the spirit in which many SCAA members went about their work.

In general, the people who first considered steps toward centralized supervision looked for conspicuous common faults and their remedy. They pointed to bad sanitation, or a lack of statistics, or manifestly cruel or foolish practices, conditions that inspection and advice might indeed correct. Only gradually did they come to think of the state government as an enterprise that might require a unified direction. When the Morrow Commission held that efficient financial management was a motive for centralization, it was taking for granted an idea of systematic administration that was hard to imagine before 1890.

Insofar as people in this early period conceived of the organization of government, they thought in constitutional, not administrative, terms. The main organ of government in their view was the legislature. Courts existed to interpret and apply the law. The "executive branch" was simply the governor, who saw that the law was enforced and who watched over the public interest. His services as watchman included an annual message to the legislature and the power—very important as described in the constitution—to call out and direct the state militia. For the rest, there was a congeries of institutions, agencies, commissions, and boards, set up to do specific jobs. They reported to the governor as the formal head of state, but their main business was with the legislature, which controlled their legal authority and their appropriations. Nothing in the character of these ad hoc agencies suggested that the governor was to direct them toward a common end.

In practice, the constitutionally separate powers were more or less linked by political parties. In this regard the governor was important because of his powers of appointment. Appointments meant patronage, patronage meant party (or factional) strength, party strength meant legislative ascendancy and all its rewards. The connection was well known and widely deplored. The device of putting state charitable and correctional institutions under the administration of unpaid managers, like private philanthropies, was supposed to keep them free of political corruption. In theory, the state executive was a caretaker and overseer; in practice, a spoilsman. In neither case was he viewed as an executive in an administrative hierarchy.

The Abbett Regime

By 1890, however, it was possible to conceive of the congeries of state agencies as a centralized administrative machine, for the governor who took office then did just that. His name was Leon Abbett. He was born and raised in Philadelphia, the son of a journeyman hatter of English Quaker descent; his mother's family came from Cumberland County in South Jersey. After graduation from high school he clerked for a lawyer and was admitted to the bar. He did not serve in the Civil War. His political career began when he moved to Hoboken in 1862. The next year, when he was twenty-seven, he became corporation counsel, and in 1864 and 1865 he was assemblyman. Then he moved across the city line into Jersey City, where he also became corporation counsel and assemblyman and president of the Board of Education. Already he was a distinguished man in the Democratic Party; in 1875–1877 he represented Hudson County in the state senate and his colleagues elected him their president.[13]

Abbett became the leading expert on constitutional law relating to municipalities. As a political leader he spoke for the great cities. His first notable service was to free Jersey City from the domination of corrupt state-appointed officials. He favored the bill for a Catholic protectory and when it was defeated he introduced the ill-fated "liberty of conscience" bill that would have provided Catholic chaplains in state institutions.[14]

Abbett was a Democrat, but he advanced his career by denouncing the ruling Democratic clique, the autocrats or kid-glove aristocrats of the State House, as he called them, men whose ties were with the squires of Monmouth, Morris and Sussex counties, who had grown powerful in the tutelage of railroad lobbyists. He professed to speak for urban workingmen and sought legislation in their interests; he was a leading critic of the great railroad corporations whose monopoly charters and tax privileges disadvantaged his urban constituents.[15]

Abbett was intelligent, imaginative, and bold, as his legal maneuvers in winning a measure of home rule and equal taxation showed. At one time he wanted the state to fill in the shallow reefs between Ellis Island and the Jersey shore and lease terminal rights on these new riparian lands—a rich source of income and a foothold for competitors of existing transportation enterprises. His political style was extraordinarily energetic, democratic, and audacious. His enemies thought him an unprincipled demagogue, a Ben Butler or John Peter Altgeld. Opposed by rich corporations, he found financial support among brewers and saloon interests (whose legal counsel he was), race track operators, and other disreputable but potent elements such as might well support an unprincipled demagogue.[16]

But mostly Abbett relied on party organization. In an energetic and very successful gubernatorial campaign in 1883, he bluntly promised to reorganize the party, rewarding those who worked before election for it and him. His victory and the significant railroad and labor legislation of his administration testified to effective leadership and party discipline.[17]

According to an acquaintance and close student of his career, Abbett was not primarily interested in becoming governor; his ambition was to have the legislature name him to the United States Senate when an occasion arose, shortly after his term ended. (Governors served three years and could not succeed themselves.) In this he was frustrated by factional opponents who were backed by the railroad lobby. His disappointment won him popular support, however, and his political allies grew in strength. In 1890, he again took office as governor and turned to perfecting an organization that would not fail to carry him to a senatorship.[18]

Abbett's bold plan was to reorganize the machinery of government somewhat as he had organized the party machinery. He would use the governor's patronage to employ men who were vassals rather than mere allies, and he would reorganize the congeries of boards and commissions so that they would respond to his direction. He had moved in this way during his first term, but now, with more experience and, as it turned out, Democratic majorities in both houses of the legislature, he could better realize his ideas. He changed and fortified old agencies and created new ones.

In his own mind, probably the most important state functions were assessment, taxation, and municipal government, subjects of which he was master, but his interest extended to banking, insurance, licensing, and a state police force. He eliminated the existing boards of managers of the two state insane asylums, set up a single board in their place, and charged it with inspecting the county asylums and accounting for the state subsidies they received. He reorganized the trustees of the school fund and the managers of the State Normal School into a new State Board of Education, put it in charge of the School for the Deaf and Dumb, and increased its powers of supervision over local school districts. (In 1893 the state superintendent of schools, recently promoted from the superintendency of Jersey City schools, engineered a sweeping consolidation of local school districts that turned out of office some 3,500 trustees who had formerly managed the schools in their tiny bailiwicks.) Every institution felt his scrutiny and the force of his will.[19]

Two generations later, it would seem that Abbett's efforts were an interesting attempt to make state government rational and efficient. The organization of the State Board of Education and the subsequent reorganization of the public school districts were recognized even then as desirable. The unification of the asylums was at least reasonable; the official inspection of county asylums was long overdue. There is no evidence that the institutions suffered much in the shakeup.

Abbett's contemporaries were shocked, however. The journalist-historian who chronicled these events, who respected Abbett's ability and recognized his services, thought the reorganization "spread the Hudson County odor all over the Commonwealth"; he meant that Abbett had put into state government the spirit of party organization, discipline, and favoritism that was more and more characteristic of urban boss rule. "It was of the very essence of the scheme that the entire local machinery everywhere should be submissive and responsive to the central power," he continues. Self-respecting men would not lend themselves to such servitude, so venal hirelings filled the places. There was "a notable decline . . . in public morale" as state and cities both fell under the ascendant petty bosses that the governor called together.[20]

In the end, voting frauds and legislative scandals turned the voters against the Democrats. These were the work of Abbett's lieutenants, the chronicler says; when Abbett vetoed some of their schemes the "autocracy" was shattered, first by a palace revolution that again lost him the senatorship, and later, after the scandals got out, by a popular repudiation that put Republicans in charge of the state government for many years.[21]

So ended that attempt to centralize the administration of the state institutions. It did not deal primarily with charities and corrections; its objective was not economy and efficiency; and its model was not a reputable bureaucracy. Its model was party bossdom, its objective was to buttress a personal political machine, and it ignored the substantial problems of caring for the dependent, defective, and delinquent classes. In 1897 the mental hospitals were given separate boards again; board members continued to inspect county asylums, but their hearts were not in central supervision.[22] The Village for Epileptics, the Children's Guardians, the reformatories, and the State Tuberculosis Sanatorium were all created with separate boards, as autonomous as could be.

Centralization in the Progressive Period

Meanwhile, the SCAA continued to inspect local public institutions. It was aided by the subsidy granted it in 1892, under Governor Abbett's regime, but at the time there were only nine county organizations and their work was sporadic or perfunctory. Increasingly the State Association became the vehicle of its Board of Managers and especially its secretary, Mrs. Emily Williamson, who was for two decades the state's acknowledged leader in charitable work. She was, as one admirer put it, "a direct descendant of Jonathan Hornblower, the well known English engineer, and on her mother's side [was] descended from Sir Christopher Newport, of Newport News fame; her mother was also a cousin of Charles Reade" (a popular reform-minded novelist in the fashion of Dickens). The Hornblowers lived in New York, but Emily married Benjamin Williamson, Jr., son of a chancellor and grandson of a governor of New Jersey, a lawyer with the best connections, who resided in his family mansion in old Elizabeth.[23]

The couple was childless, and Mrs. Williamson took up occupations suited to a woman of her class. She belonged to the Episcopal Church in Elizabeth, which already in the 1850's had a program of friendly visiting and constructive charity.[24] Her own pet charities were a home for aged women and a day nursery. She was a founder and secretary of the SCAA and in 1888 became secretary of the newly created institution for feebleminded women at Vineland. A biographical notice published in 1897, which she probably approved, said that she was "not theoretical or a sentimentalist," but interested in the practical aspects of philanthropy. This was typical COS doctrine, in which "sentimentalism" meant indiscriminate handouts and "theory" meant economic heresy—Christian or Marxian socialism, the single tax, or some other panacea. By "practical charity" she meant "requiring from each man and woman enough labor for self-support at least." [25] Accordingly, SCAA inspections of almshouses were intended in part to keep out loafers and to find responsible relatives for other inmates.

But experience was taking her beyond these simplicities. In 1892 she argued an urgent need to arouse people to what was obvious to anyone who inspected almshouses and jails, "the tide of increasing immorality, vice and crime, with its necessary accompaniments—degradation and pauperism," and she asked for some improved organization of philanthropists and philanthropic discussion and public education.[26] Her interest shifted to rehabilitation and prevention; in the late 1890's she helped lead the SCAA in supporting the agitation for the Board of Children's Guardians and the reformatory.

By 1900, these battles were won and after the death of her husband that spring Mrs. Williamson devoted even more of her means and energy to the work. She underwrote a full-time executive for the SCAA and worked hard beside him; in 1902 she became probation officer for Union County and organized the State Association of Probation Officers at her home. That year she was president of the first State Conference of Charities and Corrections. She was also active in the National Conference and in 1904 President Theodore Roosevelt named her a delegate to the International Prison Association which met in Budapest.

She was a beautiful woman, as her pictures show, and contemporaries thought her a "fluent and inspiring speaker," who always spoke extempore, with "that rarity among American women, a beautiful voice." She was a patron of New York University, especially its "School of Pedagogy." She was perhaps best known as a clubwoman in New York and New Jersey, president of the New Jersey State Federation of Women's Clubs in 1899–1901 and a director until 1905; she bowed out by entertaining some 550 ladies at a gala reception in the old Williamson mansion.[27]

Mrs. Williamson's life shows many of the forces and interests that came to support reform and incidentally centralization of the state's institutions during the progressive period. The SCAA had at best a few hundred members, but it was in a position to appeal to the women's clubs, who claimed eleven thousand members in 1905, and through them to the churches, for clergymen were disposed to respect the views of good ladies in their congregations that they ought to bestir themselves toward reform.[28]

The Roman Catholic clergy was a case in point, for as Catholic institutions grew in number and variety and Catholic philanthropists learned genteel ideas, there was an opportunity for common work. There were three great systems of institutions, Father Francis A. Foy, Mrs. Williamson's friend, told the State Conference of Charities and Corrections in 1902—those sponsored by Catholics, by Protestants, and by the state; they dealt with similar problems, he said, and a comparison and exchange of ideas, a systematic collection of data, were in order, "whereby the common end may be better served." [29] "There was a good deal of comment over the absence of the Trenton ministers at the recent meeting of the State Conference of Charities," observed the *Review of Charities and Corrections* in March, 1905; six priests were in attendance, but only one Protestant minister, who made the opening prayer. Protestant laymen envied the priest his authority and the extent of his influence, the *Review* continued, especially when the bishop applied himself to the cause.[30]

Father Foy hailed from Newark, where Catholics and Protestants were working together effectively, and it was in suburban Essex County that the clubwomen were best organized. The Associated Charities of Newark had a full-time executive earlier than the SCAA and local conferences of charities before the State Conference. It is no coincidence that the husbands and sons of the clubwomen were leaders of the progressive faction in state politics. Clubwomen supported reform in schools, hospitals, probation, and labor conditions, especially those touching women and children; they supported the consumers league and the settlement houses.[31]

Mrs. Caroline Alexander, who lived in the Stevens family castle at Hoboken but was related through her mother and her husband to old Princeton families, brought the State Conference of Charities to Princeton in 1911. The University, fresh from a bitter and losing battle against snobbery in its own affairs, had not hitherto paid attention to dependents and delinquents, except perhaps the sporty heirs among its students, but in this year of wonders "not only did students and professors attend and take part in the . . . meeting, but the Professors joined the other good Princeton people in offering the hospitality of their homes," which "of necessity increased the missionary results of the Conference." [32] (Austin Scott, the president of Rutgers, was on the Board of Managers of SCAA. Like Woodrow Wilson, he had been at Johns Hopkins when Hopkins professors were energizing the Baltimore COS; Scott had followed that example, but Wilson hadn't.) [33]

Next to Mrs. Williamson, the most prominent leader of the SCAA was Charlton Lewis. Born in West Chester, Pennsylvania, in 1834, the son of a lawyer, he took an A.B. at Yale when he was eighteen, studied law for two years, and spent two years preparing to enter the Methodist ministry. He was a pastor for a short time, then taught languages and mathematics at a normal school in Illinois, then served as an army chaplain during the Civil War. In 1865 he began practicing law in New York; three years later he succeeded Charles Nordhoff as editor of the *New York Post,* but in 1871 he returned to the practice of law for the rest of his life. A leading authority on insurance law, he lectured on the subject at Cornell, Columbia, and Harvard, which honored him with an LL.D. He was a director of several business corporations, including International Bell Telephone. He published several miscellaneous volumes, including a Latin dictionary and a translation of Bismarck's letters. A champion of prison reform, he was active in the New York Prison Association and its president from 1893 until his death in 1904.[34]

In his later years, Lewis resided in Morristown, and he entered the New Jersey story as chairman of the commission that recommended a reformatory in 1890 (he doubtless influenced its decision in favor of an Elmira-type institution). Governor Abbett frowned on the plan, but it happened that his successor, George Werts, was a neighbor of Lewis, a lawyer and a friend (two Cleveland Democrats to leaven the mass of Harrison Republicans). Werts pushed the reformatory bill through in 1895, and then named Lewis chairman of a commission to revise the penal laws and eliminate the old punitive and retaliatory jurisprudence. The revision of 1898 did not achieve this end, however, and until the reformatory opened Lewis bent his efforts to convince Jersey judges that the indeterminate sentence, crucial for reformatory discipline, did not eviscerate the judicial process. The organic law of the reformatory (1901) did have a version of the indeterminate sentence, and Lewis, as chairman of the Board of Managers, worked hard to make it a success and to win judges and politicians to supporting the institution.[35]

Lewis became president of the State Charities Aid Association in 1894 and served until his death. He was a balance to Mrs. Williamson, more interested in corrections than charities, an eminently conservative and respectable lawyer, whereas Mrs. Williamson was sometimes thought to be a shrill enthusiast. Lewis was thinking in terms of a system of institutions and their control. It was easy to think of correctional institutions as steps in a series, especially if one had arrangements in New York in mind. Lewis saw the situation in terms not of organizing helpers to deal with common problems, but of logical classes and relations given shape in the law, and his reflections were conspicuously lucid and interesting.

Supervision or Control?

It had never been clear whether the SCAA was to inspect and report on state as well as local public institutions. At first its members were not usually disposed to go beyond their minimum duties, and their references to state institutions were infrequent and respectful. But the campaign to establish the Board of Children's Guardians and the reformatories gave the SCAA leaders a special interest in how other state enterprises were run and how they coexisted in the government.

When, in 1899, scandals broke at the State Home for Girls, SCAA officials, much interested in reformatories and provision for young girls, undertook to investigate. For their pains Governor Foster Voorhees sharply criticized them—he was said to be especially critical of Mrs. Williamson—for assuming responsibilities beyond their prerogatives, and he defended the institution's management.[36] But the SCAA did not back down. Instead it hired an executive, William H. Allen, an energetic man who had just received a doctorate from the University of Pennsylvania. His reports said nothing new, but he pulled the material together in a different and striking way, and in February, 1902, he began the *Review of Charities and Corrections* which became a valuable commentary on events. According to this source managers of the State Home for Girls and of the Trenton State Hospital took court action to restrain the SCAA from officially visiting or inspecting state institutions.[37]

So SCAA officials learned that state functionaries wanted their critical attention no more than did local officials, and meanwhile they were learning more about how the legislature allocated funds. An editorial in the *Review* in 1903 pointed out that legislators were busy men who met for some thirty working days over a three-month session. There were committees on the several institutions, but their activity was "generally limited to a single formal visit, which, like all well-conducted social functions, [was] prepared for in advance," with everything pleasant and "company manners" in order. The appropriation committee passed on funds, relying "blindly upon brief statements made by the managers . . . during the . . . annual inquisition." As the committee met, the managers became "uneasy . . . because of the constant fear that they [would] not receive due consideration." Hence they approached committee members individually, like lobbyists, often with a distressing "lack of dignity." [38]

Later the *Review* published an account of an appropriations committee hearing. The institution's Board of Managers appeared by appointment. Many members of the committee were absent; those present requested that witnesses be very brief, as time was limited. The committeemen, "courteous and apparently friendly," asked "a few thoroughly sensible and practical questions" which indicated, however, that they had not read the institution's report and knew very little about it. The managers made their requests and asked the committee to visit and see for itself; otherwise, one witness said, they "had no right to question our judgment." At the conclusion of the statement the managers were "politely bowed out"; there was no further inquiry or visit. The managers had asked that the state pay $1,600 that had been privately advanced in the work and asked for a small, carefully calculated and justified increase. Sometime later, the appropriations committee decided by majority vote to disregard the requests. The committee chairman was not present at the meeting and many members had not heard the original request.

On the last day of the legislative session, the appropriation bill was jammed through under suspension of the rules, with no discussion. Thus, the author concluded, the action of the committee was arbitrary, without appeal, and irresponsible. "If they [the committee] have been careless or neglectful, prejudiced or parsimonious, extravagant or reckless; . . . if they have been honestly mistaken or deliberately at fault, it is no matter. . . . The unfortunate consequences of their action are none of their concern. The poor may suffer, the afflicted may be left to their misery, but no one is to blame." The managers and the paid workers, who faced the problems directly, might suffer too, "But who cares? There will be another committee . . . next year. And the managers don't have to stand the treatment if they don't want to; they can quit if they are aggrieved, and perhaps save the state some money by their action, as one of the members of the committee frankly informed me." [39]

The legislators, for their part, were aware of the difficulty about appropriations, but their ideas led toward appointing a small, paid, and responsible commission to run the state institutions. Some senators had this in mind when Governor Voorhees criticized the SCAA in 1900, and the court decision in 1901 that the Association could not inspect state institutions seemed to call for a new departure.[40] Accordingly, Senator Theodore Strong and Assemblyman Edward Gnichtel, neither of them known as advanced thinkers on the subject, offered bills proposing the creation of a salaried state board of control, appointed by the governor and Senate, that would supercede the institutional Boards of Managers.[41]

The ideas of a central board to replace institutional managers and a salaried board instead of an unpaid and voluntary body were not new. Such boards already existed in some mid-Western states (Wisconsin, Iowa, Minnesota) where a tradition of patrician charity was absent; Governor Benjamin Odell of New York, a businessman who wanted economy, had proposed a similar arrangement in 1901 and was working for it (unsuccessfully, as it proved) when Messrs. Strong and Gnichtel prepared their bills.[42]

The Strong and Gnichtel bills failed, but they focused discussion. The SCAA report for 1902 analyzed proposals for central control at length, and its report for 1903 was a well-informed description of state organization for social welfare by Dr. Frederick Howard Wines, who served during that year as the Association's secretary. Wines had been secretary of the Illinois State Board of Charities for almost thirty years, and he was the author of a standard work on punishment and reformation as well as notable statistical reports for the federal census. He was a founder of the National Conference of Charities and a distinguished man. (The first secretary of the SCAA, Dr. Allen, had resigned to become executive of the Association to Improve the Condition of the Poor, a large private agency in New York City; Wines had just finished his labors on the federal census.) These reports and discussion were digested and broadcast in the *Review* and in the public prints, and the State Conference took up the subject at its second annual meeting in 1903.[43]

The question under discussion was not whether there should be a central agency, but whether it should supervise or control and what institutions it should govern. Definitions of control and supervision differed, but the clearest formulation, by Charlton Lewis, held that "control" meant detailed day-to-day management, whereas "supervision" meant the power to inspect, investigate, recommend, and report, with no administrative functions. He made his point by a historical analysis based mostly on his understanding of events in New York and England. In general he contrasted the government of penal institutions, which had an obvious problem of discipline and were run by public officials, with the government of private charities, which were managed by unpaid boards of trustees. (He noted that state mental hospitals, schools for the handicapped, and reformatories resembled private charities in this respect.)

Improvement in jails and prisons came by the agitation of voluntary or private societies, Lewis said, but improvement in private charities came by some public inspection and supervision. There were, in this view, two logically consistent systems: control by paid public officials and supervision by voluntary associations, or control by voluntary bodies (institutional boards of managers) and supervision by public inspectors.[44]

In recent years, Lewis thought, the principle of control by unpaid or honorary volunteer boards of managers had been used more widely—in the state institutions, for example—but they, too, needed supervision. They were less inclined to peculation or cruelty, but they might be neglectful or extravagant. Their members were usually too busy to give close superintendence; often they were "enthusiasts who magnif[ied] the needs of the cases under their own eyes." Since the state could not relieve all suffering and remove all want, it needed some agency to take a comprehensive view and allocate its charitable expenditures wisely.[45]

Lewis argued that both kinds of institutional management, by paid officials and voluntary boards, needed supervision. In either case the key to successful administration was an "enlightened community public opinion," a well-informed notion of the work and its problems. He did not have in mind sensational exposés in the press or legislative investigations, but a constant and persistent critical review of the management. The supervisory officials who would contribute this review, whether paid or volunteer, had to discuss and illuminate problems of administration; they had to "simplify the work . . . so that it [might] be understood by the body of people." [46]

Applying this analysis to New Jersey, he found that it had an ineffective combination of the two systems. The state prison and the local institutions were run by paid officials, and the local institutions were supervised by the SCAA, a voluntary body that had, he said, "inadequate powers and deficient resources." The state institutions were managed by unpaid boards, but there was no one to supervise, criticize, and stimulate them, except perhaps the governor, who would have to be "omniscience itself to fulfill his office satisfactorily in this respect." [47]

The key question, he thought, was whether paid officials or voluntary boards should be directly in charge of institutions. He favored voluntary boards, because unpaid managers could be drawn from a better class of men, public-spirited men of means, and would give the work more dignity and respect than the usual sort of political jobholder. Accordingly he opposed the abolition of local boards and the creation of a board of control that would combine "legislative, executive, and judicial powers," as he put it. He favored a state supervisory board over all public institutions; he did not say whether the board should be paid, but presumably it would have employed paid inspectors. In general he agreed with Dr. Wines, who concluded that all the advantages of a central board of control could be secured by a central supervisory board; the central board of control might be (generally was, in practice) subject to political pressure, and even if it were not, the problem arose that it would not itself be subject to supervision. In the minds of both gentlemen, the real necessity was supervision and publicity, and supervision had to be separate from control.[48]

These thoughts were the essence of a bill offered in 1904 by Edward Duffield, assemblyman from Essex County and leader of the Republican majority. It provided for a seven-member Board of Charities and Corrections, appointed by governor and senate, with staggered terms to minimize political influence. The Board received no compensation. It had the power and duty to inspect every public charitable and correctional institution, local and state, and to report annually. It could prescribe the form of financial and other reports, but it had no administrative powers. It was, as the *Review* observed, an official and stronger version of the SCAA. "It is unusual," the editor commented, that the Association "ask, not that additional powers may be conferred upon [it], but that the state itself shall officially undertake the work which an ambitious, self-seeking society would have itself desired to do." [49]

When the legislature rejected this plan, the Association laid its defeat to the "peculiar organization, tradition and sentiments of the commonwealth," by which it meant that the state was "a confederation of counties." Local political views were channeled, it said, by "certain machine politicians, who are an incubus on any party [the legislature was strongly Republican], and whose influence is mainly felt in purely local concerns." [50] In 1905, the SCAA offered two new proposals. The first was a state board of guardians of the insane, which would review commitments to mental hospitals somewhat as the children's guardians reviewed commitments of children to almshouses, and would also inspect and try to coordinate state and local mental hospitals. The second was for a governor's "advisory commission," which the governor could use to visit and investigate state correctional institutions and to advise the appropriations committee.[51]

These new proposals scarcely received a hearing, but they show a good deal about the alignment of interests. Politicians—which is to say legislators—were not interested in more effective state supervision of almshouses, county asylums, and jails, for these were part of the spoils over which their organizations fought. Nor did they relish the SCAA's constant reflections on the evils of political management. On the other hand, they were impatient with the myopic enthusiasm and lobbying of the managers of state institutions; they were not convinced of the efficiency of such boards, which certainly had not prevented occasional scandals, and they were eager to try an "efficient and responsible" board, that is, one they could hire, deal with, and fire.

SCAA officials, for their part, recognized their own inadequacies as inspectors and wanted better supervision of local institutions, but they suspected that a state board of control would run state institutions as the county commissioners ran county institutions. They were not simply in favor of the status quo, however. As they saw it, the big institutions—the state prison and the state hospitals—were getting a much better hearing than the newer and smaller institutions, such as those for feebleminded women and epileptics and especially the children's guardians and the reformatory. Therefore, they wanted some sort of supervisory or advisory agency that could find out just how the money was being spent and why, and win a better hearing, as they thought, for more progressive kinds of work. What defeated the SCAA proposal was not just the machinations of local spoilsmen and state prison officials, or the suspicion of local private charities, especially religious ones, that supervision might extend to them, as it had in New York, but a disinclination on the part of established state institutions to accept oversight.

10

The Department of Charities and Corrections, 1905–1917

Leaders of the State Charities Aid Association who, in 1902–1903, formulated the concept of centralization had in mind the alternatives developed in their lifetimes. They assumed that the responsible body would be a board and asked whether it should be honorary (unpaid) and supervisory (authorized to investigate and report) or paid and charged with practical administration. They pondered its relation to local public institutions and to private or voluntary agencies that also provided for the unfortunate or dangerous. In these terms, they plainly favored an honorary and supervisory board whose powers would extend to local and certain private services. In effect, they advocated an enlarged, official and potent version of the work they were already trying to do.

The Commissioner of Charities and Corrections

The SCAA could not carry its case, and in 1905 the governor proposed a compromise which no one had discussed but which the legislature quickly passed. The measure established a single salaried commissioner of charities and corrections, appointed by the governor for a term of three years. His duties were to keep records of state wards and prisoners, to visit all institutions that housed them, to secure reports from the institutions, and to report annually. The commissioner was also empowered to approve plans for new buildings and, with the assistance of an architect, to oversee their construction. He was authorized to investigate in the governor's behalf. Finally, he was given an "advisory board" composed of the chief executives of state institutions.[1]

This plan offered something to everybody. To make it clear that he was not giving too much to the SCAA, the governor, Edward Stokes, bypassed it completely in selecting his commissioner. He chose a sixty-three-year-old clergyman, Dr. George Wight, who had at one time been superintendent of public instruction in Atlantic County and who had for many years held administrative posts in the Methodist Church, although he had had no connection with organized charity or charitable or penal reform. The appointment was politically astute. Wight was an old friend (Governor Stokes was also from South Jersey), experienced in administration and politically above suspicion, but not identified with reform. Furthermore, his appointment pleased the Methodists, who were increasingly active in the Anti-Saloon league and a threat to Republican unity.[2]

The SCAA continued to visit local institutions and to report. It did not oppose the creation of the state office, but the editor of the *Review* expressed "a shade of misgiving" that the governor had "put too modest an estimate upon the difficulties of the position," especially for a man without special qualifications.[3] He praised the commissioner's first report for modesty and discretion and for "the care which Dr. Wight has taken to avoid stealing the thunder of the individual boards, by refraining from making recommendations which will come with more grace from those who are directly responsible for the conduct of the institutions." [4]

This was faint praise, and in fact, Dr. Wight's reports were not only modest, discreet, and uncritical, but full of praise for the managers and executives of state institutions. He noted how they were encouraged by "an appreciative word." He thought people were too critical and contrasted the institutions too unfavorably with those of other states. He noted as a fundamental matter that the state had not gone into debt for their construction. He favored expanding existing institutions rather than building new ones (so did the existing institutions, of course).[5] In 1910, he observed that the state had financed $3.6 million in improvements in a little over a decade, and he advised "the earnest, influential body of philanthropists of the state" not to "overlook the fact that New Jersey levies no tax for the erection and maintenance of these institutions" other than "the tax on corporations, an uncertain source of revenue at the best and one that may finally fail." (He referred to the state's notorious practice of chartering corporations to do anything anywhere, for a small franchise tax.) [6]

The commissioner took no exception to the decision to develop the state prison rather than Rahway (1905–1907), and for years he favored enlarging the State Home for Girls rather than building a women's reformatory, although he later said he had been wrong in this opinion.[7] He convened his advisory committee regularly, but he found that the difficulties of common work were "almost insurmountable," because executive officers had to travel to and fro on the same day and their needs and interests were so various—the prison and the soldiers' homes, for example.[8] He said the meetings resulted nevertheless in a "marked and steadily growing improvement in institutional management"—this was in 1908—but he never mentioned a specific benefit. In 1909 Edward Johnstone said of a meeting of the advisory committee that it was an "excellent beginning" but he warned that the commissioner would have to "keep prodding" the executives "to get them to do their duties" with respect to committee work.[9] It is evident from the commissioner's report in 1910 that his business was routine inspection and paperwork and certainly not supervision as envisioned by Charlton Lewis and Mrs. Williamson.

In general, the commissioner's reports were more conservative than the SCAA's, and the SCAA's were more conservative than the recommendations of a commission which reported on December 15, 1908, on its inquiry into the causes of dependency and crime. The commission's study took only six months and its mandate mentioned among likely subjects strong drink, poor diet, faulty home training, immigration, the penal system, and unhealthy tenements. Its personnel included only two persons associated with charitable reform—Mrs. Williamson and Mrs. Alexander—and, for the rest, a doctor, a lawyer, a police chief, a college professor, a Methodist clergyman, and a newspaper editor.[10]

The subject of greatest popular interest in its report was the relation of booze to crime and dependency. (The Anti-Saloon league was threatening to split rural Republicans from the Germans and suburbanites of Essex County and the publicans of Atlantic City.) Another commission had recently exposed scandalous violations of the sabbatarian laws and linked them to corrupt politicians, policemen, and grand juries. It happened that the clergyman on the Dependency and Crimes Commission was a temperance lecturer, who went lengthily to the heart of things in his minority report. But the other commissioners declared themselves against blue laws and for accepting and regulating the liquor traffic. They approved a variety of other reforms: more stringent marriage laws; health education, especially about venereal disease; tougher narcotics laws; use of silver nitrate to prevent infant blindness; playgrounds for children; night schools for immigrants; regulation of cheap theaters; and abolition of corporal punishment.

These commissioners also recommended changes in institutions: The most radical, evidently based upon recent developments in New York, was to abolish local boards of managers and create a centralized board of control. Their proposed state board would be unpaid and removed as well as possible from politics; it would have powers of investigation and fiscal control, including central purchasing and collection, and it would establish committees to study industrial education and prison labor and to sponsor research (by the case history method).[11]

The SCAA in 1908 likewise expressed "a growing feeling that we shall have to adopt the principle of control" to furnish an active, efficient, and businesslike direction over state institutions, which "our present system of separate boards . . . has failed notably to supply."[12] There was disagreement on this point, however, for the *Review of Charities and Corrections* opposed a bill establishing a central board. The institutional executives strongly opposed it, too; Dr. Wight called them together and in a burst of activity organized a letter-writing campaign. The effective objection was that the proposed central purchasing agent would advertise in New York and Philadelphia and probably would order from "big companies outside New Jersey" instead of from "home industries." Since the institutions paid no taxes, the letter said, it seemed only fair that they should patronize home industries when possible. The bill passed the Senate but the Assembly crushed it.[13]

Reform on a Business Basis

It is ironic that as the tide of progressive reform rose in the years 1905–1911 the SCAA declined. In 1904 Dr. Wines resigned as secretary because the Association could not afford his services. Its expenses that year, including his salary, were $2,979.60; subscriptions to the *Review* and contributions from the county branches amounted to $650; the state contributed $600. Mrs. Williamson made up the balance, as she had done for years. Her hope had been that the paid secretary and the State Conference of Charities would increase interest and membership enough to make the society self-sustaining, but she was disappointed.[14]

When Charlton Lewis died in May 1904, Mrs. Williamson succeeded him as president of the Association and Father Foy became secretary. They were energetic people, considering their years, but they were unable to get either contributions or volunteers to develop the work much beyond their own efforts. The *Review* often noted the passing of old friends, but rarely the recruitment of new ones. Mrs. Williamson died in July 1909; three former governors and a United States Senator attended her funeral, which was a regal affair. The county courts closed and the flags flew at half-mast in Elizabeth and on Snake Hill, which she had often visited.[15] The SCAA, "dependent largely as it [had] been for many years upon [her] personality and zeal," was left "without practical leadership."[16] The *Review of Charities and Corrections* ceased publication for more than a year; Father Foy carried on as best he could as secretary, but he was failing and died in December 1910.[17]

In retrospect there were some reflections on Mrs. Williamson's leadership. Edward Johnstone privately deprecated the fact that "the charities of this state had been [her] personal ambition . . . for years."[18] Seymour Cromwell, who became president of the reorganized Association in 1911, remarked that it had "never been developed on a thorough business basis." Only one or two counties had consistently done their work, he said, and the "parent body [had] for a long time failed to cooperate with the county branches," so that "the broader objects of the association," such as initiating legislation, had "lacked . . . power and influence." The organization then had only 250 members, but Cromwell was the leader of a group of seventy-three "public-spirited citizens" who had formed an auxiliary for financial support. All together the Association raised a "small budget" of $8,000 a year, to hire an experienced secretary and office space and to pay printing bills.[19]

It is clear from the roll of members and the auxiliary, published in the *Review* for August-September, 1911, that businessmen were now more prominent than professional people or gentlewomen. Many of them belonged to the New York financial community, like Decatur Sawyer, who was also on the board of Rahway Reformatory, or Seymour Cromwell himself, who was president of the New York Stock Exchange.[20]

Of the women who carried on the older tradition, the most notable was Caroline Bayard Wittpenn. She was born in November 1859, at Castle Point, the Stevens family estate in Hoboken (which Stevens Institute of Technology now occupies). Her grandfather, John Stevens, who was treasurer and land surveyor of the revolutionary government in New Jersey, bought the estate in 1784. It originally included almost all present-day Hoboken, and to develop it Stevens undertook his famous efforts to employ steam engines in ferry boats and railways. His four sons continued these interests and became, among other things, leading figures in the Camden and Amboy (later the Pennsylvania) railroad system.

Caroline was raised amid these momentous masculine speculations in real estate, technology, and public affairs. Her father, Col. Edwin A. Stevens, was sixty when she was born, and as a child she drew close to her mother, who was much younger than her father and long survived him. Her mother was the child of a Princeton professor known for theological conservatism and brilliant conversation; he was poor by Stevens standards, however, and it is said that Caroline's mother's well-known sympathy with the needy, as well as her pervasive piety, was a result of this background.[21]

Caroline was educated by private tutors and in England; her adult love of home, garden, pets, and foxhunting, as well as her Episcopalian faith, was decidedly English in spirit. In June 1879 she married Archibald Alexander, of an old Princeton line, and the following year she bore him a namesake. The new family lived in Hoboken, still mostly owned by the Stevenses but now a populous annex of New York and Jersey City. In 1895 she separated from Mr. Alexander. The reason is unclear but the break was complete, bitter, and painful to her. She had hitherto been active in local charities and with her mother had endowed two churches and now she began to be active in the SCAA. She helped Emily Williamson revitalize it in 1900, and presently she became probation officer in Hudson County, working with girls and women. She thus saw the problems of the underprivileged in a new way, and became more and more dedicated to the work. She was on the commission that reported on dependency and crimes in 1908, and for years she led the campaign for a women's reformatory.[22]

Other attachments also led Mrs. Alexander into public life. Her son, Princeton '02, was close to Woodrow Wilson; in 1905 and 1907 he was in the state legislature, where he worked for a reformatory, among other reforms. He was a colonel on Governor Wilson's staff when typhoid struck him down while on maneuvers in 1912.[23] Mrs. Alexander was always a partisan of Wilson and was his adviser on state and national welfare problems, about which he admittedly knew little.[24] (The reformatory was founded during his administration.)

On January 6, 1916, Mrs. Alexander married H. Otto Wittpenn. He had been county supervisor during her early years as probation officer and she had supported him as reform mayor of Jersey City. Wittpenn served four terms and was a Democratic candidate for governor in 1916, but his political career ended when he broke with Frank Hague, the coming man in the Hudson County machine. He was more successful as a businessman, looking after his own manufacturing and banking interests as well as his wife's.[25]

So Mrs. Wittpenn's interests in charity, corrections, and politics, and the advantages and disappointments of her life, combined in her services. She often carried a portable altar on her travels and made an annual retreat, but she was not at all dour; she was a femininist and a suffragette—the first Democratic national committeewoman from New Jersey—but she was not inclined toward speechmaking or parading. She was a founder of the Colony Club of New York, but in her work she easily made friends in all classes. As president of the Board of Managers of the Clinton Reformatory from its founding, she represented the best in enlightened penology and charity when she was appointed to the newly organized State Board of Control in 1918.

The new SCAA secretary was Joseph Byers. The son of the Reverend A. G. Byers, a distinguished administrator of charities, he had served as chief officer of the Indiana State Reformatory, the Eastern State Penitentiary (Philadelphia), and the New York House of Refuge, and he had served as secretary of the Ohio State Board of Charities, the National Prison Association, and the National Conference of Charities and Corrections.[26]

Byers' reports on local institutions were obviously the work of an experienced man, detailed and constructively critical.[27] His reflections were notably more critical than Dr. Wight's. He observed that state and county insane asylums were overcrowded because they held more than five hundred epileptics and feebleminded who should have been elsewhere, and also because the criminal insane needed a special building (which the legislature had authorized but not financed). One fact "overshadow[ed] all others," he wrote: "the failure of the State to inform itself as to the number and character of public and private institutions, local or county, or to exercise over them any sort of supervision."[28] Dr. Wight did not mention these problems, but did find time to favor censoring movies and restricting immigration.

In 1912, Governor Wilson appointed Byers Commissioner of Charities and Corrections, and doubtless his inaugural address drew on Byers' ideas. Wilson himself had had no connection with charitable reform or state institutions (neither had his wife) but he was interested in administration. His article, "The Study of Administration," which appeared in the second volume of *The Political Science Quarterly,* in 1887, was perhaps the earliest American outline of a science of public administration. His discussion had no definite bearing on state government, however—it drew on European experience and the arguments for civil service—and he did not develop the theme in his later works.

It appeared from his first annual message, however, that the governor might reorganize the state government as he had reorganized Princeton University. He called for an "economy and efficiency commission," somewhat like the one President Taft had organized in the federal government in 1910, and New Jersey's was the first of many similar state commissions. Regarding state charitable and correctional institutions, he called for an agency that could "coordinate them" in "practical and serviceable cooperation." He had in mind chiefly the problem Byers had mentioned, of classifying and redistributing inmates, so that institutions could do the kind of work for which they were intended. He accepted the principle of separate unpaid boards of managers for each institution; he wanted to give the commissioner a small advisory board and "proper supervisory authority," similar to that which the Board of Education had recently obtained over local school systems. These suggestions were not specific; in substance he recommended simply a supervisory board, rather than a board of control, that would extend its supervision to local public institutions, as the Department of Education "supervised" local public school systems.[29]

Wilson was primarily interested in matters that bore directly on his own political destiny, however, and he did not press the issue; to do so would have further alienated the Democratic machine.[30] Meanwhile Byers discovered that Dr. Wight's records were in poor shape and he got caught up in the detail of routine inspection and paper work.[31] His leading idea about reorganization, which he shared with Cyrus Stonaker, who succeeded him as SCAA secretary, was the need to coordinate, not just supervise, local public and state institutions, to establish some rational division of labor between them.[32]

Exhibit A of the need for system, in Byers' mind, was the provision for mental defect and illness. This matter was urged upon him by Edward R. Johnstone, who was painfully aware of long waiting lists and the burdening of almshouses and asylums with inappropriate problems.[33] (He had recently organized the extension department of his school to campaign for better provision.) Byers' first study, as SCAA secretary, of the county asylums, had brought out the fact that the Essex institution expended per year per patient $33 more than Morris Plains and $37 more than Trenton, and the state institutions spent more on maintenance than New York, Ohio, and Indiana, without any better results.[34]

Following up these ideas, Byers became chairman of a Commission on the Care of Mental Defectives. Its report, in March 1914, said that state and county hospitals together held 1,067 patients above their capacity, and that the patients were badly distributed. It estimated the annual increase at 250. To house them it recommended a number of "farm colonies" (like those Johnstone was already developing) for the "dements" and a psychopathic clinic or reception hospital, like those appearing in big cities, that would provide early and voluntary treatment for recent cases, furnish a link to general practitioners, school teachers, and other groups that found and referred cases, and be a center of public information and research aimed at prevention. As for the feebleminded, the Commission found no good statistics on the size of the problem. They noted that there was no provision at all for children under six or for the very low grades. They looked forward to a great expansion of the public school system and of farm colonies.[35]

The Commission saw the proposed reception hospital, the state hospitals and other institutions, the county hospitals, and the farm colonies as parts of a system, and they asked for a state board or state officers to pull its parts together and guide its expansion. (The idea of a single correctional system, extending from probation by the county courts through county parental schools and penitentiaries and the various state institutions, to parole, also became a commonplace in these years.)[36] Byers firmly opposed further extension of the state into TB sanatoria, which he regarded as a job for counties and local health services.[37]

These were good ideas, but they did not receive much of a hearing. Governor James F. Fielder, who succeeded Wilson, took a bold stand in his inaugural in favor of enlightened penology, but he observed that there were no funds for it, and he made no demand for funds. He thought the legislators had "much neglected" the institutions and ought to visit them. He said that the managers were "for the most part conscientious men and women" and that those who weren't should resign. He awaited the report of the Economy and Efficiency Commission to suggest lines of improvement.[38] His tone was not urgent, and his later messages barely mentioned charities and corrections.

In 1915, Governor Fielder let Joseph Byers go and appointed in his place Richard Stockton, whose principal qualification was a historic name among Jersey Democrats.[39] Mr. Stockton informed him that the institutions were "in a highly satisfactory condition," that "hundreds of changes . . . could, and probably should, be made in the future," but that their "absolute requirement . . . at this time was not made evident."[40] Stockton was not the only one who thought matters were well in hand in 1915; Seymour Cromwell, the president of the SCAA, began his report by remarking that "New Jersey may rightfully claim a place with the most progressive states."[41]

What issues about state government did concern men in those days? In 1915 Governor Fielder asked for an inexpensive short session of the legislature, on the grounds that the last four sessions had "disposed of practically all matters for the public good which [had] been awaiting attention."[42] The Economy and Efficiency Commission reports recommended some concentration of state activities into departments, notably health, taxation, conservation, and labor; they did not discuss charities and corrections.[43] The New Jersey State Chamber of Commerce, organized in 1912, established a research agency that published studies pertaining to its interest: these related to a state police force, workmen's compensation, and the state budget—not, in any case, to charities and corrections. The state budget, established in 1916, proved to be a useful accounting device, but it made no immediate difference in policy or in the competition for funds. In 1916, the problem of county roads—and road-builders—came up; in this instance there was no doubt about the need for professional services under state supervision. The contrast with charities and corrections is striking.[44]

The Morrow and Earle Commissions

Governor Walter E. Edge, who took office in January, 1917, was the son of a railroad man who lived near Atlantic City. While attending high school he worked on a newspaper and in an advertising agency; before he was twenty he bought out the agency and presently he founded a daily newspaper in connection with it. His enterprises grew with the city and he became its leading citizen. At thirty-six, in 1909, he was elected to the Assembly and became Republican majority leader; in 1912 he was majority leader in the Senate and he led the Republican resurgence against Wilson. He was head of the Economy and Efficiency Commission and introduced the bills for a state budget and a central purchasing agent. He was elected governor by an overwhelming plurality, defeating H. Otto Wittpenn. He was then forty-two.

Edge offered himself to the voters as "a business man with a business plan." He wanted to convert the state government into a modern business corporation, he said in his inaugural address: the governor as business manager, the legislators as directors, the citizens as stockholders. He wanted state activities organized under a few executive departments, whose chiefs would form a cabinet. Paradoxically, he also viewed the departments as business corporations, each with its own board of public-spirited citizens, for he believed in the principle of citizen boards.

Skeptical Democrats considered these ideas an adman's rhetoric, and they were doubtless canny politics. But Edge was seriously concerned about political participation. Many people were residents rather than citizens of New Jersey, he said, especially in the metropolitan areas—they cast 50,000 more votes for president than for governor in 1916—and boards were, in his mind, a means of restoring and maintaining citizen interest. (He was thinking about their role in local affairs, too, for he was an active booster of good works in Atlantic City.) He pointed out, in his inaugural address, that state government worked three months instead of twelve months a year, although it is not clear whether he referred to the three-month legislative session or the practice, hallowed by tradition, that higher state officers spent only one day a week (Tuesday) in Trenton.[45]

The scandals at the state prison were the occasion for a reorganization Edge wanted to effect anyhow. The Prison Inquiry Commission was made up of business executives, not penologists; in any case its dominant member was Dwight Morrow. The Commission to Investigate State Charitable Institutions did not originate in a scandal (Edge praised existing boards in asking for it).[46] Ellis P. Earle, its chairman, was a peer of Morrow in the New York financial community. Edge, a member of SCAA (unlike Governors Wilson and Fielder), appointed Seymour Cromwell to the Prison Inquiry Commission, but no other member of the SCAA executive committee was so recognized. Dwight Morrow met once with an SCAA delegation, late in the game.[47] The SCAA secretary, Cyrus Stonaker, mentioned his services to the commissions and noted that their members had gained a lasting interest in the subject and were "secured for the cause," which implies that they were at first strangers to it.[48] As for Commissioner Stockton, he was not on either commission and there is little evidence that he was consulted.

Edge's intention was simple. He thought the solution to the problems of the prison—crowding, labor, and discipline—lay in road work and farm work. Convict labor looked like a money saver in building the highway system, which was a main topic of his inaugural. (He was encouraged in this thought by the highway commissioner, Richard Stevens, who was Mrs. Wittpenn's brother and a vice-president of SCAA.) Edge also thought that a state farm, worked by convicts, might supply all public institutions in the state, and that prisoners might also work on land reclamation and conservation projects.[49] He must have seen that the obstacles were the divided authority over the prison and the feebleness of the Prison Labor Commission. In any case, he wrote chairman Dickson of the Prison Inquiry Commission that he "fully expected [it] to recommend a general board whose responsibility it will be to administrate [sic] the affairs of all five . . . institutions." He expected that the existing boards "will be legislated out of office just as soon as your Commission is ready with a substitute." He was disappointed that a recommendation was not ready at that session of the legislature; by implication, he expected the Commission's deliberations to take but a few weeks.[50]

Chairman Dickson was not much interested in a reorganization; not until Dwight Morrow became chairman, on July 17, 1917, did a proposal take shape. Morrow's report relied heavily on Professor George Kirchwey for its criticisms of existing practices; Kirchwey suggested its main ideas about departmental organization (long before the various special studies were available), and he evidently wrote the final version.[51] The Commission recommended an unpaid board of control, eight members, at least two women, staggered terms; the board to appoint an expert executive to serve at its discretion; the executive to appoint six "expert deputies or bureau chiefs" to assist him in medical care, dietary, education, industrial work, statistics, and parole.[52]

These points received little discussion. Governor Edge did not even question leaving the appointment of an executive to the board. The matter that bothered him was the relation among boards. At first he looked upon the Morrow and Earle commissions as separate steps toward centralization; he expected that they each would abolish the institutional boards under their eye and substitute separate boards of charities and of corrections.[53] When the two chairmen got together, at his request, they devised other plans. Earle proposed to keep institutional boards under the central board, but to make them responsible insofar as the central board would nominate them. Edge warmed to this "rather adroit scheme," which would, he said, "remove what otherwise would have been quite some opposition" to centralization.[54] Furthermore, the two chairmen came to favor a single central board over both charities and corrections. In the end, Edge favored two central boards, for the reason that "with two boards [he] could secure for the state the service of many more people" without impairing central efficiency. He agreed to follow the Commissions' recommendation on this point, however.[55]

When the reports were presented, in January 1918, both recommended combining charitable and correctional institutions under a single unpaid board which would appoint an expert executive. Their reasoning, as stated by the Morrow Commission, was that the studies by Dr. Bernard Glueck at Sing Sing had showed that almost three-fifths of that prison population was feebleminded, psychopathic, or insane, and consequently harmed rather than helped by prison or reformatory discipline; that delinquents under twelve were cases for the Board of Children's Guardians rather than correctional institutions; and that common management could better develop and guide institutional services (medical, dietary, etc.) and the state use system.[56]

Both commissions held that there should also be subordinate boards. The Earle Commission finally recommended a small board over each type of institution (mental hospitals, soldiers' homes, etc.) headed by a member of the central board, but it did not try to explain or justify this plan. The Morrow Commission recommended retaining the several institutional boards, and it discussed the question at length under the rubric "central boards versus local boards." A central board was supposed to offer a more economical and efficient administration, it said, to establish standards for program and services, to plan and budget for the system as a whole, and, by its comprehensive study, to enlighten the public as to needed reforms in the system and in the administration of criminal justice.

Local boards, on the other hand, were supposed to "bring to [their] management a personal interest and a degree of devotion" that a central board "could not be expected to develop"; they were supposed to be more flexible and experimental and less vulnerable to political influence. The Commission professed to see merit in both sides, and offered its plan as a compromise: the central board would give common leadership, the local boards would "leave to the separate institutions the advantages of personal interest and devotion which have been important factors in their development." It cited the precedent of the State Department of Education as a combination of centralized leadership, under a citizen board and expert direction, with local participation, the whole kept free from partisan politics.[57]

The difference between the commissions on the character of subordinate boards was not very deep, and in the end Earle agreed to retaining institutional boards. As a practical matter, Nelson Gaskill, the counsel of the Morrow Commission, who had already studied the laws governing correctional institutions, drew up the organic act of the new department along the line suggested by the Morrow Commission, and it was hustled through the legislature early in 1918 with Hudson County in opposition. (Morrow personally paid Gaskill $1,500 for his study of the laws, and an assistant got $500; Morrow and Earle split the charge for Gaskill's bill-drafting service, $3,500. Morrow also paid Harry Elmer Barnes $1,262 for writing the history of the institutions and for other work and he underwrote the printing of his commission's report, two volumes totaling over eight hundred pages.)[58]

So the long discussion of centralization ended in what was generally recognized as statesmanlike and forward-looking legislation. It affirmed the ideals of citizen control and participation, nonpolitical administration, and expert professional service. It institutionalized the idea that both charitable and correctional institutions, both local and state institutions, were "interdependent parts of a single system for dealing with the allied social problems of delinquency and defectiveness,"[59] the idea that there were problems of management and service that were common to all institutions, and the idea that there ought to be some overall agency to study and criticize the whole and direct its development. *The Survey,* a national spokesman for professional social workers and their liberal friends, favored it without reservation. The business community was not disposed to question anything sponsored by Edge, Morrow, and Earle. Almost everyone else went along.[60]

A Historical Perspective

Since the Department was to keep this shape for more than four decades, these judgments were undoubtedly plausible. Considering its origin in historical perspective, however, it is possible to recognize a number of features of its creation that people did not notice at the time.

In the first place, the historic formulation of the issue that the commissions dealt with had not been simply "central boards versus local boards," but supervision versus control, in which control meant responsibility for the details of administration and supervision meant detached inspection, study, criticism, recommendation, and publicity. The experience of the nineteenth century, summarized in 1903, was that these functions should be separate. The New Jersey plan, established in 1918, combined them. Furthermore, it appears from Morrow's private correspondence that the founders were concerned more with the political acceptance of various plans than with the virtues of local boards as such.

In the second place, the historic issue took shape over four different problems: the supervision of institutions sponsored by local public officials, by private charitable associations, and by state officials, and finally the problem of coordinating them all. On paper the New Jersey plan gave the State Board wide powers of inspection and visitation. But neither commission discussed the problem of bringing supervisory powers to bear apart from state institutions and state wards in local institutions.

In the third place, the commissions did not, as a basis for their proposed reorganization, inquire into what was actually happening to people in the institutions. They visited the institutions, of course, and consulted experts about them. The Morrow Commission originated as a result of scandals about what went on in the prison; its preliminary report looked toward rectifying prisoners' grievances; and it praised a mild reformatory discipline over punitive duress. But neither report tried to give any sense of what it was like to live in an institution, whether as inmate or staff, and neither tried to analyze problems of management from this viewpoint.

These observations may be summarized in a question: Reformers of 1903 and 1918 alike wanted some centralizing device to pull together the parts of a system, to criticize it, and to rally an enlightened public opinion in favor of its humane and efficient development. Why was it that Charlton Lewis and Frederick Wines favored a supervisory agency, divorced from practical control, whereas Ellis Earle and Dwight Morrow favored a central board that would have ultimate responsibility for management as well as supervision? Why is it that Earle and Morrow did not even think to raise the question that seemed central to Lewis and Wines?

Partly, the answer lies in their historical perspectives. Both Lewis and Wines thought of government in terms of nineteenth-century constitutional history; Lewis' advocacy of supervision drew on the notion that people should not entrust administration and the criticism of administration to the same agency; it would be like combining executive and judicial functions, as he said. Were not the spoilsmen in political parties trying to combine the powers of government against the public interest? Was not the independent judiciary the great bulwark against demagogues? As for Frederick Wines, he was a capable public servant who had lost his job in Illinois at the hands of Governor John Peter Altgeld; he knew as well as anyone the interests that "control"—that is, power—attracted. Both he and Lewis were men whose acquaintance with institutions extended over decades. They had seen boards of control in action and had seen them fall prey to the spoilsmen. Their premises may have been dogmatic, but their judgment was based on experience that Edge, Morrow, and Earle could never equal.

Furthermore, their belief in supervision and publicity rested on the assumption that there was an enlightened public opinion which they could rally against the spoilsmen. If pressed on this point, they could have pointed to the Social Science Association, the National Conference of Charities and Corrections, the National Prison Association, the Charity Organization Societies, and many other groups, all of which represented the same kind of right-minded people who supported Liberal Republicans, Cleveland Democrats, and other heroes of the genteel tradition in politics.

But Lewis and Wines were old men in 1903, already relics, like the Social Science Association among societies of scholars, clergymen turned wardens, asylum doctors among real doctors, and bountiful "friendly visitors" among professional social workers. Edge, Morrow, and Earle were progressive businessmen inspired by important improvements in business administration. Edge thought the state government and its departments ought to be run like business corporations. Obviously, from Morrow's and Earle's point of view, business executives and their boards *did* combine legislative, judicial, and executive functions every day. (Some people wondered whether the new department and its hierarchy of boards and executives was more like General Motors or like AT&T.) To them the idea of supervision would connote cost accounting and expert consultation rather than judicial review and a reformers' association.

In a more immediate way, Morrow and Earle did not make an issue of supervision because the plainest fact of their inquiry, the one they didn't make explicit although it pervaded their reports, was that supervision didn't work. The state had had supervision, both official and voluntary, since 1905; in 1915 both authorities had said that on the whole matters were progressing nicely, and they had confined their suggestions to particulars. What the Morrow and Earle commissions said was that on the whole, that is, with reference to the system, a radical reorganization was necessary; there was no statement in their reflections to the effect that the system in 1917 was any more resourceful or enterprising than it had been in 1905.

The Morrow Commission did say that the state's correctional institutions were "upon the whole, fairly abreast of the penal systems of other progressive states," and it pointed out interesting or promising programs when it could. But it did not develop this idea or explain it. By "fairly abreast of other progressive states" it meant, apparently, simply that the state had separate institutions for different classes of offenders. It certainly did not mean that the reform schools were reforming or that prison discipline was properly penal. In September 1917 Morrow sent Kirchwey to the state prison to see whether the recommendations of the Commission's preliminary report had been put into effect. Kirchwey reported that the administration was still repressive, that the "negligence and unwillingness" of the prison inspectors was still obstructing the state use program, that medical and psychiatric examinations had barely begun, and that the food was still poorly prepared and served, by the same people.[61] This did not sound progressive.

The Earle Commission report, which was not printed for public circulation, was noticeably more critical of existing supervision. It found, among other things, that the commissioner's duties were numerous, but his "real powers" were "negligible," that there was "no effective co-operation between his office and the institutions," that he was "largely a figurehead," that local boards lobbied and competed for funds, with no rational study or allocation according to needs and deserts, that the overcrowding of insane asylums was "a long-recognized and increasing disgrace to the State," that in some cases "even ordinary sanitary conditions [were] lacking," and in others "buildings old, insanitary and unsafe, and veritable fire-traps, [were] housing hundreds of old and infirm people." [62] Earle's commission did not analyze responsibility for this situation, but its recommendation was, essentially, to give power and responsibility to the supervising agent.

Both commissions took for granted that supervision hadn't worked. Neither asked why, in any critical way. Neither undertook to represent the institutions or the central agency in terms of an enduring conflict of values or interests. To some extent such an analysis would have required a behavioral science that was beyond them, but for the rest the commissioners were satisfied to let bygones be bygones, to accentuate the positive.

Morrow, in particular, was reluctant to be a scandalmonger. "The study whose results are embodied in this report," his commission concluded, "has disclosed many . . . things which . . . require correction. But it has seemed . . . that these may well await the determination and recommendation of a central board." What the Commission wanted was not simply to end abuses but to devise "a plan that will hold out a reasonable hope of the prompt correction of abuses, and, what is perhaps of as great importance as anything else, that will furnish the fullest opportunity for the continuous education of the people of the State as to their responsibilities." [63]

What counted to Morrow and Earle was the long run. They did not keep quiet about problems because they wanted to cover them up. They wanted to create a situation in which good men could work together; that is what they thought they were creating. The feeling that dignified their efforts was not compassion for the suffering inmate, but security in the knowledge of the ways of power. Theirs was not the way of Dorothea Dix or even Emily Williamson. Helping people, they said, in effect, is mostly a question of getting the right management at the top and the right organization underneath it. Get your boards and bureaus straight, open up communications between professionals and an enlightened public, and the rest will follow in due course.

11

Establishing the Department, 1918–1925

Two hopeful ideas characterized the organic act of the new department. One was that the appointment of "lay" or "citizen" boards of management took welfare institutions out of politics; the other was that state agencies dealing with the dangerous or unfortunate had common problems and purposes. Members of a "lay" board did not run for office and received no pay for their work. Their motive was public spirit; their reward, honor; their qualification, presumably, eminence in business, a profession, or charitable service. As managers they employed a full-time executive, gave him their advice and support, and interpreted the agency's work to the public.

Now this principle was extended from particular institutions to the entire system. A new State Board of Control would direct a central department that would co-ordinate the whole. Members of the State Board were appointed by the governor for long and staggered terms, so that no governor could nominate a majority. The State Board, with the approval of the governor, appointed members of institutional boards. Taken together, the boards were a cadre of humane and civic-minded people who could be trusted to provide enlightened leadership and economical management, free of the distractions of partisanship, favoritism, and graft.

The centralizing work of the new department was for experience to determine, but in general the founders thought that the several institutions and agencies had similar problems which a common management might solve more economically, and—perhaps more important—that forward-looking leadership would encourage scientific and constructive programs in place of mere custody and repression.

These notions were generally clear and exciting to the founders of the Department, and who could fault them? Who would make hospitals or prisons into "political footballs," or fail to see that centralized management could bring economy, or object to prevention and rehabilitation as proper goals of the system? And yet, as the State Board took charge it discovered that when ideals inevitably become engaged in the personal and particular they become complicated almost beyond the understanding of men of good will.

The First State Board and Burdette Lewis

Democrats, a notably prickly lot, were skeptical from the first about the "nonpolitical" character of the boards. They had voted in a bloc against the reorganization plan, as Republicans had voted in a bloc for it.[1] But even staunchly Republican Mrs. Geraldine L. Thompson wrote Dwight Morrow that Governor Edge's nominations for the State Board were "a shock and a disappointment." Morrow replied that he was disappointed that Mrs. Caroline Wittpenn, Mr. Decatur Sawyer, president of the Rahway board, and Mr. Seymour Cromwell were not named; these—and Mrs. Thompson—had been his own suggestions. He observed that he knew only two of the eight nominees. Morrow, by this time involved in war work, had thought Decatur Sawyer was the man for chairman, and later explained to him that "the only thing that prevented your appointment [to the State Board] was the apparent necessity of distributing the appointments around the counties." [2] (Mrs. Wittpenn was named to the board in October 1918.)

People active in politics are also apt to be active in charitable services, and it seems plain that nomination to the boards typically involved both considerations. "If we can have a man who is considered a politician and who is known to us to be an honest one . . . we could not possibly do better for the personnel of the Board," remarked Mrs. Thompson about a possible nominee in 1919, and the thought unquestionably occurred to everyone.[3] In 1920 the Department had to reply to a charge that physicians were ignored for board memberships because they were not in politics.[4] In 1923 the term of Ogden Hammond, second chairman of the State Board and incidentally treasurer of the Republican State Committee, expired; Governor Silzer, Democrat, appointed William Kirby, of the Democratic State Committee, to succeed him.[5]

The Board's first task was to select a commissioner. This responsibility fell to a committee headed by Ellis P. Earle; after a "thorough examination of candidates," the job went to Burdette G. Lewis, formerly Commissioner of Corrections of New York City in the "reform"—anti-Tammany—administration of Mayor John Purroy Mitchel. Lewis brought a number of associates with him from out of state. As its secretary the State Board chose Barton T. Fell, formerly Republican Freeholder of Mercer County and an unsuccessful contender for nomination to sheriff in 1917.[6]

Burdette Lewis, who was to lead the Department for seven stormy years, had been born thirty-six years before in Jamestown, Pennsylvania. As a boy he worked on the farms and attended the grammar schools of this community. Presently he moved to Omaha, where he "worked [his] way through . . . High School by operating machines in a glove factory, graduating in three years, in 1901." He proceeded to work his way through the University of Nebraska in three years, then won scholarships to the University of Wisconsin and, the two years following, to Cornell. His graduate work was in political science and economics. He held a number of jobs on public commissions before he joined Mitchel's staff in 1910. He became deputy commissioner of corrections when Mitchel became mayor, in 1914, and commissioner the following year. He advised the Prison Inquiry Commission in 1917; he impressed Dwight Morrow, and, when political changes in New York forced him out of office, he became a candidate for the New Jersey commissionership.[7]

Certainly Lewis was intelligent, ambitious, and qualified for the job. He impressed people by his unsullied self-confidence, his gift for thinking in large and radical ways, and his quick-witted guard against detractors. Governor Edge, who had to approve his nomination, was impressed by his "common sense viewpoint." [8] "We have a strong Commissioner . . . to whom . . . to look for the formulation of our policies and plans," Mrs. Thompson wrote Morrow shortly after Lewis was appointed; and Morrow later wrote Governor Edge that other informed people expressed "most hearty approval" over the Department's organization, although they worried somewhat about criticism for going out of state.[9]

Lewis' manuscript autobiography and the recollections of people who knew him then suggest a man of high ideals of political democracy and a highly self-conscious devotion to popular government and the public interest. It was characteristic of the new commissioner that he should be preoccupied with "public relations." Perhaps his eight years in publicity-conscious New York politics strengthened this interest, but in any case the Morrow Commission had said that the proposed department should "furnish the fullest opportunity for the continuous education of the people of the state as to their responsibilities with respect to the institutions." [10]

Lewis thought that he was "fundamentally . . . in exactly the same position as the sales agent of a large corporation." His product was "good government"; there were, he said, two ways of "selling" it. One was "the quick method," the "method of modern advertising adopted by business" and "developed to the nth degree by the . . . nations at war." The other was "the old political method," that is, "moving along slowly, making as many friends as possible," pushing ahead "a step here and a step there," deliberately "trying to avoid any publicity . . . for fear that criticism will exceed praise." Essentially, he thought, people who chose the second method worked "without the knowledge of the people" because of "fear of them and lack of trust in them." [11]

But how could he "advertise" good government? In fact, Lewis thought, public attention focused on prisons or hospitals haphazardly, as "scandals" unfolded; although these revelations sometimes brought specific reforms, their long-run effect was a bad impression which made far-reaching reform more difficult. A wise publicity program would therefore present faults or shortcomings candidly, not spare them; it would, however, remove the spice of scandal, and it would also foster a stream of constructive and attractive "educational" materials on the work and problems of the agencies.[12]

Consequently, Lewis prevailed upon members of the State Board to contribute a private fund to employ, as director of records and information, Dr. Louis Blan, whose work was mostly preparing press releases.[13] Lewis and Blan were alert publicists and in a way their program succeeded. Clipping services and newspaper editors testified to its effect.[14] Unfortunately, some publicity backfired. The very first press release, for example, announced Lewis' practice of keeping a "log," a detailed record of daily work, and requiring his subordinates to do the same. In his mind the log showed his businesslike temper and his sense of public accountability: There it was, for all to see. His enemies thought it was all mere self-glorification and busywork; hostile Trenton papers ridiculed "Logging at Trenton" as the idea of a pretentious egotist. Lewis, confident of his rightness, thought the reproaches stemmed from disappointed office seekers or "grafters and lazy incompetents" whom he was compelled to discharge, "especially in connection with the State Prison." [15]

In 1919, Lewis and his publicity man arranged to take movies of the institutions, for educational purposes. It happened that these pictures showed prominently Mr. Newton Bugbee, then candidate for the Republican gubernatorial nomination; on investigation, it developed that Louis Blan had directed them while on leave of absence from the State Board and in Mr. Bugbee's employ. When Democrats took offense at this gesture, Lewis replied that he had no funds to pay Blan during his "leave," that the pictures in question were not "political" at all, and that Blan and the Department would be glad to make nonpolitical pictures explaining the institutions with all candidates.[16] (These and other movies were in fact widely and successfully distributed. Dr. Blan presently joined a company making educational films.) [17]

Nevertheless, the Democratic platform for 1920 pointed to poor conditions at the institutions, criticized the principle of "large, unwieldy commissions," and in particular denounced the selection of important department officers from out of state. Edward I. Edwards, head of the Democratic ticket, demanded that "discards in charge of state institutions . . . must go," and was reported to intend to "make it so uncomfortable for [board-member] friends of Edge and Bugbee . . . that they will get out." The Republican platform and candidate Bugbee defended the new order.[18]

Edwards was particularly hostile to Lewis, who felt that the Department's morale—as well as his own—was suffering. He answered the charges as best he could, but as the campaign got hotter, he asked that the State Board publicly vindicate its work. But Dwight Morrow, the Board chairman, was already "a good deal disturbed by . . . the extent to which we seem to have been projected into politics."[19] He wanted Lewis and the Board to "take absolutely no part in the public controversy."[20] When Lewis complained about one of Edwards' attacks, Morrow wrote back, "I would not pay a bit of attention to it." Should Lewis answer the charges, he said, "a hundred people will know about [the] original statement to one who knows about it now."[21] After the election the Board could make "a careful broad statement . . . about the care we took in enlisting our staff and the character of [its] work."[22]

Edwards won. As his inauguration approached, Lewis commented anxiously that of course the Department was responsible to the new governor. After all, he said, the governor could talk to Board members and "ask their hearty cooperation," and he could, of course, use his reappointing power to influence their policy.[23] Meanwhile, the Republican majority in the legislature moved to restrict the governor's power to remove Board members. Informed of their action, Dwight Morrow wrote the speaker, "quite informally and without consultation with other members of the Board," that he opposed the plan. "No member of the . . . Board wants any protection," he said. "The incoming Governor will be ex-officio a member of their Board. They are all most anxious to work . . . with him." So advised, the Republicans did not act.[24]

Governor Edwards duly denounced the principle of lay board administration and remarked that he "was informed" that the "chief function" of institutional boards was "to meet once a month and listen to . . . unimportant details." Assemblymen from Hudson and Essex introduced bills to eliminate local boards and reorganize the State Board, but these failed.[25] The Department was hardly "out of politics," but at least its personnel and policies remained undisturbed at a crucial time.

Organizing the Central Office

Meanwhile, Lewis and the Board went about setting up their Department. Its conception included the thought, partly spelled out in the organic act, that its several institutions had common problems which might benefit from central direction. Consequently, the office was not organized around types of institutions but around functional divisions. Officials and their jobs were spelled out in a detailed "administrative code" by Herbert Sands, an accountant and management consultant of Newark. All institutions provided some sort of medical care, for example, and it was expected that psychiatry would play an increasingly important part in correctional institutions; therefore, there was a "Division of Medicine and Psychiatry," which would help develop services in the several institutions and mobilize the resources of all for the benefit of each.

All institutions had to feed their inmates and most had some agricultural work, so there was a Division of Labor, Agriculture, Food and

Dietetics which planned for food needs and coordinated the farms. It also assigned inmate labor to other maintenance tasks—laundry, for example—and directed the state-use system. A third bureau was intended to standardize the common task of keeping records, to make the records available in the form of summary reports, and to furnish "information" to the Board of Control and the public (this was Dr. Blan's official duty). A Division of Inspection carried on the work of visiting certain private agencies and the local jails, in addition to its check on state-aided institutions. There were also Divisions of Administration and of Education and Parole.[26]

Such was the plan of the central office; the practice was a different matter. In fact Lewis had three important tasks: to set up a system of classification and education, to work out a system of employment for state use, and to devise methods of accounting and budgeting that would minimize the competition for funds.

Of these tasks, classification had priority. Even before the Department's organization, Dr. Henry Cotton had established a "psychiatric clinic" at Trenton State Hospital, which was intended to discover psychopaths and defectives among troublemakers at the State Prison, but the hesitation of prison officials and the war had interrupted its work. In 1918 Dr. Cotton became acting director of the Division of Education and Classification, and presently the clinic began operations again.

"Classification" was an enthusiasm of Commissioner Lewis, who had learned its possibilities during his association in New York with Dr. Katharine B. Davis, a pioneer in its development.[27] It meant a systematic collection of information about an inmate (previous record, health, aptitudes, and education) by a team of specialists (doctor, psychiatrist, psychologist, teacher, social worker) who combined their insights to devise an appropriate program of institutional treatment. Some sort of classification was an administrative necessity: the specialized correctional institutions were themselves rough classifications by sex, age, and offense. Within each of these the keepers had to have some way of assigning work and privileges and recommending parole. Generally, they had guided themselves by the inmate's past record, if he were a repeater, and his present behavior. Formal education, academic or vocational, was "graded" after the fashion of the schools; work assignments were used as punishment or privilege.[28]

Two developments made classification especially exciting to the commissioner: large-scale psychological testing by the Army had dramatized its possibilities, and Dr. Cotton's experimentation at Trenton State Hospital raised hope for the cure of mental illness. Ed Johnstone gave (without compensation) two or three days a week for a year to help organize the classification and parole services (he was also put on the new Prison Board of Managers).[29] Edgar A. Doll, a veteran of the Army testing program at Fort Dix, was hired to direct the Department's program and be the chief psychologist for the clinic.[30]

Doll began by testing inmates of the State Prison, with the general purpose of distinguishing the retarded. He concluded, contrary to expectation, that the "typical . . . prisoner compares favorably in intelligence with the average adult male in the . . . State," whatever that meant. The tests did bring out information of use to paroling authorities. In January 1920, he began systematically testing new prisoners so that they could be assigned appropriate training or work. He discovered then that he would first need to know what jobs were available, so he ordered an elaborate industrial survey of the prison. This procedure of analyzing and classifying men and jobs, later extended to other correctional institutions, was a fundamental step away from rule-of-thumb methods and toward rationalized management. Within a few years Doll could report that the populations of Jamesburg, Rahway, and the State Prison presented different problems of discipline and training: a quarter of the juveniles but only 6 per cent of the prison population were mentally deficient; the proportions of "insane and psychopathic types" were almost the reverse.[31]

Classification, appropriate education or training, and readjustment to the community (parole) were in theory all part of one process, and the original table of organization had put them in one division. In fact, parole supervision took a large staff prepared for social casework rather than clinical psychology, so in 1921 this division was split, part handling "classification and education," part supervising "parole and domestic relations." [32]

Similarly, the so-called director of the Division of Labor, Agriculture, Food and Dietetics in fact occupied himself with the state-use program, while a farm manager and a steward, supposedly under him, reported directly to the Commissioner.[33] There was in fact no Division of Administration, although an accountant, an inspector of local institutions, a collector of bad debts, and their clerical assistants were distinguished as "Sections." [34] Consultants who studied the organization of the central office in 1923, after four years, thought that it should be divided into two large divisions, one concerned with ". . . the objective welfare of the Department"—the central services of classification, education, and parole—and the other "concerned more with the business administration of the Department." [35] The consultants noted that the central office staff was able and worked with "loyalty and enthusiasm . . . engendered by . . . the Commissioner," but recommended a "business manager" to relieve the commissioner. This was the first of many similar recommendations.[36]

Business management was the perspective which two later surveys of the Department's work also took. "The plan of having functional advisers or specialists . . . to assist in working out the problems arising at various institutions is greatly to be commended," said a study in 1925. "In general, . . . the headquarters staff has been of substantial value in standardizing the routine . . . in the institutions." The principal criticism of the Department was that "a great deal more needs to be done" to make its supervision more thorough.[37] A more intensive survey four years later observed that "New Jersey is admirably adapted to this type of central control" and said that "the question to be here discussed is whether . . . a further step toward central control is desirable." Its recommendations looked forward to "the replacement [by central services] of many services now maintained independently by the various institutions." [38]

Both surveys, in short, pointed to many accomplishments of a centralized control: physical improvements judiciously made, more standardized bookkeeping, accounting, and budgeting practices, the classification, education, state-use, and parole systems. They pointed to many other benefits: better use of farm land, effective collection of claims, better schooling, useful inspection services, the beginnings of clinics for TB and mental illness. Neither survey questioned the fundamental conception of the office. Both thought an aggressive administrative policy could increase its benefits.[39]

Problems With Local Boards

Much of the Department's early history may be summarized around two factors that inhibited a more aggressive central administration: First, local institutions continued to manage their own affairs; second, the legislature never gave the Department enough money to effect its plans. In law the autonomy of local boards did not look very formidable. The State Board appointed their members, subject to the approval of the governor, and it was explicitly given the power to overrule them. Nevertheless, the very existence of the local boards testified to a reluctance to offend them in reorganizing the system, and it was recognized from the start that it would be tactless to replace long-term and dominating members. Some local boards "should undoubtedly be changed radically," Mrs. Thompson reported to Chairman Morrow as the reorganization was beginning, but "one is afraid to do too drastic things." [40]

In the past, local boards had largely occupied themselves with the contest for funds from the Appropriations Committee; under the new order they had to channel their pleas for funds through the commissioner, who was "chief budget officer," and the State Board. Doubtless other institutions quickly felt the frustration of the Board of Glen Gardner, whose chairman complained after a year that "we had better results under the old system." Credit for savings went to the State Board, he said, whereas faults were blamed on the institution's managers.[41] Observers applauded the end of "lobbying for charity" at the State House, but the business of "budgeting by compromise" within the Department became very tedious, and, since the Appropriations Committee had finally to pass on the Department's requests, people could go behind the State Board's back.[42]

The State Board set up a common system of accounting, but separate institutions kept their own accounts and varied the practice to suit their purposes. All three surveys of the Department before 1930 mentioned the desirability of centralizing the work of accounting, but the reluctance of particular institutions to surrender this important executive function prevented its accomplishment.[43]

Differences between the State Board and its institutional subordinates arose typically over a difference in perspective on a proposed change. Three episodes in the early history of the Department, involving Trenton State Hospital, Rahway Reformatory, and the State Prison, show how widely the causes—and consequences—varied.

Less than a month after it organized, the State Board learned about a serious situation at Trenton State Hospital. Since Dr. Cotton had come there, in 1907, the hospital had been under a dual management: Cotton directed medical work, while Samuel T. Atchley, formerly sheriff of Mercer County, was business manager. The law creating the Department had required a unified management, and Trenton's Board had elected Atchley chief executive. Cotton was therefore about to resign. This was interesting to the State Board because Dr. Cotton seemed to be the sort of enlightened leader they wanted to support. In 1907, they knew, he had created a sensation by successfully preferring charges of brutality against certain attendants; he proceeded to eliminate the forms of restraint used in handling violent cases. His hope was to make the old asylum into a hospital where sick people were treated, as in general hospitals.[44]

When the Earle Commission investigated charitable institutions in 1917, it had discovered a significant difference of opinion among students of mental illness. The largest group, composed mostly of hospital managers, nurses, attendants, and some of the older doctors, regarded insanity as incurable or at least very difficult to treat. They favored emphasis on relatively inexpensive and comfortable custody. They thought that "brutal" restraints, properly used, made things safer for the patient and his neighbors and easier for the attendants. Dr. Cotton's ideas were not popular with them, particularly when he began to wonder whether insanity was not the consequence of focal infection, which many physicians then suspected of leading to rheumatism, arthritis, and heart and kidney complaints.

Presently, Cotton began the laboratory study of organs and tissues taken from patients living and dead. He discovered significant foci of infection in the teeth, the tonsils, the digestive tract and other vital organs—practically everywhere he looked—and he discovered that if these infections were eliminated, usually by surgery, patients showed remarkable recovery from their "mental" symptoms. He seemed to bring the treatment of insanity back into the tradition of medicine. Employees at the hospital, however, their hands full with deranged inmates, found themselves involved in the painstaking routine of pre- and postoperative patients. A high mortality rate—30 per cent at times—further dismayed them. To complicate matters further, doctors disagreed: many psychiatrists, including some at Morris Plains, thought mental illness was psychogenic and not essentially related to somatic afflictions.[45]

Was this a question simply for the board of managers of the Trenton Hospital—who had already decided to let Cotton go—or should the State Board "interfere"? If the State Board acted, what should it do? The Board selected a committee to study the situation: Commissioner Lewis, Ellis Earle, its best-informed member on the hospitals, and Dr. John Nevin, a physician. Two things became clear to these gentlemen: First, Cotton was a thoughtful and impressive fellow, with a plausible theory, who got results. He took people who were mentally ill, even hopeless cases, discovered focal infections in them, operated—and in a significant number, the mental symptoms improved. Second, doctors themselves did not know the correct answer. No promising lead should be neglected, the State Board decided. Therefore, it asked the local board to assure Dr. Cotton the autonomy he had enjoyed before and to support him in his experiments. Meanwhile, it encouraged the staff at Morris Plains to pursue different notions of treatment. The Board stipulated that Dr. Cotton should publish his results for general criticism. This agreement was negotiated with what must have been considerable tact all around. Thus, in the eyes of the State Board, the cause of scientific rehabilitation was served, and the two hospitals were committed to a common end.[46]

This decision had two quite different consequences. Dr. Cotton's results seemed to confirm his radical theories. They were duly published in medical journals and, in 1921, in the Vanuxem Foundation Lectures at Princeton, "The Defective, Delinquent and Insane: The Relation of Focal Infections to their Causation, Treatment and Prevention." In 1922, the work received favorable national publicity in an article Commissioner Lewis wrote for the widely-read *American Review of Reviews.* Dr. Cotton and his associates were making "the winning fight against mental disease," Lewis said; exponents of the contrary—and accepted—view "that insanity is primarily a disease of the mind" had "signally failed to hold in check the alarming increase in insanity," whereas the Trenton Hospital might soon abandon its "old asylum section" or reconvert it to other uses.[47]

The other consequence was unfortunate: By "interfering" the "big board" had inevitably stirred resentment, and its decision created among many workers at the hospital dismay and suspicion, which later became material for a political attack on both Cotton and the State Board. "It was awful to work there; he was going much too far with his operating," a secretary recalled years later. "There was a young girl, she worked in the office right by the door where they had to roll the baskets past that carried the bodies and organs and stuff. One day she ran out screaming, she couldn't stand it any more."[48] Lewis thought of this feeling as simply one cost of progress. In 1922 he encouraged Dr. Marcus Curry, newly appointed director of Morris Plains, to bring "into line" staff "who have been there for years and who will very naturally question the desirability of all the new medical work." [49]

The State Board's plans for centralizing employment, education, and parole quickly ran into an obstacle at Rahway, where the outspoken and well-established Dr. Frank Moore had firm support from his board. The State Board wanted to make a good showing on its state-use program, and when Calvin Derrick, its able director of classification, education, and parole, brought in a critical study of Rahway's procedures, the Board decided to ask the Reformatory to send more boys out to road camps. Ostensibly to save money, it also moved to take parole out of the hands of the particular institution and give it to the central office. There was no logical connection between these steps, but they were linked by the fact that Dr. Moore had conceived a "deep-seated dislike" for Calvin Derrick.

A disagreement over the proposed head at Jamesburg exacerbated their difference.[50] Moore—and his board—argued that road work did not answer Rahway's reformatory purpose as well as intramural education; and he thought that the advantages of having the institution keep in touch with its parolees far exceeded any economy or efficiency of centralization. So the issue was drawn—and remained drawn. In general, Chairman Morrow "lean[ed] very strongly toward putting the whole responsibility on the local boards and letting them run the institutions." Other members of the Executive Committee, including Ellis Earle, opposed making an exception for Rahway and grew "weary of the constant opposition of Dr. Moore to everything that is suggested"; but the majority of the Board thought they ought to be "considerate" of the Rahway Board. Commissioner Lewis said therefore that he would "go very slow" on making changes.[51] Nevertheless, resentment lingered; after he resigned from the Rahway Board ten years later, Edward Duffield had to deny a report that he left because he favored greater autonomy for separate institutions.[52] And in 1932 Dr. Moore was openly advocating the breakup of the Department.

At the old State Prison things were even more difficult. Here the situation was complicated by the authority of the principal keeper, appointed by the governor rather than by the local Board of Managers. He held this anomalous position because he and his duties were mentioned in the State Constitution and therefore could not be changed by a mere statute such as had established the Department. He was responsible for the security of the prisoners and whatever that implied about their activities, work, and parole and the personnel who watched over them. The keeper's job was traditionally a political reward, not a professional's employment. It was obviously inconsistent with the ideal of professional management which had characterized state institutions even before the reorganization.[53]

There were three ways to get around this anomaly. One was a constitutional amendment; another was for the governor to surrender his appointing power in fact to the Board of Managers; a third was to provide a professional assistant who would really run the prison. But the constitution remained sacrosanct and governors would not surrender what little patronage they could claim. In 1917, Governor Edge had given the five-year job to a political associate; what the job really needed, he said, was a "politician" rather than a "penologist"—a man with "tact, leadership, organizational ability and an acquaintance with men in all walks of life." [54] When this splendid fellow's term ended, in 1922, Governor Edwards, a Democrat, discovered a suitable replacement in Joseph Hoff. Mr. Hoff had combined successful careers in business and politics; he had just completed ten years on the Civil Service Commission and was chairman of the Democratic party of Mercer County as well as its representative on the state committee.[55]

In August 1922, Keeper Hoff had to call on Trenton and State Police to put down a disturbance lasting several days. Its occasion was a prisoner's furious complaint that in the midst of peach season he had not received his fair share of peaches for dessert; when the prisoners learned that their uproar had attracted a crowd outside the walls they improved and prolonged the trouble. The real riot was quickly put down, according to Keeper Hoff, and the leaders were punished, but discipline remained poor, as they say, for two or three more days. Prisoners complained of poor food and bad treatment.[56]

Then, on October 25, the State Board wrote the managers of the prison that they had sworn testimony that the deputy keeper, center keeper, and two lesser officers of the prison were on a drunken party and joy ride on August 24, while the riots were still unsettled, and that these men and their subordinates had, without knowledge of the local board, reopened the dungeons and used leg irons to deal with the riot leaders. The State Board asked that the four men be suspended, pending an investigation at the prison. Keeper Hoff and the local board wanted to go slowly, to defer the suspension until the investigation was made. The State Board made the situation public on October 30 and called for a quick report.[57]

The knowledgeable correspondent of the *Newark News* observed that the deputy and center keepers were "two of the oldest employees . . . and both have weathered many a storm." (They had been particularly criticized during the investigation of the Morrow Commission, five years before, when they had promised to assist the new regime.) In due time the prison managers and the State Board set up a joint committee to investigate the charges, and their report, made the following June, did virtually clear the old hands of cruelty and infractions of rules. The deputy keeper was pensioned after almost thirty years as an "acceptable" officer "of the older type"; his assistant was given another chance to reform under a new assistant keeper who would be a professional penologist of the newer type. (Lewis tried unsuccessfully to get his acquaintance in New York, Warden Lawes of Sing Sing, for the job.) The joint committee also recommended "better enforcement" of regulations which were supposed to give prisoners a hearing, a degree of self-government among prisoners, an end to the dungeon and other antique cruelties, and—this in 1923—development of state use to end idleness, and more examination and transfer of "borderline" cases of insanity or mental defect.[58]

It is difficult to penetrate the fog of testimony and official press release that envelop this sort of episode, but the evidence suggests a situation in which old hands on the prison staff were blocking a program of "enlightened" penology. Handling desperate criminals was nerve-wracking, dangerous work; naturally the keepers thought they deserved primary consideration in it. Jailbirds could not be trusted, and there were times when only cruelty or terror would keep them in line. Certainly their testimony against guards could not be believed. "Petting" the convicts only made them more dangerous; it was "humiliating" for guards "to have to be timid in every step . . . for fear of being penalized." [59]

Lewis and the State Board did take testimony from prisoners, one in particular "of great intelligence and long experience in prison"; these men charged that the guards thought of convicts as "beasts" and used their power not simply to maintain order but also for "favoritism and graft," that is, to pamper well-heeled or influential convicts. Of course it would be difficult to get conclusive evidence of improper conduct, an "Ex-inmate" wrote in the *Newark News,* because officials were afraid that if one talked they would all be in trouble. It was this "old school" of keeper, the writer said, who opposed establishing decent conditions and complicated programs of classification, education, and work, and who won the inexperienced principal keepers quickly to their "practical and realistic" viewpoint.[60]

The recommendations of the joint committee plainly implied that the directives of the central office were not being followed, and it seems likely that the failure of the prison road-building program during the previous year was brought about by reluctant co-operation at the prison. In the future, the chairman of the State Board said, a "trained penologist," serving as assistant keeper, would run the prison. The keeper would remain as "titular head." [61] Shortly thereafter, Calvin Derrick, then serving as superintendent at Jamesburg, became "manager" of the prison.[62] But, as events proved, this was not a permanent solution.

Conflict between the State Board and an institutional board could develop in different ways, and for better or worse the autonomy of the local board was plainly a complication. Conflict was significant, but it was not typical. At least, the experts who surveyed the Department found plenty of solid accomplishment. In general, the institutions which were less favored by the legislature under the old system got decidedly fairer treatment, and many superintendents were glad to unload work on a man from Trenton. Mary Belle Harris, the new superintendent of Clinton Farms in 1918, was "fearful that our institution might be 'standardized' " but soon realized that "with Mrs. Wittpenn [on the

State Board] as an interpreter" the board "wished to perpetuate in each institution whatever was good" and "seemed willing to grant scope for initiative to able superintendents." [63]

Making Plans and Raising Funds

Quite apart from its difficulties in dealing with particular institutions, the State Board was trying to do an expensive job without enough money. This was evident in the absence of certain important staff men—a statistician and an office manager, for example—and in the doubling up of work or part-time employment of others. The Morrow and Earle commissions had been financed largely by private subscription, and members of the new board continued to chip in, not only for publicity but also toward the salary of such an important official as Calvin Derrick.[64]

Ultimately, everyone realized, an effective program depended upon adequate public support. Traditionally, this meant going to the legislature and begging for appropriation of what funds were available. The legislature could not plan to spend more money than was very plainly covered by income, an amount that was easy to figure because sources of income were few. Special funds and the sharing of state taxes with counties made finances complicated, but when the Department was organized, it was clear that the state, out of debt since 1902, would fit its needs to its existing resources, rather than bring its taxes into line with its needs.

This attitude was bound to conflict with the program of the new Department. In its founders' eyes, the Department was much more than an agent of business administration to co-ordinate existing institutions. There rose in their imagination a great system of institutions and agencies, each with a special function, each assisting the other, each supported by a network of local and private institutions. The system's ruling purposes were prevention and rehabilitation: discover the troublesome individual early, diagnose his trouble and cure or circumvent it, get him back home as a self-sufficient and perhaps productive citizen; eliminate haphazard commitment, miserable custody, inhumane repression; reform the criminal; cure the insane. The staff would find in the institutions great research and training centers. The inmates, for the most part, would find them a stopping place, not a permanent prison. Trouble, mental illness, or defect would first be recognized in a local institution like a clinic. The troublesome individual might be committed, but preferably he would receive outpatient treatment or help or, if he were delinquent, supervision and help by a probation officer. Actual commitment would lead, when possible, to speedy release, with aftercare or parole supervision. Pre- and postinstitutional programs would be set up by local agencies, guided perhaps by state demonstration clinics. If the problem involved school children, injured workingmen, veterans, or the public health, the Department would work as a team with appropriate authorities. Enlightened humanity raised this ideal, but true economy sanctioned it: Problems were simply too great for custodial institutions to handle in the old way.[65]

This ideal could hardly be improved today, and yet it received no single eloquent statement to which men could later point and say, "Here, this is what we are for." To some extent the reports of the Morrow and Earle commissions served this purpose, and so did occasional publications of the Department, but these documents rarely escaped the cautious locutions of official prose, and by the 1930's, no fundamental statement seemed called for. By then, responsibility and the gravity of persons and particulars had made the promise of 1919 seem very distant—almost as distant as the World Made Safe for Democracy. In any case, the ideal appeared most clearly in letters, articles, or addresses called forth by the controversies surrounding the Department's first long-range plans and their financing.

The point was that to fit New Jersey's institutions to the ideal would cost a lot of money. Repairing existing structures was the smallest part of the bill; introducing better methods in correctional institutions and building new treatment facilities in the mental institutions was a much larger expense. The State Prison was to become a classification center; the Rahway Reformatory was to take its place as a walled prison, and a new reformatory and several colonies were to provide diverse programs. Similarly, Trenton Girls' Home was to become a reception and classification center. A new psychopathic hospital, on the model of Boston Psychopathic, was to be a clearinghouse and diagnostic center; two institutions for feebleminded were to emphasize training and outpatient care. The new facilities should be so designed that "they could be used as general hospitals should delinquency decrease . . . , [and] should probation and medical treatment be substituted for the customary correctional treatment," as the State Board said, in first laying out its program. "There need be no hanging back, therefore, to see what may happen ten years from now." [66]

How much money? The plan submitted in 1919 and based on prices of that year called for $16 million, but because of rising prices in the postwar inflation, action was delayed. Raising this sum was the legislature's business, but the State Board favored a bond issue, which would allow it to plan its operations in a comprehensive way without having to go to the solons each year for appropriations. It would thus save the high costs of piecemeal construction and multiple contracting, and it would be able to budget its funds to bring the highest savings in preventive work.[67]

Bond issues for construction were a recent idea. Private businesses had sometimes financed their expansion thus, but government bonds were traditionally war bonds. The New Jersey Constitution of 1844 required that a peacetime issue over $100,000 be approved first by the legislature and then by referendum. Only one issue, in 1916, of $7 million, for highways, had been so approved, and the war had prevented its issue. When the State Board first presented its plan, two other powerful interests were seeking bond issues—$12 million for a soldiers' bonus, $28 million to build the Holland Tunnel and the Camden Bridge. The legislature gave these the nod, and the electorate approved them both in 1920.[68]

The year 1921 seemed favorable for presenting the Department's case. A sudden, sharp depression enabled the legislature to prune the amount to $14 million because of reduced prices. The program seemed to offer desirable public works to alleviate the depression. Morrow and Lewis were called to Washington to testify that this was the sort of medicine Commerce Secretary Herbert Hoover had called for to relieve unemployment.[69] As a special inducement, financing the issue was said to require no new taxes; because of anticipated operating economies, payments on the debt could be met from a sinking fund which was created by annual payments about the same as normal annual appropriations; an expected increase in state revenues and institutional earnings would make up the difference.[70]

To "sell" the public on the project, Lewis and the State Board organized a well-planned "educational" campaign. They prepared a full agenda of organizations and persons to reach; no means of reaching them was overlooked. The cost was originally estimated at $30,000. Personal visits and letters received special attention, especially from the corps of board members.[71]

As the election drew near, a hostile observer noted that Lewis had created a "gigantic political-social machine" which was swamping criticism of the plan. Politicians seemed reluctant to incur "the displeasure of Lewis' 'best people in the state.' " Even Governor Edwards, "formerly [Lewis'] sworn enemy," had approved the bond issue and "completely surrendered to the . . . political-social combine." The governor was reported actually "pleased with the Commissioner's growing power." [72]

Voters rejected the program by a margin of four to three in a light turnout. "Apathy . . . as campaign ends," reported the *Newark News;* "voters generally" showed "little interest . . . in the important question of the . . . bond issue." [73] The total vote was half that of 1920.[74] Defeat was certainly not caused by organized opposition. Only one person opposed the measure during its legislative hearings; the Newark Real Estate Board was the most important organization definitely opposed.[75]

Lewis himself said there were only two arguments against the plan: some people opposed on principle a bond issue as a means of financing improvements, others opposed any sort of spending program during a depression.[76] The *Newark News,* which supported the plan, argued that there was no real case for the supposed "economy" of a bond issue. "The honest-to-goodness" reason for a bond issue, its editorialist wrote, was "the hopeless feeling that the Legislature would [not] have brains enough and courage enough" to impose the requisite taxes directly.[77] After the bond issue lost the *News* said that voters felt that supporters of the plan "had not been frank when they stated over and over again that the . . . measure would not add . . . to . . . the burden of taxation." [78]

The trouble with this interpretation is that voters approved bond issues for roads of $40 million in 1922, $8 million in 1924, and $30 million in 1927, while the Department hesitated to put its case before the people again.[79] In fact, there seems to have been a special reluctance to entrust the $14 million to the State Board and especially to Lewis. As the Democrats were considering whether to endorse the proposal, Mrs. Wittpenn, a leader of the Democratic women, wrote Lewis that there was "serious trouble ahead" because leading Democrats "profess to believe that our Board would be supreme" in spending the money.[80]

Evidently this belief was widely held, although it was wrong, because both the Appropriations Committee and the State House Commission would have had to clear actual expenditures.[81] Ultimately the Democrats took no stand, and the proposal lost heavily in Democratic counties. In any case the *Newark News* opined that by defeating the bond issue, "voters have practically told the legislators" that the money must be raised in a way "whereby they . . . know just how much" it costs "with details as to how" it is spent.[82]

So the Department's long-range plans as well as its annual allowance were subject to the discretion of the legislature. If it is true that legislators represent, ultimately, public opinion, it appears that, despite the public relations program, opinion on the Department's plan was massively ignorant and confused. The 1920's were a period of bitter political divisions, but these did not foster an illuminating debate about the Department's means and ends. In his annual message for 1922, Governor Edward I. Edwards mentioned the Department seventh in a list of nine topics, after the question of what to do about the Morris Canal and the pressing need for better provision against forest fires.[83]

The next year Governor George S. Silzer summed up "things uppermost in the minds of the people . . . taxation, the regulation of public utilities, good roads, labor, and prohibition," the "paramount issue." [84] In general, the discussion of appropriations for welfare and correctional work was not complicated by a discussion of objectives. In 1924, for example, the governor reported that while "general funds available . . . will amount to $11 million," there were requests for "over $16 million." In this chronic situation, he said "those who have a selfish purpose to serve put great pressure behind their requests . . . and . . . usually succeed." On the other hand "notwithstanding . . . tearful pleas for . . . unfortunates . . . in our institutions," these requests "are the first . . . denied." [85]

After its defeat on the bond issue, the State Board worked out an "emergency" program. It called for a direct tax to raise $9 million over five years. The legislature early in 1923 agreed to impose a half-mill property tax, for one year, but restricted its use to the improvement of Morris Plains; when the tax was paid, however, it provided insufficient funds, and even that plan "had to be curtailed." [86]

In November 1923, the Department asked for a four-year tax and construction program; it asked for $9 million to complete the emergency program (prices were rising) and $5 million to improve service beyond emergency needs. The plan contemplated two big problems: more adequate provision for the feebleminded (two new institutions, in North Jersey) and a better break for employees, who were leaving because of low earnings and poor living conditions at those institutions that were so remote that they had to house their help. The other major addition was an "intermediate reformatory" for North Jersey, needed to supplement and reorganize the existing institutions. The important thing omitted in the "emergency" program was the central mental hospital and diagnostic center. A four-year program, funds assured in advance, would save $400,000, Lewis said.[87]

In support of its program, the Department could count on a variety of women's organizations, organized social workers, and a new Citizen's Committee for Institutional Development. These were not particularly strong allies. The last named, for example, was organized by David I. Kelly, formerly an official of the Department, then secretary of the Essex County Park Commission, where he was particularly interested in playground work. John Grier Hibben, president of Princeton, was chosen its leader at a "mass meeting" attended by 100. Six months later the Citizens announced plans for a headquarters.[88]

Presently, even these supporters appeared confused. The women's political organizations were reported divided over the question of means, the advisability of a four-year program, and the distinction between a campaign for specific legislation and a more general "educational" program.[89] From the headquarters of the Citizen's Committee came intimations, later confirmed, that it in effect opposed the four-year program and annual tax, on the grounds that they were politically inexpedient.[90]

The root of this confusion was a fundamental fact: Hudson and Essex counties paid the bulk of a state property tax and at the same time supported their own hospitals for the insane and tubercular. Essex County, for example, paid a quarter of the tax collected for Morris Plains at the same time it was spending $4 million on its own hospitals. The state paid one-half the cost of the patient's maintenance—but its subsidy fell behind inflated prices. The Essex freeholders wanted to know specifically how the county would benefit from the "proposed nine or fourteen million dollar program," whether the state contemplated taking over the county institutions, and whether any new institutions would be in Essex County.[91] In fact, county "mental hospitals" were crowded with feebleminded and senile cases that had nowhere else to go; officials often hesitated to send cases that could be transferred, such as epileptics, to the "remote, inaccessible" state institutions. Freeholders wanted institutions that would relieve their overcrowding and be convenient to North Jersey; they asked to retain part of the state tax collected in their county to spend on their own institutions.[92]

The four-year plan and tax passed the Assembly but ran into stronger opposition in the Senate. No party question was involved. Democratic senators were hostile, although Democratic Governor Silzer, like Democratic Governor Edwards before him, came to support the State Board. The Republican majority was divided: three, including Senate Leader Bright of Cape May, opposed any relief; two favored a one-year program; the other ten divided equally between a two- and four-year program. They compromised on a two-year program—which they proceeded to break into two one-year programs, pleading the need of "real information as to the absolute necessity of the entire program." [93]

The senators asked Lewis for a new list of projects, only the most necessary, in two one-year programs. They would not take the first half of the four-year program; they thought that four years was "too long for anyone to . . . plan for" and did not want to commit themselves.[94] Governor Silzer made an unprecedented radio address supporting the Department; a few days later he noted bitterly that the "way [would] be smooth" for the $9 million bond issue for bridges and tunnels, but it was impossible to get $2 million for four years for the state's wards.[95] That weekend the state's legislators, officials, and newspapermen were entertained at Atlantic City; amid such diversions Republican senators conferred, sifted the Board's program, and recommended no tax, no bond issue, and a one-year program.[96] The Republican legislative conference agreed, however, to a one-year tax for a training school for feebleminded in North Jersey. Further relief came when officials discovered "a loose million" in the Treasury (because of unexpected receipts from inheritance taxes).[97]

Whatever agreement was really made was misunderstood; the following year Republican senators professed surprise and dismay to learn that the State Board wanted the tax again and some $4 million more—that is, two more years of it.[98]

It is not clear how much this legislative supervision actually changed the Board's plans. In 1925 Lewis remarked that it was following the basic building program of 1920, but that it hoped to complete the work in 1929 instead of 1933, because the state tax furnished larger, quicker resources. He credited this success partly to the Board's "very conservative" estimate of outside costs plus 25 percent contingency.[99] "Party leaders," Lewis said, had genuinely tried to keep the Department out of "log-rolling, job-seeking politics"; political opposition came from smaller fry who wanted jobs and control of the spending; their special aims were to control the Division of Architecture and Construction (which spent the money) and the Division of State Use by getting them transferred to other departments.[100]

The Bright Commission; Lewis Resigns

Whatever the cause, the Department was certainly working against a strong current of hostility and suspicion. As early as 1922, an observer noted that Lewis had offended politicians of both parties, but they were "chary about going on record in favor of the dismissal of the Board of

Control," the only way to get him.[101] When Governor Silzer first took office, in 1923, he said he thought that Lewis and the Board of Control ran "a terrible department."[102] Hostile assemblymen charged in 1925 that the overweening domination and "dictatorial demands" of Lewis and the State Board had brought about the persistent antagonism of the legislature.[103] Swelling this opposition was a lingering doubt, often ignorant and unenlightened, about whether the Department's plans for prevention and rehabilitation were merely sentimental "fads and fancies" and not "absolutely necessary."[104] As total state appropriations doubled between 1919 and 1925, pressure grew for some review.[105]

The result was the study of state expenditures made in 1925 by the Joint Legislative Survey Commission, called the Bright Commission after its chairman, the senator from Cape May. Its report covered the state government as a whole and dealt only incidentally with the Department of Institutions and Agencies. Much of the work was done by hired experts; this was the first time the nascent science of "public administration" appeared formally in the contemplation of New Jersey's government.[106]

Bright, president of the Senate, had been the Department's sharpest Republican critic, however, and the leading Democratic senator, Alexander Simpson of Hudson County, wanted to make Burdette Lewis a campaign issue by having A. Harry Moore, the Democratic candidate for governor, demand his removal.[107] Lewis angered the senators by declaring that they had failed, before, as it proved, they had begun their work.[108]

The Commission's inquiry was, in short, hostile, and represents the worst that could be discovered. After due deliberation, the lead developed in public hearings concerned Dr. Cotton's work. A former nurse testified that patients were "Forced Under Knife"—as one headline put it—in unnecessary and experimental operations; these "Insane Hospital Horror Stories" led the following week to "New . . . Horror Tales."[109] Meeting once a week, "probers" kept the story going for two months. The *Newark News* concluded that the case for the hospital managers was "clear and convincing," although there were admittedly "mistakes . . . in treatment" and "obviously" the institution needed more and better employees.[110] The Bright Commission's published report, moreover, ignoring the sensational stories, merely suggested that the hospital provide better recreation and constructive employment for its patients.

Considering its hostile auspices, the report is remarkably favorable. It compared costs of New Jersey institutions with those elsewhere and found them high, but it discovered no serious failures. It held that the state should leave certain cases—such as truants at Jamesburg and unwed mothers at Clinton—to local communities; it also suggested reducing state appropriations by raising charges to the counties. It criticized the Department's "self-laudation," but its recommendations pointed plainly toward more effective centralization along lines the Department was working. It offered no ammunition to those who deplored "dictatorial demands." [111]

Nevertheless, as the reports were issued to the press during November 1925, their immediate effect, together with the election of A. Harry Moore and strong Democratic gains, was a considerable doubt about the Department's future. On December 19, 1925, Commissioner Lewis suddenly took an executive job with the Penney-Gwinn Corporation.[112] Senator Bright commented that "the primary object" of his commission had been to reduce taxation by getting rid of Lewis; henceforth, he said, "Appropriations could be made for practical purposes—frills and fancies cut out so the normal child can get his inning." Governor-elect Moore criticized "too much theory and extravagance" in the Department's work and suggested that the Board resign, too.[113]

Chairman Ellis Earle replied that the State Board did not intend to quit, and asked indignantly for a thorough investigation of its work. Disquieting reports continued: that Moore had many friends on local boards who were complaining of the power of the "big board"; that he favored eliminating the commissioner and having institutional superintendents report direct.[114] Even Republican legislators, it was said, thought the commissioner had more authority than he should if the Board of Control functioned properly, and they thought a smaller, short-term, well-paid commission would be more effective and responsible.[115]

When he took office, Moore favored changing the State Board to a paid commission, eliminating the commissioner and organizing a council of institutional superintendents.[116] He considered not appointing or reappointing anyone to the State Board, particularly not Mrs. Wittpenn, who, though a Democrat, had voted for his Republican opponent.[117]

But there was no change. Republicans, controlling the legislature, threatened to end the governor's power of reappointment; to forestall them, the governor agreed not to remove anyone.[118] Proposals for reorganization were ignored. Bright had, perhaps, "got Lewis"; his inquiry showed plainly the currents of mistrust and misunderstanding in which the Department had navigated for seven years. Lewis had offended many people; his public relations program was evidently a failure, although legislators continued to complain "of the system [he] built up and . . . the influence it [was] able to bear" on them.[119] After seven years, "extravagance" and "fad and fancy" had made legislators skeptical about the Department, but they did not yet choose to undo it.[120]

12

The Regime of John Ellis, 1926–1945

The State Board had little time in which to choose Lewis' successor. On January 4, 1926, when members were canvassed about leading candidates for the job, they expected to delay a choice until the governor and legislature made their policy clearer. Among the possibilities were the president of Dartmouth College, two professors at Princeton (one formerly Wilson's minister to Greece), and a man who had recently turned down an appointment as commissioner of education.[1] Meanwhile the Board fell back on a young fellow in the central office who was certainly likable, they thought, and promising, too. Perhaps, under the circumstances, it was difficult to bring a "big name" into the job; perhaps Board members agreed with some legislators that henceforth the Board should play a larger role relative to the commissioner. In any case, on February 23, 1926, they announced that their acting commissioner was made permanent.[2] Thus began the tenure of William J. Ellis, which continued until he died of cancer nineteen years later.

At first sight, Ellis' qualifications were not impressive; his coworkers were pleasantly surprised when he got the job. He had no professional reputation or training. Neither his physical appearance nor his public speech was commanding. He was born in Muncy, Pennsylvania, November 18, 1892, one of six children of a Presbyterian minister. In 1914 he was graduated from Hobart College. For the next three years he taught high school in Englewood, New Jersey, while doing graduate work at Columbia in history and economics.[3] He impressed people as an idealist, partly because of his strong feeling against entering the war.[4] Nevertheless when war came he became an officer and thus inadvertently fell into his career.

Assigned to Fort Dix, Ellis ran a post newspaper and helped Edgar Doll in the psychological testing program. In 1919, when Doll joined the Department, he brought Ellis with him. Ellis, then twenty-six, worked in the psychiatric clinic at the State Hospital and did most of the leg work in setting up the classification system in the state prison and later at Rahway. Industrious and level-headed, he did a good job; when Doll, who wanted to get back into research, went to Vineland, Ellis took his place and soon became director of classification and education. As such he was one of Lewis' principal advisers, and in fact did a good deal of Lewis' work as the latter got involved in the critical years 1924 and 1925.[5]

Ellis as Administrator

Ellis' recommendation, then, was that he already knew more about the particular institutions and the central office than anyone else. Personally he was usually pleasant, although he could be strict; he was self-effacing and rather reserved; he kept his own counsel. Beneath his unpretentious appearance was an idealist who, like many idealists, learned to love power. There was nothing vainglorious about him. He wanted results rather than a personal triumph, friends rather than enemies, in short, power rather than its appearance.

As an administrator, he saw the office in terms of persons and jobs, not offices and functions. He wanted workers who felt directly responsible to him. He was kind and considerate of his associates, interested in their lives and families. His genius was to discover and use abilities, while circumventing faults, to encourage and help rather than to criticize. In these ways he plainly modeled himself after Ed Johnstone of Vineland, whom he called "Uncle Ed" and whose protégé he was.[6]

Ellis was in that sense a team man, and years after his death he powerfully stirred the imagination of his team. All would remember a distance between him and them, but it is suggestive that each would also see his own qualities in the boss. A good-natured, sentimental woman who knew him for years recalled that he was "just a good, good man, that's all. And his wife, she just adored him." "Ellis was a tyrant!" —this from a hard-boiled, masterful man—"He had everything and everybody under his thumb. A great practical psychologist! The greatest I ever saw." A student of office politics observed that "Mr. Ellis always had a thoughtful word for you. It showed how well you stood. But he never missed a trick." An idealist: *"Ellis* was interested in *program."* A reflective man, with an analytical bent: "When a problem came up there would be a conference. Ellis would sit back, not saying much, chewing on his cigar, looking here, there, sort of half listening while the others talked and argued, keeping to himself. Then he would put his hands down on the table and say, 'All right, this is the situation.' And that *was* the situation."

As an administrator Ellis could draw on great personal gifts. One was his youth, vigor, and absorption in the work; aged thirty-four when he became commissioner, he had already spent seven years in the Department. Aided perhaps by these associations, his memory was remarkable. He was not given to hesitation or finicking discriminations. "He dictated at about two hundred words a minute," one stenographer remembered. "And he mumbled." Given a Department small and intimately known to begin with, he could, as the Department grew, unfold these gifts with cumulative effect.

When Ellis took over he did not propose to change the plan of the Department or its general theory. He would carry on the basic program of centralization and expansion as Lewis and the State Board had conceived it.[7] He had, therefore, the same practical problems Lewis faced: to minimize conflict with the local boards and grow in their confidence; to avoid occasion for criticism by the legislature and to grow in its confidence.

On both counts, the problems might have been construed as Lewis understood them, as problems in public relations. While there is no document that reveals what went on in Ellis' mind, events suggest that he characteristically saw the situation in personal and particular terms. In fact, he continued to do most of the things Lewis did, but there was a decisively different quality about the work.

Lewis had conceived of public relations as an effort to create widespread support for his work and to organize it for political pressure. He thought of himself as an "advertising man" addressing a mass audience, and as a rallying point for interested groups. Consequently, he was interested in formal public relations: a press agent; a numbered series of press releases; a campaign; using the movies, the radio, public school classes—a deliberate, imaginative use of "the mass media," as men later called them.

Ellis had little interest in formal public relations. He did not develop a systematic information service. Only twice during his term did the Department issue comprehensive reports of its work, and these were perfunctory summaries.[8] An editor once himself, he personally checked every press release, chewing his cigar and stabbing the copy with his pencil. He liked newspapermen and recruited some associates from among them; when he did hire a public relations official, in 1937, his choice was a veteran reporter in particularly good personal standing with newspapermen at Trenton.

Whatever he thought about the formalities of public relations, it is obvious that Ellis lost no chance to exercise his practical psychology in person. He spoke frequently in public; no orator, he was content to read speeches prepared by other hands, but people listened to him. He spent a good deal of time visiting the institutions; often he combined trips with unofficial stops to cultivate friends, board members, public officials. In his undramatic way he became one of the best-known men in the state.

It happened that when Ellis became commissioner in 1926 the situation seemed to call for just such a program. The Bright Commission and Governor Moore had revealed plenty of hostility toward the Department and there was much talk about changing it. But, significantly, there was no action. As a realist like Ellis must have seen, this result did not depend on a favorable "public opinion." It was the consequence of

Republican majorities in the legislature, particularly in the Senate. They might be divided among themselves, but on the whole they would support the Department, and they were not disposed to listen very much to the suggestions of a Democratic governor, or any governor at all, for that matter.

Hence, Ellis must have seen the problem quite differently from Lewis. The latter thought of creating public support that would persuade the legislators—an enormous job, considering the undeniable ignorance and apathy of the man on the street and the sinister maneuvering of "petty politicians." There is no record of what Ellis actually thought, but he characteristically might have recognized that since the Department's strength lay in the legislature, his problem was simply to win over opponents and make new friends among the men who actually made the decisions.

Since Republicans ruled the legislature, Ellis might have chosen, or might have been forced, to align himself with them. The essence of his situation was that he did not want to or need to. The Republicans were split, so Democrats sometimes held the balance of power and they managed to elect governors. Democrats were themselves split, of course. There was, in short, no coherent party organization, but only factions. The wisest course was to work with them all. This was possible because the dominant Republican faction and leadership—Walter Edge, for example—really believed in nonpartisan board control.[9] So did Ellis, passionately, because it gave him a free hand, effective autonomy. Other factions, learning that they could not have their way anyhow, had everything to gain and nothing to lose from "nonpartisan" administration.

The point is that the political situation, rather than "public opinion," supported the autonomy of the Department. Had the governor had more power, or the Democrats a proportionate representation in the legislature, or either party a cohesive organization and point of view, the results might have been different. Consciously or not Ellis understood this situation, and his personal qualities encouraged him to exploit it fully. His public relations were simply what Lewis had described as "the old political way . . . advancing a step here, a step there."[10]

Whatever the reason, the Department dropped out of the news. The State Board publicized a decision to change priorities on its building program, postponing again the psychopathic hospital that had been the key to its program for mental health. Instead it decided to build a new prison to end crowding at the State Prison and Rahway. The stated reason was an alarming rise in the convict population.[11] Perhaps it was coincidence that Ellis had been primarily interested in the prison, while Lewis had been especially proud of the mental hospitals' work; certainly opponents of "frills, fads, and fancies" would find less to criticize in a new reformatory.

The half-mill tax got past a veto in 1926.[12] As prosperity spread among the urban middle class and the shore counties in 1927, the tax whisked through easily.[13] Capitalizing on this euphoria, the board proposed a new ten-year plan to supplement the "emergency" program nearing completion.[14] The tax passed easily the following two years. Even after the crash the tax went through in 1930, and that fall the Department easily carried a $10 million bond issue to complete its program and furnish jobs to the unemployed (the old argument held up better this time).[15]

In all, Jersey's expenditures for institutional construction between 1923 and 1936 totaled almost $30 million.[16] These funds paid for the Training School at Totowa (opened 1928); the Reformatory at Annandale (opened 1929); a third mental hospital, not a central diagnostic hospital but the institution at Marlboro, built to relieve pressure on Greystone Park and the county hospitals of North Jersey (opened 1931); the Soldiers' Home at Menlo Park (opened 1932); the prison farm at Bordentown (opened 1937); and a considerable expansion of the existing plant, including provision for clinics for TB and mental illness.

Surveys of Administration, 1929 and 1932

All this was evidence of success with the legislature. Concerning the internal working of the Department evidence is equally plain. In 1929 the National Institute of Public Administration (NIPA) made a comprehensive and able study of the entire state government. Its point of departure was the problem of accounting and economy in a congeries of ninety-four independent boards and commissions, but it very quickly got into the question of finance and control. Its general conclusion was that the system was an administrative monstrosity.[17] It noted some bright spots, "due largely to the ability and initiative of department heads," but it observed that their success rested on their becoming "more or less self-contained units" which often were, correctly, it said, called "supergovernments."[18] The report singled out Ellis and noted the loyalty, morale, and individual efficiency of his staff, although it observed that his so-called bureaus were not carefully distinguished, described, or related to the overall organization.[19]

In line with its general thought that state agencies ought to be organized to make responsibility definite and supervision effective, the report recommended abolishing the institutional boards of managers. (It did not mention the State Board of Control.) Its argument was that the State Board was not really responsible; it was "not inclined" to "enforce its own mandate on local boards . . . except on rare occasions." It particularly criticized "budgeting by compromise," lack of central accounting, and awkward, unnecessary, and uneconomical diversity in institutional practices. By contrast, it pointed to the state use system, unequivocally under the State Board, as showing the "most rapid and efficient progress."[20] Senator Abell, Chairman of the State

Audit and Finance Commission, which sponsored the study, appeared at a party for Ellis and spoke informally of the high praise investigators had for the Department.[21]

Of course, Governor Morgan F. Larson and the statesmen around him felt that the NIPA report advanced "theories applicable only to a laboratory model government, not to a flesh and blood one." [22] Knowledgeable observers thought the plan "futile" because it ignored "the realities of New Jersey politics." [23] So the Department would keep a "dedicated fund," created by the special tax and then the bond issue, which the NIPA report said was bad policy; it would also keep the local boards.[24]

As the depression deepened, the realities of Jersey politics became less clear; in November 1931, Governor A. Harry Moore was swept into a second term (the constitution forbade his succeeding himself in 1928) and brought with him a Democratic Assembly. Governor Moore and his allies held that the chief executive should have more responsibility for the conduct of government. They revived the NIPA proposals, altered them somewhat, and hustled appropriate legislation through the Assembly.[25] Not only did they seek to eliminate all boards of managers, but they proposed to separate hospital and penal institutions in separate departments each under an expert. In this they followed the pattern set by New York under Governors Alfred E. Smith and Franklin D. Roosevelt—both friends of welfare and exemplary party men.[26]

In defense of this plan rose old Dr. Frank Moore, former superintendent at Rahway, who, remarking the difficulty in getting statistics, offered some which proved that New York did the job cheaper per capita. Commissioner Ellis in turn offered figures indicating that per capita costs in New Jersey were actually less and the quality of work, as indicated by discharge rates from mental hospitals, was superior.[27]

Statistical comparisons of this sort are especially slippery, but newspapers were favorable to the Department.[28] An editorial in the *Newark News* noted, in regard to the supposed efficiency of one-man control, that the Department had "the closest approach to one-man control . . . in the state government. The . . . controller is Commissioner Ellis, who has a good record." [29] The decisive fact, of course, was that the Senate remained under the control of Republicans who said the Democrats' reorganization plan was simply a patronage grab for Boss Frank Hague, for whom Moore spoke.[30]

At Governor Moore's request, Princeton University then made "a comprehensive survey of the operation of the [state] government . . . with a view to recommending economies . . . without impairing essential services." The report, submitted December 30, 1932, commended the Department's central office highly, although it, too, noticed that the formal structure was not carefully distinguished, described, or related to the organization. It also commended the system of local boards.[31]

Thus the second major inquiry in three years praised the Department's work. A year later Governor Moore lauded its "vigorous and concerted action" and "impressive demonstration of fine service and real accomplishment," its "effective cooperation" in public works programs and in achieving "important and extensive economies" of operation.[32] The governor soon became a personal friend of the Commissioner.

The depression, stretching across the years, gave a new prestige and understanding to public officials who dealt with the unfortunate. General provision for the aged came under the Department's direction, beginning with a state old-age assistance program in 1931, much expanded by joining the federal social security system in 1936.[33] Hitherto its work with dependent children, aged veterans, and the blind had seemed peripheral to the problems of prisons and asylums; during the 1930's it became conventional to think of "welfare" as a third kind of function. Reorganization plans offered in 1942 might have contemplated establishing three separate agencies instead of the two suggested in 1932. As counties and municipalities also expanded their programs, the Department staff, blessed with long tenure and good morale, became useful in all sorts of informal ways.

By the mid-thirties, the Department was not only "established" but had become a considerable power. It received universal approbation. It stood well with the legislature. Its construction plan was largely realized, not according to the original plan, but in some respects more lavishly. It enjoyed bipartisan support.[34] No charge of corruption blemished its record. There was a significant change of relations with the legislature. After the first years, Ellis rarely handled legislative business himself: well-chosen subordinates spoke for him. The drift of stories suggests that traffic between the Department and legislators had changed; instead of Department officials going to the solons one hears increasingly of legislators appearing in the Department to ask help, advice, or a favor. Office workers could easily spot the green hands who came in and asked to see "Bill" about some important matter (William J. Ellis was "John" to his friends).

Certainly the record suggests that the Department was, as its founders had hoped, "out of politics." Yet it was also ensconced in a political situation that was generally unwholesome. The root of the trouble was the antiquated constitution of 1844, which decreed that, in time, the legislature would be unrepresentative, the governor not responsible, and the whole affair held together by a patchwork of undemocratic faction and vested interest.[35] In this anarchy the Department had made itself stable, honest, effective; in this power vacuum, it was a power.

Ellis and the State Board

The main trend of political progress in the 1940's, however, was for constitutional revision in the direction of executive leadership and responsibility, and more generally, toward greater party responsibility. The surveys which had sanctioned the Department's work in 1925, 1929, and 1932 had all condemned the government organization as a whole.

Consequently the idea of "independent" or "nonpartisan" boards came under renewed criticism from sources that could not be associated with the *bête noire* of "Hague-ism." It was as part of a general attack on independent and irresponsible agencies that Governor Charles Edison in 1942 criticized the system of board control. His immediate provocation was that the State Board had ignored his suggestions about appointments to the boards; its selections "did not take sufficient account of the various walks of life and interests" in the state, he said; State Board members were "determined to keep out people who were not of their set." [36] The boards were therefore unrepresentative and not responsible to the elected head of state; they were also meaningless because, although the Department was "supposed to be run by a central board of control, . . . in actual fact it [was] run by the commissioner." He thought that the boards should have more labor leaders and representatives of minority groups—in a word, more Democrats—and said that the difficulty had been "smoldering for months." Ellis duly apologized for sending out the appointments, and pleaded a misunderstanding.[37]

It seems that both charges were substantially correct, although there was no occasion to put a partisan interpretation upon them. By 1932 Ellis had clearly pulled the Department out of the fire; thereafter no fundamental questions arose about the general scheme. Ellis' mastery of detail and "practical psychology" simply compelled his recognition as master of the house.[38]

There is no doubt, either, that Ellis found his board useful and valuable. Businessmen, lawyers, physicians, politicians, and other dignitaries who served on it were obviously helpful for their professional understanding, advice, and influence. For example Frank Fetridge, who served for years as a representative of organized labor, was helpful in explaining issues raised by unions.

Even when the Board was new and its policies not clearly determined, members were often as useful for the sanction of their prestige as for their contributions as directors. Dwight Morrow, the first chairman, preoccupied by his wartime work, attended only four of its first eighteen meetings and only one of the first ten executive committee meetings. He was reluctant to continue in this role and did so only because of the frank plea that his prestige was needed.[39]

The services of the Board were many and varied, but it appears that two members were especially important in the commissioner's view, because of their long association with the work and their zeal and ability. Ellis P. Earle had shown no particular interest in the institutions' work before he was appointed chairman of the commission which studied the state's mental hospitals and charitable agencies in 1917. Born in Brooklyn in 1860, he had attended public schools there and a private preparatory school in Elizabeth. At eighteen he began clerking in a law office; at twenty-one he married and joined his father-in-law in the business of manufacturing metal paint. At thirty-eight he retired from this business, already wealthy, and organized his own firm; presently his interests changed from mining and metals to banking (Manufacturers Trust), petroleum, insurance, and real estate.[40]

Earle was fifty-eight when he helped organize the State Board in 1918. Mrs. Thompson quickly noted that he was "thoroughly interested and refuses to see any obstacles in his path"; he headed the committee which selected the first commissioner, who was, Mrs. Thompson observed, "largely of his choice." [41] In 1922 he was elected chairman of the State Board, a position he held until his death in 1942.

The Department became a pet of his old age, and Commissioner Ellis was like a son to him. The two men were not much alike. Earle was an elegantly imposing man, never without a fresh carnation in his lapel. He was dignified—even his wife called him "Mr. Earle"—and he could be imperious. In 1923, for example, he wrote the organizer of the Citizens' Committee suggesting bluntly that the group might disband if it couldn't back the Board's four-year program.[42] A secretary was once startled to hear him scold a governor over the phone; the governor had asked to be excused from answering the telephone during a luncheon, but Earle would not be denied. "Governor," he said when the call went through, "you know I have no personal favor or political request to make. My interest is simply the welfare of the state's wards and the public interest, and if you don't put these things first now you had better learn to." [43] This is the act of a powerful and righteous man, to say the least.

What the chairman and the commissioner had in common was a clear focus on the practical, personal, particular elements of a situation, and a desire for the fact of power, not mere fame. No more than Ellis was Earle interested in an elaborate formal public relations program. Earle was a man of large affairs, and men of affairs do not, or did not then, address themselves to "the public." They reach for the phone: "Mr. Earle was always on the phone," a secretary remembers. There was a switchboard in his Wall Street office. "He would call in from New York two, three, four, five times a day to talk to Mr. Ellis." Earle was a generous entertainer, often at the Railroad Club in New York or on a trip, by private train, to his hunting lodge in Arkansas. He sent his secretary in the Department roses bright and early Christmas morning; insiders in the Department thought that if he gave a man a diamond stickpin, that man would be the next governor; he was in any case a generous campaign contributor.[44]

The responsibilities of wealth kept Earle close to Wall Street during the week, but on weekends he and Ellis would be off visiting the institutions together. Board members received copies of the monthly reports from institutional superintendents. Earle read these with close attention to detail, questioning prices or purchases, comparing them with earlier reports.

Mrs. Geraldine Livingston Thompson served on the State Board from its organization until 1957, when she entered a breathlessly active retirement. Her grandmother had been a pioneer prison reformer in New

York, and her two sisters were leaders in causes dear to reformers. Mrs. Thompson was no stranger to wealth; born in Washington Square, as a girl she played baseball with Franklin Roosevelt at Hyde Park and Staatsburg, her home, and she married Lewis Thompson, a wealthy sportsman.[45] "I don't need to listen to these investment counselors," she once told a friend, "I heard all about it when I was a little girl at the dinner table." The consciousness of wealth gave her a sense of social responsiblity, which found direction in her feminist heritage and her religious ideal of service. The only girl on the Staatsburg baseball team grew up to be a whirlwind of energy and zeal; she loved getting into things, seeing them through, taking sides, recalling and discovering the good in life, about which she had no doubts. In short, she loved life.

Mrs. Thompson's public career was divided between Republican politics—she was the first National Committeewoman from New Jersey—and philanthropy. After the Thompsons moved to Red Bank she became the moving spirit of the Monmouth County chapter of the State Charities Aid Association, its most active and successful chapter, later transformed into the Monmouth County Organization for Social Service, a superior welfare agency. She was very active in the organization of the Department in 1918, and she appears much more frequently in the correspondence of Chairman Morrow than any other board member. This early zeal continued; she became particularly interested in the local boards, defending them in principle, and diligent in recruiting their membership.[46]

There would seem to be a contradiction between Mrs. Thompson's own enthusiastic political partisanship and her unwavering belief in the principle of voluntary lay boards to keep politics out of welfare work. The solution lay in her belief in participation. "I want someone to say that no government, nor government department, nor political experiment can have more vitality than springs from community or individual support," she wrote to Dwight Morrow in 1920, asking him to address her Monmouth County organization. Success in any public undertaking, she said, had to rest on "a self-conscious effort toward practical knowledge and responsibility"; if leaders could awaken "such a spirit of service to the state and one's neighbors . . . there would be only hope for the future." [47] She did not have in mind the participation of the hired hands, who might have a personal or vested interest to promote, but rather the voluntary efforts of good citizens whose interest was unequivocally in the long-run public good. Voluntary participation in this sense was of course primarily the responsibility of people who had the opportunity and spirit for service.

Mrs. Thompson made it her business to see that the best people went into politics and also on the boards; with good people in both kinds of work there should be no conflict. She was a strenuous partisan and campaigned unhesitatingly against Franklin D. Roosevelt (whose team had always lost to the Staatsburg nine); but she cherished her friendship with Democrats such as her dear friends Caroline Alexander Wittpenn and Eleanor Roosevelt. They were her kind of Democrats, and she was pleased when Eleanor wrote Governor Moore in 1932 and 1934 asking him not to drop her from the State Board, as he had intended. (The governor reconsidered.)[48]

Supporting her interest in voluntary participation by good citizens were two realistic insights. A woman of affairs, Mrs. Thompson knew very well the importance of enlisting influential people in the good cause, and she knew from long personal experience that political appointments were political payoffs. Later she would develop reservations about the "professionals" who qualified for the work. No technical training, she thought, could substitute for the spirit of service.

Mrs. Thompson's perceptive enthusiasm for projects, ideas, and people kept matters lively, and so did the meetings of illustrious philanthropists which she often convoked for her causes. If the Commissioner and his staff might wonder "What now?" when she hove in sight, they could also see the generosity of her spirit and her quick, witty shrewdness about practical matters. Like Earle, she faithfully read the monthly superintendents' reports; she liked to see things at first hand and ranged the state to see them.

Whatever the theory of board control, Ellis found in these people a dedication and resourcefulness that matched his own. In this close, understanding, personal oversight lay the secret of the Department's morale and its achievements.

Local Boards and Institutions

Local board members were selected by the "big board," subject to the approval of the governor, which by Edison's time had become perfunctory. The procedure of selection was informal. Likely candidates were always in demand; in general, they were assigned in relation to what a particular board seemed to need, a physician, perhaps, or a woman, or a Democrat, or someone from a particular county. A candidate of course agreed to his selection, but people who really volunteered, who suggested their own appointment, were often disappointed. Reappointment by the State Board was not automatic; the members' interest and attendance were inquired into, informally. Nevertheless, longtime members were kept on even when they grew too old. Often the problem seemed to be to get a board working; old members and superintendents tended to dominate them.[49]

Ellis looked upon the institutional boards as local in a physical sense, that is, people who lived near an institution and who could see, understand, and explain a situation there which might call down criticism. Criticism often came from the neighborhood of the institution, and it was good to have reliable and well-known persons at hand to make a statement if a question arose.

Ellis did not condescend to local boards, however; his associates often got the impression that he was more solicitous of their ideas and intentions than of his own board's. When he first rose as adviser to Lewis he appeared to one institutional superintendent as "a young theorist, entirely inexperienced in the management of institutions" who caused "a widening gap" between Commissioner Lewis and the people in charge of particular institutions.[50] But certainly the complaints about centralization which Governor Moore voiced in 1926 and which echoed for a few years presently died out; they were no part of the criticism in 1932 or 1942.

Trouble with local boards was usually rooted in the superintendents, and Ellis took steps to win them over. The central office ordinarily played a large part in their choice and had at least to approve them. Ellis not only visited the institutions frequently but set aside Mondays to see his institutional executives in the office. Apart from his personal acquaintance with them, his staff, as it gained experience, brought understanding cooperation in the matters of accounts and budgeting, inspection, legal affairs, farm supervision, and the other services that were centralized.

In the work of winning over institutions, and also legislators, Ellis' principal official assistant was Francis X. "Spike" Gerry, who, as chief budget officer, visited the institutions frequently and dealt with the appropriations committee. The men complemented one another. Ellis was reserved and rather puritanical; Spike was an affable man of heroic conviviality. He was also a wizard at finding the boss an extra dollar in the shoestring budgets of the depression years.[51] The most famous of Ellis' assistants, however, was Dr. Ellen C. Potter, sometime head of the Pennsylvania Welfare Department and president of the National Conference of Social Work, who joined Ellis in 1927, when political changes cost her the Pennsylvania job. Technically, she was head of the Division of Medicine, but she was also Ellis' live line to the world of social workers and welfare councils.[52]

So, by the middle 1930's, the goals of the founders were, after a fashion, achieved. On paper, matters were not much different from the critical days of 1921, 1925, or 1932; what had happened was that the notions of board control, centralized direction and non- or bipartisan political support were realized in the memory, understanding, and harmonious expectations of a particular group of people. At the center sat the commissioner. The boards were filled with people with whom he could work. The central office was staffed largely with men he had selected, doing for him jobs he wanted done.

Close supervision did not mean interference; as time went on Ellis' staff felt quite autonomous. They were for the most part younger than the boss and enjoyed the physical and mental vitality of the early middle years; to this was added the confidence of long association and the sense of competence. Their recollections are full of office jokes, office characters, office crises somehow surmounted. There were occasional formal celebrations to bring them together. The boss didn't drink or approve of drinking, so these were decorous affairs until he left, discreetly early.

Then, with comic abruptness, the scene brightened. Once he returned unexpectedly after a few minutes—the story goes—and there was everybody at the bar. (The narrator smiles, shaking his head "No.") And sometimes, when it was plain that the boss would not return that afternoon and Their Highnesses on the Board were fashionably engaged, the public servants would display their talents in a social hour. Did good Mr. Ellis, tyrant and practical psychologist, miss that trick? Probably not; of course not. (The narrator shifts awkwardly, unwilling to give History a bad impression, unable to explain how the situation really was without getting awfully complicated about people and about how government offices or any offices for that matter work.)

The cardinal fact remained unspoken, not even, perhaps, clearly conscious: Ellis trusted his staff; they trusted him; there were problems—no mere office party or friendly drink at lunch, either—but there were also virtues and in any case there was understanding. Decades later people would ramble on, one story leading to the next, then impatiently or self-consciously gesture or sigh, saying, after a pause, "it was"—lamely, aware of the cliché—"a nice place to work."

The Problem of Public Relations

Certain impersonal factors contributed significantly to Ellis' success. Apart from the political situation, the cycle of boom and depression was favorable first to the Department's expansion and then to its stability. New Jersey was relatively well off during the depression. Its population growth was sharply reduced; inmate caseload rose, but its pressure was less than it had been in the 1920's or would be after the war. Deflation and unemployment during the depression helped the status of employees, even of the attendants in the institutions; here too problems were slighter than at any other time.

The war ended these advantages and left the plant dilapidated; the postwar boom and inflation raised a new order of difficulty. The drive for constitutional reform succeeded; in it the Department would remain unaltered, but its boards would seem increasingly anachronistic. Ellis Earle died in 1942; Reeve Schley, appointed to succeed him, was an enormously successful businessman who left a wartime position with Lend-Lease to devote his time to the Department. He had been on the Board since 1936; his selection was "regarded as assurance that . . . policies would be continued." [53] Mrs. Thompson lost none of her vigor but other old-timers on the Board did. It was always difficult to remove old people from an honorary position in which they had served with distinction. As for the younger generation, Mrs. Thompson worried over whether they would attain the influence of Mrs. Wittpenn, whether high taxes and professionalism had not blighted the spirit of service.

Ellis' death, on March 11, 1945, was a shock. He had fortunately been rewarded in his lifetime; apart from his prestige he had earned a decent salary, $10,000 a year to start, soon raised to $15,000, then, in 1929, when a private concern offered to double that, he got full maintenance in addition. Earle helped him with investments and left him a generous bequest.[54] Public service had not cost him what it has cost so many others.

His death was unexpected and, because of the personal quality of his administration, it left many ends dangling. He had done too much himself, his associates thought; he did not set up a chain of command or a bureaucratic SOP. He hesitated to fire incompetents, preferring to make the best of them and reluctant to make a fuss. He had "handled" the State Board himself, with only occasional reliance on his staff; the Board saw what happened in the office only through his eyes. No successor could take his place or find it easy to pick up where Ellis left off.

But where did Ellis leave off? That is, where was he going? In 1944 he reviewed his twenty-five years in the Department. The advances he chose to mention were the development of preventive and clinical work and of the classification system. The record he cites is impressive but includes no critical comment. Were the mental hospitals curing people? Were they notable centers of advanced research and treatment? Were their clinics substantially filling the need? Were the reformatories reforming? Was their system of classification, education, and parole really effective? How did one even measure their effectiveness or their possibilities?

Ellis' article, "Public Welfare in New Jersey, 1630–1944," published the year he died, was organized around three "historic trends": First, he said, specialized institutions were devised to handle the varieties of deviation. Second, their cost and administration were increasingly shared; private institutions became public, local institutions were supplemented or replaced by state and national agencies. Third, the specialized institutions were coordinated or integrated by some sort of centralized agency, whether local, state, or national, "so that the benefits of specialization [would] not lead to unnecessary diffusion of energy and to assure equable treatment of all types of economic and social problems." [55] From his perspective, the main tasks of the future seemed to be three: more care for the chronically ill, particularly among the aged; elaboration of social security; community programs to prevent delinquency and reduce crime. In each case, progress would involve the three levels of government in "perplexing problems of administration and control" which only experimentation and cooperation could solve.[56]

As a clue to Ellis' thinking at the end of his career, this document needs some qualification. Its true author was not Ellis, but his long-time friend and coworker, Douglas MacNeil, and its subject was "public welfare in New Jersey," not the Department. But Ellis signed and approved it, it does deal extensively with the Department, and it does not conflict with any other evidence.

In general, the article indicates how much Ellis was preoccupied in 1945 by such issues of the depression as relief, security, and the bureaucratic problems of integrating and coordinating welfare work. He mentions in passing the importance of "scientific treatment methods," the system of classification, education, and parole, and the clinics but, there is no suggestion that the programs of mental hospitals or correctional institutions had any shortcomings. The assumption is that the Department was on the right track and had only to stay there. Its achievements are not considered critically with reference to a goal; no new goals for this work are discussed. The need for further facilities is mentioned only in connection with "a post-war public works program designed to minimize the economic impact of demobilization." Nor is there any suggestion that the Department's organization, after twenty-five years, needed any reconsideration; the essay concludes with an explicit and uncompromising affirmation of the principle of a single department and the system of board control.[57]

There was, in short, mixed with Ellis' justifiable pride, a degree of complacency or a want of candor. Edward R. Cass, general secretary of the Prison Association of New York and a judicious observer, recalled that representatives of the Department "thought so well of themselves in the days of my good friend John Ellis, it was sacrilege to be critical of New Jersey in any way." [58] On the other hand, Ellis was too intelligent and secure to need false pride; facts, not appearances, were the ballast and wind by which he sailed. If we ask what large fact underlay the want of self-criticism, the answer is not that he was deluded, by himself or anyone else, into ignoring imperfections. Thinking in terms of the practical and possible, he was confident that he was achieving what he could realistically hope for.

Just as he accepted the faults of his coworkers and tried to fit them as they were into his work, so he accepted the political status of the Department and turned it to his purposes; he suited the demands he could make to the material he worked with. Just as his colleagues trusted and admired him, so did the legislators on whom he depended for funds. His administration was economical, honest, progressive; legislators could trust him, and did. At the same time, he learned not to ask for too much; he could see things both from the view of his staff and the local institutions, and also from that of governors and legislators. If there were corners to cut, he would cut them; if there were temporary halts to call, he would call them. Ellis—and Earle and Mrs. Thompson—knew the Department literally from the ground up; they had seen it grow; they had endured many crises. They could take a long view; things were going as well as could be expected. Ellis of course never delivered himself of his private thoughts, but an associate and protégé put it this way: Did the legislature ever take an intelligent, courageous, far-sighted view of the state's needs? "Hell no. . . . But that's all right. Look, I like those guys. They're my buddies. I see their point of view. They have their problems. They give us what they can, as much as they can. Things are improving, gradually. I'm not mad at anybody. We're going to be around here for a long time. That's the way I see it." Would Ellis or Spike Gerry have seen it differently?

In short, responsibility and power implied preoccupation with the administrative status quo. The system did work reasonably well. There was no pressing need for discussion of long-run ends and means or for a dramatic vision to focus issues and challenge the imagination—or the hostility—of other powers. In its external relations as in its internal organization, the Department reflected the character of its chief.

No one looking forward from 1918 would have predicted this situation. The argument about public welfare in the nineteenth century had turned on supervision or control, in which supervision meant a public discussion of problems and alternatives, a defining of ends and a candid criticism of means. This had been one purpose of the State Charities Aid Association and of the state commissioner of charities and corrections. The founders of the Department, bypassing this discussion and taking administrative control for granted, had concerned themselves with how to protect it from politics and how to minimize the risks of centralization. Even so, the Morrow Commission had emphasized that the fundamental problem was to create enlightened public opinion and support—that was the essential purpose of its lay boards—and its first executive had thought his work was analogous to that of a business executive who had to sell the public on long-run economy.

Before 1918, there had been two annual surveys of welfare work in the state, by the State Charities Aid Association and the commissioner, and each institution had published an annual report. After 1919 the state legislature ended the publication of these and all state reports, to save money, and the SCAA, considering that the new Department realized its hopes, disbanded. Henceforth, there was no regular survey of welfare organization. Division heads and institutions had to report monthly, in mimeograph form, and many institutions continued to publish annual reports in various forms. But the State Board and the Commissioner made no regular formal report at all. The State Conference of Charities continued under the sponsorship of the New Jersey Welfare Council but, like the National Conference, it became the vehicle of the expanding profession of social work, concerned largely with private agencies and services; it made no systematic survey of state welfare.

Historically, it was urban charity reformers who had promoted first the specialized state institutions and then state supervision, but as charity organization gave way to professional social work and charities aid gave way to a state department, the mutual interest faded. Social workers concerned themselves with improving the agencies they ran and, more generally, with improving social legislation. Ellis and his assistants concerned themselves primarily with administrative problems and legislative relations.

In short, there was no vehicle for a regular critical review and survey of the state's welfare organization. There was no way for the State Board to inform people of what policy questions it was confronting, if it were so inclined. Moreover, it is a striking fact that no one complained of the lack. Governors did not mention it; neither the publications of the Department nor the minutes of the State Board expressed such a need; nor, for that matter, did surveys by experts on public administration in 1925, 1929, and 1932.

There was no pressure on Ellis or the State Board to publicize policy questions and decisions, and they were free to follow their inclinations. Their inclinations are described in a thesis done in 1938 by a student at the School of Social Service Administration of the University of Chicago, on the Department's interpretation of its work. The author analyzed its publications and spoke at length with Ellis' colleagues. She was told that annual reports were "very expensive and seldom read," so the Department relied on occasional studies of particular problems. These related, she found, to crises or to the enthusiasms of the staff.[59] She was told that "people don't read but they will listen," and that Ellis encouraged his assistants to accept speaking engagements, with professional organizations or local groups.

The writer also noted the Department's efforts to help local agencies and service clubs, especially the American Legion, plan programs and exhibits; she was told that the Department favored "indirect activity" of this sort because it "often hesitates to promote plans [for action or reform] actively fearing criticism . . . that [it] is merely seeking more power and money." She concluded that the Department ought to try to reach "a broad general state audience, not known personally to [its staff]," a "more intangible, yet influentially inactive group, whose lethargy has slowed up state progress." (She acknowledged that this was difficult, because most Jerseymen belonged to metropolitan communities that were centered outside the state.)[60]

When Ellis died in 1945 the Department was solidly established, but its security did not rest upon a public understanding of its problems and possibilities, as later events showed. In any case, there is no suggestion in the record that he or the State Board expected that within a decade the central office would be organized upon different principles and the fundamental notions of a single department and board control would come under renewed questioning. Partly, these changes were efforts to create a better bureaucratic structure in the state government at large as well as in the Department. But partly they arose from a rapid accumulation of experience and insight among the professionals who ran the institutions.

The founders of the Department thought that the great obstacles to progress in public welfare lay in political interference and administrative organization. That was the lesson of their own past and the direction of their interest. It appears today, however, that the problems were not simply political or administrative, but lay in mistaken theories and untrained personnel all along the line, and in pervasive deficiencies in what social workers came to call community organization. To remove these obstacles was far beyond the means of any state welfare department, however organized; to understand them it is necessary to turn from problems at headquarters and consider the services offered by the institutions.

13

Services for the Mentally Ill, 1918–1945

In the minds of its founders, the new Department was intended to improve the administration of the several institutions and to unify their development. Its main power was the authority to submit a common budget. For the rest, the commissioner was supposed to stimulate good management in the institutions, and to this end he was authorized to employ experts to advise him on common institutional problems, such as diet and inmate labor. As for program, the founders wanted reformatories to reform and hospitals to cure, but they did not venture to say how. Good management and enlightened leadership would, presumably, clarify that problem. They evidently assumed that the superintendents and local boards would take the initiative.

When the Department issued its first public "summary report," in 1922, the "policy of treatment and prevention" was given first place among its "basic principles." [1] Treatment, as distinct from custody, was a medical notion; the idea of prevention, which neither the Morrow nor the Earle commissions had explicitly mentioned, was associated with medicine—with legislation to prevent TB, for example—and it was also gaining currency in social work, particularly with reference to casework with juvenile delinquents. In 1934, Commissioner Ellis began the Department's second summary report by referring to its "increasing emphasis on the advantages of a program of rehabilitation and prevention." [2] As Ellis well understood by that time, a program of prevention and rehabilitation required a system of community clinics or diagnostic services and aftercare, parole, or rehabilitation services that raised problems of a different order from those of intramural program and management.

What linked, or should have linked, the institutional program and the extramural program was a theory about the problem. Theories tell what to look for, what to expect and why. Programs, whether inside or outside an institution, are efforts to intervene in a situation and change it toward some desired end. In a rational program the directors answer the questions, "What do you think is wrong? What do you propose to do? What do you think will happen?" Practical men confront conditions, not theories, as they always like to say, and the situation is rarely simple or clear. Nevertheless, the questions are a reasonable beginning for a study of how the people charged with institutional programs in New Jersey did in fact go about their business, and how their experience changed their thinking.

The Mental Hospitals

When the State Board took over, hospital care for the insane was divided between two state hospitals and nine county asylums. Three of the county asylums (Gloucester, Passaic, and Salem) were specialized almshouses; two (Hudson and Essex) were comparable with the state institutions. There was no clear line of policy to relate them. The managers of Morris Plains and Trenton were notorious rivals for appropriations. Morris Plains, which drew its patients from a geographical district that included the most populous cities, held more than 2,700 patients in buildings designed to care for 1,650, and slept them in the halls at night. Trenton was less crowded, testifying in part to its managers' success with the legislature.[3] Obviously, some reorganization, some repair and new construction, was necessary. What kind of action and why? How did the theory of mental illness bear on the decision?

Theory was not much help. The rise of scientific medicine inclined doctors to look for somatic causes of mental illness as a basis for planning therapy. Working along these lines, they had discovered syphilis of the nervous system and a treatment that would arrest it. But they had not found other lesions, and it proved difficult even to define and classify the symptoms. Theory said that mental illness had a physical cause or causes, but it could not identify them. What were the implications of this situation for planning buildings?

Many people, lay and professional, concluded that mental hospitals were primarily custodial institutions, and reasoned that therefore custody ought to be as cheap and, hopefully, as pleasant as possible. Progressive psychiatrists felt that such a view would demoralize the asylum doctors. They thought that hospitalization was more successful in institutions that were medical, not overcrowded, and available for early treatment. And of course they wanted to look for better theories.

Both views were reflected in the recommendations of the commission that had reported on the problem in 1914. It had proposed two new types of institutions, different from the existing asylums. One was the farm colony, a frankly custodial institution, simple and economical, like those Ed Johnstone was promoting for the retarded. The other was the psychopathic hospital, a center devoted to intensive treatment and research, usually connected with a training hospital for a medical school, like Boston Psychopathic or the Phipps Clinic at Johns Hopkins.

A person looking ahead in 1918 might have predicted that the new

State Board would reorganize mental hospitals around these types. In 1913, the state had acquired a large farm named Annandale, in the peaceful hills of Hunterdon County, for a farm colony to relieve overcrowding at Morris Plains. Ed Johnstone had inspired the 1914 commission's report and Dr. John Nevin, on the Board of Managers of the Trenton Hospital and later on the State Board, had signed it. Commissioner Lewis, on his part, visualized the psychopathic hospital as the key to a program of institutional development, a center and clearinghouse for diagnosis, classification, intensive treatment, teaching, and publicity.[4]

In fact, the state's large investment in hospitals in the next decade went neither for farm colonies nor for a psychopathic hospital. The Annandale property was held to be too distant from Morris Plains, and no other farm colony was proposed.[5] Farm colonies would have diverted funds from the obvious needs of existing state institutions, and they would also have replaced or absorbed the custodial asylums of rural counties. On the other hand a new psychopathic hospital built, as Lewis proposed, in metropolitan North Jersey would have relegated existing institutions to a second class.

Meanwhile, the State Board asked the National Committee for Mental Hygiene to survey the mental hospitals. Its report, in 1921, revealed a degree of dilapidation and neglect that the Earle Commission had not recognized. Concerning Morris Plains, the investigators observed: "From the early days . . . , it is clear that . . . public officials have been derelict in their duties to this institution as a hospital for their fellow citizens." The committee also opposed "construction of a cheap and flimsy character"—the farm colony type. When, after the defeat of the bond issue, legislators passed a special tax for the institutions, they specifically restricted its use to expanding Morris Plains.

In a few years a sizable new hospital was built beside the old giant—a reception building and a clinic building, for treatment, large congregate dining halls to free ward space in the old Kirkbride building, new homes for professional staff and their helpers, a great new power plant, barns, greenhouses, a fire station, and many auxiliary buildings, all adding up to a fair-sized town. (In 1924 it was renamed "Greystone Park.") In a way, it was what Lewis had visualized after all: when the work was done John Ellis could brag about how "the old asylum" had become "a real hospital," and it had enlarged farms assiduously cultivated. Undoubtedly, these were new departures or improvements. But the new Greystone Park was more like the old Morris Plains than like Boston Psychopathic.[6]

The Theory of Detoxication

His hope for a program of treatment in a psychopathic hospital made Burdette Lewis interested in the work of Dr. Henry Cotton at Trenton

State Hospital. Cotton argued that it was a mistake to try to link mental illness only to lesions of the brain or nervous system. Any sort of persistent infection, perhaps chronic and unnoticed, could introduce into the blood stream toxins that could in time affect the brain. Many patients had bad teeth and tonsils, for example, no dramatic symptoms, just chronic trouble. Heal them or, more likely, remove them, and the patient's mental symptoms improved. Patient after patient cheered up, settled down, went home cured. But the cure did not always take; sometimes the symptoms recurred and the patients returned. Why? Perhaps because the infection had not been entirely removed. Sure enough, many patients appeared to have unsuspected infections in their stomachs, intestines, or colons. Get at these, generally by major and radical surgery, and the patients showed a dramatic improvement—if they survived, that is, for the mortality rate on major surgery ran well over 30 percent.

But mortality rates could improve along with operative techniques. The important thing was that by applying simple general principles of medical treatment, Dr. Cotton had opened possibilities for diagnosis and research that made a psychopathic hospital of some sort a foregone conclusion. Cotton set forth his theory in the Vanuxem Lectures, delivered at Princeton in 1921. In 1922, the American Psychiatric Association debated it; the following year he addressed the Royal Medico-Psychological Association in London, and English doctors were notably favorable toward his views.[7]

In the Department's summary report in 1922, Commissioner Lewis announced that the discharge rate for patients with functional psychoses, supposed incurable by ordinary medical means, was 65 percent to 70 percent of admissions since Cotton had begun intensive treatment in 1918, as contrasted with a ten-year average of 37 percent; he calculated that the discharges had saved more than $100,000 in costs of maintenance. He noted that Dr. Hubert Work, president of the American Medical Association, had told an audience at the Trenton Hospital that it was like "a general hospital, really the first [state mental hospital] I could approve." [8] The word spread along with the postwar interest in "shell-shock," the mental hygiene movement, and Freudian doctrines. Crowds of private patients came to Dr. Cotton for treatment. Trenton State Hospital could not handle them all, and many were not eligible for its care, so he presently had to arrange private accommodations for them. Even so the number of paying patients considerably helped the hospital's finances, and they were indisputable testimony to its service.

If Dr. Cotton was right, the consensus of medical opinion was wrong or partly wrong. Eventually a test would have to come. In March, 1924, Dr. Joseph Raycroft, the medical director of Princeton University and a member of Dr. Cotton's Board of Managers, wrote to Dr. Paul Mecray, another physician and board member, suggesting a formal investigation of the results of treatment. Some investigation was coming, he thought, and they might best arrange it under their auspices. Dr. Mecray was dubious. "As a doctor you probably know that the records of the Hospital are so incomplete that they would be of no value," he observed, and he feared "a lot of undesirable notoriety." [9]

Raycroft, like Commissioner Lewis, believed in Cotton's work, and the State Board of Control, which wanted Morris Plains to adopt similar methods, saw that validation by an independent inquiry would lend weight to their argument.[10] Raycroft accordingly planned an investigation under the auspices of Dr. Adolph Meyer, the dean of American psychiatrists, who had written a friendly but noncommittal introduction to Cotton's Vanuxem lectures. The first part of the investigation consisted of several kinds of observation of patients who had received surgical treatment, compared with patients who, for various reasons, had not undergone surgery. Dr. Phyllis Greenacre, a young associate of Dr. Meyer at the Phipps Clinic, made the study during the fall and winter of 1924–1925, when she lived at the hospital three days a week.

As she began her work, Dr. Greenacre was presented to a meeting of the hospital board. She was struck by the spirit of the meeting and the enthusiasm in the air. "A woman in the office at the hospital, a former patient, manic-depressive, very enthusiastic about Cotton's work, had put together some statistics showing very favorable results," she recalled much later. "It was an imposing document, blue binding and red tape. After the meeting Dr. Raycroft showed it to me. He said that perhaps Dr. Cotton was over-optimistic, but there had to be something there, he couldn't be entirely wrong, entirely biased." Cotton gave Dr. Greenacre complete cooperation as she went about tracking down patients and interviewing them. She sent copies of her reports to him and to Meyer.[11]

She could not believe what she found. "It was a nightmare," she recalled. "To begin with I looked over this document, and there, on the first page, were gross errors in computation. Nobody had bothered to check." Her reports on patients almost always contradicted Cotton's claims in some respect, if not entirely. Meyer read her reports and was concerned. Cotton seemed to overlook them. He remained cordial and cheerful, as if his reputation were not at stake. She wondered if he read the reports. Often, she found, patients were treated, sent home as improved and cured, then readmitted and given further treatment. They went up and down, as one would expect, but each improvement was counted as a separate case of improvement, even though the general trend was down. Sometimes the records didn't show readmissions as such, and a patient would have several files. Clinical observations were scant and inaccurate, as a basis for experimental validation of a theory, at least. Statistics were uncritical and inaccurate. And yet, most of Dr. Cotton's staff members were as enthusiastic as he. "Here were people, trained professional people, seeing things that just weren't there and saying things that simply weren't so," Dr. Greenacre recalled. "I couldn't believe it. I never recognized the force of contagion of neurotic attitudes to form a veritable group neurosis until I saw it there." [12]

Meanwhile, Senator Bright, out to get Lewis in his investigation of state expenditures, was building a sensation out of horror stories that had come to him from some disaffected employees. He called Dr. Greenacre to testify. Had Dr. Cotton abused patients? he asked her; had he deliberately falsified his results? She said he was innocent on both counts. The Senator did not ask what her own study showed; presumably he was afraid her testimony would support Cotton.[13]

On January 14, 1926, Cotton and Raycroft went to Baltimore to discuss the report with Dr. Meyer. Dr. Greenacre observed that "The immediate effect of operation is often very startling" and postoperative patients acted much improved. "The appearance and atmosphere of the ward for convalescent operative patients really resembled more closely the ward of a general hospital than that of a psychiatric institution." But her conclusions were that the operations, particularly the major surgery, were extremely risky and in the long run the patient's mental condition did not improve after surgical detoxication; it got worse. In other words, Dr. Cotton's claims were mistaken. He was hurting patients, not helping them.[14]

Meyer had gone over her report and approved it. Raycroft, much impressed, asked Cotton for a formal reply. Cotton said he would justify his claims, but he was depressed and disorganized during 1926.[15] In May 1927 he wrote Meyer and made a defense of his work. Meyer remained dubious.[16] The investigation ended there. Its later phases were not carried out. Its results were not made public, but Cotton had already sharply restricted surgery in favor of "massive irrigation" of the colon and other procedures. He also returned to his earlier interest in focal infections of the oral cavity. Meanwhile, John Ellis had become commissioner and Dr. Ambrose Dowd, a distinguished physician from Newark, had joined the State Board. Dowd, who disagreed entirely with Cotton's theories, became chairman of the "Mental Hygiene Committee" of the State Board, which thereafter bent the Department's interest and policy in different directions.[17]

Dr. Cotton's troubles were not over. Wealthy patients continued to come to him for treatment and he maintained what was in effect a private hospital for them. This raised a question of medical ethics. Should a physician, employed and given maintenance by the state, engage in private practice? No, said the organized sons of Asclepius, and they threatened to expel so unethical a character from the Mercer County Medical Association. "It's a question of financial and professional jealousy," Dr. Cotton said, but the State Board did not take the matter so lightly. It asked Commissioner Ellis to convene a meeting of experts to ponder a decision on this grave issue of policy. In due course, it barred physicians in the state employ from private practice—leaving the enforcement of the ruling to local boards.[18] Cotton resigned as of October 1930; he was made "medical director emeritus," without maintenance but with salary ($8,000), to "pursue the research and preventive phases of psychiatric services." [19]

Then, in April 1932, Commissioner Ellis sent to Dr. Emil Frankel, his director of statistics and research, a report by Dr. Cotton that new techniques had much reduced the mortality rate of operations and improved the results. Ellis asked Frankel and Dr. Ellen Potter, head of the Division of Medicine, for an analysis of this report and a comparison of the earlier conclusions reached by Dr. Greenacre and Dr. Cotton. The new analysis gave conclusions "substantially in agreement with . . . Dr. Greenacre's": the more treatment, the poorer the results; untreated patients did better. It was dated November 1932.[20] Dr. Cotton never answered it, if indeed he knew about it. He was already suffering from a heart condition and was confined in the spring of 1933; he seemed to recover, but died suddenly on May 8, a few days before his fifty-seventh birthday.

"Experience has made it necessary to qualify Dr. Cotton's major hypothesis . . . that focal infection of the teeth and colon is the primary cause of mental disease," Ellis said much later, in an article, "Psychiatric Progress in New Jersey, 1844–1944."

> It is now considered to be only one of several factors in the etiology of mental disease. Dr. Cotton's insistance [sic] upon the discovery and correction of abnormal medical and physical conditions however was responsible for a definite improvement in the patients' general condition and in promoting the utilization of all medical resources . . . as an aid to the restoration of mental health. His experiments, moreover, represent a determined and courageous effort to find an organic basis for mental diseases. . . .[21]

Marlboro State Hospital

On January 28, 1926, shortly after Commissioner Lewis resigned and Dr. Greenacre's findings became known to it, the State Board announced that it would postpone construction of a psychopathic hospital and invest instead in the new reformatory at Annandale. The reason given was a sharp rise in the population of correctional institutions, a consequence of the notorious crime waves of the time.[22] But in fact it never mentioned the psychopathic hospital again. Instead the Board's Mental Hygiene Committee began to promote psychopathic wards in general hospitals, which were quite a different matter from an expensive new institution that would serve as a clearing house and focus for a state system. Marlboro State Hospital, begun in 1929, located in Monmouth County just south of the metropolitan area, was conceived simply as a third regional hospital that would relieve crowding in existing state institutions. It represented no departures in policy, but its origin is interesting in three respects.[23]

In the first place, Marlboro was founded without any public discussion of how the state and its counties did and might divide responsibility for care of the insane. Between 1918 and 1931, when it opened, the number of patients in county hospitals had increased by half. Three of the almshouse annexes that the Earle Commission had counted as asylums had closed by 1931, but the six remaining county hospitals housed almost a third of the state's mentally ill. In 1934 the Essex and Hudson County mental hospitals, had almost as many patients as Trenton and Marlboro.

The finances of these institutions were complicated. Indigent patients who had no county settlement went to state hospitals at state expense, but if an indigent patient had a county residence, the county had to provide. (Most patients were indigent.) County officials might send him to a state hospital or keep him in a county hospital. In either case the state paid half the cost of his maintenance. The cost of maintenance varied. In 1931–1932 the daily per capita charge at Greystone Park was $1.21; Trenton, $1.28; Essex County, $1.51; Hudson County, $1.10; the others, around a dollar, except Cumberland, which was $.79. In general, the difference in cost represented differences in personnel and equipment, and the care was in this sense inequitable, the more since the State Board did not in fact exert control over the standards of county institutions. The state might have improved matters either by taking over the county hospitals as part of the state system, which is probably what Commissioner Lewis had in mind, or by setting high standards of care as a qualification for the state subsidy. The former policy would have required a state tax, which the political leadership would not venture; the latter was left to "friendly cooperation" between the state department's division of inspection and local authorities.[24] In any case the State Board went ahead with Marlboro without raising the general question of state aid and county care.

The architecture of Marlboro was interesting because it was different from the Kirkbride design of the older hospitals. "Here is an institution that looks more like a college than a place for the care of mentally sick," a visitor reported in 1933. "The old, gloomy fortress-like 'asylum' is gone. In its place are numerous smaller buildings—a hospital, a dining hall, nurses' home and a series of cottages, all in the modified English half-timbered style built on the quadrangle plan and connected by electrically lighted and heated tunnels for use in inclement weather." The cottages, built to house a hundred patients, were a means of classification, somewhat like the wards of a Kirkbride institution, and somewhat like a small separate specialized hospital. "The cottages are pleasant, light and airy," the reporter said, "and offer the patients for the first time, perhaps, surroundings that are an incentive to them to help themselves."

As for therapy, the hospital was well equipped to deal with organic complaints that contribute to mental illness, including an oxygen chamber, which, it was thought, would be useful in treating schizophrenia. Another innovation was psychoanalysis. "There has been a good deal of quackery in the . . . science which has tended to retard its use in legitimate ways," the reporter said, but the new institution had "a physician who had made a study of [it] and is capable of using it in a proper manner." The cost was put at $3,000 per bed, and maintenance at a dollar a day—both very low.[25]

A third striking feature about Marlboro was its organization, for it was put under dual management, like Trenton State Hospital, rather than under a medical superintendent, like Greystone Park. The medical director of the new institution was Dr. J. Berkeley Gordon. He was a young man, a Virginian and graduate of the Medical College of Virginia, who had interned in a naval hospital and then served as a medical officer in the Navy for three years. His wife belonged to a well-known Hudson County family, and in 1929 he came to New Jersey as resident physician at Jamesburg. Ellis made him acting medical director of Marlboro while the institution was under construction and the Board of Managers, when they were selected, agreed with his choice. Gordon was a surgeon and operated frequently in the institution's well-equipped surgery, but he never agreed with Dr. Cotton's theories. The superintendent and business manager was Robert W. Cox, a farmer and businessman who had served for ten years as superintendent of the Burlington County Mental Hospital.[26]

Business Administration and Patient Care

If the institution of dual management and a business manager–superintendent at Marlboro was Ellis' decision, as appears likely, it indicates that in his thinking the business manager was the key man in the mental hospital. Certainly this was true at Trenton, where Ellis was furnished a residence and where the old "warden," Samuel Atchley, kept matters well in hand. Even at Greystone Park, where Dr. Marcus Curry had been promoted to superintendent in 1920, the business manager was in charge of housekeeping and the kinds of administrative chores that Ellis and his assistants were primarily interested in, institutional labor and accounts, for example. Not only was the business executive closer than the medical director to the central office, but he was also closer to the legislators, because he talked the universal language of accounting and he could show tangible results: books balanced; money returned or applied, with permission, to other purposes; operations rationalized; improvements in the plant, made largely with the help of patients.

There were two goals in the eyes of Samuel Atchley and his peers—to save the taxpayers money and to keep the patients and staff busy. The goals reinforced one another in the notion of the self-sufficient institution. In 1930, the Trenton hospital employed a hundred patients in a cannery merely to preserve the produce of its farms; it had a large herd of cattle and twenty-seven horses; it employed patients not only in maintaining the grounds and plant, but also in a sizable mattress factory and carpentry shops, among other institutional industries.[27] Greystone Park had equally large enterprises; there the floral gardens, greenhouses, and dairy herd were matters of special pride. These were communities that largely fed, clothed, and sheltered themselves, and the man at the center of their operations, who decided what to grow, build and do, and how, who computed and justified the results, who realized the physicians' ideas in practical means and ends, was the business manager.

In a way, this was an elaboration of the traditional routine of the well-run asylum, given the advantage of stable leadership and expert advice from the central office, but it was also given the stimulus of more doctors and nurses and specialists, a growing professional staff, all the big new buildings, all the new equipment—nurses' quarters, laboratories with their little rituals of flame, potion, and microscope, occupational therapy rooms filled with toys, operating rooms and dental clinics bristling with gadgets, great shiny vats to cook food and efficient cafeterias to serve it, even oxygen chambers for schizophrenia—always something new to try and to look forward to.

When people said over and over again during these years that the old asylums were being transformed into modern hospitals, they were expressing not only optimism about some new therapy but also an authentic sense of excitement that one can recapture only by tracing cumulative changes here and there, in this respect and that, as they came. The innovations appeared also in the larger community, of course, but the institutional routine gave them a fixed point that made them obvious and interesting. Private families bought washing machines; mental hospitals installed great laundries.

Pervasive advances in specialization and rationalization of equipment and personnel, rather than dramatic therapies, changed the character of the mental hospitals and also the institutions for retarded and epileptic. The essential worker in these institutions was the attendant, a practical nurse and orderly who looked after the details of the patient's daily life—dressing, eating, bathing—and who also diverted (or restrained) patients on the ward and accompanied them about the hospital. He was on duty twelve hours a day, six days a week. His duties varied according to the patient's problems. Some patients were bedridden or infantile, and needed every care. Others could take care of themselves but were morose or rambunctious. Many needed to be protected against suicide or self-mutilation—castration, for example—or violence, sometimes fiendishly contrived. The number of attendants in a ward varied according to these needs. Over the attendants was a charge attendant, a sort of noncom who directed and helped them, and over him, in large institutions, was a director of ward service. Female attendants served the women's wards.

The professional staff included the doctor, who decided upon treatment and administered it, and the nurse, who assisted him and supervised treatment or medication. Nurses lived and ate separately from the attendants. Around this basic staff were the institutional druggists, cooks, laundrymen, artisans, farmers, bookkeepers, and their helpers.

In October 1925, the Department published a verbatim account of a conference between Commissioner Lewis and his institutional superintendents on the problem of staff recruitment. An instance of Lewis' policy of candid publicity, it is the most revealing document of the period. The Commissioner had two problems on his mind. He needed professional and other staff for the expansion then under way, and, of more pressing importance, Pennsylvania and New York had recently raised their attendants' salaries from $50 to $60 a month, plus maintenance, and lured away many of his workers. To meet that competition would cost $350,000 to $500,000 a year, plus the expense of an improvement of living quarters. Lewis recognized the need for higher pay and better conditions, but he recognized too the importance of other incentives. Make jobs into opportunities, he thought, by linking them to in-service training or practice-learning programs, and you will get the right people and the right spirit.[28]

Lewis pointed to examples of co-operation between industry and colleges and high schools and to the training of medical specialists and hospital executives in general hospitals. The first step, he said, was to analyze jobs and establish specifications for training. He quoted at length from the 1921 report of the State Civil Service Commission, which upheld the ideal of enlightened personnel policies, as demonstrated by private business, in encouraging efficient and responsible service. (The Commission confessed that it lacked the means to carry out these good ideas.) Lewis had in mind the job classification that John Ellis and Edgar Doll had done for his state-use system, and the star of the conference was Ed Johnstone, who told about the Vineland Training School's programs for training teachers, institutional inspectors, psychologists, and physicians, some by tuition courses and others by low-paying traineeships, and who emphasized the in-service training programs for non-professional staff that he had begun in 1911.[29]

Dr. Henry Cotton spoke to the point, for he was getting five promising applications for every interneship he could offer and many applications for graduate nurse positions, always hard to fill. Greystone Park, like Trenton, had a nurses' training school and it also took many nurses from general hospitals for special training; its social service department was accepting trainees from the New York School of Social Work and the Smith College School of Social Work, well known for its psychiatric orientation, and Dr. Curry was pleased with the trainees he was getting in occupational therapy and physical education, college people who worked at an attendant's salary to get experience and to qualify for much better-paying jobs.[30]

These were the programs the commissioner was interested in. What were the obstacles to them? First, everyone agreed, was the complicated and puzzling business of standardizing jobs. Second was the problem of connections with colleges or professional schools, for New Jersey had no school for physicians or social workers and even drew most of its teachers from other states, nor did it then have a modern state university that might have been approached to undertake these responsibilities. (The College of Agriculture at Rutgers University was helpful in arranging demonstrations and extension work and developing agricultural programs, Ed Johnstone observed; he had worked closely with Dr. Jacob G. Lipman, the South Jersey man who was its dean.)[31]

Third was the problem of housing. "A great deal of the housing that we have to offer is such that you couldn't ask any self-respecting person to go in and live," Dr. Curry said about Greystone Park. "I will be perfectly frank with you, I don't know where to turn. The people we get, we think we are working out a wonderful problem if they stay a month."[32] Cotton thought the same thing: an institution needed living accommodations such that "people can come there and feel they are decent human beings and being looked after properly."[33] Lewis observed that Warden Atchley had shown the state budget commissioner that "people were sleeping in places that were not as wholesome as a pigpen. They were attendants we were trying to keep, but we couldn't under those circumstances."[34]

The attendants were a key problem. Some of them came into the institutions willing to learn and to seek advancement, others to tide over a period of unemployment. Many—no one suggested what proportion—were floaters and drunks. "None of us ought to waste our time trying to train attendants of the kinds we usually get," Johnstone said, and Lewis' director of state use, who had tried to set up a course for attendants, said that "the present class of attendants" couldn't be taught because they had no incentive to learn and didn't want to learn. They were inferior stuff to begin with, their work was in fact discouraging and unpleasant, their real chance of advancement small.[35]

This discussion of personnel problems illuminates many developments in program during the years between the wars. Management was caught between two facts: First, it could not cure the patients; second, the principal custodians in the custodial force were in an unrewarding dead-end job that no one wanted. If the professional staff couldn't cure, however, it could at least keep the patients busy with various kinds of treatment, send them to clinics for tests and take out their infected teeth and tonsils, for example. (Such infections were "one of several factors in the etiology of mental illness," John Ellis said in 1944, and who could contradict him?)

Management could also hire specialists to give the patients exercises (physical education), to teach them games and dances (recreation) and hobbies (occupational therapy); it could hire people to help patients who were "improved" if not "cured" leave the hospital early (social service or aftercare), and of course it could employ the patients on the farms and in the shops, saving money for the state. Once established, all these activities could improve, for people were working at them all over the country, there were many things to be learned about them, and they could be rationalized and combined into a many-sided program. All this kept the patients from the attendants and the attendants from the patients and kept everyone busy transforming old asylums into modern hospitals. To get decent, self-respecting people in these jobs and hold them there, the institutions of course needed to offer decent living quarters and everything that contributed to developing loyalty to the institution.

In general, all these activities evolved out of the experience and needs of the institutions, not the stimulation of the central office, for the central office was organized around the idea of business administration, not program. It had experts on farms, diet, and accounts, but not on occupational therapy, recreation, or social work. If the founders had thought about a social worker in 1917 they thought about someone who made field studies of heredity and took case histories, which is what the first social workers employed in the state hospitals did; even in 1925 Commissioner Lewis was not clear on the difference between occupational therapy ("relief occupational work," he called it) and physical training.[36]

Everyone agreed that the problem was not just to analyze and standardize the jobs, work out training programs for them, and get help from universities in doing so, but that there was prejudice to overcome. Many young women would go into social service in the hospitals, it was remarked, except that they "still think the institutions are places of incarceration and places where they would be shut up entirely with undesirable associates." [37] In fact, the institutions as employers had to struggle not only with ignorance and prejudice about their work, but with general changes in the labor market. The floater-attendant manifested the mobility of labor as well as the demoralization of the proletariat, factors that had increasingly undermined the communal identifications and religious motives of the rural folk who had worked in the early asylums.

Similarly, the competition between state hospitals, urban general hospitals and other employers made professional skill and dignity rather than personal service the primary motive of middle-class people. Two ideas were obviously in conflict throughout the discussion. Sometimes men talked as if they were running a business and competing for skills in a wide impersonal labor market; at other times they talked as if they were trying to transform nineteenth-century paternalism to ring in graduate nurses and smooth young ladies from the Smith College School of Social Work.

In October 1925, the Civil Service Commission announced a raise in attendants' salaries (to $55 plus maintenance) and the provision of a higher rank of attendants, and most of the institutions were able to improve their living conditions in the next few years. By that time the attendant problem was diminishing as unemployment spread among unskilled workers, and by 1930 many middle-class people were suffering from the depression. As anxiety and confusion grew in the general labor force, state hospital jobs looked like positions of security, stability, and, in their modest way, opportunity. Men who were executives twenty years later often told how they began as attendants or part-time employees, never expecting a career but glad to get a job. In neither of his published reports, in 1934 or 1944, did John Ellis discuss the problem of getting and holding a labor force.

As regards the administration of the mental hospitals and patient care, the depression built up the authority of the business manager. He was the key man to cut costs in the persistent pressure for economy, and in the favorable labor market he and the medical director could demand loyalty to the institution. In some ways, good discipline improved patient care, and the stability of labor enabled medical directors to improve their therapy. But the means for therapeutic services were sharply limited, and business managers were interested more in saving the taxpayers money than in therapeutic patient care. During the depression Dr. Ellen Potter made a study of the hospital farms; her conclusion, never published, was that management in fact justified them by "cost accounting" rather than by "clinical accounting," or therapeutic value.[38]

At the Trenton hospital they liked to tell how Dr. Potter once dressed down Warden Atchley. An attendant had taken some patients from the Vroom Building, for the criminal insane, to the main building for treatment, and one of the men had run off. The attendant had faced a dilemma—if he chased the runaway, he left the others unguarded. Warden Atchley decided to get the attendant a shotgun and load it with number six birdshot, too small to injure a patient, but sufficient to make him think twice about running away and risking a fanny full of it. Dr. Potter learned about the decision and stormed out to see Atchley. "Here you have a lot of sick people and you're watching over them with a shotgun!" she shouted. The warden hadn't looked at it that way, but the little old lady was quite a party, all excited about it, and he ended the practice.[39] Presumably he invested the taxpayers' money in another attendant.

Other changes in patient care related to changes in the population. In the first place the rate of hospitalization for mental illness increased, from 226 per 100,000 in 1900 to 274 in 1930. The increase might be considered a reflection on modern life, but a study the Department published in 1928 implied that it was a sign that things were getting better: people were recognizing mental illness sooner, it was said, and recognizing the advantages of hospitalization. The "most arresting fact" revealed by the study was that insanity was "a disease of youth and middle age"; it is not clear why this was arresting, although in the context of its issue the report was intended to support a campaign for prevention and mental hygiene.[40] By 1940 the rate of hospitalization had climbed to 393, a sharp rise that Commissioner Ellis attributed to even better facilities for diagnosis and referral (a result of the state's progressive policies, he said) and—something new—to the increase of senile dementia, which he interpreted as evidence of improved health conditions and longer life.[41]

These consolatory thoughts were not much help to the institution superintendents, who had to provide for ward after ward of patients whom neither tonsilectomies nor occupational therapy would cure. On the other hand the central department was promoting "parole" and "home visiting" of patients, under the supervision of social workers. The number of patients out on good behavior, as it were, rose steadily from an average of sixty-two in the years 1914–1918 to 650 in 1930 and 1,300 in 1943. Patients on parole were supervised by routine visits twice a year by social workers from the hospital that released them (unlike parolees from correctional institutions, whose supervisors were responsible to a central bureau).[42]

In 1937 the hospitals began shock therapy, first Trenton, then the others, first with drugs, then with electricity. The shock, a painless but somehow fearsome physiological wallop, alleviated symptoms in a mysterious but dramatic way on certain kinds of patients that other treatments had not helped. At best, the symptoms disappeared after a few treatments; in most cases patients became notably more amenable to other kinds of help, and in only a few cases were the results negative. By 1943, almost four thousand patients had received complete courses of treatment, and well over two thousand had returned to their homes. It was the most promising development in twenty-five years.[43] In regard to the relation between theory and program, it is interesting because it did not develop out of the institutions' work or the central office—it was introduced from Europe into the United States—and in fact it flew in the face of the theories of detoxication and "mental hygiene" on which the State Board had based its plans.

Mental Hygiene

Mental hygiene clinics, the key to what Ellis called, rather grandly, "The New Jersey plan for the control and prevention of mental disease," [44] combined two different ideas and purposes. In one respect, they were conceived as outpatient clinics of the state mental hospitals, places where local doctors might refer patients for diagnosis and prognosis as a step toward their legal commitment, or where the hospital could follow up on patients on parole or convalescent leave. In this sense, the clinics were an arm of the state hospital, reaching into the community to attend patients before they got to the hospital and after they left. Adolph Meyer, among others, was interested in these extramural facilities and did much to encourage their appearance in New York in 1913 and Massachusetts in 1914.[45]

In New Jersey, Dr. Henry Cotton established the first clinic in 1918. Its purpose was to assist in the classification and transfer of state wards among the several institutions, but Trenton Hospital psychiatrists soon began to hold a clinic at the Mercer (general) Hospital in Trenton. At Greystone Park the work began as "an informal clinic for mental examinations" and consultation with parents and teachers in regard to behavior problems. By 1922 both hospitals considered outpatient clinics part of their regular work. (The sanatorium at Glen Gardner had meanwhile established a traveling clinic for diagnosing TB.)[46]

The second conception of the mental hygiene clinic related to work with children who appeared as behavior problems in the schools or juvenile courts. The models of this type were the clinics Dr. William Healy established in Chicago (1909) and Boston (1917), and which the National Committee on Mental Hygiene began to foster in 1920. These were sponsored by private philanthropy, courts, and schools, rather than by state mental hospitals. In 1923, the distinguished psychiatrist Dr. James Plant began to develop juvenile clinics in Essex County, in connection with its court, schools, and county mental hospital. He was interested primarily in the sociological features of mental illness and in the therapeutic possibilities of a variety of community agencies; by 1937 Essex had eight community clinics other than those under the state hospital.[47]

What held the outpatient clinic and the child guidance clinic together in the thinking of Ellis and his advisers was the idea of prevention. As men studied case histories of people who got into trouble they recognized that these serious maladjustments had many antecedents and signals, and they reasoned that if they could get to the problem people sooner their help might be more effective. If they could discover the retarded learner and the aggressive or withdrawn child early, they would be better able to forestall or accommodate retardation, delinquency, or psychosis. Beyond this hope for therapy or rehabilitation was a larger strategy. Ellis and his advisers, like everyone who thought seriously about institutions for the mentally ill and retarded, saw that popular skepticism and hopelessness about the subject were in part an unrealistic and irrational denial and rejection of unpleasant facts of life. If the clinics could bring the institutions to the people, they could dissipate some of the fear and shame that confused the work. They would be "educational" in a broad sense, improving public attitudes and support.[48]

The chief demand for mental hygiene clinics was in metropolitan North Jersey. At the same time Dr. Plant began his work in Essex County, the State Hospital at Greystone Park began to expand its outpatient social services under Mildred Hurley, a social worker who had served in the New York system, and in February 1926 it established a "traveling clinic" to serve the communities in its district. On the advice of the National Committee on Mental Hygiene, the clinic took the form of a psychiatric team that made regular visits to communities to examine and treat people referred by community agencies or those who came voluntarily.[49]

In 1927 Ellis established a Committee on Mental Hygiene of the State Board of Control, which included Dr. Ambrose Dowd of Newark, Dr. George O'Hanlon, the distinguished executive of Boss Hague's $10 million medical center in Jersey City, Dr. Augustus Knight, chief medical officer of the Metropolitan Insurance Company and a member of the Board of Managers of Greystone Park, and Dr. Raycroft. Its program was not only to improve medical work in the hospitals and encourage more traveling clinic work, but also and especially to encourage local general hospitals to establish psychiatric wards and to receive nervous and psychiatric cases in their outpatient clinics. The advantages of a program of care and treatment of nervous and mental patients in general hospitals were obvious. The services would be relatively free of the irrational attitudes toward mental disorder that handicapped the state institutions, they would be widely available and convenient, they would make internes and general practitioners familiar with psychiatry—otherwise mostly ignored in the training—and they would educate the public.[50]

Ellis promoted this idea in a number of departmental publications between 1927 and 1930, but he was never clear about the specific means of encouraging it. He seems to have expected that the state hospitals would hold their clinics in general hospitals—as they generally did—and this demonstration would lead hospital authorities to establish regular services. The doctors on his committee, all prestigious gentlemen, also called attention to the plan in committees of the State Medical Association.[51]

In fact, Ellis had neither a carrot nor a stick to move the general hospitals, but the state institutions did expand their outpatient work and traveling clinics. The most remarkable of these was the Northern New Jersey Mental Hygiene Clinic based at Greystone Park. At first it was primarily an outpatient service for adults, in the typical state hospital pattern, but the persistent demand of teachers and social workers and the interest of its executives turned it toward the child guidance pattern. In 1929, it was reorganized under Dr. Earl Fuller, a friend of Ed Johnstone who had previously run a school for retarded children in Pennsylvania. It was made an "autonomous" operation, that is, its staff did not work with hospital patients but only with community referrals, while the hospital maintained a separate social service department to help its patients and parolees.

The clinic team visited communities once or twice a month, seeing patients by appointment. It studied their case histories, examined them for retardation or emotional disorder, made diagnoses and recommendations, and sometimes followed up with casework treatment or even psychotherapy. It made extensive use of social workers in interpreting its services as well as in treating cases. Miss Hurley established notably high standards in this respect and the clinic was a field placement for students at the Smith College School of Social Work, who studied and criticized its operation in many ways. By 1940 it had become one recognized model for the extension of psychiatric clinics, originally an urban idea, into rural areas under state auspices.[52]

At the Trenton State Hospital the psychiatric team of the Bureau of Mental Hygiene, which had classified prisoners for the state institutions under the direction of the central department's Division of Classification and Education, was charged with the development of traveling clinics in 1927. Formally, it was part of the hospital social service, which did intake and outpatient care for hospital patients, but in fact it was a separate operation, closer to the central department than to the hospital management—Dr. Cotton was not interested in the dynamic psychiatry that influenced child guidance work—with notably higher qualification for its social workers than the hospital social service.[53] At Marlboro the hospital social service and the traveling clinic were better integrated, and that institution could employ the aftercare and diagnostic services maintained by the Monmouth County Organization for Social Service, Mrs. Geraldine Thompson's showcase for coordinated public health nursing and social work.[54] In 1938, the three state hospital traveling clinics held 629 sessions in twenty-seven communities and received almost four thousand visits, and except for local clinics in Essex County and Monmouth County they gave most of what service was available in the state. Only seven county or city hospitals maintained clinics.[55]

However useful and promising these clinics were, they were a disappointment of the hopes of 1927. Ellis and the State Board continued to chant about progress, but Dr. Ellen Potter confronted the situation with her usual candor. "Let us grant," she told the state League of Women Voters in 1935, "that . . . even with the best of intentions, the State Department . . . is unable, because of lack of funds, to provide all the mental-clinic services that would be used." What struck her was that existing facilities were used unequally and that "certain social agencies that should be among our most active patrons do not show any adequate awareness of the need for service." A few family welfare agencies and the juvenile court made the most referrals, she said (speaking primarily of Union County, the case at hand), but public schools and especially private physicians were evidently uninterested, dubious, or hostile. She thought that those who withheld their support, including the legislators, ought to do some "heart-searching." [56]

Dr. Henry Cotton, Jr., who became assistant director of the Trenton Hospital clinic in 1938 and its director two years later, held that it was a mistake to think that a clinic could, by recognizing psychosis at an early stage, prevent it and so reduce admissions to the state hospitals. It was true, he said, that adult psychotics were usually disturbed in early life, but it did not follow that disturbed people who came to the clinics were likely to become psychotic. The benefit of clinic service, he said, was less in "prevention" than in the immediate help it offered to people in trouble. The idea of "prevention" actually restricted the service of the clinic, because it discouraged clients by suggesting that they were potentially hospital cases. Nor did he think that clinics should be diagnostic clearinghouses or otherwise bring together all sorts of cases in a waiting room, where they might annoy or embarrass one another.[57]

What young Cotton wanted was specialized clinic services to handle different kinds of problems. One obstacle was the "traveling clinic" which made it difficult to bring clinic and patient together and forced a lumping together of services. But the main difficulty, he thought, was that general practitioners were either ignorant or distrustful of "modern dynamic psychiatry" and did not refer their cases or cooperate with the clinics. Sometimes they were afraid to lose the patient, he said; at best, if the family had means, the doctor referred the case to a private practitioner. In any case, the state psychiatrists and the physicians in general private practice were too little known to each other to work together. He also thought the clinics needed more "interpretation" to schools and courts.[58]

Like his father thirty years before and like Ellis' "mental hygiene committee" in 1927, young Cotton thought the problem was to bring hospital psychiatry into the main stream of medicine. Unlike his father, he supported the dynamic theories of psychiatry that were taught at Johns Hopkins, where he took his degree, and that had come to prevail in the child guidance and mental hygiene movement. Others were saying what he said about the state hospital clinics, for by 1940 it appeared to leaders of the national mental hygiene movement that the sort of alliance Ellis had expected, between outpatient clinics and child guidance clinics on one hand and state hospitals and general hospitals on the other, had not matured.[59]

During the war, the clinics (and hospitals) were a help to draft boards, but the emergency cut their personnel by half and greatly restricted their service. After the war the work went forward under much different conditions.[60]

Meanwhile, two features of the mental hygiene program of the 1930's had become clear. First, the hope that Ellis and his mental hygiene committee put in psychopathic wards in general hospitals was not only premature, but it allowed the Department to bypass the key questions of finding money and personnel for an expanded program. Obviously, in Ellis' thinking, the local communities, through the general hospitals, would finance the facilities and doctors as they did other kinds of medical work. Second, the clinics of the three state hospitals were organized and budgeted in different ways and served somewhat different classes of people; not until 1937 did they adopt a uniform report which gave comparable statistics on their service, and that was their "first and . . . [the] only step toward a research program in mental hygiene," as a student remarked in that year.[61] A social worker who studied the clinics of the Trenton Hospital in 1940 (and who worked closely with Dr. Raycroft) observed that the separation between the hospital social service and the mental hygiene clinic at Trenton arose because the former had earlier "developed policies and procedures which the . . . Department thought best, as a matter of policy, not to disturb."[62]

As for the Mental Hygiene Committee of the State Board of Control, Ellis proudly set forth its personnel and policy in his 1934 report; in his 1944 report he reiterated the policy, omitting an emphasis on research, but did not mention the Committee itself. When it was revived, after the war, it had its hands full.

14

The Problem of the Feebleminded, 1918–1945

If Ed Johnstone looked forward at the founding of the New Jersey Department, he saw a bright promise for his work. The intelligence tests had helped define the problem of feeblemindedness and showed its unsuspected dimensions. Goddard's heredity studies gave new certainty to old suspicions and had definite, obvious implications for public policy. The Extension Department of his school, led by his half-brother Alexander Johnson, had found a surprising audience for its message. Johnstone and his colleague, Edgar Doll, organized the Division of Classification and Education that was an important part of the new Department; his protégé John Ellis would rise through it to become commissioner. And yet, when men looked back from the 1950's on the intervening years, they saw them as a period of disappointment and frustration, a "dark age" of hopelessness and neglect.[1] The sources of this paradox were confusions in theory, policy, and practice.

Hereditary Defect and Mental Hygiene

If feeblemindedness was hereditary in most cases and the root of many social problems, the appropriate policy was, obviously, segregation or sterilization. There is no doubt that in the 1920's Johnstone and Ellis favored some sort of sexual sequestration. But in a practical sense segregation and custody were impossible. Custody required construction, but prisons and mental hospitals, which could not maintain waiting lists, had the first call on available funds for construction while the waiting lists for institutions for the feebleminded grew and grew. As for sterilization, it was recommended by experts in public administration who studied the Department's work in 1925, 1929, and 1932, but political opposition, from the Catholic Church among other groups, precluded a law to require it, the feebleminded did not volunteer to "make themselves eunuchs for the kingdom of Heaven's sake," and Johnstone himself did not think it was practical.[2]

Furthermore, the intelligence tests pointed past the seriously or obviously defective to the much larger number who were "borderline" and "dull normal." Half the population was below the norm, by definition, and for every child who might need institutional care there were many who needed help in the community; for every feebleminded child who became a public problem there were, by obvious statistical inference, many who somehow managed to bear their affliction in privacy. Dr. Edgar Doll, chief of research at the Vineland Training School after 1925, took note of the problem of distinguishing borderline cases and cases whose problem seemed to be "social" failure as much as "intellectual" failure, and turned from generalization about mental age, as measured by intelligence tests, to a painstaking analysis of the behavior of children at various ages to measure their physical and social development and to synthesize a "clinical syllabus" for the study of the entire personality.[3] With regard to policy, the intelligence tests turned attention from rather obvious and desperate misfits to a class that was both much larger and more hopeful.

Quite apart from the ramifications of intelligence testing, psychiatrists began to question the whole theory of hereditary defect. The leading psychiatrist in New Jersey, in the eyes of Burdette Lewis and the first State Board, was Dr. Cotton. In 1912, Cotton had hired social workers to take case histories and study the heredity of his patients, but by 1916 he had dismissed hereditary defect in favor of focal infections as the primary cause of mental disorder.[4] If he were right, his ideas would have important consequences for the theory of mental defect and preventive policies. Ed Johnstone was interested, of course, and in 1922 he suggested to Dr. George Stevenson, a young psychiatrist who had just joined his research staff, that Cotton's theories might be an appropriate point of departure for research.[5]

Dr. Stevenson had already decided that Cotton was on the wrong track, however. His own interest was more in "dynamic theories" and he presently left Vineland to join the National Committee on Mental Hygiene and to foster mental hygiene and child guidance clinics. His move was typical of the shift of interest of many psychiatrists and also social workers, who found a congenial role in the mental hygiene clinics and who became fascinated by the possibilities of understanding the psychology of their clients. In the short run, at least, the mental hygiene movement and the psychiatric theory of social casework diverted interest from the defective child and made "heredity work" old-fashioned.

The shift to mental hygiene puzzled and discouraged those who had worked with the feebleminded before the war. In 1928 Alexander Johnson wrote Porter Lee, the head of the New York School of Social Work and a partisan of new trends in social casework, to complain that the National Conference of Social Work was ignoring the practical problems of institutional care of the feebleminded and public policy toward them. The principal interest of psychiatrists in institutional work, he said bitterly, was the effort of "the medical trade union" to get its members into superintendencies. Johnson was particularly angry at the National Committee for Mental Hygiene, which had taken over the work he had begun in the Extension Department of Vineland Training School. It was led by "impractical medical theorists," he said, who were hedging on heredity and also the need for segregation and sterilization, which men with practical experience all recognized. He wanted Porter Lee to schedule a program by practical men, like Edward Johnstone, he suggested, who would renew the fruitful discussion of twenty years before (when he had been secretary of the conference), but he warned Lee that "the Mental Hygiene Society" would "not approve" of anyone who was not a physician.[6]

As dynamic psychiatry encouraged psychiatrists and social workers to doubt the theory of hereditary feeblemindedness, so the development of experimental psychology and educational psychology and the raising of professional standards among academic psychologists tended to divert them from an interest in mental defect. "Clinical psychology" of the sort Doll practiced was only one of many paths open to these gentlemen, and not the most promising; the American Psychological Association, not the American Association on Mental Deficiency, as the organization of institutional personnel came to be called, was their professional home.

The New Jersey Program

However these confusions appeared in later years, Johnstone and Ellis thought they were steadily engaged in constructive work. Simply to plan a procedure for classification and to establish it in the institutions was a large puzzling job with obviously useful consequences in reshuffling inmates and rationalizing programs. In general, Ellis saw the program as developing in two ways. Within the Department were a variety of institutions for the feebleminded, each fitted for a special class and function. (This was different from the mental hospitals, which took all kinds of patients from a certain geographic area.) In a larger sense the system reached out from the Department to include community agencies which would diagnose mental deficiency and help work out programs of training and supervision for those who could stay in the community or return to it. (The state mental hygiene clinics were in his mind—and in practice—as important in dealing with mental defect as with mental illness.)[7]

When the Department began its work, the state maintained an institution for feebleminded women at Vineland and a "colony" for men at New Lisbon. It also supported promising trainable boys and girls at Johnstone's Vineland Training School. In 1921 it established a second "colony," for low-grade males, at Woodbine, and in the next few years it developed academic and vocational training for the more promising cases at New Lisbon. In 1928 it opened a training school for higher-grade girls at Totowa, near Paterson in North Jersey. The new institution was planned to relieve pressure on the Vineland institutions by taking higher-grade girls and training them for community placement; it was located where need was great and the opportunity for placement good—a decided change from the "waste people on waste land" theory of the older institutions. None of the institutions took children who were epileptic or psychotic. In general, then, they were specialized according to the sex and ability of the children.

No one ever set forth and defended a policy of sexually segregated institutions—Vineland Training School took both sexes and so did the mental hospitals—but the pattern was maintained by economic necessity. The state institution at Vineland had originally been established as a custodial institution to keep the girls from reproducing, and it was able to receive state wards who had got what they could from the Vineland Training School. Johnstone had no place to send male state wards, however, so the New Lisbon colony, which he fostered, was for them. The vocational training that Totowa offered was mostly for domestic service, and it appears that as late as 1928 Ellis envisioned a series of farm colonies where older men could be more or less self-supporting. But the Department's publication of that year, "The Problem of the Feeble-Minded in New Jersey," shows an interesting contradiction between the policies of humane custody, on farm colonies, and training and supervised parole, or community control.

The largest part of this publication was "A Study of Mental Deficiency in Typical Degenerate Families," in which Elizabeth Kite followed up her investigations of fifteen years before into the "pineys." It was a story full of scandal and portentous references to "The stream of degeneracy . . . gathering force with time." [8] Edgar Doll introduced it with praise for its careful work, and he warned that automobiles and economic opportunity, extending even into the pine belt, were luring the "pineys" into situations more disastrous to themselves and others than ever before. He sharply criticized "The existing panacea for social ills . . . by removing encumbrances or by alleviating difficulties." This was "temporizing with natural selection" and ignoring the true alternatives "segregation, sterilization, rural colonies or supervised parole." [9]

These articles sound like an argument for more farm colonies, but Ellis, in an introduction, chose to emphasize "community control," that is, improved mental testing in schools and hospitals, special classes and remedial measures for those who weren't in institutions, and improved social service and parole work. He scarcely mentioned state institutions to block the hereditary curse. The Department, in his view, was a clearinghouse for information and consultation on programs and persons. (He thought that it would keep some sort of register of "degenerate stock" and that the Board of Children's Guardians would give special attention to deficient children who fell under its jurisdiction.) The only state institutions he mentioned at length were "small industrial or domestic colonies," not permanent residences but sheltered environments pending parole.[10]

The reason Ellis did not begin any new farm colonies—Woodbine was not a true colony—was the same reason he maintained long and growing waiting lists for the existing institutions—no funds. "Community control" was not simply a progressive program of prevention and rehabilitation, nor an effort to promote the idea of county welfare boards, then much in his mind in this as well as other respects, but a device to bypass the state's failure to provide even for the obvious needs on the waiting list. Community control was indeed the path of progress and it has a modern sound, but what if the Department offered its co-operation and consultation and the community did not after all establish the controls? The idea was analogous to his plan for psychiatric wards in general hospitals and it met the same practical difficulty: local authorities were slow to move and he had neither carrot nor stick to get them moving.

Meanwhile, events were turning Ellis away from theories of hereditary defect. In 1930, he was chairman of the Committee on Physically and Mentally Handicapped of the White House Conference on Child Health and Protection, and Ed Johnstone was chairman of the subcommittee on mental deficiency. By this time it was obvious that most of the "mentally defective" never came to public attention, and the heredity studies were also criticized on other scientific grounds. The Department's second pamphlet on "The Problem of the Feeble-Minded in New Jersey," in 1933, did not follow up on the "pineys." Ellis spoke in passing of "so-called hereditary type of feeble-mindedness." Edgar Doll devoted most of the pamphlet to provision in the public schools and other community controls. He began by observing that there were by conservative estimate forty thousand distinctly feebleminded people in the state, but only four thousand of them were in state institutions.

Clearly it was important to recognize and help those outside institutions, and the main agency of help was the public schools. Communities had a legal obligation to educate children between five and eighteen, he said, without excepting the mentally handicapped. Why were the schools reluctant to make special provision? People thought that state institutions should take care of the retarded, that the results of special education did not justify the costs, and that special classes fostered "unpleasant notoriety," Ellis said. He made no suggestions about overcoming this resistance. In his view the state institutions would take selected problems: lower grades, multiple handicaps, children beyond school age or from rural districts without special classes.[11]

But school boards were more inclined to contract than to expand their offerings during the depression. Ellis was caught in a dilemma: To emphasize hopelessness and the need for custody was to diminish hopefulness and the need for community control and special education—and vice versa. If anything, the emphasis on provision by local schools led him to disregard the need for more state provision and the frustration and suffering represented by the waiting list, which grew to 1,127 children in 1943, two-thirds of them low grade.[12]

The Colony for Idiots at Woodbine

Perhaps the most significant institution of the period, as regards mental defect, was the colony for low-grade male defectives. No one had planned such a place; no other state had one. The property came to the state as a gift, a windfall, in 1921. The town of Woodbine had been established in 1891, in the sandy wastes of Cape May County, as a colony for Jewish refugees, a philanthropy of the Baron de Hirsch Fund. The property in question had been an agricultural school for immigrant children who lacked the qualifications to enter state agricultural colleges.[13] After World War I, the trustees decided to abandon it in favor of scholarships to state universities, and they offered it to New Jersey for charitable purposes. Dr. Jacob G. Lipman, a distinguished alumnus and dean of the College of Agriculture at Rutgers, was a friend of Ed Johnstone's, and Johnstone saw an opportunity to use it to house very low-grade and multiple-handicap custodial cases that were complicating the work at the New Lisbon colony and Vineland Training School. As originally planned, it had the same board of managers as New Lisbon and it took patients from the older institution and also many helper boys who worked around the cottages and on the institution's farm lands.[14]

Woodbine opened in May 1921. It should have been a hell-hole, a custodial institution of the most desperate type. The inmates needed continual help or supervision in the commonest activities, feeding, dressing, bathing, and other unpleasant menial tasks of the sort parents perform for infants. But this institutional care could not offer authentic parental love and pride and its captivating vision of growth and change. The children were not normal babies, but unlovely freaks behaving in weird ways. Their bodies were less stunted than their minds; a boy of twenty might look to be nine and crawl like an infant; others were queer-looking mongoloids or pinheaded microcephalics, or blind, palsied, or deformed. The normal nastiness of cleaning up after babies increased when the babies grew heavy and bearded; the freakish quality was writ large by the scores of cases in each building, by the ugly institutional garb the children wore, and by all the other makeshift shoddiness of public charity. Over everything hung the fact of futility; these were hopeless cases, incarcerated until death came.

The physical plant was old and unsuited for its new occupants. The cowbarn became a dormitory. The place was isolated, very much so before the automobile came into use, and it was hard to find custodial personnel for these unfortunates and the helper boys, themselves a chore and trial, let alone find the professional personnel, doctors and nurses, whose services were so necessary. To complicate the matter, the State Board, "in the face of present opposition to the appointment of nonresidents," asked the local board to choose a superintendent who was a resident, a physician, and "if possible a world war veteran." [15] No such paragon appeared, however, and the institution struggled along during most of its first decade under a man whose main career interest was in corrections.

Between 1927 and 1931 the institution got four new "cottages"—barracks, a layman would call them—which permitted better classification and care of the patients. In 1929 Ed Johnstone's son, Edward L. Johnstone, became assistant superintendent. He had worked as a teacher in the institution in 1923, but the notion of teaching idiots seemed too far-fetched at the time. His idea was simple and practical. He wanted to get the children out of bed, teach them good habits and discrimination, let them play and learn in nursery and kindergarten fashion, encourage them toward self-sufficiency in caring for themselves and toward that measure of achievement of which they were capable. He would not give up hope for these hopeless people. He would discover what they could do. He convinced Ellis, somewhat to his surprise, and in 1930 he became superintendent.[16]

Obviously, a program such as he envisioned depended on the efforts of the custodial staff in the cottages and the helper boys; he needed not surgeons, psychoanalysts, or oxygen chambers but patient, friendly people. Fortunately, he was able to apply here the lessons his father taught at Vineland, especially when the depression made it possible for him, like other superintendents, to find a stable staff. By 1940, he had over half the children in some sort of classes and a teacher-training program for public school teachers who were preparing to work with the severely retarded; two-thirds of the children were engaged in some activity. Between 1923 and 1940, the program reduced "soil cases" from 45 percent to 30 percent, feeding cases from 15 percent to 4 percent and dressing cases from 47 percent to 27 percent.

This progress and the rationalization of procedures made it possible to bathe the boys once a day or oftener, instead of once a week, and much reduced the skin afflictions that troubled them, not to mention the smell and the bugs around the place; it helped control the incidence of disease and parasites among children who played with their feces and ate them. Activities were built around a sequence of children's holidays and parties. At first these were a bedlam—the children ate the decorations—but in a few years there was a striking improvement in order and discrimination.[17]

The spirit was the most impressive thing about the place. In the summer of 1935 young Ed Johnstone was incapacitated by illness—he was working too hard, his father said, supervising some large extensions to his plant that he had got from federal relief funds, helping to run the emergency relief program in Cape May County, and taking courses at Rutgers—but the institution was running itself "in the pink of condition"; the workers showed "a lovely spirit of loyalty and desire to keep things at their top pitch while 'the boss' was away." [18]

This was fatherly pride, perhaps, but a few years later Frank Walsh, the state budget commissioner, made much the same observation when he visited Woodbine as part of a routine acquaintance with the state institutions. He had just returned from Skillman Village for Epileptics, a trip he would never forget. "A tour of the buildings and cottages [of Skillman], the permanent home for innumerable patients . . . , each case more deplorable than the other, was my first shocking realization of the problems of the Department," he recalled much later. A visit to its dining quarters sent him, he said, "home to my family counting my blessings but shunning the dinner table." Then, "having partaken of little or nothing for breakfast," he journeyed to Woodbine. The contrast was striking: the children were happy, the help efficient, the spirit an inspiration. "I thought then," he said, "that if the Lord did not bless and guide so many wonderful people to dedicated careers . . . how much graver would be the problems of the Department." [19]

Woodbine and Skillman were rather comparable as custodial institutions with difficult cases; they were unenviable rivals for low per capita maintenance expenditures in the Department, ranking just above Vineland State School and the New Lisbon colony.[20] What Woodbine showed was the unpretentious possibilities of humane custody, given imagination, energy, and stable administration.

An undated engraving of the building in Trenton in which both justice and charity were dispensed in the late eighteenth century.

Rutgers University Library

FRONT VIEW OF THE STATE-PRISON AT TRENTON.

The above view, taken on the line of the Delaware and Raritan canal and the railroad to Camden, shows the front wall of the prison, the main building, in which reside the keeper and assistants, and the roofs of the corridors, in which are the cells of the prisoners

The first New Jersey State Prison opened in 1799. (*Rutgers University Library.*) The second (above), opened in 1836 and is, with numerous additions and alterations, still in use.

N.J. Dept. of Institutions and Agencies

Dorothea Lynde Dix, who came to New Jersey in 1844, sparked the movement which led to the building of the state's first hospital for the insane. Its first unit, called "Dix Hall," opened in 1848 with fifty patients. In 1882, Miss Dix returned to her "first-born," as she called the institution, and lived in an apartment in the hospital building until her death in 1887.

New York Public Library

Dr. Henry Cotton, Sr., medical director of the State Hospital at Trenton from 1907 to 1930, whose reforms, innovations, and experiments made history in the field of mental treatment.

N.J. Dept. of Institutions and Agencies

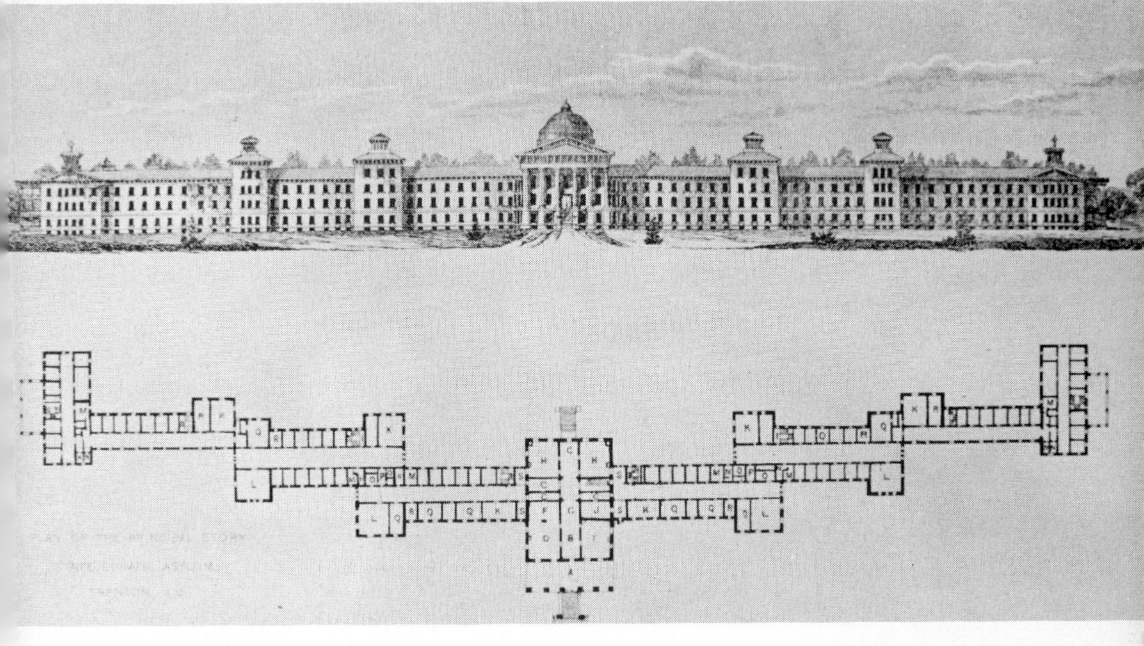

New Jersey's first institutions for the mentally ill were known as "Kirkbride Hospitals," named for their designer, Dr. Thomas S. Kirkbride, whose general plan was followed during the latter half of the nineteenth century in a number of states. The hospital at Trenton (above) shows a floor plan. The institution at Morristown below, now called Greystone Park, opened in 1876 with a capacity of 600 patients. In 1966, a staff of 1,964 cared for 4,684 patients.

New Jersey Historical Society

"Deborah Kallikak," who came to Vineland Training School, a private institution, in 1897, at the age of eight, and was transferred to Vineland State School in 1914. The picture (left) of Deborah at 17 appeared in Henry H. Goddard's *The Kallikak Family,* published in 1912; that on the right was made in 1962.

Vineland State School

Vineland State School, established in 1888, is the oldest and largest of the state's residential facilities for the mentally retarded. Its patients are females five years old and older. The average daily population is 2,000, housed in two centers, the main institution (below) and Vineland State Colony, under the same administration, about four miles away.

Vineland State School

The State Colony at New Lisbon, as it appeared about 1935. Lupin Cottage, the middle building, was erected in 1914. The institution has been greatly enlarged and now houses 1,300 mildly retarded boys and men, with a staff of 469.

From THE STORY OF FOUR MILE COLONY

The Woodbridge State School near Rahway is New Jersey's newest institution for the retarded. Opened in 1965, it cares for 1,000 severely retarded children and adults of both sexes.

Vincent G. Kling and Associates, Architects

Edward R. Johnstone, executive director of the Vineland Training School from 1898 to 1944. His work with the mentally retarded earned him an international reputation, and led to the establishment of state supported institutions following the pattern he set at the Training School. In addition, he held numerous unpaid posts on state welfare boards throughout his long career.

Courtesy of Mrs. Carol Johnstone Sharp

In 1955 the Bordentown Manual Training School was transferred from the Department of Education to that of Institutions and Agencies, and opened the following year as the Edward R. Johnstone Training and Research Center. The Johnstone program has three major objectives: the rehabilitation of retarded persons with a potential for return to their communities; training of personnel for the field of retardation; and basic and applied research. Expanded facilities will provide also for training of deaf-retarded and blind-retarded students.

N.J. Dept. of Institutions and Agencies

Mrs. Caroline Wittpenn, who was active in New Jersey welfare work for a half century. She led the campaign for the establishment of Clinton Farms State Reformatory for Women, which opened in 1913, and was a member of the first State Board of Control, established in 1918.

N.J. Dept. of Institutions and Agencies

The administration building at Clinton Farms. Vocational training and community living are stressed in this cottage-type institution for females over sixteen. There are 49 buildings on its 300 acres, and the normal population is 375.

N.J. Dept. of Institutions and Agencies

Dwight W. Morrow (above), who headed the Prison Inquiry Commission of 1917, and Ellis P. Earle (below), who was chairman of a parallel body, the Commission to Investigate State Charitable Institutions. The findings of the Morrow and Earle Commissions led to the formation of the Department of Institutions and Agencies, under the State Board of Control.

N.J. Dept. of Institutions and Agencies

Mrs. Geraldine Livingston Thompson of Red Bank, leader in the State Charities Aid Association before 1918, founder of the Monmouth County Organization for Social Service, and member of the State Board of Control from 1918 to 1957.

N.J. Dept. of Institutions and Agencies

Governor Walter E. Edge, in whose first administration, 1917–1919, prison and public welfare reform were initiated with the Morrow and Earle Commissions. "A business man with a business plan," he supported the institution of board control during his long political career in New Jersey.

N.J. Dept. of Institutions and Agencies

The State Home for Boys at Jamesburg, established in 1865, was New Jersey's first correctional institution for juveniles. Originally situated on a farm of 490 acres, it now consists of 60 buildings on 725 acres. Boys from eight to sixteen are housed in cottage units and rehabilitation plans are carried out on an individual basis.

N.J. Dept. of Institutions and Agencies

Highfields, the former home of General and Mrs. Charles A. Lindbergh, where youthful male offenders are given intensive treatment under a probationary plan. The estate was given by the Lindberghs to the state in the 1940's. The New York Foundation and the Astor Foundation started research in 1950 and in 1952 the state assumed the cost of operation, while the Astor Foundation continued to finance the research.

N.J. Dept. of Institutions and Agencies

The Turrell Residential Group Center for Girls at Allaire, with a program comparable to that of Highfields, was opened in 1960. The state's other residential group centers are located in Warren County and Ocean County.

N.J. Dept. of Institutions and Agencies

William John Ellis (left), Commissioner of Institutions and Agencies, 1926–1945.

N.J. Dept. of Institutions and Agencies

Sanford Bates (below, left), Commissioner, 1945–1954, and John Tramburg (below, right) who served as Commissioner from 1955 to 1963.

N.J. Dept. of Institutions and Agencies

The Diagnostic Center at Menlo Park, for the presentence examination of defendants before the courts. Some patients are also referred by private organizations or physicians. A complete physical, mental, and social inventory is taken for every person examined to determine the best treatment for cure or rehabilitation. The Center examines 500 inpatients and 2,000 outpatients annually.

Eugene S. Griggs

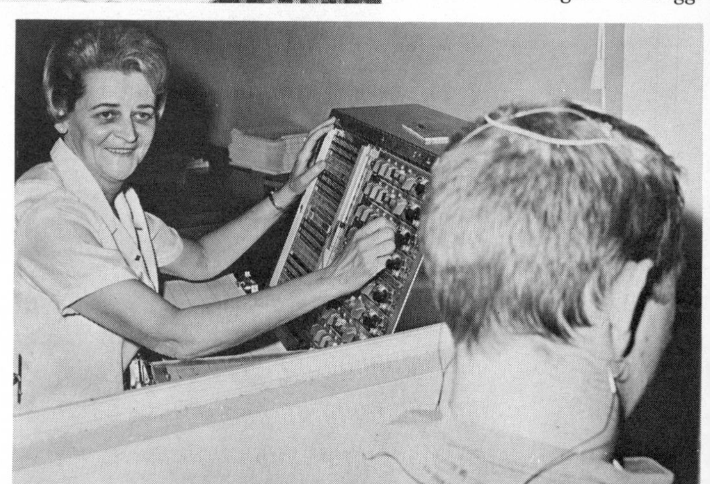

A nurse gives an encephalogram to a patient at Menlo Park.

Asbury Park Press

The New Jersey Home for Disabled Soldiers, also at Menlo Park, has 80 infirmary beds and 120 domiciliary beds. Established in 1866 at Newark, and moved twice, it was established on this 126-acre site in 1929. On the grounds of this institution the Rahway Prison Farm maintains a minimum custody camp housing 50 inmates. Other camp branches of the prison are at Marlborough State Hospital and on the grounds of the Rahway Prison.

N.J. Dept. of Institutions and Agencies

15

Correctional Theory and Practice, 1918–1945

In March 1917, while he was commissioner of corrections of the City of New York, Burdette Lewis summarized his view of criminology and penology in a volume in "Harper's Modern Science Series" called *The Offender and His Relations to Law and Society*. The title suggested two of his leading ideas, that the offender was the proper focus of attention and that his treatment was related to something more complicated than the court and the prison, that is, to society. These ideas were neither original nor critically stated, but they showed an open-minded, experimental temper and a breadth of vision that was to characterize Lewis' efforts in New Jersey.

Lewis on the Offender

With regard to the character of the offender, Lewis noted the traditional theory that criminals had allowed their sinful impulses to rule them, and he acknowledged, contrary to the opinions of "idealistic radicals," that some criminals were indeed willful scoundrels. He also acknowledged that criminologists like Lombroso were right in holding that sometimes the criminal was "bad because of his physical or mental make-up," and that some offenders were clearly pathological deviants. But most offenders were neither evil-minded nor pathological, he said; the typical criminal was a more or less passive vehicle for influences of heredity and environment and "we cannot determine exactly how far he is responsible for his shortcomings." [1]

With respect to the theory of institutions, he was satisfied to define four purposes of punishment. The traditional purpose was *retribution*, he said; in this regard the subject of attention was the offense, rather than the offender, and the problem was somehow to make the punishment fit the crime. By *deterrence* he understood an example that would discourage would-be criminals; by *prevention*, the protective custody, as it were, of habitual offenders. Retribution, deterrence, and prevention were purposes that applied, he thought, to evil-minded and pathological offenders. The fourth purpose, reform, applied to that large group who were not willful villains or congenital deviants, who would return to the community and who might benefit from a program designed to counter the bad influences that had worked upon them.[2]

A critical thinker might have gone on to analyze these ideas, to ask, for example, how far the notion of moral guilt and retribution was consistent with the scientific notion of impersonal influences and re-education, or to inquire into the empirical evidence for the theories. Instead, Lewis passed quickly to a fact that was, to him, obvious and paramount: whatever the refinement of theory, judges and wardens could bring a great deal more knowledge to bear on their decisions about the offender than they usually did. Reformers attached a great importance to changes in legal procedure and organization, he said, but judges in any setup needed a variety of definite and accurate information that they did not usually have. Reformers fostered various systems of penal discipline, but practical administrators needed to know about doctors and medicine, food and sanitation, schooling and industrial employment, and so forth, in their bearing on the offender. In short, whatever the refinement of theory or the formality of organization, judge and warden needed expert help to construct a diagnosis and plan a program.[3]

From this proposition Lewis moved into an extensive discussion of what information was relevant, who might collect it, and how the judge and warden might assemble and consider it. This process he called "classification." It employed experts to study the offender and then put their insights together to work up a program suited to his individual needs. The agency to collect facts he called a "laboratory" or "clearinghouse." The models in his mind were the psychopathic institute or clinic Dr. William Healy had established to help the Juvenile Court in Chicago, the Bureau of Social Hygiene attached to the State Reformatory for Women at Bedford Hills, New York, and the proposed detention home for women offenders in New York City, where courtrooms and medical facilities would be in the same building as the detention rooms. He was also thinking of personnel work in private industry.

After the trial court had determined guilt, Lewis thought, the offender should go to the clearinghouse for study; acting on the information collected in the study, the judge would put him on probation, under expert and constructive oversight, or sentence him to prison. Lewis envisioned the imprisonment as planned by an inclusive department with specialized facilities for different classes and easy transfer among them. The sentence should be indeterminate, he said, with the date of release set by institutional authorities when an appropriate program was completed and the experts thought the offender was ready for parole.[4]

The "relation of the offender to society," mentioned in his title, was a question of impersonal influences, social, psychological, and biological, that were not clear, but which a study of the offender might illuminate;

his idea here was that the information and insights accumulated in the necessary process of disposing of offenders might feed back into social theory so as to clarify the nature of the impersonal forces and make possible a degree of social control and prevention, somewhat as the study of individual illnesses made possible programs of public health.[5]

What is impressive about this discussion is the enthusiasm with which Lewis moves from what is to what ought to be and his focus on practical administration, for all his ideas were drawn from particular experiments actually going forward around New York, and what he did was to pull them together. In his eyes the New Jersey institutions must have seemed like a small and rather backward show (he did not mention any of them among his examples of progress). They included two institutions for juveniles, two reformatories, and the state prison. The several institutions did not have much in the way of expert service and they were not linked together in a common purpose. The plan of the new Department, which called for experts on medicine, classification, education, institutional labor, and parole, was in line with his thinking, however—George Kirchwey, who formulated it, was also thinking about developments in New York. So was the Morrow Commission's notion that the problems of delinquency and dependence were linked and therefore charitable and correctional institutions ought to be parts of a common system, for clearly this implied some sort of clearinghouse for assignment and transfer among the institutions.

In the practical business of establishing expert services and a comprehensive system Lewis faced three rather different problems. With respect to the juvenile institutions and the reformatory for women, the problem was to repair their neglect under the old system and to get a stable and progressive staff, but he felt no doubts about what needed to be done. With respect to the Rahway reformatory there was some question about means and ends, complicated by bad feeling between the superintendent, supported by his local board, and the central office. In the case of the prison there was a large question of means and ends, complicated by outright hostility and a conflict of powers.

The Homes for Juveniles

Mary Belle Harris became superintendent of the State Home for Girls in May 1919, and her published reminiscences of the next five years give a lively sense of the problems of the new Department and the work of developing a program in an institution. Miss Harris fell unexpectedly into her career. She took a Ph.D. at the University of Chicago in Sanskrit and then became an expert on numismatics; she was also a talented musician. In 1914 Katharine Davis, also a Chicago Ph.D., made her superintendent of the Women's Workhouse on Blackwell's Island. In 1918 Mrs. Wittpenn brought her to Clinton Farms. She soon left for war work and when she returned Mrs. Wittpenn, on the State Board, and

Commissioner Lewis, her former boss in New York, asked her to take the girls' home. It was a mess, they said, and they hoped it might become, under her direction, the clearinghouse for female offenders.[6]

"I accepted the new position, feeling quite confident that with my long and varied experience I could cope with the situation successfully," Miss Harris recalled. But her experience had been with older women and in institutions that were in order.[7] The Morrow inquiry had found the girls' home "among the best institutions of its kind in the country," but when Miss Harris arrived it had not had a superintendent for a year and had been out of control for months. She was not prepared for the frenzied violence of juveniles cutting loose. The core of the problem appeared to be a number of girls who were emotionally disturbed—the Morrow Commission had mentioned their presence—and a larger number who were feebleminded.

Under ordinary conditions the disturbed girls would have been isolated and the feebleminded would have fitted themselves into an orderly routine, but conditions were not ordinary. Escapes were a persistent problem, since the institution was unfenced, unguarded, and part of Trenton. Many girls had a practice of running out to help look for escapees. There was no place to isolate troublemakers; strong rooms had been dismantled (before there was anything to take their place) and the girls had learned to tear the plaster off the walls and literally claw their way from room to room (the place looked like the ruins of Ypres, a visitor said). The girls learned that Miss Harris had forbidden rough stuff, so they were unrestrained by fear. Meanwhile the staff was leaving.[8]

Miss Harris desperately recruited help from her friends and had thirteen disturbed girls transferred to the State Hospital, and matters settled down, on the surface. In a few months there was a serious fire in one of the old buildings—all firetraps—and she sent to the county jail six girls who had confessed to arson. Their arrest became the occasion for a political attack on the girls' home and ultimately on the Department. The result was that county officials decided to return the girls to the Home just as a court decided that the thirteen psychopaths were illegally committed to the State Hospital and a girl who had gone berserk and homicidal had to be returned from the State Prison, where the keeper reported that she "was tearing down [its] morale."

Miss Harris arranged to commit the homicidal girl to Vineland State School; she (and her managers) paroled the psychopaths, assuming that they'd be back, but not right away or all together, and meanwhile she rushed work on new strong rooms. The arsonists were held at the jail after all, and they carried on so that the newspapers stopped charging her with severity—sending tender adolescents to jail—and complained about lack of severity. But when Commissioner Lewis conducted a public investigation, during which Miss Harris testified that she had resorted to spanking, as authorized by the board—"administered by the physician and nurse, with a rubber overshoe, and not upon the bare skin"—and that it had quieted the girls so that everyone could get some sleep, the papers returned to the theme of cruelty.[9]

The episode is significant because it shows the difficulties of juvenile institutions and people's expectations about them. Reflecting on it, Miss Harris said she regarded corporal punishment as "inexcusable and an admission of failure," but that "the experience made me humble and less critical of others who are caught in a situation of a similar nature." [10] Meanwhile she worked to improve the situation, that is, to develop services and a program so obviously lacking. She had little to begin with. Although half the girls were sex offenders, they had not been tested for venereal disease; tests showed that there were scores of cases instead of the ten mentioned in the most recent report, and many of them had lived in the institution for years. Miss Harris devised a classification system, with help from the central department, and arranged a variety of assignments for the girls. She tried especially to organize activities that would encourage their interest and participation, music and dramatics, for example, and ceremonial graduations to parole. Most of all, she was interested in student government, in which the girls elected officers who were supposed to exercise a good influence by their authority.[11]

When Miss Harris left the institution on New Year's Day, 1925, its plant was much improved, its staff was larger and better paid, with specialists to help the superintendent plan and conduct a rationalized and many-sided program. The stated purpose of the program was not to punish, but to encourage participation, training, and self-discipline. Miss Harris left, she said, because experts from the central office were giving her too much paper work and too little initiative; they were criticizing her academic and industrial program. The doctors were disagreeing, and whatever the right and wrong of the case, it was clear that the day of the professional and the expert was at hand in the institution's life. As for Miss Harris, she became superintendent of the federal women's prison then being built, and many of her assistants also had successful careers in institutional work.[12]

According to the Morrow Commission, the State Home for Boys at Jamesburg deserved "little but commendation" for its "external or material aspects," but its spirit was that of a "stern military regime" that made the children worse rather than better, and its services—medicine, education, recreation, cottage supervision—were poor. "Obviously what is needed is a radical change in the spirit of administration," the commissioners said.[13]

A new Board of Managers was appointed in 1918 by the State Board of Control. Its report for 1921 was an account of its stewardship. Unlike the Morrow Commission it had found that the plant had been much neglected, and it reported great improvement in that respect. It had doubled the salary of the superintendent, to $5,000 plus maintenance, and raised the pay of other employees to reduce their turnover. It characterized the medical care of the previous regime as "unpardonable neglect" and mentioned among other good results a marked decrease in skin and scalp diseases, which had often been epidemic. It criticized the institution's large farm as inappropriate for the needs of the boys' training, and described a general revision of program—a classification procedure feeding into an integrated program of academic and industrial education, sports, and recreation. It announced the end of "the old repressive method of discipline" which had "as its main purpose making life simple and easy for employees, rather than benefiting the boys," and the arrival of modern practices intended "to make the boys capable of becoming self-directing free citizens" by "participating in the direction and discipline of the institution." [14]

The instrument of the change was Calvin Derrick. A graduate of normal schools and Columbia Teachers College, he had been a teacher and a principal before turning to corrections. He had served as superintendent of schools of Auburn Prison, superintendent of a George Junior Republic, superintendent of the Preston School of Industry in California, warden of Westchester County penitentiary and acting warden at Sing Sing. Lewis, who had known Derrick in New York, hired him as director of education and parole and part-time, then full-time, superintendent at Jamesburg.[15] The story of his administration is one of establishing and reworking the procedures his Board of Managers confidently saluted, trying to make the form into substance.

Jamesburg was one of five similar institutions selected in 1929 for study by the United States Children's Bureau, which published a detailed account of their program and an analysis of their results. The authors were favorably impressed by everything about the boys' home. They approved the plant, especially "the hamlet," an isolated unit for disturbed and problem boys, and the residences for the staff, practically all of whom lived on the grounds. The academic qualifications and interests of the staff and its teamwork impressed them. "Even a casual visitor would have observed that [it] included some interesting personalities and that a great deal of rather original work, some of it more or less experimental . . . , was being done. This is only possible where there is . . . administrative leadership and where the workers receive encouragement from those in authority," they wrote.[16] They approved the effort to individualize treatment by the variety of formal training, sports, hobbies, and recreation, and the discipline.

Derrick's presidential address before the American Prison Association in 1934 was an interesting comment on his career. "Active workers" in penology "are quite prone to become pessimistic," he said. "Because of [our] intense interest and close application to the work . . . , we become . . . painfully conscious of the drawbacks, the handicaps . . . , and it seems to us perfectly obvious that if only a certain few things could be accomplished . . . the fulfillment of plans and dreams would take place; and we marvel at society's slowness of comprehension, at the legislators' indifference and at the taxpayers' willingness to continue paying the bills that could, in our reasoning, so easily be cut." Against this pessimism he placed what seemed indisputable to him, the clarification of ideals and the fundamental progress in prison management and programs intended to rehabilitate, and here he voiced the realistic pride of a man who has made an idea into a team and a process. (He evidently did not feel so heavily the impositions that caused Mary Belle Harris to leave.) [17]

Derrick noted especially the role of "the scientific group" in collecting and interpreting facts and considering programs. In this connection, he paused to comment on the publications of Sheldon and Eleanor Glueck, which indicated that even superior "treatment" in institutions was mostly a failure. "It might be of interest to you to know that your President was deeply moved and challenged by [their] book 'One Thousand Delinquent Boys,'" he said. "His first impulse was to resign and go into deep retirement." Instead he asked Emil Frankel, director of statistics and research for the New Jersey Department, to study the careers of 1,000 boys released consecutively from Jamesburg. Frankel's study showed, he said, that "somewhere between 55 percent and 69 percent . . . conducted themselves pretty well" and only 28 percent committed serious delinquencies, which encouraged him and convinced him "that we are not all groping in the dark and that constructive results do come from our work." [18]

The Children's Bureau study, which was published the following year, but which was based on an earlier and smaller sample, did credit Jamesburg with the smallest proportion of failures of the five institutions, 31 percent, but classified the remainder about equally between "successful" and "doubtful." The most striking conclusion of its study, however, was that all the institutions had approximately the same results.[19]

Clinton Reformatory

The State Reformatory for Women at Clinton yielded to no one in its enlightened spirit. Its plant had been neglected under the old system, but with Mrs. Wittpenn on the State Board and progressive penologists from New York in charge of the new Department, it got a better break. Many people came to visit and all left to applaud it. Their published accounts are much alike, almost like program notes on a show. Act one was the charming old farmhouse which became the superintendent's residence, fire in the grate and curtains at the window. Act two was the cottages, spic and span and homey, with dining rooms where waitresses served the food (part of their vocational training). "The 'cells' are either dormitories or little white rooms," an Englishwoman reported in the *Manchester Guardian* in 1920. "They are light, bright, prettily furnished in a plain way—rather as might be rooms in a Swiss hotel." [20]

The cottages were scattered around the grounds, with no bars, fences, or walls to mar their pastoral setting. "Except for the absence of bicycles you might mistake Clinton for the Vassar campus," a reporter—male—wrote in 1940.[21] Act three was a visit to the maternity cottage and its heartwarming bevy of madonnas, most of them too young for Vassar and many of them coffee-colored, a touch of Gauguin in Hunterdon County. Act four was Mrs. Wittpenn's chapel, where the sinners trooped to worship, in the old days, with heads covered and faces veiled. Act five was the girls in the Negro cottage singing those beautiful old hymns at the vesper hour.

The theme of the show, and in a way the theme of the institution, was the goodness of people. "Some of the girls and women . . . have committed murder; some are thieves. All have long sentences," the Englishwoman said, "yet the majority are not locked in their rooms." Indeed, the girls governed themselves, acting with "moderation and fairness" and "the greatest effort . . . to avoid what are called . . . stoolpigeons." This was before 1929, when many hardened offenders previously held in the State Prison were finally moved to Clinton. But the tough ones hadn't changed matters, the reporter said in 1940; they proved to be especially reliable and many were student officers "in what to the layman would appear to be a fabulous system of self-government."

Often the visitors wondered, when they learned that the honor girl passing by was a famous murderer and she was escorting a probationer who had spent most of her years in custody, how the "fabulous" plan could work. The thought involved stereotypes about the offender that scientific penology was only beginning to debunk, the notion that a delinquent's offense would be an indication of his behavior as an inmate, for example, or that older, "hardened and serious" offenders were harder to manage than crowds of coltish adolescents. (The classifiers found that emotionally unstable individuals were much more numerous in juvenile than in adult institutions.) From this viewpoint, the population of Clinton was relatively mature and stable, and it was also relatively small, between two and three hundred during the years 1929–1938. Many girls had committed the crime of illegitimate pregnancy, and the institution was in this respect a welfare agency where judges who had no other community resource would send poor girls. (Rich girls in trouble didn't get to the judge, of course.)

The policy at Clinton—an appeal to honor and responsibility, to participation and self-discipline—allowed its officers to capitalize on the relatively manageable qualities of its population. But it is obvious to anyone who tries to reconstruct the inner history of the institution that the morale and self-discipline envisioned in the program did not generate themselves. An opportunity to do right was also an opportunity to do wrong; every freedom and responsibility was subject to abuse; inescapably the officers ran risks, ultimately the risk of public misunderstanding and criticism. Self-government and participation were never simply that, they were of necessity stimulated and supervised with imagination, resourcefulness, tact, and, of course, firmness, in every aspect of the institution's life. With so many points at which it could go wrong, the enlightened reformatory policy, professed and practiced at Clinton much more than at the homes for juveniles, laid a great demand upon the facilities and the staff.

Much depended on the superintendent. The system seems to have worked for May Caughey, who got it going, but not for her successor, and for Mary Belle Harris, during her brief term in 1918, but not for her successors.[22] When Edna Mahan showed up in August 1928 to begin her reign she found ornamental iron grilles on some cottage windows and other restraints that did not accord with her idea of an open institution; when she had them removed there was a rash of escapes before the girls settled down. There was also a hose for "hydrotherapy" and evidence of other punishments that she deemed improper. The inmate government was working poorly, ridden by cliques and favoritism. Dr. Ellen Potter, who had temporarily filled the position before Miss Mahan's advent, had struck on the expedient of taking girls for automobile rides as a reward and incentive.[23]

Miss Mahan, then only six years out of the University of California, had worked for the California Bureau of Juvenile Research and served as probation officer for the Juvenile Court of Los Angeles and superintendent of the Los Angeles County Detention Home. From this staging area of Enlightenment on the west coast she had moved to the Harvard Law School Survey of Criminal Justice, in Boston, where she was associated with the Gluecks and Felix Frankfurter, among others, and where she joined the admirers of Miriam Van Waters, the Queen of Enlightenment. Miss Mahan became the youngest, best-looking superintendent around the country, with her own regal poise, confidence, and commanding zeal, a "rare combination of administrative skill and philosophic insight," as John Ellis put it, who "made an outstanding demonstration of the extent to which inmate participation is possible in a correctional program." [24]

Miss Mahan got a full-time physician for her institution in 1930 and also graduate nurses instead of the midwives who had hitherto delivered babies, and she brought in new teachers, more of them, with better qualifications. She had "a little difficulty" with her board in making the changes—they were not prepared for so critical a view—but presently she won them over and the staff too. She was helped in the work by an improved plant, four substantial buildings that opened between 1927 and 1930, and by the favorable labor market of the depression. Here, as at Jamesburg and most institutions, the staff lived on the grounds, which was convenient since they were on duty almost continuously, at least in the cottages. John Ellis was like a father to her, she said. By the time she was thirty she had matters well in hand in running a nationally recognized institution, and decades later those years would seem wonderfully simple to her.[25]

Rahway and Annandale

The men's reformatory at Rahway came off well in the Morrow Commission's report in 1917. Its efficient administration and material aspects were "of the first order," the commissioners reported, and they "doubted whether many elementary schools in the country are better, in point of equipment, in the quality of the teaching staff or in the efficiency of instruction." They criticized it on three counts: its discipline was too severe, like a prison, they said (they recommended a new trial of self-government, which Superintendent Frank Moore had already tried and discarded); its psychological testing was unsatisfactory; and its industrial education poorly developed.[26]

Dr. Moore, its superintendent since 1909, was not to be sold on self-government, however, and he was not pleased when Lewis' man Calvin Derrick criticized his educational program and proposed to remove parole supervision from the institution and centralize it, or when people from Trenton began to suggest how he could improve his psychological testing and to tell him how best to fit his charges into the state use program.[27]

Rahway was supposed to be "one of the 'show places' among the institutions of the State," the Bright Committee said in 1925, but it did not live up to its billing. The schooling was "old style academic type with practically no correlation to the shop work"; men averaging twenty-one years of age received a kind of instruction given to children of six to fourteen. Vocational training was incompetently taught, the Committee said, without any enthusiasm or sense of its importance. Discipline was old-fashioned; prisoners seemed to have little confidence in the administration and no contact with the warden; they did not understand the credit-rating system as well as the Jamesburg boys understood their new point-scoring system.[28] For its part, the State Board had recently turned down Dr. Moore's request for a pay raise, as it would refuse a later request in 1928; meanwhile, after considerable discussion, it prevailed upon him to discontinue the "rule of silence" in his institution.[29] In 1929 he resigned, and so did three of his board members.[30]

Whatever Dr. Moore's inclinations, the fact was, as he had said for many years, that the depressing prison architecture of Rahway inhibited an enlightened discipline. From the first, Commissioner Lewis and his associates had in mind to make it the state prison and turn the old Trenton plant into a reception and classification center. To replace or supplement Rahway they planned a new reformatory that would be everything Rahway was not. This was Annandale Farms, built in 1926–1929 on a hilltop neighboring Clinton and opened in April 1929.

Rahway boys had already farmed the land (it was also a camp for their road gangs) and they built the new institution. Even so it was a very expensive showplace. The public administration experts who reported on the state government in 1929 observed that it was costing seven times as much as the buildings at the prison farm at Leesburg, then under construction, which were also minimum security and appropriate for a reformatory in their judgment. They thought the Department might better spend more money on preventive activities and other types of institutions, but, they said, the policy question did not and could not come up because expenditures for Annandale came from the "dedicated fund" raised by the half-mill tax, which could be spent only for that purpose. The situation was a case in point for their argument against dedicated funds.[31]

The prison farm at Leesburg had simple structures of concrete blocks, whereas Annandale had substantial and carefully designed buildings, faced with handsome native stone, quarried by the boys on the site. The new reformatory embodied two central ideas—first, that it would take only good security risks among young offenders, and second, that it would house them in cottages, separate units designed for fifty to seventy boys and organized variously to meet the needs and dispositions of more or less homogeneous groups. There was a cottage for newcomers, for example, who were in time promoted through a series of cottages with increasing privileges, culminating in an "honor cottage" for boys near parole, or perhaps in a cottage for parole violators. There were also other bases of classification, related to the program of the particular cottage. In general, the enterprise was a step toward individualization of treatment as suggested by scientific classification and study of the offender.

The cottages and other buildings of the community were laid out in an orderly way on the hilltop and looked like a residential school, without a wall or fence to mar the "campus." The scene was a striking contrast with the stone walls and cell blocks of Rahway. The spirit was different, too. Some officers wore uniforms and Sam Browne belts, but others did not, and no one carried a weapon. There was very little formal education of the old-fashioned elementary school type; instead the management made a deliberate effort to employ work and informal agencies—clubs, hobbies, and sports—to engage the boys. Sydney Souter, Jr., who worked out the educational plan and who presently became superintendent, had worked at a boys' camp sponsored by Ellis Earle and was much interested in recreation, especially sports, as an outlet for emotion and as a character-building agency. (John Ellis approved this idea heartily; a small man, he was an apostle of YMCA fitness and liked rugged athletic types, whom he boldly challenged to ping-pong, and as a sometime high school teacher he thought that boys learned more English in debating or current events than in academic exercises.)[32]

The difficulty at Annandale, like that of all the enlightened institutions, was discipline, for repressive policies had at least the merit that they made things simple and safe for the custodians, whereas an enlightened, nonrepressive philosophy might encourage self-discipline and re-education but might also stimulate escapes and fights. Group tension among Annandale boys erupted in a race riot in September 1930, just a five-minute scrap, the authorities said, ended long before the state police arrived; but four months later state police were called again to put down a more serious fight in which nine boys were injured—along with some officers—and nine boys escaped. The escapees were simply running away from the fight, the superintendent said, which is to say they were chased out of the institution because they didn't feel safe there. (The excitement spread to the neighboring hilltop; three Clinton girls ran away that night.) [33]

At Annandale, like Clinton and the institutions for juveniles, the management had to balance a professional, and to some extent a public, interest in a hopeful reformatory discipline against the notoriety and public hostility aroused by trouble and escapes. So thought Dr. F. Lovell Bixby, the Department's expert on classification and education, when he went with Ellis to investigate the Annandale riot, and it seemed to him that some hypocrisy was inevitable in the situation. He did not think that New Jersey institutions were so bad in this respect, however, when, a few years later, he made a national survey of juvenile institutions for the Osborne Association and came back "sick, just sick," because of the covert brutality he could see beneath the pious surface.[34] And in 1941, twelve years after it opened, the eminent Dr. William Healy described Annandale's program at length as the "outstanding example" of an enlightened reformatory discipline in the United States.[35]

Classification and Parole

The Department's policies about classification and parole ran into the established practices of particular institutions, and since the State Board was not inclined to press matters, the results were often less than hoped for. Its classification plan furnished "admirable material for discussion of [its] work," the Joint Legislative Survey Committee reported in 1925. "Presumably it is in effect through all of the institutions. Upon going more closely into the matter, however, the working out of the program is found to exist in part on paper only. . . . The foundations not being complete, it is not surprising to find that the educational and industrial superstructure can be substantially improved upon." [36]

Conditions were especially difficult at the State Prison, where the keeper was eager to assert his autonomy from the experts of the central department and where punitive attitudes prevailed without much qualification. Concerned about escapes from the State Prison in 1926—and dubious about the enlightened penologists in the Department—Governor A. Harry Moore called a hearing in June 1926, with the prison managers, the warden, and Commissioner Ellis. "I think we have got to the point where prison reform . . . has swung too far to the other side," he told them. "We don't have penal institutions any more." He was particularly opposed to coddling or pampering second offenders. "We must make them sorry they are there. If it doesn't make them sorry, our whole system falls down." Ellis assured him that the State Prison was "feared by prisoners generally" and there was no coddling there.[37] In 1926, the "flat sentence" law went into effect, a punitive measure, the very opposite of the indeterminate sentence law on which progressive penology depended.[38]

Ellis had established the classification system, such as it was, and he was determined to make it work.[39] By 1929 he had friendly superintendents in all the reformatories: Derrick at Jamesburg, Mahan at Clinton, George Giger, who had been his inspector in the central office, at Annandale, Mark Kimberling at Rahway, and he would soon have Mrs. Kate Burr Johnson, a graduate of the New York School of Social Work and sometime commissioner of public welfare of North Carolina, at the girls' home. He put the revision of classification under Dr. Ellen Potter, but the work quickly shifted to Dr. F. Lovell Bixby, whom he had just hired for that purpose and who would figure largely in the history of the Department.

Bixby, a New Englander, had majored in psychology at Clark University, a leader in that discipline, taken a Ph.D. at Cornell under the psychologist Titchener, taught there for a year (1926–1927), and then gone to Rice Institute as associate professor. Texas weather was not to his taste, however, and when it came down to it he did not see any promising line of research in Titchener's direction, physiological psychology. He heard that Ellis was looking for a chief clinical psychologist and applied for the job. He was not much interested in clinical psychology, but he had worked as an attendant at East Gardner State Colony in Massachusetts, in an experimental program for rehabilitating chronics, a powerful experience, and in Texas he had been called upon to administer tests at a children's home. Moreover, Ellis told him the job would be at the prison, and he had taken a stimulating course in criminology at Clark from Harry Elmer Barnes, then fresh from his work for the Morrow Commission. He told Ellis, and Derrick, Doll, and Johnstone, that he didn't know what "classification" meant, but they received him warmly and he went to work in 1929.[40]

There were two difficulties in making the system work, he found. One, the classifiers did not transform their information into a diagnosis and plan, or, two, if they did, their report was filed with no follow-through. What was needed was a standard operating procedure that would define participants, roles, records, questions, decisions, and review. What he did was simply to spell things out and put them together, and his *Procedure for Classification,* which the State Board approved and circulated to the institutions on November 25, 1930, was later made the procedure of the federal Bureau of Prisons, which employed him to write its manual on the subject. It presently became standard in American prisons and reformatories.[41]

The plan provided for the reception and quarantine of the inmate and his examination. It established a committee, under the institutional superintendent or his deputy, which included designated staff officials—in effect, all those with expert knowledge and a point of view—to compile a classification summary in prescribed form. The officials then met to consider and decide specific questions about transfer, custodial requirement, medical care, and program, to record their decisions in a definite way, and to review cases every six months, until they were ready and able to justify parole.[42] This procedure was the most notable contribution New Jersey had made to the history of penology.

Meanwhile, in 1930, John Ellis sent Bixby to the State Prison to get the system working there. The prison had a classification procedure for work assignments, which Ellis himself had devised, but the keeper and his subordinates wouldn't pay any attention to it and couldn't be coerced, at least not without a fuss. "Ellis told me I didn't have any authority but I was expected to have plenty of influence," Bixby recalled much later.

> In practice work assignments were made as rewards or perquisites in the traditional way, by the men in charge at the center desk, a tough old deputy keeper who knew what he wanted and why, and a convict clerk, a lifer, very intelligent and able. If a classification committee made assignments, they would lose this power, so they weren't cooperative. They wouldn't let me past the desk, for example, except under guard, so I was put in a little office with my shoeboxes full of cards.
>
> The first step was to replace the convict clerk, who never should have had that kind of authority. When we got the prison managers to replace him he was broken-hearted. He came to me and said he'd given the prison his best and asked if he hadn't done a good job, which he had, within reason, because he knew the jobs and the men well. He was depressed and upset and I warned the deputy keeper to look after him. But they didn't, and he presently blew up, got into a fight, killed a guard and was killed himself. Too bad, but my prediction impressed the deputy keeper. It happened, too, that I wrote up an account of the incident which I showed him. It wasn't a formal report or anything but his name was in it and I discovered that, like a lot of old prison men, he was rather superstitiously afraid of written documents with names in them. Anyhow my stock went up around there.
>
> Sometime later I got a chance to show how the system could work. The court of pardons held its regular semi-annual meeting and, because the flat-sentence law had virtually eliminated parole by the managers, pardon or parole by the court of pardons was the only way to clear the prison. The court was mostly laymen, politicians, and you couldn't tell what they would do, but every six months there was a sort of general jail delivery that left the prison labor force disorganized. That's why the convict clerk had been so useful. He could step

in and reassign people quickly, so as to keep things running. The new civilian clerk didn't know anything about this, of course, so at this point I showed the principal keeper my shoeboxes, showed him what he needed to know and how he could get a classification committee to use it. In the circumstances it seemed like a businesslike procedure, not just more red tape from the central department, and he was willing to try it. So we were in.[43]

Classification was important not only for work assignments, education, and other aspects of institutional life, but also for parole. Properly carried out, the procedure established guidelines and goals that enabled the classification committee to make deliberate, expert recommendations to the Board of Managers, which, under the Department's organic act, retained the power of parole. In 1919 parole agents, hitherto attached to institutions, were assigned to the central office and covered a district rather than an institution. (The prison had its own parole officer, however, appointed by the keeper and completely separate from the central office.) The report of the National Institute of Public Administration (1929) criticized the practice of parole by institutional managers—it favored a single paid board—and also criticized the parole supervision as inadequate and inefficient.[44]

The improvement of classification procedures was a partial remedy for the first complaint, because a committee of professionals screened the candidates for parole, but the Department made no effort to eliminate the managers from the final decision. Shortly after the NIPA report Ellis got more funds for better parole supervision—more workers, better qualified. When Winthrop Lane studied the Department's parole procedure for the National Commission on Law Observance and Enforcement (the Wickersham Commission) in 1931, he concluded that both theory and practice were excellent. Decisions of the committees were taken on "the inmate's real personality, prospects, and behavior," he wrote, "and not (as is so often the case) on the basis of his history of delinquencies or court record." Committee meetings had none of "that attitude of hostility, indignation, conventional and heavy moral censure which interferes with the judgments of many institutional heads. . . . On the contrary the point of view and atmosphere seemed to be that of a clinic at which specialists . . . were pooling the information . . . , coming to the best conclusions they could and recommending the treatment they thought most likely to succeed."[45]

Parole was much cheaper than custody, so there was an economic motive to support it. Between 1930 and 1935 the number of prisoners, including those in the boys' and girls' homes, fell from 4,079 to 3,962, but the number of parolees under supervision rose from about 3,500 to 5,188.[46] Given a rational procedure and organization, the principal difficulty with parole was personnel—not much of a problem as the depression fell.

Employment and Program

The classification committee could make a refined analysis of the offender's needs and capabilities, suggesting what kind of treatment and program were most appropriate, but it could not provide the means for a program. In fact, its options for program were few. In the homes for juveniles and, to a lesser extent, the reformatories, the management was legally required to provide schooling and it was therefore justified in employing teachers and even in developing extracurricular activities, sports and hobbies, to keep the children busy. The criticism of Rahway's "old-fashioned" education and Calvin Derrick's interest in informal education and character-building reflected the interest of professional educators in child-centered teaching as opposed to academic formalism. At the prison, however, and to a lesser degree at Rahway, management had no such legal obligation and punitive attitudes inhibited diversion that might be risky or merely pleasant. For older offenders the problem of idleness called for a solution that was at once discipline, education, and diversion: work, hard labor.

The problem of prison labor had largely occupied the Morrow Commission. It had fully endorsed the policy of state use, which the state had adopted in principle in 1911. The idea of state use appealed to many people. It affirmed the desirability of prison labor, it saved the taxpayer money, it eliminated or at least restricted the competition of convicts with honest labor. What it didn't do, as prison officials complained, was employ the prisoners. To favor state use was easy; to establish it and make it work were difficult.[47]

The Morrow Commission did not consider this objection in general, but it did recommend ways of expanding the market. Its principal hopes were road work, other public work (for example, conservation), farm work, and, for intramural industries, license tags and school furniture, which combined a number of useful trades in production for a large public market.[48]

All the correctional institutions had farms by 1917, Rahway and the prison had sent out road gangs, and there was obviously a need for highways and conservation projects. In fact, the prison farms at Leesburg and Annandale were at first land improvement—conservation—projects. Road work did not appeal to prison officials, however. Few of their wards were eligible for a minimum security detail, in their view, and these men also had to work the farm.[49] At Rahway the management considered road work secondary to education, academic and industrial; it, too, had farms to staff. In the view of highway officials, convict labor was a complication and it happened that private contractors—as politically active and sophisticated a group as there was—had plenty of cheap labor and were bidding low in the 1920's.[50] Finally, federal legislation in 1933 in effect eliminated convict road work.

Institutional farms, unlike road work, offered the possibility of several degrees of security. Rahway's was outside its walls, the Leesburg institution, like Annandale, was minimum security, and in 1937 the Department opened a medium security prison farm at Bordentown, which took good risks from the State Prison. These developments depended upon the improvement in classification, which included a considered judgment about the offender's security needs, and also on the fact that minimum and medium security installations were much cheaper to build than cell blocks.

In the original plan for the central department the employment of prisoners was the responsibility of a director of labor, agriculture, food, and dietetics in charge of a Division of State Use. In fact, the farms were managed quite differently from the prison industries. Most of the institutions had established farms, so the "farm supervisor" from the central office had to work with them. In general, he tried to relate their production to dietary needs on one hand and soil conditions on the other, and to develop them in a mutually productive way. At the small and new institutions that could not afford a skilled manager he was especially helpful. (Donald Rice, farm supervisor from 1920 to 1923, recalled that "At the girls' home they had some Greek teacher [Mary Belle Harris] who didn't know *any*thing about running a farm.") [51]

Because the farm supervisor rode the marvelous engine of government-sponsored scientific research, so much better than any research about human problems, it is an irony of the Department's history that its farm crops flourished better than its human wards. Ellis reported in 1944 that the value of farm products had increased from $695,000 to $1,163,000 in the past decade (he did not mention the changing price level). Potato production at Leesburg increased from 235 bushels per acre in 1934 to 264 in 1942, he said, while at Trenton it was 352 bushels per acre. Milk production had steadily increased, and the average cow produced 9,842 pounds a year compared with 7,624 pounds twenty years before. In 1944, he said, institutional farms produced 7½ cents worth of the 26½ cents allowed for food per person per day (persons included inmates and staff in all institutions)—a considerable accomplishment.[52]

This farm production employed prisoners (as well as the mentally ill and retarded), but in practice it was distinguished from the "state-use industries" which employed prisoners (and some other inmates) in manufacturing enterprises. Unlike the farming operations, state-use industries were centralized in the sense that the director of state use and his staff decided what to make, where, and how, kept the accounts, and marketed the product. Since he had an unlimited supply of convict labor and he was by law preferred vendor to all public agencies in the state, at prices he set, his job looked easy. His "capital" was a grant of $200,000 from the legislature, plus $247,000 worth of equipment supplied him prior to 1926, plus what "profit" he could turn in making and selling products. He was, accordingly, able to plan his business without an annual trip to the legislature for appropriations. His market was the state purchasing agent, established in 1916, who received orders from all state institutions and agencies and had first to offer them to state use, which could release or take them.

The job was, in fact, difficult. The market was small, made smaller by the increasing productivity of modern machinery and by political pressures. In practice, there was considerable higgling about prices and the Division limited its production to appease political, business, or labor interests. The director was the manager of a corporation that did business in many different lines; the diversification made for high capital investment and high costs of supervision. As for personnel, the supervisory jobs were civil service, subject to red tape and irrelevancies like veterans' preference; the inmate labor force was difficult to begin with and hedged about by requirements of custody and program. The classification committee was a help in assigning labor, but it worked first of all for the institutional management, which took the best people for its own maintenance work.[53]

So the Department never manufactured school furniture: The enterprise would have involved a large capital investment, competition, in effect, with a very competitive industry, and negotiation with municipal officials. License tags, on the contrary, were not competitive and required much hand labor, since each set was different, and traffic signs and various chains for the highway department were new industries that state use could move into. It also developed printing, within limits negotiated with the printing industry.

Still the Bright Committee reported in 1925 that the shops were idle and that the Division was "merely 'playing' at production." It gave four reasons: insufficient orders, lack of materials, poor co-ordination between shop and institutional schedules, and fear of producing a surplus. It favored state use as a policy (what alternative was there?), but it made no suggestion for new lines of work. It did not mention school furniture. It said the great need was "keen and capable business management of the highest type," an "expert administrator" associated with "an expert accountant of the highest caliber." [54]

Ellis found this managerial paragon in 1926 in the person of Maxwell Rockhill. At least the National Institute of Public Administration reported in 1929 that the State Use Division would make "an important contribution to modern penology" by its program when the plan was "completely organized." [55] A tangible measure of success was the increase of its revolving fund (capital) to well over $1 million in 1932, plus substantial increases in the value of its equipment after depreciation.[56]

The achievement is interesting because Max Rockhill was not, by all accounts, a hard-driving managerial type. He was a mild, kindly man who had served in the Department as director of parole from 1921 to 1926. He loved children—his own marriage was childless—and he was active in the Boy Scout movement. As member and president of the Jamesburg Board of Managers for thirty-seven years he helped Derrick work out its remarkable scouting organization. He was a close friend of

Ellis and well acquainted with Trenton businessmen and club men. He and Ellis certainly persuaded the public administration experts in 1929, but these gentlemen were looking for evidence of the advantages of centralized control and responsibility.[57] The experts from Princeton who studied the Department in 1932 were interested in saving money, however, and they had some reservations. The overall profits of the enterprise—the growth of the revolving fund—despite many losing industries, were consequences of high prices charged in an uncompetitive situation, they observed. In some cases the Division had reduced prices on printing orders by 50 percent when the purchasing agent had got comparative outside bids.[58]

In his summary report for 1923–1933 Ellis claimed that the system produced goods at less than the market price, but he gave no examples (he also said it had "the wholehearted support of both employers and organized labor").[59] There was no official study of the matter between 1932 and 1957. In 1938, an unofficial student of the Division's work observed that its largest sales were auto tags and traffic signs, but it sold fully 70 percent of its products to institutions and agencies within the Department (the largest order was clothing for the Board of Children's Guardians). The student's question was whether state use saved the state money; she said she could not tell, because the standards and specifications were not adequate for an objective judgment. She did not discuss its noneconomic benefits, but her figures show that in 1937 state use employed less than one-third of the prison population, less than half the Rahway population, and less than one-third of the Annandale population.[60] Ellis never published official figures on idleness, however, nor did he even mention the problem in his reports.

Preventing Delinquency

In mid-1932, as the depression deepened, Calvin Derrick was puzzled because he had two hundred fewer boys than two years before. Juvenile institutions in other states showed the same trend, he discovered, but he found no clear explanation. He guessed that in New Jersey "well organized social work" was holding down court referrals, and there was "a definite tendency on the part of courts and probation officers to minimize rather than exaggerate minor offenses." He thought that Governor Moore's request that judges commit as few boys as possible had had an effect. Moreover, he thought the depression had helped, because children were getting more supervision at home, and service clubs and churches were emphasizing recreational and character-building agencies.[61]

He might also have mentioned a specific dissatisfaction with "reform schools," a sentiment which had prompted the Children's Bureau study of their results. In May 1925, Bishop T. J. Walsh had told a convention of the Knights of Columbus that Jamesburg (and other reformatory institutions) simply didn't reform boys or prepare them for citizenship, and he asked the Knights to help encourage probation instead of reform schools.[62] Later that year the Bright Committee had objected strongly to the practice of sending truants to Jamesburg; it thought that local truant officers, social workers, and parental schools should handle the truant problem.[63] There had been an official survey of probation in 1928 that had led in 1929 to a reorganization of the juvenile courts, to make them distinct from a police magistrate's court and more like a welfare agency. (It put probation officers under civil service.)[64]

Derrick was nevertheless observing from his vantage point a rising tide of interest in children and their problems which had the sources he mentioned. It was confused and not primarily concerned with delinquency, but it drew the attention of great social organizations—schools, churches, police, welfare agencies, character-building agencies, service clubs, and rural social organizations—and of the professions that served them. In the schools of social work, which addressed themselves most directly to the generic features of these activities and their organization, "social group work" and "community organization" came to be considered professional methods alongside social casework, while casework set a standard for services in schools, probation and parole, as well as in family service, child welfare, hospital, and child guidance work.[65]

The relation between general services for children and the prevention of juvenile delinquency had a notable focus in New Jersey in the extraordinary effort of Boss Frank Hague to reduce delinquency in Jersey City. The Boss, like the Bishop, had no use for reform schools. In 1931 he established a Bureau of Special Service in his school system under an assistant superintendent of schools. Its purposes were to identify and diagnose physical and mental problems, to improve facilities for special education for problem children, and to expand recreational facilities on school property.

The Bureau had a large staff, including the personnel of a child guidance clinic plus ophthalmologist, otologist, a large corps of special and visiting teachers, attendance officers, recreation instructors, and a special detail of police officers. It took referrals from school principals and the police, examined them for handicaps and problems, gave them appropriate remedial work, conferred with their parents, and followed up its suggestions with visits from teachers or the special policemen. It referred children to the juvenile court only if there were a definite legal problem, and the court itself had a large well-paid staff of probation officers. It claimed to have reduced the number of Jersey City children committed to state institutions by 90 percent between 1930 and 1937, and it was the model for similar agencies in Passaic and Long Branch.[66]

This was an impressive operation, as dear to Boss Hague as his fabulous medical center. At the New Jersey Conference on Crime, held in March, 1935, Dr. Thomas Hopkins, his bureau chief, claimed to "have done . . . more than has been done anywhere in the United States in the coordination of agencies bearing on child welfare and delinquency prevention.[67] Hague promoted the Juvenile Delinquency Commission, organized the next year, and helped get it $133,000 in research funds, which made its report the most elaborate social research on delinquency in the decade.[68]

The Commission did describe the Jersey City operation at length and praised its school and clinic work, but it was skeptical about its most publicized feature, the special police detail. The policemen were supposed to handle complaints about juveniles by seeking them out and taking them to their families, by-passing the police court and working with the Bureau of Special Service attached to the schools. This arrangement was, in the Commission's view, a substitute for the Juvenile Court and proper social casework, which policemen, however carefully selected and briefed, could hardly offer. The Commission acknowledged the Bureau's successes, and granted that an agency attached to the schools was likely to encounter less hostility from parents than an agency identified with courts of law, but it suggested that the Bureau's achievements owed more to its spirit than to its organization.[69]

The Commission recommended co-ordinating councils at the state and local levels, rather than the Jersey City organization. It proposed a state children's commission that would include the heads of the state Departments of Labor, Education, and Health, the commissioner of the Department of Institutions and Agencies, the superintendent of state police, the governor, and five citizens. It wanted this body to conduct research, mostly through its member agencies, publish the results, and set standards for local children's agencies. The local councils would be sponsored by counties or big cities and would include a freeholder, Juvenile Court judge, probation officer, sheriff, superintendent of schools, representative of the Board of Children's Guardians, and representatives of other public and private agencies. These local agencies would provide a child adjustment service, substantially a child guidance or mental hygiene clinic, as a center for referrals and advice.

The co-ordinating council, so conceived, was based on a famous experiment in Los Angeles and exemplified by a council in Union County (Elizabeth). It was supposed to include a greater variety of agencies than the special service bureau of the Jersey City type, to be more adaptable, because it built on existing programs and achievements, and to be more "educational" in arousing and informing public interest.[70]

John Ellis was an important member of the Commission and his co-worker Douglas MacNeil supervised the research, so the report sets forth his ideas on the theory of delinquency and steps to control it. The report discarded single-factor theories, of course, and pointed to a "wide range of causal factors": mental or physical problems, unwholesome parental care, unfortunate associations, unsatisfactory school experience, and "community factors"—poverty, movies, literature, business morality, and political morality. The common element in these factors was that "children who become delinquent . . . lack satisfactory human relationships." As a practical matter the conditions and responses of their delinquent behavior were very complex, the Commission said, and individuals responded differently in similar situations.

The practical conclusion was that, to nip delinquency in the bud, "individual factors [had to] be classified and wise preventive and corrective action taken through the study of individuals, particularly at the time when they show the first symptoms of maladjustment." [71] It was this thought that led to the recommendation for child adjustment centers. As for offenders between sixteen and twenty-one the Commission suggested that they go to the Juvenile Court, and that the Court make a mandatory clinical study and report before it decided on probation or commitment.[72]

The Commission also discussed institutional care of delinquent children. Its main emphasis in this respect was the need for county detention homes for children, to keep them out of the police station and jail. As for state institutions, the Commission stated that they were planned to permit the classification of individuals and "to develop an individualized program for each offender." [73] The report acknowledged that the "cliché" that institutions for juveniles were "prep schools for prison" was "sometimes valid." It did not pursue the point, however, except to report that inmates of the state institutions for juveniles were "almost unanimous" in saying that the institutions were helping them; those who had graduated to prison claimed that they had been harmed in juvenile institutions, the Commission said, but they explained this as a consequence of the stigma that the community placed on reform school boys after their release.[74]

The Commission did recommend a new state institution, for study of "emotionally disturbed children" pending their foster home placement. It is not clear what this institution would do, except that it would receive children who were not delinquent, psychotic, or retarded; it would not be a residential institution or treatment center, but it would be a sort of detention home and diagnostic center for the Board of Children's Guardians.[75]

In short, the Commission's report in 1939 differed in some ways from Burdette Lewis' account of the offender, published in 1917. The emphasis on faulty human relationships in the etiology of delinquency was new; so was the emphasis on community programs drawing on a variety of agencies and the idea of social casework. But both documents held that the causes of delinquency were many and complex, that the first task in a rational program was to identify their pattern in the individual, by "classification," that both judge and warden, both probation officer and correctional staff, needed this information and that there had to be appropriate agencies to gather it, that when the information was assembled and interpreted the authorities needed appropriate agencies and alternatives to "individualize" treatment.

In a historical view, the Department addressed itself during the 1920's to classification among and within institutions; during the 1930's it tried to promote classification before commitment by child adjustment clinics and social casework sponsored by juvenile courts. (In 1935 a law made it possible for judges to commit delinquents to institutions for classification and study, pending their sentence; this was called a "classification commitment.") [76]

In applying the notion of classification the Department ran into two difficulties. First of all, however refined the classification of the offender, the facilities and personnel for treatment or program were inadequate; second, there was no conclusive evidence that the work was bringing good results, nor even any clear idea of how "individualized treatment" was supposed to bring about good results. Until psychologists or psychiatrists and sociologists came up with better theories and a correctional staff learned how to apply them and got the tools, the idea of classification was perforce of limited value.

What was clear was that experts acknowledged that the New Jersey Department was on the right track. States that did not have a variety of institutions, or a central organization of them, or standard qualifications for personnel protected by civil service, that had only the rudiments of a classification procedure, a state-use system, an education or recreation program, a parole system, that had no clinics or community programs to undertake work with predelinquent children and probationers—all these had much to learn from New Jersey, as the proceedings of the American Prison Association or Fred Haynes' *American Prison System,* published in 1939, plainly showed.

Meanwhile, population remained low in juvenile homes and even in the reformatories during the depression. It increased as prosperity returned after 1938, but by 1943 the delinquents were busy at work or war (male delinquents, that is; Clinton had to rise to the emergency). As corrections seemed well in hand, the depression crisis pulled Ellis' attention, and his coworkers', in other directions. When F. Lovell Bixby returned to the Department in 1946 to look after its correctional work, after twelve years with the Osborne Association and the federal Bureau of Prisons, two things struck him forcibly. One was that, compared with 1933, nobody in the central office was much interested in corrections; the other that "those welfare operations, old age assistance and child welfare and that stuff, had moved from the wings to the center of the stage." [77]

16

From Charity to Public Welfare, 1918–1945

In the years when the New Jersey Department was conceived and organized, the general name of its concerns changed significantly. The old name—the name of the supervisory agency that the state had established in 1905, for example—was "charities and corrections"; it pointed to the local almshouse and jail and to the private and public agencies intended to supplement or supplant them. The new name, "public welfare," was first applied to departments in the government of Midwestern cities (Kansas City, 1910) and states (Illinois, 1917). It was intended to connote preventive social casework, rehabilitation, and democratic service, as opposed to a condescending attitude and palliative or punitive institutions.[1]

Charity and Casework

The organic Act of 1918 styled the New Jersey Department Charities and Corrections, and since its founders endorsed the idea of rehabilitation, one might expect that they would quickly change its name to public welfare. Instead the name was changed in 1919 to Department of Institutions and Agencies, and thus it remained.[2] Whatever its faults, the name reflected the founders' interest in managing institutions. Burdette Lewis was interested primarily in corrections and secondarily in public administration; he had had no experience with the family service and child welfare agencies that were developing constructive casework. Insofar as Lewis concerned himself with charitable institutions, he supported Dr. Cotton, who looked forward to hospital treatment rather than extramural provision, and who opposed the dynamic psychology that progressive caseworkers were applying.

John Ellis was also a corrections man; his primary interest was classification as a device for rationalizing institutional management, and his mentor, besides Lewis, was Ed Johnstone, whose ambition was to transform custodial institutions into schools and laboratories. Lewis and Ellis had first of all to pull the boards and superintendents of the several institutions into a team and to steer the Department through its difficulties with the legislature. Neither inclination nor the pressure of events led them to pay attention to the Department's agencies for constructive casework.

Among the Department's institutions were two veterans' homes—really almshouses and nursing homes—but they had no program of casework with the aged, and their population fell steadily between 1919 and 1933, when it stood at 241.[3] Three agencies did attempt to do casework with state wards outside institutions. Closest to the commissioners' hearts was the Division of Parole in the central office, which supervised parolees from the state homes, the reformatories, and institutions for the mentally retarded (but not the State Prison). But the commissioners naturally viewed its work as the final process of institutionalization, rather than a program of rehabilitation in the community.[4]

A second casework agency was the Commission for the Blind, which helped its clients by home teaching, vocational and recreational services, and beginning in 1922, financial assistance to the needy blind. It was a small operation (in 1933 it taught 653 persons and administered 369 pensions) with its office and manual training shop in Newark, quite separate from the central office in every respect.[5]

The largest agency attempting preventive or constructive casework was the State Board of Children's Guardians. Its standing in the founders' eyes is suggested by the fact that it was not discussed in the Department's first "Four Year Summary Report" in 1923. Its office was in Jersey City, not Trenton, and as late as 1929 experts from the National Institute of Public Administration described it as "practically a law unto itself in the handling of its funds and its problems." [6]

When it was set up, the Board of Children's Guardians had been progressive because of its policy of state guardianship and foster home placement, instead of institutional care, for "dependent children," that is, children who would otherwise have entered almshouses. Later, it also placed neglected or delinquent children who were committed to it by judges who deemed the children's homes and families unsuitable. In 1910, it began to place children with their own mothers as well as in foster homes, and this "home life" program had grown rapidly after 1913, when mothers—widows—were allowed to apply for help before they and their children were committed to the almshouse.[7]

Both the foster home program, for children without a suitable family, and the home life program, for families without a breadwinner, were intended to substitute constructive supervision for almshouse charity. The Board's "social investigators" were in touch with poor-law officials and judges who committed the children or families to its care, with the private child-care and child-placement agencies that also helped poor children and their families, and with the variety of professions and institutions that got involved in "child welfare." It was, therefore, in a strategic position to lead in the general improvement of services to children, and it is significant that studies of the state's organization for social welfare made during the 1920's observed that New Jersey was lacking in this respect.

The United States Children's Bureau published in 1927 a series of studies of the agency, made at the request of the State Board of Control. The Bureau's experts found that it was doing a good job, considering its difficulties, but that it was badly understaffed and its staff was underpaid. (Frances Day, its executive, earned $4,200 in 1925, much less than the superintendent at Jamesburg.) The Board of Children's Guardians had itself freely acknowledged these problems in its reports for 1918 and 1919, but the new Department, fighting to meet the grave need for new construction, had not found means to give it a more adequate staff.[8]

As a result, the experts said, the agency was unable to recruit the trained and qualified personnel that had become available because of the development of professional education for social work. Its operations were centralized at Jersey City and agents worked in various localities at various tasks as they arose, a policy that made continuity of service to communities and to the children impossible. In the dependent children's program, Miss Day and her assistant felt that their staff "were not sufficiently trained or experienced to be entrusted with the preparation and execution of a complete program for any child," so they made all the decisions themselves.[9]

Child Welfare and County Organization

Even more serious than these administrative problems, in the experts' view, was the agency's inability to work for improvement of services in the local communities of the state.[10] This criticism grew out of a central argument in contemporary discussions of public welfare, namely, that preventive work and rehabilitation required the integration of local services. The Charity Organization Societies had sounded the theme a generation before; what was new in the 1920's was an emphasis on public agencies and integration at the county level.

The instrument of integration, in the new view, was a county welfare board (perhaps a single executive). Services to be integrated were probation, connected with the County Court (or Juvenile or Domestic Relations Court); the truant officer and special teachers or classes under the county superintendent of schools; public child welfare services (including the programs administered in New Jersey by the Board of Children's Guardians); parks and recreation; parole supervision; public health services, including nurses and clinics; the county almshouse, now called "welfare house" and conceived as a nursing home for feeble old folks and the chronically ill; and—here lay a great difficulty—the administration of public outdoor relief. The county welfare board was devised so that small rural communities could share their problems and resources and together, at the county level, provide expert professional services they could not otherwise afford. It built on the success and promise of rural consolidated schools and agricultural extension work.[11]

It happened that a successful and interesting experiment along these lines was going forward in New Jersey—the Monmouth County Organization for Social Service. It had begun in 1912 as a chapter of the State Charities Aid Association, after an investigation into the operation of the poor law and charitable work in the county had shown that private and public charity was unorganized, demoralized, and ineffective, that truancy was common and unheeded, and that services to children were negligible.[12]

Monmouth County had a striking variety of people, even for New Jersey. Its prominent localities in 1912 were seaside resorts—Asbury Park, still a Methodist resort, and Long Branch and Sea Bright, which catered to fun-loving cosmopolitans. Frequent trains served these people and also the residents who commuted to New York and Philadelphia. The county seat was Freehold, in a prosperous agricultural section, but adjacent areas were sandy and infertile, farmed by "the Italian, Pole, or Hebrew, or the indigenous 'poor white.'" Many poor Negroes worked as servants, and in the salty inlets around the resorts lived "fisher folk and oyster and clam diggers" whose "primitive modes of life and simple social standards naturally result[ed] from their isolated existence" and who reminded people of the unfortunate "pineys."[13]

The agglomeration of rich man, poor man, and solid freeholder, of cosmopolitan and rural isolate, also existed in other Jersey counties, like Morris and Mercer. What was distinctive about Monmouth was the presence of Mrs. Geraldine Thompson of Brookdale Farm and Red Bank. It was she who had financed the investigation that revealed the failure of public spirit and philanthropic enterprise in the county, and she who solicited, bearded, collared, and organized the fortunate ones, her fine friends, until the Monmouth County chapter of the State Charities Aid Association was larger, richer, and more influential than the parent body. When the State Association disbanded in 1918, supposing that the new state Department would solve all problems, the Monmouth chapter became the Monmouth County Organization for Social Service.[14]

Its practical work was originally conceived as related to health and hygiene and developed through public schools and public health nurses. It conducted studies to determine needs and established experimental programs to demonstrate their value. In 1913, it began a campaign for a much-needed county TB hospital and clinics, which finally opened in 1921. In 1914, it paid the salary of a county school attendance officer. In 1915, it financed a study of the needs of retarded children in the public schools and it contributed to the salary of a full-time probation officer. In 1916, it employed a public health nurse. In 1917, it supported a "supervisor of child study" on the staff of the county superintendent of schools. In 1919, it employed John L. Montgomery, who had been in probation and corrections work in California, as its executive secretary, and he was presently appointed "county adjuster," in which capacity he made legal and financial arrangements for commitments to state charitable institutions.

In its various enterprises, the Monmouth County Organization worked closely with national agencies like the Red Cross, the Tuberculosis Association, and the National Committee on Mental Hygiene, which established an experimental traveling clinic in the county in 1921. It also handled investigations, family casework, and aftercare and parole for people committed to state institutions, as well as assisting and encouraging probation. It showed the need and possibilities of county organization of social services, and a study of it published by the United States Children's Bureau in 1922 concluded that "It is probable that the next few years will witness the development of similar organizations in the several counties of the State." [15]

As if to bear out this prediction, a committee of the state legislature in 1923 brought in a report which led to a revision of the state poor law in 1924. Its most important provision permitted counties to institute nonsalaried County Welfare Boards, which would appoint an executive to manage the county almshouse and administer outdoor poor relief according to principles of social casework. Once established, its promoters thought, the county welfare board would become a logical agency to integrate probation, parole, aftercare, health, school, and other child welfare services, which were obviously linked and overlapping in practice.[16]

The counties did not act on this "permission," however, and there matters stood when John Ellis became commissioner in 1926. Whatever he knew or cared about the subject then, events were to push it upon him. The Children's Bureau studies, published in 1927, criticized the Board of Children's Guardians for its failure to lead private agencies and the community toward integrated programs, and the Bureau's experts observed that, "unlike most progressive departments of public welfare," New Jersey's Department had no division responsible for child welfare, or community organization, or education and publicity, and that the county welfare board system was a dead letter.[17] That same year, 1927, Ellis engaged as director of medicine Dr. Ellen Potter, who, as commissioner of public welfare in Pennsylvania, had used her position to promote County Welfare Boards in that state, and in fact Ellis employed her as his representative among social work agencies.[18]

Reorganizing the Children's Guardians

Neither Ellis nor his Board nor the Board of Children's Guardians published any thoughts on the situation, but in retrospect it seems that by 1927 three considerations must have been paramount in Ellis' mind. First, the children's agency was a large and growing enterprise, substantially outside the interests and function of his office, and much criticized for what it did and didn't do. Second, professionals in child welfare thought that the key to preventive work was the integration of children's services. Mrs. Thompson's MCOSS had won national recognition for its efforts in this direction; furthermore the mental hygiene clinic that interested Ellis was a key diagnostic agency for problem children and for probation. Third, work with children was obviously related to work with adults—their parents—and the county welfare board seemed to be the appropriate agency for bringing all the services to bear on common problems. Incidentally, the county welfare board applied the principle of an unpaid honorary citizen board, such as the state Department and its several institutions boasted, to local welfare concerns, to minimize the hunt for political spoils.

Reasoning from these considerations, Ellis might have envisioned a system of county welfare boards that administered child welfare—and adult—services, employing a professional staff of social workers, special teachers and nurses, with the state Department acting to set standards, supervise, advise, and encourage. Accordingly one might expect that he and the State Board would put a person in charge of developing such a program, preparing public opinion, and drafting legislation. And this is in some measure what happened; Ellen Potter was a logical choice to develop such a program and the Department did, in the next few years, issue some publications related to the subject.

The earliest of these, dated June 1929, entitled "County and State Welfare Work in New Jersey," was interesting, however, because it avoided the question. Ellis took the occasion to endorse the poor law revision of 1924 for providing for "constructive family rehabilitation" and "the prevention of pauperism through social work" but he did not specifically mention the county welfare board or discuss the thinking that supported it. The publication was simply a directory of social agencies in the state, a useful document such as the Department had not thought to issue before.[19] Later that year, experts from the National Institute of Public Administration recommended a more active state program in encouraging community social work services and suggested that this effort might come through expanded child welfare programs emanating from a division of the central office. They specifically recommended that such a division take over the work of the Board of Children's Guardians.[20]

It is likely that Ellis and the State Board were reluctant to act so long as Frances Day was running the children's agency, because of her long service and because she was close to her own Board, which had from the beginning worked at administration and, in effect, supplemented the short-handed staff as well as determined policy.[21] It happened that Miss Day became fatally ill late in 1929, however, and the State Board undertook a critical review of the agency's work, advised by a new superintendent, Elizabeth Wyatt. She reported that the caseworkers were inadequately trained and poorly supervised, so they made mistakes that led to rehearings that clogged court calendars, and that their service to the families and wards was poor.[22] (This was much stronger criticism than the federal Children's Bureau had published.) On April 10, 1930, Ellis summarized the needs: more competent staff, more representative board, more decentralized management (closer to the counties and private agencies), and more effective organization of the work. The State Board accordingly proposed a reorganization intended to meet these needs, and moved the agency's headquarters to Trenton.[23]

Part of the reorganization was the upgrading of civil service standards for social workers, to include at least two years of college and appropriate courses in sociology and psychology, plus experience and desirable personal qualities. Because of the move and the new standards, half the workers were replaced in the next year. The other main point of reorganization was the institution of district offices, each with a staff of workers who were assigned definite and continuing caseloads.[24]

But the striking thing about the reorganization, in retrospect, is that Ellis and the State Board maintained the traditional pattern of an "agency" under a local board, and they did not take the opportunity to establish a child welfare and community organization division of the sort recommended by the United States Children's Bureau, the National Institute of Public Administration, and the experience of other states. Nor did they even discuss the possibility in public. Obviously, there were considerations that weighed against such a move, and it is possible to guess at what they were. First of all there was little political support for the county welfare board, and much opposition from those who stood to lose by a professional and nonpolitical administration of local relief. Certainly if the existing poor-law officials had wanted such boards, they could and would have established them.

Furthermore, to establish a division of welfare or child welfare in the central office would violate the logic of its organization. The divisions of the central office handled administrative functions, such as accounts, not types of institutions or problems; to set up a division on welfare, supposed to supervise local welfare agencies, would have suggested analogous divisions of corrections and mental hospitals and possibly the break-up of the Department.

There were two points at which the Department did influence local agencies. It had a Division of Inspection, which inspected local jails and almshouses, but which investigated by request for the most part and made recommendations rather than applied sanctions. A Division of Medicine inspected and licensed private hospitals, mental hospitals, and nursing homes, and in 1927 the law was strengthened by including a penalty clause. Moreover, a "field agent" attached to the central office—not to the Board of Children's Guardians—inspected child-saving institutions and counseled them, pursuant to a law of 1922, but the Department did not have power to license them and did not ask for it.[25]

In short, for Ellis and the State Board to have proposed in 1930 a division of child welfare would have required a change in their administrative thinking; such a division would have assumed the existence of county welfare boards, which were not politically popular, or it would have involved turning the state's parole and child-welfare services over to some politically-oriented regime. Even Mrs. Thompson's Monmouth County organization was not a county welfare board but a private agency, something like what social workers were beginning to call a community welfare council. The integration of services at the local level sounded fine in theory, but in practice it may well have sounded to Ellis and his board like something Boss Hague would promote in Jersey City. On either count, the cardinal consideration, in Ellis' view, would have been to protect his own Department and its service from outright political interference. It was therefore better to keep things as they were, not to try anything new and fancy.

Meanwhile, the depression was giving a different dimension to the problems of child welfare and community organization for social service.

The Pension Survey Commission

The story of unemployment relief in New Jersey during the depression has been told at length in other volumes.[26] In the present context, the relevant question is, how did it look to Ellis and his Board, with regard to the work of their Department?

Like other people, they saw the problem in the perspective of the poor law. According to the Poor Law of 1924, relief fell into two classes. One was permanent or indoor relief for people who needed long-term assistance, like the chronically sick, the insane, or dependent children. The other was temporary outdoor relief given to the poor in their homes because it was cheaper or more dignified than indoor relief. Its recipients were typically afflicted by an emergency—an accident, illness, or unemployment—that would presumably soon pass. In this class also fell provision for transients, vagrants, the homeless and friendless, and the shiftless or undeserving who might also be sent to the jail or workhouse.[27]

Massive long-term unemployment, such as the depression brought, did not fit either category. The published thoughts of Ellis and his co-workers give no indication that they had any inkling of how serious or prolonged the depression would be until the fact was long evident. Accordingly they seem to have looked upon mass unemployment as a special emergency relief problem, akin to temporary outdoor relief but related to an unusual economic crisis and not to the personal and family difficulties of the typical outdoor relief case. Their reflections about the Department's role in the crisis must have run something like this: "The economic emergency is so serious and widespread as to be a problem for emergency legislation with a temporary and probably political administrative machine to handle it. But the emergency will pass and then we shall still encounter our old problems." [28]

Meanwhile the main problem in Ellis' mind as the depression broke was that of converting the institutions to more centralized and efficient management, on one hand, and of winning over legislators on the other (the most serious attempt to break up the Department came with the Democratic ascendancy in 1932). Therefore, he probably thought of the depression as primarily an occasion for economies, for economizing would both bring the institutions into line and win over legislators. The depression did not have great immediate effect upon his institutions. The most dramatic change was the increase in cases under the Board of Children's Guardians, which rose from 13,321 in 1926 to 27,508 in 1931—a factor of the administrative difficulties of that agency.[29]

A new connection between the Department and local relief began when, in 1930, the legislature established a Pension Survey Commission to study the problem of old age dependency and pensions. The movement for pensions—very advanced at the time in neighboring Pennsylvania—had considerable and growing political support. Ellis was a member of the Commission, which noted the number of aged people on poor relief who were treated like temporary or emergency cases, although they constituted in fact a class of permanent outdoor relief. It also reported that local overseers of the poor were untrained and in most cases part-time, and that their work was inept and wasteful. The Commission recommended two legislative remedies. One made county welfare boards mandatory (not simply permissive) and put them in charge of both indoor and outdoor relief in the county. The other established a system of old age pensions, heavily subsidized by the state but administered by the new county welfare boards under state supervision.[30] Ellis supported these ideas in a pamphlet dated March 1931, which was his first explicit statement on the idea of a welfare board.[31]

The action of the legislature on these recommendations was characteristic. Legislators, unwilling to affront the local overseers of the poor and their supporters by requiring that new boards take over their work, refused to make the boards mandatory. (Proposals to establish the county welfare boards, offered as referenda in the elections of November 1931 and supported by Republican leaders, were defeated in every county but three, Camden, Warren, and Morris.) [32] They did establish a state old age pension, however, and they did require that the county establish a board to handle the pensions. That much, at least, was taken from the local overseers.[33]

To be eligible for a pension, the applicant had to be seventy and to have both a legal settlement in a county and a residence of fifteen years in the state. He had to be in good health, since the provision was for outdoor relief. He had to be without any legally responsible relatives who could support him and without an estate of more than $3,000. He had to agree to reimburse the state and county out of his estate (the cost of his funeral was limited toward this end). Furthermore, if his need resulted from the unemployment of relatives, he was ineligible until his situation "took on an aspect of permanency"—the assumption being that the unemployment of responsible relatives was a temporary or emergency matter.[34]

In practice, an old person who needed outdoor relief applied to the county Old Age Pension Board. The Board employed an investigator to collect facts on eligibility and need, then decided whether to grant a pension and how much. The state paid three-quarters of the amount granted, up to a maximum of a dollar a day; the county paid the balance. The state set standards and rules for investigation and the budgeting of needs, and supervised their administration by means of a new Division of Old Age Relief in the Department of Institutions and Agencies. The grand result of this law, which went into effect in July 1932, was that the pension supplemented the existing resources of needy old people "to the end that the recipient is relieved for the present at small cost," as John Ellis said in 1934, and "his progress toward complete dependency . . . is arrested." The program was administered so economically that the careful estimates of the Pension Survey Commission were proved mistaken: it had guessed that 12,250 persons would receive aid averaging $25 per month; in fact, after two years 7,688 persons were receiving an average grant of $15.16 per month.[35] The state's contribution came from a "dedicated fund" created out of receipts from the state inheritance tax.[36]

So boards for the administration of old age relief were established in all counties, and in 1935 Ellis praised their work and urged that counties extend their work to all outdoor relief, management of the welfare house, and the general coordination of welfare activities.[37]

Meanwhile, in 1932 the Pension Survey Commission had brought out a report which led to changes in the work of the children's guardians. The Commission was struck by the fact that one of the programs administered by the agency was much more expensive and growing more rapidly than the other. This was the dependent child or foster home placement program, which cost $215 per year per child, as compared with $134 for the home life program. Upon investigation, the Commission learned that many children were ineligible for the home life program—the cheaper one—because their fathers were still living, although absent or unable to support the family; other children were assigned to the dependency program, even though the "foster parents" were their own mothers, because the program allowed authorities to make larger grants. Accordingly, the eligibility requirements for home life were made more realistic and geared to better investigation and casework.

One might expect that the Commission would have taken the occasion to put this work of investigation and supervision upon the county boards set up to handle old age pensions, which did the same work for their clients. Instead, the Commission made a peculiar distinction. It reasoned that the home life program was cheaper because the county court had taken part in the decision, whereas the dependency program was more expensive because, once the determination of dependency had been made, the Board of Children's Guardians decided how much to give (within legal limits, of course). The Commission therefore decided to have the county court make all decisions, on the basis of information supplied it by the Board. A representative of the freeholders also had to take part. Presumably this would keep social workers from being too generous with the taxpayers' money, but the procedure threw a heavy burden of administration on the courts. To relieve the burden, the court could appoint a "referee" to handle some kinds of cases. The result of this legislation was to give local communities a larger part in the granting of aid, not through the local overseers of the poor or through the county welfare board, but through the county court and a representative of the freeholders.[38]

Social Security and Categorical Relief

The Social Security Act of 1935 did not make as much difference in the administration of welfare in New Jersey as it did in most other states. The Act established two kinds of programs. One, social insurance for old age and unemployment, fell outside the Department's purview. The other, categorical relief, or federal grants-in-aid for certain categories (types) of persons needing outdoor relief, namely the aged, the blind, and dependent children, fitted handily into existing state programs.

Since the Department did need some legislation to qualify its programs for federal grants-in-aid, Ellis might have taken the occasion to iron out an anomaly in his administrative organization. The older agencies—the Board of Children's Guardians and the Commission for the Blind—administered their programs directly, although county officials participated in the determination of eligibility and needs (and paid the pensions). The new program, old age relief (called old age assistance after 1936), was administered by county welfare boards under the supervision of a division in Ellis' office. Since Ellis favored the administration and integration of casework services under county welfare boards, he might have taken the opportunity to reorganize the older agencies on the model of the newer. He did not. To reconstruct the older agencies he would have had to eliminate their Boards of Managers, for the Division of Old Age Assistance did not have a board. (The county welfare boards were supposed to afford citizen participation.) Perhaps he feared charges of empire-building or perhaps he was simply reluctant to complicate the business of rewriting the law. In any case, he instructed Irving Engelman, who drew the legislative bills, to make the minimum changes necessary.[39]

With regard to the Board of Children's Guardians, the minimum change was to liberalize the eligibility requirements, to change the formula for payments to account for federal grants, and to establish a new service for rural areas, which would provide diagnostic and casework service and in general stimulate local community interest in and provision for children. The workers who carried out the latter mission were employed by county welfare boards but the Board of Children's Guardians supervised them and reimbursed the counties to the extent of half their salaries and expenses.[40]

This was another step toward administration by county boards and it was part of a reorganization of the agency's work by its new chief, Joseph Alloway, in 1936. Alloway, a sometime public relations man from Philadelphia, had come to Ellis' attention as secretary of the Pension Survey Commission, and Ellis had put him in charge of setting up the old age pension program. In this capacity he established close ties with the county welfare boards that administered it. His gift for administration impressed Ellis and soon became evident in the organization of the children's guardians. In addition to the new Division of Child Welfare, for rural areas, he set up central divisions for health, statistics, finance, and clothing, and strengthened and decentralized the district offices. He also put much thought into the agency's reports as a medium of public relations and he took steps toward "staff development." [41]

The need for staff development arose from the fact that civil service job specifications and salaries were too low to attract trained social workers, and, more fundamentally, from the fact that there was no certified standard for professional social work (as the head of the state Civil Service observed in 1934, when he met with the state Association of Social Workers and others in an effort to establish one).[42] There had always been some sort of organized orientation for the caseworkers, but until 1935 it took the form of staff meetings which dealt with such matters as the workers' use of cosmetics, smoking, clothes, and "manners" with clients, officials, and the public. In 1935, the eminent Dr. James Plant of Newark lectured to the workers on child problems and mental hygiene, and the agency began granting educational leaves of absence. Alloway had in mind a regular program managed by a training supervisor and a division of social service in his office, but he was unable to get the division started before 1939 and the course was not offered until 1942, when it was soon dropped because of the difficulty of travel in wartime.

A study of these efforts by Mrs. Carolin Hughes, a student at the New York School of Social Work who later became the agency's training supervisor, pointed to a misunderstanding between administrative officials and caseworkers, despite a recognition of the fact and efforts to overcome it. She noted that in November 1945 only five of the ten members of the central office staff had any graduate study in social work and only one had completed graduate training in social work. In the field, less than half the workers had finished college and less than a fifth had any graduate courses in social work. Turnover was an urgent problem, then as in the past.[43]

The misunderstanding Mrs. Hughes referred to, between administration and service, reflected the fact that practical administrators in public welfare thought in terms of getting a definite volume of work done in a limited time, in relation to appropriations or sharing of funds, for example, with prescribed records to show for it, whereas the social work guild was interested in refined casework along lines developed in private agencies that thought of relief as merely a means to some sort of rehabilitation.[44]

Ellis himself was unprepared to understand the social workers' point of view, and none of his agency executives were technically social workers. Characteristically he looked past the formality of office and preparation to men and jobs. He wanted men of affairs who could get along with legislators and local officials; he could recognize them and judge their work. Alloway was such a man, and so was Marc Dowdell, who had been a newspaper man in Trenton before entering the state service as Alloway's assistant in 1934, who succeeded Alloway as chief of old age assistance and who was one of Ellis' principal speechwriters.[45] Other career men who undertook the administration of welfare programs in these years were lawyers, like Irving Engelman and Edwin Hann, Jr. Dr. Ellen Potter, Ellis' representative to professional social work, had nothing to do with drafting or administering welfare programs in the Department.[46] Ellis was very critical of the "utopianism" of some social workers and their ignorance of economics and administration, which, he thought, "shocks economists, businessmen, legislators, and others who might be helpful under favorable circumstances."[47]

General Relief and Municipal Aid

The really central problems about public assistance in the later years of the depression, in Ellis' mind, were related to administration of general relief. From 1933 to 1936, the federal government had made large emergency grants to the state Emergency Relief Administration, which had in turn subsidized outdoor poor relief of the unemployed. President Roosevelt's advisers had favored work relief—wage payments for public work—over a dole, however, and in 1935 they decided to get the federal government out of "this business of relief"—to stop subsidizing state and local agencies—and instead to develop large-scale public works programs directed from Washington. In a way, they established another category, the employable unemployed, and proposed to help it with work relief; the unemployable—the aged, blind, and dependent children—would get public assistance by the new "categorical relief" programs, and unfortunates who got neither work relief nor categorical relief would fall under general poor relief, administered by localities under the poor law.[48]

It was apparent to the New Jersey legislature that the federal work relief projects would not support all the employables and that the federally-assisted categorical relief programs would not provide for all the unemployables, and it followed that local outdoor relief (general relief) would continue to be a large undertaking. As a practical matter, many municipalities would need some state aid in financing this relief, and along with the financial assistance some supervision to make sure that decisions about giving relief were made, recorded, and followed up in a businesslike way. Since many families on poor relief would also have a member or two eligible for a categorical program (and hence a federal subvention), it would be convenient and efficient to have investigations and programs integrated, and it was possible, in an integrated and large-scale program, to employ or develop skilled social work in its administration. In short, the logic that pointed to administration of all relief by county welfare boards in 1924 and 1932 seemed even more convincing in 1936 and 1937.

The great question early in 1936, therefore, when the federal government stopped subsidies to the state Emergency Relief Administration, was what kind of agency would follow it. Ellis' idea, embodied in a bill drawn for him by Irving Engelman, was for administration by county welfare boards under state supervision. The bill was defeated in the Assembly by a vote of 25–23.[49] Instead the legislature established a State Financial Assistance Commission which would allocate an "equalization fund" among the municipalities for emergency relief. The fund was accumulated by transfer of other state funds and by sale of bonds—not a stable financial base. What was equalized was the ability of municipalities to raise funds to relieve their poor. If their taxes exceeded a certain proportion of their property valuation, the state underwrote the balance of their needs.[50]

So, instead of incorporating the administration of outdoor relief into the work of Ellis' department and the existing county welfare boards, as every expert opinion recommended, the legislators chose to keep alive an emergency type of organization that ran from a new state agency, the Financial Assistance Commission, directly to municipal authorities. The argument for the new arrangement was that if the municipal officials administered the program they would keep expenses low, and that officials appointed locally as part of local government would make better judges of needs and quicker sources of relief than some finicking social worker in a county office.[51]

Since the state Financial Assistance Commission was made up of elected officials and its staff was exempt from civil service, as were most of the local officials who administered aid, it is possible to interpret the decision as simply an effort by politicians to maintain the spoils system. It also gave form to the assumption that the depression was an emergency and the problem of large-scale outdoor relief did not merit the dignity of a permanent addition to the state Civil Service and its welfare department.[52] What is clear is that the municipalities did not want outdoor poor relief administered by county welfare boards. In large municipalities the work was a political plum; in small municipalities it was hardly worth bothering about (several municipalities did not participate in the state assistance program because their expenditures for relief were so small). However much the large and small, or rural and urban, municipalities might disagree on substantial issues, they could agree on the dogma of local autonomy. And autonomy it was, for the state commission in practice contented itself with the allocation of funds, made few demands about administration and practically none about service.[53]

Since Ellis and the State Board were supposedly above politics and supposed to give the state overall leadership in welfare matters, it is a striking fact that their record shows very little in the way of outspoken support for a more enlightened order. A social worker who studied the Department's public relations in 1938 mentioned its efforts to get better administration of relief. "There were indications," at the time she wrote, "that the politicians were ready for a decentralized system [i.e., by county welfare boards] which would be placed in the Department of Institutions and Agencies." The principal means to promote this end, she said, had been that the Department had established "friendly relations with the county departments and local overseers . . . demonstrating [its] stability . . . and its friendly intentions." She did not mention formal public support, however, or any active campaign.[54]

Two investigations of "emergency relief"—neither by Ellis or his Board—kept the question alive.[55] In 1940, there was a reorganization which put the operation under a single full-time director of municipal aid and put the local officials under civil service, but it did not give administration to county welfare boards and supervision to Ellis' department.[56]

The problems and policies of welfare administration in the state as of 1940 were admirably and critically described in Paul Tutt Stafford's *Government and the Needy, A Study of Public Assistance in New Jersey*. Stafford, a professor of political science at Princeton, had written his dissertation on the administrative organization of the state Department of Institutions and Agencies and made himself a close student of state and local services. His study drew on the resources of the Federal Writer's Project for historical studies of poor relief and on grants from the Brookings Institute and Princeton for a first-hand examination of its administration. It is the sort of study the state Board of Control of Institutions and Agencies might have made or sponsored, if it had been willing to confront the problems in a candid and critical way.

In Stafford's view, the depression had forced a transition from old-fashioned poor relief to modern public assistance. The former was traditionally a part-time, casual enterprise to meet a peripheral problem. The latter was, potentially at least, a professional well-organized service to meet a problem that had become central. The existing order represented a series of compromises or expedients showing steps in the transition. It had two major weaknesses, he thought. First was a diffusion of responsibility among different levels of government, such that services which should have been integrated and comprehensive were left to the insight and energy of a variety of officials who mistook small parts for large wholes. This carving up of relief functions not only made the service ineffective but made popular understanding and control difficult, so ultimate political responsibility was ignored. "There are probably not more than a score of laymen and policy-making political representatives in the entire state who know the present system's ramifications or can identify in a general way the various organizations involved," Stafford observed; "the system literally defies public comprehension; it is a source of mystery to most legislators." [57]

The second weakness he saw was the lack of administrative and financial stability in the system; that is, the officials could not think ahead and plan efficiently simply because their tasks and resources were conceived in terms of a passing emergency. The exception to the rule, he thought, and the best feature of the system, was the administration of categorical relief, which had a stable financial base of shared funds and full-time professional administration and supervision.[58]

The solution he proposed was to finance and administer all relief—direct and work, emergency and poor-law, indoor and outdoor—in the general pattern of the categorical programs. He wanted the federal government to make a contribution and supervise the states, the state governments to make a contribution and supervise the local governments, the local governments to make a contribution and administer the program under regular civil service procedures. Specifically, he favored an integrated program of public assistance under the state Department of Institutions and Agencies; local services he proposed to transfer from the municipality to the county except for populous municipalities that could support regular services.[59]

By some coincidence, these thoughts are similar to those Ellis voiced at a conference on relief held in April 1940. Ellis, too, recommended that the federal grant-in-aid program for categorical relief be extended in principle to cover work relief (then a federal responsibility) and general assistance (local poor relief). He pointed to the advantages this would have for intake, classification, and certification of cases, for finance and recording, for fact finding and research, and especially for determining and meeting needs. Given a comprehensive policy and initiative, he said, states could organize their finances and personnel to remove "this issue of human welfare . . . from the vicissitudes and vagaries of partisan political expediency." [60]

In short, by 1940 the question of integrating services in county welfare boards was subordinated to the question of integrating federal work relief and local public assistance, on the assumption that mass unemployment was not an emergency but a permanent condition. While in theory, as Stafford looked at it, for example, the county welfare board was the best device for integration, he was willing to concede that populous municipalities might have organizations separate from the county. The fact was that the political interests that favored municipal, rather than county, administration had prevailed. The state administrator of municipal aid appointed in 1940, Charles Erdman, a professor of political science at Princeton University and mayor of the Borough of Princeton, gave the municipal poor relief officials aggressive and able leadership.[61]

Unresolved Issues

Just as men had begun to think that large-scale unemployment was permanent, the wartime prosperity began and removed the pressure for radical reorganization. In June 1943, Ellis was called upon to publish his thoughts on the future as part of the report of a state Commission on Postwar Economic Welfare. He mentioned first his Department's need for construction and maintenance, then for new institutions. He proposed local health centers and clinics for rehabilitation and for people on public assistance; he looked forward to federal aid in their construction and also in developing some form of health insurance. (These suggestions probably stemmed from the interests of Dr. Ellen Potter.) Finally, and briefly, he mentioned the need for a restudy of public assistance laws. He notably did not discuss the question of integrating public assistance or the county welfare boards.[62]

By contrast, the statement of Mr. Erdman, head of the State Municipal Aid Administration, was explicit about the service needs in public assistance and appropriate measures to meet them, all to be coordinated at the "community or local level" under state supervision and guidance; by implication he looked forward to a reorganization of existing categorical programs at the municipal, instead of the county, level under his agency, not Ellis'.[63]

In 1944, therefore, matters stood much as they had in 1934. Of the categorical programs, old age assistance was administered by county welfare boards under state supervision, and so was aid to the blind (after 1939), but aid to dependent children was administered directly by the State Board of Children's Guardians through district offices, and there were services for crippled children administered by a special commission outside the Department.[64] Outdoor poor relief was still administered mostly by local officials, now incorporated into civil service and organized under a separate state agency. The notion of a responsible and comprehensive state policy integrating the several kinds of outdoor relief and services for the needy, and relating these to the extramural programs of prevention, aftercare and rehabilitation, with which they were in fact closely linked, was ignored. A "look to the future" which Ellis published in 1945 scarcely mentioned the problem and certainly did not analyze it.[65]

To summarize with regard to the theory of welfare administration between 1918 and 1945, there were two new ideas that the New Jersey Department had difficulty incorporating. One held that problem people were somehow maladjusted and that the appropriate way to handle them was by individualized social casework by a community agency at an early stage in their difficulties. It was further held that these difficulties characteristically involved family disorganization, and might best be treated in that context, and that children in the formative years ought to be a special object of attention.

These ideas developed among professional social workers in family service and child welfare agencies in the big cities and in professional schools that trained social workers. In detail they were confused and unimpressive, but they were supported by popular interest in child development and mental hygiene, they gave new force to old ideas about prevention and rehabilitation, and they had obvious ramifications for work with delinquents and the mentally ill or retarded as well as those who primarily needed material relief. As the New Jersey Department was set up, however, there was no one responsible for exploring these ideas or promoting them. There was some consideration of their importance with respect to parole, to aftercare for mental patients, and to mental hygiene clinics, but these matters were generally tangential and peripheral to the Department's concern with institutional management.

In the second place, there was a shift in the direction of the theory of public administration. The founders of the Department had addressed themselves to shortcomings in the management of the state's charitable and correctional institutions. They concluded that what was needed was a management that was unified, so that it could deal with common problems in a systematic way and speak with a single voice, and that was nonpolitical, operated by career officials under the general guidance of honorary citizen boards. They wanted citizen participation, which was afforded by the boards, and they recognized a problem of overcentralization, which was solved by the existence of institutional boards. The newer theories of welfare administration, however, related to the development of extramural services and citizen participation at the local level, and held that a state department should foster and guide this activity. This line of thought was worked out most clearly with regard to child welfare, but it also applied to extramural programs for state institutions, mental hygiene clinics, social service and aftercare programs, for example, or delinquency prevention, probation, and parole services. In this view, the work of a state department was to develop programs, intramural and extramural, and business management and professional or career leadership in institutions were more or less taken for granted in passing.

Ellis was interested in developing programs, of course, and in an informal way he was very much interested in establishing friendly working relations with individuals and groups at work in local communities. But his primary and formal commitment to institutional management determined his perspective on these matters. He thought that the Department should relate to the communities through its institutions, that the mental hygiene clinics should be attached to mental hospitals, for example, and he never did see his way clear even to transfer child welfare services from district offices to county welfare boards.

If he had been primarily interested in developing local services, Ellis might have gone to the political leadership or the public and asked for a carrot and a stick—financial aid and strong powers to inspect or license, for example—to get the local communities moving. There is no evidence that he ever contemplated such direct action. For one thing, to whom might he have turned? To Boss Hague, the anti-Hague Democrats, the Hague Republicans, the anti-Hague Republicans, to the governor or the legislature, or to some special pressure group such as his predecessor Burdette Lewis had tried to organize? The lesson of Ellis' first decade of leadership, which guided his second, was to let politics alone so that politicians would let his Department alone, to lead as best he could without giving orders, contradicting anyone, or suggesting that the Department, the politicians, or the people of the state had important responsibilities that were not met or recognized. If Ellis and his Board could have worked on the state level as Mrs. Thompson did in Monmouth County, organizing people and groups and getting them to work together, the story might have been much different. But they could not.

Perhaps Ellis (and his Board, for they were formally in charge) would have talked more about human needs and responsibilities if they had felt that they really had effective programs to sell. But the fact was that, given an ideal political situation and a responsive and responsible public—given, that is, a moral consensus—there was simply no scientific consensus on who the problem people were, what their problems were, or how to help them. Was mental illness a consequence of organic lesions or poor "mental hygiene"? Was a mental hygiene clinic supposed to keep people out of the asylum or simply to help people who were confused and suffering? Was mental retardation a genetic fault or a judgment of social inadequacy? Should correctional institutions punish, re-educate, or resocialize, and in any case, how? What could social workers really do and how could you tell a good social worker from a bad one? In a way, all the practical problems of administration rested on scientific theories that were confused and dubious.

By the nature of their tasks and the perspective of their historical situation, Ellis and his Board addressed themselves to problems of administrative organization and political interference, rather than to problems of scientific theory, untrained personnel, and community organization.

Certainly Ellis and his Board never published anything pointing to the need or opportunity for research in the programs they were responsible for. Once Ellis did reveal his thinking on the subject, however, and his remarks show that he recognized some of the limitations under which he labored. The occasion was a celebration in 1931 of the twenty-fifth anniversary of the laboratory at the Vineland Training School. Dr. Henry Cotton had recently retired as medical director at Trenton State Hospital to devote himself to research, and Ellis was bemused by the situation. "People who should have been patient and understanding, and who should have withheld hasty judgments have not done so" in Dr. Cotton's case, he said. This statement was certainly less than the whole truth about Cotton's difficulties, but Ellis made an interesting comment: "More is gained by speaking frankly about the limitations of [research in public institutions] than by trying to make extravagant claims," and he went on to say something that was never said frankly in any official report during his administration.

> Public institutions, generally, either have not had the vision of what could be done [by research] or have not been able to "sell" their vision and ideal and purposes to the people who supply the money. When it has been attempted, too often the character and calibre [sic] of the personnel has not been of the right sort or the environment has not been suitable.

"One or two states have . . . buildings, and have obtained competent [research] personnel," he went on, but he did not believe that they had been "able to give the kind of 'aura' to their situation that makes for the most hopeful sort of situation." Research required a "spirit of adventure" and a "complete freedom" that was possible only in a university, he thought.[66]

This argument might have led Ellis to the conclusion that somehow someone in the Department should be engaging academicians in research related to its programs, but there was neither provision in his budget for any such office nor clear direction as to where to turn or for what. The state did not provide for its needs in higher education, even for the professional education of school teachers; it chose to draw upon institutions in neighboring states rather than to develop its own colleges and professional schools. There was no proper state university that Ellis might have asked to train the personnel he needed—doctors, social workers, specialists in public welfare administration and criminology—or that he might have asked to do scientific work for him, as the College of Agriculture at Rutgers trained specialists and did research for Jersey farmers.

The history of the services of the New Jersey Department between 1918 and 1945 reveals how much of the work lay outside the institutions and how much it depended upon the general development of theory and professional skill. Increasingly, the success of its work lay in inducing local communities to provide extramural services and integrated programs and in inducing organized professions and the scientific community to take more interest in its work.

The demand laid upon the Department in 1918 was to keep public welfare away from the spoilsmen and make it businesslike; the institution of board control, so prominent in its organization, was a combination of the nineteenth-century notion of well-to-do philanthropists and the twentieth-century notion of boards of directors of business corporations. By 1945, the class of genteel reformers and philanthropic heroines was nearing extinction, however; the science of administration was not the prerogative of businessmen alone, and the ideas of public welfare and professional service had largely supplanted the older ideas of charity and correction. The demand in 1945 was that particular kinds of service be measured against standards that were set by national professional associations and a national scholarly community and resources that were enlarged by the federal government and by national voluntary associations for research and publicity.

As the New Jersey Department turned to face the crisis of postwar expansion following wartime neglect, the heritage of its administration in these crucial matters was not especially helpful.

17

Postwar Problems

Two events mark 1945 as a year of transition for the Department: the death of William John Ellis and the end of the war. Ellis' administration drew so much on his personal gifts—his "practical psychology" and extraordinary memory, for example—that his successors inevitably brought divergent personal styles to the job. The postwar years raised problems that differed from those between 1930 and 1945. In some respects they were like those of the earlier postwar period, the 1920's, but the similarities were hard to see across the years, even if one had been inclined and prepared to look for them. Certainly circumstances of the 1950's prompted questions that were familiar to a student of the 1920's or of the generation before that: questions about the organization of state services, their supervision and control, their relation to local public agencies, to associations of volunteer philanthropists or reformers, to professional workers and their science, and more generally to the groups and interests in the state whose opinions and moral commitments were the foundation of political support.

By 1958, there was enough concern about the structure and work of the Department to call forth a special study commission, which set out to review the system suggested by the Morrow and Earle commissions forty years before. In a practical sense, the interesting thing about its report, published the following year, was its recommendations. But in historical perspective the report, and the situation leading to it, offer an instructive comparison with earlier efforts to understand and prescribe for the state's organization for social welfare.

Old Problems and New

In most respects, the peculiar structure of the New Jersey Department—its comprehensive character and its lay boards—made the position of the commissioner quite strong. The boards protected him from direct intervention by political spoilsmen, and they were a vehicle of constructive interest for and interpretation by the laymen who made them up. In theory, the commissioner (and the State Board) had ample authority to institute policies and programs of unusual breadth and flexibility, comprehending almost all the state's welfare institutions. In practice, however, the commissioner had to deal with local institutions that were jealous of their prerogatives and autonomy, and he had to get funds from a legislature or an electorate whose political leaders had no direct responsibility for his operations. Neither institutions nor politicians could dictate to him, but he, for his part, could not dictate to them. The politicians were too divided and the institutions too isolated to offer constructive alternatives to his leadership, but he and his Board had to weigh decisions so as to minimize disagreement and conflict.

It was this situation, as well as his natural inclination and the tutelage of "Uncle Ed" Johnstone, that brought out Ellis' "practical psychology" and his willingness to postpone a public confrontation of issues such as his predecessor had tried; and it was the depression that secured his power. The constant pressure for "economy"—holding down expenditures—was a lever to move the institutions, and his office was well organized to oversee their business administration. In the political stalemate of the depression years, the board system allowed him to get along with all sides. In any case, since to economize was to make do, to hold the line, Ellis found that he did not have to ask for much, and there was little pressure on him to ask for more. That was one secret of his success.

After the war this situation changed. The phenomenal and unexpected growth of the state's population and many special factors, such as the improvement of medical care and the increase in family disorganization, caused sharp increases in the Department's caseload, and the cases that got to the institutions tended increasingly to be very difficult or hopeless. There was, consequently, a need for new facilities and staff. But the postwar inflation put the state government at a disadvantage in recruiting staff and providing construction; housing for the senile and schools for the retarded drew on the pool of resources that supplied housing and schools for normal people.

Moreover, interested parties said with increasing conviction that the need was not simply to catch up or keep up with the population, but also to establish higher standards of service and large new services. The general ideas behind these demands were familiar and hardly disputed—prevention, rehabilitation, the dignity and rights of the persons in need—but they found new voices and urgency in these years. There were new sources of standards and support: the federal government and the philanthropic foundations, which drew large new means, directly or indirectly, from the federal tax laws of the depression and war years; national associations for health and welfare and professional organizations of many kinds, which influenced the federal government and philanthropic foundations; the great apparatus of research and communication, taking shape primarily in the universities but also in other settings, which furnished insights and ideas for the practical-minded.

None of these influences was entirely new, but they grew so fast, in so many reciprocal ways, as to constitute a new environment for the Department. Around it rose a variety of citizen groups that saw, in many different, partial and confused perspectives, the gaps between scientific understanding and public policy, public policy and public programs, and whose plea in the 1950's was not to make do or hold the line, but to do more, to ask more, than anyone had seriously suggested in the 1930's.

There were many favorable factors in meeting the new challenge. The state had many well-established and prosperous industries and it was a leader in such growth industries as chemicals and pharmaceuticals. In per capita income and education its citizenry ranked among the highest in the nation. The social divisions that had affected its welfare institutions before 1930—between urban and rural, foreign-born and native, Catholic and Protestant—were diminishing, and on all sides there was a more realistic and sympathetic attitude toward the state services. This was true in particular of private charities and welfare agencies and their supporters, whose organization and methods had gone forward during the war and afterward because of the improvement in community chests and councils, who found a forum in the annual conferences and activities of the New Jersey Welfare Council, and who were able to offer the public services more general support and constructive criticism than in prewar years.

Among the hopeful factors, not least was the esteem in which the Department was held, in state and out. When it was necessary to replace Commissioner Ellis, the State Board quickly found a man of wide experience and national reputation, Sanford Bates. Bates, on his part, came to the job thinking that "John Ellis had a pretty respectable operation going there and [he] wasn't disposed to change anything very much." [1] There is no record that anyone was thinking differently at that time.

Commissioner Sanford Bates

Sanford Bates was born in Boston in 1884. He attended English High School there and night classes at the YMCA until he received an LL.B. from Northeastern University in 1906. He was elected in 1912 to the state legislature, serving as representative and later senator, and it seemed that he had found his career in the law and Republican politics. In 1918, he became commissioner of penal institutions in Boston, however, and the following year Governor Calvin Coolidge asked him to head the State Department of Corrections, a job he held for ten years. In 1929, President Hoover made him head of the federal prison system and in the next nine years, under Hoover and Roosevelt, he expanded and developed that system into a model for the country. He resigned in 1937 to become executive director of the Boys Clubs of America, a job which paid half again as much as his federal position and left him more free to lecture and teach (at the New York School of Social Work, among other places). His professional interest in the work was its relation to crime prevention, but he became dissatisfied with it and left when Governor Lehman of New York asked him to become parole commissioner there, a job he held until he came to the New Jersey Department on June 1, 1945.[2]

Many offices and honors in associations for corrections and social work testified to Bates' reputation. His book, *Prisons and Beyond* (1936), set forth his doctrine that since most prisoners return to society, prison life (and parole) ought to prepare them for their return. This was a familiar idea, and the "paraphernalia of reform" and principles of administration he described were also familiar—a career service and classification and individualization of program, for example. What gave weight to his presentation was that he was a doer who had founded a system of institutions that actually put these honored ideas into practice. As for his knowledge of New Jersey, he had known and admired both Burdette Lewis and John Ellis, and he had always looked with interest upon their plan of organizing common services in functional divisions, an arrangement which in some respects resembled what he had done in Washington.[3]

When he came to Trenton, Bates was almost sixty-one, nine years older than the man he replaced. Tall, heavy-set, and ruddy, he worked as long hours as Ellis. He struck his new coworkers as a man who liked long conferences, more of a talker than Ellis, full of stories with morals, some funny, some stern. He could be entertaining and inspirational, but no one described him as a "great practical psychologist."

The words that came most frequently to his admirers involved "principle." "Mr. Bates was more of a broad thinker than Mr. Ellis," remarked a secretary who knew them both well. "He thought more about general organization and principles as such. It was his legal training, I suppose. And he was *very* New England." "Bates had an ethical quality," according to a more skeptical observer. "He really thought that what was strictly right in the immediate situation was always best in the long run." "That Bates wasn't afraid of anybody, he wouldn't buy anybody"—this from an admirer—"I've heard him stand up to 'em all—politicians, businessmen, union men, doctors, judges, everybody." A disgruntled subordinate, a friend of Ellis', conceded that "if you could sell the old man on your case he would give you a kind of support that Ellis never would. John would wait to see how the wind was blowing; Bates would go to bat for you."

Bates' strong sense of personal responsibility and interest in formal procedures often struck his associates as egotism. "He was Mr. Big Commissioner, everything had to go through him," one observer noted. "To get to see him you first made an appointment with his secretary," a subordinate recalled. "The interview, when it finally took place, was likely to be a long cross-examination, and then he took a long time to decide. When you made another appointment to discuss the matter further, you had to go over the whole thing again, and justify points you thought were already settled. So I learned, better get it in writing." Such comments make an unintentional contrast with Ellis' self-effacing manner, his marvelous memory, and his speedy decisions. They also suggest how much Ellis had thought in terms of particular men and assignments: It must have been difficult for a stranger to see how problems, jobs, and people fitted together in the office.

As for the institutions, Ellis had relied on his direct relation with their superintendents and officials to give them a common direction, and he had hesitated to push them into common patterns of formal organization, so there were inevitably confusing idiosyncrasies in their administration. This was all quite different from the system Bates had built in Washington for the far-flung federal prisons, where he had few administrative precedents to complicate affairs, no local boards to celebrate variety of administration, and where only three men reported directly to him. It often seemed to the new commissioner that elementary procedures were inadequate. "How often have I seen him read a report," recalled a long-time associate, "and then throw it down on the desk and say 'That's not the way to do it, that's just not right at all!' " The gesture meant that, while Bates approved the general organization of the Department, many details of its operation left him puzzled and impatient. It was not long before innovations gave form to his own ideas.

Problems of Internal Organization

Ellis' way of welding the several institutions together might be characterized as an omniscient and paternalistic empiricism. His reliance on personal acquaintance was formalized in the regular Monday visits his superintendents made and his own frequent field trips, as well as the formality of monthly reports and annual budget hearings. Bates, unable to draw on long personal acquaintance and inexperienced in the administration of mental hospitals and public assistance programs, felt a need for expert consultation and help. His first departure was to establish three new "deputy commissioners" in the fields of corrections, welfare, and mental health. He regarded them as people who would filter and investigate problems within their jurisdiction, form a policy-making administrative group for the Department, represent it at professional meetings, and promote new programs. They were his assistants, not subordinates in a chain of command, and they differed in this respect from a fourth deputy commissioner, Francis ("Spike") Gerry, who since 1937 had been formally in charge of administration.[4] But Ellis had not developed the office of deputy commissioner and it would have been out of character for him to establish intermediaries of this sort.

As for the budget, Bates needed no expert advice here: His hearings, formal, detailed, and long, took up most of two months. The budget was, he thought, a review of the year's work and "an opportunity to dig pretty deeply into the philosophy and administrative capacity of the superintendent and his assistants." It was also a necessary check on officers who did not have ordinary incentives to economize. "I really think that one of my chief contributions to the Department was illustrating to some of the men already on the staff that there was a real science to budget-making," he observed much later, and he recognized that "no doubt this may have irritated some of the superintendents." Associates complained that he was "too conscientious," he said, or that he "did not 'get along' with people." [5] Certainly the budget was even more important as a means of information and control for Bates than for Ellis.

The new commissioner made two other notable efforts to bring together the central office and the scattered institutions. For one thing, he encouraged conferences of personnel who held similar jobs (business managers or psychologists, for example) and conferences of board members with common interests, including a grand dinner that assembled them all.[6] For another, he realized a plan, already some years old, for a departmental magazine, the *Welfare Reporter,* which, since the Department published no regular reports, became the principal historical record of its work. As first conceived, it was a monthly news magazine of twenty-four pages, intended largely to build "a stronger unity and *esprit de corps*" among employees and board members but partly to inform the "general public," especially makers of public opinion and officials of other state agencies.[7]

The focus on personnel is significant, for it soon became clear that holding and recruiting staff would be a major concern. There was no personnel officer in the Department as originally planned. Recruitment was, in theory, the business of particular hiring agencies and the state Civil Service Commission; in fact, it was not a problem during the depression and it was disorganized by the war.

As the postwar situation took shape, it became evident that the old-time fear of political spoilsmen, which led state civil service commissions to suspect executives of political motives, had insulated the commissions to some extent from the needs of operating departments, made them slow to comprehend the vagaries and shifts of job classification, and left them out of touch with training centers for professional staff. Accordingly, in April 1945, the Department hired a man to improve its liaison with the state Civil Service Commission. This was Raymond F. Male, a young man who had been with the state commission and who was a doctoral student at Princeton under the eminent William Carpenter, sometime head of the commission. Male, a slight man who looked even younger than he was, was brainy, enthusiastic, articulate, and energetic, and Bates presently made him head of a new division of personnel.[8]

As in the 1920's, the labor problem involved both unskilled and professional workers. The situation of the custodial workers at the mental hospitals and institutions for the retarded was particularly difficult. An effort to unionize the workers at the Trenton State Hospital in April

1942 had brought forth these demands: an eight-hour day, instead of twelve; minimum pay of $80 per month instead of $50, and the option of a cash settlement for maintenance; better food; rotating jobs; seniority rights; grievance procedures. In a report on the situation Ellis had argued that civil service and the merit system, not unions and seniority, ought to protect the workers and assure them of fair conditions.[9]

As in the 1920's, it was neither unions nor civil service, but a tight labor market and competition from institutions in neighboring states that finally brought improvement—the eight-hour day in September 1945 and, presently, higher wages.[10] The eight-hour day forced many institutions to hire three shifts in place of two and to reorganize their care where it had depended on family-type supervision. It meant that more workers had to live off the grounds. Since the turnover was high and many vacancies were never filled, it forced the Department into energetic campaigns to recruit workers and new experiments with in-service training that would, it was hoped, give incentive and a better civil service classification to the more promising workers. The state anti-discrimination act, passed in 1945, opened these jobs to Negroes, who soon took them in large numbers. The work of planning and supervising these changes, as well as recruiting, training, and reclassifying the employees, fell inevitably upon the central office, particularly on Ray Male.[11] The problem of recruiting professional staff is best discussed in relation to particular programs, but it also fell upon the central office.[12]

In short, personnel problems after the war forced a reorganization of the labor force in most of the institutions, broke up the tradition that most workers lived at the institution in a sort of big family, and forced the central office to take increasing responsibility for recruitment, training, and personnel policy generally.[13] A comparable difficulty in the 1920's had been relieved by the depression. Now the Cold War, the Korean War, the continued growth of population, inflation, and widespread prosperity afforded no such quietus.

Constitutional Changes

Meanwhile, a new constitution, reflecting changes in the social structure of the state, presented a threat to the character of the Department. The movement to reorganize the state government had begun under Governor Wilson in 1912, when its slogan was "economy and efficiency" and its practical ideas were the executive budget, civil service, and the nonpartisan administrative board, all devices to take politics out of government. In the 1940's, the slogan was executive control and responsibility, and one practical idea was to increase the governor's powers and make them more flexible, so that he could test his ideas and the electorate could, in turn, test him.[14]

In 1940 began a new and determined effort to revise the old constitution of 1844. It was supported by governors of both parties, but defeated, at first, by the traditional factionalism of rural and urban Republicans, Hague and anti-Hague Democrats, Catholics and Protestants. But the question would not rest. The Committee for Constitutional Revision, which pressed it, was an unlikely amalgam of, among other groups, the American Federation of Labor, the CIO, six women's organizations (including the League of Women Voters, the State Federation of Women's Clubs, and the American Association of University Women), the New Jersey Taxpayers Association, and the Association of Real Estate Boards.

What held these diverse groups together was their urban associations, which made them think that strong and active state government would improve everyone's lot, and a body of ideas about public administration that academics had, over two decades, hammered into a semblance of science. In this perspective, the old factionalism was unenlightened but understandable, and its issues were negotiable in the interest of a long-run improvement. For their part, the factions had nothing constructive to offer and no professors of political science to give them dignity and authority: Without strong principles, they could be approached and persuaded.[15]

In 1947, newly-elected Governor Alfred Driscoll, a Republican supported by a Republican legislature, arranged a constitutional convention and managed it so as to minimize factionalism. The constitution that resulted was an imperfect instrument of representative government —it continued the inequitable apportionment of the State Senate and resolved some key issues by arbitrary compromise—but it gave form to many enlightened ideas and its very compromises showed that the traditional factions were willing to resolve their disagreements in a common good. Both parties endorsed it; the electorate ratified it in November by a large majority.[16]

The constitutional convention, and the legislative enactments that reorganized the government on the new principles, were a major concern of Commissioner Bates and the State Board for more than a year. There were two lines of argument that bore upon the Department. One held that all executive departments ought in principle to be led by men directly responsible to the governor, and that boards like the State Board of Control contradicted this principle. The other held that the Department as it stood might better be divided into two or more departments, each under an expert head. On his record, Bates might well have agreed with both arguments, for he had managed single-interest departments of correction in both Massachusetts and Washington, under direct political control, by officials of both parties, without honorary citizen boards to protect—or complicate—his administration.[17]

Despite his success in politically responsible departments, Bates was keenly aware of the tenuous character of penal reform, so vulnerable to apathy and "the recurrent blight of partisan politics," and he knew from experience how agencies for welfare and mental hygiene could help criminals and their families.[18] He was, therefore, disposed to defend the New Jersey arrangement, and of course Reeve Schley and Mrs. Geraldine Thompson, the dominant members of his Board, were entirely opposed to change.[19]

There were three general arguments in favor of the status quo. First was the old argument against political interference, with a new accent on supporting professionalism rather than frustrating spoilsmen: The work of the Department, it was said, involved professional services that needed special protection not given to highway engineers or public health officials. Second was the belief, inherited from the Department's founders, that since the services were related in many ways, they would flourish better under unified direction. Third was the argument that the Department, like the Department of Agriculture, also under a board and also seeking special status, had been "undeniably well-run." The convention delegates reckoned that the opposition of partisans of the two departments was not worth contesting, so they provided that executive departments should have a single head appointed by the governor unless otherwise provided by law, and the law—the reorganization acts—continued the old system. In some respects the governor did gain more control: he was empowered to approve the Board's choice of a commissioner, to remove him after a hearing, and to approve its appointments to local boards.[20]

So, in the constitutional reorganization of 1947–1948, the structure of the Department was vindicated as an exception to the general trend. But the long discussion was a distraction at a critical time, and it made the commissioner hesitate to give his new deputies any direct administrative authority, lest he seem to set a precedent for the separation of their work into autonomous departments.[21]

The Bond Issues

Next to the campaign to keep the Department unchanged in the constitutional reorganization, Bates advised his Board in June 1947, the most important problem before them was to support a bond issue for "long delayed but vitally necessary construction." [22] In this respect, the Department's needs ran athwart a system of state finance that was peculiar and troublesome. It was the boast of New Jersey's political leaders that in per capita income their constituents stood fourth in the nation, but in per capita state taxes they stood lowest. What state taxes there were fell on public utilities, notably the railroads, and on business corporations, inheritances, and a miscellany of items including cigarettes, alcoholic beverages, motor vehicles and fuels, and horse racing. This was a narrow tax base for a state that was among the most urban and industrial in the nation, but the political leaders made "no new taxes" a battle cry.

The fact was that the low state taxes were balanced by high local taxes on property; the citizen's total tax burden—state and local—approximated that of neighboring states. The net result was that the state government's low income necessarily restricted its services. Furthermore, the constitution of 1947, like the one it replaced, required a popular referendum on any sizable state borrowing. In short, if the Department were to get money for construction, it would have to convince not only the state legislators, but also the electorate.[23]

The minimal character of state provision was most obvious in the field of higher education. In the late 1940's less than half the college students who were residents of the state attended college there. Rutgers was just beginning to change from a liberal arts college with an agricultural school to a modern state university, and the six state teachers colleges did not begin to meet the state's need for public school teachers.[24] Accordingly, it occurred to many groups that had recently supported constitutional revision that a great bond issue to finance state construction for both education and welfare was in order. With the needs so plain and partisans of both education and welfare at work, the prospect for approval would be bright. The legislators agreed to propose an issue of $50 million, to go on the ballot in November 1948. Both political parties and many state organizations endorsed it.[25]

The result was a decisive defeat. In retrospect, it appeared that many Jerseymen, Catholics in particular, had reservations about aiding Rutgers, which had a traditional tie to the Dutch Reformed Church and only fourteen public members among its fifty-six trustees. Moreover, the Taxpayers Association strongly opposed the bond issue; it doubted the need and in any case it favored a pay-as-you-go policy, avoiding high interest charges. Since the legislature was unlikely to vote new taxes for a pay-as-you-go policy, the defeat meant at least another year's delay in construction.[26]

In 1949, the legislature proposed another referendum, for $25 million for welfare institutions alone.[27] Determined not to lose this one, the commissioner and the State Board undertook an active campaign. They raised some money—about $7,000—from private sources for advertising, but mostly their efforts were to mobilize the Boards of Managers and welfare workers into county committees and to arrange for support by statewide associations. In particular, the Department submitted its list of 101 projects to a thorough study by representatives of the Taxpayers Association; these gentlemen, officials of large corporations whose services were contributed for the job, not only supported the issue, but observed that it would meet only half the existing need, and that as soon as it was spent a second bond issue would be needed.[28]

The strenuous campaign, the support of the Taxpayers, and the absence of organized opposition resulted in a two-to-one victory in the referendum. (Bonds for a veterans' bonus and aid to housing were defeated at the same time.)[29] In the spring of 1950 contracts were let and construction begun.[30] In 1952, the voters agreed to an additional $25 million issue to finish the program. Again there was no organized opposition and this time the referendum carried by four to one.[31]

The successful bond drives were evidence of popular support for the

Department. The 1949 campaign in particular seemed like a turning point, the first time since the 1920's that the Department had tried to get across to the people of the state a lively sense of their unmet responsibilities in regard to its wards—and the people had responded.[32] In retrospect, however, there were some decided qualifications on the achievement.

First of all, the Taxpayers' and later studies revealed the desperate state to which delays in construction had reduced the institutions. Compared with their rated capacity, the three mental hospitals were overcrowded by 45 percent, institutions for the mentally retarded by more than 25 percent (with long waiting lists), and correctional institutions by 27 percent. Obviously, such overcrowding not only brought out the worst in the institutional round of life—eating, sleeping, bathing, occupations, exercise—but it also minimized the possibility of rehabilitation. At worst it was a cruel risk to life. The fire hazard was terrific in many institutions—this was what first caught the eye of the Taxpayers' study group—particularly at Greystone Park, with its seventy-year-old wood-and-plaster interiors and wooden stairs and roof (the hospital fire department had an average of one alarm a week in and around the locked wards). Even at Marlboro State Hospital, which had fire-resistant construction, the water supply was too small for minimum protection. Crowded quarters caused a continuous risk of contagion and epidemic, especially since neither the mental hospitals nor the institutions for the retarded had adequate provision for isolating the tuberculous.[33]

In 1951, when the threat of new state taxes caused political leaders to demand new efforts at economy, Reeve Schley, the chairman of the State Board, made the strongest official statement that body ever issued about the niggardliness of the state's provision for its wards. General hospitals spent $15–$18 per day per patient, he said; state mental hospitals spent about $2.50. At Veterans Administration mental hospitals the employees and patients were equal in number; in state mental hospitals the ratio was one to four or five. To bring the staff at Greystone Park up to standards set by the American Psychiatric Association would have required 1,400 additional employees. The gross cost of raw food for people in the state's institutions was 47 cents per day, of which the inmates themselves raised 13 cents' worth. The cost of clothing per person per year was $19.96. Poor wages and working conditions and housing which he called "indefensible" in some cases, resulted in turnover and vacancies that necessarily harmed the state's wards. The fault, he said, lay not with budget authorities, but with the state's fiscal policy.[34] In this perspective, in so rich and favored a state, the successful bond issues strike one as too little and too late.

Moreover, the campaign for them revealed much about the state of public opinion. The Morrow Commission had hoped above all that the plan of the Department would "furnish the fullest opportunity for the continuous education of the people of the State as to their responsibilities,"[35] but certainly the campaign for the bond issues had nothing to do with continuous education: it was an emergency measure to meet a crisis. The Morrow Commission had ignored the practical question of how the new Department was to inform the people of their responsibility. Presumably the citizen boards were the means of communication, but in fact in 1949 (as in the 1920's) the burden of the campaign fell on the commissioner and his staff, who worked night and day for months. They won their cause, but the episode raises the question whether this sort of affair was really their job. The commissioner had a full-time administrative position; his ordinary and expected role in fund-raising was to make a budget and justify it to the appropriate authorities. He was not hired as a public relations man, and neither in Massachusetts nor in Washington had his duties involved responsibility for a large-scale bond drive.

Finally, it is clear that the bonds were needed to catch up, not to step ahead, and the whole argument about them turned on the need for improving existing institutions. The key document in winning public support, the Taxpayers' study, was prepared by a draftsman and two engineers. They were experts on fire hazards, steam boilers, and plant maintenance—subjects that largely occupied them in the report—but they were not prepared to see these matters as aspects of a service. With regard to the service they simply repeated the views of their guides. In the immediate context, that was perhaps enough: obviously, rehabilitation was good, it was economical in the long run, and overcrowding and inadequate facilities diminished efficiency in many ways.

But the technique and possibility of rehabilitation, the service the institution gave, were not an engineer's business, any more than were the indignity, frustration, and suffering that their investigation revealed. They saw and reported on construction projects and weighed their economy against alternate construction projects and long-run trends in institutional population (reasonable economy in the taxpayer's interest made 10 percent overcrowding tolerable, they said).[36] It was a significant change in the 1950's, however, that public discussion of the Department's character and work shifted from the perspective of experts in public administration or experts in industrial engineering to the perspective of people who were primarily interested in the quality of the services the state afforded.

18

New Perspectives on Corrections, 1945–1954

The system of correctional institutions in 1945 gave shape to three ideas. Most important was "classification" and a means of "individualized treatment." The several institutions were themselves a gross segregation by age, sex, and offense, and within the institutions a classification committee worked out assignments to quarters, work, education, and other services by an expert study of the individual. A second general idea was that the several institutions had common interests as regards both program and management, and that, moreover, the correctional institutions overlapped services for the mentally retarded and ill and dependent children. This thought was the rationale of the single department combining all services. Finally, the officials of the system were supposed to be expert career men, and it was the function of Boards of Managers to protect them from politics and to give them the support of enlightened laymen.

Many commendations of New Jersey correctional institutions were evidence that they were on the right track, and in his "look to the future" in 1945 John Ellis had not suggested any changes in their organization or any new institutions. Nevertheless, the role of the Department was unclear in two respects. For one thing, as the Morrow Commission had originally envisioned the system, the state institutions were part of a larger system that began in the community with local law enforcement and institutions, and ended in the community with parole. The new department was given power to inspect local jails, for example, and Burdette Lewis had planned a central agency for presentence study of the offender. But in practice Ellis had not tried to develop his formal authority over local institutions, and although the Juvenile Delinquency Commission of 1939 had strongly recommended state supervision of probation to improve the service, Ellis did not press the issue because he was reluctant to antagonize the county courts.[1]

Nor was there a single official, other than the commissioner himself, whose business was to oversee and direct the programs of the several institutions. The person most directly interested in broad questions of correctional program was the director of classification and education, the job Ellis and F. Lovell Bixby had held. In 1945, however, the director of classification was a psychologist whose primary interest was in the retarded. At least so it seemed to Dr. Bixby, when Bates brought him back to the Department in June 1945, as deputy commissioner in charge of corrections and parole.[2]

Unfinished Business

Parole, one of Bates' particular interests, was an example of the loose organization of the Department. There were in practice three methods of parole. Reformatory inmates, who had, for the most part, indeterminate sentences, were paroled by the Board of Managers of the institutions and supervised by parole officers working out of the central office. This arrangement led to various standards and practices in the several institutions, and the increasing demand for parole officers (and probation officers, whose work is similar) and the rising standards for their training made personnel problems especially difficult in this service.

The two other modes of parole involved the State Prison. Convicts there had determinate sentences, minimum and maximum terms. Ordinarily a convict became eligible for parole by the prison's Board of Managers at the expiration of his minimum term less commutation time for good behavior and diligence. Since judges tended to put minimum and maximum terms rather close together, partly to forestall an early parole, this ordinary process was likely to take a long time. Meanwhile, however, there was a second way to get released from prison. Prisoners who showed evidence of a change of character or who thought their sentences were too harsh could seek a pardon from a Court of Pardons composed of judges and laymen. Technically, this court exercised the governor's power of clemency, but since it could grant either full pardons or conditional licenses to be at liberty, it was in effect a paroling agency unrestricted by the minimum sentence or by other limitations upon the ordinary paroling agency. In fact, it granted four or five releases to every one granted by the Board of Managers.[3]

This two-headed arrangement was peculiar, and so was the fact that parolees from the State Prison were under supervision of officers from the Prison; parole officers from the central Department had nothing to do with them. The sanction for these arrangements was the state constitution of 1844, which had recognized the power to pardon long before modern parole was developed, and which, according to judicial interpretation, gave the keeper of the State Prison undivided control over the security and discipline of the convicts, including parolees.

The autonomy of the prison keeper had been an obstruction to central control from the first, although in the later years of Ellis' administration he had managed to avoid conflict. This situation was not to last. Two weeks after he took office Bates transmitted to the State Board a review of parole work at the State Prison. There were over nine hundred convicts on parole with only two field officers to supervise them, the report said. The positions were used as a promotion for custodial officers, not a professional's employment, and supervision from the central office was nominal. As a result, preparole investigation and parole supervision were perfunctory, case records were minimal, and the classification and training programs at the prison had suffered. Bates asked that the central office take over this work and employ eight additional officers to handle it.[4]

The advisability of the move seemed obvious, but of course the State Board had first to confer with the prison Board of Managers and they with the principal keeper, who was appointed by the governor (not the prison managers) and who was, at this time, John L. ("Sparrow") O'Hara, a penologist by virtue of service on the Trenton police force and the Democratic state committee.[5] In January 1946, to resolve everyone's doubts, the State Board got an opinion from the attorney general that the prison might constitutionally avail itself of the facilities of the central Department, and finally, in July 1946, a year after the action began, the work was transferred.[6] The *Newark News* reported that the Prison Board had waited until the conclusion of Keeper O'Hara's term to "relinquish this prerogative."[7]

Meanwhile, Bixby had reorganized the Department's parole officers into nine districts, each under a supervisor whose business was to maintain casework standards and to develop relations with community social service agencies and employers. He also recodified rules and procedures.[8] The result was a strengthening of parole services, but its general significance was in the increased centralization of operations on one hand and the establishment of a decentralized field service, a district office in continuous touch with community agencies, on the other.

The centralization of parole did not touch the paroling power of the Court of Pardons, however, and in June 1946 a new principal keeper had taken office who was not inclined to surrender any more prerogatives. He was George W. Page, a businessman and politician from Trenton who had swung Mercer County, normally a Democratic stronghold, behind Republican Governor E. Walter Edge in 1944. An amiable, popular man, he was no penologist, and Bates accordingly protested his nomination, to no avail. Page responded by bluntly affirming his constitutional autonomy.[9]

The constitutional convention of 1947 was, therefore, an opportunity as well as a threat for the Department: it was an occasion to change the status of the keeper and to end the jurisdiction of the Court of Pardons. In both respects Bates and the State Board were successful: The new constitution did not mention the keeper or a court of pardons. A new paid Parole Board was organized in 1948 to handle all cases on minimum-maximum sentence, and it was recognized that after Page's term expired, in 1951, the prison managers, not the governor, would appoint the keeper. Thus the new constitution ended two obstacles to centralization that had hung fire for thirty years.

New Directions

The interest in child welfare and juvenile delinquency, which had created the Juvenile Delinquency Study Commission in 1936, continued and grew after the war. The Commission's report (1939) had emphasized the principle of state-local collaboration in delinquency prevention. It had proposed a new state children's agency, made up of heads of state departments concerned with youth problems together with a citizens' panel representing nongovernmental agencies. The interested state departments, in its view, were Education, Institutions and Agencies, Health, Labor, and the State Police, who were presumed also to influence their counterparts on the local level. The growing corps of juvenile court officials, probation officers, and social workers in private agencies accounted for the persistence of the interest. The problem was that services were spotty and unorganized. The hope was that a central agency of state officials and laymen would help local communities to organize and improve their services.[10]

Ellis was much interested in this problem (his "look to the future" mentioned possibilities in delinquency prevention); so was Bates, who had worked with the Boys Clubs. Accordingly, in September 1945 the State Board established a Division of Community Services for Delinquency Prevention, under the direction of Douglas MacNeil, who had served the Juvenile Delinquency Study Commission as research director and was assistant director of Ellis' Division of Statistics and Research and, in fact, Ellis' handyman for community relations. The new Division was supposed to collect facts on delinquency and prevention and make them available; in addition, it was to advise and consult with local agencies in establishing or improving coordination of services for children in trouble; and beyond that, it was to send field representatives into communities to help them study their situation and do "something of what we call a 'hit-and-run' community organization job." [11]

The original idea was that communities would establish local committees or councils of officials and the state commission and its staff would work with them. But as of 1947, MacNeil and his assistants had no state commission to serve and the local communities had held back from organizing "because of uncertainty regarding [its] legal propriety . . . , or because of interdepartmental jealousies or for want of energetic promotion." [12]

Then, in 1947, MacNeil got some state and local agencies to advise and collaborate with. The legislature authorized local communities to set up Youth Guidance Councils, thus settling any doubts as to their legality, and named the Division of Community Services as a consulting agency for them. Moreover, Governor Driscoll called a statewide Conference on Youth, modeled after the White House Children's Conferences and intended to follow up a National Conference for the Prevention and Control of Juvenile Delinquency. MacNeil's office organized this conference and later served as staff for an agency that grew out of it, a "Governor's Committee on Youth," which included state department heads and a citizens' panel, and which was to follow up on the conference and prepare for participation in the approaching White House Conference in 1950.[13]

By 1949 it looked as though the recommendations of 1939 for a state agency and local agencies to coordinate services were realized, and MacNeil was working up standards for juvenile court statistics and other basic research data hitherto scattered or neglected. He had published in 1948 an index of community vulnerability to social breakdown, which he thought would identify and classify the particular problems of different cities, and he had other research projects going to help in evaluation and future planning.[14]

With the mechanisms of interagency cooperation and citizen participation established and a trained and interested staff available for consultation, research, and community organization, the day looked bright. Obviously, MacNeil thought, the mechanisms needed the energy of civic spirit to work, and he knew by long experience that it would be "difficult to arouse public sentiment to the degree of warmth needed."[15] But it must have seemed to him then that the old ideal of state leadership in state-local collaboration was soon to be realized in new ways, and certainly the White House Children's Conference of 1950, with its new emphasis on large-scale grass-roots participation, which he himself largely organized in New Jersey, encouraged him in this hope.

The Diagnostic Center

Two new institutions for delinquents, the Diagnostic Center at Menlo Park and the Residential Treatment Center at Highfields, also manifested the continuing interest in juveniles and their problems. The Diagnostic Center was essentially a clinical laboratory to help judges by a presentence study of cases. The idea had entered into the early thinking about the Department. Burdette Lewis had envisioned a "clearinghouse" for the offender as an agency for the study and disposal of court cases and inmates; he had proposed a "central psychopathic hospital" as its site, and although this idea was discarded in the 1920's, the famous classification system in New Jersey correctional institutions was a trunk from the same root.[16] In 1935, moreover, the legislature had authorized judges to take advantage of the institutions' facilities by making "classification commitments" to them for short-term study prior to sentence. The procedure was used for the mentally ill and retarded, but mostly for delinquents; it offered judges both a resource for advice and the occasion to give offenders a "taste of institutionalization" that might have a deterrent effect.[17]

In theory, there were other resources available to the judges, of course—their own probation departments and local mental hygiene clinics. Ellis had hoped that the latter would provide diagnostic services for the courts as well as for social agencies, schools, and his institutions. When the clinics did not develop adequately, the Juvenile Delinquency Commission in 1939 and Ellis himself in 1943 recommended a state-sponsored "child study institute for use in classification of problem children and the planning of . . . treatment . . . to check tendencies toward juvenile delinquency." After the war David Nimmo, judge of the Juvenile and Domestic Relations Court of Hudson County, and other juvenile court judges won the support of Governors Edge and Driscoll and, together with them, the legislature.[18]

The new institution, which was dedicated on November 30, 1949, considerably broadened the idea of a "classification commitment," however. For one thing, since it was neither a correctional institution nor a mental hospital, it was presumed to avoid the stigma of the older procedure. It took referrals from social agencies and private individuals, as well as courts and state institutions; it served offenders and non-offenders, adults and children, inpatients and outpatients.[19] (A law regarding sex offenders, passed in 1949, when many states were acting on this subject, named the new center as the place for their study.)[20]

The center's facilities were much more elaborate than those of any existing clinic: a handsome building, modern inside and out, with accommodations for fifty-six residents and facilities for many outpatients. Its director, Dr. Ralph Brancale, was a psychiatrist; his staff included psychologists, social workers, nurses, and people to run the laboratories and machines (including a polygraph or lie detector).[21] The cost of the buildings was $1.2 million (the Juvenile Delinquency Study Commission had estimated $100,000), of which the federal government paid a third, under the Hill-Burton Act.[22] The cost of service was paid by users—courts, agencies, or individuals.

In the history of classification procedures in the Department, the Diagnostic Center marked a transition from "descriptive" psychological testing—of intelligence, for example—to diagnosing and even treating the dynamics of motivation. The staff used interviewing, projective tests, hypnoanalysis and narcoanalysis in studying their patients and preparing their recommendations. As they reflected on their work, trying to link their clinical pictures of the offenders to the older styles of evaluation and prescription, they drew back. On one hand, "classification" struck Dr. Brancale as "sterile . . . a labelling procedure"; on the other hand, without it "clinical thinking" became "loose and irresponsible," lacking a framework for scientific analysis. His own ideas on the subject, after six years at the Center, were "admittedly crude and sketchy," at best "an orientation and a starting point" toward "a really satisfactory classification of the offender."[23]

The modesty of his claim reflected an improved scientific acumen in psychology, the result of many trials and errors, and Brancale took for granted a distinction between classification as an administrative necessity and classification as a comprehensive scheme of diagnostic categories. The typical procedure, he thought, was "little more than a check list of the inmate's deficiencies and assets, with specific recommendations for rectifying or exploiting each specific finding," and he criticized the assumption behind this procedure, "that an atomistically constructed picture of the patient's assets and liabilities," forced into "a hodgepodge semblance of personality structure," would "automatically provide the basis for a prescription of treatment which is expected to solve all of the offender's problems." [24] Thus did the insights of dynamic theories of motivation raise questions about the hopes and practices of the 1920's.

Highfields: Guided Group Interaction

The second new institution for juveniles gave a radical form to this sort of criticism. Its origin, according to Dr. Bixby, who was one of its founders, was the idea of a special program for troublesome boys, in an institution in which a small group of inmates and custodians would live and work together. His work as director of classification and education in the early 1930's had convinced him that the impersonal reformatory regime and repressive atmosphere that he saw were not helpful, and neither was the tactic of transferring troublemakers among institutions. He thought that only people could help people, and he imagined a program that was small and intensive, where supervision would be close, earnest, and include every aspect of group life. He encouraged such a program at Rahway and later when he was warden of the federal reformatory at Chillicothe, but he was unable to isolate the group or avoid the prison atmosphere.[25]

Came the war and Bixby became assistant director of the Army's Correction Division. There were many military delinquents, of course, and since their manpower and the personnel to guard them was at a premium, the Army wanted to get them back to duty in a hurry. The commander of the Rehabilitation Center at Fort Knox was, consequently, willing to experiment with advanced techniques of "group psychotherapy" which had been practiced in various settings on a small scale in the 1930's. He employed a psychiatrist, the psychiatrist trained a few assistants, and they worked out a program that was so unmilitary that Bixby was sent to investigate it. He was impressed, as were other investigators, and it was later extended to all Army rehabilitation centers.[26]

When he returned to New Jersey after the war, Bixby wanted to try group therapy in the reformatories, so he brought in Lloyd W. McCorkle, a young sociologist who had helped run the military program. The project, which began in 1947, was called "guided group interaction" to avoid the connotations of psychotherapy. "Group interaction" referred to the reciprocal attitudes and acts among individuals who spent much time together. As sociologists analyzed the prison community, distinguishing statuses and roles, they realized how much inmates were involved with each other and how their relationships with their peers and their keepers tended to confirm and reinforce their anti-social ideas, to eclipse the efforts at treatment and guidance that were offered them. One hope of "group therapy" was that penologists could structure and guide this life so that the expectations and pressures of living together would play a constructive role in reform.[27]

Psychotherapy got into the picture because clinical studies of offenders showed that they rationalized and justified their behavior in terms of a notion of their character that was usually confused and mistaken. Since the delinquents often did not understand what they were really like or what their real problems were, the typical reformatory discipline—repressive, didactic, and inspirational—did not touch the source of their behavior. Psychotherapy also suggested that if delinquents could talk about their problems and examine their behavior in a permissive and candid dialogue, they might improve their understanding and try to attain their ends by getting along with other people and staying out of trouble. Especially was this possible if a wise and tactful counselor could "guide" the dialogue by clarifying and organizing its points as they emerged. There were occasions for this sort of therapeutic interview in reformatories, of course, on an individual basis, with the chaplain, psychologist, parole officer, social workers, or the warden himself, but they were much limited by the lack of qualified personnel and the formal setting. The idea of "group therapy" was that group discussion of problems would be more economical, in a way less formal, and that the ferment of the discussion might carry over into the life of the institution.[28]

The first "guided group interaction" programs in New Jersey reformatories, then, were regular but informal discussions by groups of some twenty-five inmates who met for an hour three times a week, and who were encouraged "to express themselves freely regarding their own problems and feelings and those of their peers," with Lieutenant McCorkle in the chair to guide them.[29]

The business of guiding discussions was difficult—even the coherent, significant parts that were published as examples were hard to follow—and there were many problems in organizing the classes and fitting them into the institutional routine, so that when McCorkle left in 1948 to teach in the Maxwell School at Syracuse University the programs languished.

These ventures were merely innovations in the ordinary educational program of the reformatories—special classes, as it were. The new institution at Highfields, however, was designed from the first to realize fully the principle of guided group interaction. Its immediate cause was peculiar. In June 1949, a group of judges had questioned the indeterminate sentence law, under which they committed convicts to reformatories where the managers, who had the power of parole, held them for periods averaging twelve to eighteen months and could hold them much longer. The judges doubted the wisdom and justice of this policy, and recommended, among other things, a law permitting them to impose short fixed-term sentences of three to six months. Bates and Bixby stoutly defended the indeterminate sentence—offenders with another type of sentence would disrupt the ordinary reformatory discipline—but it occurred to Bixby that short sentences might have great value in many cases if they were treated in a separate unit with an intensive program.[30]

What Bixby had in mind was his old idea of a residential center for intensive treatment, with two significant changes. First, he would have the boys committed as a condition of probation, rather than as prisoners, and in this way the unit would minimize the coercive features of a reformatory. Second, he would base the program on the development of informal group relations, with group psychotherapy playing an important part. Specifically, he proposed that the Department make Highfields (the former Lindbergh country estate, which had been donated to the State) into a residence for a few boys—no more than twenty-five—who would come for a stay of three to six months and then would return to the community to finish their probationary period. The project would not only satisfy the judges and be a worthwhile experiment, he observed, but it would be cheaper than sending the boys to reformatories and it involved "such a relatively small investment" that he told Bates he "did not see how we can afford not to do it." [31]

In June 1949, even a small investment was beyond reach, but then Samuel Lewisohn, a New Yorker and a long-time patron of enlightened penology, approached Bates about subsidizing an experiment and in the event got substantial private support from the New York Foundation for a two-year trial. Mr. and Mrs. Douglas MacNeil also made a grant, and Barklie Henry, on the Board of Managers of the Diagnostic Center, interested his friends in the Vincent Astor Foundation in supporting a research study of its results. While the foundations were considering their grants, the state refurbished the property, which began to receive boys on July 1, 1950.[32]

Highfields in operation had no guards or precautions against escape and only two general prohibitions: boys could not leave the grounds without an adult, nor could they converse with female patients at the state hospital where they worked. Their jobs at the hospital were real work, in the kitchen or on the farm, for which they earned fifty cents a day. They also took turns at doing chores around Highfields, for which they were not paid. They rose at 6 A.M. on weekdays, ate and straightened up until they left for work at 7:30, worked from 8:00 until noon and from 1:00 P.M. until 4:30. Every night but Thursday and Saturday they attended guided group interaction sessions, conducted by the director for two groups, from 7:00 to 8:30 and from 8:30 to 10. On Saturday they cleaned house and went to the nearby village of Hopewell to run errands or they played outdoor games. Sunday they could attend a town church, accompanied by an adult, and they received visitors from noon until 7:00 P.M. They were free to leave the grounds during these hours with an adult.

Six people made up the staff: the director, the cottage supervisors (a handyman and a cook), and a "sociological intern" or trainee, all lived on the grounds; the work supervisor and a secretary did not. The atmosphere was deliberately lenient, accepting, and supportive, but, on the other hand, there was little privacy for the boys; all their behavior was observed as a "mode of adjustment" somehow related to a boy's self-image and to his problems, and all was grist for the mill of the group discussions. At first the boys were suspicious of the leader and guarded in their responses, but as the director patiently waited out the silences and rode out the storms, a process of testing began in which hostility and aggression became more and more frank and personal and discussion became disorderly. Presently, however, the group began to take the leader at his word and to test one another, and gradually the mutual criticism and comment among the boys led to a friendly interest in one another's "progress" with their "problems." [33]

As the boys were induced to see themselves as others saw them, to recognize the purposes and conditions of their behavior, and to try new roles for themselves, the situation became charged with emotion. "It is a universal observation that therapeutic changes in the personality are accompanied by increased anxiety and tension," says an account of the institution's treatment philosophy, but at Highfields the inmate cannot "hide and lick wounds" as he can in civilian life. He lives "with the same people with whom he has shared intimate revelations, frequently against his will and in spite of all attempts at control and disguises." If group treatment is to be effective it "must take the risk of becoming a manufactory of human projectiles let loose in a social situation which already has all the aspects of a human arsenal." [34]

One could not fail to admire the tact, poise, and candor and the experimental temper of the men who set out to create and control this ferment and who made it work. Work it did: Critical comparisons showed that its graduates did consistently better than control groups, and its success continued after Albert Elias, a sometime intern, replaced McCorkle as director in 1952, and showed that its ideas and methods could be transmitted.[35]

Accordingly, Highfields was taken over by the state in 1952 and became the model for several similar centers. Its limitations were obvious. It performed a very specialized function, possible only with support from a large department. It depended for a work situation, emergency medical care, and business office services on the nearby state hospital (The State Neuro-Psychiatric Institute, formerly Skillman Village for Epileptics), and other state institutions did its laundry and provided other medical care. It also depended on the services and co-operation of judges and probation officers from all over the state. More profoundly, it ran the risk that its informal organization and impromptu administration would be cast into a bureaucratic and institutional mold.

In this connection, it was passing strange that its sponsors rejected a proposal to establish a local board of managers, holding that a status directly under the director of corrections would give them more discretion and flexibility.[36] Thus the most progressive and eccentric state institution deliberately declined to get involved in the system of board control that had been set up, in theory, to protect the individuality of the several institutions from the myopia of centralizing bureaucrats.

Correctional Institutions: Problems and Programs

The thinking behind Highfields illuminated two problems of correctional institutions in the postwar years. Highfields, like probation, kept hopeful cases out of the reformatory; the consequence was that reformatory inmates were increasingly unpromising, disturbed or retarded, with long histories of trouble. Moreover, because its residents came as a condition of probation, Highfields avoided the dilemma of reformatory officials, who were expected to combine friendly help with punitive restraint. In the past, reformatory officials had straddled these purposes by conceiving of their institutions as a substitute home, as in the case of the "state homes" for boys and girls under sixteen, or as a sort of special school and workshop for older delinquents where, in any case, the inmates would learn good habits in a program more or less tailored to their individual needs. The increasingly difficult character of the population and new theories of crime and punishment both undermined the rationale of existing programs.

The effect of probation and other community resources for handling delinquents was evident at the time of the bond drive in 1949. The state homes for juveniles were both occupied below capacity, and the Diagnostic Center, which opened that year, took as residents many children who would otherwise have gone to them for classification commitments. The men's reformatories, by contrast, were overcrowded, Annandale by 25 percent and Bordentown, the former prison farm which became a reformatory in 1948, by 16 percent. The state prison was 30 percent overcrowded, and Clinton Farms Reformatory for Women, which took both reformatory and prison commitments and had a maternity hospital, was overcrowded by 80 percent.[37] A comparison of Annandale boys showed that 10 percent of the inmates of 1939 had committed offenses at the age of eleven or under; in 1951 the figure was 26 percent. Twenty-seven percent of the inmates of 1939 had been on probation; in 1951 the figure was 74 per cent. Four per cent of the inmates had a record of escapes in 1939, 20 per cent in 1951.[38] Moreover, the reformatory population in 1949 or 1951 was born during the years of low birth rates in the 1930's. The high birth rates of the 1940's would put the reformatories in the same position as junior high and high schools—with no double sessions and no dropouts to relieve the pressure.

Clinton Farms was especially hard hit because of its tradition of an honor system and student government. An orientation pamphlet written by inmate editors in 1950 quoted a statement "from the earliest days" to show how the system still worked, after thirty-five years: "Honor methods have developed such a spirit of responsibility," the old document read, ". . . that often three or four months go past without a single case of serious discipline. . . . The woman who has to be disciplined and locked [in her room] is boycotted by the rest of the women . . . and after she has apologized and come out of her room is made to feel she must work again for the good of the place before she can secure the friendship of the other women." "All for one and one for all," an appeal to inmate responsibility and initiative, was the spirit of the honor system, the authors said; the hierarchy of "probies," honor girls, and student officers was designed to give privilege and responsibility to inmates who showed themselves worthy.[39]

Overcrowding strained this system in every way. "It is difficult to maintain morale when women have to be herded together," Superintendent Edna Mahan reported in 1946, when much worse was still to come. "There are more runaways because there are too few supervisors to give adequate supervision or the individual attention necessary to spot the discontented and disgruntled." "Serious problem cases"—the "impulsive unpredictable ones and the sex deviates"—increased disproportionately, so she asked for a new maximum security wing to segregate them and more social work and psychiatric service ("real therapy instead of diagnosis") to handle them.[40] She got the maximum security installation in 1952, as a result of the bond drive. It stood in the midst of the campus, evidence that the honor system and team spirit did not reach many of the new problems. (As for Annandale, it ended its history as an "open" institution when it was fenced in 1954.)

Despite its difficulties, Clinton continued to be a symbol of courageous modernity for many people. Miss Molly Mellonby, who visited there in 1952 as a member of the British Prison Commission, thought it "the most considerable achievement she had seen" in America. She noted that when Miss Mahan had first come Clinton had held only 170 women, and it was possible for her and her staff to know them all fairly well, whereas at the time of her visit there were more than four hundred inmates. "Not only is it impossible for [Miss Mahan] and her staff to have the same knowledge of this large number," she wrote,

> but it is very difficult to infuse them with the same community spirit. . . . One would be tempted to say, in fact, that it was impossible were it not that it is still to a remarkable extent achieved, but no doubt less perfectly and at a cost, I suspect, of wear and tear and general strain on the staff that should not be disregarded. . . . The standard, set from the top, of serenity and confidence, was a high one, but it must be a struggle to maintain it in the face of increasing difficulties.[41]

Miss Mellonby expressed reservations about the power of the lay Board of Managers, but she was impressed by its functioning. Most Board members had served many years, she observed, "and devote so much time to the work that they are completely in the picture and obviously know the Superintendent, the staff and inmates so well, and have such confidence in the policy of the former, that difficulties are most unlikely to arise." [42] In the view of this critical observer, then, Clinton was quite a place; but her description emphasized the personal role of its superintendent in its functioning.

The other reformatories had never relied on the honor system and student government as much as Clinton, and the changes in population impelled their superintendents to look to changes in formal education for a better program. Ordinary academic and vocational education seemed increasingly irrelevant to the needs of their wards. What they wanted was a kind of instruction aimed directly at the problems and interests of the inmates. Albert Wagner, the superintendent of Bordentown reformatory, called in 1950 for "social education" to "develop positive attitudes and desirable social conduct, rather than academic mastery or the acquisition of special skills"; it would, he said, aim at "improving the individual's ability to live with himself, see things as they really are, accept other individuals with understanding, and . . . cope with ordinary . . . social situations." [43]

In its focus on the inmate's self-image and his attitudes, social education was like "guided group interaction," and it was developed in the reformatories in 1950 just as Highfields went into operation. The differences were that guided group interaction had its roots in group psychotherapy and focused on individual personality problems, whereas social education dealt with common attitudes and situations in a didactic and systematic way. Guided group interaction, as practiced at Highfields, depended upon the skill of a discussion leader-therapist; social education was conceived in terms of definite points to learn, definite courses of study and particular teaching methods—matters that educators could formalize into a curriculum and program.

Social education drew on the expertise of teachers, not therapists, and it was an aspect of the widespread interest in "life adjustment" courses during those years. Like progressive education generally, it began with a critical study of the interests and possibilities of the students. Here was much matter for sober reflection. Charles Perrine, in a D.Ed. thesis at Rutgers in 1954, "Social Adjustment Interests of Delinquent Males in New Jersey Reformatories," summarized what the best scientific tests of attitude showed about the boys, and set the problem social education would have to confront. The boys thought that "only saps work for a living," he said; they took only casual jobs, for spending money. They sought immediate gratifications with no forethought. They lacked respect for authority and believed that "if it's legal, it ain't fun." They could not distinguish right and wrong. They suffered from "feelings of hostility, rejection, insecurity, inferiority and over-dependence" and swung from "unwarranted feelings of worthlessness and despair" to foolishly unrealistic aspirations. "Disturbances in the psychosexual sphere" led them to unwholesome aggression or passive perversion. They had no sense of belonging to anything. They misunderstood the basic organization of society and the "rights and duties of responsible citizenship in a democracy." [44]

What social education had to offer this forlorn crew was simply modest courses about specific practical problems of ordinary life. "The school program . . . is probably different than any you have had contact with before," a pamphlet for Annandale inmates stated in 1955. "The whole purpose is to teach people such important things as: getting along with other people, how to apply for a job, spending money wisely, etc." [45] Shop training was retooled as a "guidance procedure" related to social education and parole placement, which explored the boy's aptitudes and interests and gave elementary practical instruction.[46]

In this respect, as in others, the improvement lay in a refinement of specific objectives and methods. Thc models were programs in New York and in the federal government's reformatories, and Bixby and Donald Goff, a sociologist in the division of classification and education, worked them out with the professional staff of the several institutions.[47] The long-term objective was a definite sequence with carefully planned orientation and prerelease courses at either end of an indeterminate "treatment-activity" period, which, as instituted at Annandale in 1958, reduced the average stay of fifteen to eighteen months by a third.[48] The more intensive program and shorter stay helped to keep down the overcrowding, as the war babies came of age, and meanwhile, in December 1954, Annandale planted a seedling, a forestry camp that the CCC had once occupied at High Point State Park. Conducted together with the state Department of Conservation, it was a minimum security camp for boys near release, intended, it was said, to help them bridge the gap from institutional life to freedom.[49]

The Prison Riots of 1952

While public interest in juvenile delinquency encouraged reformatory officials to experiment with new institutions and intensive programs, the situation at the prison was moving toward an explosion. The prison had three branches in 1952: the old fortress in Trenton, opened in 1836; the "prison farm" at Rahway, opened in 1902 as a reformatory, which changed its role in 1948; and a minimum security farm at Leesburg in South Jersey. Between them, the two walled institutions held over two thousand inmates, more than all the reformatories combined. The old prison held men with long sentences for serious crimes or repeaters. In theory, they were the worst cases for custody and discipline. In fact, the ordinary majority were not especially troublesome, but the prison was the "dumping ground" of the state system, and the crowd included a disproportionate number of "insane or near-insane, mental defectives, unstable psychopaths, some . . . highly assaultive, . . . sexual psychopaths, passive homosexuals, aggressive 'wolves' with long records of fights . . . , escape artists, agitators, and 'incorrigibles' of all ages." [50]

Prison authorities had meager resources to handle these troublemakers. The institution was too small and its antiquated construction made surveillance difficult (three or four men in a cell behind solid walls and doors) and life unpleasant (prisoners complained of sewer gas and rats); the yard was so crowded that active sports were unmanageable.[51] Human resources were also meager. At the time of the riots half the guards were on temporary appointment, and many were too old or too young to take the civil service examination; in 1951 there was a turnover of 75 percent among them; for several years all the senior correction officers were on an acting basis. The reason was simple—low salaries. What held the operation together were workers who had entered the service in the depression and remained in spite of discouragement because they expected that some day the career man would be suitably rewarded.[52]

As for program, two-thirds of the prisoners at Trenton were employed in state use or maintenance, which was heavily overstaffed; the other third were idle. Idle prisoners were allowed in the yard from 1:30 to 3:00 P.M. and from 5:00 to 7:00 P.M. on weekdays, weather permitting (the State couldn't afford to pay guards for the evening stint, so the convicts paid them out of their welfare fund). On weekends yard time was 1:00 to 3:00 P.M. For the rest, the school, library, and other constructive activities were "virtually non-existent" and professional staff was lacking for any sort of rehabilitation and even for classification.[53]

Most correctional institutions in these years were crowded with troublesome cases and undermanned by an underpaid staff, but particular circumstances plagued the prison. The parole law of 1948 proved to be inequitable in some respects; the parole board was slow to go into operation and prisoners thought it did not give them a fair hearing. (Involuntary idleness in the prison aggravated this problem by denying inmates "work time" in commutation of their sentence.)[54] An experienced warden might have managed the available resources in a more imaginative and effective way, but the politician-businessman Governor Edge appointed held on until January 1951. There followed a nine-month search for a professional who would take the job. It finally fell to the acting warden, William H. Carty, who had worked at the prison for thirty-three years. Unfortunately, on November 2, 1951, the day after his appointment was made permanent, a seriously disturbed inmate assaulted him, broke his jaw in five places and sent him to the hospital for two months. During 1951, in short, the prison lacked decisive leadership and meanwhile the staff was insecure and turning over.[55]

When Carty took over, Bates and Bixby encouraged him to curtail "hobby shop" activities, which convict entrepreneurs had organized into a sizable business, because the convicts were shipping the products (souvenir knick-knacks) across state lines in violation of federal statute. Prisoners had put the income from this and other sources "on deposit" and transferred it freely among themselves. Often they spent it at the commissary, where they could supplement or even supplant the prison diet. (It was against the rules to cook in the cells, but the commissary sold raw food anyhow.)[56]

Warden Carty tightened up discipline with grim severity, pushed by an article in the *Newark Star Ledger* for January 2, 1952, headed "INSIDE TRENTON PRISON—Dope, Sex, Booze, Dice—And Rule by Convicts." Reportedly based on interviews with disgruntled guards, it made sensational charges of lax discipline. A committee of the prison Board of Managers investigated the charges. Some officers testified that the disciplinary court had failed to support them adequately, but in general the Board found no substantiation of the sensational charges. Instead they found it "amazing . . . that the prison operates so well with such a great proportion of inexperienced officers."[57]

The Board issued its report on Monday, March 31, 1952. As luck had it, on the preceding Saturday night, near midnight, some fifty-two men in the segregation wing of the prison began to riot, howling and tearing out the fixtures in their cells. The guard retreated, under orders, and soon the men were out of their cells. Some surrendered the next day; the rest held out until Monday night. The segregation wing was a prison within a prison for especially disturbed and dangerous cases, however, and it was possible to believe that the riot was a fortuitous explosion of disturbed individuals that had "little to do with conditions or practices in the prison as a whole."[58]

Later there were minor incidents with fractious inmates at Trenton and at Bordentown, signs of high tension, but on the morning of April 15 a planned riot broke out in the prison print shop. Sixty-nine prisoners took part; they captured four guards as hostages and supplied themselves with food and makeshift weapons. They held out for four days. Warden Carty, suspecting trouble, had moved some convict leaders to Rahway. The rumor spread that guards had beaten them severely and a sort of sympathy riot began at the prison farm; 231 men took nine guards as hostage and barricaded themselves on a second floor. This demonstration lasted more than five days.[59]

Riot leaders demanded an investigation of the prison and parole system by outsiders, among other things, and Governor Driscoll accordingly appointed a distinguished committee of inquiry. It included Judge Harry Heher, of the New Jersey Supreme Court, Stanley Ashe, a well-known warden from Pennsylvania, and Austin MacCormick, a professor of criminology at the University of California, head of the Osborne Association, and sometime subordinate of Bates in the federal Bureau of Prisons. Their report, dated November 21, 1952, said that obvious deficiencies in plant, personnel, and program were "basic" factors of the riots. They created an "explosive situation" which "any spark" might have set off, either by "spontaneous combustion" or by "deliberate lighting of the fuse by inmate agitators."[60] The committee made a number of specific recommendations about the parole system and the program, but the real solution, they said, was for the state to give "the administrators of long experience and proven competence now directing the State Department of Institutions and Agencies" the wherewithal to do their job.[61]

Perspectives on the Riots

Meanwhile prison riots had occurred across the country, and in November 1952 Peg and Walter McGraw, two industrious journalists, began to put together a radio series on the subject. Their inquiries brought out "a frightening indictment of our prison system" which blamed, not the malfeasance or folly of prison officials, but public ignorance and apathy. This was no scoop, they realized—it was substantially the conclusion of the investigating committee in New Jersey, for example—but as reporters they discovered some peculiar features about the responses of officials.[62]

Early in their work, the McGraws interviewed the eminent Sanford Bates, for example, and they remarked that his main concern was that accounts of the riots and their causes would ignore the great majority of convicts who made no trouble and the faithful guards who watched over them. The riots did not show a need for reform at Trenton State Prison, he said; riots were only possible, in fact, where an enlightened system gave inmates a modicum of freedom and resources. What was the reason for the riots, then, if not a need for reform? the McGraws asked. Bates pondered the question. "I think it's spring fever," he told them. "You can quote me on that any time." In addition to the season he pointed to "the general unrest in the world." [63]

The reporters were puzzled. The Commissioner seemed almost to defend the old prison. "Why doesn't he just come out and say it's a rat hole and ought to be eliminated?" Mrs. McGraw asked her husband. "Why doesn't he use the publicity to get rid of it and get funds for a new prison?" Perhaps, her husband mused, it was politics; perhaps he was somehow protecting the people with ultimate responsibility, the Board of Managers or the governor. But that did not make much sense.[64]

They asked permission to talk to guards and convicts at the prison, to get different points of view; they talked to guards, who all said what the Commissioner had said, but they could not talk to inmates; in fact, Bates asked them to promise not to talk to inmates. The McGraws tracked down some ex-inmates and interviewed them on prison conditions; they said little that the investigating committee did not confirm in its official report, but they said it pungently, and the McGraws used the tapes of their interviews in the show. Then, as they prepared the final production, Bates asked to hear it. The audition was a trauma. The Commissioner was incensed by the taped interviews with ex-inmates; he felt that his word was contradicted by convicted felons; he thought he recognized one spokesman as a riot leader; the riot leader was clearly out to embarrass him, he said, and so were the McGraws; it was an

American tradition that anonymous critics could not condemn anyone in such a fashion. . . .[65]

In the end the show went on, somewhat altered by Bates' protests. The McGraws were still puzzled. "Why does he resist allowing the public to know why a new prison is urgently needed?" they asked themselves. No theory made sense. They were not attacking the Commissioner, whom they admired; they were "attacking a system, but he had made it a personal war." "Maybe," Mrs. McGraw suggested at last, "he's just a real good fighter." [66]

The event seemed to justify the McGraws; the riots served to emphasize difficulties and needs that the authorities themselves had long pointed to, but now there was action. Lloyd McCorkle was brought in as associate warden to develop the program. There were improvements in parole law and administration. Yard time was increased and the state found funds to pay the guards for the added duty. Guards' salaries were raised. Money was put aside from the bond issue to build an up-to-date maximum security prison outside Trenton.[67] But those concerned were sure that these immediate gains were long-run losses. Bates thought the riots would, in the long run, "not only injure [the prisoners'] own chance of emergence but . . . impair the public confidence in the efficacy of humane prison practices." [68]

The investigating committee, for its part, was careful to distinguish "between a valid basis for grievances and a valid method of reacting to them." It is true, the committee said, that riots sometimes lead to overdue improvements, but their "long-range effect is detrimental to prisoners and correctional services designed to help them. Public opinion is inevitably stiffened against offenders by demonstrations . . . that cause the average citizen to feel that all prisoners are dangerous wild beasts and should be kept under rigid repression." [69]

Lloyd McCorkle, who succeeded Carty as warden when the latter went on sick leave, took a different view of the prisoners' grievances. One of his tasks was to talk with inmate leaders—to keep them talking, in fact; it was an enlightening dialogue. Then, two months after he took over, he faced another riot. This time a few prisoners tried to saw through window bars opening on a public street. They failed, but they had taken three hostages and they stirred up a demonstration. McCorkle ordered guards to force their way into the wing, shooting submachine guns at the ceiling. Two prisoners were injured by ricochets, but the insurrection quickly ended.[70]

These dramatic events served to focus his reflections about the old dilemma of punishment versus reform: How can you help a man become a self-directing law-abiding citizen by imposing a punitive regimentation on him? The dilemma, he said, implied that custody was "a rather sordid punitive operation" by which inmates were "perpetually locked, counted, and controlled"; by contrast, treatment and welfare looked like "attempts to introduce freedom and dignity" into a custodial regime. But this contrast, he said, "misses the central reality of the inmate's life in prison."

"The reality," McCorkle continued, in his report as warden for the year 1953–1954, "is simply this":

> The welfare of the individual inmate, to say nothing of his psychological freedom and dignity, does not importantly depend on how much education, recreation, and consultation he receives but rather depends on how he manages to live and relate with other inmates who constitute his crucial and only meaningful world. It is what he experiences in this world; how he attains satisfactions from it, how he avoids its pernicious effects—how, in a word, he survives in it that determines his adjustment and decides whether he will emerge from prison with an intact or shattered integrity. The significant impact of institutional officials is therefore not in terms of their relations with the inmate alone, but in terms of a total effect on the social world in which he is inextricably enmeshed. In these terms, an evaluation of the institution's contribution to the welfare of its inmates may not realistically be made with the typical institutional platitudes and statistics about hours of recreation, treatment, and education. The evaluation must rather be made in terms of how the prison authorities are affecting the total social climate, how successful they are in enabling the less hostile persons to advance themselves, how successfully they are protecting these people from intimidation or exploitation by the more anti-social inmates, how effectively they curb and frustrate the lying, swindling, and covert violence which is always under the surface of the inmate social world. The efficient custodian now emerges from the role of restrictor and becomes the one who safeguards inmate welfare. . . . A control system which is lax enough to permit thievery and intimidation must eventually result in a deterioration and vicious circle.[71]

On the surface, this argument was different from McCorkle's practice at Highfields, which sought to eliminate the custodian and to encourage self-expression and the trial of new social roles, rather than to impose strict outer conformity to institutional rules. To be sure, the theories and policies dealt with different kinds of offenders, selections of the most and least promising, as it were, in different situations. What made the ideas consistent was a well-informed systematic analysis of the social structure of the different institutions, by which custody, services, and treatment were related to a "total social climate" according to a frame of reference that was as large and explicit as could be.[72]

The ideas about personality and social structure on which McCorkle drew were not his own invention, but part of the growing literature on behavioral science and criminology which he had studied at several institutions of higher learning, including the University of Chicago and New York University, a center of scholarship in criminology where he took a Ph.D. in 1952. McCorkle based his own contributions to this literature largely on practical experience; what especially dignified his thinking was an effort to overcome the "peculiar, almost unbridgeable remoteness" between scholarly theories and the phenomena of crime and punishment. The criminologist, he said, was like "a doctor who cannot even locate his patients until they reach the hospital" and then finds himself "denied access to the wards." [73]

In 1955, Gresham Sykes, a sociologist at Princeton, undertook a study of the social system of the Trenton State Prison. For three years he read documents, visited, talked to prisoners and guards, and administered formal questionnaires. In this effort "to gain access to the thoughts and life of captives and captors" he became aware of the problem of prison officials. "Careers, jobs and reputations depend on the efficient functioning of the prison," he said, "and what is a familiar administrative problem for the prison bureaucracy can become a scandal of mismanagement if it is made public." Fortunately, he found ready co-operation and little reticence at Trenton; "of particular worth," he said, were the "many long discussions" with the warden, Dr. McCorkle, who was "as much a student of the prison as its chief administrator." [74]

Not that the doctors agreed. Dr. Sykes suggested that Dr. McCorkle's celebration of custody might be a rationalization of the use of extreme measures "to avoid any events which would excite public indignation," and he doubted whether strict conformity with prison rules increased the inmate's readiness to conform to civilian moral standards.[75] He was still more skeptical of the "powder keg" theory of the prison riots, which the investigating committee had affirmed. In his own view, the power of the keepers necessarily had a fatal defect, in that it depended on some degree of uncoerced co-operation by inmates which forced officials into minor compromises of the strict rule. The compromises, eroding the authority of the guards, led to other compromises, and inmate leaders came to exert increasing control by unofficial terror and largesse. It was to the advantage of these inmate leaders, like the guards, to prevent incidents, but they found it difficult to do so; occasional dramatic events wrote large the fearful compromise of authority, and the administration, by tightening discipline, unsettled the inmate leaders and disturbed the uneasy compromise. Then the way was open for unstable and violent types to assert themselves as inmate leaders.

Prison riots in general appeared to be part of a cycle from tension to accommodation back to tension—perhaps riot. The instability was rooted in a contradiction in prison life: the custodians could not exert the total power expected by the public; neither could they control the slide into compromise; the public would not tolerate informal, unofficial control of the institution by inmate leaders, and of course would not tolerate an open breach with the authorities.[76]

Whatever the merit of his analysis, Dr. Sykes offered an interesting "postscript to reformers." "Present knowledge of human behavior is sufficient to let us say that whatever the influence of imprisonment on the man held captive may be, it will be a product of the patterns of social interaction which the prisoner enters into day after day, year after year, and not of the details of prison architecture, brief exhortations to reform, or sporadic public attacks on the 'prison problem.' " Any effort to reform the prison, and thus the criminal, he went on, "which ignores the social system of the prison is as futile as the labors of Sisyphus." The extent to which men could influence and change the social system of the prison was, in his view, the central issue—that, and not the recalcitrance of the individual inmate.[77] So the clergymen, lawyers, and philanthropists who had directed the course of prison reform in New Jersey gave way to the sociologists of interaction, and "the central reality of prison life" appeared to be much different from the formality of administration that had occupied the Morrow Commission in 1917.

19

Services for the Retarded: The Parents' Movement

The spread and improvement of mental testing after 1920 had made it evident that most of the "feebleminded" somehow made their way in the community, and this viewpoint weakened the presumption that they were inherently social problems. In April 1931, the New Jersey Conference on Child Health and Protection resolved that community diagnostic clinics, special public school classes, and "community care"—supervision and service—should be the mainstays of a program for the mentally handicapped, with institutional care reserved for selected cases and purposes.[1] This idea fitted in with Ellis' hopes for the county welfare board, mental hygiene clinics, and delinquency prevention, but, like them, its promise was not realized in the 1930's.

Toward Community Care

There were two general obstacles to a more enlightened policy toward mental deficients. One was the elementary question of defining the category. When the intelligence tests were first devised, it seemed that mental age and IQ were the bases of diagnosis, but thoughtful scientists like Edgar Doll, who had been chief psychologist in the New Jersey Department before he became director of research at the Vineland Training School from 1925 to 1949, realized that social incompetence was the practical test and that "intelligence" had a social as well as a biological matrix. The confusion appeared in the use of new names that made no valid distinction: "mentally deficient," which became popular in the 1930's, a politer version of "feebleminded" and "mentally defective"; and "retarded," which became popular in the 1940's and connoted slow learning or development rather than organic defect. Gradually, it became clear that some people inherited poor mental capacity but others suffered from accidents of gestation or birth, and also that "mental deficiency" stood to its particular forms as "fever" stood to "influenza" or "typhoid"—it referred to a symptom rather than a disease.[2]

The second problem was that, because diagnosis was indefinite, agencies that might have felt a clear responsibility did not. Obviously, the schools were best prepared to screen intellectual retardation, but in fact, diagnostic clinics were run mostly by mental hospitals in New Jersey and case-finders were often juvenile courts or welfare agencies that dealt with problem people. After diagnosis the appropriate service was a special class in the public school, or a state training school, or a private training school. Since none of these resources was adequate, the provision was often a waiting list. After training, the appropriate community service was some sort of supervision, by public or private agencies, and perhaps some special job training and placement, along the lines of the vocational rehabilitation of the physically handicapped. Finally came a need for some custodial provision for the aging deficient who had outlived his family.

The agencies that were responsible for these services included family service and child welfare agencies, public schools, state training schools, mental hospitals, juvenile courts, probation and parole offices, vocational rehabilitation and employment agencies, and public assistance. In each case these agencies had paramount and unmet responsibilities for normal people; mental deficients were, in most people's thinking, the least promising cases, and so they proved to be expendable.[3]

However much John Ellis would have liked to take leadership in promoting community care, his Department was simply not set up for community organization. His executive closest to the subject was Dr. Lloyd Yepsen, director of the Division of Classification and Education from 1934 until 1952. Yepsen had taken an M.A. in psychology at Ohio State in 1921 (under H. H. Goddard), served as chief clinician at Vineland Training School from 1921 to 1929, returned to Ohio State to earn a Ph.D. in 1931, and served as clinical psychologist for the North Jersey mental hygiene clinics.[4] His official duties in the Department pertained to the institutions, of course, and in this respect he had his hands full. The business of psychological testing, central to classification, had to be standardized and supervised, and he also had to define the general role of psychologists and their competence, which was still an open question. As late as 1939, J. Quinter Holsopple, chief psychologist under Yepsen, observed that the great variation in psychological service in the several institutions raised a question as to its efficiency and that was before the psychologists began to use projective tests and to practice therapy, as they would do in the 1940's.[5]

There was nothing about Yepsen's official position that directed his attention to the retarded (his predecessor, Dr. Bixby, had been in corrections), but his associations at Vineland kept him interested in the subject and especially in the need for better community understanding and organization. To this end he said and did what he could. In 1940, he arranged an institute at the North Jersey Training School at Totowa to enlist the social agencies of the great cities in the cause.[6] The next year Ellis reiterated the possibilities of community care, with a new emphasis on home training for children too young for school, on foster homes instead of institutional care (an idea Edgar Doll had imported from Europe), and on the unsolved problem of coordinating local resources.[7]

The war directed attention elsewhere, but many high-grade deficients found employment and made clear the possibilities in this line. Two long-range factors worked to increase Yepsen's problems, however. The rising birth rate, after the decline of the 1930's, increased the number of cases, and the introduction of antibiotics during the war years selectively increased the survival of many low-grade defectives who had, in the past, succumbed to respiratory ailments. On both counts the waiting list for institutions grew. Since Yepsen's office had the responsibility to compile the list and assign cases to institutions as openings appeared, he was kept painfully aware of unmet needs. Hence, in September 1943, at the suggestion of young Ed Johnstone, he began an experiment with home training for families on the waiting list from North Jersey. Parents found the program—a visiting teacher—very helpful, and as it happened, almost half the families in the experimental group decided that they wanted to keep their children after all.[8]

Yepsen told the 1949 Governors' Conference on Exceptional Children that New Jersey had five home teachers, each serving at least twenty-five children, each child representing a saving of $11,500 per year over institutional care. His talk also mentioned the usefulness of parent groups, like those he had helped organize among families on his waiting list; but it is plain that at that time he did not imagine that the parents would become an independent and wonderfully effective force in the long-delayed movement toward community care.[9]

The Association for Retarded Children

In October 1946, a letter appeared in the *Bergen Evening Record* from a woman who said that she had a retarded child and who appealed to other parents in her situation to get in touch with her. (It is ironic, in view of the consequence, that the editor did not want to print her name, which was Mrs. Laura Blossfeld.) A dozen readers responded; Dr. Yepsen met with them and furnished a mailing list of other prospects. Forty parents organized themselves in Paterson in June 1947. Some of them, from Newark, formed a second group in September 1948, and a third appeared in the Raritan Valley at the same time. Much encouraged, after their initial awkwardness, the founders decided to organize on a systematic basis, and before long there were active groups in most counties. In June 1949, their representatives met at Dr. Yepsen's home to form a state-wide organization, and the Department prepared a manual for forming new units.[10]

Meanwhile, the possibilities of a parents' organization were brought before the American Association for Mental Deficiency (AAMD) at its convention in 1947, and little groups showed up all around the country, in Washington, California, Minnesota, Illinois, Massachusetts, and (in 1949) in New York. As secretary of the Association (president in 1947–1949), Dr. Yepsen was eager to spread the word and invite parents to AAMD meetings, and under these auspices a national association of parents was established in 1950. Lee Marino, president of the New Jersey Association, was chairman of the first national convention, and Mrs. Fitzhugh W. (Elizabeth) Boggs, who, like Marino, was from Essex County, was on the national Board of Directors.[11]

The parents' association grew so fast and worked so well that it threw into relief the changing circumstances of the 1930's and 1940's. It was one of several similar organizations that involved a measure of self-help for afflicted families, like the National Foundation for Infantile Paralysis, which had proved so successful in the 1930's. The depression and war limited opportunities for this sort of association, but postwar prosperity and middle-class leisure opened the field wide. Moreover, the improved survival of low-grade deficients brought an increased likelihood that middle-class parents would become involved, since low-grade "accidental" cases are distributed at random in all social classes. Finally, the outlook of parents was changing, partly because informed opinion was increasingly critical of doctrines of a hereditary curse, partly because of an increasing candor about their problem (Pearl Buck and Mrs. Roy Rogers, among others, wrote eloquent books about their retarded children), but partly because of the obvious neglect by community agencies that might have helped.

The New Jersey leaders showed extraordinary initiative and energy both in organizing parents and in devising practical services. Their initial purpose was simply to share experiences and listen to advice from experts, but they quickly began to provide pleasant surprises for their children, in and out of institutions, and to charter buses to visit the South Jersey institutions. In July 1949, the Essex County group opened a diagnostic and guidance clinic for retarded children. It met at first in the Fuld Neighborhood House in Newark; Dr. Antoinette Friend, the head worker at Fuld, acted as its administrator; its staff included a pediatrician, a psychologist, and, as needed, a psychiatrist, who examined the child, and a social worker who interviewed the parents. Later other groups undertook this project. In October 1950, Elizabeth Boggs, who was educational projects director of the Essex group, set up a class for severely retarded children in Fuld House, and five others, mostly in church buildings, were begun within a year. Later the group arranged religious education for the children, nurseries for preschool children, canteens for teenagers, Boy Scout troops, a summer camp, and a sheltered workshop, among other ventures.[12] Other county groups developed services to suit their particular needs and resources.

It was exciting that so few people, volunteers working part time, could achieve so much with so little. In 1953, there were some 1,400 members in the state; a fund drive the previous year had raised $39,000. Both membership and fund-drive income rose—the latter sharply—but not until 1957 did the state organization have a full-time professional executive.[13] In the meantime, parents had put together what resources they could find—a room in a church, an amateur teacher, donations from philanthropists (the Turrell Fund was an important contributor)—and their achievements gave form to their abilities and to the relief, dignity, and hope they found in a situation that had been only a desperate burden for earlier generations.

In the process, they made themselves well-informed critics of every aspect of service, and they realized increasingly how great and unjust was the neglect of the retarded. They presently outgrew the role Dr. Yepsen had imagined for them. On the local level, he had hoped at first that they would simply reduce the burden of the waiting list and perhaps help the institutions. Aware of potential embarrassment from naïve enthusiasm or angry criticism, he arranged a staff adviser for each unit. On the national level, he envisioned the parents as a fund-raising and publicity section of the AAMD, serving the professionals, similar to the work of lay volunteers in the Heart Association. But it soon became evident that the parents were not to be a docile auxiliary. Both the local and national groups became independent and autonomous forces.[14]

Much of the New Jersey organization's interest focused on state agencies. The Essex clinic embodied a criticism of existing mental hygiene clinics—most of them state-operated—in two ways. First, the existing clinics were too crowded, of course, unable to serve the parents more effectively if they had wanted to. Second, they did not particularly want to serve the retarded. Their interest was primarily in emotionally disturbed children who might benefit from psychotherapy. Children diagnosed as mentally deficient were directed to a residential school, without much further guidance to child or parent. Family doctors, psychologists, teachers, and social workers who were not especially prepared to deal with the retarded often lumped their problems under the global diagnosis that implied a hopeless dismissal. The parents, however, wanted guidance and help. They strongly supported the view that "intelligence" had an emotional, as well as a biological and social, matrix, that emotional confusion much impaired the intellectual performance of their children, and that they deserved psychotherapy as much as other children. (Experts diagnosed emotional disturbance by interview, mental retardation mostly by standardized test, so it was sometimes difficult to see the correlation.)[15]

What most annoyed the parents was the failure of school districts to provide for the deficient, despite a clear legal obligation. School boards said that children whose IQ fell below 50 were not educable, and consequently were the responsibility of the state. The state institutions said they had no room. One purpose of the private classes the parents arranged was to show the possibilities of classroom training for the lower level. But public school classes for higher-grade children were far from satisfactory, and the state institutions for the retarded suffered particularly from the overcrowding and understaffing of the postwar years. (The parents became active and effective workers in the bond drives.) Despite many calls for action over a generation, the state had only makeshift provision for "defective delinquents," a very difficult class; the result was that judges committed them to correctional institutions, where they received little practical help and in any case seriously complicated the programs.[16]

When the retardate had received what training was offered and looked for a job, the employment agencies that served normal people were unprepared to help and uninterested, even hostile. Since he was handicapped, he might have been eligible for services offered to the physically handicapped, but these were organized mostly by surgeons for the rehabilitation of injured workers or soldiers and not prepared to help people whose handicap was mental.[17] As for the agencies that had to relieve the destitution of the unemployed retardate, social workers in private agencies, like psychiatrists, usually recommended institutional placement and let it go at that; public assistance offered no special provision for these children who never grew up. Nor did public recreation agencies have programs for children who were distinctly subnormal.

Everywhere they looked, parents saw ignorance and oversight in the definition of services so as to exclude the mentally deficient. Authorities like Ellis and Yepsen had been talking for years about the need for more and better provision, but no one had listened. What struck the parents, however, was not simply that their unfortunate children needed more help, but that they had a right to it, that public and community agencies that ignored them were ignoring an obligation.

Apart from their efforts at mutual aid and self-help, the parents took it upon themselves to present their case to particular social agencies and public authorities, and because they were well-informed, serious and practical-minded advocates, they received a hearing. At their request, a State Commission to Study the Problems and Needs of Mentally Deficient Persons was authorized in June 1950. The Commission, which included two legislators, a psychologist, a journalist, a social worker, Lee Marino and Dr. Yepsen (who acted as secretary), began meeting the following January. Its report, in February 1954, was a thorough and critical review of the subject.

Only a third of the report discussed state institutions. Priority went to general problems of public ignorance, research, personnel, and community services, especially education. Early in the movement Yepsen would have settled for state support of the classes parents had established, but the parents, and the Commission, were resolved that the children should receive a free and appropriate public education by right. This proposition was the heart of a bill John Shannon, a Newark school teacher and assemblyman, who was on the Commission, offered in the 1953 legislature. Defeated then, it was enacted in the "Beadleston Laws" of 1954, which revised previous legislation on the education of physically and mentally handicapped children.[18]

With respect to the mentally handicapped, the law required the commissioner of education to define three classes: the educable, who would receive a special education for more or less independent lives in the community; the trainable, who, although severely retarded, were capable of a degree of training for self-help; and the nontrainable, who could not benefit from classroom instruction. The law obliged each local board of education to arrange for the examination of its children and to provide for the two upper groups (perhaps in classes sponsored jointly with other communities). The state set standards for the examiners and the classes and offered financial aid to districts that met them. A "director of special education" in the state Department of Education worked with boards and administrators in establishing the classes.

The results were dramatic. By the school year 1956–1957 classes for the educable had increased from 280 to 565, classes for the trainable from seven to 122; many classes were in rural areas previously unserved. As opponents had warned, the new requirements caused an unprecedented scramble for the limited supply of psychologists and specially trained teachers. The situation forced large increases in training in the state's colleges and energetic recruitment elsewhere.[19] The Beadleston Acts were the most important consequence of the parents' agitation.

As for state institutions, the Commission found that only "devotion and self-sacrifice" had enabled their workers to bear the state's "policy of low salaries and small staffs." Most cottages afforded "only a minimum of custodial care," the Commission said, and as a start it recommended increasing the number of attendants by 50 percent and raising salaries to the level paid correction officers.[20]

The Commission criticized the "hierarchy" of the institutional staff and asked for in-service training, staff conferences, and other incentives for cottage workers. It criticized the policy of staff living at the institution—subsidized maintenance instead of proper salaries—and it suggested that superintendents take new jobs every four or five years, to give them new perspectives and bring them into closer touch with university and research centers. It noted that the structure of the Department obscured "direct and simple lines of communication" between institutions and the central office, and it asked for a review of the Department's goals, structure, and organization. It approved the home training program, but observed that it was much understaffed; it observed that the Department's Bureau of Inspection, which inspected private mental hospitals, was unable to inspect private schools for the retarded.[21]

Apart from these specific criticisms, it seemed to the commissioners that no one in the Department had the responsibility to oversee services for the mentally deficient or to stimulate new programs or the research, specialized training, or public information on which long-term improvement depended. The commissioners noted that after their work began there were many improvements "merely because an official agency [had] been asking questions and focussing attention." Among these was a Bureau of Mental Deficiency, set up in the Department under Dr. Yepsen, which took over admissions and home training from the Division of Classification and Education, and supervision of children on home visits from the Division of Correction and Parole. The Commission also took some credit for a new bureau of mental health research in the Department.[22]

The Reorganization of 1955

At the beginning of 1954, Dr. Yepsen left the central office to become superintendent at New Lisbon (he died of cancer the following year), and Dr. Maurice Kott became chief of the Bureau of Mental Deficiency. Kott had entered the state service in 1937 as an intern psychologist at Annandale and Trenton State Hospital; he later served as psychologist for the Mental Hygiene Bureau attached to that hospital, as a cottage supervisor at New Lisbon, as psychologist in the army, and as chief psychologist in the central office.

Kott's experience had led him to believe that there was a fatal gap between what the professional staff in an institution talked about and what the custodial staff did, and a second gap between what the central office experts talked about and what the institutional staff did. His professional identification led him to support the narrow view of a psychologist as a man qualified by academic discipline—a solid Ph.D.—and the broad view of a psychologist as researcher and therapist as well as tester and diagnostician. He was therefore disposed to take a critical view of both policy and administration within his bailiwick, and he was critical too of the older view that the mentally deficient were unfortunate people who ought first of all to be kept happy by good-hearted custodians; on his view they were "people, not pets," with a right to a joblike performance from the people who served them.[23]

In the climate created by the parents' organization these ideas found ready support, and in the fall of 1955 he announced a significant expansion of the Department's program. A new institution, the Edward R. Johnstone Training and Research Center in Bordentown, was set up to develop intensive training programs for various classes of children, to train cottage workers, teachers, psychologists, and social workers, and to be a center of research. Like Highfields, the new institution did not have a board of managers, in this case because Governor Robert B. Meyner opposed it.[24] A second development was a reorganization of "field services"—investigation of applications, casework with deficients and their families before and after institutionalization, home teaching, and consultation and public information for local communities. The reorganization contemplated a greatly increased staff of social workers and home teachers, organized in three regional offices.[25]

Both developments gave shape to the thought that mental deficiency in itself was not sufficient ground for commitment to an institution, that commitment was not a resignation to lifelong custody, that state officials ought actively to promote personnel training and community organization to make these hopes possible, and research to clarify and perhaps solve the problems. There were of course many obstacles in working out the new programs, but it seemed to everyone concerned that 1954 and 1955 were a turning point, when the ghost of the Kallikaks ceased to haunt public policy and airy visions of community care became administrative problems.

20

Mental Hygiene and Hospitals, 1945–1954

In 1945, more than half the Department's wards were in mental hospitals, which were by far its largest investment in plant and professional staff. When Bates became commissioner this great enterprise was in an emergency that was obvious, but it also faced great changes that were obscure.

"Five years ago it would have seemed to us an impossibility that [Greystone Park State Hospital] could continue to function as a curative hospital with the number of patients increased by two hundred while the professional personnel was reduced practically one-half and the non-professional personnel even more," reported Dr. Marcus Curry in 1945, and his managers observed that only affiliate nurses (who visited the hospital as part of their training) and conscientious objectors (assigned there in place of military duty) had kept the institution going.[1] At Marlboro State Hospital during that year there were twenty-five attendants to fill two hundred positions (a hundred conscientious objectors were due to leave) and thirteen graduate nurses to fill fifty-one positions.[2]

Shortly after he took office, Bates convened the Mental Hygiene Committee of the State Board of Control, which had not met for some time, together with some of his staff and consultants. The discussion turned mostly on restoring the institutions to their prewar levels. The Committee looked forward to expanding shock therapy and aftercare, to some special provision for the increasing number of senile cases ("people are now unwilling to accept almshouse standards for the care of the aged and any mental impairment is considered adequate reason for mental hospital care," they said), and, finally, they looked forward to a new state hospital. Taken together, these steps would relieve overcrowding, they thought.

For the rest, the Committee again endorsed the "New Jersey Plan," first set down in 1927, for psychiatric wards in general hospitals, and they recommended doubling the resources of mental hygiene clinics working out of the state hospitals. These steps would, they thought, help take care of the needs of emotionally disturbed veterans. The Committee noted a "persistent shortage" of psychiatrists, which it blamed on the indifference of medical schools, but it was pleased that the state hospitals were approved for resident training in psychiatry. It noted that in the whole nation there were only five schools accredited for training psychiatric social workers, two of which sent students to the North Jersey Mental Hygiene Clinics for field training.[3]

The Committee's discussion and conclusions did not differ essentially from those of the Committee on Mental Diseases of the New Jersey Health and Welfare Conference, which had studied the state's programs in 1939. That Committee had found that the state's preventive and curative program was "far in advance of the general average" because its work was "conducted by a single well-co-ordinated state department."[4] But it would soon appear that those prewar standards, the "general average," embodied a timid complacency.

The Changing Role of the Central Office

There was in these years an increasingly sympathetic view of mental illness. Partly this was because of the influence of dynamic psychologies on literature and social science, partly because of their influence on child training, child guidance, and education. Even physicians, pediatricians especially, began to heed the old complaint that psychiatry was ignored in their training and practice. This popular interest was not readily transformed into higher appropriations or a powerful association of reformers, but it was reflected in the development of extramural practice in psychiatry, which was mostly for people who could afford it. In 1953, there were 118 psychiatrists in private practice or clinic work in New Jersey, compared with only forty-five in the state hospitals.[5]

Psychiatric casualties in the war gave a new focus to this interest; after the war Congress poured resources into hospitals for them. The policies of these Veterans Administration facilities, determined by expert advisory committees, established a standard of treatment and service far above that of the state hospitals. They created new markets for psychiatrists, psychologists, and social workers and stimulated professional training and research.[6]

In 1946, Congress passed the National Mental Health Act, sponsored by the National Committee on Mental Hygiene, which established a center for information and research (later the National Institute of Mental Health, NIMH), and authorized grants for research, professional training, and community mental health programs. The act was intended to stimulate action by public health authorities, not state hospitals, although in New Jersey the Department of Institutions and Agencies administered the programs, because of its system of mental hygiene clinics based on state hospitals.[7]

Finally, the Council of State Governments, undergoing an expansion of its work, made systematic and critical studies of state mental health services. Its expert advisers on the subject said what the advisers to the VA and NIMH had said, but now the message got across to governors and politicians with the stamp of sound public administration.[8] Taken together, the increase of public interest, the VA hospitals, the NIMH, and the Council changed the climate in which state mental health programs operated. Whereas during the depression the problem was to hold the line, to economize, after the war it was to invest money in new programs. The old talk about prevention, cure, and community services was implemented by practical plans. Since the pressure for change came mostly from outside the existing state system, it fell to the central office to develop the new programs.

To be sure, the scope of the new demands did not become evident for several years, but in any case Commissioner Bates had had no experience at running mental hospitals, nor any professional association with medical men or mental hygiene. (Shortly after taking office he toured Greystone Park; unprepared for what he saw—the dreariness, hopelessness, and apathy of the back wards—he was sick for two days afterward.) [9] Nor was the Mental Hygiene Committee of the State Board of Control likely to be of much help in interpreting the future. Its influential members were old men, like Dr. Joseph Raycroft of the Trenton State Hospital Board of Managers or Dr. Arthur P. Hasking, for decades county physician and adjuster of Hudson County. At no time during his tenure did Bates have a psychiatrist on his State Board, as Ellis had had Dr. Ambrose Dowd; nor were any lay members especially distinguished in the field of mental health. Consequently, his deputy commissioner for mental hygiene and hospitals was to be a crucial adviser.

The first man to hold the job bore a familiar name and face, Dr. Henry Cotton, Jr. He had much to recommend him, including his long association with Trenton State Hospital, where he grew up, professional training at Johns Hopkins and its Phipps Clinic, his management of the Trenton hospital's mental hygiene clinics, which were close to the central office, and his experience as a hospital executive in the Army. After the war he had returned to the Department as a psychiatric consultant, and in a few months Bates made him deputy commissioner. His task was liaison between the commissioner and the mental hospitals, the state training schools for mental deficients, and the hospitals for tuberculous and epileptics. He was supposed to encourage high standards of treatment, service, and staff training in them; to attend to psychiatric service in all institutions; to develop the mental hygiene clinics; to oversee the inspection of county and private mental hospitals and general hospitals, and to advise with Dr. Bixby on parole from mental hospitals. He later became responsible for administering programs under the National Mental Health Act and federal aid for hospital construction.[10]

As "liaison man," he did not have any direct authority or any professional staff (the Division of Mental Hygiene and Hospitals consisted of Cotton and a secretary). He quickly cleared up one anomaly of the past, when the medical director rather than the business manager was made superintendent of the hospitals at Trenton and Marlboro. Ellis had always resisted this step, but Bates was amenable to it. For the rest, Cotton found his status difficult. Superintendents, used to dealing directly with Ellis, did not like to go through an intermediary, and the narrow resources of money and, especially, personnel on all sides made innovation difficult. Unfortunately, young Dr. Cotton also had private troubles, and one day in June 1949, at the age of forty, to the astonishment of his coworkers, he took his own life.[11]

For more than eight months the office was not filled; then Dr. Edward Humphries took over. Forty-five years old at the time, he had taken his M.D. at Columbia and his psychiatric training at the New York State Psychiatric Institute and hospital. From 1933 to 1942 he engaged in research in mental deficiency at the New York state institution at Letchworth Village. From 1940 to 1948 he had edited the *American Journal of Mental Deficiency,* and he was president of the American Association for Mental Deficiency in 1948–1949 (succeeding Dr. Yepsen in that position). From 1944 until he came to the Department in March 1949, he had been chief of the Bureau of Prevention and Education in the Ohio state system, where his duties had included fostering a state research program, state-supported professional training programs, and community programs.[12] A thoughtful man, he made some innovations in New Jersey and proposed some far-reaching plans (to use county hospitals as receiving hospitals, for example), but they struck Bates as impracticable, and he left quietly in March 1953, after four years.[13]

The office was then empty for nine months before Dr. E. Newton Pleasants came to fill it. Dr. Pleasants had been clinical director of Marlboro State Hospital prior to 1948, superintendent of the state hospital at Raleigh, North Carolina (1948–1952), and assistant superintendent of the Essex County mental hospital until he came to the Department in January 1954, six months before Bates retired.[14] By this time the Division of Mental Hygiene and Hospitals included staff positions in psychiatric social work and community services, a chief of medical services (somatic medicine, for all institutions—the successor to Ellis' old Division of Medicine), three new institutions plus the Diagnostic Center, which was autonomous, however, and the Bureau of Mental Deficiency, which was also largely autonomous. There was also a new Mental Health Research Center, whose director reported directly to Bates, not Pleasants. In short, the Department's efforts in the field were growing numerous and complicated.[15]

Meanwhile, Bates was occupied with elementary problems of institutional life. The foremost of these was overcrowding. In 1946, he arranged with the Navy to use its vacated barracks at Mercer Airport, in West Trenton, as temporary quarters for senile patients.[16] This makeshift lasted from April 1947 to June 1955, when the 680 patients then in residence (502 women, 178 men) were moved to the new state hospital at Ancora. Bates' principal work in this respect was the bond drives of 1949 and 1952; four-fifths of the funds so raised went for mental hospitals or institutions for the mentally deficient.

In other ways he interested himself in patient welfare. In 1946, he arranged surveys of fire hazards which led to safety measures and later much impressed the representatives of the Taxpayers Association.[17] Two years later he insisted that budget officials eliminate a policy whereby they deducted the cost of employees' food from their salaries, but held this sum in the treasury rather than adding it to food expenditures, so that inmates, rather than the state, had been subsidizing the maintenance of the staff. (In 1948 this tactic reduced the per diem expenditure for food that actually reached the inmates from 38 cents to 29 cents.) He also checked to see that inmates got the diet and menu that was authorized for them.[18] He promoted the placement of senile patients in foster home care and the "paroling" of mental patients under supervision.[19] These various improvements arose out of Bates' familiarity with institutional management and budgeting; they involved inmates of all institutions and did not require any particular knowledge of psychiatry.

To help relieve the personnel shortage at the mental hospitals, Bates and his personnel director, Raymond F. Male, worked out a new position, that of psychiatric technician, which stood somewhere between the traditional jobs of attendant and nurse. Candidates took a civil service examination to become eligible, then received a year's training—some three hundred hours of formal instruction, plus supervised study, clinical teaching, and supervised ward experience. The state paid them to take the course (which was also approved and subsidized for veterans' training by the VA). There were two programs, leading to two grades of technician. If successful, candidates earned more than attendants and became part of the civil service. The general plan, to "squeeze up" ward personnel, was widely praised (by the National Mental Health Foundation, the organization of wartime conscientious objectors who had worked on the wards, among others), but it proved difficult to recruit candidates and to hold them in the program. (Almost half dropped out, and many resigned after graduation, mostly to take better-paying jobs.)[20] Bates credited this program, which got under way in 1947, "largely to the ingenuity and persistence of Mr. Raymond Male"; he did not mention the Division of Mental Hygiene and Hospitals in connection with it.[21]

The Child Treatment Center

The Arthur Brisbane Child Treatment Center began in July 1940 as a children's unit at Marlboro State Hospital. The problem of emotionally disturbed children had always been difficult. They were clearly behavior problems, withdrawn or destructive, but it did not seem right to condemn them, as it were, to an insane asylum or to expose them to exploitation by adult lunatics. They were sometimes sent to institutions for mental deficients (often the diagnosis was plausible) or, if they got into trouble, to correctional schools for juveniles. After mental hygiene or child guidance clinics developed in the 1920's, the children often appeared in them. There they were diagnosed and sometimes treated in accord with dynamic psychology.

This mental hygiene emphasis on psychotherapy was, of course, rather precious in the view of most asylum psychiatrists, but on the other hand it did not seem right to classify children according to adult behavior symptoms or to subject them to somatic therapies. Meanwhile, a number of residential orphanages, losing their traditional function because of the practice of foster home placement, turned to caring for these difficult children, who obviously needed a special environment. In these settings, among others, group psychotherapy had developed in the 1930's; it was this sort of institution that the New Jersey Juvenile Study Commission of 1939 had recommended, and that the Diagnostic Center was intended to be, for children who came before the courts.[22]

The original children's unit at Marlboro was for those who had been committed to mental hospitals. Its director, Dr. Georges H. Lussier, was a native of Quebec Province and a graduate of the medical school of the University of Montreal. He served for a year at Danvers State Hospital, in Massachusetts, and in 1926 came to Polk State School in Pennsylvania, where he specialized in the care of feebleminded and epileptic children and took charge of the mental hygiene clinics. He stayed there for a decade, except for a year of postgraduate study in neuropsychiatry and child guidance at the University of Pennsylvania. In 1936 he became head of the men's service at Marlboro State Hospital. Experienced in both hospital psychiatry and child psychiatry, he was put in charge of developing the new operation.[23] As matters turned out, the unit was never filled to capacity. Doctors and parents were reluctant to sign legal papers of commitment (often there was considerable doubt as to whether children were legally insane, of course), and welfare agencies and mental hygiene clinics also hesitated to recommend children for mental hospital treatment even of this special character. Consequently many children who might have benefited from the treatment never came for it.[24]

In 1944 Mrs. Arthur Brisbane, widow of the famous newspaperman, and her children donated to the state their beautiful home and estate at Allaire, in Monmouth County near the sea. Originally, they intended it for the rehabilitation of veterans, but at the suggestion of the State Board it was made into a residential treatment center for emotionally disturbed children and the Marlboro children were moved to it in November 1946. The following June it became a separate service, with its own board of managers. Its organic act (P. L. 1947, ch. 252) said that it should provide observation, care, and treatment for minor children who were seriously maladjusted, with or without psychosis. Admission was voluntary, upon application of parent or guardian to the Division of Classification and Education in the central department, which screened and assigned children and maintained a waiting list, as it did for the training schools for mental deficients.

The Division could also transfer children from any other state institution, including the Board of Children's Guardians. Since the institution held only fifty or sixty children, it accepted only those between five and twelve years of age (between the special problems of very young children and of adolescents) who had no special problem of mental or physical handicap, and who did not suffer from advanced psychosis—the most treatable cases. Patients or public authorities paid on the same basis as for mental hospital care. The maximum fee for private patients was $20 per week.[25]

What the center offered the children was a protected environment, free of the pressures and tensions of their usual social lives, in which experts could study their behavior carefully and administer appropriate therapy. Treatment included individual, group, and play therapy and occasionally narcotherapy. At first it included electroshock therapy, the standby of adult institutions, but the shocks proved not to help kiddies. Dr. Lussier believed that every aspect of life bore upon therapy. He and most of the staff lived at the institution, and he personally saw to it that the "group supervisors" (attendants) and other employees deliberately worked toward a therapeutic milieu (as the practice was later called). The program of formal education was based on the public school curriculum, with special and very small classes. (Many of the children were nonreaders.) Discharge was by extended home visit, as for adults, when appropriate. Otherwise, when the child became twelve he was returned to his parents or sent to other responsible agencies.[26]

The center was unique among state institutions and in 1951 it was one of a dozen similar treatment centers, mostly private and experimental, selected for description by the Child Welfare League of America. The study made no critical evaluations but Dr. Lussier in a concluding "critique" noted that the budget of his institution "in no way" reflected its work and observed that it could not "be compared with privately endowed centers where financial assistance and budgets are of no question." He looked forward, he said, to employing a full-time psychiatrist to help him with professional care, an additional psychologist (his psychologist was not only a tester but a teacher and therapist), three social workers (at the time he had none, since the one he had employed had been paid by the federal Children's Bureau and the state had not yet picked up the cost), and an additional teacher.

Dr. Lussier's budgetary restrictions became clear in a comparison of per capita costs at the institutions studied: Brisbane's expenditure, $2,099, was about three-fifths of the next lowest and less than a third of that of the two most expensive institutions, which were also state-financed, as it happened, in California and Michigan, and which were tied in with state programs of research and professional training. As Dr. Lussier remarked, his location, which was a fine residence for the children, was "remote from teaching centers in metropolitan areas where professional personnel would be available on a voluntary basis." [27] Although it was plainly a useful and promising innovation, the Arthur Brisbane Child Treatment Center at Allaire had not thrown all New Jersey traditions to the wind.

The Neuro-Psychiatric Institute

The passage of decades had made Skillman Village for Epileptics an anomaly. From its start, in 1898, it had been a medical institution, but its doctor-superintendents had never found the time or means, if they had the inclination, to investigate epilepsy in a scientific way. The condition was assumed to be hereditary (New Jersey law forbade epileptics to marry) and to be degenerative; both assumptions fostered the notion of custody. Nevertheless, doctors in Boston and other centers of research had discovered improved anticonvulsant drugs that could control the symptoms and allow the afflicted a nearly normal life. A plan of parole under supervision began at Skillman in 1935 and during the wartime labor shortage many people who had come to the village as children and grown up there were able to leave and work outside.[28]

The anomaly was that if a perfect anticonvulsant drug had appeared (and none of the drugs was perfect, of course) many patients at Skillman had plural disabilities that would have required continued care or other kinds of treatment. Many were psychotic or mentally deficient and unmanageable. (There were two locked buildings on the site.) Others were physically handicapped or really degenerated, perhaps because of their affliction or because of their prolonged custodial care. The place was not especially overcrowded, but it was disadvantaged in the postwar labor market. The forty-eight-hour week forced it to recruit employees from neighboring communities, but its rural setting was distant from its labor market. To complicate the labor problem the antiquated buildings made surveillance, maintenance, and food service difficult, and under an administration which began in 1948, patients were told that because they were really sick people they did not have to accept work assignments around the institution.[29]

Obviously custodial, dilapidated, and troublesome, the place was hard to justify in the bond drive, and Bates was concerned about it. In 1951, he sent young Ed Johnstone, who had made a success out of the difficult and remote institution for idiots at Woodbine, to look it over. After a three-months' study, Johnstone reported on its problems of plant and personnel, but what struck him most was that the administration had no central direction in mind, so that cross purposes and personal antagonisms obstructed its service. He made some practical suggestions, among them that the Board of Managers learn more about what was happening, but his concluding thought was that perhaps any administration was doomed to frustration, since the patients had so many different problems tied together under the name epilepsy. He observed that most other states had eliminated special institutions for epileptics and asked whether authorities might not do well to redefine Skillman's function.[30]

A similar question was being raised outside the Department by a committee of the Medical Society of New Jersey. These gentlemen recognized that convulsive disorders were a serious business, afflicting about ½ percent of the population, but they could see that improved drugs could give these patients a nearly normal life, if the doctors and patients knew about them, and if the patients could solve their other problems. One obstacle was the notion of a hereditary curse, which current research held to be much exaggerated. In 1950, the doctors devised a plan for education and a consultation-demonstration service and presented it to the New Jersey Society for Crippled Children and Adults—the Easter Seal Society—for financial backing. A small program was organized in 1951. It was mostly education, at first—disseminating literature and arranging institutes—but the co-ordinator received a grant from a federal government agency to study clinics for epileptics, such as one that the Easter Seal Society had established in Ohio. The general subject was of growing interest also to child welfare workers, since convulsive disorders in children qualified them for special services for the handicapped.[31] From these perspectives too a custodial institution for epileptics was hard to justify.

Three other problems became pressing at about the same time. One was the growing number of children with advanced psychosis, who were not eligible for Brisbane and were out of place in wards for adults. Another was narcotics addicts; a third, the increase in the number of alcoholics. What these various unfortunates had in common was that the mental hospitals did not want them and no one knew much about their condition. Consequently, the idea occurred to Bates and his advisers to collect them all at Skillman, together with the hard core of the epileptic group, and hire people to do research on them.

After much consultation and deliberation, the State Board on July 1, 1952, issued a directive for a radical reorganization of Skillman along these lines. Management (but not the Board of Managers) was to be changed, inmates were to be reclassified and reassigned, hospital and laboratory facilities furnished, and the plant refurbished to receive its new problems.[32] It might seem that the plan exchanged a heterogeneous lot of epileptics for an even more heterogeneous assortment of cases, but whereas the old regime had been custodial, the new would be chosen and equipped to breathe the hopeful and critical spirit of research into the place. Thus Skillman Village, the old idea of a happy residence, gave way to the Neuro-Psychiatric Institute, the new idea of a workshop for scientists.

The new superintendent, Dr. Robert S. Garber, was forty years old, a graduate of Jefferson Medical College who also taught there, and a diplomate of the American Board of Psychiatry and Neurology. He had come to Trenton State Hospital as a resident physician in 1938 and quickly rose to assistant medical director; he was respected as both an administrator and a researcher.[33] In June 1953, Dr. Nolan D. C. Lewis, an eminent physician, biochemist, and research scientist recently retired from the New York Psychiatric Institute, was engaged at the new institution as director of research. Dr. Garber set about reclassifying patients (half went to mental hospitals, many of the rest went home) and arranging in-service training for the staff; Dr. Lewis planned the laboratories and facilities (he contributed his own extensive library), began to recruit a staff, and visited the mental hospitals to stimulate research in them.

To implement the return of epileptics to the community, Dr. Garber arranged for the Department to pay the salaries of physicians and other staff to carry on the community consultation and traveling clinic service which the Easter Seal Society had planned and largely underwritten. The service was guided by an Advisory Council including representatives of the Medical Society, the Easter Seal Society, and state Departments of Institutions, Health, Education, and Labor. The state Department of Health loaned electro-encephalographic machines to the hospitals which the traveling clinic visited, one in each of the four public health districts in the state; it also paid part of the cost of the technicians to run them and drew on its resources for public relations and public health nursing to support the program. Not until March 1954 was it possible to find personnel to get the traveling clinic operating, but the net result was that the Neuro-Psychiatric Institute, the Department of Health, and the Easter Seal Society put together a field service that was so effective that admissions to the institution on account of epilepsy were reduced from 250 a year before the reorganization to a total of twenty in three years after July 1953. (The Beadleston Laws, passed in 1954, were a help to epileptic as well as retarded children.) [34]

Gradually, the Institute took its new form, but it proved difficult to find and hire scientists who were interested in epilepsy or the other subjects assigned it by law. One difficulty was financial, as Dr. Lewis observed when he resigned in 1957. In New York, he said, he had for seventeen years disposed of $1.5 million a year for research projects; his New Jersey budget was $50,000, which employed four scientists and two secretaries. Penny-pinching pushed the research program below operating efficiency, he said, and the state should either be willing to spend or to quit. He deplored the "short-sighted" opinion of "some New Jersey citizens that we should let New York or Philadelphia do the research and let New Jersey use the results." [35] But as it turned out, the lures toward more research, including grants from NIMH and from private drug companies, and a growing sense of its dignity and importance, inside the Department and out, would keep the program alive.

Ancora

The third institution for the mentally ill begun under Bates' administration, Ancora State Hospital, had been projected twenty-five years before, but additions to existing hospitals, the makeshift of the naval barracks, and overcrowding had postponed it. In the list of projects presented to the Taxpayers Association for the bond drive of 1949 it appeared as a 1,500-bed hospital costing $15 million. At that, it would have been a quarter the size of Greystone Park and half the size of Marlboro.[36] Intended to serve the southern counties as a fourth regional hospital, it was built on land donated by Camden County and Winslow Township at the edge of the Jersey pine barrens, midway between Camden and Atlantic City. Construction began in May 1952.

State hospitals tend to grow bigger and more expensive than planned. At Ancora's dedication, October 27, 1955, the plan called for an institution to house 2,178 patients in nine substantial buildings (no "cottages" here), plus service buildings, flanked by residences for professional staff on the south and "employees" on the north, all adding up to a self-contained community and representing an expense of $22 million, almost half the amount raised by both bond drives. Its superintendent, appointed shortly before the dedication, was Dr. Harry H. Brunt, a young man who had become an army psychiatrist immediately after taking his M.D. at the University of Pennsylvania and who had later done postgraduate work in a VA hospital. A diplomate of the American Board of Psychiatry and Neurology, he was on the teaching staff of the medical schools of the University of Pennsylvania and Jefferson Medical College. He entered the state service at Trenton State Hospital, then became assistant superintendent of the reorganized Neuro-Psychiatric Institute before coming to Ancora.[37]

In April 1955, the new hospital received its first patients, transferred (under state police escort) from Trenton. Their new abode offered fine protection against the elements, with subterranean tunnels between the buildings. It had a built-in public address system to bind the little community together and a "radio control system" for quick checks on its citizens. The patients found the wards subdivided by "dwarf walls," which, it was said, gave them a measure of privacy without interfering with their supervision. The walls were painted soft pastel colors and the ceilings had acoustical lining to keep the noise level low, a blessing in a mental hospital. A prerelease building was in the planning stages.

Thus quietly did Ancora take its place among the state hospitals, after long travail. From the start men were divided about it. When Governor Alfred Driscoll laid the cornerstone, in March 1953, he said it was a tragedy that it had not been built twenty-five years before, but he gave the legislature credit for having played "a tremendously important part in making New Jersey the leader among states in the care of its less fortunate citizens." He spoke of the "great glory of the movement from the dark days when mentally sick persons were thrown into dark holes to the bright future of tomorrow when they would be returned to useful society to carry their own weight and the spiritual entities that made the individual a reflection of God's will." Ancora symbolized this movement in another way, he said; it was "the best flowering of the private enterprise system." "The real sign of the system," the Governor continued, "is the interest it takes in the welfare of all our citizens in contrast to the iron curtain countries where the state determines welfare." [38]

But when Governor Robert B. Meyner came to dedicate the new institution, nineteen months later, he did not see in it a symbol of progress or the Cold War. He thought it was "a monument to mankind's failure to find the answers to the problems of mental illness in our complex modern society." He said he fervently hoped that he would live to see the day when states would stop building brick-and-mortar symbols of the failure. He suggested a review of old-age assistance laws to find ways to keep the aged out of mental hospitals. He urged a greater effort toward prevention and rehabilitation. He regretted that the state spent so little on research. He recognized that a new approach would cost money, but he said it offered the hope of breaking the cycle of overcrowding and more building, and the hope "that Ancora would be our *last* dedication of a giant state mental hospital." [39] In such wise did the great institution become a straw that showed how the political wind was shifting direction.

Community Services for the Mentally Ill

The National Mental Health Act of 1946, which was passed to encourage the development of community services as well as research and professional training, bypassed the traditional state hospitals to encourage state departments of public health to administer its programs. New Jersey, together with a few other states, mostly with separate departments of mental hygiene, was an exception to this rule, because the mental hygiene clinics working out of its state hospitals were taken as evidence that the Department did have an interest in fostering a broad program of community services.[40]

There had never been any critical thinking in New Jersey as to how these clinics were supposed to develop community services. Historically, they had two quite different jobs. One was to serve the institution as an arm reaching out into the community, for diagnosis and aftercare of prospective or paroled mental hospital patients. The other was to serve community agencies by consultation and advice, especially by diagnosing problem people (primarily children) who came to the attention of the agencies. But how were these two functions supposed to encourage the development and expansion of community services?

The thinking, never explicit, seems to have been as follows: Personnel of the state clinics would visit communities and talk to people (officials, mostly) who might be interested in their service. In time, school administrators, juvenile court judges, social workers, clergymen, and others would see that problem people might suffer poor mental health; they would send them to the clinics for diagnosis and perhaps treatment. Especially crucial were the doctors; by holding the clinics in general hospitals, the Department would show local doctors the importance of mental hygiene in the treatment of somatic illnesses, and the benefit of treating mentally ill patients with the same facility and objectivity with which they treated their ordinary patients.

Once the mental hygiene clinics had demonstrated their benefit, teachers, judges, social workers, and physicians would say to the people who managed and financed schools, courts, social agencies, and general hospitals, "We need this service." The authorities, moved by the demand, would consider the question, and at this point the staff of the state clinics would be available to help formulate the need and the plan. In short, the mental hygiene clinics were to demonstrate the need and possibilities of community services for the mentally ill, and, more generally, to educate the public, especially the relevant professional groups, in regard to the whole problem of mental illness.[41]

The argument was plausible, and if someone had asked for evidence to support it he might have been referred to a few clinics founded under local auspices, especially in Essex County, where the eminent psychiatrist James S. Plant had developed clinics tied to the school systems. But it is obvious that the special problems of the depression and the war kept Ellis from actively promoting the clinics, and there is no evidence that he was inclined to do so in any case.

A survey of the clinics early in 1946 revealed that they had lost half their prewar personnel and had long waiting lists. A Department committee that recommended their expansion mentioned some budgetable costs: psychiatrist, $6,000 a year; psychologist, $3,600; psychiatric social worker, $3,000. The committee went on to discuss the practical questions of location and management. Clinics should be under the Department's supervision, it said, to assure high standards. They should rest on the understanding and co-operation of local doctors. Local authorities should provide adequate office space—preferably in hospitals. Clinics should segregate the mentally deficient and institutional parolees from other patients; otherwise "many mental hygiene clinic patients and their relatives [would] not co-operate fully or [would] refuse further . . . clinic help." The main emphasis was on psychiatric wards in general hospitals.[42]

There is little sense of urgency in this document, but within a few years it became apparent that it was impossible to recruit personnel even to restore the prewar level of service. The North Jersey Mental Hygiene Clinic, the most successful prewar operation, got along mostly with part-time help, and in 1949 ceased to be a field placement for social workers from Smith College.[43]

In September 1949, Dr. Luman Tenney, director of the Trenton Hospital clinics, described his work in terms of frustration. The clinics were trying to do too much, he said, and perhaps doing more harm than good. In the effort to serve, they took too many referrals. The referring agencies did not furnish good case histories or material, so the clinic staff had either to dig up the information or to diagnose on misleading information; the result was long delay and faulty work. When recommendations were made the communities did not have resources to implement them. He observed that, according to estimates of the National Committee for Mental Hygiene, the area he served should have eleven full-time clinic teams, supported by a network of public and private social agencies. He had two. He recognized that it would be impossible to approximate that standard because there simply were not enough trained personnel available "even if our State pay scales were comparable to those of private agencies and the Veterans Administration." [44]

There were, Dr. Tenney thought, three hopeful features of the situation. One was the school system, which was willing to consider a mental hygiene approach toward behavior problems, but which had neither the staff—the psychologists—nor the program, in most places, to do much. A second was the use of funds under the National Mental Health Act, which helped subsidize his staff and helped Camden County equip a clinic. Finally, he thought, the "newly formed State Mental Hygiene Society and its county units" might "improve public understanding of the need and purpose of mental hygiene clinics." [45]

The state mental hygiene association, which would indeed play a part in developing community services, was slow to appear in New Jersey, despite the fact that Clifford Beers, for decades the leader of the National Committee for Mental Hygiene, and many other important figures in the movement, like Dr. James Plant and Dr. George Stevenson, were residents of the state. Ellis himself was a director of the National Committee in the 1930's, but he rarely called these gentlemen into his councils, and he once told Dr. Stevenson that he didn't think the state needed a mental hygiene organization.[46] During the war a local organization began in Union County, however, to support a mental hygiene clinic there, and another began shortly in Monmouth County, where social services were relatively well organized.

In 1947, the New Jersey Welfare Council called together citizens interested in county mental health programs; there followed a series of regional meetings for organization, and the state association was established in 1948. Clergymen were often leaders in these local groups; so were wartime conscientious objectors, who had usually been moved by religious scruples and who had founded their own national organization to help mental patients; so were social workers and the relatives of patients, not to mention the patients themselves (Clifford Beers had been a mental patient).[47]

The organization was not a mass movement, but it established a group of people who were interested and informed critics of mental health services and partisans of improved community services. In 1952, they sponsored a law which allowed local officials to subsidize clinics which were not under full control of government. Soon after its passage the Mercer County freeholders appropriated $30,000 to a child guidance center which also received support from the United Fund and from various private institutions and agencies. Other localities followed this pattern, so that by 1955 there were seven clinics in the area Dr. Tenney served, several others a-borning, his own appropriations had been doubled in five years, and there was an officer in the state Department whose job it was to stimulate communities to take action. It looked as though the demonstration clinics were finally beginning to get results.[48]

The state hospitals, for their part, were trying more actively to encourage community support. "Psychiatric hospitals are in their present plight because the people, by and large, want them that way," Dr. J. Berkeley Gordon, the superintendent of Marlboro State Hospital, told a medical conference in 1952. Their basic problem—"a heartbreaking job," he felt—was public relations. The first step, he thought, was to have a scientifically sound institution. The next was to get its staff out to talk to people, and to get outsiders in to see for themselves. He noted the particular value for this purpose of acquaintance with clergymen, but his chief enthusiasm was for a volunteer women's auxiliary, such as all the New Jersey state mental hospitals had organized in 1948 and 1949.

Speaking of Marlboro's auxiliary, Dr. Gordon said that at first the staff was concerned "lest the ladies might, in their well-meaning ignorance, attempt to dictate hospital policies or through naïveté take at face value the plausible stories of paranoid patients." But careful screening and a "short indoctrination course" forestalled these problems. The ladies proved to be a considerable help around the place, he said, and soon they were able to inform their husbands and acquaintances that "Patients are *not* beaten and brutally treated, they are *not* kept in the hospitals as semi-slaves to work without pay; they are *not* the subjects of cruel experimentation or sexual indignities; and the doctors who work in these hospitals are *not* lazy, incompetent, indifferent political appointees." Finally, he mentioned the growing mental hygiene societies as valuable in enlightening public opinion. What the enlightened public would do, he hoped, was furnish more money. "There is nothing the matter with our psychiatric hospitals that a few million dollars won't fix," he concluded—meaning, of course, "a few million for each hospital." [49]

While the New Jersey Association for Mental Health did stimulate local services and work for larger state appropriations, it was also the springboard for a sharp attack on the omnibus structure of the New Jersey Department. Dr George Stevenson, one of its leaders and medical director of the National Association, discussing "New Jersey's contributions to psychiatry" in the *Journal of the Medical Society of New Jersey* in 1953, complained about "an absence of total state planning," which he blamed for the great size of its state hospitals, two or three times what experts thought was proper, for the persistence of county asylums, and for the unsystematic development of state mental hygiene clinics, attached as they were to separate hospitals.[50] In June 1954, the Association passed a resolution advocating the establishment of a separate Department of Mental Health.[51]

That December, in an angry speech, Dr. Stevenson took the case before the annual conference of the New Jersey Welfare Council. Speaking as a member of the Board of Managers of Marlboro State Hospital, he observed that the Board's duties and responsibility were not clear. It passed on the parole of inmates, which was not, in his opinion, its proper work, but it did not hear or discuss the budget of its clinics, which was an appropriate job. It was supposed to be responsible to the State Board of Control, but, he said, "It makes no report to that board, nor does it in fact receive guidance and supervision from it." The arrangement seemed only to confuse the line of authority from the commissioner to the superintendent, and to diffuse responsibility.

Dr. Stevenson favored the system in Massachusetts, which had a separate Department of Mental Hygiene under a single director. He pointed to the excellence of its research and training programs in attracting personnel, whereas two of the New Jersey hospitals had recently lost their accreditation for training residencies. He disputed the argument that an omnibus department brought the integration of various services; integration was most effective, he thought, in an interdepartmental committee between agencies with clear technical and administrative authority and responsibility. As for the state Board's role in protecting institutions from political interference, he thought that true protection came from inner strength in the institutions, a highly professional character and tradition, such as had enabled the Massachusetts system to flourish despite political storms.[52]

The Welfare Council did not, in its resolutions, call for a reorganization of the Department. The significance of the criticism was that it came under the auspices of an association of private citizens that was in a position to compare the situation in all states, that could not be called political, and that could not be ignored; and the focus of its criticism was less what had been done than what had not been done. Within a year, however, political and scientific developments were to offer irresistible incentives to a more active role by the central department as regards both hospital care and community services.

21

Assistance and Services: Problems of Organization

In John Ellis' thinking, the model for a public assistance program was old-age assistance, in which federal, state, and local (county) governments all paid a share, and which county welfare boards administered, under supervision of the state Department, which in turn met conditions attached to federal grants-in-aid. The outlook, on this view, was to organize the other programs in this fashion, to centralize general assistance (old-fashioned municipal poor relief) under the county welfare board, and to decentralize the categorical programs for dependent children and the blind, which were administered by state agencies, to the county welfare boards with state supervision. On the surface, these did not look like difficult tasks. The state agencies were certainly subordinate to the State Board; there was already legislation enabling municipalities to transfer their general assistance to the county.

Ellis was not inclined to push for a change, either upon his Department's agencies or upon the local poor-law officials, and wartime prosperity removed any pressure for action. The State Board never published any thoughts on the general question, but Ellis' publications in 1940 and 1943 show that the problem of local poor relief—the heart of the matter—was linked in his mind to the problem of federal work relief. Obviously, the three kinds of relief—work relief for the unemployed, categorical relief for the aged, dependent children and the blind, and general assistance—were related.

From Ellis' viewpoint, it was difficult to plan at the state level when the federal government's spending for work relief depended on the whim of Congress. Therefore, he thought, the federal government ought to decentralize work relief among the states, as it had done with the categorical programs and the original emergency relief legislation, so that federal, state, and local government would participate in financing, planning, and administering a unified system, with the county welfare board in charge of most direct service.[1] If this is the relation he looked forward to, it made sense for him to hold off on a confrontation with municipal poor-law officials, on the ground that the postwar depression, which everyone expected, would bring the federal government into local relief.

Integrating Public Assistance

There matters stood when Sanford Bates became commissioner. Like Ellis, he had had no official connection or experience with public assistance programs, but whereas Ellis grew up with the system, and Joseph Alloway and Marc Dowdell, who directed the principal welfare agencies, were his men, Bates did not have this personal acquaintance. As deputy commissioner for welfare he chose Dr. Ellen Potter. She was a grand character, recently president of the National Conference of Social Work; her official position, Director of Medicine, had put her in touch with the growing problem of chronic illness and its relation to public assistance, and she had acted as Ellis' representative to the social work community—but she was nearly seventy-five years old when she became deputy commissioner, and she was hardly prepared to advise Bates on the political and legal problems of integrating assistance. Bates had to face the immediate questions of the constitutional convention and the bond drive, which diverted his attention from the question of welfare organization.

In his personal attitude Bates was conservative, perhaps not more so than Ellis, but full of New England home truths about personal responsibility and self-reliance, suspicious of welfare handouts that might undermine those virtues, and deeply conscious of his obligation to give economical service to the taxpayers. His background in corrections made him interested in Douglas MacNeil's efforts at community organization for delinquency prevention, but otherwise he scarcely mentioned the welfare agencies of his Department in his first annual report to the State Board.[2]

In the first issue of the *Welfare Reporter,* Bates offered a general interpretation of the Department's work that sounded a theme he would often repeat: the proportion of citizens of New Jersey receiving categorical assistance was among the lowest of any state, but the grants were relatively high. He took issue with the opinion that these figures showed a hard-hearted policy or administration. In his judgment, they showed "that the people of New Jersey have been trained in habits of thrift, self-reliance and industry." (The grants were actually lower than in comparable states.)[3] In this article he quoted Paul Stafford's study of public assistance in New Jersey, *Government and the Needy;* Stafford's whole point was the crying need for reorganization, but Bates used only a quote on the danger of government paternalism for individual initiative and self-reliance.[4] In June 1946, he was quoted as opposing the integration of the categorical programs in a single agency, on the grounds that existing state agencies were doing well and a reorganization might expose them to political controversy.[5]

Like Ellis, Bates was dubious about social workers. Addressing the northeastern conference of the American Public Welfare Association in 1948, he commented on his recent reading about public welfare. He criticized a social worker's opinion that investigations of eligibility were mostly a waste of time and cut down on necessary services. He criticized Edith Abbott's proposal of a universal old-age pension in place of old-age assistance with a means test. He agreed with the opinion, in a publication of the United States Chamber of Commerce, that professional social workers failed to take well-rounded and balanced views on social issues. He approved a report by the Civic Association of Baltimore that "blamed the Federal Security Administration and the schools of social work for a wrong philosophy which highlights the theory that the client is always right." He approved a statement emphasizing that work was better than relief or pensions and that "gave recognition to the system of free enterprise as being our American heritage which we must not throw away through inadvertance [sic]." He urged that progress in the field of welfare might "even be consistent with cutting down relief and compressing its applicability." (At the close of the session, it was reported, "One young woman said to another, 'That sounded to me like the old theory of lesser eligibility dressed up for the new look.' ") [6]

For their part, social workers in New Jersey were increasingly dissatisfied with the state's welfare organization. Their forum, the New Jersey Welfare Council, drew its main strength from progressive (that is, professionalized) private agencies organized into community chests and councils, together with the professional-minded public agencies, both county and municipal, and, of course, workers in the state services. Social workers thought the assistance grants were too small, based on meager and unformalized conceptions of adequacy; they were dubious about narrow eligibility rules, about residence and relatives' support, for example, and administrative procedures that trifled with the feelings of the needy; they were particularly critical of the separation of categorical programs and general assistance, and in favor of their integration. These points were subjects of resolutions by their annual conference in November, 1948.

Bates, commenting from the floor on one discussion, observed that it was futile to ask appropriation committees for more funds for grants until the taxpayers were willing to pay more taxes (taxpayers had just defeated his first bid for a bond issue), and the director of welfare for West Orange defended municipal administration of poor relief on the grounds that municipal officers did not have a ceiling on grants and could be more generous than officials of a county-administered categorical program.[7]

In his report to the State Board in June 1949, Bates remarked that there had been "pressure from Washington . . . and, to some extent, from some of the private social agencies in and around Newark" to integrate the three types of categorical assistance and also to bring municipal poor relief under the Department's control. He did not see any clear advantage in the first proposal; he thought that the transfer of municipal relief might result in lower administrative costs. "But," he added, "there are strong political reasons why our local relief should be left to the immediate locality." He noted considerable progress toward integration of the categories within the Department, including among other things a budget manual for granting assistance, which Dr. Potter had prepared, and "printed notices . . . for the information of the public, in order that what little confusion may exist as to where an applicant might go for any particular kind of relief can be eliminated." He also noted that outside experts had, at the suggestion of the Department, prepared a study for Governor Driscoll on the further integration of welfare activities; the report had not yet been published, he said, but he had "been advised" that the experts had given "thorough approval to this Department and the way in which we have been administering these services." [8]

The Bane-May Report

The study in question had been requested by the League of Women Voters and the Welfare Council, as well as the Department, and it came in the wake of a proposal to integrate the welfare services of state and local governments in a separate department in the reorganization under the new constitution.[9] The experts were Frank Bane and Geoffrey May, of the Council of State Governments—eminent authorities indeed—and their summary, when the report was published, was forcefully crisp. The structure of public assistance in New Jersey, they said, was

> in part out-moded, in general complicated and expensive. Two state departments are involved. . . . Two sets of local officials are involved in related work, with separate channels to separate state departments. And there are eight different but related systems of welfare administration in the state. There are four types of aid administered or supervised by the State Department of Institutions and Agencies, each with a different set of administrative and financial relationships between the counties and the . . . department. There are four individual systems by which aid is offered not by the counties but by the municipalities, largely in cooperation with the State Department of Conservation and Economic Development.

The result was that county and municipal services overlapped, requiring duplicate efforts, while state supervision over the municipalities was "sometimes weak" or "completely absent"; consequently, there was an improperly variable treatment of individuals in need, an "entrenchment of differing administrative interests," and an expenditure for administration that was "at . . . or near the top of all states." Narrow eligibility requirements for categorical assistance caused many cases to fall on local relief, with a loss of federal participation in the payments, and the requirement of municipal settlement wasted administrative time and money.[10]

The central problem, the experts thought, was municipal poor relief. According to the reorganization of 1940, the State Municipal Aid Administration, in the Department of Conservation and Development, granted a subsidy to municipal poor relief officials, on condition that it "supervise" their administration. The most common arrangement, in 328 of the state's 566 municipalities, was that the state paid 40 percent of authorized expenditures. But fourteen municipalities had elected to have the state pay all their assistance grants, according to its own rules, in return for giving the state the proceeds of a one-mill welfare tax; in these cases, however, the municipalities hired and paid the officials who actually performed the service. Two counties had a semblance of a county system of general relief. A fourth group of municipalities, about a third of the whole number, mostly small and unpopulous, elected not to receive any state reimbursement and hence were entirely unsupervised. The supervision, in any case, was mostly fiscal, the experts found, and the professional training and service of the officials were, with some exceptions, poor.[11]

The experts were more respectful of the county-state programs, but they observed some duplication between the state agencies for children and the blind and the county welfare boards. They were not much impressed by the state's claim of low expenditures but high grants in its categorical programs. If a state aided only the most needy applicants, they said, of course its grants would be high, especially in urban places where living costs were high. They also observed that the high proportion of industrial workers covered by social insurance would reduce the need for public assistance.[12]

There were several ways to judge the relative cost of administration, Bane and May said. Bates' executives chose to compare it with the amount of assistance grants and with the total state population, which measures made it look small. They thought a more fair and accurate measure was administrative cost per case-month, including both categorical relief and general assistance. On this basis all administrative costs were very high. Old-age assistance cost more to administer than in any other state, and general assistance, by the municipalities, cost far more to administer than in any other state—$16.10 compared with $10.41 in New York, the second highest, and $7.25, the national average.[13]

As for the administrative organization of the state's welfare functions, Bane and May thought the Department of Institutions and Agencies was "actually not an operating unit" but "a federation of operating entities." The commissioner had no direct control over the agencies for children or the blind, which had separate Boards of Managers; his "deputy commissioner" had neither authority nor responsibility for administration; he had no direct channel to workers in the field. Each state agency had its own field services, with little procedural co-ordination among them; each agency sent out its own rulings and instructions, but these were not numbered or indexed to make a welfare manual.

"It is all too easy to criticize these arrangements," the experts said, but the situation did not show, in their judgment, that "past and present commissioners . . . have . . . failed to understand the principles of administration." Some of the "weakness" was, in their opinion, that the commissioner had no legal authority to direct all the programs of his own department. Some was the local tradition that agencies and counties "tend to consider themselves at least semi-autonomous." Some might be "self-protective: The Department is large and contains various functions that might be separated from it." The experts also expressed doubts about the institution of the State Board of Control. It was supposed to protect the work from political mismanagement, they knew, but they thought that "good public administration is as important as good public welfare" and that the answer to political mismanagement was "not in preventing a governor from running an executive function but in choosing a governor who will run it properly." [14]

In their practical recommendations the experts agreed with the old argument: Integrate welfare programs under the Department of Institutions and Agencies and the county welfare boards, they said, and put state officials to supervising the counties; have the state and county share equally in all categorical programs and also in general assistance. "There is little that is original in this report," they observed. "The strength of our suggestions lies in the fact that they have long been understood by informed groups, that their adoption is only a matter of time in any case." [15]

The difficulty, they recognized, was that, while all the contending parties favored "integration," they wanted to integrate different things. The Board of Child Welfare (as the Children's Guardians were called after 1948) held that services for children should be together. The Commission for the Blind believed in a single program—prevention, financial assistance, education, rehabilitation—for their wards. The New Jersey Welfare Council wanted to integrate the granting of assistance—the general procedure of receiving and investigating applications, budgeting grants, and casework with the family in need—under county welfare boards, leaving special problems of children or the blind to special consultants or workers. The New Jersey Municipal Welfare Employees Association agreed that welfare programs ought to be integrated around the assistance function, but they favored consolidation at "a democratic local base" as opposed to "totalitarian" dictation from above.[16]

The Division of Welfare

The importance of these diverse opinions became clear when Governor Driscoll finally released the Bane-May Report, in January 1950, along with a recommendation for consolidation. The legislature transferred the function of subsidizing and supervising general relief from the Department of Conservation to the Department of Institutions and

Agencies, but it did not choose to alter the plan of administration by local officials, which had been the essential complaint. The operation was attached to the Bureau of Old-Age Assistance, the only change being a reduction of a third in its appropriation and the necessity to reduce the existing staff.[17]

Meanwhile, the State Board introduced a new feature in the Department's organization. This was a Division of Welfare, which had at its head the deputy commissioner of welfare acting in an executive rather than an advisory role, and which included under his direction all the categorical programs and the newly-transferred program of aid to the municipalities. The change in administrative structure was a large departure in theory from the older pattern of functional divisions such as classification, accounting, and medicine, but in practice the existing agencies did not change their business and their executives continued to report to their Boards of Managers.[18]

Meanwhile, in September 1949, Dr. Ellen Potter resigned, and Bates appointed Elmer V. Andrews to succeed her and run the new division. Andrews, forty-two, had a B.S. and M.A. from the University of New Hampshire. His background was in public administration. In 1939 he had gone to work for the Social Security Administration in his state; two years later he became assistant to the commissioner of public welfare of New Hampshire; he was appointed commissioner in 1942 and served until he came to New Jersey.[19] An unassuming, deferential man, he believed that the "greatest weakness of administration" in public welfare was public ignorance about the dilemmas of the work—the demand to increase service beyond the means of the staff, or to grant adequate aid without sufficient appropriation.[20] But if the new deputy commissioner hoped to develop a program of systematic public information on welfare problems in New Jersey, to illuminate the problem of integration, perhaps, he was evidently disappointed.

The issue of integrating public assistance came to a crisis in February 1951. After the Bane-May Report was published, Bates had asked Marc Dowdell, the head of old-age assistance, and Irving Engelman, his assistant, to draw up a bill embodying its ideas about reorganization. The bill, designated A-17, took the form of a revision of state welfare laws, a much needed codification in itself, and it included provision for an important new category made possible by amendments to the Social Security Act in 1950, namely, aid to the totally and permanently disabled.

The bill proposed to take this fourth category of cases away from local poor relief and place it with other federally aided programs under county welfare boards. It did not abolish local relief, as the Bane-May Report had suggested, but left it optional with the municipalities. It changed the formula for all assistance programs so that state and local government shared equally. It assigned the assistance functions in child welfare and aid to the blind to the county welfare boards (a concession from Bates). Its financial effect was to reduce direct costs to counties and municipalities and increase the contributions of the state government. Governor Driscoll supported the bill warmly and Bates made a lucid and persuasive case for it in committee hearing.[21]

Opposition was strong but diverse. Municipal officials attacked any infringement on home rule; the CIO and some private agencies opposed a reimbursement provision which they thought too restrictive; the Commission for the Blind and its well-organized supporters and the Board of Child Welfare and its particular friends opposed the separation of assistance from these agencies.[22] Ultimately the bill was defeated, although a program of aid for the totally and permanently disabled was enacted.[23]

Unwilling to leave the matter there, the legislature provided for a new commission to study the subject. It included members of both houses of the legislature and private citizens; its chairman was Walter L. Kidde, a well-known businessman prominent for many years in welfare organizations and sometime president of the New Jersey Welfare Council. The Kidde Commission reviewed the issues at length and came up with a bill that followed closely the recommendations of the Bane-May Report and the defeated A-17. Its principal change was a further concession to the home-rule party and a hedging on whether strikers could receive emergency aid. But the concessions did not satisfy the municipal aid officials, and they also alienated Bates. He had "agreed to go along with" the transfer of assistance functions to the county welfare boards "on the understanding . . . that that was part of the complete integration of all welfare services," he said, but the Kidde Commission's bill did not establish integration of general assistance; therefore he was opposed.[24]

Its proposals defeated, the Commission tried again in 1954. Mr. Kidde by this time was exasperated by the opposition from both sides, that is, the Department and the municipal officials; it represented, he thought, simple resistance to change. He was particularly annoyed by the "blind fear and emotion" of municipal officials. "We are accused of failing to show cause for changes," he said. "Perhaps the time may have come to stop pulling punches and to make some of these criticisms. I hesitate very strongly to do it, but . . . it may be necessary." [25]

There the matter stood. Another commission, five years later, would comment again on the "startling lack of coordination and unity of function in the categorical programs," the weak supervision of municipal relief, and the organization of the Division of Welfare—"actually a federation of operating units rather than an operating unit in itself." It would suggest again the old reorganization: integration of public assistance under county welfare boards with state supervision; a direct line of authority from commissioner to bureau chiefs and to the field; equal sharing of costs between county and state.[26] By that time, however, a number of other aspects of integration had come to the fore.

Expanding Child Welfare Services

When people called for the "integration of welfare services" in the 1940's they usually had in mind the consolidation of public assistance in the county welfare board, but increasingly in the postwar years another problem of organizing services came to the fore. It involved the "co-ordination" of agencies that were set up to handle the normal problems of normal people, as it were, and in general it was a consequence of the fact that these agencies, for education, health, and law enforcement, were taking enlarged views of their work. The general issue came into focus in relation to child welfare, where it was part of delinquency prevention, mental hygiene, and "preventive and protective" services for children, and in dealing with the aged, where it was linked especially to chronic illness and hospitalization.

The report of the Juvenile Study Commission in 1939 had made the point that a sound preventive program depended on some integration of the school and various health clinics as well as the police and Juvenile Court, and beyond these institutions lay the need to control unwholesome influences and bolster wholesome influences. But what machinery could co-ordinate and direct the community's institutions toward these grand ends? Boss Hague was proud of his program based on the public schools and the police; others favored a voluntary confederation of public and private agencies for mutual direction. Many people looked for leadership to the Juvenile Court, which was in a strategic position to catch trouble early. In any case, the co-ordinating machinery was conceived as local. When Douglas MacNeil said the work of his Division of Community Services for Delinquency Prevention was "a hit-and-run job of community organization," his assumption was that he was to alert local leaders to the needs and possibilities of bringing together local services.

Since the state Department had no authority over local courts and probation, or over any other local agency, its interest in co-ordinating local services arose in three contexts. The courts committed troublesome children to its institutions; it supervised the children when they returned to the community on parole; and the courts sometimes committed children to the Board of Children's Guardians for foster home placement instead of sending them to institutions. One might expect that someone would have made a case for integrating probation and parole services, since they were similar, but neither the Department nor the courts chose to do so.

The work of the Board of Children's Guardians was different from that of children's agencies in many states. It had been set up to keep children out of almshouses. This it did by assuming legal guardianship over them, then delegating their care to foster families. Foster homes were supposed to be more wholesome than institutions, and the Board was supposed to try to restore the children to their natural parents.

But judges committed the children to the agency, and legally ended the authority of the parents. After 1910, the judges could also commit delinquent children for foster home placement.

Then, in 1913, the Board was given charge of a "home life" program, the New Jersey version of a mother's pension, which was a precedent for Aid to Dependent Children (ADC) under the Social Security Act. This was a public assistance program, a category of poor relief, and the Board of Children's Guardians did not become the legal guardians of these children, but simply investigated and supervised the grant of relief. Home life grants had quickly become a much larger program than guardianship, and the demand for integration of public assistance under county welfare boards referred to it alone. Under all plans for integration, the program of guardianship and foster home care was to stay with the agency, and the state government was even supposed to take over the cost of supporting the children under it—a sweetener for the counties, which had formerly paid the bill.

With regard to both guardianship and home life the agency was, in 1945, primarily engaged in direct service. It placed and supervised children and granted aid through its own employees. In many other states—those deemed progressive—the state children's agency did not, as its main work, directly serve children. Instead, it supervised local agencies, public and private, which did the actual work. It set standards for them and guided or pushed them toward the standard.[27]

The proposal to have county welfare boards handle home life under state supervision was in line with this thinking. As for the guardianship program, the significant thing about it in the 1940's was that it depended on court commitments. Before the agency could help a child, a judge had to find that its parents were incapable of caring for it. But to separate a child from his family, to make him a ward of the state, was a grave decision. Increasingly judges looked for other dispositions, and increasingly social workers in child welfare and family service agencies tried to get to the family in the early stages of its difficulty, before it became a court case.

During the depression, when public programs dispensed almost all financial aid, private agencies had perforce to apply themselves to casework with their clients, and this interest was stimulated and supported by the professional schools of social work. Consequently, preventive and protective services grew in importance. These private services, which offered counseling and other help, were a first line of defense against family breakdown. They could reach the family before it got to court, or the judge could refer cases to them, or they could go into court in behalf of neglected and delinquent children, and the judge could commit the child to them or make some less formal arrangement. It became more and more clear in the 1930's and 1940's that the Board of Children's Guardians was a residual agency. In the cities it took cases that private agencies could not handle or rejected. It largely served the rural areas, where there were no private agencies.

To obtain a subvention under the Social Security Act, the Board had set up a Division of Child Services to encourage and assist the development of child welfare services in rural places, and, informally, the agency's managers and staff were of course active in the improvement and coordination of children's services. But it was not primarily or officially a leadership agency. Its first job was to serve the children in its programs. In this respect, the wartime prosperity somewhat lightened its burdens; its labor force of female caseworkers was less disorganized than the custodial force of institutions, and since it maintained no plant, it had no problem of dilapidation. When Bates took office his pressing problems lay elsewhere.

But troublous times lay ahead. The wartime baby boom, including many illegitimate births, increased the case load, and inflation caught the agency in a double squeeze. The cost of child care rose faster than the state increased allowances for foster care, and the competition for social workers increased their selling power faster than the state agency, working through civil service, could increase its buying power. There was an improvement in private agencies and other community resources with regard to preventive and protective services, but the state program, the residual program, grew disproportionately. The cumulative result, very evident by 1950, was a vicious cycle of heavy case loads, inexperienced workers, difficulties in finding foster homes, and high turnover among the workers.[28] There were improvements: more professional supervision in the district offices and programs of orientation, in-service training, and educational leaves for the caseworkers.[29] Difficult as the situation was, the agency offered more promise to children, in the minds of Bates and his advisers, than did service by county welfare boards, which were even farther from professional norms—which is why Bates was dubious about surrendering the home life program.

In some ways, the Board tried new roles. Its Division of Child Welfare Services, which had begun by paying a social worker to do casework in rural counties, changed its policy in 1946. Thereafter, the rural county welfare boards employed the caseworker under state supervision, and the county shared the cost with the state and federal government. (Unfortunately not many counties undertook the service.) In 1949, the Board developed an experimental homemaker service, designed to give short-term emergency care when a mother was incapacitated or absent, so that the children would not have to go into a foster home. It was also stimulated by a federal grant and administered by the counties.[30]

These were steps toward state encouragement and supervision of local public services, and at its meeting in November 1950, the New Jersey Welfare Council came out strongly for more work of this sort and more services to children without court commitment.[31] The Board accordingly expanded its work in inspecting and advising agencies and institutions serving children and unmarried mothers, and in approving agencies that offered children for adoption.[32] Later that year, after Bates had failed in the attempt to get a revision of the Welfare Code, there was a revision of the child welfare section which added an important new program. This was "care and custody," that is, casework supervision and even foster home placement, offered to a child and family on the request of the parents rather than on commitment from a court.

The new law made it possible for the Board to initiate preventive or protective service in the fashion of private agencies. It recognized that the state had a responsibility to provide services to children in need, whether or not they were dependent or delinquent. Since it required that the state agency act only when private and voluntary services were not available, it put the Board in a position to encourage the development and coordination of private agencies, and in fact required it to do so. In general, the new law shifted the state's emphasis from the child's eligibility for state service to his need for help, and directed the state agency either to stimulate or to supply preventive and protective services for all children.[33]

A Permanent State Youth Agency

The new child welfare law held much promise for improved state leadership in this area, but the problem of inadequate funds to hire caseworkers and compensate foster families increased during the early 1950's. The demand grew for a new agency, like those in New York and other states, that would plan and co-ordinate programs for children and youth, at the state as well as the local level.

If things had worked out as Douglas MacNeil had expected in 1950, the state agency would have been the Governor's Committee on Youth, which included heads of state departments and private citizens appointed by Governor Driscoll to prepare for the White House Conference in that year; the local agencies would have been the Municipal Youth Guidance Councils authorized by legislation of 1947 and made up of public officials and private citizens engaged in services to juveniles on a local level; his own Division of Community Services for Delinquency Prevention would have consisted of a staff for research and consultation to serve both state and local groups.[34]

MacNeil worked hard on organizing widespread participation in the White House Conference, and the preconference report, *Children and Youth in New Jersey* (1949), is the best general survey of the manifold aspects of child welfare work in the state until that time. But the Governor's Committee did not continue to function after the conference, and the Municipal Youth Guidance Councils languished.[35]

The legislature established in 1954 a Juvenile Delinquency Study Commission, including members of both houses and private citizens (none associated with the Department of Institutions and Agencies or its Board of Control) and a research director, Alan S. Meyer. The Commission was continued for six and a half years—in 1957 it became the Youth Study Commission, in recognition of the breadth of its inquiries—and its reports to the legislature during this period were widely distributed. Its public hearings, energetically summoned by the chairman, Mrs. Arthur Vervaet, brought out a wide range of expert opinion. Its primary interest was delinquency, but it covered the whole range of children's services, from particular state programs, such as Highfields or foster home care, to such subjects as child labor and school dropouts.[36]

The Commission's publications brought out in many ways the diversity of state and local, public and private, programs that bore on the problems of youth and how they developed in isolation and sometimes at cross-purposes. Toward the end of its work, it focused on the case for a state co-ordinating agency, which it felt was the foremost need. It had in mind an unpaid board of citizens and a small professional staff, who would plan and assist a continuous program of study and research on the needs and problems of juveniles, evaluate and coordinate state and local services, and help these agencies plan. The proposed board would report annually to the governor and otherwise publicize its studies and reflections, and act as a clearinghouse and consultant for any interested party. Since it was to study and evaluate the work of operating departments, as well as co-ordinate them, that is, bring their staffs together to clarify and solve mutual interests and problems, it was to be a division in the Department of State, responsible directly to the governor and deliberately removed from operating departments such as Education and Institutions and Agencies.[37]

Meanwhile, a new administration in the Department of Institutions and Agencies had replaced MacNeil's Division of Community Services by consultants for community organization in corrections and mental health, and early in 1959 his associate, Mrs. Pauline Thyfault, had become executive secretary of the New Jersey committee that arranged the state's participation in the 1960 White House Conference on Children and Youth. This in itself was a large-scale job of community organization, much larger than the work in 1950. It involved recruiting a state committee and county committees, dividing them into a host of subcommittees to study and discuss various subjects, then pulling together the committees' work and summarizing it in a volume. More than five thousand people took part in the activity. To aid their deliberations, a Committee on Research and Resources, under MacNeil's direction, prepared a guide and a handbook, full of helpful hints and information, including a useful collection of relevant statistics and a list of some seventy civic and professional organizations that the county committees might consult or draw on.[38]

This Committee, like the legislative Youth Study Commission, named as its first priority the strengthening and co-ordinating of community planning. It saw three alternatives. One was a permanent commission, somewhat in its own image, and somewhat like what MacNeil had hoped would follow up the work of the 1950 Conference. A second possibility was a nongovernmental agency, something like the New Jersey Welfare Council, with state officials participating in its planning features but not in its "organized efforts to secure public endorsement of its program."

A third was a continuing interdepartmental body of state officials. The Committee made no proposal for municipal planning and co-ordinating agencies, like the municipal youth guidance councils, but it urged citizens to participate more in the life of their communities.[39]

None of these proposals was what the Youth Study Commission would recommend as a permanent youth agency—they did not involve the notion of a small official body separate from operating departments and in a sense passing judgments upon them, and responsible to the governor—but it was clear that people on all sides were looking for some new state agency to co-ordinate their welfare programs.

The State and the Sick Poor

Traditionally, the care of the sick poor was the business of local poor relief. The specific institution in cities was the hospital, financed by municipal or county taxes, by private philanthropy, or by both. At first the hospital was a sort of specialized almshouse, a place of quarantine and care for transients. The improvement of scientific medicine in the late nineteenth century—largely in connection with the observation and treatment of hospital patients—made it more specialized as a place of intensive treatment for acute illness. This development sharpened a distinction between acute and chronic illness, which required for the most part long-term nursing care. The general hospital took short-term acute cases; the municipal and county almshouses were filled with the chronic sick, especially since they were likely to be old people who had no family to care for them.

The state was not involved in local poor relief, in New Jersey, except that state institutions took special cases out of the local almshouses, hospitals, and jails. There were three state institutions that helped the sick poor. First were the mental hospitals, which antedated the modern general hospital. Second were the veterans' homes, which appeared after the Civil War and were quasi-medical institutions to protect homeless and sick veterans from the misfortunes of charity. Third was the state tuberculosis sanitorium. Since the state never found the means to care for all the mental patients or for most of the TB patients, it developed a system of subsidies to county hospitals for these purposes. This was a sort of state grant-in-aid, and one important job of Ellis' accounting office was to clear the payments. But this responsibility did not in practice involve the setting of standards of care or the supervision of the local institutions.[40]

At first it seemed that the state might extend this policy of subsidies to local medical institutions for all sorts of chronic illness. In 1911, the legislature authorized state aid to private hospitals that cared for incurable cases; but in 1913 the act was repealed because of two objections, one that the care of the sick poor was the responsibility of local communities, not the state, the other that public subsidies to private institutions were a priori a mistake. The assumption behind both arguments was that a policy of state subsidies opened the state treasury to unprincipled raids by local agencies, public and private.[41] The idea that state aid might be a device to extend or improve services—the idea of the grant-in-aid as it appeared in the Social Security Act and developed after 1935—was not a consideration. A New Jersey commission to study state and county aid to general hospitals reported in 1929 that the existing system of county and municipal support was sufficient and state aid was not needed.[42]

Aid to dependent children, to the blind, and to the aged, subsidized by the state, involved it incidentally in the provision of medical care for these classes. If they needed help, the social worker was supposed to see that they got it. For the most part, workers simply referred clients to the hospitals and clinics that served the needy poor. If an aged person were in an insitution for chronic illness, however, he was not eligible for old-age assistance, which was considered to be a form of outdoor relief, and therefore he fell upon municipal relief, that is, the almshouse or hospital.

There were two other state-aided programs, not under the Department of Institutions and Agencies, that involved the state in medical care to some extent. In 1919, New Jersey established a Rehabilitation Commission to arrange or provide, in its own clinics, therapy for physically handicapped people who might be restored to self-support. In large measure, this agency helped workers injured in industrial accidents, so it was located in the Labor Department. But the program offered many people a constructive alternative to dependency or institutionalization on poor relief.[43] In 1926, the state established and contributed to a Crippled Children's Commission which carried on the admirable work that fraternal organizations, notably the Elks, had done for the care and treatment of children who might otherwise have become almshouse or general hospital cases. The fraternal orders largely financed the work, together with the counties. After 1935 the federal government provided matching funds, and it grew rapidly.[44]

For the rest, the care of the sick poor fell upon local agencies, and events conspired to make it an increasing burden. For one thing, the costs of medical and nursing care rose along with the improvement in standards. For another, the number of chronically ill increased, along with the proportion of aged in the community. Moreover, the passing of the rural homestead and the separation of generations in family life made it more difficult for relatives to care for the aged. If old folks became "senile," it was possible to put them in mental hospitals, where they received relatively inexpensive care subsidized by the state; this was one reason that state mental hospitals became so crowded in the 1940's. By this time it was evident that the state would have to take a somewhat larger part in medical care. Its obligation to assist the aged poor required that it provide for their health needs, which often involved some sort of continuous medical care in a hospital or an alternative to a hospital, such as a nursing home or a mental hospital. Since hospital beds were scarce and expensive to maintain, the state tried both to encourage the provision of more beds and to find inexpensive substitutes.

Thus was forged the main link between public assistance by the state, medical care, and the general demand for hospital beds. There was another link that became increasingly clear: many families were self-supporting or independent except for the risk of expensive illness and hospitalization, and they seemed to need a special form of public assistance, for medical indigency, as it were. To some extent they could protect themselves by hospitalization insurance, which grew popular among middle-class people in the late 1930's and later became a fringe benefit in labor contracts. But many people, and those most in need, stood outside these plans.

If a helpless aged person, or any case of chronic illness, came before the poor-law officials in the 1920's, they had three alternatives. One was to pay a visiting nurse to help the person in his home; second was to find a new residence for him, a boarding home, perhaps, or a nursing home; third was to send him to a hospital or almshouse. The Division of Medicine of the Department of Institutions and Agencies had the power to inspect these institutions, except the private general hospitals. For the most part, its inspection and supervision were advisory. If a community wished to change an old-style poor farm to a new-style welfare house, the Division would advise local authorities on architecture and equipment as well as service. In 1927, it was empowered to license (not merely inspect) nursing homes, but these were mostly for paying patients. The cheapest and best provision for the indigent aged and chronic sick seemed to be the welfare house.[45]

The advent of state old-age pensions changed this outlook. They offered a sizable subsidy to cases that could be kept on outdoor relief, out of the institution. Under the federal Social Security Act of 1935 a similar policy obtained. Consequently, the county welfare boards, which handled old-age assistance (OAA), began to try to place their clients in boarding or nursing homes, which were not considered institutions, so they would be eligible for state and federal financing. The difficulty with this scheme was that assistance grants did not meet the charges, or even the costs, of private nursing or boarding home care, although these places often took welfare cases when it suited them. Consequently, there were two pressures on the system, first to increase OAA payments to cover the cost of residential care, second to allow payment for aged and chronically ill persons in institutions, especially in county welfare houses.[46] The state authorized more generous payments for OAA in 1943, but they continued to be less than private patients were charged and less than the nursing homes needed to stay in business, or so they said.

The Department of Institutions and Agencies suggested in 1946 that the state declare that it had a responsibility to help local communities and private agencies care for the chronic sick, and in 1947 its Division of Old-Age Assistance recommended three kinds of state subsidy: one for the operating costs of public institutions for this class, another for a new category of public assistance, similar to old-age assistance but covering the chronic sick who were under sixty-five, a third to provide visiting nurses or housekeepers to help the sick in their own homes.[47]

The obstacle to these ideas was that the state had no funds for them. In May 1947, Governor Driscoll told a meeting of county welfare officials that his administration was "vitally interested in the care of the chronically ill," but that new programs would require new taxes and it was "perfectly clear that we have reached the end of our rope so far as our present finances are concerned." He did not suggest any new taxes, of course. Bates, who spoke later, mentioned as possibilities for action more construction of facilities, state subsidies for institutions and for individuals (another assistance program), and better home-care programs. He made no suggestions about how the state might finance the aid, although he mentioned the possibility of federal assistance.[48] Bates himself was skeptical about the wisdom of encouraging institutional care—the old almshouse under a new name, he feared.[49]

Then, in 1948, state officials found something they could do without spending money. This was a revision of the unemployment compensation law to allow benefits to workers who were unemployed because of temporary illness or disability that occurred outside the employers' premises. In effect, the revision was a sort of compulsory sickness insurance financed by workers' contributions and administered through the labor department. It was a promising kind of program, but of course did not touch the problem of long-term illness and did not help the aged.[50]

In the long run, it was the promise of federal matching funds that pushed the state into action. The first occasion was the Hospital Survey and Construction Act, the Hill-Burton Act, which offered federal grants-in-aid to hospital projects under certain conditions. One prerequisite was that a state agency survey existing facilities and needs. Another was that the state establish standards of maintenance and operation and enforce them under a licensing law. The estimate of hospital needs included beds for mental patients, TB patients, and the chronic sick. In New Jersey, the Department of Institutions and Agencies was put in charge of the survey, and in 1947, after a bitter fight in the legislature, its Division of Medicine was empowered to license private general hospitals.[51]

By January 1948, the Department had set up an Advisory Council and formulated a plan for construction. (Its first stage included assistance to the new state Diagnostic Center and a TB unit at Greystone Park.) The federal grant-in-aid was for one-third of costs, including not only construction but consultants' fees and equipment. Some state governments supplemented the federal grants with their own matching funds, usually a third of the cost, so the local sponsor had to provide only a third, but in New Jersey this was impossible, of course.[52]

The original plan proposed to allocate 30 percent of the federal funds each to projects for general hospitals, public mental hospitals, and chronic illness facilities, and 10 percent to "public health centers." [53] The actual expenditures for the first five years followed a different pattern, however: general hospital projects got 62 percent, mental hospitals 25 percent, and chronic ill facilities 11 percent, with 2 percent going for hospitals for communicable diseases.[54] The significant thing was that the pressure of federal matching funds had brought about a state plan, and state standards and a licensing authority, that would otherwise probably have been long delayed.

In 1950, Congress amended the Social Security Act to provide a fourth category of federally aided public assistance—aid to the permanently and totally disabled. In effect, this category included the disabled and chronic sick who were too young to be eligible for old-age assistance and who had hitherto fallen on local poor relief. The New Jersey statute (P. L. 1951, ch. 139) put the work of administration on the county welfare boards, with supervision by the Bureau of Assistance (formerly Division of Old-Age Assistance) in the central Department.[55]

The 1950 amendments also allowed federal participation in assistance payments to people in public institutions, such as welfare houses (not mental hospitals or TB asylums, however); and it authorized the federal government to share in the payments for medical care for people in the categories it aided. These features set the stage for a major shift in the relation between public assistance and medical care: If the state chose to adopt them, the assistance agencies were put in the position of having to set standards of service for the medical care they purchased for their clients, whether the care was in public agencies, such as a welfare house, or by physicians, clinics, or hospitals that served the individuals on assistance. In other words, if the state were to share costs of medical care for public assistance clients, so that it could take advantage of the new federal matching funds, it had to say how much it would pay for what kind of service. This was a much more complicated and controversial matter than simply "inspecting" medical facilities.

Here, then, was another argument for the integration of public assistance programs under the county welfare board, since the budgeting and planning of medical care for clients involved a degree of expertise in casework that untrained and part-time municipal officials could scarcely offer. The Kidde Commission, which had been appointed to study the integration of welfare following the defeat of A-17 in 1951, discussed the question at length, and went so far as to propose a new fifth category, "hospitalization assistance." Hospitalization assistance would allow the state and counties (and hopefully the federal government) to share the hospital costs of people who were not on public assistance but were unable to pay the high costs of hospital care.

In fact, Kidde argued, the hospitals were taking care of these people, they had definite policies about the medically indigent, and they were passing the cost of their care on to other parties. To some extent, local taxpayers paid—directly in the case of public hospitals, indirectly in the form of municipal or county grants to private general hospitals. Often the grants to private general hospitals were in the form of lump sums, not related to specific services, much as a philanthropist would donate money to the hospital. To some extent, private patients paid the cost of care of the indigent, because the hospital overcharged them to make up its deficit. To some extent, local philanthropists paid the bill, by their contributions to the hospital or to the community chest which helped support the hospital. To some extent, the State paid, for services to dependent children, the aged, and the blind in its categorical programs.

If one considered the variety of ways in which the costs were computed and the bills made out, the billing arranged and the payments made, the situation was inevitably cumbersome and inefficient. In its place Kidde wanted to establish a system whereby a single public agency, the county welfare board, paid for medical care for people on public assistance and the "medically indigent," according to realistic charges for actual services rendered.[56]

These suggestions supported his Commission's general recommendation to integrate federally assisted categories under county welfare boards, and, together with a program of "hospitalization assistance," they would have removed many relief cases from municipal officials. (Among other things their proposal eliminated municipal residence requirements that had hitherto governed the municipalities' responsibility for assistance to the sick.) The Commission also favored a reimbursement policy, whereby welfare officials might recover all or part of the assistance paid if a recipient became prosperous during the next six years. They proposed that the reimbursement policy be liberal and fair, of course, but the idea alienated unions and social workers as much as their other proposals alienated municipal and state officials and other partisans of the status quo.[57]

Problems of Organizing Services

Before 1950, state leadership in thinking about the chronic sick and the aged rested mostly with the Department of Institutions and Agencies. It, not the Department of Health, became the planning and licensing agency under the Hill-Burton Act. In the years 1948–1950, the Department of Health was reorganized under the new constitution, however, and thereafter it took a much more active role. The reorganization eliminated a form of board control and put the Department under a single commissioner appointed by the governor. The governor also appointed a Public Health Council, an unpaid board of eight persons (including at least two physicians and a dentist) whose duties were to advise the commissioner on public health and the work of his Department, to investigate public health activities, and to amend the Sanitary Code, which regulated local public health work. The commissioner organized his Department into six divisions that were for the most part supposed to provide consultation, information, and stimulation to local services, rather than direct services to individuals. The Department brought its influence to bear on local health authorities through the medium of four district offices.[58]

The main problem of the new Health Department was to push the municipal Boards of Health into combining into larger jurisdictions so they could afford qualified full-time staff (as late as 1954 there was no qualified licensed public health official in over two-thirds of the municipalities) and to coordinate the services offered by nongovernmental agencies, school districts, counties, and the state.[59] The problem with regard to local agencies was analogous to the problem of integrating welfare, and there were common interests between the two departments: The Health Department stimulated TB control programs, which had once been left to traveling clinics from the state sanitarium at Glen Gardner, and it worked with the Neuro-Psychiatric Institute in encouraging activities in behalf of epileptics.

In 1952, the Department established a Division of Chronic Illness Control, which distributed literature and arranged training courses related to treatment of cancer, heart disease, and other ailments, and did some research (supported by federal, not state, funds).[60] It also sponsored a Governor's Conference on the Prevention of Chronic Illness at Trenton in December 1952, and it became interested in the health problems of the aged. Dr. Daniel Bergsma, the commissioner of health, was on the New Jersey Old Age Study Commission which was appointed in 1955 (so was a woman from the Extension Division of Rutgers, but the Commission included no member of the Department of Institutions and Agencies or its Board of Control). Bergsma helped prepare a public hearing on the subject in December 1955, which was published in his Department's monthly periodical, and the Department later published papers from a Governor's Conference on the Aging held in 1959.[61]

The report of the Old Age Study Commission, published in 1957, was not primarily a study of public assistance or chronic illness. It looked at the situation of all aging people, with chapters on their needs for income, health, education, recreation, religion, and housing. The chapter on income emphasized the possibilities and values of continued employment for those who wanted it, and the significance of private (company-sponsored) retirement programs for older workers, as well as their Social Security retirement income and old-age assistance. Its discussion of health emphasized programs for prevention and rehabilitation, counseling, and mental hygiene. (Its discussion of boarding and nursing homes came mostly under "housing.") Everywhere they looked, the commissioners found two great needs, first to collect facts and sponsor research on matters pertaining to the aging, and second to stimulate and coordinate existing programs. Toward these ends the commissioners proposed a permanent commission set up as a division in the Department of State, a Citizen Council on Aging, to enlist and rally private agencies in the field, and community councils, to help stimulate and coordinate activities in local communities.[62]

A Division of Aging based on these ideas was established in May 1958. "With no precedent at either the state or federal level," it undertook to relate "generalized concern for older people to concrete action programs." Its work was mostly fact collecting and publishing, public relations, and community organization. It planned a Governor's Conference on the Aging in 1959 and the state's participation in a White House Conference on Aging in 1961.[63] Eone Harger, its director, was a sometime member of the State Board of Control and much of her division's work was done together with the staff of the Departments of Institutions and Agencies and Health. But in general the new enterprise gave form to the thought that the state's organization for social welfare needed an agency to study, report, and stimulate programs by pulling together resources scattered in many places in the government and among voluntary agencies. It was conceived as reporting directly to the governor, deliberately separated from operating departments such as Institutions and Agencies and Health. It was the model for the Division of Youth that the Youth Study Commission would propose in 1961, and both proposals were an indication of a growing interest in program and in action by the governor and by local communities. These ideas were shaped by the spirit that had led to the constitutional reorganization of 1947.[64]

For the rest, the leading questions about integrating welfare programs were unresolved during the 1950's. These were first, the integration of categorical programs under county welfare boards; second, the integration of general assistance (municipal poor relief) under county welfare boards; and third, the systematizing of medical payments for people on public assistance and those who were medically indigent, on the basis of a reimbursable cost formula for actual services. Nevertheless, the Department's welfare work was much altered during the decade because of new programs and the administrative detail they involved. A synopsis of these may indicate the changing scope of its work.

First was the administration of state financial assistance to municipal welfare departments, taken over from the Department of Conservation in 1950. This was primarily fiscal supervision, but it was open to development. In 1951, the Board of Child Welfare inaugurated its "care" program, which greatly increased the state's responsibility for child welfare services. During that same year the people who handled old-age assistance expanded their work to include the total disability program. Both agencies became involved in medical care for their clients, as "third parties" who made purchases or arrangements with vendors of medical care. This business grew large in the case of people receiving old-age assistance when it became permissible to pay for their care in public institutions, and welfare officials paid increasing attention to the non-medical aspects of the institutional care they were approving for their clients.[65] The Division of Inspection much increased its work to include a growing number and variety of sheltered care institutions.[66] The net result was discussion about and formulation of standards and procedures that did much to minimize the lack of formal integration.

As for the financing of public medical care, a commission that reported on the subject in 1959 reiterated the thinking of the Kidde Commission as to an accounting for costs and a system of payments for actual services. They added the thought that, since welfare agencies were now in the business of budgeting and planning medical care for their clients, they needed professional consultation. To this end, they proposed that the Division of Welfare establish a medical unit to advise it and to give consultation and supervision to the work of county welfare boards. They also emphasized the importance of medical consultants in interpreting the programs to medical organizations, and the importance of medical social workers, public health nurses, and homemaker services in establishing effective and economical home-care programs. In conclusion, they quoted with approval a statement that set forth a significant shift in thinking about public medical care "from provision of some medical treatment and minimal custodial care to . . . a wide range of protective, curative and rehabilitative health services; and from reluctant acceptance of paupers to eligibility of all persons needing basic income maintenance and increasingly of medically needy people." [67]

This conclusion also epitomized the changing views of social workers, administrators, and their allies with regard to the general relation between assistance and service. Until there was substantial political support for much larger public expenditures, discussion was perforce limited to administrative changes, and in New Jersey at least, it was difficult to formulate the problems so as to generate constructive popular interest at the local or state level.

22

Transition: The Tramburg Administration, 1955–1959

Between the retirement of Commissioner Sanford Bates in 1954 and the report of the Commission to Study the Department of Institutions and Agencies in 1959 there was a marked change in thinking about the Department's work and in its internal organization. People who lived through the change tended to think of it in personal terms. But in historical perspective—even the short perspective of this study—it appears that the transition was related to larger social and intellectual changes that were independent of what particular officials thought and did.

The New Jersey Committee on Children and Youth, in its preparation for the White House Conference of 1960, summed up social changes under four headings: high mobility and dispersion of population; continued high birth rate; prosperity, somewhat balanced by chronic unemployment in some areas; and inflation. It was possible, the Committee thought, to define three distinctive areas of the state: the older urban places, where population was declining but where Negro and Puerto Rican neighborhoods were growing rapidly; a broad band of suburbia, characterized by small developments housing people of similar income and ethnic background; and rural sections, not yet suburban.

These diverse places were alike, however, the Committee thought, in their lack of a sense of community and their confusion of values. In some ways society was more homogeneous than in the past: the Committee did not mention the traditional conflict between native and foreign-born, rural and urban. Instead it observed that rural and urban ways of thought were inharmoniously mixed, and that there was "a lack of agreement on basic matters" between generations. The automobile and the mass media were blending all groups and places into supermetropolitan districts that had lost their roots and community spirit, the Committee reported. There was "an increased understanding [of group identifications and relations] on a theoretical level, but an absence of any overall organizational strength for pulling groups together." These were the phenomena that led the Committee to put its highest priorities on parent education, family counseling services, citizen participation, and social planning and co-ordination of services.[1]

The immediate political consequence of the dispersion of population, the Committee observed, was a sudden need for increased local services, particularly for education, highways, and water and sanitation; the demand put a burden on the local real estate tax, already the highest in the nation, and on local government.[2] At the same time, it might have mentioned the taxes levied by the federal government to finance foreign aid, the Cold War, and the huge war debt, for these remained painfully high and obvious.

In this situation, when economic prosperity seemed to be undermined by high taxes and inflation and by the cost of the Cold War, there spread a sense of disappointment, frustration, anger, betrayal; the fear and suspicion of an international Communist conspiracy was directed at liberal programs for the "welfare state"—as the phrase went in the 1950's. Welfare stateism seemed to many people like a socialist threat to the free enterprise system; it certainly threatened new, higher taxes and more regulation. In short, the demand for more and better social services in the decade after the war encountered a persistent and angry hostility that ran from earnest fiscal conservatism to cynical red-baiting.

This general situation was everywhere difficult with relation to the role of state government, and particularly difficult in New Jersey. The pattern of progress in social services after the war was that the federal government would make a grant-in-aid for service and set minimum standards for a state plan; the state would formulate the plan and supervise the grant, often with its own contribution; and local agencies would contribute and actually administer the service. In general, that is, the federal and state governments would stimulate local action. In this arrangement the state played a key role as organizer and intermediary. It required, therefore, increasing resources, to match federal grants and to finance planning, consulting, or supervisory services. But the traditional tax structure of New Jersey, which financed most services out of local real estate taxes, left the state little means for leadership. According to a study of state finances published by the Council of State Governments, New Jersey collected a smaller proportion of the total of state and local taxes in 1954 than in 1942 and the smallest proportion of any state; the average per capita revenue of state governments rose in these years by 27 percent, but New Jersey's rose not at all.[3]

Low state taxes were, of course, the boast of New Jersey politicians, and conservatives in the state, as elsewhere, were dubious about the whole system of federal grants-in-aid. Alfred Driscoll, governor from 1947 to 1954, was particularly concerned to hold down taxes and improve economy in government. His successful work for a new constitution and a reorganization of the state government reflected a conservative's horror of waste and mismanagement—the sentiment of the Hoover Commission. He was dubious about national encroachments on state prerogatives and autonomy, fearful of a national bureaucracy that would be neither representative nor free. He was particularly dubious about federal grants-in-aid. Citizens of New Jersey earned high incomes, he said, and paid high income taxes to the federal government; the government returned a proportion of this money to the state in grants-in-aid, but a larger proportion went to other states; and the part that was returned to New Jersey induced the state government to raise more tax money from the citizens as matching funds. If Jerseymen didn't have to pay such high income taxes, he said, they would have more money to spend on their local and state government, without the surcharges of a federal bureaucracy. Why not, therefore, have the national government get out of these programs and leave them to the states?

Governor Driscoll was particularly annoyed because New Jersey did not have a state income tax, and did not compete with the federal government for that tax resource, and yet the federal government made no adjustment to reward this meritorious self-restraint, but actually penalized it and, by allowing taxes as deductions, rewarded those states that had income taxes.[4] The question of allocating tax sources was serious; it loomed large in the mind of General Eisenhower and his advisers in 1952, and it was no coincidence that Governor Driscoll was one of Eisenhower's warmest supporters.

Commissioner Bates was in agreement with Governor Driscoll, as his testimony in Washington on the Social Security Amendments of 1950 showed. Like many conservatives, Bates looked forward to an increase in social insurance (financed by payroll taxes) rather than public assistance (financed by general taxation); he was especially proud of the fact that New Jersey had relatively few people in its categorical relief programs.[5] He had little sympathy with the kind of social work thinking that found expression in the federal agencies, or with the stream of regulations and memoranda that they contributed to his workload.

It would be wrong to say that Governor Driscoll was not interested in the state's social services—both bond issues were passed during his administration, with his support—but his concern was economy, to improve budget controls and civil service rather than to expand and develop the services. Insofar as he encouraged state action, he was preoccupied by the problems of state aid to education and to highways (the New Jersey Turnpike and the Garden State Parkway, two achievements of his administration, were self-liquidating toll roads). In his valedictory he mentioned ten needs for improvement: education, highways, and water supply came first, and a program for the chronic sick and reorganization of public welfare came eighth and ninth. (Recreation facilities were tenth.) [6]

Driscoll's successor, Governor Robert B. Meyner, was of course interested in economy and administrative efficiency, but he was more willing than Driscoll to expand services, which he looked upon as a natural concomitant of social development rather than a drag upon free enterprise. He preached no sermons on the dangers of federal encroachments. Like Driscoll, he moved first to meet needs in education—a much-enlarged program of state aid to local districts—and highways, but he also favored new programs for mental health and retardation, and in all respects he looked for federal aid to help get things moving.[7]

Governor Meyner was limited by his own pledge against either a sales tax or a personal income tax, and by the unrepresentative legislature, which had Republican majorities in both houses. But he felt that people were behind his idea of more active state government, that if his proposals could get a fair hearing before legislative committees instead of a summary dismissal by a legislative caucus ("basement government," he called it), he would win; and the election of 1957, which returned him by a handsome margin with an overwhelming majority in the Assembly and a notable gain even in the Senate, seemed to bear him out.[8] It was clear, in any case, that Governor Meyner was inclined to think of state services more in terms of adequacy than of money costs and taxes, and this general view was sanctioned by unimpeachably conservative experts who recognized that a proper measure of economy and efficiency must include both aspects.[9]

The Central Office in Transition

There were three trends in the character of the central office that became especially marked after 1945. One was the growing importance of its welfare functions, carried over from the depression and, in the 1950's, involved in the public discussion of problems of youth and aging. In 1920, three people in ten on the Department's case load were in welfare programs; in 1959, the figure was almost seven in ten. Second was the increase in staff supposed to stimulate intramural programs and help in research and planning—an expansion of the original idea of central office experts in classification, education, and medicine. Third was the increase of staff to handle extramural activities related to the institutions—"field services" or consultant or supervisory services, or people directly engaged in community organization.

The general result of these trends was to bring together many people whose appointments depended on professional training and certification and whose careers lay in a profession rather than a particular institution, who measured their standing by professional honors, publications in professional journals, and employment as consultants and researchers. A student of the documentary record observes (with a sigh) the swells of jargon in their ruminations. There was also much sophisticated fussing about professional areas of competence and other problems of role definition in a bureaucracy, related to civil service classification, to prestige, and ultimately to service.

The conception of professional experts in a rational bureaucracy had been central in the thinking of the founders of the Department, but the founders had thought of administration in terms of their experience in business, and of professionals in contrast with political spoilsmen. After 1945, however, thinking about administration involved more general ideas of bureaucracy, related to experience in the armed services or the government. Burdette Lewis, the Department's first commissioner, had studied public administration, but John Ellis was technically an amateur. He played by ear and drew his close associates from journalism, business, and politics. He could hire experts in accounting, farm management, architecture, law, and medicine, but he would hardly have identified the consultants who appeared in the office between 1945 and 1959, except perhaps for clinical psychologists. Of course, he needed experts and judged them shrewdly, by all accounts, but the spirit of his administration was to put together the man and the job, not the certified expert and the office.

An observer in the late 1950's saw a pervasive disharmony between staff who identified with the older regime, the depression years, and those who came into prominence after the war. Old hands thought of their peers as real gentlemen or at least wonderful people, people who really understood how the Department worked. They thought of the newer crew as lacking in "heart and soul," interested in academic theories instead of real facts, deficient in loyalty and even manners ("Well, he's a bright, brash young man, rather pushy, don't you think?"), disrespectful and unappreciative of the past. The newer people, on their part, did tend to think that real progress began about 1945 and was introduced from elsewhere. They did not usually intend an invidious comparison with the past, but they applied ideas and standards that had been developed and refined in larger contexts and transmitted by their professional education.

As commissioner, Sanford Bates straddled this transition. On one side his reputation rested upon his service in Massachusetts, New York, and the federal government and it extended to all nations; his original purpose in appointing deputy commissioners—to advise him on policy, to represent the Department among professionals, and to stimulate progressive programs—foreshadowed the work the newer staff was to do; and of course he hired many new people. On the other side, Bates was older than Ellis and belonged to the passing generation; he was a lawyer turned penologist, an upright administrator amid politicians rather than a spokesman for a professional interest, a builder with a sharp eye for site selection and construction costs rather than a technician contemplating a web of services. He was conservative temperamentally as well as politically, not inclined to make drastic changes, not much in sympathy with the lines of speculation the postwar professionals were bringing to bear. Often they thought he was too defensive about the existing order, too reluctant to change.

Add to this ambivalence an unfortunate coincidence: Many veterans on his staff suffered from personal problems or sickness that made their efforts unreliable. The cheerful active characters of 1930 or 1935 were tired and shaky twenty years later. Perhaps some should have been fired, but Ellis had not fired them; they were in fact real gentlemen or at least wonderful people; they did really understand how the Department worked. Bates respected their loyalty and often undertook to carry part of their work himself. The whole operation was notably aging; many superintendents were near retirement, along with their boards. The State Board was full of senior citizens during Bates' administration. In April 1953, William T. Read, a former legislator and political official, retired after sixteen years because of advanced age, he said, and Dr. Harold W. Dodds, the president of Princeton University, retired aften seventeen years because he could no longer balance the demands on his time. In May 1957, there was a sad scene when Reeve Schley, 75, who had been on the State Board since 1936, was stricken while speaking at a testimonial dinner for Mrs. Geraldine Thompson, who was retiring after a term that began in 1918.[10]

In March 1956, the state integrated its retirement system with federal Social Security, and more than 220 employees of the Department found it necessary or advantageous to retire, causing a large turnover and shifting of jobs.[11] By this time the new commissioner was on the scene and making changes among his assistants. On both counts, at all levels, the old hands were disappearing with unwonted speed.

A Time of Troubles

In the early 1950's the Department encountered considerable criticism. Some came from people interested in mental health services, care of the retarded, child welfare, or the integration of public assistance, who wondered whether their interests were neglected in the omnibus Department. But some was frankly political and arose in the wake of the constitutional reorganization and the bond issues.

Unlike Ellis, Bates undertook to negotiate directly with the legislators. This was a job he was accustomed to, for which his budget-minded approach and conservative temper suited him. But the New Jersey legislators proved hard to get along with. In his report to the State Board in 1949, he felt it necessary to refute charges that the Department was "empire-building," and he observed that "a small group of senators" had defeated three important Department bills (one would have made the warden of the state prison responsible to the Board of Managers, thus implementing the new constitution).[12] In 1950, as the building program got under way, the Division of Architecture was transferred to the Treasury Department, a step which Bates opposed and which obliged him to discharge a number of employees who had "practically nothing to do with architecture" but had been "placed in the division for convenience."[13]

Then, in 1953, Bates found himself at odds with Robert B. Meyner, the Democratic candidate for governor. One of Meyner's advisers was Raymond F. Male, the young man whom Bates had put in charge of personnel work. Male's efforts, especially the psychiatric technician program, had won him a reputation, but he and Bates became estranged, and early in 1952 he went to New York as administrative director of the

National Association for Mental Health (of which Dr. George Stevenson was medical director). He presently joined Meyner's entourage and worked up material that gave the candidate grounds to charge that "political interference" had "hamstrung expenditures" for new construction. Reeve Schley and Bates, angered by this turn of events, called for a "showdown," as the newspapers put it. A two-hour conference among Meyner, Bates, and Schley led Meyner to concede "an unfortunate use of language" and Schley to declare that some "erroneous interpretations" had been cleared up.[14]

Despite the embarrassment of this confrontation, Meyner went on to win the election and took office the following January. The situation confirmed the doubts that some people had about the special status accorded the Department in the reorganization: Bates was a cabinet officer who was not appointed by the governor and out of sympathy with many of the governor's ideas. In May, Bates confirmed rumors that he would retire on his seventieth birthday, July 17, 1954. Meyner commented that he was considering breaking the omnibus Department into three, for corrections, mental health, and welfare.[15] Meanwhile, the appointment of a new commissioner rested with the State Board, although the governor, under the new constitution, had to approve it.

A year elapsed after Bates announced his retirement before a successor was named. Meanwhile, Dr. Bixby served as acting commissioner. ("Spike" Gerry, the senior deputy commissioner, retired on June 1, 1954, because of ill health and died in October, at fifty-eight.)[16] Bixby was a partisan of the New Jersey system of local boards. He recognized its difficulties, that it took a great deal of patience and persuasion to get things done, but he thought that it insured a continuity and stability of policy that straight-line administrative organization fatally lacked.[17]

The new governor and his advisers thought differently. "Working in the office of the Governor has given me a better picture of welfare administration in New Jersey than I ever had during seven years in the department most concerned with these problems," Ray Male told the New Jersey Welfare Council late in 1954. There was, he thought, "a hardening of the categories"—a reference to the argument about integrating public assistance. The "welfare picture" looked like something "in our old family album," posed formal portraits of individual members but never a group portrait of the whole family.[18]

Meyner himself noted in January 1955 that he had exercised an active supervision of the Department, visiting the institutions and conferring frequently with Schley and Bixby, and that he frequently discussed the idea of three separate departments and the elimination of board control.[19] He postponed investing in a new state prison, to replace the old fortress recently troubled by riots; it might last five more years, he said. He recommended investing two million dollars in a new attack on mental disease, beginning with the addition of six hundred new staff members, on the basis of a Civil Service survey of ward care in late 1954, and a stronger emphasis on research (here he recommended $1.5

million for converting facilities into the research and training center for the retarded at Bordentown), and he was pleased that the Department had requested $262,000 for research, compared with $50,000 for the current year.[20]

In April 1955, Meyner and Frank Walsh, the acting president of the State Board, announced that John Tramburg of Wisconsin would become commissioner in July. (Schley, the president of the Board, was on his annual winter vacation in Florida at the time of the announcement.)[21] Then, in July, Mr. Schley asked not to be re-elected president; Walsh succeeded him, but in a few months he asked to be relieved of the responsibility, and the board elected its newest member, Lloyd B. Wescott, in his place.[22] And so appeared the three men who would shape the Department's work for several years. They were an unlikely combination: Governor Meyner, a gray-flannel Democrat, young, astute, ambitious; John Tramburg, an amiable, quizzical bear of a man, a country schoolmaster turned social worker; and Lloyd Wescott, a rich dairyman, a goateed squire, lean, quick-moving, soft-spoken. But all three saw eye-to-eye about the Department, they were energetic and hard-working, and in their several ways they were parts of the transition.

John W. Tramburg

The new commissioner was born on February 28, 1913, in Fall River, Wisconsin. He came of college age in the depression and in 1935 was graduated from the State Teachers College at Whitewater. He taught school for a year, then became educational adviser in a CCC camp. In 1937, he enrolled in the School of Social Service Administration of the University of Chicago, and thus became the first executive of the Department to have formal training in social work. From 1939 to 1942 he was a probation officer for the Juvenile Court of Washington, D. C.; in 1941–1942 he also attended the law school of Columbus University in Washington. He was a navy officer for the next three years.

After the war, Tramburg returned to Washington as assistant superintendent of a home for juveniles. In 1948, at thirty-five, he became director of public welfare for the District of Columbia, in charge of its institutions, public assistance, mental health, and child welfare programs. Two years later he was made director of the Wisconsin Department of Public Welfare, which included state correctional institutions, mental hospitals, and public assistance and child welfare programs, and which had just undergone a reorganization.[23]

In November 1953, Tramburg was granted a leave of absence from Wisconsin to become federal commissioner of social security. The appointment drew applause from the editors of the *Social Service Review,* a leading journal of social work, who had been concerned about the direction the new Eisenhower administration might take. In Wisconsin, they said, Tramburg had "won high praise" and "showed himself to be a man of imagination and courage, . . . who was able to win support

. . . in unexpected quarters." They also noted with approval that he "showed an appreciation of the value of workers with professional education, and he succeeded in attracting probably more than the state's fair share to Wisconsin"—a matter they knew about, since the School of Social Service Administration, which published the journal, was the largest source of trained workers in the West.[24]

While Tramburg was in Washington, in May 1954, Reeve Schley called on him to ask if he would be interested in the New Jersey job. He said he had promised the Wisconsin board that he would return, which he did in August. "Tramburg straightened out a lot of real problems for us," Nelson Rockefeller, the President's special assistant, said in commendation.[25] In February 1955, Tramburg was approached again about the New Jersey job, and this time he was more receptive. He asked the Board members who interviewed him about salary levels in the Department, staff-patient ratios, and budget procedures. They were not conversant with these matters, he found, but they seemed willing to support progressive policies (the commissioner's salary was going up from $15,000 to $18,000 plus maintenance, among other things). He also asked about the position of institutional boards of managers, since he'd had to deal with only one board in Wisconsin. Because he was a registered Republican, he asked to meet Governor Meyner, and he felt satisfied that politics would be no obstacle.[26]

Certainly the new commissioner's experience, both in practical casework and in administration, was admirable qualification for his new job. He was no scholar or writer, and his utterances tended to be clusters of rhetorical questions and gnomic banter, but he plainly had a commitment to professional social work and a critical temper. In October 1955, the New Jersey Welfare Council asked him to speak on the subject "social work inventory." It was "like writing out the dimensions of the Golden Rule," he said, and his list was full of half-failures and half-successes. "Principles have completely different meaning to . . . people in the field." "Accountability, yes—but what do we count?" Prevention and research were a distant hope and a nice thought. Formulas for computing assistance made even well-informed people stutter. Public reporting was poor, but confidential records were made public. Agencies were not working together.

There was a long list of difficulties, but his conclusion was optimistic: we may yet abolish poverty. What the inventory showed most, he thought, was the need for alertness, the "essence of public welfare administration." The diagnosis and prescription were not academic or even clear, but they accurately revealed him as a confident man with a zest for administration, willing to trust others as he trusted himself.[27] The State Board had no particular advice or instructions to offer him; Meyner asked that he implement his (Meyner's) recent proposals for expanded mental health programs.[28]

In some ways, it was a good time to take office: There were no crises in sight like the postwar labor problem and inflation or the constitutional reorganization; the bond drives were won and construction mostly completed; the new state institutions and welfare programs were in orbit, and the status of the warden of the prison was resolved; the whole state government was functioning better as a result of the new constitution; Rutgers, the State University, opened a School of Social Work in 1955, under Dean Wayne Vasey, an expert on public welfare; the political situation was relatively stable, with Meyner settled into office and the election two years away; nationally, the Korean War was settled, the red scare diminishing, and inflation slowing down; and a growing public interest in welfare problems was manifest in the associations for the mentally ill and deficient and the commissions on youth and aging. Accordingly, Tramburg was able to turn his attention to problems of internal organization and, if not solve them, at least bring them into focus.

Reorganizing the Central Office

When Tramburg took charge, the work of the central office was organized according to two divergent principles, sometimes called functional and operational. The original plan, for functional divisions, assumed that each division advised on a particular function, such as state use, medical care, or classification, that was common to all sorts of institutions. It assumed that the experts in charge of these divisions were employed by the commissioner to advise him and the institutional superintendents. They were not links in a chain of command. On this arrangement Bates had superimposed "deputy commissioners," who were more or less in charge of the different classes of work the Department did, with delinquents, mentally disordered, and dependents. They, too, were liaison men and advisers, however, not links in a chain of command.

Then, in 1950, in response to the discussion over the integration of welfare, Bates had established a Division of Welfare, which collected all the Department's welfare agencies under the deputy commissioner for welfare, and which was, in theory, an operating division with a chain of command that ran from the commissioner through his deputy to operating agencies. In 1953, there was a change of official titles in the Department, to bring its nomenclature into line with other departments under the new constitution. Deputy commissioners were thenceforth called directors, and the former divisions were called bureaus (Bureau of Classification, or State Use). Bureaus that could easily be identified with a particular kind of service were put under directors, for example the Bureau of Parole under the director of corrections and the Bureau of Accounts under the director of administration. Other bureaus, such as State Use and Inspection, continued to report directly to the commissioner.[29]

The arrangement sounds confusing, and it was. The Wisconsin Department of Public Welfare, by contrast, had five divisions, four of them operational (public assistance, child welfare, corrections, and mental hygiene) and the fifth for business management. This arrangement was not Tramburg's doing—it took form in a reorganization of that department in 1939—but it was the pattern he had in mind.[30] In general, the organization into operating divisions gave recognition to the increasing complexity of administering the services, and the expanding role of the central office in formulating program objectives for the institutions and in inspection, consultation, and community organization. Most of the offices in the operating divisions were new; most of the original functional divisions of the Department could be subsumed under the rubric of business management or more vaguely "administration," and they now were clearly only part of its job. It was this trend, to operating divisions, that Tramburg undertook to develop.

In part, the solution was easy: Regroup the appropriate bureaus of the central office into new divisions of correction and mental health, in some cases changing or dividing their work to suit their new position, and give the directors of correction and mental health direct authority over them. This was done during 1955–1956.[31] In part, however, it was difficult, because the commissioner and his division director did not have direct formal authority over the institutions or agencies. If a superintendent chose to ignore what the division director wanted, the matter went from the director to the commissioner to the State Board, which consulted with the institution board and might either try compromise or order compliance. In short, the institutional boards stood between the central office and the superintendent, or the superintendent stood between the central office and his institutional board.

Conceivably, the public-spirited citizens who made up the local boards might have resigned their power or invited stronger leadership from the State Board, or the superintendents might have asked to work directly under the division director, but history records that institutional boards and superintendents made no such moves. To change the system, after four decades, therefore required that some authority say that it wasn't working well and defend the thesis against righteous indignation. That position would assume some antagonism between the aims and interests of the directors and their advisers and the superintendents and their staffs, between the State Board and the local boards, and no one was eager to explore this subject.

Meanwhile, there was much for division directors to do that was clearly within their power, as developments in the next few years showed, and the Commissioner had other changes in mind for the central office. Like his predecessors, he devoted much time to the budget. In his own view, his emphasis was on program rather than prudent management. "The thing to look for," he once observed, "is, how does the superintendent justify the request? Does he think in terms of, say, keeping up the plant, or does he start with people and make a case based on their needs? Of course he has to keep up the plant, but how does he work out his priorities?" [32] Two factors lent him support in his emphasis on program: First, it was what Governor Meyner wanted to hear (so long as it did not involve a broad-based tax, at least), and after 1957 Meyner's influence was increased by a Democratic majority in the Assembly. Second, Tramburg's rural background and manner gave him "a quick rapport with the representatives from rural New Jersey on both sides of the political aisle"—a useful quality in his situation.[33]

One thing that struck Tramburg at the beginning was the lack of published reports on the Department's work. He saw a need for a regular summary and began annual reports in 1956, but he was frankly uncertain about their form. The report for 1956 was a collection of mimeographed reports, fastened together without continuous pagination. The next few versions were selective and decorative, organized around the idea of "trends," but they included no general discussion by Tramburg or the State Board. The report for 1960 and thereafter was an issue of *The Welfare Reporter,* the departmental publication. The *Reporter* changed in 1957 from a monthly, featuring news and pictures aimed primarily at personnel and board members, to a scholarly-type quarterly, no pictures, no news, but substantial articles on departmental policies and programs intended for persons in the community. Taken together, the annual report and the quarterly offered more systematic information than had hitherto been made public about the Department's work.

Expanding Mental Health Services: Clinics

The movement for improved services to the mentally disordered, which came on one hand from volunteer organizations and on the other from the Council of State Governments and the Governors' Conferences by way of Governor Meyner, bore fruit in the fiscal year 1955–1956 in an extraordinary appropriation for $3.1 million. Almost half of this went for refurbishing the old buildings that became the Johnstone Training and Research Center. The remainder went toward the establishment of field services for the mentally deficient; toward continuing the program of basic research at the Neuro-Psychiatric Institute; toward expanding a program of "family care" for mental patients who could live in private homes; toward hiring more nurses for the mental hospitals; and toward purchase of the tranquilizing drugs that were just showing their promise. Over a half million dollars was returned unspent; most of it was allocated to hire people, but the personnel was not available.[34]

As director of the Division of Mental Health and Hospitals, Tramburg brought in Dr. V. Terrell Davis. It was frequently mentioned that Dr. Davis was a native of Long Branch and attended public schools in Trenton. He took an M.D. at Washington University in St. Louis in 1936, and his residencies and employment were mostly with the United States Public Health Service. Like most of the new executives, his wartime experience was crucial. "I was at a big hospital in Texas when they began to bring in psychiatric casualties from Guadalcanal," he recalled. "It was an eye-opener. We saw ward after ward of men with classic schizophrenic reactions, but they weren't like the typical mental hospital patients. They came from all sorts of backgrounds, no hereditary disposition, no history of childhood withdrawal, no prior symptoms. You could really believe that they were sick people, people who ought to have medical treatment." [35]

Dr. Davis was certified in psychiatry in 1946 by the American Board of Psychiatry and Neurology and the following year he became chief of psychiatry at the U. S. Marine Hospital, Ellis Island, and later at the Public Health Hospital on Staten Island. His work included developing a psychiatric residency program and training programs for nurses, psychologists, and psychiatric social workers. He was chief psychiatric consultant for the Public Health Service and familiar with the progressive programs of New York State. He was notably successful in developing outpatient and community clinics in Staten Island. From 1948 to 1953 he received training in psychoanalysis at the William Alanson White Institute in New York. Then, in 1954, he resigned to take a four-job package in Tramburg's department in Wisconsin, as assistant director of the Division of Mental Hygiene, associate professor of psychiatry at the University of Wisconsin medical school, assistant director of the Wisconsin Psychiatric Institute, and clinical director of the Wisconsin Diagnostic Center. When he came to New Jersey, in February 1956, his salary was $20,000, higher than Tramburg's, although it did not include maintenance.[36]

Dr. Davis' first large task was to develop a program in which the state would subsidize and encourage community mental health clinics. Meyner was behind the idea, which was already realized in New York and Pennsylvania. So was the Welfare Council. All the professional societies and such diverse groups as the Republican Women, the Camden County Mayors' Association, and the AFL-CIO testified for it. Davis and his advisers drew up the bill, modeled largely on those of New York and Minnesota, and in July 1957 it passed the legislature without a dissent (P. L. 1957, ch. 146).

The incentive to get the local communities moving on the program was a state grant-in-aid offered to local sponsors. The sponsors might be public agencies or private nonprofit corporations or a combination of the two. They had to plan the project and to arrange to raise at least half the funds, from whatever sources they could find. Then they had to get the plan approved by a County Mental Health Board, which was provided for under the act as an important community organization feature. This County Mental Health Board was to be appointed by the freeholders (the county administrative body) and to include not more than twelve residents. They would serve without compensation and would include representatives of the County Welfare Board, local boards of health, school boards, the Medical Society, and the Mental Health

Association. Their business was to pass on projects with regard to local needs and interests, to act as a planning and integrating body, not as a sponsor.

After the County Mental Health Board gave its approval, it passed the project on to the Department of Institutions and Agencies, which checked it against state requirements—minimum standards for personnel and administration—and which administered the state grant. The Department was also supposed to furnish consultants and technical assistance to county boards and local sponsors. To guide its policies, the State Board appointed a seven-member State Mental Health Advisory Council, including by statute two representatives of the Freeholders' Association, and others to represent the state League of Municipalities, the state Mental Health Association, and the professions of psychiatry, psychology, and social work. At the end of the first year seventeen clinics were receiving aid; in the next two years the number rose to thirty-seven, with five more planned.[37]

The state grant-in-aid was for half the expenditures up to a limit of twenty cents multiplied by the population of the county. The logic of the figure was that there should be a clinic for every 100,000 persons; a clinic would cost $40,000 per year, and the subsidy would amount to half of that. Moreover, since the total state appropriation for the projects was only $340,000, including $90,000 offered by the federal government, it was clear that authorities would have to be selective about the projects offered them. (New York offered a grant of up to a dollar per capita.) Accordingly, Davis and his advisers made an important policy decision: The state would foster community mental health clinics intended mostly for child guidance, with somewhat expanded consultation to community agencies. The significance of the decision was that it set aside the historic pattern of traveling clinics based on the state hospitals, and in effect put them out of the child guidance business.

There were three advantages to the program envisioned in the 1957 legislation, Dr. Davis thought. First and most important, the communities would feel a deeper sense of responsibility and commitment than had been apparent in the operations of the state-sponsored clinics, which had been unable to engender much active participation by local citizens in planning or interpreting their work. Second, experience showed that practitioners interested in child guidance functioned differently from those concerned with adult outpatients from the mental hospitals. Third, Dr. Davis wanted to improve the continuity between the care that mental patients received inside and outside the institution.

Consequently, in July 1958, Dr. Davis got the State Board to rule that each hospital should develop an outpatient department served by physicians on the inpatient service. He recognized that the hospitals were often at some distance from people who would need outpatient service, but he observed that patients would be within fifty miles of a facility and he hoped to minimize the difficulty by telephone consultations with local doctors and special arrangements for transportation. (He mentioned in passing the possibilities of increased use of psychiatric wards in general hospitals, that might perform many functions of the regional state hospitals—he had set up such a unit in the Staten Island hospital—but evidently experience had postponed the realization of this idea.)[38]

The Open Hospital

The plan to reorganize outpatient clinics and bring them closer to inpatient services was one aspect of a changing view of the mental hospital that came into prominence in these years. Its sources were hospital care in England, where Dr. Maxwell Jones coined the phrase "the therapeutic community" to denote one of its features, and American sociological studies of the mental hospital. The sociologists found that in the asylums, as in the prisons, the paramount circumstance of the inmate's life was the way he got along with other patients and his custodians in the ward, in the everyday round of life, and they argued that the hierarchical and authoritarian social organization of asylum life were more important and harmful than the various medical treatments were beneficial.[39]

This sociological critique merged with medical critiques of the organization of service in mental hospitals. Custodial care represented an attitude that focused on the patient's liabilities, Dr. Davis said in a talk to the New Jersey Neuro-Psychiatric Association shortly after he took office, whereas a sound medical approach would emphasize his "assets" as well, "inasmuch as we are able to recognize now that this is the major area of variation and that we all have our liabilities" in the sphere of our emotional reactions. The programs associated with "therapeutic patient care" were, in this view, efforts to capitalize on the patient's assets, to get him moving and, hopefully, out of the hospital. In the field of management, he said, medical directors should no longer be the exclusive or even primary source of new developments, but they should take cues and leads from the staff and program specialists who actually worked with the patients.[40]

In May 1958, seven psychiatrists from the New Jersey system, including the medical directors, had the opportunity, courtesy of the Milbank Memorial Fund, to visit mental hospitals in the British Isles for three weeks. What struck them most forcibly, according to a published report of their impressions, was "the humanistic attitude toward the psychiatric invalid" which "permeated all phases of hospital practice." Its objective expression was the small, low-standing buildings and the small wards with ample living space, an insistence on privacy in sleeping arrangements and bathrooms, many amenities of life, such as rugs, drapes, white table linen and complete flatware service, clothes that were individually selected and tailored (if the patient could not provide his own), and well-furnished day rooms, recreational facilities, and places of worship. Humanistic concern was also evident in the constant, friendly, and respectful relations between staff and patients (staff spent little time in office work and record-keeping) and the prominence given the nursing staff in working with patients (unlike the hierarchical organization back home).

With regard to administration, the visitors were impressed by the integration of mental health and other medical services, mediated by the National Health Service, and by the general assumption that the hospital psychiatrist was a medical doctor rather than "a warden charged with safeguarding society against atypical behavior and protecting the patient at all costs against his destructive impulses"—an assumption also expressed in the commitment laws and procedures. The visitors were impressed, too, by the system of lump-sum appropriations and retrospective justification of the budget, and by the high proportion of expenditures on direct services to patients, at the expense of modernization of plant and equipment.[41]

As for the clinical programs, many of the New Jersey psychiatrists had believed that the open-door policy meant that "the wards were simply unlocked and the patients allowed freedom to come and go as they chose." They found that visible restraints—window guards and fences—were absent or inconspicuous, that the staff relied on drugs and moral controls to restrain the patients (supported, in some cases, by a few locked wards, for British psychiatrists were divided on whether the institution should be completely open), and that there were degrees of permissiveness or parole allowed the patient. The English doctors advised that the opening of doors had to be well prepared and that it depended on a tolerance of deviant behavior in the community. For the rest, the visitors observed that there was no formal psychotherapy, and that the shock treatments were mild by American standards; the emphasis was on brief intensive treatment and quick return to the community, and the doctors noticed that there were many failures and readmissions.[42]

Therapeutic patient care and the open hospital became watchwords to identify and encourage many programs in the mental hospitals. Some were already under way and needed only recognition and support. Others depended on hiring new personnel or making organizational changes; many were easy to establish in form but in practice ran against the grain of existing attitudes and routines. In November 1959, Dr. Davis reported to the annual conference of the Milbank Memorial Fund on how the visit to England had stimulated progress. He noted many changes in the organization of the hospitals. Most important in his eyes was the organization of the medical staff into self-governing committees that took responsibility for carrying out professional policies, after the fashion of the organization of general hospitals and contrary to the tradition of a strictly authoritative administration by the medical director. (All but one of the public mental hospitals in New Jersey had lost accreditation in 1958, largely because of inadequate staff organization, he said, but this was the consequence, quite proper, of applying the standards of general hospitals; when the mental hospitals could qualify under the new standards they would be well ahead of the past.)

There was an experiment going forward at Ancora to divide the big hospitals into several smaller units, each giving the whole range of services, but sharing utilities and some resources. There were efforts to give nurses more authority in partnership with doctors. A state commission had been established to review commitment procedures and other laws. Laundry and farming operations had been eliminated as major functions of hospital administration. There was an effort to increase and co-ordinate patient activities—recreation, occupational therapy, education, and library service—drawing largely on volunteer assistants.[43]

As for relations between the mental hospitals and the community, he pointed to the outpatient clinics, with expanded work staffs, which were supposed to be a resource for consultation and mental health education; and to efforts by nursing and social work consultants to establish liaison with public health nurses and social work resources in the community, which would make it possible to transfer more cases to family care. To establish liaison with the community was an old idea, easier said than done, but the hopeful and determined tone of Dr. Davis' presentation arose from the fact that now there were people charged with the responsibility of effectuating these proposals and other people charged with stimulating and supervising them; there was an investment as well as a pious hope.

Along with the ideas of therapeutic patient care and the open hospital came an increased emphasis on research and training. The annual report for 1957–1958 gave priority to these subjects and Dr. John B. K. Smith, director of professional education at Trenton State Hospital, in an article published that year, could take it for granted that psychiatry had three major tasks, that research and education were as important as service.[44]

It was not long since authorities had considered these three functions to be somewhat antagonistic. For example, when two state hospitals had lost their accreditation in 1952, Sanford Bates had commented that "Important as it is to provide training centers . . . , this Department has always considered [that] its primary obligation [is] to provide safe, decent and skillful care for the overcrowded number [sic] of patients that are being sent to us." It was his view that "It is strictly the concern of National associations, colleges and universities to extend to psychiatrists their primary training in order that they can come to us capable of doing work for which they are called, and [not to] rely upon overburdened hospitals to, in addition to their other duties, carry on these training centers." [45] By 1958, however, it was argued that "It is necessary to train skilled personnel or do without them," and it was further thought that a lively research program was necessary to attract and hold able people.[46]

As for research, Douglas MacNeil, then chief of the Bureau of Social

Research, compiled a list of 101 projects under way in mid-1958. Many were carried on in the new Johnstone Center, in the Neuro-Psychiatric Institute, or in the institutions for the mentally ill or deficient, but all institutions were represented; most were on psychiatry or clinical psychology, but other disciplines were represented (six were by social workers).[47]

The *Welfare Reporter* was filled with reports of research, critiques of research, and articles about research and administration and the administrative aspects of research. "The Federal government . . . has had so many agencies granting funds or actually doing research that an applicant may well become confused without a guide book as he attempts to select the appropriate bureau or department to whom he might sell his project," Dr. Maurice Kott wrote in 1960, and private foundations also had large-scale granting programs; but it was important nevertheless for the state government to finance research, he thought, so that its peculiar operations and functions would not escape critical attention. But how to justify the project to budget authorities, how to budget expenses in advance, how to organize the staff, how to relate it to services and training, how to get results recorded and cumulated, to minimize duplication—all these were practical problems.[48]

The Division of Correction and Parole

The Division of Correction and Parole, which was organized under Dr. Bixby shortly after Tramburg took office, had three bureaus: Parole, State Use, which employed mostly prison labor, and Corrections. The last named was the analogue of the consultants employed in mental health. Its duties were to advise and supervise the institutions with regard to their classification and treatment programs, and to help local communities develop programs of delinquency prevention. It had also to inspect county jails and municipal lockups (an activity which was required by law but which had often been ignored for want of staff), and to provide transportation for parole violators and other prisoners inside and outside the state. In practice, the Bureau had a skeleton staff: Dr. Donald Goff, a sociologist, its chief, plus an assistant for consultation, and three or four corrections officers.

The big question about program when the Bureau took over was what to do about the State Home for Boys at Jamesburg. There were three general problems at the institution. First, it took a wide age range, from eight to fifteen. Second, it was a dumping ground for difficult children, disturbed children who had passed their twelfth birthday and were no longer eligible for the Arthur Brisbane Child Treatment Center, for example, or antisocial mental deficients for whom there was no place at New Lisbon. Third, the original idea that Jamesburg would provide a home for children who needed discipline was plainly archaic: The children needed therapy more than discipline and in any case it was difficult to find suitable houseparents at the starting salary of $2,520.

The employees turned over rapidly, and often they felt they had to resort to "unacceptable disciplinary practices," as the phrase goes. In one bad week in 1956 two boys suffered skull fractures, for which employees were indicted for assault. Bixby and others from the central office conducted an investigation which showed, according to the president of the institution's Board of Managers, "that there seemed to be a greater pattern of tolerance of corporal punishment than I think any of us were aware of." [49]

The situation was presently investigated at length by a special committee of the State Senate. The senators found it scandalous, and one of them, Malcolm Forbes, who was soon to be the Republican candidate for governor, was especially intent upon fixing responsibility. For almost forty years authorities had thought that it was a bad policy to mix boys under twelve with teenagers, but nothing had been done. Why? he asked the president of the local board. Who was supposed to say or do something? Well, the president replied, it was the responsibility of the State Board. How did it happen that there were bad phases at Jamesburg that escaped the attention of the local board—who was responsible for that? "I do not think that the Board was fully taken into the confidence of . . . either the administration within the Institution or the Central Office," the president said. Why?

> I don't attribute this to anybody's desire to do anything dishonest or lacking in integrity [said the president], I attribute it to the fact that over a period of time the whole operation of the Department . . . became very sloppy. That's part of the reason.
>
> I think the people just didn't appreciate the fact that when a new member comes on a board of managers, he may be a businessman or a housewife or a school teacher or something else, and he suddenly . . . gets a letter that he's been nominated. . . . They don't know right off the bat what they are supposed to do and the indoctrination or briefing of them has been almost non-existent, so that they really don't know what a very responsible function they have under the law. And nobody tells them.[50]

The Department had, of course, regularly made its plea for staff and facilities before the legislature, including the senators, but now the tragedy provided the means and occasion for a reorganization of the Jamesburg program. The size of living groups was reduced and each cottage assigned a particular kind of problem: aggressive boys, who needed control, in one; passive boys, who needed support, in another, and so forth. The cottages were put under the supervision of cottage masters, not substitute parents or professional social workers (they cost too much), but knowledgeable and mature persons who could carry out therapeutic principles under professional guidance. In general the program was restructured around the diversity of cottages and the quality and climate of their group relations, and in all this the influence of Highfields was apparent. But the essence of the change was that salaries were raised to the level of corrections officers in the adult prisons, and more staff was employed, so there was better supervision.[51]

As for the Bureau of State Use, it held a key to the important problem of idle prisoners. The system had fared well in the depression, when raw materials were cheap and instructor-supervisors easy to hire, but the postwar inflation had reversed these conditions and meanwhile the equipment had become increasingly dilapidated. Three things brought its difficulties to Commissioner Bates' attention in 1952: the retirement of its long-time chief; the prison riots, which highlighted the problem of idleness and destroyed much equipment; and a new state policy of changing auto license plates every five years instead of annually, which ruined one of its best industries. Dr. Bixby, who temporarily held the job of director, was displeased by its organization, which in his view divided responsibility between state-use officials and the wardens and which also failed to tie in with the correctional program.[52]

John C. Bonnell, a production engineer who was appointed director of the Bureau, was displeased by the industrial discipline, the antiquity of the equipment (the knitting industry at Vineland State School was using machinery installed in the 1920's), and the quality of the products.[53] Moreover, the work did not have many friends. It was diversified and restricted so as to minimize competition, but at some point it had to compete with civilian business. It was set up to sell to state agencies, and in many cases its products and service were tailored to their needs, but there were inevitably complaints on many accounts. Consequently, Bates appointed an Advisory Council, of a sort he had found useful in the federal system, to advise Bonnell and interpret the Division's work.[54]

But opposition was never stilled, and in 1956, when state use was moved into the Division of Correction, there were a number of bills presented to limit its work. The advisory committee thereupon asked the Taxpayers Association to make a study of the system and recommendations about it. The Association's report, published in August 1957, made a strong defense of production for state use and a general endorsement of operating policies. Among other things, it criticized the extent to which the earnings of the system had been used to pay for functions that were not properly chargeable to it—some expenses of institutional operation and the cost of the *Welfare Reporter,* for example.[55] The report made numerous recommendations about personnel and marketing, which were soon adopted, and in general it was a powerful support for the work.[56]

At the same time, the changing scene in the mental hospitals and schools for the retarded allowed the Bureau to abandon the industries in them or turn the work over to details of prisoners. Consequently, the work of farming and laundering was done by minimum security prisoners and there was a renewed effort to find appropriate tasks for the maximum security prisoners, who were now clearly the core of the problem.[57] So by discarding the idea of the self-sufficient institution, in which the business manager employed patients on farms and laundries, the mental hospitals and training schools furnished an unexpected market for the labor of the young men who were crowding into its reformatories and prison. It was a happy coincidence in the Department's history.

In reviewing the development of programs in the 1950's—fostered not only under the Divisions of Mental Health and Corrections, which Tramburg had set up, but also in the Division of Welfare, in which he was especially interested, and in the Bureau of Mental Deficiency, which established its field services and the Johnstone Research and Training Center after his tenure began—it is apparent that the boards of managers of particular institutions had taken little part in them, and that organizations for welfare in other states and in the federal government had moved ahead without "local" or even "central" boards. By 1958, Tramburg, Wescott, and Meyner believed it was time for a change. The law, and historical tradition, took this question out of the hands of partisan politicians and power-seeking bureaucrats, however, and laid it upon a nonpartisan citizen body which would, like the Morrow and Earle Commissions forty years before, collect and digest the wisdom of the community.

23

The Study Commission of 1959: Historical Perspectives

Lloyd Wescott, like John Tramburg, came from Wisconsin, born there in 1907 and educated in the schools of Ripon and at Ripon College. He was a modern dairy farmer, a pioneer in scientific modes of breeding and schemes to dry hay and save labor. The first co-operative breeding unit in America had its headquarters on his farm and took advantage of his experiments in the freezing of semen, and he was an officer of many dairymen's associations. In 1942, the Board of Managers at Clinton Reformatory was thought to need a dairyman, to advise on the institutional farm, and he was appointed to assist its deliberations. He liked public service and he certainly had the means and energy for it. Here, as in dairying, he looked for the new idea, the scientific advance, the organization for mutual advantage. He was a founder and president of the Hunterdon County Medical Center, a modern diagnostic center and general hospital and an ultramodern concept of medical care for a rural area. He was also president of the Karen Horney Psychiatric Clinic in New York. Governor Meyner had appointed him to several agricultural committees and in 1956 made him a member of the newly organized Board of Governors of Rutgers University, which was supposed to oversee its conversion to a true state university. But he resigned this position when the State Board elected him its president.[1]

Wescott was not a patient man as regards public affairs and not given to memorializing traditions. "It was this damned genuflecting to the past that got me," he once recalled. "The 'New Jersey system,' New Jersey the leader in this or that, the grand work being done in New Jersey. Well, it just wasn't that good, I didn't think." He had been on the Board at Clinton and seen how overcrowding and low salaries had compromised its operation. "The neglect of that institution, and the others, by the late 'forties, was a scandal. It was public irresponsibility." The bond drives were a turning point, but they were mostly catching up with neglect, he thought. His acquaintance with modern hospital practice and psychiatry did not lead him to believe that New Jersey was showing the way. There were promising new institutions and developments, to be sure, but no ground for complacency.[2]

Although recognizing a value in citizen boards, Wescott thought the New Jersey system confused their functions. "On one hand, the law says that local boards shall have control of and responsibility for local institutions. On the other hand, it says that the State Board has control and ultimate authority. Who has the authority? What authority?" When the situation at Jamesburg came to light, the question arose as to who had appointed the superintendent, he recalled. "The local board said the central office made the selection. Tramburg and Bixby said the local board did." Both parties had a hand; neither was clearly responsible. "Here is a medical institution," he said of another situation. "It has patients who aren't getting treatment. And what is on the board's mind? They want a fire house for their fire engine. Is that what boards are for?" To Wescott, the New Jersey system of state and local boards looked like a "weak-kneed compromise," a "bit of political expediency." [3]

In January 1957, Governor Meyner announced that two officials of the Department had asked him to appoint a commission to study its legal framework and organization, particularly the system of board control, and Wescott was reported to be preparing an examination that would make possible an evaluation along the lines of the Hoover Commission reports.[4] The matter hung fire for a year. Then on January 17, 1958, Meyner named the Commission. Its chairman was Archibald Stevens Alexander, grandson of Caroline Bayard Stevens Alexander Wittpenn, the doyenne of the Department's early history. Alexander, a prominent Democrat, sometime state treasurer and unsuccessful candidate for senator, was chairman of the Board of Governors of Rutgers. His associates included Jane Stretch, the editor of *The Camden Courier-Post;* Barklie Henry, a New York banker who resided in Princeton and who had served energetically on the Board of the Diagnostic Center and the State Board; and three eminent lawyers, Edward S. Greenbaum and William H. Jackson of Princeton, and Raymond A. Brown of Jersey City.

The Rockefeller Brothers Fund contributed $23,650 to finance the work, so that the Commission could pay its expenses and hire a small staff, namely Professor Richard T. Frost, a young political scientist at Princeton, and the well-known journalist Lucy Freeman. Its principal research methods were to visit the institutions and agencies, talk with their boards and officials, and listen to testimony from all sorts of experts and interested parties. (It did not hold formal hearings or take verbatim transcripts, "in the interest of obtaining the full and frank views of those with whom it . . . met.") Its work occupied nineteen months; its report was released on September 3, 1959.[5]

The commissioners held, as their main point, that the structure of the Department was partly obsolete. Its founders, they said, had intended in 1918 to establish central direction of state institutions and, by the system of board control, to enlist the support of enlightened citizens and minimize the influence of spoilsmen. The Department had achieved these ends, but over the years impersonal forces had altered the context of its work. Its case load had grown much larger and more costly, and the system now included many new programs and institutions. Progress in scientific and social thought had brought about enlarged conceptions of the services it offered, and many voluntary and professional associations had appeared to give voice to the new ideas.

Changes in government had put many prerogatives of an institution under central control: its budget, its personnel classifications and policies, its farm and industrial operations, even its precautions against fire and its dietary. In this perspective, the old system seemed too restricted: it had been conceived in terms of managing and co-ordinating a few state institutions, largely custodial in nature, the commissioners said, rather than in terms of fostering and guiding a variety of services in which any particular institution was only one resource among many and many resources were extramural, operated by public or private agencies in the community. The institutional boards had been conceived as business managers and public-spirited philanthropists, rather than as intermediaries with scientific, philanthropic, and other interested publics.[6]

The understanding that state institutions handled only a fraction of the state's welfare problems—that patients in mental hospitals were only a fraction of those that suffered mental disabilities, for example—led the commissioners to their central constructive idea: the "web of services."

> We feel that there will never be adequate organization of personal care services . . . until there is an adequate structure linking the essential services in what resembles a web more than a chain. One test of the structure will be whether, when trouble asserts itself in a home anywhere in the State, the procedures undertaken will flow into each other as simply as if the case were being handled by a single agency, when in fact, State, County, municipal and private agencies and institutions may all be deeply involved and participating.[7]

The metaphor of undertaking procedures that flow through structures that resemble webs more than chains was mixed, but the thought was a recurrent feature of the Commission's recommendations for the various services. With respect to care of the mentally ill, the commissioners were enthusiastic over the idea of the open hospital and the possibilities of extramural facilities, and they urged that the state increase its contribution to local mental health facilities, to get the communities moving faster. They envisioned the Department taking primary responsibility to "blue-print and refine . . . integrated programs providing a full circle of services" so as to fill the "gaps in the web" with more "way stations." To do this would require that it co-operate with existing agencies and associations interested in the service. The commissioners recommended that the state subsidize research and training programs more adequately, so that the way stations would be able to hire trained personnel, currently in extremely short supply, and everyone would have a fund of critical thinking to draw on; and that it "reinforce" its "standard-setting . . . and . . . inspection activities . . . to insure effective Statewide services." [8]

Service to the mentally retarded obviously involved a web of services, because problems began in early childhood and the afflicted would probably need some degree of public help all their lives. The Commission favored state aid and guidance in fostering special community services in schools and clinics, and also for vocational training and placement. Those retardates who were also aggressive, who often got in trouble with the law and became "defective delinquents" in a correctional institution, were in special need of a variety of services to recognize and remedy their deficiencies. This service, too, was much in need of research and personnel, the Commission found, and it urged the state to develop its programs toward these ends.[9]

With regard to correctional programs, the commissioners drew upon the reports of the Youth Study Commission that showed how the state might foster and guide services for preventing crime. They observed that there were eight times as many persons on probation as in institutions, but that, because probation was under the county courts, the work was poorly done in many counties. (The average case load was over 150, three times what the National Probation and Parole Association thought was proper for good supervision.) The Commission did not recommend that the state administer probation (together with parole). It did recommend a stick and a carrot to get the local communities moving: The stick was that the Administrative Office of the courts, established in 1948 to advise the chief justice on judicial operations in the state, be authorized to set and enforce standards. The carrot was that the state offer matching funds, like those for community mental health facilities, to help counties maintain adequate standards.

The commissioners thought that state aid to improve probation would be a good bargain because it would minimize expensive institutional care and new construction. In general, they envisioned the state's taking "over-all responsibility" to improve local preventive and noninstitutional resources, by working with all relevant agencies, state and local, public and private.[10]

As for the web of services in public assistance, the commissioners unequivocally endorsed the judgment of the Bane-May report (1949) and the Kidde Commission (1953) that the assistance function—granting relief—be integrated under County Welfare Boards, with the states and counties sharing equally in the nonfederal costs. They saw no merit in the oft-repeated arguments that general assistance ought to remain with the communities or that the Board of Child Welfare stood between its clients and inept if not corrupt administration by counties. The Commission also recommended that the Department receive greater powers to approve and supervise private charitable associations and institutions, since these were obviously important parts of the web.[11]

Citizen Participation: Board Control

The thought that the state should help fabricate a web of services led the Commission to take for granted that the Department should be organized into operating divisions, with their characteristic emphasis on research and training personnel, planning and programs, consultation and supervision inside and outside the state institutions, and community organization. This sort of organization required freedom for action on the part of professional administrators, and the commissioners noted that the trend in state welfare administration had been away from board control, toward centralized control of institutions under a single board and then toward a department headed by a single professional administrator. Moreover, the services "considered by the professionals as being among the best in the country" had "in all cases . . . a direct line of administrative authority from the Commissioner down."

The New Jersey system of board control, however, made the commissioner's position anomalous in two ways: the State Board cut across the line of authority between the governor and the commissioner, so that he was "in the . . . administration but not of it"; and, of course, the local boards cut across the line between the commissioner and the executives of institutions. The Study Commission observed that each of the four heads of the Department had been "of outstanding calibre, . . . trained or experienced in . . . professional work. Few states have been so fortunate." On the other hand, it said, "the anomalous role of the local institution and agency heads has caused confusion and conflict during the forty year experience under the Morrow system." [12]

The basic idea of the Boards of Managers, the commissioners thought, was to enlist the support of laymen and volunteers. They believed that lay participation was more important now than ever, but that its function had changed. It was no longer proper, they thought, for laymen to invest their energy in administrative detail, such as the management of institutions implied. Many aspects of management had properly been centralized in the commissioner and his assistants, and institutional "policies" had to be conceived centrally in terms of an interdependent system of institutions. On the other hand, the commissioners thought, the great work of recognizing and perfecting the web of services, of co-ordinating scattered efforts, different scientific disciplines, different publics and remote communities, was a challenge to imagination and energy that required more lay participation, not less.

Accordingly, the Study Commission, or the majority of its membership, proposed two major changes. One was to give the commissioner of the Department power to appoint heads of institutions and agencies, to give him direct authority and responsibility for management. All the members agreed on that. They disagreed on a proposal to redefine the duties of local boards so as to eliminate the function of management, making them inspectors, advisers, publicists, and interpreters. In this role, board members would be able, it was supposed, to turn to developing the web of services: to encourage community ties and to establish liaison with community agencies; to stimulate interest and research through university, foundation, or other connections; to study and support the service, particularly in regard to making and justifying the budget. Moreover, the majority wanted to change the authority to parole convicts on indeterminate sentence from the local boards to a separate board, made up of delegates from the several local boards.[13]

So thought Miss Stretch and Messrs. Barklie Henry, Greenbaum, and Brown; but the chairman (Mr. Alexander) and Mr. Jackson dissented. They thought that it was sufficient to give the commissioner power to appoint institutional executives, that there was still a role for local boards in management and in formulating local policies and that to eliminate it would vitiate the boards. It was their opinion that local boards, while sometimes an obstacle to progress, had often been in the right, because they were better acquainted with local conditions. They also objected to the majority's proposals about parole, holding that the Department should either continue the present system but prescribe certain common standards, or give the business to a paid parole board, like that which paroled convicts with determinate sentences.[14]

Both sides agreed that all the boards could function better, and recommended better "indoctrination" of their members, more formal organization to focus responsibility, and a limitation of the terms of members so as to avoid the embarrassment of discharging long-time members. They also proposed a new sort of board, a "divisional council," composed of delegates from local boards who would advise on general problems of a division, and other devices, like the annual program and dinner that Bates had tried, to bring board members and executives together.[15]

Such were the conclusions of prolonged and earnest study of the New Jersey system after forty years. The majority recommendations seemed too "drastic" to the dissenters, but certainly one can imagine much more drastic proposals, such as eliminating the local boards and the State Board, leaving welfare administration to politicians and professionals and allowing them to encourage citizen participation as it suited their interests and needs. It was certainly true, as the Commission said, that citizen interest was important, but it did not follow that having 154 citizens on boards of twenty-two institutions and agencies was a proper form of participation. The commissioners might have argued that the proper role of citizen boards was to oversee local services (like the county welfare boards or mental health boards), or to oversee a particular kind of service (like the proposed divisional councils), or to take the part of a class of people who needed a variety of services (such as children, the aged, or the retarded). They might have argued that these forms of citizen participation and others better answered to the needs of the time than local boards, and that the question of local boards was not very important.

What made the status of local boards important, of course, was the fact that it involved a change in the law and a judgment about the service of many citizens who had served on the boards, and whose service, it was said over and over again, had contributed much to the leadership of the state's institutions. (If the local boards had been composed of employees or inmates, the question would have been quickly resolved.) It was respect for the sensibility of board members that shaped the Commission's view of the history of the Department. On the one hand, the commissioners ascribed the obsolescence of the system to impersonal forces; on the other it passed over references to "confusion and conflict" without any description or analysis.

Their view was reasonable as far as it went, and it went far enough to serve their purpose as leaders of public opinion. But a critical reconstruction of the Department's history brings out also the importance of the particular individuals who guided the course of events, and of other impersonal forces that the Commission did not mention.

The Commission summarized its view of the change in forty years as "the difference between the old philosophy of custodial institutions and the philosophy of a closely co-ordinated family of institutional and community services" (another metaphor for the "web of services"). In a way this is misleading. The idea of a web of services is, after all, not difficult to conceive. From the first, people who were interested in "charities and correction" realized that the human problems of deprivation, demoralization, dependency, and delinquency were linked and complex, and that there was a need to bring many and various resources to bear in helping an individual. By 1930, social workers had developed more or less critical methods of casework and community organization that were deliberately intended to deal with these aspects of the problem. Nor was it difficult to see that local and state institutions were related and ought to be part of a system. Certainly the Morrow Commission recognized the significance of extramural facilities for delinquents, of local institutions, and of the relation between charitable and correctional institutions, and so did Burdette Lewis and Ed Johnstone and John Ellis, their protégé. Certainly, by 1930, the notions of county welfare boards, mental hygiene clinics, community care of the retarded, and the importance of research were all formulated. In the 1930's, Boss Hague was developing what was perhaps the most impressive web of services in the state for delinquency prevention and medical care. The experts in public administration who investigated the state government in 1929 and 1932 recognized the significance of research, prevention, and community institutions. Therefore, the question arises, why was the progress so slow?

The Boards and the Transition

In a historical perspective, there were three sources of confusion and delay in realizing the ideal of a web of services. In the first place, the idea of the web was based on logically prior and more general ideas of prevention, treatment, and rehabilitation, and consequently it involved more or less scientific theories about a problem and how to handle it. But the scientific theories on which the Department operated its institutions were at best imperfect. What was needed in this respect was research, and scientific research depended upon the presence of a body of studious people with a critical and experimental temper and with an opportunity to test their ideas. The Boards of Managers might conceivably have furnished such a group, and to some extent individual members did advise on scientific matters. But the basic improvement in this respect was the development of professional associations that were formed around university training.

The Boards of Managers might have offered (or published) candid criticism of the institutions' work, but in fact the candid and experimental temper was found in the universities and developed by scholars who worked there in an established scientific tradition. Of course these men needed some opportunity to test their ideas, and state institutions, safeguarded by their Boards of Managers, might have provided these laboratories, somewhat as the Vineland Training School did, or the Highfields project. But, as it happened, New Jersey had neither a state nor a private university that trained the professionals its welfare services needed, and, in any case, universities in other states usually developed their research and training programs in institutions that were separate from a state system. Consequently, the New Jersey institutions were, for the most part, left out of this vital circle.

A second source of confusion lay in the problem of defining standards of care and treatment. From a humanitarian viewpoint, that is, simply with regard to the well-being of public wards, standards are important because they define a moral obligation, the level of service that public authorities feel they ought to provide. But standards are also important in an economic sense, because they define the unit and quality of service that public authorities are paying for. The lay Boards of Managers, local and state, might well have addressed themselves to this question, which involved the public conscience and was central to policy. Of course, standards were developed for people in institutions and on public assistance—all sorts of standards, for diet, clothing, professional personnel and civil service, and so forth. But the Boards of Managers did not play a large role in formulating or evaluating them. To learn what was considered a proper caseload for a parole officer or a proper staff organization for the care of mental patients, one did not consult the reports of boards, but the publications of professional associations or other interested parties.

The moral force behind the Beadleston Acts, for example, was the belief that public authorities owed handicapped children a quality of education comparable to that which they afforded to normal children. There had been state laws to this effect, but they had been ignored until the parents' association (not the boards of institutions or the State

Board) had raised the question. Often, in fact, the definition of standards took form when the federal government arranged to use a local or state facility or offered a grant-in-aid, and then the guidelines were worked out by professional people. In respect to standard-setting, therefore, the problems were to organize an alert and active professional association and to bring its case before public authorities. This was manifestly easiest to do at the national level, in the federal government. The federal prison system, the federally aided categorical assistance programs, and the VA mental hospitals were all cases in point.

The third source of confusion in realizing the vision of a web of services, and perhaps the most important, was the problem of the carrot and the stick, the devices to get local communities to support the services that made up the web. That the carrot usually suggested was a program of state subsidies to public and private institutions suggests a paradox: Early charity reformers had generally opposed public subsidies, but in the 1950's reformers favored them. Why? And related to that question is another: Why was it necessary to find a carrot and a stick in the first place? Why didn't the local communities provide the necessary or important facilities on their own initiative, as the charity organizers of 1900 expected and as even Commissioner Ellis, in the 1930's, expected them to do? It is convenient to answer these questions in terms of broad historical trends—changing attitudes toward government and toward paupers, defectives, or delinquents, for example—but it is also possible to relate the changes to the character and interests of specific groups of people in the community.

The founders of charity reform in New Jersey, the people who supported the Charity Organization Societies, the State Charities Aid Association, and the state Conferences of Charities and Correction, were for the most part rich people who felt a religious and patrician obligation to help the unfortunate. There were doubtless elements of snobbery, guilt, and class interest in their efforts, but in any case they were solicited on every hand to be generous. The Charity Organization Society gave form to their interest because it was a defense against their being duped by unscrupulous solicitors, and it appealed to an intelligent and well-informed interest in help that was discriminating and efficient.

The charity organizers could easily see that the almshouse and jail were undiscriminating and inefficient and exploited by politicians, especially in the larger cities. Public charity, in this view, meant waste, corruption, and, of course, higher taxes. Therefore, the reformers favored private charities at the local level, especially those run along discriminating and efficient lines, and they also favored state institutions, which were managed, like the private charities, by honorary unpaid boards of managers, and somewhat removed from political control.

By the 1920's, this situation had changed, at least in the sizable cities. The older spirit of patrician philanthropy and genteel charity organization gave way to the community chest, which was directed by local businessmen and appealed for support to the whole community, and to the federation of more or less professional social work enterprises. The civic-minded business and professional class who were backing the community chest and social work were also supporting ideas about economy and efficiency in public administration. The New Jersey Department of Institutions and Agencies was one product of this line of thought. It was set up relatively early, however, before speculation about public administration had come to favor clear lines of authority and to oppose unpaid administrative boards. (The latter note was sounded in the report of the National Institute of Public Administration on the state government in 1929, but the preponderance of informed and critical opinion at that time probably still favored citizen boards.) [16] To the businessmen and professional people who planned the Department, and served in it and on its boards, the boards did not look much different from those that directed avatars of progress like business corporations, community chests, or, for that matter, public schools. Certainly most professional social workers, who were oriented toward private agencies, favored the institution of board control.

A significant characteristic of these people was that they all came from a small sector of society—the urban business and professional class—and even within their class they were not very numerous or influential. It is difficult, of course, to measure how effective they were, but the wartime Red Cross drives, which were a model for the later community chest campaigns, suggest a standard of what a really strong and effective organization might do.

Conversely, the leaders of the urban working people and the rural towns, insofar as these groups had organization and leadership, were not much interested in progressive welfare policies, public or private. The social base of a more enlightened welfare policy was therefore narrow and it was weakened by the fact that the political alignment in the state made the urban business and professional class largely dependent upon the support of people of moderate means, especially in the small towns and rural sections. This was important because any attempt to improve services in a large way required more taxes, and most taxes in the 1920's and 1930's were levied by local governments on real estate for local services. Even state construction in the 1920's was financed by a state property tax.

The property tax was a poor source of revenue for welfare programs, because it was not progressive and it was difficult to increase. It fell on a small part of the wealth of people whose income was from salaries, profits, or fees, and it fell most directly and heavily on home owners of moderate means and farmers. It also happened, because of the antiquated constitution, that these people were heavily overrepresented in the legislature. Consequently, the enlightened and civic-minded faction of the business and professional class was linked politically with a much larger and more potent group whose ideas about welfare services were characterized by pastoral simplicity.

To complicate matters, the demands for other state and local services, particularly highways and education, were rapidly increasing in the 1920's. It was obvious that welfare programs and agencies would be a poor third in this competition for public funds, but circumstances peculiar to New Jersey gave unusual strength to the other two. Good highways were an economic advantage to farmers, to the resort towns and to owners of real estate generally, and it happened also that highways were handily financed by user taxes (gasoline and license). Moreover, it happened that out-of-state drivers, en route to New York, Philadelphia, or the seashore, paid a large share of the gasoline tax.

As for education, it too was an asset to real estate values, in the more select suburbs, at least, and it was a ladder of social mobility whereby people could nourish aspirations for their children. Furthermore, it was possible for school boards, by paying a small premium to teachers, to draw on the educational resources of New York and Pennsylvania and to ignore the responsibility of the state for teacher training and higher education generally. Consequently, the very high local property taxes in New Jersey—at least in the cities and suburbs—represented a deliberate and rather generous investment in local primary and secondary schools. But every expenditure on the schools increased the difficulty of spreading the local property tax to cover welfare services.

The answer to financing welfare programs was a broad-based state tax, but the federal income tax, rising steadily through the depression and the war, seemed to pre-empt the most likely means. A state sales tax, tried in mid-depression, showed politicians that the opposition was overwhelming.[17] Meanwhile, the hostility and anxiety aroused by New Deal programs found a peculiar focus in New Jersey because Boss Hague, the tribune of the masses in Hudson County and the bête noire of solid citizens elsewhere, was President Roosevelt's strong ally. (Boss Hague financed his own welfare programs, in medical care and delinquency prevention, out of local property taxes, which were the highest in the state.) The result was that the civic-minded and enlightened members of the business and professional class, who were willing to support progressive welfare programs, became even more dependent politically upon small-town and rural elements, at the same time that the great expansion of public welfare during the depression seemed to incapacitate the private agencies, which they had traditionally supported, and perhaps to furnish a nucleus for a sinister new political organization of public pensioners.

The Department of Institutions and Agencies was, in these turbulent years, formally nonpartisan and free of the spoils system, but its leaders —Lewis and Ellis and the great majority of board members—were members of the business and professional class. They represented its progressive side and certainly were not spokesmen for a narrow class interest or political program. But they were not likely to ignore the concerns of their class, and especially the importance of frugal administration, free from political abuse. This was a reasonable concern. Able leaders, like Governors Edge and Driscoll, gave it a forceful direction, and the Democratic governors of the depression and war years offered no constructive alternative. The fundamental condition of welfare administration in New Jersey before 1945, boards or no boards, was the paucity of tax resources, but the leaders of the Department, whether professionals or board members, were not disposed to discuss the state's fiscal policy, even with regard to the adequacy or enlargement of the service their institutions rendered.

In the years after the war, enlightened attitudes toward welfare programs spread among business and professional people. For one thing, new recruits to their ranks, and those most familiar with welfare problems, recognized the importance of prevention and rehabilitation and the possibilities of the web of services. These groups were proportionally small but numerically sizable, and in their professional associations and the other civic organizations they supported, such as the League of Women Voters, they found a voice. Meanwhile experience in the depression and the war had undermined the older skepticism and fear about government spending and about public welfare programs, doubts that had inhibited their support during the 1920's and 1930's.

Not only was the enlightened element of the business and professional class larger and better organized, but it was no longer so closely tied to the metropolitan suburbs and the Republican Party; its members could often find common ground with leaders of ethnic minorities and labor leaders; it was much easier for them to support Robert Meyner, the "gray-flannel Democrat," who was, incidentally, no commuter to Manhattan but an upward-mobile small-town lawyer from Phillipsburg, on the upper Delaware, than to support the vassals of Boss Hague who had been offered them in earlier years.

The support for enlightened welfare programs, which was always primarily among these people, spread; the services received an increasingly sympathetic hearing, although opposition remained lively among other groups, of course. There were, in the years between 1945 and 1959, perhaps a score of presentations about New Jersey state institutions in national magazines and other mass media, all of which described and praised the more service-minded and progressive institutions, such as the Diagnostic Center, the Brisbane Child Treatment Center, or Highfields, and these, together with general discussions of social problems and welfare programs, must have encouraged among their audiences a more favorable disposition toward prevention, rehabilitation, and the idea of a web of services.

The emphasis in these presentations was on program, however, and for the most part they ignored questions of finance or taxes. In the 1950's it was apparent that the business and professional class, more willing than ever to support enlightened services, was being pushed from many directions toward supporting a broad-based tax to finance the services. There was no broad-based support for the tax, as yet, so their political leaders were forced into evasions that were comic, if one ignored the suffering they entailed. Governor Meyner was both in favor of better services and pledged against a personal income tax or sales tax.[18] The Study Commission report, in 1959, made a strong and enthusiastic case for spending more money on state programs and state grants-in-aid to local service—there was no dissent at all on these ideas—but no one raised the question of how much it would all cost and the report did not suggest that the state's fiscal policy had any historical bearing on its organization for social welfare or on their own "design for the future."

The Boards of Managers might have taken a lead in the postwar years in defining and debating this fundamental fiscal problem. Many members did as individuals, and collectively the boards were a cadre in the bond drives of 1949 and 1952. But a bond drive for institutional construction is different from a campaign for a broad-based tax to finance enlarged and improved services. By this time, the tradition was set that boards did not discuss public policies in public, but stuck to their institutions, and the moot question before the Study Commission was still whether the boards should continue to appoint superintendents and otherwise engage in managerial functions.

To summarize, there were in 1918 three problems in the way of realizing the ideal of a web of services. One was to formulate improved scientific theories as a basis for the programs of prevention, treatment, and rehabilitation. Another was to develop and clarify standards, which were a device to give form to the conscience of public authorities and to give an accountable dimension to the service rendered. A third was to find and support an adequate fiscal base for the services. The Boards of Managers were not in a good position to do much about any of these problems, which depended on conditions largely beyond their control, interest, or even comprehension. The problem to which the Study Commission addressed itself, that of organizing a web of services, a variety of resources, state and local, public and private, into an interdependent series of way stations, was, of course, an important aspect of these related problems, and it raised the question, how, as a practical matter, can leaders at the state level get leaders in the communities to establish and support the parts of the web that were so essential to the whole scheme?

The Carrot and the Stick

The problem of getting local communities to act was more basic than the need for a broad-based tax. The citizens who participated in preparing for the White House Children's Conference of 1960 described it, in the report of their deliberations, as a diminishing of shared values, a loss of the sense of community, a social disorganization that was the consequence of the mobility and dispersion of the population and of social change so rapid that it separated the generations. The terms suggest that they thought the problem was getting worse as well as changing character but they made no attempt to measure it. It was this observation about social life as it affected children that led these civic-minded people to put their highest priorities for action on agencies for planning and community organization and on citizen participation, and it led them also to recommend a restudy and possible reorganization of local government and to support a broad-based tax, which would, in their view, enable state agencies to encourage community organization and citizen participation.[19]

This observation is an ironic comment on the argument in the 1950's that integration of welfare (and health) services at the county level would violate the grand old New Jersey tradition of "home rule." In the view of these people, at least, there was no home rule to speak of. Politically, of course, the argument for home rule rationalized the concern of taxpayers in unpopulous townships that their inclusion in larger units would mean higher taxes, and of municipal officials that they would lose their jobs to professional or full-time workers from the county seat. It is an interesting fact that during the immediate postwar years a third of the townships did not elect to take state financial aid for their general assistance programs: it shows that the welfare problems that plagued cities and suburbs had not yet become serious to the rural townships.[20] Many localities were disorganized by social change, but many others, unpopulous but politically potent, were still removed from the problems and the scientific and organizational approach to them that gave currency to the idea of a web of services.

To a historian, it is not at all clear whether society in New Jersey in the 1950's was more dispersed, disorganized, or impotent than it had been in earlier generations. The professional societies and citizen groups who made themselves heard on public policy were certainly manifestations of organization, and the spread of mass culture to the countryside, and of gray-flannel Democrats to Phillipsburg, was evidence of a diminishing of social divisions. (The report to the White House Conference had likened the uprooted quality of life in the decade to the conditions which had confronted immigrant children and their parents in earlier generations.) Be that as it may, the social history of the state is full of examples of the difficulty of arousing and sustaining a sense of community or civic spirit on either a local or a state level. Episode after episode reveals how a precious few public-spirited and philanthropic people challenged massive apathy and neglect about welfare programs, how a few public servants worked amid galling frustration and indignity to help the public wards, and how cruel deprivation and brutality often dishonored the ideals of patient, kindly, and efficient service.

This aspect of the state's social history stands in contrast with its main theme, the story of the people who managed to carve out careers more or less suited to their ability, foresight, industry, and luck, who became or remained prosperous and powerful, who did not lack for fellowship and associations for mutual advantage, who made the comfortable homes and busy towns and farms, and who found much to be complacent and conservative about. But of course the two themes are related. The mobility, dispersion of population, and the disorganized uprooted quality of life, the absence of plan and of community spirit, are the unwholesome consequences of a large measure of individual freedom. The individuals and families who were pursuing their careers, making their homes, and elaborating their interests were incidentally failing to participate in community life and to plan and support, among other things, the web of services for the unfortunate and dangerous who sometimes appeared at the periphery of their freeholds.

Postscript: The Study Commission and the War on Poverty

The Study Commission's report had no dramatic impact on welfare administration. Its significance as a conclusion to this history lies in its central concerns rather than in its practical results. Its charge was to examine the administrative structure of the Department, and its perspective—determined by its informants—was that of experts in the services. *Given these programs and agencies,* it asked, *how can we organize them to better advantage?* Its answers—epitomized in the notion of the web of services—pointed to the needs of experts: research, trained personnel, and "community organization" to facilitate their work. Political support for the requisite investment in these improvements was growing, but it was still insufficient and unfocused.

Meanwhile, the inadequacies of public welfare generally were receiving attention in a different context, that of national economic policy. Among economists, the fear of inflation that had characterized President Eisenhower's advisers was giving way to concern about the increase in "hard-core unemployment" and its concentration, along with related welfare problems, in pockets of poverty. In 1958, John Kenneth Galbraith's *The Affluent Society* made a strong case for larger expenditure on social services; in 1962, Michael Harrington's *The Other America* dramatized the plight of the new poor, who, he thought, suffered novel handicaps. These best-selling books, and others like them, appealed to business and professional people and enlarged the support for "welfare state" measures, and property owners interested in urban renewal or area redevelopment also came to favor active federal programs.

The new poor themselves were notably absent from the early stages of this discussion—both Galbraith and Harrington had remarked on their fecklessness—but presently the leaders of the civil rights movement turned from their moral and legal successes to seeking improvements in services that could help their constituents, and gave many of these people a voice. The broad tendency of this sentiment was toward a "war on poverty" in which "economic opportunity" rather than public welfare was the theme, and the militant poor, once aroused, were no more respectful of welfare administrators than the local taxpayers' associations had been. But within a few years after the Study Commission reported, a new demand for better services was evident and increasing.

In view of the history of state institutions in New Jersey, the discussion of poverty in the 1960's brought into relief the separation between general economic policy, determined at the national level, and welfare administration, organized and directed under state law. It is a striking fact that never in the first forty years of the Department had its leaders, lay or professional, published any reflections on the relation between national economic policy and the programs they administered. Until the great depression pushed the federal government into active "countercyclical measures" (as economists came to call them), there were few options to provoke discussion, and insofar as questions of national policy were defined in terms of freedom versus regulation, the personal inclinations and affiliations of the Department's leaders favored laissez-faire views. They could not ignore the federal relief measures during the depression, but, like almost everyone else, they looked upon them as "emergency" programs, temporary and separated from their responsibility. By 1940, when it appeared that mass unemployment was a permanent condition of welfare administration, John Ellis did offer some constructive suggestions for combining work relief and public assistance, but high employment during and after World War II removed the urgency of the problem.

By 1942, therefore, this depression-born link between state welfare administration and national economic policy was broken, and federal work relief projects played little part in the "war on poverty" of the mid-1960's. Moreover, the State Board had no direct responsibility for or connection with the social insurances—old age, survivors, or unemployment—which became, in the 1940's, primary resources against economic dependency. The Board was not authorized to comment on these programs, although they were related in many ways to its services; in 1960 as in 1940 it was preoccupied by balancing vested interests related to its services. In this context arose the varieties of expertise and the questions of theory and practice that have been discussed in this history, and to which the inquiry in 1959 addressed itself. Charged to survey "the state's organization for social welfare," the Study Commission had no mandate nor historical precedent to consider questions about the reduction of unemployment, the relation of social insurance to public assistance, the connection between economic deprivation and crime or mental disorder, or the role of social services in promoting equal opportunities and conserving human resources.

The founders of the Department hoped that its most important function would be to "educate the people of the State as to their responsibilities" with respect to its work, but after forty years it appeared that its problems were so involved with technical questions and institutional vested interests, with vagaries of scientific theory and administrative responsibility, that any general program of "education" was out of the question. In the 1950's, state leaders were talking instead about "community organization" to encourage the participation of local groups and integrate particular services. Their proposals—many of them summarized by the Study Commission—were well-informed and practical, but they were much more modest than grand programs to educate people to their responsibilities.

On the other hand, it appeared from the experience of the depression and of the "war against poverty" in the 1960's that public attitudes toward welfare programs moved with larger currents of opinion on the performance of the economy, and that these tides of opinion, related to national politics and focused and formed by nationwide media of communication, had significant consequences for welfare administration. From time to time, one might hypothesize, coalitions of the underprivileged and their sympathizers would take form around demands that the federal government act when other agencies could not or would not, and these demands would create a political climate in which improvement and innovation in welfare programs were possible.

If the main factor of progress is a national wave of concern about the economy, it may be that the wisest course for welfare administrators, philanthropists, and social workers is not to try to generate the wave, as some would have it, but rather to prepare themselves to ride it to best advantage when it comes. Certainly their ideals will gain clarity and currency as their technical competence improves, and insofar as the leaders and workers in the New Jersey Department of Institutions and Agencies have confronted in a candid and critical way their problems of technical competence, so tortuous and discouraging, they have done a worthy service for their wards and for their—and our—ideals of humanity and science.

Notes

Abbreviations Used in the Notes

Acts	*Acts of the . . . Legislature of the State of New Jersey*
Assembly Journal	*Minutes of Votes and Proceedings of the . . . General Assembly of the State of New Jersey*
DCC	[New Jersey] Department of Charities and Corrections
Leg. Docs.	*New Jersey Legislative Documents*
NJDIA	New Jersey Department of Institutions and Agencies
SCAA	[New Jersey] State Charities Aid Association
NJRCC	*New Jersey Review of Charities and Corrections*
Senate Journal	*Journal of the . . . Senate of the State of New Jersey*

NOTES FOR CHAPTER 1

[1] John E. Pomfret, *The New Jersey Proprietors and Their Lands* (Princeton: D. Van Nostrand, 1964), pp. 3, 44, 83–87, 107–108; Richard P. McCormick, *New Jersey from Colony to State* (Princeton: D. Van Nostrand, 1964), pp. 59–61.

[2] Julian P. Boyd, ed., *Fundamental Laws and Constitutions of New Jersey* (Princeton: D. Van Nostrand, 1964) is a convenient collection of documents; on the importance of freeholders, see pp. 55, 61–63, 76–78, 83–89; McCormick, pp. 55–56; Rudolph J. Vecoli, *The People of New Jersey* (Princeton: D. Van Nostrand, 1965), pp. 33, 64.

[3] Marcus Jernegan, *Laboring and Dependent Classes in Colonial America 1607–1783* (New York: Frederick Ungar, 1960), pp. 45–50; Richard B. Morris, *Government and Labor in Early America* (New York: Columbia University Press, 1946), pp. 310–314, 513–517; Abbott Emerson Smith, *Colonists in Bondage: White Servitude and Convict Labor in America 1607–1776* (Chapel Hill: University of North Carolina Press, 1947), pp. 3–25.

[4] Smith, pp. 34–35.

[5] Wallace N. Jamison, *Religion in New Jersey: A Brief History* (Princeton: D. Van Nostrand, 1964), pp. 11–27; Thomas Jefferson Wertenbaker, *The Founding of American Civilization: The Middle Colonies* (New York: Scribner's, 1949), pp. 82, 126–127, 163, 196; Sydney V. James, *A People Among Peoples: Quaker Benevolence in Eighteenth-Century America* (Cambridge: Harvard University Press, 1963), pp. 23, 32–36.

[6] Brian Tierney, *Medieval Poor Law* (Berkeley: University of California Press, 1959), pp. 128–132; E. M. Leonard, *The Early History of English Poor Relief* (Cambridge: University Press, 1900), pp. 9–10, 17–21; William James Ashley, *An Introduction to English Economic History and Theory* (London: Longmans, Green, 1914), pp. 359–361.

[7] John L. Rankin, "Newark Town Government from 1666–1833," *Proceedings of the New Jersey Historical Society,* 3d ser., X (1915), 12; E. F. Hatfield, *History of Elizabeth, New Jersey* (New York, 1868), p. 222; Boyd, p. 151.

[8] Samuel Allinson, *Acts of the General Assembly of the Province of New Jersey* (Burlington, N. J., 1776), p. 8.

[9] Paul Tutt Stafford, *Government and the Needy: A Study of Public Assistance in New Jersey* (Princeton: Princeton University Press, 1941), pp. 30–34; Andrew D. Mellick, Jr., *Lesser Crossroads,* ed. Hubert G. Schmidt (New Brunswick: Rutgers University Press, 1941), pp. 370–372.

[10] Allinson, pp. 85–86.

[11] *Ibid.,* p. 119.

[12] *Ibid.,* p. 222.

[13] *Ibid.,* pp. 179–186, 198–202.

[14] Leonard, pp. 30–36, 65; Morris, pp. 1–3, 14.

[15] Allinson, p. 222.

[16] *Ibid.*, pp. 417.

[17] The following analysis is drawn from the law, Allinson, pp. 403–419; see also Stafford, pp. 41–45.

[18] Stafford, pp. 33–34, 43.

[19] Boyd, pp. 58–59, 83–89.

[20] [N. J.] Prison Inquiry Commission, *Report,* Vol. II, *A History of the Penal, Reformatory and Correctional Institutions of the State of New Jersey, Analytical and Documentary,* by Harry E. Barnes (Trenton: MacCrellish and Quigley, 1917), pp. 21–27; Henry Clay Reed, "Chapters in a History of Crime and Punishment in New Jersey" (Ms. Ph.D. diss., Princeton, 1939), pp. 32–48, 64–67, 85a–85e.

[21] Reed, pp. 63, 369–374, 397–398, 412–413, 427–449; Arthur D. Pierce, *Smugglers' Woods: Jaunts and Journeys in Colonial and Revolutionary New Jersey* (New Brunswick: Rutgers University Press, 1960), pp. 9–12, 16–19, 25–26.

[22] Reed, pp. 289, 299–300, 322–335, 422, 499.

[23] *Ibid.*, pp. 85b–85c; Smith, pp. 264, 274–276; Harry B. Weiss and Grace M. Weiss, *An Introduction to Crime and Punishment in Colonial New Jersey* (Trenton: Pasttimes Press, 1960), pp. 91–95.

[24] Reed, pp. 537, 544, 549–553; Smith, p. 275.

[25] Henry S. Cooley, *A Study of Slavery in New Jersey* (Baltimore: Johns Hopkins University Press, 1896), pp. 12, 35, 39–40.

[26] Reed, pp. 85b–85e; Weiss, pp. 7–8, 38.

[27] Reed, pp. 86–87, 277–282.

[28] *Ibid.*, pp. 498, 537, 549–552.

[29] Adrian C. Leiby, *The Early Dutch and Swedish Settlers of New Jersey* (Princeton: D. Van Nostrand, 1964), pp. 77–79, 98–101, 105–107, 117–118; Vecoli, pp. 16–17, 21–22; Wertenbaker, pp. 13, 25, 100–102.

[30] Jamison, pp. 54–56; McCormick, pp. 92–93; James, pp. 28–32.

[31] Jamison, pp. 38–43; McCormick, p. 96.

[32] McCormick, pp. 58–63, 69–70, 77–78.

[33] J. Hector St. John de Crèvecoeur, *Letters from an American Farmer* (New York: E. P. Dutton, 1957), pp. 17–21, 37–40, 44–47, 64.

[34] Frederick B. Tolles, "Introduction," *The Journal of John Woolman and A Plea for the Poor* (New York: Corinth Books, 1961), pp. vii, ix–x.

[35] Mellick, pp. 20–21, 389–391; for the breakdown of New England settlements in New Jersey, see Wertenbaker, pp. 139–142.

[36] Reed, pp. 137–146.

[37] Richard P. McCormick, *Experiment in Independence: New Jersey in the Critical Period, 1781–1789* (New Brunswick: Rutgers University Press, 1950), pp. 20–22; Morris, pp. 513–518.

[38] McCormick, *Experiment in Independence,* pp. 22–23, 69–71, 95–98.

[39] Cooley, pp. 20–22, 31.

[40] *Ibid.*, pp. 45–47.

[41] *Ibid.*, pp. 25–27; Mellick, pp. 372–381.

[42] Stafford, pp. 40–41, 69–70.

[43] *Laws of the State of New Jersey; Revised and Published . . . by William Paterson* (Newark, 1800), pp. 32, 270, 378.

[44] Carl Bridenbaugh, *Cities in the Wilderness: The First Century of Urban Life in America 1625–1742* (New York: Knopf, 1955), pp. 235–237, 394–395; James, pp. 47–48.

[45] These facts were established by an examination of municipal records: Stafford, pp. 52–65; *Revised Statutes of New Jersey, 1821,* p. 695.

[46] Stafford, pp. 65–67; *Revision of the Statutes of New Jersey Published under the Authority of the Legislature by Virtue of an Act Approved April 4, 1871* (Trenton: John Murphy, 1877), pp. 833–845.

[47] Nelson Burr, *Education in New Jersey, 1630–1871* (Princeton: Princeton University Press, 1942), pp. 19, 51, 83–85, 113, 126, 150–151.

[48] Burr, pp. 54, 58, 62, 69–70, 72–73, 221–222.

[49] *Ibid.,* pp. 227–228, 238–239.

[50] *Ibid.,* pp. 240–242.

[51] *Ibid.,* pp. 234, 244–248.

[52] *Ibid.,* pp. 299–300.

[53] *Acts,* 1838, p. 82.

[54] Burr, pp. 247, 251–252, 258, 259.

[55] *Ibid.,* pp. 266, 271, 277, 280–281.

[56] *Ibid.,* pp. 245–246, 276, 300–301; *Assembly Journal,* 1838, pp. 42–45.

[57] Roscoe L. West, *Elementary Education in New Jersey: A History* (Princeton: D. Van Nostrand, 1964), pp. 26–27, 34–36, 40–46.

NOTES FOR CHAPTER 2

[1] "Historical Address," *NJRCC,* October, 1903, p. 154. See also Thomas Cushing and Charles E. Sheppard, *History of the Counties of Gloucester, Salem, and Cumberland, New Jersey . . .* (Philadelphia: Evarts & Peck, 1883), pp. 114–116, 325–326; *Model Jail of the Olden Time; Designs for "A Debtors Gaol and Workhouse for Felons" for Burlington County . . . by Robert Mills, Architect, Philadelphia, May, 1808* (Russell Sage Foundation, Department of Delinquency and Penology, Pub. no. 2, 1928).

[2] Henry Clay Reed, "Chapters in a History of Crime and Punishment in New Jersey" (Ph.D. thesis, Princeton, 1939), pp. 55–59, 302, 388, 549–550.

[3] [N. J.] Prison Inquiry Commission, *Report,* Vol. II, *A History of the Penal, Reformatory and Correctional Institutions of the State of New Jersey, Analytical and Documentary,* by Harry E. Barnes (Trenton: MacCrellish and Quigley, 1917), pp. 46–48.

[4] Barnes, pp. 44–45, 47–48. The legislature could relieve sheriffs of responsibility for losses in jailbreaks: see *The State Gazette and New Jersey Advertiser* (Trenton), Feb. 6, 1798.

[5] Reed, pp. 37, 50, 71–72.

[6] Richard P. McCormick, *Experiment in Independence: New Jersey in the Critical Period, 1781–1789* (New Brunswick: Rutgers University Press, 1950), pp. 90 n. 70, 82, 97–98.

[7] Barnes, pp. 32–35; Harry Elmer Barnes, *The Evolution of Penology in Pennsylvania: A Study in American Social History* (Indianapolis: Bobbs-Merrill, 1927), pp. 27–37.

[8] Reed, pp. 75–82, 85b–85c.

[9] Barnes, *Evolution of Penology,* pp. 80–102.

[10] *Ibid.,* pp. 83–84; Orlando F. Lewis, *The Development of American Prisons and Prison Customs . . . 1776–1845* (The Prison Association of New York [1922]), pp. 43–44.

[11] Gertrude Wood, *William Paterson of New Jersey, 1745–1806* (Fair Lawn: Fair Lawn Press, 1933), pp. 118–119; a debate over the criminal code appears in *The State Gazette and New Jersey Advertiser* (Trenton), Feb. 6, 1798; the code is in *The Laws of the State of New Jersey, Revised and Published . . . by William Paterson* (Newark, 1800), pp. 208–221. The law authorizing the prison is *Acts,* 1797, pp. 189–190.

[12] The organic act of the prison is *Acts,* 1798, p. 280, reprinted in Barnes, *History of Penal . . . Institutions of . . . New Jersey,* pp. 371–377.

[13] Barnes, *History,* pp. 371, 373–374, 377.

[14] Negley K. Teeters, *They were in Prison: A History of the Pennsylvania Prison Society* (Philadelphia: Winston, 1937), pp. 22–24.

[15] Barnes, *History,* p. 378.

[16] A description of the building is in the *Journal of the* [New Jersey] *Legislative Council . . . 1798,* pp. 16–17; see also Lewis, pp. 44, 49.

[17] Barnes, *History,* p. 61; Barnes, *Evolution,* pp. 122–124; Lewis, p. 28.

[18] Barnes, *History,* pp. 59, 63, 420–421.

[19] *Ibid.,* pp. 66, 67–68; Negley K. Teeters, *The Cradle of the Penitentiary: The Walnut Street Jail at Philadelphia, 1773–1835* (Pennsylvania Prison Society, 1955), pp. 44–45.

[20] Barnes, *History,* pp. 404–405.

[21] *Ibid.,* pp. 410–411.

[22] On the Society for Useful Manufactures see Joseph S. Davis, *Essays in the Earlier History of American Corporations* (Cambridge: Harvard University Press, 1917), I, 386–387. The prison cost $41,000; the bridge at Trenton, completed in 1806, cost $180,000: Wheaton J. Lane, *From Indian Trail to Iron Horse: Travel and Transportation in New Jersey, 1620–1860* (Princeton: Princeton University Press, 1939), p. 126.

[23] *Assembly Journal,* 1804, pp. 147–155.

[24] *Assembly Journal,* 1812 (2d sitting), pp. 133–135; *Assembly Journal,* 1813, p. 76; *The Trenton Banking Company: A History of the First Century of Its Existence . . .* (Trenton, 1904), p. 74.

[25] *Assembly Journal,* 1818, pp. 130–136.

[26] Boston Prison Discipline Society, *Report,* 1826, p. 36.

[27] Walter D. Lewis, *From Newgate to Dannemora: The Rise of the Penitentiary in New York, 1796–1848* (Ithaca: Cornell University Press, 1964), pp. 90–93.

[28] *Assembly Journal,* 1830, pp. 186–187, 190–191.

[29] Negley K. Teeters and John D. Shearer, *The Prison at Philadelphia: Cherry Hill . . .* (New York: Columbia University Press, 1957), pp. 3–4, 17–23.

[30] "Report of the Joint Committee . . . on . . . a New State Prison," *Journal of the* [N. J.] *Legislative Council . . . 1833,* pp. 66–67.

[31] *Ibid.,* pp. 68–69.

[32] *Ibid.,* pp. 71–72.

[33] Orlando Lewis, *Development,* p. 192.

[34] *Letters on the Pennsylvania System of Solitary Imprisonment* (2d ed., Philadelphia, 1837), pp. 29–31.

[35] Reprinted, Barnes, *History,* p. 449; see also p. 91.

[36] *Ibid.,* pp. 88, 90; O. Lewis, *Development,* p. 193.

[37] "Physician's Report," *Journal of the Legislative Council . . . 1839,* p. 83.

[38] "Physician's Report," *Assembly Journal,* 1841–1842, p. 192.

[39] Reprinted, Barnes, *History,* p. 456.

[40] Reprinted, *Ibid.,* pp. 459–461.

[41] Dorothea Dix, *Remarks on Prison and Prison Discipline in the United States* (Boston: Munroe and Francis, 1845), pp. 24, 54.

[42] *Ibid.,* pp. 24, 38.

[43] Reprinted, Barnes, *History,* pp. 488–489.

[44] *Ibid.,* pp. 489–490.

[45] *Ibid.,* pp. 155–156.

[46] *Ibid.,* pp. 96, 475–477.

[47] *Ibid.,* pp. 477, 114–115.

[48] Richard P. McCormick, *The History of Voting in New Jersey: A Study of the Development of Election Machinery, 1664–1911* (New Brunswick: Rutgers University Press, 1953), pp. 87–91, 123–125.

[49] Lane, pp. 284–286, 326, 369–370.

[50] Barnes, *History,* p. 73.

[51] "Reports of the Committee of the Majority and Minority on the House of Refuge," reprinted in *ibid.,* pp. 570–579.

[52] *Ibid.,* pp. 69–72; the report of the investigation of 1830 is reprinted on pp. 396–423.

[53] *Ibid.,* pp. 101–102.

[54] *Ibid.,* pp. 103–104.

[55] *Ibid.,* pp. 126–127, 521.

[56] *Ibid.,* pp. 117–118.

[57] *Ibid.,* pp. 91, 104; Lane, pp. 309, 323.

NOTES FOR CHAPTER 3

[1] James Parker, *Conductor Generalis, or, the Office, Duty and Authority of Justices of the Peace* (Woodbridge, 1764), p. 287.

[2] John Locke, *An Essay Concerning Human Understanding,* Alexander Campbell Fraser, ed. (New York: Dover, 1959), I, 210.

[3] Edouard Seguin, *Idiocy* (New York: Teachers College, Columbia University, 1907), pp. 39–40.

[4] *Ibid.,* pp. 47–56.

[5] Albert Deutsch, *The Mentally Ill in America: A History of Their Care and*

Treatment from Colonial Times (2d ed., New York: Columbia University Press, 1949), pp. 332–336.

[6] The basic law is an act of November 21, 1794, in *The Laws of the State of New Jersey, revised and published . . . by William Paterson* (Newark, 1800), pp. 125, 190. Other important acts governing the mentally disordered are *Acts,* 1804, pp. 328–331, and *Acts,* 1819–1820, pp. 91–95.

[7] Parker, pp. 287, 451.

[8] See the organic act of the Asylum, *Acts,* 1847, p. 29.

[9] Parker, pp. 287, 451.

[10] Deutsch, pp. 78–80.

[11] Kathleen Jones, *Lunacy, Law and Conscience, 1744–1845: The Social History of the Care of the Insane* (London: Routledge & Kegan Paul, 1955), pp. 31, 34, 39, 131; Deutsch, pp. 89–91.

[12] Deutsch, pp. 137–143; Norman Dain, *Concepts of Insanity in the United States, 1789–1865* (New Brunswick: Rutgers University Press, 1964), pp. 12–14, 50–52, 167–168. The other state institutions were in Vermont, 1836; Ohio, 1838; Tennessee and Maine, 1840; Georgia and New Hampshire, 1842.

[13] David L. Cowen, *Medicine and Health in New Jersey: A History* (Princeton: D. Van Nostrand, 1964), pp. 10, 14, 69–74.

[14] *Journal of the* [N. J.] *Legislative Council,* 1839–1840, p. 286; *Assembly Journal,* 1840, pp. 444–445; Henry M. Hurd, *Institutional Care of the Insane in the United States* (4 vols.; Baltimore: The Johns Hopkins Press, 1916), III, 58.

[15] *Assembly Journal,* 1840, pp. 449, 464.

[16] *Ibid.,* pp. 450, 455, 464.

[17] *Assembly Journal,* 1840–1841, p. 522.

[18] *Ibid.,* pp. 402, 442–443.

[19] *Journal of the* [N. J.] *Legislative Council,* 1842, p. 167.

[20] *Acts,* 1843, p. 512.

[21] Her famous "Memorial" is in the *Senate Journal,* 1845, pp. 175–219.

[22] Francis Tiffany, *Life of Dorothea Lynde Dix* (Boston: Houghton Mifflin, 1892), p. 115; Helen E. Marshall, *Dorothea Dix, Forgotten Samaritan* (Chapel Hill: University of North Carolina Press, 1937), pp. 104–108.

[23] Marshall, pp. 246, 250.

[24] Earl D. Bond, *Dr. Kirkbride and His Mental Hospital* (Philadelphia: J. B. Lippincott, 1947), pp. 9–30.

[25] *Ibid.,* pp. 31–32.

[26] *Ibid.,* pp. 32–35; Deutsch, pp. 191–192.

[27] "Biographical notes," ms. in the library of the Trenton State Hospital; Minutes of the Board of Managers, Trenton State Hospital, April 6 and 19, 1847.

[28] Buttolph's mentor, Dr. Amariah Brigham, was a partisan of phrenology: Dain, pp. 61–62, 163. On phrenology generally, see John D. Davies, *Phrenology: Fad and Science. A 19th Century American Crusade* (New Haven: Yale University Press, 1955).

[29] N. J. State Lunatic Asylum, *Annual Report,* 1848, pp. 29–30; H. A. Buttolph, "Insanity and Mental Derangement," *Senate Journal,* 1853, App. pp. 110–138;

H. A. Buttolph, "Insanity or Mental Derangement; Remarks on Its Nature, Causes, Classification, Pathology, and Symptomatic Forms" (his address as president of the Association of Medical Superintendents in 1887), in the library of the Trenton State Hospital.

[30] N. J. State Lunatic Asylum, *Annual Report,* 1852, pp. 19–20; H. A. Buttolph, "Historical and Descriptive Account of the New Jersey State Lunatic Asylum at Trenton," ms., Trenton State Hospital.

[31] Bond, pp. 34–35.

[32] N. J. State Mental Hospital at Trenton, *Annual Report,* 1897, p. 52.

[33] N. J. State Lunatic Asylum, *Annual Report,* 1849, in *Senate Journal,* 1849, p. 63.

[34] "Bylaws . . . State Lunatic Asylum, 1848," ms. in the library of the Trenton State Hospital.

[35] N. J. State Lunatic Asylum, *Annual Report,* 1857, p. 40; *Ibid.,* 1858, p. 14.

[36] Cf. N. J. State Lunatic Asylum, *Annual Report,* 1853, in *Senate Journal,* 1853, Appendix, pp. 97, 109.

[37] "An act to provide for the organization of the State lunatic asylum . . . ," *Acts,* 1847, pp. 24–25, 28 (sec. 20–22, 36); cf. N. J. State Lunatic Asylum, *Annual Report,* 1864, p. 12.

[38] N. J. State Lunatic Asylum, *Annual Report,* 1850, pp. 27–28.

[39] *Ibid.,* 1850, p. 10.

[40] *Acts,* 1847, pp. 24–26 (sec. 17, 20, 21, 27, 28).

[41] Governor's message, *Senate Journal,* 1851, pp. 18–19; N. J. State Lunatic Asylum, *Annual Report,* 1851, in *Senate Journal,* 1851, pp. 44–45, 53.

[42] N. J. State Lunatic Asylum, *Annual Report,* 1850, pp. 28–29.

[43] N. J. State Lunatic Asylum, *Annual Report,* 1849, pp. 62–63; Governor's message, *Senate Journal,* 1851, pp. 18–19.

[44] N. J. State Lunatic Asylum, *Annual Report,* 1850, in *Senate Journal,* 1851, pp. 56–58; *Ibid.,* 1853, in *Senate Journal,* 1853, p. 97.

[45] *Acts,* 1848, p. 214; N. J. State Lunatic Asylum, *Annual Report,* 1849, in *Senate Journal,* 1849, pp. 89–93.

[46] N. J. State Lunatic Asylum, *Annual Report,* 1853, in *Senate Journal,* 1853, App. pp. 97–98, 109.

[47] State Sanitary Commission, *Report,* 1866, pp. 36–37.

[48] N. J. State Lunatic Asylum, *Annual Report,* 1868, pp. 19–20.

[49] *Ibid.,* p. 19; N. J. State Lunatic Asylum, *Annual Report,* 1876, p. 16.

[50] N. J. State Lunatic Asylum, *Annual Report,* 1852, p. 16.

[51] N. J. State Lunatic Asylum, *Annual Report,* 1868, p. 20; *Ibid.,* 1871, pp. 11–13.

[52] *Ibid.,* 1858, pp. 540–541; *ibid.,* 1864, p. 12.

[53] *Ibid.,* 1867, p. 26; *ibid.,* 1869, pp. 21–22.

[54] *Ibid.,* 1871, pp. 11–13; *ibid.,* 1872, p. 5.

[55] Deutsch, pp. 132–135, 147–157; those who denounced "the cult of curability" overdramatized it: see Dain, pp. 114, 202–203.

[56] N. J. State Lunatic Asylum, *Annual Report,* 1853, p. 23.

NOTES FOR CHAPTER 4

[1] John E. Brush, *The Population of New Jersey* (New Brunswick: Rutgers University Press, 1956), pp. 16–18, 32–35.

[2] John E. Bebout and Ronald J. Grele, *Where Cities Meet: The Urbanization of New Jersey* (Princeton: D. Van Nostrand, 1964), pp. 30–35, 43; Francis B. Lee, *New Jersey as a Colony and as a State* (4 vols.; New York: Publishing Society of New Jersey, 1903), IV, 243–245.

[3] Lee, IV, 274–279.

[4] *Ibid.*, pp. 264–267; Harold F. Wilson, *The Jersey Shore: A Social and Economic History of the Counties of Atlantic, Cape May, Monmouth, and Ocean* (3 vols.; New York: Lewis Publishing Co., 1953), I, 406–408, 413, 518–525; II, 712–715; Jennie Barnes Pope, "The Old Iron Industry," William Starr Myers, ed., *The Story of New Jersey* (5 vols.; New York: Lewis Historical Publishing Co., 1945), ch. 4; Hubert G. Schmidt, *Rural Hunterdon: An Agricultural History* (New Brunswick: Rutgers University Press, 1946), pp. 8–10, 51–52, 64, 216–221; cf. George Weller, "The Jackson Whites," *A New Jersey Reader*, Henry C. Beck, ed. (New Brunswick: Rutgers University Press, 1961), pp. 69–83.

[5] William E. Sackett, *Modern Battles of Trenton . . .* (2 vols.; Trenton: John L. Murphy, Printer, 1895, and New York: Neale Publishing Co., 1914), I, 19–23, 48–64, 184–186, 195, 208; Ransom E. Noble, Jr., *New Jersey Progressivism Before Wilson* (Princeton: Princeton University Press, 1946), pp. 1–11, 21–25, 100–121.

[6] Sackett, I, 86–90; Noble, *loc. cit.;* Bebout and Grele, pp. 37–39.

[7] "Foreign Blood in New Jersey," *NJRCC,* Oct. 1903, pp. 157–158, states the reformers' views of the population; Mary B. Sayler, "Housing Conditions in Jersey City," *Annals of the American Academy of Political and Social Science,* January 1903 supplement; Rudolph J. Vecoli, *The People of New Jersey* (Princeton: D. Van Nostrand, 1965), pp. 102–103, 136–137, 153–157.

[8] Duane Lockard, *The New Jersey Governor: A Study in Political Power* (Princeton: D. Van Nostrand, 1964), pp. 71–76; Vecoli, pp. 163–172; John E. Bebout, *Party Alignment in New Jersey, Especially Since 1925* (M.A. thesis, Rutgers University, May 1938), pp. 94–97.

[9] Charities incorporated before 1877 are handily recorded in John Hood, *Index of the Colonial and State Laws of New Jersey . . .* (Trenton: John L. Murphy, 1877), under the rubrics "Associations," "Asylums," "Charitable and benevolent societies," "Hospitals," etc.; on Catholic charities see "The Catholic Factor in New Jersey Charities," *NJRCC,* March 1902, p. 26, and a detailed list in *NJRCC,* October 1903, pp. 160–163; Elizabeth Delaney, "Poor Relief in Elizabeth, New Jersey . . ." (M.A. thesis, Rutgers University Library, 1937), pp. 85–87, 155–205; on hospitals see David L. Cowen, *Medicine and Health in New Jersey: A History* (Princeton: D. Van Nostrand, 1964), pp. 91–97.

[10] Delaney, pp. 31, 121–123, 126.

[11] *Ibid.,* pp. 137–143.

[12] *Ibid.,* pp. 145–148.

[13] *NJRCC,* Dec. 1902, p. 215; see also July–August 1902, pp. 123–128; May 1903, pp. 77–78.

[14] "Pauperism," Bureau of Statistics of Labor and Industries of New Jersey, *Fifth Annual Report,* 1883, pp. 373–374, 377–378.

[15] *Ibid.,* pp. 378, 407–408, 385–387; see also Paul Tutt Stafford, *Government and the Needy: A Study of Public Assistance in New Jersey* (Princeton: Princeton University Press, 1941), pp. 52–72.

[16] "Pauperism," p. 395.

[17] *Ibid.,* p. 407.

[18] *Ibid.,* p. 407.

[19] *Ibid.,* p. 408; see also Council of State Charities and Corrections, *Second Annual Report,* 1885, pp. 13–14.

[20] The general shift of interest from pauperism to poverty is the theme of Robert H. Bremner, *From the Depths: The Discovery of Poverty in the United States* (New York: New York University Press, 1956), see pp. 123–128.

[21] Aaron I. Abell, *The Urban Impact on American Protestantism, 1865–1900* (Cambridge: Harvard University Press, 1943), pp. 11–14, 55, 118–135; Herbert A. Wisbey, Jr., *Soldiers Without Swords: A History of the Salvation Army in the United States* (New York: Macmillan, 1955), pp. 17, 25, 33; Delaney, pp. 158–165; C. Howard Hopkins, *History of the Y.M.C.A. in North America* (New York: Association Press, 1951), pp. 23, 40–41.

[22] Daniel T. McColgan, *A Century of Charity* (2 vols.; Milwaukee: Bruce Publishing Co., 1951), I, 190–194.

[23] *NJRCC,* September–October 1902, p. 152; December 1902, p. 208; March–April 1903, p. 58; August–September 1903, pp. 124–125; February 1906, pp. 85–86.

[24] "Charity Organization in New Jersey," *NJRCC,* February 1902, p. 16; "Private Initiative," *NJRCC,* June–July 1903, p. 111.

[25] "Pauperism," p. 411; *Child Welfare in New Jersey, Part I* (U. S. Children's Bureau Publication 174, Washington, D. C., 1927), pp. 8–9 (an account of the SCAA evidently based on interviews with survivors); on the SCAA in New York, see David M. Schneider and Albert Deutsch, *The History of Public Welfare in New York State, 1867–1940* (Chicago: University of Chicago Press, 1941), pp. 20–22, 24.

[26] "Charity as an Art," *NJRCC,* November 1903, p. 182; *NJRCC,* May 1906, pp. 196–197; in general, see Frank D. Watson, *The Charity Organization Movement in the United States: A Study in American Philanthropy* (New York: Macmillan Co., 1922), pp. 211–221.

[27] E.g., SCAA, *Annual Report,* 1887, p. 30, and *Annual Report,* 1891, pp. 8–9; *NJRCC,* November 1903, pp. 176–178.

[28] E.g. *NJRCC,* February 1902, pp. 10–11, 15–16; March–April 1903, p. 25; August–September 1903, p. 132; April 1905, p. 105; SCAA, *Annual Report,* 1913, pp. 14–15.

[29] The laws establishing probation are *Acts,* 1900, p. 289; *Acts,* 1906, p. 104.

[30] *Assembly Journal,* 1811, 2d sitting, p. 100.

[31] *Acts,* 1874, pp. 34–35; on federal pensions see William H. Glasson, *Federal*

Military Pensions in the United States (New York: Oxford University Press, 1918).

[32] According to Hood, p. 99.

[33] *Acts,* 1865, pp. 551–552; 1866, pp. 249–251; 1867, pp. 214–215; 1868, p. 768; *Assembly Journal,* 1876, joint resolutions 3 and 4.

[34] *Acts,* 1866, pp. 955–959; 1867, pp. 824–825.

[35] Governor [Theodore] Randolph, *Message,* January 11, 1870, pp. 20–21; Governor [Joel] Parker, *Message,* January 12, 1875, n.p. On the role of the federal government in state domiciliary care, see Gustavus A. Weber and Laurence F. Schmeckebier, *The Veterans' Administration, Its History, Activities, and Organization* (Washington: Brookings Institution, 1934), pp. 86–87, 279.

[36] Governor [George] Werts, *Message,* January 14, 1896, n.p.

[37] Martha Chickering, "An Early Experiment in State Aid to the Aged, California, 1883–95," *Social Service Review,* XII (March 1938): 41.

[38] Homer Folks, *The Care of Destitute, Neglected and Delinquent Children* (New York: Macmillan Co., 1907), p. 101.

[39] President's Commission on Veterans' Pensions, Staff Report No. 1, *The Historical Development of Veterans' Benefits in the United States . . .* (Washington: Government Printing Office, 1956), pp. 3–4, 13, 14–15, 24.

NOTES FOR CHAPTER 5

[1] Homer Folks, *The Care of Destitute, Neglected, and Delinquent Children* (New York: Macmillan Co., 1907), pp. 8, 39–42; Grace Abbott, *The Child and the State* (2 vols.; Chicago: University of Chicago Press, 1938), I, 189–194.

[2] See *infra,* p. 38. The Essex County institution was authorized by *Acts,* 1857, p. 204. Magistrates or parents could commit boys under fifteen, who were then subject to indenture as under the poor law.

[3] *Report of the Commissioners on the Reform of Juvenile Offenders, Leg. Docs.,* 1865, Doc. 13, reprinted in *Report of the* [N. J.] *Prison Inquiry Commission, Volume II. A History of the Penal, Reformatory and Correctional Institutions of the State of New Jersey, Analytical and Documentary,* by Harry E. Barnes (Trenton: MacCrellish and Quigley, 1917), II, 579–588.

[4] *Ibid.,* pp. 581–582.

[5] "The Relation of Coal to Crime," *NJRCC,* March 1905, pp. 52–53.

[6] *Report of the Commissioners on the Reform of Juvenile Offenders,* p. 583.

[7] *Ibid.,* pp. 584, 587.

[8] *Ibid.,* pp. 584–585, 587.

[9] *Report to the Legislature of the Joint Committee on the Reform School, Leg. Docs.,* 1886, Doc. 42, reprinted in Barnes, pp. 588–592; see also Barnes, pp. 246–247, 255.

[10] Nelson R. Burr, *Education in New Jersey, 1630–1871* (Princeton: Princeton University Press, 1942), pp. 274–277.

[11] John O'Grady, *Catholic Charities in the United States: History and Problems* (Washington: National Conference of Catholic Charities, 1930), pp. 112–117; David M. Schneider and Albert Deutsch, *The History of Public Welfare*

in New York State, 1867–1940 (Chicago: University of Chicago Press, 1941), p. 73.

[12] William E. Sackett, *Modern Battles of Trenton . . .* (2 vols.; Trenton: John L. Murphy, Printer, 1895, and New York: Neale Publishing Co., 1914), I, 112–116.

[13] *Ibid.*, pp. 116–117.

[14] *Acts*, 1888, p. 188.

[15] At first the commitment procedure was designed to keep children out of jail and even out of the police and criminal courts, but these enlightened provisions were abandoned in practice. Robert Flemming, "The Child Offender in New Jersey," *Justice and the Child in New Jersey. Report of the* [New Jersey] *Juvenile Delinquency Commission* (Trenton, 1939), pp. 39–40. Mr. Flemming, a distinguished lawyer, served for decades on the Board of Children's Guardians.

[16] Barnes, pp. 247–248.

[17] *Report to the Legislature of the Joint Committee on the Reform School*, 1886, quoted in Barnes, p. 590.

[18] "Report of the Committee on the Industrial School for Girls," *Assembly Journal*, 1900, pp. 452–454; Barnes, pp. 263–266.

[19] Ellis R. Meeker, quoted in *The Elizabeth* [N. J.] *Daily Journal*, March 13, 1900, p. 1; see also March 14, 1900, p. 5.

[20] Barnes, pp. 266–269. The legislature reorganized both the boys' and the girls' reform schools and renamed them "State Homes": *Acts*, 1900, p. 176 (boys), p. 481 (girls). The boards of managers received the power to parole inmates, as well as bind them out or discharge them.

[21] *NJRCC*, June 1904, pp. 112–113.

[22] SCAA, *Twenty-ninth Annual Report*, 1914, pp. 23–24.

[23] *NJRCC*, March–April 1903, p. 48; June–July 1903, p. 118.

[24] Caroline Bayard Colgate, *Off the Straight and Narrow* (New York: Lee Furman, Inc., 1917), pp. 61–62, 70–74, 83, 91.

[25] *Report to the Legislature of the Joint Committee on the Reform School*, 1886, quoted in Barnes, pp. 589, 592.

[26] Folks, pp. 103–105, 83–85; *Report of the Delegate from New Jersey to the National Conference of Charities and Corrections . . . 1881, Leg. Docs.*, 1881, Doc. 24, pp. 1–4.

[27] [N. J.] Bureau of Statistics of Labor and Industries, *Fifth Annual Report*, 1883, pp. 411–413; SCAA, *First Annual Report*, 1886, p. 23.

[28] SCAA, *Fourth Annual Report*, 1889, p. 7; *Fifth Annual Report*, 1890, pp. 8–9, 17–18.

[29] Folks, p. 81.

[30] *Report of the New Jersey Commission on Defective, Delinquent and Dependent Children, and their Care, to the Legislature, Session of 1898. Leg. Docs.*, 1898, No. 43, pp. 3, 19–20, 23; SCAA, *Twelfth Annual Report*, 1897, pp. 9–13.

[31] *Report of the New Jersey Commission on Defective, Delinquent and Dependent Children, and their Care, Leg. Docs.*, 1898, No. 43, pp. 3, 20.

[32] *Ibid.*, pp. 4–7, 29–30, 33–35.

[33] *Report of the New Jersey Commission on Defective, Delinquent, and Dependent Children, and their Care, Leg. Docs.*, 1899, No. 35, pp. 11–13, 19–21;

Paul Tutt Stafford, *State Welfare Administration in New Jersey* (Princeton University Department of Political Science, 1934), pp. 109–110.

[34] *New York Morning Journal,* March 7, 1898, quoted in Patricia Charash Levine, "The Origins of the State of New Jersey Board of Children's Guardians" (M.S. thesis, New Jersey State Teachers College, Newark, 1953), p. 119. The overseer was Mr. John Hewitt.

[35] *Ibid.,* p. 120.

[36] Levine, pp. 62–66.

[37] *Ibid.,* pp. 66, 89–90, 110.

[38] *Ibid.,* pp. 68–69, 114–115.

[39] *Ibid.,* pp. 110, 114; *Report of the . . . Commission . . . 1899,* pp. 6–7.

[40] Sackett, II, 87–89.

[41] *Ibid.,* II, 89–90.

[42] SCAA, *Eleventh Annual Report,* 1896, p. 33.

[43] *Report of the . . . Commission . . . 1899,* pp. 17–18; SCAA, *Fifth Annual Report,* 1890, p. 18.

[44] *Hoboken Observer,* April 20, 1901, quoted in Levine, p. 131.

[45] *Acts,* 1899, p. 362.

[46] Levine, pp. 78–79, 85–86; *Child Welfare in New Jersey, Part II* (U. S. Children's Bureau Publication No. 175, Washington, 1927), p. 6; Stafford, p. 110.

[47] *Hoboken Observer,* April 12, 1901, quoted in Levine, pp. 127–129.

[48] Levine, pp. 88–90; *Acts,* 1902, p. 547.

[49] SCAA, *Thirteenth Annual Report,* 1898, pp. 7, 9.

[50] *New Jersey Conference of Charities and Corrections,* 1902, pp. 34, 38.

[51] *NJRCC,* March 1902, p. 27; *New Jersey Conference of Charities and Corrections,* 1904, p. 127; O'Grady, p. 418.

[52] Levine, pp. 79–80.

[53] *Hoboken Observer,* April 29 and 30, 1901, quoted in Levine, pp. 132–133.

[54] New Jersey State Board of Children's Guardians, *Annual Report,* 1911, p. 4; *Child Welfare in New Jersey. Part 2* (U. S. Children's Bureau Publication No. 175, Washington, 1927), p. 4.

[55] Francis Day, "What New Jersey Has Done for its Dependent Children," *NJRCC,* February 1911, pp. 19–21.

[56] "The First Fifty Years in the Life of an Agency," *Welfare Reporter* (NJDIA), November 1949, p. 5.

[57] N. J. State Board of Children's Guardians, *Annual Report,* 1911, p. 4; *ibid.,* 1913, p. 5; SCAA, *Twenty-ninth Annual Report,* 1914, p. 8; Stafford, p. 133. The "Widow's pension" law is *Acts,* 1913, p. 578.

[58] SCAA, *Twenty-ninth Annual Report,* 1914, p. 26; *Acts,* 1915, p. 444 (part of an important general child welfare act).

[59] N. J. State Board of Children's Guardians, *Annual Report,* 1918, p. 4; 1919, p. 3.

NOTES FOR CHAPTER 6

[1] David M. Schneider, *The History of Public Welfare in New York State, 1609–1866* (Chicago: University of Chicago Press, 1938), pp. 201–203; Harry

Best, *The Deaf: Their Position in Society and the Provision for their Education in the United States* (New York: Thomas Y. Crowell Co., 1914), pp. 139–141, 165, 226, 233.

[2] *Acts,* 1821, p. 3; 1830, pp. 113, 314; 1838, p. 82; 1853, p. 139; 1873, p. 45.

[3] Schneider, pp. 371–372; Harry Best, *The Blind: Their Condition and the Work Being Done for Them in the United States* (New York: Macmillan Co., 1919), pp. 266–267, 289–290, 330–331.

[4] *Acts,* 1836, p. 305; 1837, p. 79; 1843, p. 59; *Rev. Stat.,* 1847, p. 406; *Acts,* 1860, p. 689; 1864, p. 311; 1865, p. 796; 1873, p. 45.

[5] *Assembly Journal,* 1872, pp. 152–154, 1188–1190.

[6] *Report of the Commissioners on the Deaf and Dumb, Blind and Feeble-minded, Leg. Docs.,* 1874, No. 23, p. 9.

[7] *Ibid.,* pp. 19–21.

[8] *Senate Journal,* 1874, pp. 27–28.

[9] *Acts,* 1874, pp. 133–134; *Senate Journal,* 1876, p. 37.

[10] Comptroller of the Treasury, *Annual Report . . . 1874, Leg. Docs.,* 1875, pp. 35–36.

[11] William E. Sackett, *Modern Battles of Trenton . . .* (2 vols.; Trenton: John L. Murphy, Printer, 1895, and New York: Neale Publishing Co., 1914), I, 78–80, 112; Schneider, p. 371.

[12] *Acts,* 1882, pp. 259–263.

[13] *Acts,* 1891, p. 164; 1911, p. 513.

[14] *Acts,* 1895, p. 753; Comptroller of the Treasury, *Annual Report . . . 1895–1896,* pp. 54–55.

[15] Best, *The Blind,* pp. 469–470, 747. The Arthur Home later received state aid: *Acts,* 1916, p. 279.

[16] *Acts,* 1908, p. 731; 1909, p. 208; 1911, p. 114; Best, *The Blind,* pp. 684–686, 688–689.

[17] *Acts,* 1911, p. 513; 1912, p. 585; Lydia Hayes, "The Work of the New Jersey Commission for the Blind," *NJRCC,* February 1911, pp. 17–19.

[18] On Stephen Garrison's proposal of 1847, see *The Training School* [Bulletin], June 1908, p. 6. The subsidy for indigent retarded was authorized by *Acts,* 1860, p. 240. The School was then called "The Pennsylvania Training School for Feeble-minded Children," see Elwyn Training School, *One-Hundredth Annual Report,* 1951–1952, pp. 9–10.

[19] I[saac] N. Kerlin, *The Mind Unveiled* (Philadelphia: A. Hunt & Son, 1850), pp. 53–54.

[20] *Ibid.,* p. x.

[21] *Ibid.,* pp. xi, xii.

[22] *Ibid.,* pp. 143, 146, 147.

[23] *Report of the Commissioners on the Deaf and Dumb, Blind and Feeble-minded,* pp. 19–21.

[24] *The Training School* [Bulletin], June 1908, pp. 3–6; September 1920, pp. 73–75.

[25] New Jersey Training School for Feeble-minded Children at Vineland, *Annual Report,* 1897, includes the best statement of Garrison's ideal.

[26] David M. Schneider and Albert Deutsch, *The History of Public Welfare*

in New York State, 1867–1940 (Chicago: University of Chicago Press, 1941), pp. 98–99.

[27] New Jersey Institution for Feeble-minded Women, *Annual Report,* 1889, p. 8. *Acts,* 1888, p. 157, authorized the governor to remove "indigent and feeble-minded females" to a "home" where they were kept "entirely separate from the other sex." The organic act of the State School is *Acts,* 1888, p. 267.

[28] Governor John Griggs, Message, January 11, 1898, in *Leg. Docs.,* 1898, pp. 14–15; New Jersey Institution for Feeble-minded Women, *Annual Report,* 1897, pp. 8–9; 1898, p. 12.

[29] Governor George T. Werts, Message, January 14, 1896, *Assembly Journal,* 1896, pp. 17–18; New Jersey State Village for Epileptics, *Annual Report,* 1898, pp. 1–2, 8; 1902, p. 3.

[30] "Edward R. Johnstone," *Welfare Reporter* (NJDIA), February 1947, p. 7; Alexander Johnson, *Adventures in Social Welfare . . .* (Fort Wayne: The author, 1923), pp. 181, 187, 188.

[31] E. R. Johnstone to Alexander Johnson, June 18, 1915, in possession of E. L. Johnstone, Fort Lauderdale, Fla.

[32] The articles were scattered through volumes 17–19 of *The Training School Bulletin;* Edward R. Johnstone, *Dear Robinson:—Letters on Getting Along With Folks* (Vineland: The Training School, 1923).

[33] *The Training School Bulletin,* March 1922, p. 147.

[34] Johnson, pp. 13, 85, 366.

[35] Walter S. Cornell and Louis Nussbaum, "The FM Club: An Historical Sketch," *The Training School Bulletin,* April 1952, pp. 17–22.

[36] Edgar Doll, ed., *Twenty-five Years: A Memorial Volume . . .* (Training School at Vineland, Department of Research Series, No. 2, 1932), pp. 6–9, 55–56.

[37] H. H. Goddard, "In the Beginning," *Training School Bulletin,* December 1943, p. 154.

[38] H. H. Goddard, "Two Months Among European Institutions for the Mental Defectives," *The Training School* [Bulletin], July 1908, p. 15.

[39] Goddard, "In the Beginning," p. 155.

[40] H. H. Goddard, *Feeble-mindedness: Its Causes and Consequences* (New York: Macmillan Co., 1916), pp. 2, 5–6, 19, 573, 583–585; *Twenty-five Years: A Memorial Volume,* pp. 58–59, 61.

[41] Henry H. Goddard, *The Kallikak Family: A Study in the Heredity of Feeble-mindedness* (New York: Macmillan Co., 1912), pp. 13–19, 29–30, 99–100, 111–115.

[42] E. Kite, "Two Brothers," *Survey,* 27 (March 2, 1912): 1861–1864; "Unto the Third Generation," *Survey,* 28 (September 28, 1912): 789–791; "The Pineys," *Survey,* 31 (October 4, 1913): 7–13, 38–40 and *passim.*

[43] E. R. Johnstone, "What Are We Trying to Do," *The Training School* [Bulletin], August 1908, pp. 3–9.

[44] *Acts,* 1904, p. 270.

[45] *Acts,* 1909, p. 126; 1911, p. 513.

[46] Mark H. Haller, *Eugenics: Hereditarian Attitudes in American Thought*

(New Brunswick: Rutgers University Press, 1963), pp. 125–126, 136; *Acts,* 1911, pp. 513, 353; Johnson, p. 414.

[47] Joseph Byers, *The Village of Happiness: The Story of the Training School* (Vineland: n.p., 1934), pp. 76–80.

[48] Johnson, pp. 391–392, 413–414; Byers, pp. 86–90; Haller, pp. 113–114.

NOTES FOR CHAPTER 7

[1] State Asylum at Morristown, *Annual Report,* 1888, p. 11, summarizes these developments.

[2] United States Census Office, *Compendium of the Tenth Census, 1880,* p. 1678; New Jersey Commission on the Care of Mental Defectives, "Report," *Assembly Journal,* 1914, pp. 395–396.

[3] Conference of Boards of Public Charities [National Conference on Social Welfare], *Proceedings,* 1876, pp. 13, 115–116.

[4] *Acts,* 187, p. 73; 1876, p. 144. Jane East, *The Essex County, New Jersey, Asylum for the Insane, 1872–1910* (M.A. thesis, University of Chicago School of Social Service Administration, June 1940), pp. 31–32, 36, 42, 76.

[5] Henry M. Hurd, ed., *The Institutional Care of the Insane in the United States and Canada* (4 vols.; Baltimore: Johns Hopkins University Press, 1916), III, 98–100, 105; East, pp. 6–16, 50, 66, 74.

[6] East, pp. 15–21.

[7] *Ibid.,* pp. 21, 32–33, 77.

[8] William E. Sackett, *Modern Battles of Trenton . . .* (2 vols., Trenton: John L. Murphy, Printer, 1895, and New York: Neale Publishing Co., 1914), I, 78, 102–105, 155. Governor Joseph Bedle, Message, January 8, 1878, *Leg. Docs.* 1878, No. 4, pp. 8, 16.

[9] East, pp. 52, 56–57.

[10] Albert Deutsch, *The Mentally Ill in America . . .* (rev. ed., New York: Columbia University Press, 1949), pp. 231–233.

[11] Deutsch, pp. 249, 254–256.

[12] Joint Committee on Lunatic Asylums, "Report," *Senate Journal,* 1880, pp. 163–169.

[13] Joint Committee to Investigate County Asylums, "Report," *Senate Journal,* 1881, pp. 998–1002.

[14] Deutsch, pp. 276–286, 291–299.

[15] East, pp. 56–58, 60–62, 89–91.

[16] H. A. Buttolph, "Remarks on the Organization and Management of Hospitals . . . for the Insane. Under Single and Dual Heads," *The Alienist and Neurologist,* October 1887, pp. 7–9.

[17] *Acts,* 1893, p. 207; 1894, p. 266. East, pp. 96–97; State Hospitals of New Jersey, *Annual Report,* 1896, p. 8.

[18] This analysis is based on interviews with staff whose acquaintance with the hospitals began before 1920, including several second-generation workers.

[19] Buttolph, pp. 7–8.

[20] Francis B. Lee, ed., *Genealogical and Personal Memoir of Mercer County, New Jersey* (2 vols.; New York: Lewis Publishing Co., 1907), I, 200–201.

[21] Clippings from Trenton papers for November 27, 1901, in scrapbook at Trenton State Hospital; see also SCAA, *Sixth Annual Report,* 1891, pp. 25–26; *Thirteenth* [i.e. Fourteenth] *Annual Report,* 1899, pp. 10–11; State Hospitals of New Jersey, *Annual Report,* 1896, pp. 13–15; DCC, *Annual Report,* 1909, p. 5; *ibid.,* 1910, p. 6.

[22] Buttolph, pp. 8–9.

[23] Special Committee to Investigate the Management, Government, and Discipline of the State Asylum at Morristown, "Report," *Senate Journal,* 1899, pp. 58–73; Hurd, pp. 88–89.

[24] Committee of the Board of Managers, quoted in Trenton papers, November 27, 1901, clippings in scrapbook at Trenton State Hospital.

[25] East, pp. 62–64.

[26] *Psychogram* (Greystone Park State Hospital, January 1920), pp. 3–5.

[27] See *infra,* p. 105.

[28] E. R. Johnstone to Alexander Johnson, June 18, 1915, in possession of Mr. E. L. Johnstone, Fort Lauderdale, Fla.

[29] New Jersey State Village for Epileptics, *Annual Report,* 1898, p. 8; *ibid.,* 1908, p. 7.

[30] J. E. Wallace Wallin, "A Personalized Story of the First State-Supported Psychological Clinic in New Jersey," *Welfare Reporter* (NJDIA), October 1960, pp. 149–151.

[31] *Ibid.,* pp. 155–156, 159.

[32] *Ibid.,* pp. 157, 160.

[33] "Henry A. Cotton," *American Journal of Psychiatry,* XIII, 921 (January 1934), obituary by Dr. Adolph Meyer, Cotton's mentor, who gives a sympathetic appraisal but errs in the year of birth; *National Cyclopedia of American Biography,* XXIV, p. 388.

[34] H. A. Cotton, "A Review of the Progress of Modern Psychiatry," *Journal of the Medical Society of New Jersey,* July 1908, pp. 74–78.

[35] Charlotte Louise Hammell, "The New Jersey State Hospital at Trenton, 1848 to 1908" (M.A. thesis, University of Chicago School of Social Service Administration, 1938), pp. 75–76. Dr. Ward had served at Trenton for 40 years.

[36] Trenton State Hospital, Minutes of the Board of Managers, October 18, 1907.

[37] Charlotte Billington, "The New Jersey State Hospital for the Insane, at Trenton, 1908–1940" (M.A. thesis, University of Chicago School of Social Service Administration, 1941), p. 36. The Hospital still has its earliest volumes of case records.

[38] *Ibid.,* p. 31.

[39] *Ibid.,* pp. 38–39. The publications are available in the State Library under the title "Collected Papers by the Medical Staff of the New Jersey State Hospital, Trenton," Volume 1, 1907–1911; Volume 2, 1912–1913, with a third volume, 1919–1931.

[40] Donald Rice, interview, April 15, 1961; Dr. Harold Magee, interview, March 10, 1961.

[41] Billington, pp. 38–43.

[42] Trenton State Hospital, *Annual Report,* 1916, p. 13.

[43] Richard H. Shryock, *The National Tuberculosis Association, 1904–1954: A Study of the Voluntary Health Movement in the United States* (New York: National Tuberculosis Association, 1957), pp. 25–28.

[44] *Ibid.,* pp. 49–57.

[45] *Ibid.,* pp. 76, 123–124; NJRCC, April 1906, pp. 131, 140.

[46] NJRCC, May 1902, p. 108; *Manual of the Legislature of New Jersey,* 1918, p. 102; *Acts,* 1902, p. 395.

[47] NJRCC, March 1904, p. 40; DCC, *Annual Report,* 1906, p. 22.

[48] NJRCC, April 1906, pp. 131–132, 140.

[49] *Acts,* 1907, p. 421.

[50] State Tuberculosis Commission, "Report," *Senate Journal,* 1910, pp. 138–140; DCC, *Annual Report,* 1913, pp. 13–14.

[51] *Acts,* 1910, p. 129; 1912, pp. 348–349; SCAA, *Twenty-sixth Annual Report,* 1911, p. 9.

[52] SCAA, *Twenty-ninth Annual Report,* 1914, pp. 17–19.

[53] *Acts,* 1911, p. 201; 1913, p. 22; SCAA, *Twenty-sixth Annual Report,* 1911, p. 9; *Twenty-seventh Annual Report,* 1912, p. 6.

[54] New Jersey. Commission to Investigate State Charitable Institutions, 1917, *Report* (ms., Trenton State Library), pp. 6, 8.

[55] SCAA, *Twenty-ninth Annual Report,* 1914, p. 13; Dayton D. McKean, *The Boss: The Hague Machine in Action* (New York: Houghton Mifflin, 1940), pp. 166–171.

[56] SCAA, *Twenty-ninth Annual Report,* 1914, pp. 29–30; 1916, pp. 27–29, 37, 46.

[57] NJRCC, March–April 1903, pp. 51–52; SCAA, *Twenty-sixth Annual Report,* 1911, p. 9.

NOTES FOR CHAPTER 8

[1] New Jersey Prison Inquiry Commission, *Report . . . January 1, 1918* (Trenton: n.p., 1917), I, 11.

[2] Quoted, E[noch]. C. Wines and T[heodore]. W. Dwight, *Report on Prisons and Reformatories of the United States and Canada . . .* (Albany, N. Y.: Van Benthuysen and Sons, 1867), pp. 314–315.

[3] *Report of the Commissioners to Examine the Various Systems of Prison Discipline and Propose an Improved Plan . . . , Leg. Docs.,* 1869, reprinted in N. J. Prison Inquiry Commission, *Report,* Vol. II, *A History of the Penal, Reformatory, and Correctional Institutions of the State of New Jersey, Analytical and Documentary,* by Harry E. Barnes (Trenton, N. J.: MacCrellish and Quigley, 1917), p. 534. (Volume I comments on jails on pp. 25–28 and makes an extensive statistical analysis of their prisoners for the years 1912–1917.)

[4] Prison Inquiry Commission, pp. 26–27.

[5] NJRCC, July–August 1902, pp. 136–137; December 1902, pp. 208–209; March–April 1903, pp. 50–51.

[6] Quoted in Barnes, pp. 521, 522.

[7] *Ibid.*, pp. 158, 517, 518, 531.

[8] *Ibid.*, pp. 522, 523, 531.

[9] *Ibid.*, pp. 519–520.

[10] *Ibid.*, pp. 150–151; William E. Sackett, *Modern Battles of Trenton . . .* (2 vols.; Trenton: John L. Murphy, Printer, 1895, and New York: Neale Publishing Co., 1914), I, pp. 157–158.

[11] Quoted in Barnes, pp. 553, 525.

[12] On the general issue, see Blake McKelvey, *American Prisons: A Study in American Social History Prior to 1915* (Chicago: University of Chicago Press, 1936), pp. 94–96.

[13] *Report of the Commission on Prison Labor of the State of New Jersey, Leg. Docs.*, 1880, reprinted in Barnes, pp. 498, 500.

[14] *Ibid.*, pp. 500–501.

[15] *Acts*, 1881, p. 230; *Report of the Special Committee of the General Assembly of 1883 on Contract Prison Labor, Leg. Docs.*, 1884, Doc. No. 39; McKelvey, pp. 94–96.

[16] *Acts*, 1884, pp. 21, 230; Barnes, pp. 146–148.

[17] NJRCC, June 1902, p. 94; October 1904, pp. 211–212.

[18] Quoted, Barnes, pp. 526–527.

[19] Barnes, pp. 526–527, 152–153, 507–508.

[20] *Ibid.*, pp. 169–170.

[21] Prison Inquiry Commission, pp. 60–62.

[22] *Ibid.*, pp. 62–65, 73.

[23] Barnes, pp. 531–532.

[24] *Ibid.*, pp. 532–533.

[25] *Ibid.*, pp. 533, 535–537; McKelvey, pp. 60–61.

[26] Barnes, p. 533.

[27] *Report of the Commissioners on the Prison System of New Jersey, and on an Intermediate Prison*, 1878, reprinted in Barnes, pp. 600, 602, 606–608.

[28] Barnes, pp. 154, 194. The early support for a reformatory for women came from Quaker groups and the Women's Christian Temperance Union (WCTU): *Senate Journal*, 1887, pp. 713–714.

[29] Report of the Commissioners on a State Reformatory, *Assembly Journal*, 1890, pp. 783–791, reprinted in Barnes, pp. 612–618.

[30] Barnes, pp. 287–289; NJRCC, May 1904, pp. 86–87; April 1905, p. 103.

[31] Barnes, pp. 290–294.

[32] New Jersey State Reformatory at Rahway, *Annual Report*, 1916, pp. 13–14.

[33] Prison Inquiry Commission, pp. 47, 49–50.

[34] Barnes, p. 306; NJRCC, June–July 1903, p. 118; May 1911, p. 6.

[35] NJRCC, September–October 1902, p. 156.

[36] *Report of the Women's Reformatory Commission*, 1904, *Leg. Docs.*, 1904, No. 57, reprinted in Barnes, pp. 628–631.

[37] New Jersey State Reformatory for Women, *Annual Report*, 1914, pp. 8–9.

[38] *Ibid., Annual Report*, 1916, p. 4.

[39] SCAA, *Thirtieth Annual Report*, 1915, pp. 26–28.

[40] *Loc. cit.;* N. J. State Reformatory for Women, *Annual Report,* 1914, p. 5; 1916, pp. 3–4.

[41] Prison Inquiry Commission, pp. 51–53.

[42] *Ibid.,* pp. 55, 130–135.

[43] *Ibid.,* p. 131; Barnes, pp. 221, 223.

[44] Prison Inquiry Commission, p. 134.

[45] *Ibid.,* pp. 160–161; Barnes, p. 223.

[46] Prison Inquiry Commission, pp. 57–58, 84–85, 137–138.

[47] Barnes, pp. 187, 198, 549.

[48] *Ibid.,* pp. 190–192.

[49] *Report of the Dependency and Crimes Commission,* 1908, pp. 16–17.

[50] Prison Inquiry Commission, p. 73.

[51] *Newark News,* November 18, 1916, p. 6; Barnes, pp. 187–189.

[52] *New York Times,* January 13, 1917, p. 15; *American Labor Yearbook,* 1916 (New York: Rand School of Social Science, 1917), pp. 46–47.

[53] Caroline Bayard Colgate, *Off the Straight and Narrow* (New York: Lee Furman, Inc., 1937), pp. 96–100.

[54] *Newark News,* January 29, 1917, p. 1.

[55] Prison Inquiry Commission, pp. 81–85, 92.

[56] *Newark News,* June 13, 1917, p. 9; Nelson Gaskill to George Kirchwey, September 24, 1917, copy in papers of Dwight W. Morrow, Amherst College Library.

[57] Prison Inquiry Commission, pp. 3–5; *Newark News,* June 27, 1917, p. 1; July 23, 1917, p. 1; September 10, 1917, p. 1.

[58] *Newark News,* July 18, 1917, p. 1; William Dickson to Governor Walter Edge, June 27, 1917, July 17, 1917, copies in Morrow papers.

[59] William Dickson to Commissioner, n.d. [ca. January 24, 1917] Morrow papers.

[60] Morrow to Dickson, January 30, 1917, Morrow papers.

[61] J. A. H. Hopkins to Morrow, August 14, 1917; Morrow to Hopkins, August 23, 1917; Hopkins to Morrow, September 4, 1917, Morrow papers.

[62] *Newark News,* July 19, 1917, p. 10.

[63] George Kirchwey to Morrow, July 30, 1917, and August 22, 1917 (two letters), Morrow papers.

[64] Prison Inquiry Commission, pp. 8–9.

[65] Morrow to Governor Walter E. Edge, September 14, 1917.

[66] Morrow to Kirchwey, November 26, 1917; parts of the report were published under Kirchwey's name in the *Journal of Criminal Law and Criminology,* IX (August 1918), 207–239.

[67] Prison Inquiry Commission, pp. 19–20, 72–77.

[68] *Ibid.,* pp. 72, 77.

[69] *Ibid.* pp. 65–67.

[70] *Ibid.,* pp. 31–32, 53–54, 56; Barnes, p. 233.

[71] Barnes, pp. 233–234; Prison Inquiry Commission, pp. 13, 19, 69.

[72] Prison Inquiry Commission, p. 19; Barnes, p. 558.

[73] Quoted, Barnes, pp. 523, 525.

[74] Quoted, *Newark News,* June 13, 1917, p. 9.

[75] Barnes, pp. 231, 159.

[76] Charlton Lewis, "False Sentiment the Bane of Penal Law," NJRCC, November 1903, pp. 173–179. This address was given before the National Prison Congress at Louisville in 1903; the "false sentiment" is the passion for retribution through penal law.

[77] Colgate, p. 100.

NOTES FOR CHAPTER 9

[1] "Charity Organization in New Jersey," NJRCC, February 1902, pp. 15–16.

[2] David M. Schneider and Albert Deutsch, *The History of Public Welfare in New York State, 1867–1940* (Chicago: University of Chicago Press, 1941), pp. 20–22; New Jersey Bureau of Labor Statistics, *Annual Report,* 1883, pp. 411–412; SCAA, *Twenty-eighth Annual Report,* 1913, pp. 16–17; *Child Welfare in New Jersey. Part I* (U. S. Children's Bureau, Pub. No. 174, Washington, 1927), pp. 8–9.

[3] Robert W. Kelso, *The History of Public Poor Relief in Massachusetts, 1620–1920* (Boston and New York: Houghton Mifflin Co., 1922), pp. 143–152; Schneider and Deutsch, pp. 14–15, 18–19. On the general development, see Sophonisba P. Breckinridge, *Public Welfare Administration in the United States: Select Documents* (Second edition; Chicago: University of Chicago Press, 1938), pp. 237–243; and Frank J. Bruno, with chapters by Louis Towley, *Trends in Social Work, 1874–1956 . . .* (New York: Columbia University Press, 1957), pp. 31–43.

[4] State Sanitary Commission, *Report,* 1866; State Health Commission, *Report,* 1874; New Jersey State Board of Health, *Annual Report,* 1882, pp. 117, 120.

[5] Reprinted in New Jersey Prison Inquiry Commission, *Report,* Vol. II, *A History of the Penal, Reformatory and Correctional Institutions of the State of New Jersey, Analytical and Documentary,* by Harry E. Barnes (Trenton: MacCrellish and Quigley, 1917), pp. 610–611.

[6] *Report of the Delegate to the National Conference of Charities and Corrections . . . 1881, Leg. Docs.,* 1882, Vol. I, Doc. No. 24; *Report of . . . Delegates to the National Conference of Charities and Corrections . . . 1882, Leg. Docs.,* 1883, Vol. III, Doc. No. 28.

[7] *Acts,* 1883, p. 249.

[8] New Jersey State Council of Charities and Corrections, *Annual Report,* 1886, pp. 3–4, 10–11, 13–15. Governors continued to appoint members to the moribund council, however, until it was abolished in 1896 (*Acts,* 1896, p. 179).

[9] *Acts,* 1886, p. 231; SCAA, *Seventh Annual Report,* 1892, pp. 11–12.

[10] *New York Times,* January 14, 1900, p. 13.

[11] SCAA *Seventh Annual Report,* 1892, p. 12.

[12] NJRCC, January 1911, pp. 19–21.

[13] On Leon Abbett see *Dictionary of American Biography* (20 vols.; New York: Scribner, 1928–1937), I, 223–224; *National Cyclopedia of American Biography* (42 vols.; New York: James White, 1892–), I, 458–459; William E.

Sackett, *Modern Battles of Trenton . . .* (2 vols.; Trenton: John L. Murphy, Printer, 1895, and New York: Neale Publishing Co., 1914), I, 223–224.

[14] Sackett, pp. 224, 114–115.

[15] *Ibid.*, pp. 124–127, 144–145, 224–225, 231–232.

[16] *Ibid.*, pp. 82–85, 288, 383–384.

[17] *Ibid.*, pp. 218, 220.

[18] *Ibid.*, pp. 210, 264, 267, 282, 356–357.

[19] *Ibid.*, pp. 357–365, 80–82. The reorganization of the asylums was authorized by *Acts*, 1891, p. 168; Abbett discusses it in his *Second Annual Message* (n.p., 1892), January 12, 1892, pp. 31–32.

[20] Sackett, p. 368.

[21] *Ibid.*, pp. 383, 388, 395.

[22] *Acts*, 1897, p. 447.

[23] F[rederick]. W. Ricord, ed., *History of Union County, New Jersey* (Newark: East Jersey History Co., 1897), pp. 297–298; *Elizabeth* [N. J.] *Daily Journal*, July 13, 1909, p. 10; *Proceedings of the New Jersey Historical Society*, N.S. I (1916), 104.

[24] Elizabeth Delaney, "Poor Relief in Elizabeth, New Jersey . . ." (M.A. thesis, Rutgers University, 1937), pp. 162–172.

[25] Ricord, pp. 297–298.

[26] SCAA, *Seventh Annual Report*, 1892, p. 12.

[27] Ricord, p. 298; *Elizabeth Daily Journal*, July 13, 1909, p. 10.

[28] NJRCC, February 1902, p. 15; March–April 1903, p. 30; November 1905, p. 242.

[29] NJRCC, March 1902, p. 26.

[30] NJRCC, March 1905, pp. 55–57.

[31] E.g., NJRCC, February 1902, p. 15; May 1903, p. 90; February 1906, pp. 71, 73; November 1905, p. 242.

[32] NJRCC, April 1911, p. 28.

[33] Charles Hirschfeld, *Baltimore, 1870–1900: Studies in Social History* (Baltimore: Johns Hopkins Press, 1941), pp. 138–139, 144, 159–160; "Scott, Austin," *Dictionary of American Biography*, XVI, pp. 486–487.

[34] "Charlton Lewis," *National Cyclopedia of American Biography*, XXXVIII, 549–550; NJRCC, June 1904, pp. 97–98.

[35] Barnes, pp. 616–617, 173–174, 285; Charlton Lewis, "The Indeterminate Sentence," SCAA, *Thirteenth* [i.e., Fourteenth] *Annual Report*, 1899, pp. 17–32; Charlton Lewis, "False Sentiment the Bane of Penal Law," NJRCC, November 1903, pp. 173–179.

[36] *New York Times*, January 14, 1900, p. 13.

[37] NJRCC, November 1904, pp. 160–161; February 1905, p. 22; *New York Times*, June 29, 1901, p. 9.

[38] NJRCC, December 1903, pp. 206–207.

[39] NJRCC, April 1904, pp. 63–64.

[40] Governor Foster Voorhees, Annual Message, *Manual of the Legislature of New Jersey . . . 1900* (Trenton: T. F. Fitzgerald, n.d.), p. 455; *New York Times*, January 14, 1900, p. 13, June 29, 1901, p. 9.

[41] NJRCC, May 1903, p. 85.

[42] Schneider and Deutsch, pp. 138–139.

[43] SCAA, *Eighteenth Annual Report,* 1903, pp. 13–14; NJRCC, May 1903, pp. 74, 93; May 1904, pp. 84–85.

[44] Charlton Lewis, "The Need and Best Methods of State Supervision of Charities and Corrections," New Jersey Conference of Charities and Correction, *Proceedings,* 1903, pp. 57–68, also in NJRCC, March–April 1903, pp. 31–38.

[45] NJRCC, March–April 1903, pp. 32–33.

[46] *Ibid.,* pp. 34–35.

[47] *Ibid.,* p. 34.

[48] *Ibid.,* pp. 35–37.

[49] NJRCC, January 1904, pp. 241–242.

[50] NJRCC, April 1904, p. 66; May 1904, p. 85.

[51] NJRCC, January 1905, pp. 194–195.

NOTES FOR CHAPTER 10

[1] *Acts,* 1905, p. 92.

[2] NJRCC, May 1905, p. 131; February 1906, pp. 60–63; Methodist Episcopal Church, Conference, New Jersey, *Yearbook and Minutes, 81st Session* (Philadelphia, 1917), p. 138.

[3] NJRCC, May 1905, p. 131.

[4] NJRCC, January 1906, p. 23.

[5] DCC, *Annual Report,* 1908, pp. 4–5, 10–12.

[6] DCC, *Annual Report,* 1910, p. 5.

[7] DCC, *Annual Report,* 1909, p. 13.

[8] DCC, *Annual Report,* 1907, p. 24.

[9] *The Training School* [Bulletin], VI (1909): 172–173.

[10] *Acts,* 1908, p. 209; NJRCC, May 1908, p. 158; William E. Sackett, *Modern Battles of Trenton . . .* (2 vols., Trenton: John L. Murphy, Printer, 1895, and New York: Neale Publishing Co., 1914), II, 280.

[11] Sackett, II, 277–281; NJRCC, December 1908, p. 310; [N. J.] Commission to Investigate the Causes of Dependency and Criminality, *Report* (Trenton, 1909), pp. 3–6.

[12] SCAA, *Twenty-third Annual Report,* 1908, pp. 8–10.

[13] NJRCC, December 1908, p. 296; April 1909, pp. 462–463; May 1909, p. 487.

[14] NJRCC, May 1904, pp. 84–85.

[15] *Elizabeth* [N. J.] *Daily Journal,* July 14, 1909, p. 1, July 15, 1909, p. 1.

[16] SCAA, *Twenty-fifth Annual Report,* 1910–1911, p. 5.

[17] NJRCC, January 1911, pp. 2, 3, 6.

[18] E. R. Johnstone to Alexander Johnson, June 18, 1915, in possession of Mr. Edward L. Johnstone, Fort Lauderdale, Florida.

[19] NJRCC, April 1911, pp. 11–12.

[20] NJRCC, August–September 1911, pp. 16–19.

[21] J. J. Scannell, ed., *Scannell's New Jersey's First Citizens and State Guide,* V (1925), 732.

[22] *Ibid.; Jersey Journal* [Jersey City], December 5, 1932, p. 8; letter from Archibald Alexander (first husband) to the editor of the *New York Times,* February 14, 1915, Sec. III, p. 2; interview with Archibald Stevens Alexander (grandson), August 16, 1961.

[23] *Jersey Journal,* August 31, 1912, pp. 1, 4.

[24] *New York Times,* January 27, 1913, pp. 1 and 2, gives an account of a meeting at Mrs. Alexander's home at which she brought together President-elect Wilson and leading social workers.

[25] *New York Times,* July 26, 1931, p. 18; July 29, 1931, p. 19.

[26] NJRCC, January 1911, p. 4.

[27] *Ibid.,* pp. 10–18.

[28] SCAA, *Twenty-fifth Annual Report,* 1910–1911, p. 5.

[29] Governor Woodrow Wilson, First Annual Message, January 9, 1912, *Senate Journal,* 1912, p. 16; Gustavus A. Weber, *Organized Efforts for the Improvement of Methods of Administration in the United States* (New York: D. Appleton and Co., 1919), pp. 84–86, 114–119.

[30] John M. Blum, *Joe Tumulty and the Wilson Era* (Boston: Houghton Mifflin, 1951), pp. 32–40.

[31] DCC, *Annual Report,* 1912, pp. 14–17; *ibid.,* 1913, pp. 4, 8–9, 11.

[32] DCC, *Annual Report,* 1912, pp. 6–12.

[33] *The Training School* [Bulletin], April 1908, p. 3.

[34] NJRCC, February 1911, pp. 1–3.

[35] N. J. Commission on the Care of Mental Defectives, "Report," *Assembly Journal,* 1914, pp. 394–411.

[36] DCC, *Annual Report,* 1912, pp. 6–7; SCAA, *Twenty-ninth Annual Report,* 1914, pp. 4–7.

[37] DCC, *Annual Report,* 1913, pp. 13–14.

[38] Governor James Fielder, Inaugural Address, January 20, 1914, *Senate Journal,* 1914, pp. 36–38.

[39] *Manual of the Legislature of New Jersey,* 1916 (Trenton: Thomas F. Fitzgerald, n.d.), p. 394.

[40] DCC, *Annual Report,* 1915, p. 3.

[41] SCAA, *Thirtieth Annual Report,* 1915, p. 4.

[42] Governor James Fielder, First Annual Message, January 12, 1915, *Manual of the Legislature of New Jersey,* 1915 (Trenton: Thomas F. Fitzgerald, n.d.), p. 637.

[43] N. J. Economy and Efficiency Commission, *Second Report* (Trenton: MacCrellish, 1914).

[44] Governor James F. Fielder, Second Annual Message, January 11, 1916, *Manual of the Legislature of New Jersey,* 1916 (Trenton: Thomas F. Fitzgerald, n.d.), pp. 600–602.

[45] Governor Walter E. Edge, Inaugural Address, *Senate Journal,* 1917, pp. 34–36; Walter E. Edge, *Jerseyman's Journal* (Princeton: Princeton University Press, 1948), pp. 27–28, 89.

[46] *Senate Journal,* 1917, pp. 225–227.

[47] Dwight Morrow to Seymour Cromwell, October 30, 1917, Dwight Morrow papers, Amherst College Library.

[48] SCAA, *Thirty-second Annual Report,* 1917, p. 11.

[49] Governor Walter E. Edge, Inaugural Address, *Senate Journal,* 1917, pp. 48–50.

[50] Walter E. Edge to William Dickson, March 7, 1917, copy, Morrow papers.

[51] George Kirchwey to Dwight Morrow, July 30, 1917, and two letters dated August 22, 1917; Memorandum from Dwight Morrow to George Kirchwey, November 26, 1917, Morrow papers. A large section of the report appeared under Kirchwey's name in the *Journal of Criminal Law and Criminology,* IX (August 1918), 207–239.

[52] [N. J.] Prison Inquiry Commission, *Report,* Vol. I (Trenton: n.p., 1917), pp. 74–75.

[53] Walter E. Edge to Dwight Morrow, October 15, 1917, Morrow papers.

[54] Edge to Morrow, November 14 and 28, 1917.

[55] Edge to Morrow, November 28, 1917; Walter Edge to Ellis P. Earle, December 3, 1917, copy, Morrow papers.

[56] Prison Inquiry Commission, pp. 20, 43–44, 67, 71.

[57] N. J. Commission to Investigate State Charitable Institutions, 1918, *Report* (ms., New Jersey State Library), pp. 11–12; Prison Inquiry Commission, pp. 65–70.

[58] Dwight Morrow to Ellis P. Earle, February 6, 1918; Morrow to F. J. Faulks, October 6, 1917; Morrow to Harry E. Barnes, January 18, 1918, Morrow papers. The organic law of the department is chapter 147, Acts of 1918; the vote is in *Assembly Journal,* 1918, pp. 600–601, and *Senate Journal,* 1918, pp. 427–428.

[59] Prison Inquiry Commission, p. 67.

[60] *The Survey,* March 2, 1918, pp. 590–594; March 16, 1918, p. 658; July 13, 1918, p. 434.

[61] George Kirchwey to Dwight Morrow, September 22, 1917, Morrow papers.

[62] N. J. Commission to Investigate State Charitable Institutions, pp. 5–9.

[63] Prison Inquiry Commission, pp. 77, 69.

NOTES FOR CHAPTER 11

[1] *Newark Evening News,* February 19, 1918, p. 17.

[2] Geraldine Thompson to Dwight Morrow, March 16, 1918; Morrow to Thompson, April 16, 1918; Dwight Morrow to Decatur Sawyer, July 10, 1918; Dwight Morrow papers, Amherst College Library.

[3] Geraldine Thompson to Dwight Morrow, May 6, 1919, Morrow papers.

[4] *Newark Evening News,* December 16, 1920, p. 15.

[5] *Manual of the Legislature of New Jersey,* 1922, p. 426; *Manual of the Legislature of New Jersey,* 1925, p. 423.

[6] *Newark Evening News,* May 8, 1918, p. 9.

[7] "Burdette Gibson Lewis," *National Cyclopedia of American Biography* (42 vols.; New York: James White, 1892–), Current Vol. E, 256–257; "Record of Training and Experience of Burdette G. Lewis," mimeographed, Burdette G. Lewis papers, New Jersey State Library, Trenton; Burdette Lewis, ms. *Autobiography,* "The Truth Shall Make You Free," pp. 2–3, "The Human Side

of War Nitrates," pp. 2, 8–9, Lewis papers; A. H. Springer to Ogden H. Hammond, May 1, 1918, Morrow papers; Edward R. Cass to author, December 30, 1958.

[8] *Newark Evening News,* May 8, 1918, p. 9.

[9] Geraldine Thompson to Dwight Morrow, May 23, 1918; Dwight Morrow to Governor Walter E. Edge, July 12, 1918, Morrow papers.

[10] New Jersey Prison Inquiry Commission, *Report* (Trenton: n.p., 1917), I, 69.

[11] Burdette Lewis to Seymour Cromwell, September 5, 1918, copy, Morrow papers.

[12] *Ibid.;* Lewis, "The Truth Shall Make You Free," pp. 3–7, Lewis papers; B. G. Lewis, "The Single Department Plan," National Conference of Social Work, *Proceedings,* 1924, pp. 565–566.

[13] Burdette Lewis to Dwight Morrow, July 30, 1920, and August 4, 1920, Morrow papers; Lewis, "The Truth Shall Make You Free," pp. 6–7, Lewis papers.

[14] Burdette Lewis to Dwight Morrow, March 28, 1919, and November 29, 1919, Morrow papers.

[15] Lewis, "The Truth Shall Make You Free," pp. 7–10, Lewis papers; *Newark Evening News,* editorial, December 19, 1925, p. 11.

[16] Burdette Lewis to Caroline Wittpenn, August 30, 1919, copy, Morrow papers.

[17] Louis Blan to Burdette Lewis, March 13, 1920, copy, Morrow papers.

[18] Burdette Lewis to Dwight Morrow, October 3, 1919, October 28, 1919, and November 1, 1919, Morrow papers; *Trenton Times,* October 28, 1919, p. 1.

[19] Dwight Morrow to Geraldine Thompson, September 6, 1919, Morrow papers.

[20] Dwight Morrow to Burdette Lewis, October 4, 1919, Morrow papers.

[21] Dwight Morrow to Burdette Lewis, October 29, 1919, Morrow papers.

[22] Dwight Morrow to Burdette Lewis, October 30, 1919, Morrow papers.

[23] *Newark Evening News,* January 6, 1920, p. 15.

[24] Dwight Morrow to W. Irving Glover, January 13, 1920; W. Irving Glover to Dwight Morrow, January 14, 1920; Ogden H. Hammond to Dwight Morrow. January 20, 1920, Morrow papers.

[25] Governor Edward Edwards, Special Message, *Senate Journal,* 1920, p. 397; *Assembly Journal,* 1920, Assembly Bills No. 331 and 401.

[26] "Four Year Summary," *The Quarterly* (NJDIA), April 1923, pp. 17–18; Herbert R. Sands, "Administrative Code, Department of Institutions and Agencies, 1918," typescript, New Jersey State Library, Trenton.

[27] Mary B. Harris, *I Knew Them in Prison* (New York: Viking Press, 1936), pp. 74–76, 190.

[28] Calvin Derrick, "A Report on the Present Parole and School System and Classification System, August 5, 1918," copy, Morrow papers.

[29] *The Training School Bulletin* (Vineland Training School), September 1921, pp. 66–67, and December 1922, p. 118.

[30] On classification, see "Four Year Summary," *The Quarterly,* April 1923, p. 29; New Jersey State Prison, *Report,* 1919, pp. 7, 55; B. G. Lewis, "The

Employment of Prisoners in New Jersey," *The Quarterly,* October 1922, pp. 1–2.

[31] New Jersey State Prison, *Biennial Report,* 1920–1921, pp. 95–100; Edgar A. Doll, "Study of the Individual as a Basis for Institutional Treatment," *The Quarterly,* October 1922, pp. 10–11.

[32] "Organization Survey," *The Quarterly,* July 1923, pp. 21, 24; Maxwell Rockhill, "Why the Bureau of Domestic Relations is . . . Associated with the Bureau of Parole," *The Quarterly,* October 1922, p. 3.

[33] "Organization Survey," *The Quarterly,* July 1923, pp. 13–14.

[34] *Ibid.,* p. 12.

[35] *Ibid.,* p. 13.

[36] *Ibid.,* pp. 11–13.

[37] [N. J.] Joint Legislative Survey Committee, *Reports . . . Trenton, December 9, 1925* (Trenton: MacCrellish, 1925), p. 312.

[38] [National Institute of Public Administration], *Report on a Survey of the Organization and Administration of the State Government of New Jersey . . . Trenton, 1930* (Trenton: MacCrellish, 1930), pp. 169, 164.

[39] *Ibid.,* p. 164; Joint Legislative Survey Committee, p. 312.

[40] Geraldine Thompson to Dwight Morrow, May 23, 1918, Morrow papers.

[41] *Newark Evening News,* October 10, 1919, p. 6.

[42] *Newark Evening News,* January 20, 1919, p. 17, and January 22, 1919, p. 8; "Four Year Summary," *The Quarterly,* April 1923, p. 18; *Newark Evening News,* February 7, 1925, p. 7; National Institute of Public Administration, p. 166.

[43] "Organization Survey," *The Quarterly,* July 1923, pp. 56–57; Joint Legislative Survey Committee, p. 313; National Institute of Public Administration, pp. 194–196.

[44] Burdette Lewis, ms. autobiography, "The Road to Mental Health," pp. 1–2, Lewis papers.

[45] *Ibid.;* Statement of Mrs. Francis Van Dyke, a social worker at Trenton State Hospital, to A. H. Springer, secretary to Dwight Morrow, "Memorandum," June 18, 1919, and letter from Dwight Morrow to Mrs. Francis Van Dyke, July 15, 1919, Morrow papers.

[46] Lewis, "The Road to Mental Health," pp. 1–2.

[47] Burdette Lewis, "The Winning Fight Against Mental Disease," *American Review of Reviews,* April 1922, pp. 411, 416, 418; Henry A. Cotton, *The Defective, Delinquent and Insane: The Relation of Focal Infections to Their Causation, Treatment, and Prevention* (Princeton: Princeton University Press, 1921), pp. 111–122.

[48] Mrs. Agnes Trier, interview, July 21, 1959.

[49] Burdette Lewis, "Log," December 21, 1922, Lewis papers.

[50] Geraldine Thompson to Dwight Morrow, June 10, 1919, Morrow papers.

[51] Geraldine Thompson to Dwight Morrow, June 10, 1919; Dwight Morrow to Ellis P. Earle, June 14, 1919; Burdette Lewis to Frank Moore, March 22, 1919 (copy); Burdette Lewis to Dwight Morrow, March 22 and July 17, 1919; Edward D. Duffield to Burdette Lewis, July 23, 1919 (copy), Morrow papers.

[52] *Newark Evening News,* January 20, 1930, p. 1; January 22, 1930, p. 4.

[53] Burdette Lewis to Dwight Morrow, July 11, 1919, and appended "Opinion of the Attorney General," Morrow papers.

[54] *Newark Evening News,* January 29, 1917, p. 2.

[55] *Manual of the Legislature,* 1922, p. 381.

[56] *Newark Evening News,* August 22, 1922, p. 2, and August 23, 1922, p. 1.

[57] *Newark Evening News,* October 30, 1922, p. 1.

[58] *Ibid.; Newark Evening News,* June 22, 1923, p. 1.

[59] Letter from "A prison employee of five years" to the editor, *Newark Evening News,* June 22, 1923, p. 13.

[60] *Newark Evening News,* June 22, 1923, p. 13; Burdette Lewis, ms. autobiography, "Planning Progress," pp. 2-F, 2-G, Lewis papers.

[61] *Newark Evening News,* June 23, 1923, p. 2, also editorial, p. 9.

[62] *New York Times,* July 31, 1923, p. 17.

[63] Harris, p. 109.

[64] Burdette Lewis, "The Truth Shall Make You Free," p. 5.

[65] Burdette Lewis, "Governmental Cooperation Without Control," *The Quarterly,* January 1923, p. 7; "Four Year Summary," *The Quarterly,* April 1923, pp. 7–14; Burdette Lewis, "Environment, Heredity, and Individualism," *The Quarterly,* October 1924, pp. 11–16.

[66] Burdette Lewis, "Address before Family Social Workers, Sept. 19, 1921, at YWCA, Newark," Lewis papers; Burdette Lewis to Dwight Morrow, December 17, 1919, and September 21, 1921, Morrow papers.

[67] Burdette Lewis, "Planning Progress," pp. 6–7.

[68] Amos Tilton, "Constitutional Limitations on the Creation of State Debt," *New Jersey Constitutional Convention of 1947* (5 vols.; Trenton, 1949–1953), II, 1712–14.

[69] *Newark Evening News,* September 29 and 30, 1921, clippings, Lewis papers.

[70] *Newark Evening News,* September 16, 1921, editorial, clipping, Lewis papers.

[71] Lewis's "Log" for 1921 shows in detail how he directed the program and his papers include records of the drive; an "Agenda for conference on educational campaign" and a letter from Burdette Lewis to A. L. Bowen, February 2, 1922, in the Lewis papers, are particularly revealing.

[72] *Trenton Evening Times,* September 13, 1921, clipping, Lewis papers.

[73] *Newark Evening News,* November 8, 1921, p. 1.

[74] *Manual of the Legislature,* 1921, p. 530; *Manual of the Legislature,* 1922, p. 508.

[75] *Newark Evening News,* March 23, 1920, p. 14, and October 21, 1921, p. 7.

[76] Burdette Lewis to A. L. Bowen, February 2, 1922, Lewis papers.

[77] *Newark Evening News,* editorial, October 26, 1921, clipping, Lewis papers.

[78] *Newark Evening News,* November 9, 1921, p. 8

[79] Tilton, p. 1714.

[80] Caroline Wittpenn to Burdette Lewis, undated [October 2, 1921], Lewis papers.

[81] Lewis, "Address before Family Social Workers," Lewis papers.

[82] *Newark Evening News,* editorial, November 9, 1921, p. 8.

[83] Governor Edward I. Edwards, Second Annual Message, *Senate Journal,* 1922, pp. 14–17.

[84] Governor George S. Silzer, Inaugural Address, *Senate Journal,* 1923, pp. 63, 76.

[85] Governor George S. Silzer, First Annual Message, *Manual of the Legislature,* 1924, pp. 570–571.

[86] *Newark Evening News,* February 28, 1923, p. 8; George S. Silzer, Second Annual Message, *Assembly Journal,* 1925, pp. 25–27.

[87] *Newark Evening News,* November 16, 1923, p. 14; December 23, 1923, p. 1.

[88] *Newark Evening News,* March 3, 1923, p. 3; May 15, 1923, p. 8; May 16, 1923, p. 1; November 2, 1923, p. X-6.

[89] *Newark Evening News,* September 10, 1923, p. 9.

[90] *Newark Evening News,* December 1, 1923, p. 19; January 5, 1924, p. 19.

[91] *Newark Evening News,* January 21, 1924, p. 4.

[92] *Newark Evening News,* December 13, 1923, p. 16; February 12, 1924, p. 4; February 13, 1924, p. 20.

[93] *Newark Evening News,* February 23, 1924, p. 1.

[94] *Ibid.;* February 26, 1924, p. 4.

[95] *Newark Evening News,* February 26, 1924, p. 4; February 28, 1924, p. 4; March 1, 1924, p. 17.

[96] *Newark Evening News,* March 3, 1924, p. 1.

[97] *Newark Evening News,* March 4, 1924, p. 2.

[98] *Newark Evening News,* January 20, 1925, p. 5.

[99] *Newark Evening News,* March 16, 1925, p. 7.

[100] *Newark Evening News,* June 3, 1925, p. 2.

[101] *Newark Evening News,* December 29, 1922, p. 15.

[102] *Newark Evening News,* January 7, 1924, p. 9.

[103] *Newark Evening News,* February 10, 1925, p. 5.

[104] See, for example, *Newark Evening News,* March 23, 1920, p. 14; letter to the editor, November 7, 1921, p. 8; February 23, 1924, p. 1.

[105] Joint Legislative Survey Committee, p. 6.

[106] *Ibid.,* pp. 435–442; *Jersey Journal* [Jersey City], July 3, 1925, p. 1, and July 10, 1925, p. 4; *Newark Evening News,* July 23, 1925, p. 1. The "Organization Survey" in 1923 was by a firm of public accountants: see *The Quarterly,* July 1923.

[107] *Jersey Journal,* July 10, 1925, p. 6.

[108] *Newark Evening News,* May 27, 1925, p. 1.

[109] *Jersey Journal,* July 23, 1925, p. 15, and editorial, p. 21; July 30, 1925, p. 9.

[110] *Newark Evening News,* September 24, 1925, editorial, p. 13.

[111] Joint Legislative Survey Committee, pp. 435–442; *Newark Evening News,* November 30, 1925, p. 2.

[112] Dwight Morrow wrote a recommendation for Lewis only three days before he resigned: Dwight Morrow to Ralph Gwinn, December 16, 1925, Morrow papers.

[113] *Newark Evening News,* December 19, 1925, p. 1.

[114] *Newark Evening News,* December 21, 1925, p. 1.

[115] *Newark Evening News,* December 23, 1925, p. 4.

[116] *Newark Evening News,* January 26, 1926, p. 4.

[117] *Newark Evening News,* January 14, 1926, p. 1.

[118] *Newark Evening News,* February 26, 1926, p. 2; November 15, 1926, p. 1.

[119] *Newark Evening News,* December 19, 1925, editorial, p. 11; December 23, 1925, p. 4.

[120] *Newark Evening News,* February 24, 1926, p. 4.

NOTES FOR CHAPTER 12

[1] *Newark Evening News,* January 4, 1926, p. 6.

[2] *Newark Evening News,* February 24, 1926, p. 2.

[3] *Newark Evening News,* March 12, 1945, p. 22 (Ellis' obituary); "William John Ellis," *National Cyclopedia of American Biography* (42 vols.; New York: James White, 1892–), XXXIV, 105–106.

[4] Harry Elmer Barnes to author, July 26, 1958.

[5] *Welfare Reporter* (NJDIA), December 1946, p. 3; Mrs. Agnes Trier, interview, July 21, 1959.

[6] Interviews with Marc Dowdell, February 25, 1959; Douglas MacNeil, November 26, 1958; and Edward L. Johnstone, March 8, 1961.

[7] W. J. Ellis, "The New Jersey Plan," *Welfare Magazine* (Illinois Department of Public Welfare), January 1927, pp. 5–6.

[8] These were NJDIA, *Summary Report, 1923–1933, and Handbook* (Trenton: The Department, 1934), and NJDIA, *A Report, 1934–1943, and Handbook* (Trenton: The Department, 1944).

[9] Dayton D. McKean, *Pressures on the Legislature of New Jersey* (New York: Columbia University Press, 1938), pp. 32–33; Dayton D. McKean, *The Boss: The Hague Machine in Action* (Boston: Houghton Mifflin, 1940), pp. 55–57, 67–89; Walter E. Edge, *Jerseyman's Journal . . .* (Princeton: Princeton University Press, 1948), pp. 252–254.

[10] See above, ch. 11, note 11.

[11] *Newark Evening News,* January 28, 1926, p. 4; February 24, 1926, p. 4. Cf. Lewis' statement on the importance of the hospital, *Newark Evening News,* March 16, 1925, p. 7.

[12] *Newark Evening News,* April 2, 1926, p. 1.

[13] *Newark Evening News,* March 1, 1927, p. 4; March 22, 1927, p. 6.

[14] *Newark Evening News,* April 22, 1927, p. 11.

[15] *Newark Evening News,* April 9, 1930, p. 5; *Manual of the Legislature,* 1931, p. 564.

[16] N. J. State Budget Department, *New Jersey State Government Functions,* 1933, pp. 50–51; the figure was compiled from expenditures reported in *New Jersey State Government Functions,* 1939.

[17] [National Institute of Public Administration], *Report on a Survey of the Organization and Administration of the State Government of New Jersey* (Trenton: MacCrellish, 1930), pp. 7–9.

[18] *Ibid.,* p. 10.

[19] *Ibid.,* pp. 175–179.

[20] *Ibid.,* pp. 165–169.

[21] *Newark Evening News,* November 19, 1930, p. II-5.

[22] *Newark Evening News,* March 25, 1930, p. 4.

[23] *Newark Evening News,* January 13, 1930, p. 6.

[24] National Institute of Public Administration, pp. 192–193.

[25] *Assembly Journal,* 1932, pp. 830, 832.

[26] David M. Schneider and Albert Deutsch, *The History of Public Welfare in New York State, 1867–1940* (Chicago: University of Chicago Press, 1941), pp. 272–275.

[27] *Newark Evening News,* April 14, 1932, pp. 4, X-15; *Trenton Evening Times,* April 14, 1932, p. 1.

[28] Editorials, *Trenton State Gazette,* April 14, 1932; *Trenton Evening Times,* April 14, 1932; *Newark Evening News,* April 16, 1932: clippings in the files of the New Jersey Welfare Council, Newark, New Jersey, for 1932. The Welfare Council supported the Department.

[29] *Newark Evening News,* editorial, March 16, 1932, p. 10.

[30] *Newark Evening News,* December 17, 1931, p. 15.

[31] School of Public and International Affairs of Princeton University, *Report on a Survey of Administration and Expenditures of the State Government of New Jersey . . .* (n.p., 1932), pp. 4–5, 129–130, 148–150; hereafter referred to as *Princeton Survey.*

[32] Governor A. Harry Moore, Second Annual Message, *Senate Journal,* 1934, p. 19.

[33] On these developments, see below, Ch. 16.

[34] *Princeton Survey,* pp. 129–136; McKean, *Pressures on the Legislature of New Jersey,* pp. 142–143; Paul Tutt Stafford, *State Welfare Administration in New Jersey* (Dept. of Political Science, Princeton University [1934]), p. 46.

[35] Charles R. Erdman, Jr., *The New Jersey Constitution—a Barrier to Governmental Economy and Efficiency* (Princeton: Princeton University Press, 1934), pp. 3–6; Edge, pp. 258, 261; Julian P. Boyd, ed., *Fundamental Laws and Constitutions of New Jersey, 1664–1964* (Princeton: D. Van Nostrand, 1964), p. 37.

[36] *Newark Evening News,* February 18, 1943, p. 1.

[37] *Newark Evening News,* February 25, 1943, p. 2.

[38] See, for example, Governor Edge's statement in the *Newark Evening News,* March 12, 1945, pp. 8, 22.

[39] "Memorandum of meetings held by State Board . . . March 1918–August 1919," and letter from Dwight Morrow to Governor Walter Edge, February 4, 1919, papers of Dwight Morrow, Amherst College Library.

[40] Earle's obituary, *New York Times,* October 13, 1942, p. 23.

[41] Geraldine Thompson to Dwight Morrow, May 23, 1918, Morrow papers.

[42] *Newark Evening News,* December 18, 1923, p. 14.

[43] Mrs. Elizabeth Feehan, interview, November 24, 1958.

[44] Mrs. Agnes Trier, interview, July 21, 1959.

[45] *New York Times,* March 2, 1957, p. 22; *Welfare Reporter,* April 1957, p. 3.

[46] Interviews with Douglas MacNeil, August 28, 1958, and Elizabeth Feehan, November 24, 1958; *Welfare Reporter,* April 1957, pp. 3–4.

[47] Geraldine Thompson to Dwight Morrow, May 31, 1920, Morrow papers.

[48] *Newark Evening News,* June 14, 1933, p. 8, and April 27, 1934, p. 20. Mrs.

Thompson had irked Governor Moore by helping to frustrate his intention to remove her friend, Mrs. Caroline Wittpenn, from the State Board. Mrs. Wittpenn, a leading Democrat, had supported Moore's Republican opponent for governor, and when her term on the Board expired, Moore appointed someone else in her place. Mrs. Thompson worked to enlarge the Board to nine members so that the next Governor, Morgan F. Larson, a Republican, could add Mrs. Wittpenn to the Board again. Moore returned to office in 1932, in time to veto Mrs. Thompson's reappointment to the Board. *Newark Evening News,* January 10, 1933, p. 5.

[49] Interviews with Douglas MacNeil, August 28, 1958, and Agnes Trier, July 21, 1959; these were the staff members most directly involved with Board appointments. Appointments also occupy much of the record of Board meetings.

[50] Mary B. Harris, *I Knew Them in Prison* (New York: Viking Press, 1936), p. 237.

[51] *Welfare Reporter,* November 1954, p. 7 (Mr. Gerry's obituary); interviews with Cantwell Walsh, March 4, 1959; Eugene Urbaniak, August 2, 1961, and Sanford Bates, March 3, 1959.

[52] Obituaries of Dr. Potter are American Medical Association, *Journal,* CLVI (April 19, 1958), 2062; *New York Times,* February 10, 1958, p. 23; *Social Service Review,* XXXII (September 1958), 301–302; Emil Frankel, interview, February 18, 1959; Phyllis Morely, "Interpretation of Public Welfare Administration in the New Jersey Department of Institutions and Agencies" (M.A. thesis, School of Social Service Administration, University of Chicago, 1938), pp. 81, 86, 88.

[53] *Newark Evening News,* November 21, 1942, p. B-7, and February 25, 1943, p. 2; "Reeve Schley," *National Cyclopedia of American Biography,* XLV, 412–413.

[54] *Newark Evening News,* October 27, 1929, p. 2; Agnes Trier, interview, July 21, 1959.

[55] William J. Ellis, "Public Welfare in New Jersey," *The Story of New Jersey,* William S. Myers, ed. (5 vols.; New York: Lewis Historical Pub. Co., 1945), II, 84–85.

[56] *Ibid.,* pp. 81–83.

[57] *Ibid.,* pp. 42–44, 48–49, 85.

[58] Edward R. Cass to author, December 30, 1958.

[59] Morely, pp. 93, 98.

[60] *Ibid.,* pp. 84–88, 98.

NOTES FOR CHAPTER 13

[1] "Four Year Summary," *The Quarterly* (NJDIA), April 1923, p. 5.

[2] NJDIA, *Summary Report, 1923–1933, and Handbook* (Trenton: The Department, 1934), p. 1.

[3] New Jersey Commission to Investigate State Charitable Institutions, *Report,* 1918 (ms., New Jersey State Library, Trenton), pp. 1–2, 7–8; SCAA, *Thirty-first Annual Report,* 1916, pp. 12–16.

[4] Commission on the Care of Mental Defectives, "Report," *Assembly Journal,* 1914, pp. 397–399, 408–410; Burdette Lewis, "Presidential Address, State Conference of Social Welfare," *The Quarterly,* October 1924, pp. 12–13.

[5] *Newark Evening News,* October 20, 1919, p. 8.

[6] I have been unable to find a copy of the survey; all quotations in this paragraph are from W. J. Ellis, "What the Half-Mill Tax Has Accomplished to Date," *The Quarterly,* July 1927, n.p.

[7] Henry A. Cotton, *The Defective, Delinquent and Insane; The Relation of Focal Infections to Their Causation, Treatment, and Prevention* (Princeton: Princeton University Press, 1921), pp. 1, 14–17, 35; B. G. Lewis, "The Winning Fight Against Mental Illness," *American Review of Reviews,* April 1922, pp. 411–418.

[8] *The Quarterly,* April 1923, pp. 32–34.

[9] These letters and others cited below in this section are bound with the "Trenton State Hospital Survey—1924–1926. Made by Dr. Phylis [sic] Greenacre with the cooperation of Dr. Adolph Meyer . . . ," in the library of the Bureau of Social Research, NJDIA: Joseph Raycroft to Paul Mecray, March 11, 1924; Mecray to Raycroft, March 24, 1924.

[10] New Jersey State Board of Control, NJDIA, Minutes, July 23, 1924, p. 11 (in the State Board office).

[11] Dr. Phyllis Greenacre, interview, May 2, 1961.

[12] *Ibid.;* letter from Dr. Phyllis Greenacre to author, May 16, 1961.

[13] Dr. Phyllis Greenacre, interview, May 2, 1961.

[14] "Trenton State Hospital Survey—1924–1926," pp. 37, 24–25.

[15] Adolph Meyer to Joseph Raycroft, January 18, 1926; Raycroft to Meyer, January 28, 1926 and October 28, 1926, in "Trenton State Hospital Survey."

[16] Henry Cotton to Adolph Meyer, May 28, 1927; Adolph Meyer to Joseph Raycroft, June 4, 1927, "Trenton State Hospital Survey."

[17] *Summary Report 1923–1933,* p. 53.

[18] *Trenton Evening Times,* April 10, 1930, p. 1; *Newark Evening News,* June 28, 1930, p. 2.

[19] State Board of Control, Minutes, July 29, 1930, p. 12; September 16, 1930, p. 8.

[20] Division of Statistics and Research and Division of Medicine, "Study of 'end results' of 645 major operative cases and 407 non-operative cases treated at Trenton State Hospital 1918–1932, with comparisons of studies made by Dr. Greenacre and Dr. Cotton, November, 1932" (ms., Division of Social Research Library, NJDIA).

[21] W. J. Ellis, *Psychiatric Progress in New Jersey, 1844–1944* (Trenton: The Department, 1944), pp. 10–11.

[22] *Newark Evening News,* January 28, 1926, p. 4.

[23] *Summary Report 1923–1933,* p. 52.

[24] Paul T. Stafford, *State Welfare Administration in New Jersey* (Princeton University Department of Political Science, 1934), pp. 74–75, 93–96; NJDIA, *A Report 1934–1943 and Handbook,* pp. 31, 55–56.

[25] Elma Johnston, "New Jersey's Insane Receive New Deal," *Trenton Sunday Times-Advertiser,* August 27, 1933, III, 1–2.

[26] *Ibid.;* State Board of Control, Minutes, October 28, 1930, p. 5; February 27, 1931, p. 3; June 23, 1931, p. 9.

[27] Donald Rice, "The occupation of patients at the Trenton State Hospital has therapeutic and economic value, April 28, 1930" (ms., Trenton State Hospital); Donald Rice, interview, April 14, 1961.

[28] "Institutions and Universities as Co-operative Training Schools," *The Quarterly,* July–October 1925, pp. 7–31, 38–39.

[29] *Ibid.,* pp. 13–17.

[30] *Ibid.,* pp. 17, 34.

[31] *Ibid.,* pp. 19, 28, 15.

[32] *Ibid.,* p. 18

[33] *Ibid.,* p. 23

[34] *Ibid.,* p. 37.

[35] *Ibid.,* pp. 19, 31–32.

[36] *Ibid.,* p. 34.

[37] *Ibid.,* pp. 24, 36.

[38] Dr. George Stevenson, interview, April 22, 1961.

[39] Donald Rice, interview, April 14, 1961.

[40] Emil Frankel, *The Increase of Mental Disease in New Jersey* (NJDIA Pub. No. 13, Trenton, 1938), pp. 2–3.

[41] NJDIA, *Report 1934–1943,* pp. 47–49.

[42] Charlotte Billington, "The New Jersey State Hospital for the Insane at Trenton, 1908–1940" (M.A. thesis, School of Social Service Administration, University of Chicago, 1941), pp. 87–91.

[43] NJDIA, *Report 1934–1943,* pp. 50–52.

[44] W. J. Ellis, "The New Jersey Plan," *Welfare Magazine* (Illinois Department of Public Welfare), January 1927, pp. 5–6; W. J. Ellis, *The New Jersey Plan for the Control and Prevention of Mental Disease* (NJDIA Pub. No. 29, Trenton, 1935).

[45] Helen L. Witmer, *Psychiatric Clinics for Children, with Special Reference to State Programs* (New York: The Commonwealth Fund, 1940), pp. 43–44.

[46] Ellis, *Psychiatric Progress in New Jersey,* pp. 17–18.

[47] John N. Boyd, "The Development and Organization of State Mental Hygiene Service as Administered through Community Clinics in New Jersey" (M.A. thesis, School of Social Service Administration, University of Chicago, 1937), p. 25; George S. Stevenson, "New Jersey's Contributions to Psychiatric Progress," *Journal of the Medical Society of New Jersey,* L (September 1953), 413.

[48] Emil Frankel and Thomas B. Kidner, *The Care and Treatment of Nervous and Mental Patients in General Hospitals* (NJDIA Pub. No. 18, October 1929), pp. 3–4; *Newark Evening News,* November 29, 1929, p. 26.

[49] Ellis, *Psychiatric Progress in New Jersey,* p. 18; Mildred Hurley, interview, June 5, 1961.

[50] Frankel and Kidner, pp. 3–4.

[51] W. J. Ellis, "State Policy of Cooperating in the Development of Psychiatric Facilities in Local General Hospitals," *Hospital Social Service,* XXII (1930), 297, 301.

[52] Witmer, pp. 132–149.

[53] Billington, pp. 94–97.

[54] Boyd, p. 123; Sylvia Maude Behrman, "Mental Hygiene Services Under State Departments of Health" (M.A. thesis, School of Social Service Administration, University of Chicago, 1943), pp. 86–87.

[55] New Jersey Health and Welfare Conference, Committee on Mental Diseases, *Report* (mimeographed, 1939, in the State Library at Trenton), p. 16.

[56] Ellen Potter, "Local Responsibility for a Mental Hygiene Program," *Mental Hygiene,* XIX (April 1935), 203, 205–206.

[57] Henry A. Cotton, Jr., "Scope and Purpose of the State Mental Hygiene Clinic," *Mental Hygiene,* XXIV (April 1940), 178–179, 180, 183.

[58] *Ibid.,* pp. 185–188.

[59] Witmer, pp. 245–256, 390–396.

[60] Ellis, *Psychiatric Progress in New Jersey,* p. 19; "Report of the Committee on the Expansion and Development of State Mental Hygiene Clinics, March 30, 1946" (mimeographed, in the files of the Division of Mental Health and Hospitals, NJDIA), n.p.

[61] Boyd, pp. 123, 127.

[62] Billington, p. 97.

NOTES FOR CHAPTER 14

[1] George Stevenson, "Where and Whither in Mental Deficiency," *American Journal of Mental Deficiency,* LII (July 1947), 43–47.

[2] [N. J.] Joint Legislative Survey Committee, *Reports* (Trenton: MacCrellish, 1925), p. 369; [National Institute of Public Administration], *Report on a Survey of the Organization and Administration of the State Government* (Trenton: MacCrellish, 1930), p. 189; School of Public and International Affairs of Princeton University, *Report on a Survey of Administration and Expenditures of the State Government of New Jersey . . .* (n.p., 1932), p. 146 (hereafter referred to as *Princeton Survey*); *The Problem of the Feeble-minded in New Jersey* (NJDIA Pub. No. 14, Trenton, 1928), pp. 41–42; Dayton D. McKean, *Pressures on the Legislature of New Jersey* (New York: Columbia University Press, 1938), pp. 74–75, 91.

[3] Edgar A. Doll, "The Outlook for Research," *Twenty-five Years: A Memorial Volume in Commemoration of the Twenty-fifth Anniversary of the Vineland Laboratory, 1906–1931* (Vineland Training School, Department of Research Series Pub. No. 2, 1932), pp. 41–42.

[4] Charlotte Billington, "The New Jersey State Hospital for the Insane at Trenton, 1908–1940" (M.A. thesis, School of Social Service Administration, University of Chicago, 1941), p. 43.

[5] Dr. George S. Stevenson, interview, April 8, 1961.

[6] Alexander Johnson to Porter Lee, May 12, 1928, in the papers of Edward R. Johnstone, in possession of Edward L. Johnstone, Fort Lauderdale, Florida. This letter is a first draft, and it is not clear whether or in what form it was mailed.

[7] *The Problem of the Feeble-minded in New Jersey* (1928), pp. 5–6; NJDIA, *Summary Report 1923–1933 and Handbook* (Trenton: The Department, 1934), pp. 58–62.

[8] *The Problem of the Feeble-minded* (1928), pp. 26, 32.

[9] *Ibid.*, pp. 14–15.

[10] *Ibid.*, pp. 5–6.

[11] Edgar A. Doll, *The Problem of the Feeble-minded in New Jersey* (NJDIA Pub. No. 23, Trenton, 1933), pp. 13, 15–16.

[12] NJDIA, *Report 1934–1943 and Handbook* (Trenton: The Department, 1944), pp. 60, 68.

[13] NJRCC, March 1902, pp. 29–32.

[14] NJDIA, *Welfare Reporter,* July 1946, p. 17.

[15] State Board of Control, NJDIA, Minutes, April 22, 1921 (in State Board office).

[16] E. L. Johnstone, interview, March 8, 1961.

[17] Harry von Bulow, "A Twenty-Year Report of the Woodbine Colony, 1920–1940" (ms. in the files of the Colony); E. L. Johnstone, "Dear Robinson Replies," *Training School Bulletin* (Vineland, N. J.), November 1938, pp. 144–148; December 1938, pp. 158–160; March 1939, pp. 11–15; E. L. Johnstone, "The Training of Low-Grade Mental Deficients at Woodbine State Colony," *Training School Bulletin,* February 1941, pp. 178–185.

[18] Edward R. Johnstone to Alexander Johnson, August 31, 1935 and October 3, 1935, Johnstone papers.

[19] Frank E. Walsh, statement to the Essex County Unit of the New Jersey Association for Retarded Children, November 8, 1956, in possession of Mrs. Fitzhugh Boggs, Upper Montclair, New Jersey.

[20] NJDIA, *Report 1934–1943,* pp. 66, 69–71, 128.

NOTES FOR CHAPTER 15

[1] Burdette G. Lewis, *The Offender and His Relations to Law and Society* (New York: Harper, 1917), pp. 6–8.

[2] *Ibid.*, pp. 5, 52–54.

[3] *Ibid.*, pp. 29–30, 54–57.

[4] *Ibid.*, pp. 102–107, 181–182, 113, 116–117, 175–178.

[5] *Ibid.*, pp. 253–254, 312–313.

[6] Mary Belle Harris, *I Knew Them in Prison* (New York: Viking Press, 1936), pp. viii–ix, 5–6, 97, 137–138.

[7] *Ibid.*, p. 138.

[8] *Ibid.*, pp. 138–140, 142–146, 153; New Jersey Prison Inquiry Commission, *Report* (Trenton, n.p., 1917), I, 45.

[9] Harris, pp. 146–157.

[10] *Ibid.*, p. 156.

[11] *Ibid.*, pp. 165–166, 191–192, 196–197, 222–223.

[12] *Ibid.*, pp. 235, 237, 241.

[13] Prison Inquiry Commission, I, 42–43.

[14] New Jersey State Home for Boys, Jamesburg, *Annual Report,* 1921, pp. 8–9, 11, 13, 17.

[15] Alida Bowler and Ruth Bloodgood, *Institutional Treatment of Delinquent Boys. Part I. Treatment Programs of Five State Institutions* (U. S. Children's Bureau Pub. No. 288, Washington, 1935), p. 91.

[16] *Ibid.,* pp. 91, 94.

[17] Calvin Derrick, "Presidential Address," American Prison Association, *Proceedings,* 1934, pp. 3–6.

[18] *Ibid.,* pp. 11–13.

[19] Alida Bowler and Ruth Bloodgood, *Institutional Treatment of Delinquent Boys. Part II. A Study of 751 Boys* (U. S. Children's Bureau Pub. No. 230, Washington, 1936), p. 98.

[20] *Manchester Guardian,* February 12, 1920, clipping, scrapbook, Clinton Farms.

[21] Frederick Woltman, *New York World-Telegram,* November 29, 1940, clipping, scrapbook, Clinton Farms.

[22] Harris, pp. 100–101.

[23] Edna Mahan, interview, July 17, 1961.

[24] William J. Ellis, "Public Welfare in New Jersey," *The Story of New Jersey,* William S. Myers, ed. (5 vols.; New York: Lewis Historical Publishing Co., 1945), II, 33.

[25] Edna Mahan, interview, July 17, 1961.

[26] Prison Inquiry Commission, pp. 47–50.

[27] Geraldine Thompson to Dwight Morrow, June 10, 1919; Burdette Lewis to Dwight Morrow, July 17, 1919, papers of Dwight Morrow, Amherst College Library.

[28] [N. J.] Joint Legislative Survey Committee, *Reports* (Trenton: MacCrellish, 1925), pp. 319–321, 393–394.

[29] State Board of Control, NJDIA, Minutes, January 23, 1924, p. 2; January 24, 1928, p. 5; February 28, 1928, p. 5 (in the office of the State Board).

[30] State Board of Control, Minutes, May 28, 1929, pp. 9–13.

[31] [National Institute of Public Administration], *Report on a Survey of the Organization and Administration of the State Government . . .* (Trenton: n.p., 1930), pp. 192–194.

[32] Sydney Souter, Jr., "A Recreation Program and Its Relation to Institutional Administration," American Prison Association, *Proceedings,* 1932, pp. 360–361; W. J. Ellis, "Correction and Adjustment Through Education," American Prison Association, *Proceedings,* 1933, pp. 191–192.

[33] *New York Times,* September 7, 1930, p. 19; September 8, 1930, p. 21; January 28, 1931, p. 1; January 29, 1931, p. 48.

[34] F. Lovell Bixby, interview, July 3, 1961.

[35] William Healy and Benedict S. Alper, *Criminal Youth and the Borstal System* (New York: The Commonwealth Fund, 1941), pp. 49–53, 237.

[36] Joint Legislative Survey Committee, p. 316.

[37] "Hearing held June 2, 1926, before Governor A. Harry Moore, on the prison situation" (ms., files of the NJDIA Division of Correction).

[38] *Acts,* 1926, p. 357 (repeals maximum-minimum sentence).

[39] W. J. Ellis, "Classification as the Basis for Institutional Training, Treatment, and Parole," American Prison Association, *Proceedings,* 1929, pp. 189–194.

[40] F. Lovell Bixby, interview, July 3, 1961.

[41] For a full discussion of the classification work in New Jersey and its significance in the 1930's, see Fred E. Haynes, *The American Prison System* (New York: McGraw-Hill, 1939), pp. 232–246, 251.

[42] F. L. Bixby, "The Relation of Classification to Penal Administration," American Prison Association, *Proceedings,* 1930, pp. 391–397; F. L. Bixby, "Relation of Classification to Institutional Administration," American Prison Association, *Proceedings,* 1932, pp. 111–112.

[43] F. Lovell Bixby, interview, July 3, 1961.

[44] National Institute of Public Administration, pp. 226–231.

[45] Winthrop D. Lane, "Parole Procedure in New Jersey" (Report to the National Commission on Law Observance and Enforcement [the Wickersham Commission], mimeographed, in the files of the NJDIA Division of Correction), pp. 26–27, 50. See also *Journal of Criminal Law and Criminology,* XXII (September 1931), 390–392.

[46] NJDIA, *Summary Report 1923–1933,* pp. 34, 85; NJDIA, *Report 1934–1943,* pp. 122, 127.

[47] Haynes, pp. 311–313.

[48] Prison Inquiry Commission, I, 154–161.

[49] New Jersey State Prison, *Biennial Report,* 1920–1921, pp. 20–23, 29.

[50] National Institute of Public Administration, pp. 289, 290–291.

[51] Donald Rice, interview, April 14, 1961.

[52] NJDIA, *Report 1934–1943,* pp. 17, 20, 22.

[53] John Bonnell, interview, July 12, 1961.

[54] Joint Legislative Survey Committee, pp. 339–341.

[55] National Institute of Public Administration, pp. 197–198.

[56] *Princeton Survey,* pp. 83–84.

[57] National Institute of Public Administration, p. 198.

[58] *Princeton Survey,* pp. 85–86.

[59] NJDIA *Summary Report 1923–1933,* pp. 43, 47.

[60] Grace Kastelansky, "Some Fiscal Aspects of the State-Use System of Prison Employment in New Jersey" (M.A. thesis, Rutgers University, 1938), pp. 30, 48–56, 75–76.

[61] New Jersey State Home for Boys, Jamesburg, *Annual Report,* 1931–1932, p. 7.

[62] *New York Times,* May 20, 1925, p. 4.

[63] Joint Legislative Survey Committee, p. 403.

[64] New Jersey Juvenile Delinquency Commission, *Justice and the Child in New Jersey* (Union City: Hudson Dispatch, 1939), pp. 139, 161.

[65] Ernest V. Hollis and Alice L. Taylor, *Social Work Education in the United States* (New York: Columbia University Press, 1951), pp. 11–18.

[66] Juvenile Delinquency Commission, pp. 198–208; Dayton D. McKean, *The Boss: The Hague Machine in Action* (Boston: Houghton Mifflin, 1940), pp. 221–225.

[67] New Jersey Conference on Crime, *Abstracts of Addresses and Discussions . . .* ([Trenton]: n.p., 1935), pp. 44–45.

[68] Juvenile Delinquency Commission, pp. viii, 217–220.

[69] *Ibid.,* pp. 123–128, 207–208.

[70] *Ibid.,* pp. 10–16; Ellen Potter, "Local Responsibility for a Mental-Hygiene Program," *Mental Hygiene,* XIX (April 1935), 202.

[71] Juvenile Delinquency Commission, p. 105.

[72] *Ibid.,* p. 18.

[73] *Ibid.,* p. 196.

[74] *Ibid.,* pp. 190, 196.

[75] *Ibid.,* p. 17.

[76] *Acts,* 1935, p. 752.

[77] F. Lovell Bixby, interview, July 3, 1961.

NOTES FOR CHAPTER 16

[1] Howard W. Odum and D. Willard, *Systems of Public Welfare* (Chapel Hill: University of North Carolina Press, 1925), pp. 4–6, 31–32, 219.

[2] *Acts,* 1919, ch. 97.

[3] NJDIA, *Summary Report 1923–1933 and Handbook* (Trenton: The Department, 1934), pp. 65–67, 92.

[4] *Ibid.,* pp. 31–37; Cornelia Meytrott, "County Organization for Child Welfare in the State of New Jersey," *County Organization for Child Care and Protection* (U. S. Children's Bureau Pub. No. 107, Washington, 1922), pp. 75–76.

[5] NJDIA, *Summary Report 1923–1933,* pp. 80–81.

[6] [National Institute of Public Administration], *Report on a Survey of the Organization and Administration of the State Government of New Jersey . . .* (Trenton: MacCrellish, 1930), p. 176. The revised poor law is *Acts,* 1924, ch. 132.

[7] See above, pp. 94, 96.

[8] *Child Welfare in New Jersey. Part 1* (U. S. Children's Bureau Pub. No. 174, Washington, 1927), pp. 48, 49; *Child Welfare in New Jersey. Part 2* (U. S. Children's Bureau Pub. No. 175, Washington, 1927), pp. 15, 52, 64, 120–121.

[9] *Child Welfare in New Jersey. Part 2,* pp. 18, 20, 53, 64–65, 120, 122.

[10] *Ibid.,* pp. 13, 25, 122.

[11] *County Organization for Child Care and Protection,* pp. 1–17; Odum and Willard, pp. 212–235.

[12] Meytrott, pp. 81–82.

[13] *Ibid.,* p. 80.

[14] *Ibid.,* p. 81.

[15] *Ibid.,* p. 91.

[16] Paul Tutt Stafford, *State Welfare Administration in New Jersey* (Princeton University Department of Political Science [1934]), pp. 92–94; *Child Welfare in New Jersey. Part 4* (U. S. Children's Bureau Pub. No. 180, Washington, 1927), pp. 22–23.

[17] *Child Welfare in New Jersey. Part 1,* pp. 36–37; *Child Welfare in New Jersey. Part 2,* pp. 13, 25, 122.

[18] Odum and Willard, pp. 153–171; *Newark Evening News,* May 6, 1927, p. 8; National Institute of Public Administration, p. 191; Ellen Potter, "Coordination and Development of Welfare Service in the County," *Social Service Review,* VI (1932), 452–462.

[19] *County and State Welfare Work in New Jersey* (NJDIA Pub. No. 17, Trenton, June 1929), pp. 5, 7–8.

[20] National Institute of Public Administration, pp. 175–176, 190–191.

[21] Janet Barkhorn, "A History of the New Jersey State Board of Children's Guardians from its Inception in 1899" (M.A. thesis, Fordham University School of Social Service, 1947), p. 70.

[22] NJDIA, State Board of Control, Minutes, December 17, 1929, pp. 2–3; March 25, 1930, pp. 3–5 (in the office of the State Board).

[23] State Board minutes, April 10, 1930, p. 3; May 27, 1930, pp. 2–3.

[24] Barkhorn, pp. 72–74.

[25] The licensing of private medical institutions was established by *Acts,* 1927, p. 247; the inspection of child-saving institutions, by *Acts,* 1922, pp. 178–180. Accounts of this work appear in *Child Welfare in New Jersey. Part 1,* pp. 8–9; *Summary Report 1923–1933,* pp. 39–42.

[26] Douglas H. MacNeil, *Seven Years of Unemployment Relief in New Jersey, 1930–1936* (Washington: Social Science Research Council, 1938); Paul Tutt Stafford, *Government and the Needy: A Study of Public Assistance in New Jersey* (Princeton: Princeton University Press, 1941).

[27] *Acts,* 1924, pp. 252–298.

[28] W. J. Ellis, Presidential Addresses, American Public Welfare Association, *Social Service Review,* VI (September 1932), 485–486, and VII (September 1933), 489–490.

[29] NJDIA, *Summary Report 1923–1933,* p. 93.

[30] New Jersey Pension Survey Commission, *Report No. 1* ([Trenton]: n.p., 1931), pp. 11–12, 14, 16, 19–21.

[31] *The County Welfare Board . . .* (NJDIA Pub. No. 20, Trenton, March 1931).

[32] *New York Times,* April 4, 1931, p. 15; November 5, 1931, p. 3; Stafford, *State Welfare Administration,* p. 100.

[33] *Acts,* 1931, p. 530.

[34] NJDIA, *Summary Report 1923–1933,* pp. 50–51, 113.

[35] *Ibid.,* pp. 50–51.

[36] Stafford, *State Welfare Administration,* pp. 100–102.

[37] NJDIA Division of Old Age Relief, *Two-year Report, 1933 and 1934* (NJDIA Pub. No. 28, Trenton, 1935), pp. 5–7.

[38] New Jersey Pension Survey Commission, *Report No. 5, State Care of Dependent Children in New Jersey* (n.p., 1932), pp. 3–4, 49; Stafford, *State Welfare Administration,* pp. 120–123.

[39] Irving Engelman, interview, August 4, 1961. A well-informed critical study is Robert Lansdale, *The Administration of Old-Age Assistance in Three States* (Chicago: Public Administration Service, 1936).

[40] Barkhorn, pp. 52–53.

[41] *Ibid.,* pp. 76–79, 81; Edwin Hann, Jr., interview, August 2, 1961.

[42] *Compass* (National Association of Social Workers), December 1934, pp. 2–3.

[43] Carolin [sic] A. Hughes, "Staff Development in a Public Agency" (M.S.W. thesis, New York School of Social Work, Columbia University, 1945), pp. 7, 10–13, 45–46, 51–52, 60–62.

[44] *Ibid.*, pp. 45–47; Edwin Hann, Jr., interview, August 2, 1961.

[45] NJDIA, *Welfare Reporter,* September 1954, p. 1.

[46] Irving Engelman, interview, August 4, 1961; Edwin Hann, Jr., interview, August 2, 1961.

[47] W. J. Ellis, "Public Welfare Administration and the Skills it Demands," National Conference of Social Work, *Proceedings,* 1936, pp. 512–513.

[48] Josephine Chapin Brown, *Public Relief 1929–1939* (New York: Henry Holt and Co., 1940), pp. 149–170.

[49] Irving Engelman, interview, August 4, 1961; *Assembly Journal,* 1936, pp. 726–727.

[50] Stafford, *Government and the Needy,* pp. 110–115.

[51] *Ibid.*, pp. 110–111; Irving Engelman, interview, August 4, 1961.

[52] Stafford, *Government and the Needy,* p. 265.

[53] *Ibid.*, pp. 180–181.

[54] Phyllis Morely, "Interpretation of Public Welfare Administration in the New Jersey Department of Institutions and Agencies" (M.A. thesis, School of Social Service Administration, University of Chicago, 1938), pp. 95–96.

[55] New Jersey Unemployment Relief Commission, *Reports* (Trenton: MacCrellish, 1938 and 1939); New Jersey Legislature. Joint Emergency Relief Committee, *Report on an Investigation of Relief Administration in New Jersey* (n.p., February 1940) (sometimes cited as "Glover Report").

[56] Stafford, *Government and the Needy,* pp. 113–115, 182–187.

[57] *Ibid.*, p. 273.

[58] *Ibid.*, pp. 274–275.

[59] *Ibid.*, pp. 284–292.

[60] W. J. Ellis, "Extent and Nature of the Present Relief Problem," *State Government,* May 1940, p. 103.

[61] Stafford, *Government and the Needy,* pp. 186–187; *New York Times,* July 2, 1940, p. 14 and July 10, 1940, p. 15.

[62] New Jersey State Commission on Post-War Economic Welfare, *A New Jersey Program for the Post-War Period, First Report . . . February 28, 1944* (Trenton: n.p., 1944), pp. iv, 74–75.

[63] *Ibid.*, pp. 75–77.

[64] Stafford, *Government and the Needy,* p. 206n.

[65] W. J. Ellis, "Public Welfare in New Jersey, 1630–1944," *The Story of New Jersey,* William Starr Myers, ed. (5 vols.; New York: Lewis Historical Publishing Co., 1945), II, 81–86.

[66] Edgar A. Doll, ed., *Twenty-five Years: A Memorial Volume in Commemoration of the Twenty-fifth Anniversary of the Vineland Laboratory, 1906–1931* (Vineland Training School: Department of Research Series, No. 2, 1932), pp. 20–22.

NOTES FOR CHAPTER 17

[1] Sanford Bates, interview, February 25, 1959.

[2] *Current Biography* (New York: Wilson, 1940–), January 1961, pp. 8–10.

[3] Sanford Bates, *Prisons and Beyond* (New York: Macmillan, 1936), pp. 149–174, 204–205; letter from Sanford Bates to author, November 22, 1963.

[4] *Welfare Reporter* (NJDIA), July 1946, p. 19.

[5] Letter from Sanford Bates to author, November 22, 1963.

[6] *Welfare Reporter,* July 1946, p. 7; February 1948, pp. 3–4.

[7] *Welfare Reporter,* April 1947, p. 19.

[8] *Welfare Reporter,* September 1946, pp. 15, 17.

[9] "Memorandum submitted on behalf of the State Board of Control of Institutions and Agencies to the Governor's Special Committee established to study working conditions in state service" (mimeographed, n.p., n.d. [July 1942]), files, Bureau of Legal Affairs, NJDIA; *Newark Evening News,* November 22, 1942, p. 1.

[10] *Newark Evening News,* August 23, 1945, p. 9; September 28, 1945, p. 12.

[11] See his articles in the *Welfare Reporter,* February 1947, p. 21; March 1947, pp. 17–18; May 1947, pp. 18–19; March 1948, p. 22; March 1949, pp. 16–17. The anti-discrimination law is *Acts,* 1945, Ch. 169.

[12] *Welfare Reporter,* April 1948, p. 22.

[13] *Welfare Reporter,* March 1951, p. 7; April 1957, p. 4; *Newark Evening News,* March 24, 1957, p. 21.

[14] Council of State Governments, *Reorganizing State Government: A Report on Administrative Management in the States and a Review of Recent Trends in Reorganization* (Chicago: The Council, 1950), pp. 3–5, 146.

[15] Richard N. Baisden, *Charter for New Jersey: The New Jersey Constitutional Convention of 1947* (Trenton: Division of the State Library, Archives and History, New Jersey Department of Education, 1952), pp. 5–8, 16, 105–107; Bennett M. Rich, *The Government and Administration of New Jersey* (New York: Thomas Y. Crowell Co., 1957), pp. 19–22, 25–26, 35.

[16] Baisden, pp. 10, 108–109; Rich, pp. 29–36; Julian P. Boyd, ed., *Fundamental Laws and Constitutions of New Jersey, 1664–1964* (Princeton: D. Van Nostrand Co., 1964), pp. 46–50 (a copy of the Constitution is on pp. 193–233).

[17] Baisden, pp. 18–20; State of New Jersey, *Constitutional Convention of 1947* . . . (5 vols.; Trenton, n.p., 1949–1953), V, 37–40, 100, 478–479, 500–504.

[18] Bates, pp. 125, 240, 269.

[19] Letter from Sanford Bates to author, November 22, 1963.

[20] Baisden, pp. 19–20; Report from Sanford Bates to Members of the State Board of Control, May 19, 1948, NJDIA State Board of Control minutes in the Board office; the reorganization act is *Acts,* 1948, p. 147.

[21] Letter from Sanford Bates to author, November 22, 1963; F. Lovell Bixby, interview, July 5, 1961.

[22] Report from Sanford Bates to State Board, June 24, 1947, p. 8, in Board minutes.

[23] Rich, pp. 4, 6, 124–126, 140, 150–151; Morris Beck, "Government Finance in New Jersey," *The Economy of New Jersey, A Report Prepared for the Department of Conservation and Economic Development of the State of New Jersey,* by A Group of Rutgers Scholars under the Direction of Professor Salomon J. Flink (New Brunswick: Rutgers University Press, 1958), pp. 560–561, 578.

[24] Rich, pp. 212–214.

[25] *The Welfare Reporter* for October 1948 describes the needs.

[26] *Newark Evening News,* November 15, 1948, p. 4; November 24, 1948, p. 4.

[27] *Newark Evening News,* March 14, 1949, p. 1.

[28] *Newark Evening News,* September 16, 1949, p. 21; New Jersey Taxpayers Association, *New Jersey's Institutional Needs . . .* (n.p., n.d. [1949]), pp. 4–5, 31; *Welfare Reporter,* October 1949 (bond drive issue); April 1950, p. 14; letter from Sanford Bates to author, November 22, 1963.

[29] *Newark Evening News,* November 9, 1949, p. 1.

[30] *Newark Evening News,* April 11, 1950, p. 35.

[31] *Newark Evening News,* March 20, 1952, p. 21; October 21, 1952, p. 10; *Welfare Reporter,* November 1952, pp. 1–2.

[32] Lloyd Wescott, interview, August 9, 1961.

[33] New Jersey Taxpayers Association, pp. 14–22, 26.

[34] *Welfare Reporter,* February 1951, p. 4.

[35] New Jersey Prison Inquiry Commission, *Report* (Trenton: n.p., 1917), I, 69.

[36] New Jersey Taxpayers Association, pp. 1, 26–28, 29, Appendix.

NOTES FOR CHAPTER 18

[1] New Jersey Juvenile Delinquency Commission, *Justice and the Child in New Jersey* (n.p., November 1939), p. 176; F. Lovell Bixby, interview, July 3, 1961.

[2] F. Lovell Bixby, interview, July 3, 1961.

[3] *Ibid.;* "A Review of the Policies and Procedures of the Parole Bureau of the New Jersey State Prison . . . June 1945," appendix to the minutes of the NJDIA State Board of Control, July 10, 1945, pp. 2–3; testimony of Sanford Bates in State of New Jersey, *Constitutional Convention of 1947 . . .* (5 vols.; Trenton, n.p., 1949–1953), V, 177–190.

[4] Report from Sanford Bates to the State Board of Control, June 18, 1945, in State Board office; State Board of Control, minutes, July 10, 1945.

[5] *Welfare Reporter,* August 1946, p. 6; *Manual of the Legislature,* 1945, p. 332.

[6] State Board of Control, minutes, January 22, 1946, p. 22; July 2, 1946, p. 13.

[7] *Newark Evening News,* June 12, 1946, p. 25.

[8] State Board of Control, minutes, August 26, 1947, p. 8 and appendix.

[9] *Manual of the Legislature,* 1947, p. 348; F. Lovell Bixby, interview, July 3, 1961.

[10] N. J. Juvenile Delinquency Commission, pp. 10–12.

[11] Douglas MacNeil, "Two and One-Half Years of State-Local Collaboration

in Delinquency Prevention," National Probation and Parole Association, *Yearbook,* 1948 (n.p., 1949), pp. 252–255; D. MacNeil, "State Government and the Prevention of Delinquency," *State Government,* XXII (May 1949), 142–144.

[12] MacNeil, "Two and One-Half Years," p. 254.

[13] New Jersey Governor's Committee on Youth, *Children and Youth in New Jersey* (n.p., 1949), pp. 1–4, 95–101.

[14] MacNeil, "Two and One-Half Years," p. 261.

[15] *Ibid.,* p. 262.

[16] Burdette G. Lewis, *The Offender and His Relations to Law and Society* (New York: Harper, 1917), pp. 105–117.

[17] "Thirteen Years . . . of Diagnostic Service," *Welfare Reporter,* September 1949, pp. 9–10.

[18] N. J. Juvenile Delinquency Commission, p. 17; Sanford Bates, "Diagnostic Center to Serve Courts," *Welfare Reporter,* September 1949, pp. 3–6.

[19] The organic law includes a statement of philosophy and procedures: *Revised Statutes, Cumulative Supplement,* Section 30: 4A-1 to 30: 4A-17. (The original legislation was *Acts,* 1946, ch. 118, and 1947, ch. 238.)

[20] *Acts,* 1949, ch. 20.

[21] *Welfare Reporter,* September 1949, p. 11.

[22] NJDIA, *New Jersey Builds Hospitals . . .* (Trenton, 1953), pp. 33–34.

[23] Ralph Brancale, "Problems of Classification," *Welfare Reporter,* March 1956, pp. 11–13 (reprinted from *National Probation and Parole Association Journal,* October 1955); Maurice Kott, "The Post-War Decade, 1946–1956," *Welfare Reporter,* October 1960, p. 200.

[24] Ralph Brancale, "Psychiatric and Psychological Services," *Contemporary Correction,* Paul W. Tappan, ed. (New York: McGraw-Hill Co., 1951), p. 193.

[25] F. Lovell Bixby, interview, July 5, 1961.

[26] *Ibid.;* Lloyd W. McCorkle, Albert Elias, and F. Lovell Bixby, *The Highfields Story: An Experimental Treatment Project for Youthful Offenders* (New York: Henry Holt and Co., 1958), p. 9.

[27] Lloyd W. McCorkle, "Group Therapy," *Contemporary Correction,* pp. 214–215.

[28] *Ibid.;* F. Lovell Bixby and Lloyd W. McCorkle, "A Recorded Presentation of a Program of Guided Group Interaction in New Jersey Correctional Institutions," American Prison Association, *Proceedings,* 1948, p. 190.

[29] Bixby and McCorkle, p. 190.

[30] McCorkle, Elias, and Bixby, pp. 173–174.

[31] *Ibid.,* pp. 174–175.

[32] *Ibid.,* pp. ix, 179–180.

[33] *Ibid.,* pp. 74–75.

[34] *Ibid.,* pp. 76–77.

[35] *Ibid.,* pp. vii–viii, 149–151.

[36] *Ibid.,* pp. 154–155.

[37] New Jersey Taxpayers Association (see above, p. 450, n. 28), p. 18.

[38] Donald Goff, "The Effects of Changed Social Conditions on the Annandale Population" (mimeographed, September 23, 1952, files of the Division of Classification and Education), n.p.

[39] *About You . . . and Clinton Farms* (Clinton Farms Reformatory, 1950), pp. 14–18.

[40] New Jersey Reformatory for Women, *Annual Report*, 1945–1946, pp. 8–9.

[41] Molly Mellonby, "Reformatory for Women—Clinton Farms, New Jersey," typescript, files at Clinton Farms.

[42] *Ibid.*

[43] Albert Wagner, "Are We Don Quixotes in Correctional Education?" *Journal of Correctional Education,* I (January 1950), 16.

[44] Charles J. Perrine, "Social Adjustment Interests of Delinquent Males in New Jersey Reformatories" (D.Ed. thesis, Rutgers University, 1954), pp. 202–203.

[45] *About Annandale Farms* (New Jersey Reformatory, Annandale, N. J., 1955), p. 8.

[46] John Bishop, "Pre-Vocational Training in Social Re-Education," *Journal of Correctional Education,* II (April 1952), 32.

[47] Price Chenault, "Education," *Contemporary Correction,* p. 231.

[48] New Jersey Reformatory, Annandale, *Annual Report,* 1957–1958, appendix, "The Revised Program."

[49] Charles Houston, "Forest Conservation," *Welfare Reporter,* March 1955, pp. 1–2, 10.

[50] New Jersey Committee to Examine and Investigate the Prison and Parole Systems of New Jersey, *Report . . . November 21, 1952* (n.p., 1952), pp. 30–31.

[51] *Ibid.,* pp. 14–15, 17.

[52] *Ibid.,* pp. 45–46, 52.

[53] *Ibid.,* pp. 34, 37–38, 44.

[54] *Ibid.,* pp. 81–83.

[55] *Ibid.,* pp. 60–61.

[56] *Ibid.,* pp. 164–166.

[57] *Ibid.,* p. 149.

[58] *Ibid.,* pp. 3, 10, 131.

[59] *Ibid.,* pp. 4, 11–12, 133–134.

[60] *Ibid.,* p. 9.

[61] *Ibid.,* pp. 113–115.

[62] Peg and Walter McGraw, *Assignment: Prison Riots* (New York: Henry Holt and Co., 1954), p. 2.

[63] *Ibid.,* pp. 14–16.

[64] *Ibid.,* pp. 40–41.

[65] *Ibid.,* pp. 16–18, 31–41, 254–256.

[66] *Ibid.,* pp. 263–264.

[67] N. J. Committee to Examine and Investigate the Prison and Parole Systems, pp. 103–109.

[68] *Ibid.,* pp. 141–142.

[69] *Ibid.,* p. 12.

[70] *Ibid.,* pp. 110–113; Lloyd McCorkle, interview, November 21, 1959.

[71] Quoted in Gresham Sykes, *The Society of Captives* (Princeton: Princeton University Press, 1958), pp. 36–37; see also Richard R. Korn and Lloyd W.

McCorkle, *Criminology and Penology* (New York: Henry Holt and Co., 1959), pp. 473–474.

[72] Korn and McCorkle, pp. 27–42.

[73] *Ibid.*, p. 597.

[74] Sykes, pp. xix, 135.

[75] *Ibid.*, pp. 33, 37.

[76] *Ibid.*, pp. 126–129.

[77] *Ibid.*, p. 134.

NOTES FOR CHAPTER 19

[1] The Conference resolutions are quoted in Edgar A. Doll, *The Problem of The Feeble-Minded in New Jersey: The Relation of the Public Schools to the Public Institutions* (NJDIA Pub. No. 23, Trenton, February 1933), pp. 28–31.

[2] Stanley P. Davies, *The Mentally Retarded in Society* (New York: Columbia Univ. Press, 1959), pp. 85–92.

[3] George Stevenson, "Where and Whither in Mental Deficiency," *American Journal of Mental Deficiency,* LII (July 1947), 44–46.

[4] Biographical notices of Dr. Yepsen, *American Journal of Mental Deficiency,* LIII (July 1948), 14, and *Welfare Reporter,* July 1955, p. 6.

[5] J. Quinter Holsopple, "1919–1939: A Historical Note," *Welfare Reporter,* October 1960, pp. 179–180; Anna S. Starr, "Notes on the Early Development of the Rutgers Psychological Clinic," *ibid.,* pp. 182–183; Maurice Kott, "The Post-War Decade, 1946–1956," *ibid.,* pp. 199–200.

[6] Lloyd Yepsen, "New Jersey's State Institutional Program," *Training School Bulletin* (Vineland Training School), December 1940, p. 147.

[7] W. J. Ellis, "State Program for the Care of the Mentally Deficient," *American Journal of Mental Deficiency,* XLVI (January 1941), 421, 426–428; Edgar Doll, "Foster Care for Mental Defectives," *Training School Bulletin,* February 1940, pp. 193–205.

[8] Miriam Lernerd, "The Institutional Program for the Mentally Deficient in New Jersey," *Training School Bulletin,* June 1945, pp. 61–63; Lloyd Yepsen and Vincentz Cianci, "Home Training for Mentally Deficient Children in New Jersey," *Training School Bulletin,* April 1946, pp. 21–26; letter from Edward L. Johnstone to author, April 16, 1965.

[9] Lloyd Yepsen, "Where We Stand at Present in Care of Mentally Deficient," *Welfare Reporter,* August 1949, pp. 6–7.

[10] New Jersey Association for Retarded Children, *Resources for Retarded Children in New Jersey* (3rd ed., The Association, 1960), p. 1; New Jersey Association for Retarded Children, *Ten Years of the Essex Unit: Headlines and Sidelights* [Newark, 1958], p. 1.

[11] "How It All Started," *Children Limited* (National Association for Retarded Children), August–September 1960, p. 3.

[12] *Ten Years of the Essex Unit, passim.*

[13] New Jersey Association for Retarded Children, *Resources for Retarded Children,* p. 3.

[14] Mrs. Elizabeth Boggs, interview, October 14, 1960.

[15] Letter from Elizabeth Boggs to author, October 24, 1960; Stevenson, p. 45.

[16] New Jersey Commission to Study the Problems and Needs of Mentally Deficient Persons, *Mental Deficiency in New Jersey* (Trenton, n.p., 1954), pp. 87–88, 92–93, 133–136.

[17] Henry Kessler, "Rehabilitation in New Jersey," *Journal of the Medical Society of New Jersey,* L (September 1953), 423–426; Henry A. Brodkin, "New Jersey Service to the Physically Handicapped," *ibid.,* L (April 1953), 135–137.

[18] *Acts,* 1954, Ch. 178 (the mentally handicapped) and Ch. 179 (the physically handicapped).

[19] New Jersey Association for Retarded Children, *Resources for Retarded Children,* pp. 2–3.

[20] N. J. Commission to Study the Needs and Problems of Mentally Deficient Persons, pp. 108–109, 111.

[21] *Ibid.,* pp. 113–115, 103–105, 42–43, 119, 69–70.

[22] *Ibid.,* pp. 10–12, 35–36.

[23] *Welfare Reporter,* November 1952, p. 5; *ibid.,* January 1954, p. 12; Maurice Kott, "The Post-War Decade," pp. 200–201; letter from Maurice Kott to author, August 23, 1960; Maurice Kott, interview, October 18, 1960.

[24] F. Lovell Bixby, interview, July 5, 1961; the organic act of the Johnstone Training and Research Center is *Acts,* 1955, Ch. 208.

[25] *Welfare Reporter,* October 1955, pp. 5–7.

NOTES FOR CHAPTER 20

[1] Greystone Park State Hospital, *Annual Report,* 1945, pp. 17, 34–35.

[2] *Newark Evening News,* December 13, 1945, p. C-15.

[3] NJDIA State Board of Control, Mental Hygiene Committee, minutes, June 25, 1945, in the office of the State Board.

[4] New Jersey Health and Welfare Conference, Sub-Committee on Mental Diseases, *Report . . . May 11, 1939* (mimeographed, The Conference, 1939), pp. 9–11, and letter of transmittal.

[5] George S. Stevenson, "New Jersey's Contribution to Psychiatric Progress," *Journal of the Medical Society of New Jersey,* L (September 1953), 414–415.

[6] George S. Stevenson, *Mental Health Planning for Social Action* (New York: McGraw-Hill Co., 1956), pp. 82–91.

[7] Council of State Governments, *The Mental Health Programs of the Forty-Eight States* (Chicago: the Council, 1950), pp. 82–86.

[8] *Ibid.,* pp. 1–2, 44–45.

[9] Sanford Bates, interview, March 3, 1959.

[10] *Welfare Reporter* (NJDIA), July 1946, p. 19; July 1948, p. 3.

[11] *Welfare Reporter,* July 1948, p. 3; Mrs. Rose O'Brien, interview, April 21, 1961. (Mrs. O'Brien was secretary to the Deputy Commissioner.)

[12] *American Journal of Mental Deficiency,* LIV (July 1949), 7–10.

[13] *Welfare Reporter,* April 1953, p. 3; Rose O'Brien, interview, April 21, 1961.

[14] *Welfare Reporter,* January 1954, p. 2.

[15] For the structure of the Division, and the Department, as of 1954, see *Your Department of Institutions and Agencies* (NJDIA Pub. No. 56, April 1954).

[16] Report from Sanford Bates to Members of the State Board of Control, May 17, 1946, in the office of the State Board. (This was in effect Bates' annual report.)

[17] *Ibid.*

[18] Report from Sanford Bates to the Members of the State Board of Control, May 19, 1948, in the office of the State Board.

[19] Report from Sanford Bates to the State Board of Control, June 13, 1949, in the office of the State Board; Annette Trumbull, "Foster Home Care for Patients," *Welfare Reporter,* April 1953, pp. 9–10.

[20] *Welfare Reporter,* March 1947, pp. 15–16; J. S. Eberhardt, "Better Ward Patient Care: The Psychiatric Technician Training Program," *Welfare Reporter,* October 1958, pp. 185–189.

[21] Report from Sanford Bates to Members of the State Board of Control, June 24, 1947, in the office of the State Board.

[22] Joseph H. Reid and Helen R. Hagan, *Residential Treatment of Emotionally Disturbed Children: A Descriptive Study* (New York: Child Welfare League of America, 1952), pp. iii, v–vi.

[23] *Welfare Reporter,* February 1940, p. 3.

[24] Reid and Hagan, p. 1; George H. Lussier, "Allaire," *Welfare Reporter,* November 1950, p. 3.

[25] Reid and Hagan, pp. 2–3, 6–7, 18–19.

[26] *Ibid.,* pp. 7–16; Lussier, pp. 3–4, 17–18.

[27] Reid and Hagan, pp. 19–20, 306.

[28] Albert Piggott, "Progress in Treating Epilepsy," *Welfare Reporter,* April 1947, p. 13.

[29] E. L. Johnstone, "Skillman Report," typescript, copy in possession of Mr. Johnstone, Fort Lauderdale, Florida.

[30] *Ibid.*

[31] Michael Goodman, "Serving the Needs of the Epileptic in New Jersey," *Welfare Reporter,* April 1958, pp. 76, 79.

[32] The reorganization is described in the appendix to the minutes of the State Board of Control for July 1, 1952; see also *Welfare Reporter,* November 1952, p. 2. The new organic law is *Acts,* 1953, Ch. 122.

[33] *Welfare Reporter,* November 1952, pp. 5, 7.

[34] Goodman, pp. 79–82.

[35] *Welfare Reporter,* April 1957, p. 6.

[36] New Jersey State Taxpayers Association, *New Jersey's Institutional Needs* . . . (n.p., n.d. [1949]), pp. 13, 18.

[37] *Welfare Reporter,* December 1954, pp. 2–4.

[38] Quoted, *Welfare Reporter,* April 1953, p. 1.

[39] Quoted, *Welfare Reporter,* December 1954, p. 1.

[40] Council of State Governments, pp. 85–90.

[41] NJDIA, *Summary Report 1923–1933 and Handbook* (Trenton: The Department, 1934), pp. 8–9, 12–13; William J. Ellis, *Psychiatric Progress in New Jersey, 1844–1944* (Trenton: The Department, 1944), pp. 17–18.

[42] "Report of the Committee on the Expansion and Development of State Mental Hygiene Clinics, March 30, 1946," files, Division of Mental Hygiene and Hospitals.

[43] Mildred Hurley, interview, June 5, 1961.

[44] Luman Tenney, "Mental Hygiene Clinics Hampered by Lack of Community Resources," *Welfare Reporter,* September 1949, pp. 16–18.

[45] *Ibid.,* pp. 17–18.

[46] Dr. George S. Stevenson, interview, April 18, 1961.

[47] *Ibid.;* Robert D. Smith, "State Mental Hygiene Society Proposed," *Welfare Reporter,* April 1948, pp. 6–8.

[48] Robert Myers, "Mental Hygiene Clinics in New Jersey," *Welfare Reporter,* April 1955, pp. 1–2.

[49] J. Berkeley Gordon, "Problems of Psychiatric Hospitals," *Journal of the Medical Society of New Jersey,* L (March 1953), 101–104.

[50] Stevenson, "New Jersey's Contributions to Psychiatry," pp. 412, 414, 416.

[51] *Welfare Reporter,* June 1954, p. 10.

[52] Typescript of the address in possession of Dr. George S. Stevenson, Red Bank, N. J.

NOTES FOR CHAPTER 21

[1] W. J. Ellis, "Extent and Nature of the Present Relief Problem," *State Government,* May 1940, p. 103; W. J. Ellis, "The Case for State-Local Administration," *Public Administration Review,* I (Spring 1941), 233–239.

[2] Report from Sanford Bates to the Members of the State Board of Control, May 17, 1946, in the office of the State Board.

[3] Sanford Bates, "Protection and Prevention," *Welfare Reporter,* May 1946, p. 4; *Welfare Reporter,* June 1946, p. 11, compares grants in New Jersey, Connecticut and Massachusetts.

[4] *Ibid.,* p. 4; see above, pp. 282–283.

[5] *Welfare Reporter,* June 1946, p. 12.

[6] "Welfare Administrators Disagree on Purposes of Public Assistance," *Welfare Reporter,* September 1948, pp. 3–4.

[7] *Welfare Reporter,* January 1949, pp. 5–7.

[8] Report from Sanford Bates to Members of the State Board of Control, June 13, 1949, in the office of the State Board.

[9] *Welfare Reporter,* January 1949, p. 5; Frank Bane and Geoffrey May, *Public Welfare in New Jersey: A Structural Analysis* (Trenton, n.p., 1949), pp. 64–65.

[10] Bane and May, pp. 1–4.

[11] *Ibid.,* pp. 17–23, 35–39.

[12] *Ibid.,* pp. 24–25, 8–9, 54.

[13] *Ibid.,* pp. 10–11.

[14] *Ibid.,* pp. 26–28, 67.

[15] *Ibid.*, pp. 68–71, 77.

[16] *Ibid.*, pp. 60–64.

[17] Report from Sanford Bates to Members of the State Board of Control, June 26, 1950, in the office of the State Board.

[18] *Ibid.; Welfare Reporter,* July 1950, p. 7.

[19] *Welfare Reporter,* September 1949, p. 13.

[20] Elmer V. Andrews, "The Impact of Public Opinion on Public Welfare," *Welfare Reporter,* pp. 4–5.

[21] Bates' remarks were published in the *Welfare Reporter,* May 1951, pp. 5–7, 14–17.

[22] *Public Hearing on Assembly Bill No. 17 before Assembly Standing Committee on Judiciary . . . February 23, 1951,* manuscript, New Jersey State Library; Irving Engelman, interview, August 4, 1961.

[23] *Acts,* 1951, Ch. 139; 1952, Ch. 24.

[24] Commission to Study the Administration of Welfare in New Jersey, *Report . . .* (Trenton: MacCrellish, 1953), pp. 1–5; *Public Hearing on Assembly Bills Nos. 448, 449, 450 . . . April 7, 1953,* manuscript, New Jersey State Library, pp. 33–34.

[25] *Public Hearing on Assembly Bill No. 227 . . . May 6, 1954,* manuscript, New Jersey State Library, pp. 60–64.

[26] [N. J.] Commission to Study the Department of Institutions and Agencies, *The State's Organization for Social Welfare in New Jersey* (n.p., n.d. [1959]), pp. 42–43, 48–50.

[27] See Kathryn Welch, *The Meaning of State Supervision in the Social Protection of Children* (U. S. Children's Bureau Pub. No. 252, Washington, 1940).

[28] *Welfare Reporter,* July 1949, pp. 6–7; January 1950, pp. 9–10.

[29] Carolin Hughes, "State Board of Child Welfare," *Welfare Reporter,* March 1949, pp. 6–8.

[30] Helen King, "State Board Now Offers to Rural Families Casework Services," *Welfare Reporter,* November 1949, pp. 13–14.

[31] *Welfare Reporter,* January 1951, pp. 12–13.

[32] *Ibid.*, p. 16.

[33] *Acts,* 1951, Ch. 138; *Welfare Reporter,* August 1951, pp. 3–4, 17; Edwin F. Hann, Jr., "First Year's Experience with a New Investment in Children," *Child Welfare,* December 1954, pp. 9–11, 16–17.

[34] New Jersey Governor's Committee on Youth, *Children and Youth in New Jersey* (Trenton, n.p., 1949), pp. 4, 82.

[35] New Jersey Committee on Children and Youth, *New Jersey Children in a Changing World* (mimeographed, n.p., February 1960), Ch. VII, pp. 2, 15–17.

[36] New Jersey Youth Study Commission, *Final Report: Action for Children and Youth* (mimeographed, n.p., June 1961), pp. 1, 34–36.

[37] New Jersey Youth Study Commission, *Why New Jersey Needs a Permanent Youth Agency, An Interim Report* (mimeographed, n.p., 1961), pp. 4–6.

[38] New Jersey Committee on Children and Youth, *New Jersey Children in a Changing World,* Ch. X, pp. 1–2.

[39] *Ibid.*, "Priorities," pp. 1–2.

[40] Paul T. Stafford, *State Welfare Administration in New Jersey* (Department of Political Science, Princeton, 1933), pp. 91, 98–99.

[41] *Acts,* 1911, Ch. 138; SCAA, *Twenty-fifth Annual Report,* 1910–1911, p. 9; *Acts,* 1913, Ch. 10.

[42] Stafford, p. 105, n. 23.

[43] [National Institute of Public Administration], *Report on a Survey of the Organization and Administration of the State Government of New Jersey . . .* (Trenton: MacCrellish, 1930), pp. 158–161.

[44] *Welfare Reporter,* March 1947, pp. 5–7; "Historical Survey Including Legal Provisions, 1926–1946," New Jersey State Crippled Children Commission, *Report,* 1946, pp. 11–19.

[45] Ellen Potter, "How Can A Program for Care of the Chronically Ill and Aged be Integrated? A Case Report of Experience in One State," *Public Welfare,* I (November 1943), 326–332.

[46] *Ibid.; Welfare Reporter,* March 1947, p. 9; *Welfare Reporter,* July 1947, pp. 11–13.

[47] NJDIA, Bureau of Social Research, *Chronic Disease in New Jersey 1931–1953: A Review* (mimeographed, September 1953), p. 2; Emil Frankel, "Planning for the Long-Term Patient," *Welfare Reporter,* June 1947, pp. 5–6.

[48] *Welfare Reporter,* June 1947, pp. 3–4.

[49] *Welfare Reporter,* September 1948, p. 4.

[50] *Acts,* 1948, Ch. 109, 110; W. S. Conklin, "New Jersey Temporary Disability Benefits Law," *Welfare Reporter,* December 1948, pp. 22–23.

[51] Report from Sanford Bates to the Members of the State Board of Control, June 24, 1947, in the office of the State Board; *Acts,* 1947, Ch. 340.

[52] E. A. Mooney, "Construction Program," *Welfare Reporter,* December 1948, pp. 15–17.

[53] *Newark Evening News,* December 30, 1947, p. C 24.

[54] *Welfare Reporter,* August–October 1953, p. 6.

[55] *Welfare Reporter,* August 1951, pp. 4, 13.

[56] Walter L. Kidde, "A Streamlined Public Welfare Program for New Jersey," *New Jersey Municipalities,* January 1953, pp. 10–12; Commission to Study the Administration of Welfare in New Jersey (1953), pp. 21–26.

[57] *Ibid.*

[58] Bennett M. Rich, *The Government and Administration of New Jersey* (New York: Thomas Y. Crowell Co., 1957), pp. 221–225.

[59] *Ibid.,* pp. 225–226.

[60] *Ibid.,* pp. 231–232.

[61] Daniel Bergsma, "Fifty Years of Progress in Public Health," *Journal of the Medical Society of New Jersey,* L (September 1953), 420; Daniel Bergsma, "The New Jersey Program for the Prevention of Chronic Illness," *Public Health News* (New Jersey State Department of Health), February 1956, pp. 37–40 and *passim; Public Health News,* August 1959, *passim.*

[62] New Jersey Old Age Study Commission, *A Positive Policy Toward Aging* (Trenton, n.p., February 1957), pp. 200–211.

[63] New Jersey Department of State, Division of Aging, *Triennial Report,* May 1958 to May 1961 (mimeographed, 1961), pp. 1, 7, 15, 22.

[64] New Jersey Youth Study Commission, *What Kind of a Permanent Youth Agency for New Jersey?* (29th Public Hearing, mimeographed, July 1960), p. 30A.

[65] Irving Engelman, "Improving Institutional Care for the Aged," *Welfare Reporter,* July 1958, p. 105; Gertrude Lotwin, *A State Revises its Assistance Standard* (U. S. Department of Health, Education and Welfare, Public Assistance Report No. 39, 1959); Gladys White, *State Methods for Determining Need in the ADC Program* (U. S. Department of Health, Education and Welfare, Public Assistance Report No. 43, 1961).

[66] F. Spencer Smith, "Sheltered Care for Boarding Homes," *Welfare Reporter,* September 1955, p. 5; F. Spencer Smith, "Licensed Nursing Homes," *Welfare Reporter,* April 1956, pp. 3-4.

[67] New Jersey Commission to Study the Administration of Public Medical Care, *Report and Recommendations* (Trenton, n.p., 1959), pp. 9, 13-14, 20, 48-49.

NOTES FOR CHAPTER 22

[1] New Jersey Committee on Children and Youth, *New Jersey Children in a Changing World* (mimeographed, n.p., February 1960), Ch. II, pp. 1-2, 6-7; Ch. VI, pp. 11-15; "Priorities," pp. 1-4.

[2] *Ibid.,* Ch. II, p. 8.

[3] Council of State Governments, *State Finances, 1942 and 1954* (Chicago: The Council, 1956), pp. 12-14.

[4] Governor Alfred E. Driscoll, messages to the legislature, *Senate Journal,* 1947, pp. 70-72, and *Senate Journal,* 1948, pp. 31-33.

[5] *Welfare Reporter* (NJDIA), April 1950, pp. 3-5.

[6] Governor Alfred E. Driscoll, message to the legislature, *Senate Journal,* 1954, pp. 27-28.

[7] Governor Robert B. Meyner, message, *Senate Journal,* 1956, pp. 29, 32.

[8] Governor Robert B. Meyner, message, *Senate Journal,* 1958, pp. 21-22.

[9] Bennett M. Rich, *The Government and Administration of New Jersey* (New York: Thomas Y. Crowell Co., 1957), pp. 124-125, 396-397.

[10] *Welfare Reporter,* April 1957, p. 3.

[11] *Welfare Reporter,* April 1956, p. 5.

[12] Report from Sanford Bates to Members of the State Board of Control, June 13, 1949, in the office of the State Board.

[13] Report from Sanford Bates to Members of the State Board of Control, June 26, 1950, in the office of the State Board.

[14] *Newark Evening News,* September 25, 1953, p. 32; October 3, 1953, p. 5; October 23, 1953, p. 6.

[15] *Newark Evening News,* May 14, 1954, p. 1; May 20, 1954, p. 1

[16] *Welfare Reporter,* November 1954, p. 7.

[17] F. Lovell Bixby, interview, July 3, 1961.

[18] Quoted, *Welfare Reporter,* January 1955, pp. 1-2.

[19] Governor Robert B. Meyner, message, *Senate Journal,* 1955, p. 37.

[20] *Second Supplementary Budget Message of Robert B. Meyner . . . Trenton, New Jersey, March 21, 1955,* pp. 3–10.

[21] *Welfare Reporter,* May 1955, p. 3.

[22] *Welfare Reporter,* October 1956, p. 5.

[23] *Welfare Reporter,* May 1955, pp. 3–4. Mr. Tramburg died of a heart attack in Trenton on January 14, 1963. *Public Welfare,* April 1963, pp. 3–4, has an extended obituary.

[24] *Social Service Review,* XXVIII (March 1954), 89.

[25] John W. Tramburg, interview, August 10, 1961; *Welfare Reporter,* May 1955, p. 4.

[26] John W. Tramburg, interview, August 10, 1961.

[27] *Welfare Reporter,* October 1955, pp. 4–5.

[28] John W. Tramburg, interview, August 10, 1961.

[29] *Welfare Reporter,* August–October 1953, p. 11; a diagram of the administrative structure appears in *Your Department of Institutions and Agencies* (NJDIA Pub. No. 56, April 1954).

[30] Wisconsin State Department of Public Welfare, *Conserving Human Resources in Wisconsin. Biennial Report . . . July 1, 1952, to June 30, 1954* (n.p., 1954), pp. 7–8.

[31] NJDIA, *Summary Report, 1955–1956* (mimeographed, The Department, 1956), reports of Divisions.

[32] John W. Tramburg, interview, August 10, 1961.

[33] Letter from Lloyd W. McCorkle to author, August 26, 1964.

[34] NJDIA, *Summary Report, 1955–1956,* "Division of Mental Health and Hospitals," unpaged.

[35] V. Terrell Davis, interview, June 7, 1961; *Welfare Reporter,* November 1955, pp. 3–4.

[36] *Welfare Reporter,* November 1955, pp. 3–4.

[37] Thomas McGinnis, "Some Practical Considerations of the Community Mental Health Services Act," *Welfare Reporter,* July 1958, pp. 116–118; *Welfare Reporter,* April 1961, p. 52.

[38] V. Terrell Davis, "The Developing Pattern of Services for the Psychotic Patient in New Jersey," *Welfare Reporter,* July 1960, pp. 99–101; V. T. Davis, "New Approaches to Mental Health Programming," *Welfare Reporter,* January 1962, pp. 3–5.

[39] Maxwell Jones, *et al., The Therapeutic Community . . .* (New York: Basic Books, 1953); Alfred H. Stanton and Morris S. Schwartz, *The Mental Hospital . . .* (New York: Basic Books, 1954); Milton Greenblatt, ed., *The Patient and the Mental Hospital* (Glencoe, Illinois: The Free Press, 1957).

[40] V. Terrell Davis, "The Mental Health Program of New Jersey," manuscript, files of the Division of Mental Health and Hospitals.

[41] Paul Haun, "A Report on British Psychiatry: Consensus," *Welfare Reporter,* January 1959, pp. 3–9.

[42] Robert Bennett, "Clinical Programs," *Welfare Reporter,* January 1959, pp. 16–23.

[43] V. Terrell Davis, "Benefits Gained by State Hospital System from Study

Tours Abroad," manuscript, files of the Division of Mental Health and Hospitals.

[44] J. B. K. Smith, "Horizons of Mental Illness," *Welfare Reporter,* January 1958, p. 44.

[45] NJDIA, *Accomplishments of the Department of Institutions and Agencies* (mimeographed, October 16, 1952), p. 7.

[46] NJDIA, *Annual Report,* 1958, p. 6; Smith, p. 44.

[47] *Welfare Reporter,* July 1958, pp. 137–143.

[48] Maurice G. Kott, "Administrative Aspects of Research in Mental Retardation," *Welfare Reporter,* January 1960, pp. 12–14; Douglas MacNeil, "Research and Administration," *Welfare Reporter,* July 1958, pp. 99, 102–104.

[49] New Jersey Legislature. Senate. Special Committee to Investigate and Study the State Home for Boys at Jamesburg. *First Public Hearing,* February 5, 1957 (manuscript, New Jersey State Library), p. 20A.

[50] *Ibid.,* pp. 4A–5A; 21A–22A.

[51] F. Lovell Bixby, "Changed Attitudes Towards the Correction of Youthful Offenders," *Welfare Reporter,* May 1956, pp. 3–4, 7; F. Lovell Bixby, interview, July 3, 1961.

[52] Memo from F. Lovell Bixby to Sanford Bates, October 22, 1952, manuscript, files of the Division of Correction.

[53] John C. Bonnell, interview, July 12, 1961.

[54] John C. Bonnell, *Mobilizing Public Support for Prison Programs. Paper presented to the . . . 90th Congress of Correction, Denver, Colorado* (n.p., October 1960), pp. 3–4.

[55] New Jersey State Taxpayers Association, *Improving State Use Industries* (Trenton, n.p., 1957), pp. 45–46, 1–2.

[56] Jane Barus, "Improving State Use Industries," *Welfare Reporter,* October 1958, pp. 159–160.

[57] NJDIA, *Annual Report,* 1958, pp. 15, 19.

NOTES FOR CHAPTER 23

[1] *Welfare Reporter* (NJDIA), October 1956, p. 5.

[2] Lloyd Wescott, interview, August 9, 1961.

[3] *Ibid.*

[4] *Newark Evening News,* January 15, 1957, p. 17; January 27, 1957, p. 22.

[5] [N. J.] Commission to Study the Department of Institutions and Agencies, *The State's Organization for Social Welfare, 1959* (n.p., 1959), pp. 88–90, 2–3; Richard T. Frost, "The New Jersey Institutions Case," *Cases in State and Local Government,* Richard T. Frost, ed. (Englewood Cliffs, N. J.: Prentice-Hall, 1961), pp. 219–236, is a participant's account of the Commission's deliberations.

[6] Commission to Study the Department of Institutions and Agencies, pp. 4–6, 56–59.

[7] *Ibid.,* p. 64.

[8] *Ibid.*, pp. 14–18, 23–24.

[9] *Ibid.*, pp. 18–22.

[10] *Ibid.*, pp. 25–28, 35–36.

[11] *Ibid.*, pp. 37–38, 45–46.

[12] *Ibid.*, pp. 58–59, 61–62.

[13] *Ibid.*, pp. 62–64, 68–70, 32–34.

[14] *Ibid.*, pp. 73–76.

[15] *Ibid.*, pp. 66–70.

[16] See Arthur C. Millspaugh, *Public Welfare Organization* (Washington, D. C.: Brookings Institution, 1935), pp. 541–545.

[17] Dayton D. McKean, *Pressures on the Legislature of New Jersey* (New York: Columbia University Press, 1938), pp. 154–187, has a good analysis of the political storm over the sales tax in 1936.

[18] See Meyner's message, *Senate Journal,* 1958, pp. 149–150, also *New York Times,* March 3, 1957, p. 44, and December 4, 1957, p. 32; Paul J. Strayer, *New Jersey's Financial Problem* (New Brunswick: Rutgers University Press, 1960), pp. 3–7, 95–96, is an indignant statement and demand for leadership.

[19] New Jersey Committee on Children and Youth, *New Jersey Children in a Changing World* (mimeographed, n.p., February 1960), Ch. II, pp. 4–8, and "Priorities," pp. 1–2, 7–8.

[20] Commission to Study the Department of Institutions and Agencies, p. 42, n. 1.

A Note on Sources

A Note on Sources

I. Primary sources

Two collections of papers illuminate the founding and early years of the Department: The papers of Dwight Morrow, in the Amherst College Library, include his correspondence as chairman of the Prison Inquiry Commission and as first chairman of the State Board of Control, from 1918 to 1920. Because he was unable to attend many meetings of the State Board, his correspondence is full. The papers of Burdette G. Lewis, commissioner of the Department from 1918 to 1925, in the State Archives, include correspondence, "logs" of his daily work, clippings, and copies of a manuscript autobiographical narrative in the manner of Lincoln Steffens which has several chapters describing his years in New Jersey.

I had unrestricted access to records of the central office of the Department. It had no formal archive and its records were not retained or organized for historical research, but secretaries directed me to files that seemed to have historical importance, which brought out many situations that I would otherwise have missed. The Bureau of Statistics and Research had collections of institutional reports and many miscellaneous items, such as scrapbooks and reprints, in its files. The complete minutes of meetings of the State Board of Control are available in its office, with a most useful card index. This office also has monthly reports by central office executives. The several institutions have miscellaneous "historical" files in addition to the records of their boards.

A basic source about all public institutions is the law. The New Jersey Legislature met annually and published its enactments under the title *Acts of the . . . Legislature of the State of New Jersey*. There were occasional compilations and revisions in 1811, 1821, 1833, 1847, 1877, 1896, 1911, 1925, and 1937. The revision of 1911 is annotated, and laws since 1939 are handily set out in *New Jersey Statutes Annotated* (St. Paul, Minn.: West Publishing Co., 1939–). A guide to the annual session laws before 1877 is John Hood, *Index of Colonial and State Laws Between the Years 1663 and 1877 Inclusive* (Trenton: J. L. Murphy, 1877). The *Senate Journal* and *Minutes of Assembly* give dates of action that lead a researcher to newspaper accounts. They also include messages (and vetoes) from the governor, resolutions, and sometimes petitions. These materials are indexed separately from the legislative business in the back of each volume.

New Jersey Law Reports, going back to 1790, are valuable sources about the interpretation and administration of the law; they have a subject index to each volume, and recent compilations of the law often refer to important cases.

As the business of state government increased in the nineteenth century, the legislative journals became repositories for a variety of reports, and beginning in 1861 these were mostly separated into volumes of *Legislative Documents,* which were continued until 1918. The indispensable guide to these and other official publications is Adelaide R. Hasse, *Index of Economic Material in Documents of the States of the United States: New Jersey, 1789–1904* (Washington: Carnegie Institution of Washington, 1914), in which matters relating to welfare institutions are presented under the rubric "Maintenance." Dorothy F. Lucas, *Bibliography of New Jersey Official Reports, 1905–1945* (Trenton: N. J. State Department of Education, Division of State Library, Archives, and History, 1947), with a *Supplement, 1945–1960* (1961), carries Hasse's work forward in less elaborate fashion. Many important official publications are also mentioned in the *Public Affairs Information Service,* which begins in 1915 and grows steadily more valuable, and, of course, includes many items other than official publications. The *Index to Legal Periodicals* is a guide to that increasing body of cogent analysis and interpretation.

The *Legislative Documents* include official reports of the State Charities Aid Association (1886–1917) and the Department of Charities and Corrections (1906–1917). *The Report of the Prison Inquiry* (Morrow) *Commission* (Trenton, 1917) was printed at the expense of its members; the *Report of the* (Earle) *Commission to Investigate State Charitable Institutions* (1917), the other investigation which led to the creation of the State Department of Institutions and Agencies in 1918, survives only as a typewritten manuscript in the State Library.

The public reports of the State Department of Institutions and Agencies were irregular. A brief "Four Year Summary of Reports" appeared as the April, 1923, issue of *The Quarterly,* a periodical published occasionally by the Department from 1922 to 1927, which also included news about its organization and work. The Department later published a *Summary Report, 1923–1933, and Handbook* (Trenton, 1934) and a *Report, 1934–1943, and Handbook* (Trenton, 1944). From 1946 to 1950 Commissioner Sanford Bates made an annual report to the State Board in the form of a mimeographed letter or memo, which is available in the office of the Board, and after 1945 *The Welfare Reporter,* a monthly magazine, covered the Department's work and activities. A mimeographed annual report appeared in 1955–1956, and a regular printed annual report began in 1957. In 1958 the *Welfare Reporter* changed from a monthly to a more scholarly-type quarterly; since 1960 it has included the annual report. Issues of the *Welfare Reporter* of particular historical interest are: "50 Years of Psychological Services in the New Jersey State Department of Institutions and Agencies, 1910–1960," October, 1960, and "65 Years of Service to Children in New Jersey," July, 1964.

In recent years the State Library has collected many unpublished legislative documents, including some transcripts of hearings; these are indexed in its catalog.

The annual messages of the governor, and sometimes the statements by newly elected presiding officers of the legislature, present the work of institutions and the Department in the context of general political concerns. Much factual information can be gleaned from the governor's budget message, after 1916, and from the publications of the budget department and the Civil Service Commission. There were three surveys of the state government, with expert attention to the Department's work, between 1925 and 1932: Joint Legislative Survey Commission, *Report* (Trenton, 1925); National Institute of Public Administration, *Report on a Survey of the Organization and Administration of the State Government of New Jersey . . .* (Trenton, 1929), and Princeton University, School of Public and International Affairs, *Report on a Survey of Administration and Expenditures of the State Government of New Jersey . . .* ([Princeton], 1932).

The *Reports* of the Pension Survey Commission (1931–1932) include much valuable information, particularly the fifth, which deals with the work of the Board of Children's Guardians. *Justice and the Child in New Jersey,* the report of the Juvenile Delinquency Commission (Trenton, 1939), includes historical and statistical information. These commissions were the forerunners of many that provided, after 1945, a storehouse of facts and critical opinion. Among these were the Governor's Committee on Children and Youth, *Children and Youth in New Jersey* ([Trenton?], 1949); New Jersey Committee on Children and Youth, *New Jersey Children in a Changing World* (n.p., 1960); The New Jersey Commission to Study the Problems and Needs of Mentally Deficient Persons, *Mental Deficiency in New Jersey. . . .* (Trenton, 1954); The New Jersey Youth Study Commission, which issued forty-nine reports of hearings and publications between 1954 and 1961, concluding with *Action for Children and Youth* ([Trenton?], 1961), with a useful cumulative index; The New Jersey State Old Age Study Commission, *A Positive Policy Toward Aging* ([Trenton], 1957); New Jersey State Commission on Mental Health, *Toward Mental Health in New Jersey* ([Trenton?], 1961); New Jersey Commission to Study the Administration of Public Medical Care, *Report and Recommendations* ([Trenton], 1959); and, of course, the Commission to Study the Department of Institutions and Agencies, *The State's Organization for Social Welfare in New Jersey* (Trenton, 1959).

The New Jersey Welfare Council, the successor to the State Conference of Charities and Corrections, has in its office in Newark various materials of historical interest, which at the time of my research were unclassified and difficult to use. Inasmuch as the Council brought together representatives of private agencies and professional social work and ventured to oversee the whole of the state's social welfare enterprises and to influence the legislature, its history should have a high priority for future research.

From 1902 to 1909 and in 1911 the State Charities Aid Association published in addition to its annual report a monthly (often bi-monthly) *Review of Charities and Corrections,* a running commentary on a variety of social and political affairs. My systematic newspaper coverage began in 1913 and relied heavily on the morgue of the *Newark Evening News,* to which I had access, and the *New York Times,* which gave space to New Jersey stories that would interest commuters and which was conveniently indexed. Among the serials and journals that I checked for New Jersey material or background were: the *Proceedings* of the National Conference of Social Welfare and its predecessor organizations; *The Survey; Proceedings* of the American Correctional (formerly Prison) Association; the *Yearbook* of the National Probation and Parole Association; *Mental Hygiene; Social Service Review; State Government; Public Welfare; United States Government Publications: Monthly Catalog* (a convenient guide to a variety of publications about New Jersey made under federal auspices, by the Children's Bureau, for example); and *The Training School Bulletin,* published by the Training School at Vineland, which gave good coverage to state programs for the mentally deficient and also included wise commentary on state affairs by Edward R. Johnstone.

Of exceptional value were unpublished theses and research projects in schools of social work, especially at Columbia University, Fordham, and the University of Chicago. Some were formal histories, but most were studies of aspects of services or administration; many of the authors were past or present employees or otherwise well acquainted with the operations, and whatever the scientific merit of their analyses, their descriptions are eye-witness accounts of features that rarely appear in formal reports or investigations.

Much of my research was in the form of interviews, which I mention under acknowledgments.

II. Secondary works

My subject involves many features of social life that have substantial historical literatures. The most useful single guide to material related directly to New Jersey is Nelson R. Burr, *A Narrative and Descriptive Bibliography of New Jersey* (Princeton: D. Van Nostrand, 1964), a volume in "The New Jersey Historical Series," which was planned to commemorate the state's tercentenary, and in the bibliographies of other books in the series, notably *The People of New Jersey,* by Rudolph J. Vecoli; *Medicine and Health in New Jersey,* by David L. Cowen; *Where Cities Meet: The Urbanization of New Jersey,* by John E. Bebout and Ronald J. Grele; *The New Jersey Governor: A Study in Political Power,* by Duane Lockard; *Religion in New Jersey: A Brief History,* by Wallace N. Jamison; and *Organized Labor in New Jersey,* by Leo Troy. These works came too late to facilitate my own research, although I have sometimes cited them in my documentation. Useful as the series is, it does not add up to historical interpretations of the main institutional systems of the state—the class structure, voluntary associations, the economy, or even the polity. In effect its volumes are substantial but disparate essays which supplement but do not supplant two earlier collections of essays that have passed for general histories of the state: *New Jersey: A History,* edited by Irving S. Kull (6 vols.; New York: American Historical Society, 1930–1932); and *The Story of New Jersey,* edited by William Starr Myers (5 vols.; New York: Lewis Publishing Co., 1945). The latter includes an article on "Public Welfare in New Jersey, 1630–1944," signed by William J. Ellis, which I discuss in my text.

General works that discuss the relation between the labor force, poor relief, and crime in the colonial period are Richard B. Morris, *Government and Labor in Early America* (New York: Columbia University Press, 1946); Abbott Emerson Smith, *Colonists in Bondage: White Servitude and Convict Labor in*

America, 1607–1776 (Chapel Hill: University of North Carolina Press, 1947); and Carl Bridenbaugh, *Cities in the Wilderness: The First Century of Urban Life in America, 1625–1742* (2nd ed.; New York: Knopf, 1955) and *Cities in Revolt: Urban Life in America, 1743–1776* (New York: Knopf, 1955). In my delineation of the rural democracy two works were especially useful: Harold F. Wilson, *The Jersey Shore: A Social and Economic History of the Counties of Atlantic, Cape May, Monmouth, and Ocean* (3 vols.; New York: Lewis Publishing Co., 1953) and Hubert G. Schmidt, *Rural Hunterdon, An Agricultural History* (New Brunswick: Rutgers University Press, 1945). On the economic development of the state before the Civil War, I found Wheaton J. Lane, *From Indian Trail to Iron Horse: Travel and Transportation in New Jersey, 1620–1860* (Princeton: Princeton University Press, 1939), of broader significance than its title implies, and there are summary discussions in the volumes edited by Kull and Myers. My views of politics in relation to local welfare institutions rest upon the admirable analyses of Richard P. McCormick in *New Jersey from Colony to State, 1609–1789* (Princeton: Van Nostrand, 1964); *Experiment in Independence: New Jersey in the Critical Period, 1781–1789* (New Brunswick: Rutgers University Press, 1950), and *The History of Voting in New Jersey: A Study of the Development of Election Machinery, 1664–1911* (New Brunswick: Rutgers University Press, 1953), which goes beyond its title.

My discussion of welfare institutions in the rural society draws on Paul Stafford, *Government and the Needy: A Study of Public Assistance in New Jersey* (Princeton: Princeton University Press, 1941), which incorporates the results of an extensive study of local archives conducted under the WPA; Harry Elmer Barnes, *A History of the Penal, Reformatory, and Correctional Institutions of the State of New Jersey, Analytical and Documentary,* which he did as Volume II of the *Report of the Prison Inquiry Commission* (Trenton: MacCrellish, 1917), which I discuss in my text, and also his later book, *The Evolution of Penology in Pennsylvania: A Study in American Social History* (Indianapolis: Bobbs-Merrill, 1927); Henry Clay Reed, "Chapters in a History of Crime and Punishment in New Jersey" (Ph.D. thesis, Princeton, 1939), which is based on court records and includes an important chapter on church discipline as a social control. Sydney V. James, *A People Among Peoples: Quaker Benevolence in Eighteenth Century America* (Cambridge: Harvard University Press, 1963) makes a thoughtful analysis of the sectarian charity and humanitarian enterprises of Friends in New Jersey as elsewhere. Nelson Burr, *Education in New Jersey, 1630–1871* (Princeton: Princeton University Press, 1942), notes the relationship between public education, private charity, and philanthropy, and the political contests it engendered.

Histories of public welfare in other states are mostly chronologies of legislative and administrative precedents, unredeemed by analysis. The best of them are in the series of "Social Service Monographs," published by the School of Social Service Administration of the University of Chicago, and listed together with non-historical volumes under that title in Baer's *Titles in Series.* I found some perspective in the best of the Chicago volumes, David Schneider, *A History of Public Welfare in New York State,* 1607–1867 (Chicago: University of Chicago Press, 1938) and David Schneider and Albert Deutsch, *A History of*

Public Welfare in New York State, 1867–1940 (Chicago: University of Chicago Press, 1941), and in William C. Heffner, *History of Poor Relief Legislation in Pennsylvania, 1682–1913* (Cleona, Pa.: Holzapfel Pub. Co., 1913).

On the development of the poor law and the rise of state institutions in the nineteenth century, the most important general works are Sophonisba P. Breckinridge, *Public Welfare Administration: Select Documents* (2nd ed.; Chicago: University of Chicago Press, 1938); Edith Abbott, *Public Assistance* (Chicago: University of Chicago Press, 1940); and Grace Abbott, *The Child and the State* (2 vols.; Chicago: University of Chicago Press, 1938), which are compendiums of documents with commentary. General trends in public welfare in the years before 1930 are summarized in Howard W. Odum and D. W. Willard, eds., *Systems of Public Welfare* (Chapel Hill: University of North Carolina Press, 1925); in several chapters of that most useful work, *Recent Social Trends in the United States: Report of the President's Research Committee on Social Trends* (2 vols.; New York: McGraw-Hill Co., 1933), and in various articles in *The Encyclopedia of Social Sciences.* The general impact of the depression on public welfare is described in Josephine Brown, *Public Relief, 1929–1939* (New York: Henry Holt, 1940) and in Marietta Stevenson, *Public Welfare Administration* (New York: Macmillan, 1938).

The rise of professional social work is the subject of Kathleen Woodroofe, *From Charity to Social Work in England and America* (Toronto: University of Toronto Press, 1962) and of Roy Lubove, *The Professional Altruist: The Emergence of Social Work as a Career, 1880–1930* (Cambridge: Harvard University Press, 1965), a thoughtful analysis. Nathan E. Cohen, *Social Work in the American Tradition* (New York: Dryden, 1958) includes chapters and bibliography on the profession since 1930. *The Encyclopedia of Social Work* (New York: National Association of Social Workers, 1965), and its predecessor, *The Social Work Yearbook,* published biennially from 1929 to 1960, presents authoritative short articles on welfare institutions and professional interests. In the large literature on social reform since 1890 two works have particular bearing on welfare agencies: Robert Bremner, *From the Depths: The Discovery of Poverty in the United States* (New York: New York University Press, 1956), and Clarke Chambers, *Seedtime of Reform: American Social Service and Social Action, 1918–1933* (Minneapolis: University of Minnesota Press, 1963). Robert Bremner's *American Philanthropy* (Chicago: University of Chicago Press, 1960) is a brief account of various voluntary agencies, with an extensive bibliography.

On the general development of corrections in the nineteenth century, Blake McKelvey, *American Prisons: A Study in American Social History Prior to 1915* (Chicago: University of Chicago Press, 1936) may be supplemented by Negley V. Teeters and John D. Shearer, *The Prison at Philadelphia: Cherry Hill* (New York: Columbia University Press, 1957), on the Pennsylvania system, and Walter D. Lewis, *From Newgate to Dannemora: The Rise of the Penitentiary in New York, 1796–1848* (Ithaca: Cornell University Press, 1964), on the Auburn system, a thoughtful interpretation. On the treatment of mental disorders the principal secondary works are: Henry M. Hurd, *Institutional Care of the Insane in the United States* (4 vols.; Baltimore: Johns Hopkins Press, 1916); Albert Deutsch,

The Mentally Ill in America: A History of Their Care and Treatment from Colonial Times (Rev. ed.; New York: Columbia University Press, 1949), and *One Hundred Years of American Psychiatry* (New York: Published by Columbia University Press for the American Psychiatric Association, 1944). Notable recent works on special subjects are Norman Dain, *Concepts of Insanity in the United States, 1789–1865* (New Brunswick: Rutgers University Press, 1964), and Mark H. Haller, *Eugenics: Hereditarian Attitudes in American Thought* (New Brunswick: Rutgers University Press, 1963), on views of mental deficiency.

My analysis of political alignments in urban industrial New Jersey, as they bore upon public welfare administration, draws upon: William E. Sackett, *Modern Battles of Trenton . . . 1868 to 1894* (Trenton: John L. Murphy, Printer, 1895) and *Modern Battles of Trenton. Volume II, Werts to Wilson* (New York, Neale Publishing Co., 1914); Ransom E. Noble, *New Jersey Progressivism Before Wilson* (Princeton: Princeton University Press, 1946); Arthur S. Link, *Wilson: The Road to the White House* (Princeton: Princeton University Press, 1947); John M. Blum, *Joe Tumulty and the Wilson Era* (Boston: Houghton Mifflin, 1951); Walter E. Edge, *Jerseyman's Journal: Fifty Years of American Business and Politics* (Princeton: Princeton University Press, 1948); Dayton D. McKean, *Pressures on the Legislature of New Jersey* (New York: Columbia University Press, 1938), and *The Boss: The Hague Machine in Action* (Boston: Houghton Mifflin Co., 1940), an exposé rather than an analysis. These books, like the tradition of political history from which they derive, focus on contests and personalities and say little about the practical nature of services or their administrative development.

As for the state's welfare institutions, Barnes' *History of the Penal . . . Institutions* and the *Report of the Prison Inquiry Commission,* with its appendixes, carry that story to 1918; Stafford's *Government and the Needy* traces developments in public assistance until 1940, and his earlier work, *State Welfare Administration in New Jersey,* a Ph.D. thesis published by the Department of Political Science, Princeton University, 1934, describes the development of state welfare administration. Stafford's historical interpretations are narrowly institutional, but his analysis of formalities is always admirably clear. Martin W. Stanton, "A History of Public Poor Relief in New Jersey, 1609–1934" (Ph.D. thesis, Fordham University, 1934), has information on the relation of public and private agencies. On emergency programs during the Depression, see Douglas MacNeil, *Seven Years of Unemployment Relief in New Jersey, 1930–1936* (Washington: Social Science Research Council, 1938), which includes discussions of local and private agencies.

For developments in the state since 1945 I found most useful *The Economy of New Jersey,* A Report Prepared for the Department of Conservation and Economic Development of the State of New Jersey. By A Group of Rutgers Scholars under the Direction of Professor Salomon J. Flink (New Brunswick: Rutgers University Press, 1958); and Bennett M. Rich, *The Government and Administration of New Jersey* (New York: Thomas Y. Crowell, 1957). Several volumes of the "New Jersey Historical Series" touch on the social history of the recent period, notably John E. Bebout and Ronald J. Grele, *Where Cities*

Meet: The Urbanization of New Jersey, and there is much relevant information in the *New York Metropolitan Region Study,* published in nine volumes by the Harvard University Press (1959–1961).

There are very useful files of biographical references at the Rutgers University Library and the State Library at Trenton. *The Manual of the Legislature of New Jersey,* issued annually after 1872, includes thumbnail biographies of many state officials, annual messages of the governors, election returns and much other information.

Index

Index